Crisis in the Later Middle Ages

THE MEDIEVAL COUNTRYSIDE

Previously published volumes in this series are listed at the back of the book.

VOLUME 13

Crisis in the Later Middle Ages

Beyond the Postan-Duby Paradigm

Edited by

John Drendel

BREPOLS

British Library Cataloguing in Publication Data

A catalogue record for this book is available from the British Library.

D/2015/0095/50
ISBN: 978-2-503-54742-8
e-ISBN: 978-2-503-54829-6
Printed in the EU on acid-free paper

In memory of
Richard Britnell and John Munro

Contents

Illustrations

Figures

Map

Tables

Introduction

John Drendel

The papers in this collection inaugurated a series of five conferences held between 2002 and 2009 which have renewed our understanding of the medieval economy at the turn of the fourteenth century. The 2002 meeting in Montreal was conceived as a wide-ranging discussion of a model of crisis in the later Middle Ages which Michael Postan and Georges Duby made the dominant paradigm for understanding the economy in this period. The papers brought to the fore some of the principal critiques of this model and opened up in particular the pertinance for the Mediterranean world of a model of crisis based upon northern Europe.[1] Subsequent meetings in Rome and Madrid followed up on the latter by pursuing the questions proposed in Montreal within the context of the western Mediterranean. Thus the meeting in Rome in 2004 addressed the question of whether food shortages in the Mediterranean could be understood properly within an interpretive schema dominated by an event, the Great Famine of 1315–22, which the Midi did not suffer.[2] In Madrid in 2005, attention turned to the role of small towns and local markets in integrating the Mediterranean economy, a theme which historians of the North have pursued as an alternative to the crisis model.[3] Two years later

[1] 'Postan-Duby: Le destin d'un paradigm historique/The Destiny of an Historical Paradigm', Montreal, 10–12 October 2002.

[2] 'Les disettes dans la conjoncture de 1300 en Méditerranée occidentale', Rome, 27–28 February 2004, published as Bourin, Drendel, and Menant, *Les disettes dans la conjoncture de 1300*.

[3] 'Dinámicas comerciales del mundo rural: actores, redes y productos / Dynamiques commerciales du monde rural: acteurs, réseaux, produits', Madrid, 17–20 October 2005, to be

John Drendel (drendel.john@uqam.ca) is professor of medieval history at the Université du Québec à Montréal.

Crisis in the Later Middle Ages: Beyond the Postan-Duby Paradigm, ed. by John Drendel, TMC 13 (Turnhout: Brepols, 2015) 1–13 BREPOLS PUBLISHERS 10.1484/M.TMC.5.103781

in Madrid participants approached the question of commercialization in the Mediterranean from the monetary perspective.[4] However, the first conference in Montreal, whose papers are presented here, encompassed studies from all of western Europe, with the explicit intention of assessing the lag between the revision of Postan's ideas among the historians of medieval England represented in this collection and his more enduring influence on the Continent. This volume thus represents a milestone in that its authors address critically for the first time since the 1970s how the Ricardian-Malthusian model elaborated by Michael Postan for England was applied to western Europe as a whole.

Georges Duby was most influential in ensuring the success of Postan's analysis of crisis, notably through his magisterial synthesis, published in 1962, *L'économie rurale et la vie des campagnes dans l'Occident médiéval*.[5] Duby's subtle analyses, elegant style, and ambitious scope — the work examines all of western Europe between the ninth and the fifteenth centuries — brought international recognition both to him and to the field of rural history. In the 1970s in France the text was a pillar for students preparing the prestigious *agrégation* in medieval history. As such, it formed the attitudes of an entire generation of French medievalists, and not without good cause. Duby spun a seamless narrative from a bibliography of over 640 works on Italy, Germany, Spain, the Low Countries, and Scandinavia. England alone was represented by 115 bibliographical entries, most of which were monographs. In the pages of *L'économie rurale*, students in France — and no doubt many of their lecturers — encountered for the first time the work of scholars like Michael Postan, Ambrose Raftis, Evgeny Kosminsky, and Wilhelm Abel. From the perspective of this volume, perhaps the best way of measuring its impact is to consider how long Duby's arguments have held sway. Aside from the attacks led by Robert Brenner and Guy Bois against Malthusian determinism from a Marxist perspective in the late 1970s, French historians had by and large accepted Duby's presentation of the later Middles Ages in *L'économie rurale* until our meeting in Montreal.[6] This is remarkable

published as Bourin, Menant, and To Figueras, *Echanges, prélèvements et consommation dans le monde rural*.

[4] 'Moneda, crédito y fiscalidad en el mundo rural / Monnaie, crédit et fiscalité dans le monde rural', Madrid, 8–10 February 2007, to be published together with papers from the 2005 Madrid conference in Bourin, Menant, and To Figueras, *Echanges, prélèvements et consommation dans le monde rural*.

[5] Duby, *L'économie rurale*; Duby, *Rural Economy*, trans. by Postan.

[6] Bois, *Crise du féodalisme*; Phillipp Schofield's essay in this volume resumes the principal elements of the Marxist critique of Malthusianism, generally referred to as 'the Brenner Debate'

for three reasons. First, French medievalists have taken Duby to task on other issues, notably his pessimistic view of Carolingian agrarian productivity and the chronology and rapidity of the 'feudal transition' between the ninth and the twelfth centuries.[7] The second reason is that Duby's interpretation of the later Middle Ages relies upon Michael Postan, and while the Postan paradigm still dominates British historiography, it nevertheless drew serious criticism from historians of Britain from the start.[8] Finally, Duby based this model of agrarian crisis on studies of northern Europe and extended it to a Mediterranean Europe with a radically different climate and ecology.[9] Thus the discordance between the dearth of debate in France over ideas contested for decades in Britain lies at the heart of these essays. The contributions on England explore the ideas of Duby and Postan from synthetic perspectives while most of the papers concerning the Continent are works of original research which re-examine the Postan-Duby model in light of specific cases. The participants honour Georges Duby, in the same way historians of England have always admired Michael Postan — through the penetrating light of criticism. Georges Duby put no conclusion at the end of *L'économie rurale* in the hope that others might rapidly move beyond his insights.[10] That time has now come.

Readers of Georges Duby's major works might well perceive the historian of Cluny as having only an indirect knowledge of the later Middle Ages. That is not, however, the case. Between 1952 and 1970, and in particular while writing *L'économie rurale*, Duby taught at the Université d'Aix-Marseille where he worked with Edouard Baratier who headed the departmental archives in Marseille. Baratier's archival work represented a remarkable opportunity for both historians, for he had the task of organizing one of the largest holdings of medieval records in France. The Archives départementales des Bouches-

after the name of one of its principal protaganists, Brenner, *The Brenner Debate*, ed. by Aston and others; for one critical appraisal of Duby's approach, see Hélias, 'Le vocabulaire de Georges Duby'. The article in this volume by Erik Thoen and Tim Soens vigorously renews the 'Brenner' approach.

[7] Jean-Pierre Devroey succinctly summarizes the debate over Carolingian seed-ratios in Devroey, *Économie rurale et société*, pp. 112–17; Barthélemy, *La mutation de l'an mil a-t-elle eu lieu?*

[8] Barbara Harvey was an early and insistent critic: Harvey, 'The Population Trend in England'; Harvey, 'Introduction'; for an overview of the debate in Britain, see Hatcher and Bailey, *Modelling the Middle Ages*; Dyer and Schofield, 'Recent Work on the Agrarian History of Medieval Britain'.

[9] A difference explored in the conferences on the 'Conjoncture de 1300' and summarized in Bourin and others, 'Les campagnes'.

[10] Duby, *L'histoire continue*, p. 97.

du-Rhône is the repository of the sole surviving administrative registers of the Angevin kingdom of Naples, the legacy of Aix's role as capital of the county of Provence. In addition, this archive shelters thousands of notarial registers, the largest and oldest notarial *fonds* extant in France, as well as an abundance of ecclesiastical cartularies, charters, and local records from towns and villages.[11] Duby and Baratier used these records in their own work and guided a generation of talented students — Joseph Shatzmiller, Michel Hébert, Louis Stouff, Monique Zerner, and Noël Coulet, among others — in local studies which today comprise some of the most significant monographs from the postwar period in France.[12] Duby himself published several local studies, including three articles based upon the Hospitaler cartulary of 1338, one of the more interesting documents brought to light by Baratier.[13] Duby did indeed have more than general knowledge of primary sources concerning the period upon which the articles in this volume focus, knowledge derived both from his research alone and in collaboration with Baratier, as well as from the work of students they supervised.

With this in mind, let us reread *L'économie rurale* on the period 1200–1348 in order to measure the importance and influence of Duby's ideas about this period. First of all, Duby insisted that agriculture was the fundamental engine of economic growth, challenging medievalists like Robert Lopez and Philippe Wolff who, following the footsteps of Henri Pirenne, focused upon the leading role of commerce and towns in developing the medieval economy.[14] Duby seems to have been particularly influenced by Reginald Lennard, cited forty-seven times, who argued that Domesday England had a highly structured landscaped carefully organized to maximize agrarian production. Evgeny Kosminsky's portrayal of a peasantry struggling with lords over the control of surplus suffuses

[11] Bautier and Sornay, *Les sources de l'histoire économique et sociale du Moyen Âge*, I.

[12] Shatzmiller, *Recherches sur la communauté juive*; Hébert, *Tarascon au XIVe siècle*; Beaucage, *Visites générales des commanderies*; Stouff, *Arles à la fin du Moyen Âge*; Zerner, *Le cadastre, le pouvoir et la terre*; Coulet, *Aix en Provence*. See also Duby, 'Recherches récentes sur la vie rurale'. Baratier and Duby attracted many foreign students, Canadians like Beaucage and Hébert, but also students from the Eastern bloc, whose work fills the pages of *Provence Historique* and the *Cahiers de CESM*. In particular, see Poppe, *Economie et société d'un bourg provençal*.

[13] Duby, 'Techniques et rendements agricoles'; Duby, 'Note sur les corvées'; Duby, 'La seigneurie et l'économie paysanne'.

[14] Duby, *L'histoire continue*, p. 12. After 1945 Philippe Wolff embodied the Pirenne tradition; his immensely influential study of Toulouse launched the postwar school of urban medievel history, a role played in English-language historiography by Robert Lopez: Wolff, *Commerce et marchands de Toulouse*; Lopez, *The Commercial Revolution of the Middle Ages*.

Duby's brutal portrait of seigneurial domination after *l'an mil*.[15] Yet his analyses elide raw ideological underpinnings, notably in the passages, arguably among the best in the book, which attribute the progress of cultivation in the long thirteenth century to the interplay of efficient manorial management, improvements in tools and agronomic techniques, and improved seed selection.[16] The underlying argument is that manorial agriculture was the source of improvements in medieval agriculture at the expense of peasant initiative — the prevailing line of thought among British historians until recently.[17] At this point in his narration, Duby evokes the end of essarts and 'surpeuplement' after 1250 and introduces Postan's Ricardian-Malthusian model as an explanation for agrarian decline before the Black Death.[18]

Our volume includes a report by the late Richard Britnell from a bench in Postan's Cambridge classroom about the argument for a Malthusian crisis before the plague, while the late John Munro, in one of his last articles, unravels the more neglected analysis which Postan applied to the crisis after 1350. What I would like to emphasize here is how skilfully Duby adapted Postan's ideas, particularly in his chapter on the 'rise of exchange'. He noted the role of the town as an escape valve for growing population pressure in the countryside, and he carefully outlined the growing orientation of thirteenth-century agriculture towards urban markets.[19] Duby was quite aware of how a market economy was spreading through the European countryside, propelled by a demand for foodstuffs and raw materials, particularly those provided by animal husbandry. The need for meat, skins, wood, and iron brought merchants into the highest valleys of the Pyrenees, upland Provence, and the Alps. Regional specialization in cereals, sheep, and cattle accompanied a growing division of local labour in response to growing rural demand for goods fabricated from metal, leather, and cloth. Duby suggested that exchange was a factor which rendered more tolerable 'extraordinary' rural overpopulation.[20] Thus he hedged his Malthusianism

[15] Duby, *L'économie rurale*, pp. 401–05.

[16] Duby, *L'économie rurale*, pp. 133–207.

[17] Anne DeWindt brings to the fore this critique of Duby in her contribution to this volume, with an abundant bibliography.

[18] Duby, *L'économie rurale*, pp. 216–19.

[19] Duby, *L'économie rurale*, pp. 223–24.

[20] 'La spécialisation progressive de certains paysans dans la production de denrées marchandes rendit possible l'extraordinaire entassement de population sur les tenures pulvérisées': Duby, *L'économie rurale*, p. 259.

in a way which actually anticipated many of the revisions which British historians of the 'commercialization' school have brought forward in opposition to Postan; unfortunately French historians never followed up his lead.

The frontal attack upon Postan's analysis of a demographic crisis in the countryside came in 1966, when Barbara Harvey published a critique of the notion of 'overpopulation' in pre-plague England. She cited many examples, based upon local studies, which showed that population growth had not stalled in England before the Great Famine.[21] The accumulation of studies by others which followed gave rise to a 'counter-paradigm' for the crisis of the fourteenth century which emphasized the role of markets both in overcoming Malthusian pressures by increasing agricultural production through specialization and in ultimately creating the crisis through their failures. Elements of this model can be found in a prescient *Annales* article which Edouard Perroy published in 1949.[22] Perroy argued before even Postan that overpopulation was a factor in provoking the economic crisis of the fourteenth century before the Black Death. However Perroy's argument was not monocausal, and indeed he suggested that the interaction in France and England between war taxation and monetary mutations was just as important as demography in perturbing the economic viability of agriculture after the Great Famine. The central role of markets implicit in this thesis was furthur developed by Harry Miskimin, who took Perroy's analysis of the price scissors between falling grain prices and rising labour costs after 1317 and applied it to the diverging price movements of those same commodities and urban cost structures after the Black Death. Miskimin's analysis of the structure of markets linking town and countryside underscored their failure as an articulating mechanism of crisis, even though between 1962 and 1969 he had come accept the thesis of overpopulation on the eve of the Great Famine. This focus on markets thus linked the destiny of the urban economy to that of the countryside and posed the question of the countryside's integration into a market economy.[23]

Market integration as a driver of specialization and productivity in the period 1250–1350 was the focus of studies from England beginning in the late

[21] Harvey, 'The Population Trend in England'.

[22] Perroy, 'A l'origine d'une économie contractée'.

[23] In a famous article written in 1962 with Robert Lopez, Miskimin gave rather little importance to demography other than as an index of growth, and he placed the population peak at the eve of the Black Death; eight years later, Postan had influenced his views. Lopez and Miskimin, 'The Economic Depression of the Renaissance', p. 416; Miskimin, *The Economy of Early Renaissance Europe*, pp. 23, 78–80 (failure of markets), pp. 30, 90 (price scissors).

1980s which have been well summarized elsewhere. I will simply mention here a few milestones.[24] The critique of Postan's argument that overpopulation led to declining yields on marginal lands was met by Mark Bailey's pioneer study of the intensive use of ecological niches on marginal lands in the fourteenth century. Bruce Campbell developed an impressive body of data demonstrating the diversification and specialization of demesne agriculture, particularly in the catchment basin drained by London's urban demand. James Masschaele argued that lords profited from peasant agriculture by creating a vast network of local markets, rather than by expropriating surplus through feudal levies. The result was that markets had so penetrated the rural economy by 1300 that peasants marketed in the aggregate a greater surplus of grain and wool than did their masters. John Langdon explained the rapid increase in horses in thirteenth-century peasant agriculture not by the advantages gained by plowing more quickly, but rather by the desire of small producers to reach as many local markets as possible by decreasing the time it took to transport their produce. A steady increase in the money supply from the end of the twelfth century supported widening and deepening of markets. Richard Britnell drew together the different empirical elements of these studies into a 'commercialization' model worthy of Adam Smith, which fully rejected the notion that the rural economy depended upon the crude relationship between surface cultivated and population growth. Britnell did not believe that the English economy could have broken through the 'Malthusian ceiling' in the fourteenth century; his point rather is that the limitations to growth were those imposed by immature and inefficient economic institutions. However, even these flawed markets connected rural society to the larger world in a way that allowed peasant initiative to play a leading role in the economy.[25]

Georges Duby's interpretation of the crisis also recognized the importance of markets in a way that modulated the influences of Postan's Malthusianism. Duby had an insight into how specialization — a Smithian approach to understanding the medieval countryside — weakened Postan's interpretation, but in the end, his own perspective on the impact of markets and exchange is deeply pessimistic. He saw the introduction of money into the peasant economy in the

[24] Hatcher and Bailey, *Modelling the Middle Ages*; Dyer and Schofield, 'Recent Work on the Agrarian History of Medieval Britain'; Campbell, 'The Agrarian Problem'; Bourin and others, 'Les campagnes'.

[25] Bailey, *A Marginal Economy?*; Masschaele, *Peasants, Merchants and Markets*; Langdon, *Horses, Oxen and Technological Innovation*; Britnell, *The Commercialisation of English Society*; Britnell, 'Specialization of Work in England'; Britnell, *Britain and Ireland 1050–1530.*

later twelfth century as a lever which rich peasants and townspeople used to drive the countryside into debt and poverty, an analysis close to that of Phillipp Schofield in this volume. Inflation eroded seigneurial dues, but peasants borrowed to purchase livestock and plows, cloth and salt, to pay taxes and to purchase limitations on customary payments from their lords. The crushing burden of debt resulted in the expropriation of peasant land by 'kulaks', lords, and merchants.[26] This pessimism is never expressed as determinism, but as Schofield points out in his contribution to this volume, Postan's own work on the peasant land market oscillated between a Leninist and a Chayanovian perspective. The former influenced Duby, and from this viewpoint it was difficult for him to imagine peasants, even rich ones, producing surplus on the scale envisioned by the protagonists of the commercialization model.

The essays in this volume approach the paradigm of Postan and Duby from two perspectives. First a series of synthetic articles by Richard Britnell, John Munro, John Langdon, Thierry Pécout, Christopher Dyer, and Phillipp Schofield continue the historiographical debate over the crisis model, not only in Great Britain but also in the Mediterranean region and the Low Countries as well. Britnell and Munro, as I noted, profit from two decades of revision of the Postan thesis before and after the Black Death to explain why it failed to account for historical change in both periods. Schofield examines the role of the land market and debt in Postan's writings, which Duby integrated into his analysis, and he shows how the corrosive effects of commercialization on village society continue to nourish critics of the commercialization model. Langdon proposes a Shumpeterian analysis of the rural economy, arguing against the existence of the 'innovation ceiling' implicit in Postan's Malthusian schema. Dyer examines how Postan's neglect of the role small towns played in the rural economy undermines his arguments and discusses the many important links which recent research has illuminated between urban centers and the countryside in Britain. Pécout provides a long view of the historiographical use of the concept of 'crisis' with respect to the later Middle Ages since the beginning of the twentieth century and shows how the nature of those crises evolved from political to demographic and, most recently, back to a political-institutional analysis.

A second series of empirical studies based upon original research shows the direction taken by critics of Postan and Duby in recent years. Anne DeWindt, an early and brilliant student of Ambrose Raftis, enlarges upon the concept of 'peasant agency', which Raftis believed to be incompatible with the deter-

[26] Duby, *L'économie rurale*, p. 491.

minism of Postan's Malthusianism, and shows how 'agency' actually functioned in the villages of Ramsey Abbey. Many local studies support her own empirical evidence that peasant initiative played the determining role in the later medieval rural economy, more often than not with the complicity of lords. Erik Thoen and Tim Soens, in a complex, finely etched study, reject both the Malthusian and 'commercial' models for interpreting Flanders, arguably the most highly integrated market of the Middle Age, in favour of the Marxist approach of Robert Brenner and Guy Bois. They emphasize the capacity of aristocratic elites to use feudal institutions as instruments of surplus extraction.

Case studies from France suggest that facts on the ground run far ahead of a French historiography still influenced by Georges Duby. Laure Verdon's detailed analysis of *capbreus*, records of peasant holdings of the King of Majorca in the late thirteenth century, describes rational strategies of land purchase and exchange which advanced household wealth, and she argues that these strategies, rather than desperation, lay behind the *capbreus* transactions. They therefore should not be interpreted as evidence of peasantry in crisis in Old Catalonia at the end of the thirteenth century. Francine Michaud examines the labour market in Marseille after the Black Death and finds that salaries stagnated after 1370, after accounting for inflation; furthermore, employers advantageously shifted from salaried labour to apprenticeship. Demographic decline did not translate into an improved market for urban labourers, many of whom continued to emigrate from the countryside until the end of the century. Salaried labour is the concern of Philippe Bernardi as well. His study of the notarial contracts and accounts of the Avignon papacy shows that industry in the Provençal countryside — medium- and large-scale production of raw materials like plaster, tiles, and finished and semi-finished cut stone — generated jobs for a lot of peasants. The notion that specialization in the village was limited to a few blacksmiths dependent upon the local demand is no longer tenable; a diversified rural economy, integrated by urban demand into regional markets, multiplied employment opportunities in the countryside both before and after the Black Death.[27] Monique Bourin integrates several of these factors — peasant initiative, the labour market, and rural industry — in a wide-ranging study of the Bezier plain in the first half of the fourteenth century. Here, continuing demographic expansion and an active land market encouraged artisans and notables to invest in land. Those investments stimulated peasants to

[27] See most recently Minovez and others, *Les industries rurales dans l'Europe médiévale et moderne*.

cultivate vineyards, an intensive crop, particularly on marginal lands poorly adapted to grain cultivation, while textiles provided an increasing number of employment opportunities. What is most remarkable about the Languedocian example is the lucidity of the consuls of Narbonne who articulate and quantify the employment and savings created by increasing the added value of textiles through technological innovation. Their perception was not one of crisis but rather of the opportunities and the risks created by a complex economy at the mercy of shortsighted royal fiscal policies. Constance Berman re-examines Duby's perception of crisis in the manorial economy before and after the Black Death from the perspective of female Cistercian convents. In the Paris region, these houses prospered at least until the most destructive phases of the Hundred Years War. Indeed, some even benefited from the woes of the more traditional male establishments.

Together, these studies point towards a new horizon for social history beyond the limits which the powerful erudition of Georges Duby and Michael Postan tended to impose. The contributors of the papers in this volume share the heady experience of exploring that new horizon. Their vision, expressed in these papers, is one of a medieval society in which economic and social threads wove together town and country in a complex web extending to the furthest reaches of the 'margin' in the highlands of the Mediterranean and the heaths of England. They argue that the invisible hand of Adam Smith as well as institutions of social power should displace the positive checks of Thomas Malthus as arbiters of human destiny, a destiny which invidual agency had the power to transform. In order to understand the later medieval crisis, our attention must shift to the interactions among exchange, power, and culture in all of their bewildering complexity, particularly in rural society under stress during the fourteenth century. The papers here lay the foundation for these new avenues of approach.

Bibliography

Bailey, Mark, *A Marginal Economy? East Anglian Breckland in the Later Middle Ages* (Cambridge: Cambridge University Press, 1989)

Barthélemy, Dominique, *La mutation de l'an mil a-t-elle eu lieu? Servage et chevalerie dans la France des xe et xie siècles* (Paris: Hachette, 1997)

Bautier, Robert-Henri, and Janine Sornay, *Les sources de l'histoire économique et sociale du Moyen Âge*, I: *Provence, Comtat Venaissin, Dauphiné, Savoie* (Paris: CNRS, 1968)

Beaucage, Benoît, ed., *Visites générales des commanderies de l'ordre des hospitaliers dépendantes du grand prieuré de Saint-Gilles (1338)* (Aix-en-Provence: Université de Provence, 1982)

Bois, Guy, *Crise du féodalisme* (Paris: Presses de la Fondation Nationale des Sciences Politiques, 1981)

Bourin, Monique, François Menant, Sandro Carocci, and Lluis To Figueras, 'Les campagnes de la méditerranée occidentale autour de 1300; tensions destructrices, tensions novatrices', *Annales: Histoire, Sciences Sociales*, 66 (2011), 633–704

Bourin, Monique, John Drendel, and François Menant, eds, *Les disettes dans la conjoncture de 1300 en Méditerranée occidentale: La conjoncture de 1300 en Méditerranée occidentale*, Collection de l'Ecole Française de Rome, 450 (Roma: Ecole Française de Rome, 2012)

Bourin, Monique, François Menant, and Lluis To Figueras, eds, *Echanges, prélèvements et consommation dans le monde rural: Actes des colloques de Madrid (17–19 octobre 2005 et 8–10 février 2007), La conjoncture de 1300 en Méditerranée occidentale, II* (Rome: Ecole Française de Rome, 2014)

Brenner, Robert, *The Brenner Debate: Agrarian Class Structure and Economic Development in Pre-Industrial Europe* ed. by Trevor Aston and others (Cambridge: Cambridge University Press, 1985)

Britnell, Richard, *Britain and Ireland 1050–1530: Economy and Society* (Oxford: Oxford University Press, 2004)

——, *The Commercialisation of English Society* (Cambridge: Cambridge University Press, 1993)

——, 'Specialization of Work in England, 1100–1300', *Economic History Review*, 54 (2001), 1–16

Campbell, Bruce M. S., 'The Agrarian Problem of the Early Fourteenth Century', *Past and Present*, 188 (2005), 3–70

Coulet, Noël, *Aix en Provence: Espace et relations d'une capitale (milieu xive – milieu xve s.)* (Aix-en-Provence: Université de Provence, 1988)

Devroey, Jean-Pierre, *Économie rurale et société dans l'Europe Franque (vi^e–ixe siècles)* (Paris: Histoire Belin Sup, 2003)

Duby, Georges, *L'économie rurale et la vie des campagnes dans l'Occident Médiéval (France, Angleterre, Empire, ixe–xve siècles): Essai de synthèse et perspectives de recherches*, 2 vols (Paris: Aubier, 1962)

——, *L'histoire continue* (Paris: Odile Jacob, 1991)

——, 'Note sur les corvées dans les Alpes du sud en 1338', in *Études d'histoire du droit privé offertes à Pierre Petot* (Paris: Montchrestien, 1959), pp. 141–46

——, 'Recherches récentes sur la vie rurale en Provence au XIVe siècle', *Provence Historique*, 15 (1965), 97–111

——, *Rural Economy and Country Life in the Medieval West*, trans. by Cynthia Postan (Columbia: University of South Carolina Press, 1968

——, 'La seigneurie et l'économie paysanne, Alpes du Sud, 1338', *Etudes Rurales*, 2 (1961), 5–36

——, 'Techniques et rendements agricoles dans les Alpes du sid en 1338', *Annales du Midi*, 70 (1958), 403–13

Dyer, Christopher, and Phillip Schofield, 'Recent Work on the Agrarian History of Medieval Britain', in *The Rural History of Medieval European Societies: Trends and Perspectives*, ed. by Isabel Alfonso, The Medieval Countryside, 1 (Brepols: Turnhout, 2007), pp. 29–47

Hatcher, John, and Mark Bailey, eds, *Modelling the Middle Ages: The History and Theory of England's Economic Development* (Oxford: Oxford University Press, 2001)

Harvey, Barbara, 'Introduction: The "Crisis" of the Early Fourteenth Century', in *Before the Black Death: Studies in the 'Crisis' of the Early Fourteenth Century*, ed. by Bruce M. S. Campbell (Manchester: Manchester University Press, 1991), pp. 1–24

——, 'The Population Trend in England Between 1300 and 1348', *Transactions of the Royal Historical Society*, 5th ser., 16 (1966), 23–42

Hébert, Michel, *Tarascon au XIVe siècle* (Aix-en-Provence: Edisud, 1977)

Helas, Jean-Claude, 'Le vocabulaire de Georges Duby dans *L'économie rurale et la vie des campagnes dans l'Occident médiéval*', in *Les territoires du médiéviste*, ed. by Benoît Cursente and Mireille Mousnier (Rennes: Presses Universitaires de Rennes, 2005), pp. 45–70

Langdon, John, *Horses, Oxen and Technological Innovation: The Use of Draught Animals in English Farming from 1066 to 1500* (Cambridge: Cambridge University Press, 1986)

Lopez, Robert, *The Commercial Revolution of the Middle Ages, 950–1350* (Englewood Cliffs: Prentice-Hall, 1971)

Lopez, Robert, and Harry Miskimin, 'The Economic Depression of the Renaissance', *Economist History Review*, 14 (1962), 408–26

Masschaele, James, *Peasants, Merchants and Markets: Inland Trade in Medieval England, 1150–1350* (New York: St Martin's Press, 1997)

Minovez, Jean-Michel, and others, eds, *Les industries rurales dans l'Europe médiévale et moderne: actes des 33e Journées Internationales d'Histoire de Flaran, 7–8 Octobre 2011* (Toulouse: Presses universitaires du Mirail, 2013)

Miskimin, Harry, *The Economy of Early Renaissance Europe, 1300–1460* (Englewood Cliffs: Prentice-Hall, 1969)

Perroy, Édouard, 'A l'origine d'une économie contractée: les crises du XIVe siècle', *Annales: Économies, Sociétés, Civilisations*, 4 (1949), 167–82

Poppe, Danuta, *Economie et société d'un bourg provençal au XIVe siècle: Reillanne en haute Provence*, trans. by Danuta Poppe and others (Wrocław: Académie Polonaise des Sciences, Institut d'histoire de la culture matérielle, 1980)

Shatzmiller, Joseph, *Recherches sur la communauté juive de Manosque au Moyen Âge, 1241–1329* (Paris: Mouton, 1973)

Stouff, Louis, *Arles à la fin du Moyen Âge* (Aix-en-Provence: Université de Provence, 1986)

Wolff, Philippe, *Commerce et marchands de Toulouse (vers 1350 – vers 1450)* (Paris: Plon, 1954)

Zerner, Monique, *Le cadastre, le pouvoir et la terre: Le Comtat Venaissin pontifical au début du XVe siècle*, Collection de l'École Française de Rome, 174 (Roma: École Française de Rome, 1993)

Commercialization, Stagnation, and Crisis, 1250–1350

Richard Britnell

Over the last fifty years the medieval economy has been one of the liveliest areas in English history, despite the relatively small number of specialists engaged in the subject. The spectrum of ideas, and the sheer volume of evidence, is much greater than it was in 1963, when I began to study the rural economy and society of the thirteenth century as a member of Michael Postan's undergraduate Special Subject class in Cambridge. At that time Postan in England and Georges Duby in France both had considerable (though not uncontested) influence, and although they differed in detail there was considerable overlap in their analysis of change. Postan strongly recommended to his students Duby's synthesis, *L'économie rurale* (1962), which was later translated by his wife, Cynthia Postan, into English.[1] This paper aims to assess how the hypotheses of Postan and Duby, but especially the former, have been affected since the 1960s by research on England before the Black Death, concentrating on the implications of the so-called commercialization model or models.

The ideas of Postan and Duby were firmly founded in empirical observation. Neither historian was primarily a theorist; both had a clear sense of the importance of statistical evidence for their arguments. Duby's work on the society and the economy of the Macon region is a masterpiece of close analysis of historical evidence, and the arguments of *L'économie rurale* are buttressed with a rich collection of textual, cartographic, and statistical support. Postan's own researches

[1] Duby, *L'économie rurale*; Duby, *Rural Economy*, trans. by Postan.

Richard Britnell (1944–2013) was emeritus professor of history at the University of Durham, where he taught from 1966.

Crisis in the Later Middle Ages: Beyond the Postan-Duby Paradigm, ed. by John Drendel, TMC 13 (Turnhout: Brepols, 2015) 15–34 BREPOLS PUBLISHERS 10.1484/M.TMC.5.103782

in this area did not produce a substantial monograph, but he was able to rely on the prolonged empirical research of others. A principal source of inspiration was the work of Sir William Beveridge, whose compilation of statistics relating to prices, wages, and crop yields, notably from the Winchester pipe rolls, was one of the most solid foundations on which Postan's ideas were founded.[2] By the 1960s there were other major studies of medieval England, firmly based on documentary evidence, which directly contributed to the formulation of his model. The most significant were perhaps Edward Miller's study of the estates of Ely Cathedral,[3] Ambrose Raftis's study of the Ramsey Abbey estates,[4] Herbert Hallam's work on the Lincolnshire fenlands,[5] and Jan Titow's doctoral thesis on the Winchester bishopric estates.[6] Postan drew valued support for his ideas concerning the state of the peasantry from Eugene Kosminsky's statistical findings from the Hundred Rolls.[7] He also had a rich background in the writings of Russian, French, and German economic historians.

Postan's hypotheses about the thirteenth century were founded upon an impressive array of data. He was able to claim substantial support for his most important conclusions, though this was inevitably in the hazardous form of local evidence from particular estates rather than aggregated national statistics. The relevant factual evidence can be subsumed into eleven main propositions, which were also accepted by Duby.[8] (1) Population rose during the thirteenth century.[9] (2) Agriculture became more commercialized on many estates and market demand for cereals grew.[10] (3) Between about 1080 and 1250 there was extensive clearance of woodland, as well as drainage of coastal marshes

[2] Beveridge, 'The Yield and Price of Corn'; Beveridge, 'Wages in the Winchester Manors'; Britnell, 'The Winchester Pipe Rolls'.

[3] Miller, *The Abbey and Bishopric of Ely*.

[4] Raftis, *The Estates of Ramsey Abbey*.

[5] Hallam, *The New Lands of Elloe*; Hallam, 'Population Density'.

[6] Titow, *Land and Population*; Titow, 'Some Differences between Manors'; Titow, 'Some Evidence of the Thirteenth-Century Population Increase'; Postan and Titow, 'Heriots and Prices'.

[7] Kosminsky, *Studies in the Agrarian History*.

[8] For further reference to these eleven propositions, see Britnell, 'Agriculture, Marketing and Rural Change', pp. 108–09.

[9] Postan, 'Medieval Agrarian Society', p. 563; Postan, *The Medieval Economy and Society*, pp. 27, 31; Duby, *Rural Economy*, trans. by Postan, pp. 119–20.

[10] Postan, 'Medieval Agrarian Society', pp. 581–84; Postan, *The Medieval Economy and Society*, pp. 99–101, 104; Duby, *Rural Economy*, trans. by Postan, chap. 4.

and inland marshes, with the object of increasing agricultural output. This was followed by a slowing down of such activity in the later thirteenth century because most of the land available for clearance or drainage was peripheral to main areas of settlement and often of inferior quality.[11] (4) Livestock densities were too low to provide adequate manure for the extended arable husbandry of the later thirteenth century.[12] (5) Arable acreages on some large estates, such as those of the bishopric of Winchester and Ramsey Abbey, began to contract well before the Black Death.[13] (6) Grain yields on the Winchester bishopric demesnes and elsewhere were declining in the later thirteenth century.[14] (7) About 45 per cent of recorded rural tenancies were too small to provide a family with subsistence, which implies, taking urban populations into account, that well over half the population was not self-sufficient for the provision of basic necessities.[15] (8) Around 1300 population peaked at a level appreciably higher than that of earlier centuries.[16] (9) Land hunger in the late thirteenth century is attested by high prices for land, increasing labour services, rising seigneurial exactions from customary tenures, and the ease with which landlords were able to find tenants.[17] (10) Prices during the thirteenth century were more volatile than wages and rising faster.[18] (11) Food supply was precarious at the height of the medieval peak of population, death rates rose, and the famine of 1315–18 was the most severe of the thirteenth and fourteenth centuries.[19] Together these

[11] Postan, 'Medieval Agrarian Society', pp. 549–52, 559; Postan, *The Medieval Economy and Society*, pp. 18–23; Duby, *Rural Economy*, trans. by Postan, pp. 67–75, 86–87.

[12] Postan, 'Medieval Agrarian Society', pp. 554–56; Postan, *The Medieval Economy and Society*, pp. 57–59; Duby, *Rural Economy*, trans. by Postan, p. 104.

[13] Postan, 'Medieval Agrarian Society', p. 559; Postan, *The Medieval Economy and Society*, p. 105; Duby, *Rural Economy*, trans. by Postan, p. 261.

[14] Postan, 'Medieval Agrarian Society', pp. 557–58; Postan, *The Medieval Economy and Society*, pp. 23–25, 61–64; Duby, *Rural Economy*, trans. by Postan, p. 101.

[15] Postan, 'Medieval Agrarian Society', pp. 612, 619, 622–24; Postan, *The Medieval Economy and Society*, pp. 130, 132–34; Duby, *Rural Economy*, trans. by Postan, pp. 123–24.

[16] Postan, 'Medieval Agrarian Society', pp. 561–62; Postan, *The Medieval Economy and Society*, pp. 32–33; Duby, *Rural Economy*, trans. by Postan, p. 124.

[17] Postan, 'Medieval Agrarian Society', pp. 552–54; Postan, *The Medieval Economy and Society*, pp. 33, 150–51; Duby, *Rural Economy*, trans. by Postan, pp. 239–42, 251–52, 257–58.

[18] Postan, 'Medieval Agrarian Society', pp. 566–67; Postan, *The Medieval Economy and Society*, pp. 36, 230–43; Duby, *Rural Economy*, trans. by Postan, pp. 123, 263–64.

[19] Postan, 'Medieval Agrarian Society', pp. 564–65; Postan, *The Medieval Economy and Society*, pp. 33–34; Duby, *Rural Economy*, trans. by Postan, pp. 123–24.

findings suggested that during the later thirteenth century the possibilities for further investment in agriculture were running out, that population was growing at the expense of per capita resource levels and welfare standards, and that this helps to explain the famines of the early fourteenth century.

Some of the relevant observations have gained further support from research conducted since 1963. Though queried by Anthony Bridbury, who would transpose Postan's Malthusian crisis back to the eleventh century,[20] the first proposition, that population was rising during the thirteenth century, is hardly controversial; a recent analysis makes it a principal feature of the century to be explained.[21] The growing commercialization of agriculture is similarly uncontroversial, having been a leading topic of research for several decades.[22] The third proposition, including the chronology of forest clearance and drainage adopted by Postan, has been supported by a number of local studies.[23] It is generally accepted that by 1300 the arable resources of England were stretched to a point where further extensive growth was difficult to achieve.[24] There is little to shake the seventh proposition above, that during the thirteenth century a growing number of peasant holdings were too small to provide an adequate livelihood.[25] The eighth proposition is similarly secure. Remarkably high local populations by both earlier and later standards have been documented in numerous studies, particularly in East Anglia and Essex.[26] Indeed, it is still an open question whether the total English population in 1300 was higher than at any later point before the eighteenth century.[27] The ninth proposition, relating to land hunger, remains a normal element in descriptions of the later thirteenth and earlier fourteenth centuries, despite challenges to Postan's

[20] Bridbury, *The English Economy*, p. 124; Bridbury, *Medieval England*, pp. 107, 170.

[21] Langdon and Masschaele, 'Commercial Activity and Population Growth'. See also Campbell, *English Seigniorial Agriculture*, pp. 406–10.

[22] Britnell, *The Commercialisation of English Society*, 2nd edn, esp. pp. 115–23; Campbell, 'Measuring the Commercialisation'.

[23] King, *Peterborough Abbey, 1086–1310*, pp. 81–84; Raftis, *Assart Data and Land Values*.

[24] Campbell, *English Seigniorial Agriculture*, pp. 386–90.

[25] E.g. Bailey, *Medieval Suffolk*, pp. 43, 55, 58–64; Campbell, 'The Agrarian Problem', pp. 50–60; Kitsikopoulos, 'Standards of Living'; Schofield, *Peasant and Community*, pp. 24–25.

[26] Campbell, 'Population Pressure, Inheritance', p. 92; Poos, *A Rural Society after the Black Death*, pp. 33–34; Smith, 'Human Resources', p. 198.

[27] Smith, 'Demographic Developments', pp. 47–50; Smith, 'Plagues and Peoples', pp. 179–81. For an estimated English population of 5.5 million in 1300, using Campbell's estimation procedure, see Stone, 'The Consumption of Field Crops', pp. 19–21.

interpretation of rising rents and entry fines. Postan used rising seigneurial exactions as prima facie economic evidence of the rising demand for land and would have considered the fact that land hunger can be better demonstrated in other ways as all to the good. Evidence that the customary element in peasant land tenure protected tenants and prevented the returns to landlords from rising as high as market values is damaging to Marxist analysis rather than to the population-resources model, which can accommodate it.[28] Falling real wages, and a weakening of the bargaining power of wage earners in the late thirteenth century, as in the tenth proposition, are established by David Farmer's statistical research,[29] as well as by some estate studies.[30] Even if trends in real wages are not a true indication of family earnings, they imply diminishing returns to labour.[31] Occupational specialization outside agriculture can hardly have been a major source of productivity growth in an economy where so much employment was seasonal or casual.[32] Until these observations are better explained by reference to some alternative hypotheses, a problematic relationship between population, resources, and investment will need to be built into any satisfactory interpretation of the thirteenth-century economy.

One of the chief areas of uncertainty over the years has been the absolute size of England's population at its peak, but this debate is barely helpful for resolving the problems at issue. No figure was ever central to Postan's arguments about the English economy. He supposed the population around 1300 was understated by Josiah Cox Russell's estimate, chiefly because he thought Russell had underestimated the population in 1377. Lecturing on the subject in 1963 he was prepared to allow a population of 4.5 million at the time of the poll taxes of 1377–81, to which he would have added at least 30 per cent to allow for the affects of the Black Death, together with other allowances for population losses before 1348 as well as possible additional losses between 1349 and 1377. This implies a population of possibly over 6.0 million at the start of the century. However, Postan emphatically rejected the idea either that a figure for total population could be reliably established or that it was a nec-

[28] E.g. Campbell, 'The Agrarian Problem', pp. 60–70; Dyer, *Making a Living in the Middle Ages*, pp. 182–83.

[29] Farmer, 'Prices and Wages [1000–1355]', pp. 772–78.

[30] Page, 'Challenging Custom'; Rush, 'The Impact of Commercialization'. See also Campbell, 'The Agrarian Problem', p. 65; Campbell, 'The Land', pp. 216–17.

[31] Langdon and Masschaele, 'Commercial Activity and Population Growth', pp. 71–72.

[32] Britnell, 'Specialization of Work in England'.

essary element in his argument. What was important was the changing relationship between population and resources of land and knowledge. He ought to be taken at his word on this issue.[33] Since 1963 estimates of population in 1300 have gone in all directions, some even higher than 6.0 million, some very much lower, and there is currently little prospect of agreement.[34] This ongoing debate about absolute population size matters in the context of some statistical ventures, such as estimating the level of urbanization.[35] It is nevertheless unrewarding as a criticism of Postan's ideas. Estimates of total English population that build in assumptions about the relationship between population and resources are of tangential importance, since any argument to the effect that the kingdom's arable resources were cultivated to about their limit around 1300 is an argument in Postan's favour, regardless of the implied size of population.

However, some of Postan's core propositions, notably those listed above as the fourth, fifth, sixth, and eleventh, have been effectively challenged by more recent research. The notion that soils might be impoverished by failure to replace necessary nutrients has received support from the evidence of Cuxham (Oxfordshire), but the implied cause is not that of Postan's fourth proposition, as listed above.[36] Analysis of a wider range of manorial evidence has weakened the case for supposing that the productivity of arable farming on manorial demesnes was compromised by falling numbers of animals, partly because 'the net effect of the changes taking place within the pastoral sector over the period 1250–1349 was to maintain livestock numbers in a state of dynamic equilibrium'.[37] Postan overestimated the number of animals required by good practice and oversimplified the relationship between investment in herds and investment in arable farming.[38] It is doubtful whether the livestock ratio in peasant farming was as inadequate for productivity as Postan's arguments imply.[39] The fifth proposition (declining arable acreage on some demesnes) is strictly

[33] The arguments he used then were subsequently published in almost identical form in Postan, *The Medieval Economy and Society*, pp. 29–31. See, too, the comments in Postan, 'Medieval Agrarian Society', pp. 561–63.

[34] For the range, see Campbell, *English Seigniorial Agriculture*, pp. 402–04.

[35] Britnell, 'Commercialisation and Economic Development', pp. 11–12.

[36] Newman and Harvey, 'Did Soil Fertility Decline?'.

[37] Campbell, *English Seigniorial Agriculture*, pp. 173–75.

[38] Biddick, *The Other Economy*, pp. 2–4, 130; Campbell, 'Agricultural Progress', pp. 29–31; Campbell, *English Seigniorial Agriculture*, pp. 173, 176.

[39] Bailey, *A Marginal Economy?*, pp. 93–94; Hare, *A Prospering Society*, pp. 57–58.

correct, but contracting arable husbandry was far from universal before 1315.[40] In addition, the implications that might be drawn from it to support Postan's notion that soils were becoming impoverished can be contested on numerous grounds. Even Raftis's account of declining sown acreages on Ramsey estates attributed them to the superior profitability of pasture farming rather than to falling productivity in cereals cultivation.[41] Despite numerous isolated references to *terra debilis* in our sources, the available evidence is not sufficient to support the idea that the quality of the soil was deteriorating generally. The sixth, closely related, proposition (declining crop yields) was important to Postan because it formed the best support for his hypothesis of declining agricultural productivity. He attributed this partly to the ploughing up of poorer soils, partly to the deterioration in the ratio of pasture to arable husbandry, but partly also to a deterioration of soils through overcropping.[42] However, there are serious objections to using changes in yield ratios as evidence of declining overall agrarian productivity. Bruce Campbell has emphasized the limited value of crop-yield ratios in this respect. Even for measuring crop yields, he prefers to employ weighted aggregate grain yields per seed, rather than separate yields for different cereals, which obstruct comparisons between different demesnes and obscure the overall analysis of change.[43] Campbell has also shown that declining arable productivity cannot be regarded as a universal feature of thirteenth-century agriculture; between 1250 and 1350 they are calculated to have risen on the documented demesnes of Norfolk.[44] The eleventh of the propositions is currently arguable but unproven, even though the fact that repeated famines caused crisis mortality is not in question.[45] Though we might expect the number of those vulnerable to dearth and famine to be raised through increasing market dependency, as implied by the second, seventh, and tenth propositions, and though this might result in an upward trend in mortality rates as argued by Postan, it remains an open question whether this was in fact the case.[46]

[40] Campbell, *English Seigniorial Agriculture*, pp. 232–34.

[41] Raftis, *The Estates of Ramsey Abbey*, pp. 161–63.

[42] Postan, *The Medieval Economy and Society*, pp. 58–64.

[43] Campbell, *English Seigniorial Agriculture*, p. 322.

[44] Campbell, 'Land, Labour, Livestock', pp. 161–64; Campbell and Overton, 'A New Perspective on Medieval and Early Modern Agriculture', pp. 70, 74. There is a brief general overview and literature survey in Jordan, *The Great Famine*, pp. 25–31.

[45] E.g. Bailey, 'Peasant Welfare in England', pp. 238–41.

[46] Smith, 'Demographic Developments', pp. 52–61.

The Postan Model as a Case of Overreaching and Oversimplification

One of the recurrent lines of criticism of Postan's ideas is that his generalizations are overextended both in time and space. His attempt to explain declining population in the fourteenth century by postulating a permanent decline in the fertility of the soil is, on current evidence, the weakest part of the population-resources model.[47] In effect the model will only explain a cessation or deceleration of growth in particular regions during the later thirteenth century. The extension of the concept of falling agricultural productivity to account for fourteenth- and fifteenth-century agrarian contraction was overambitious and is itself questionable. The abandonment of this idea has serious implications for the wider relevance of Postan's model. If there was no significant undermining of the quality of the soil in the thirteenth century, there is no explanation within this model for a long-term decline in population, or for the economic problems of the fourteenth and fifteenth centuries. Even Postan's keenest supporters would probably acknowledge that this sacrifice is one that has to be made. The model is overplayed in trying to account for so much history at once.

Postan also overextended the applicability of his model in space. If the principal constraint on economic growth were the balance between population and land, it is very remarkable that the same chronology of growth and contraction is characteristic of so much of western Europe. To what extent do the explanations that Postan derives from southern English evidence fit the evidence for other places with a similar course of development? The circumstances of Ireland, for example, were very different, since the possibilities of arable expansion there were greater than in England between the Anglo-Norman conquests of 1169–72 and the later thirteenth century. The pattern of Irish settlement was very unlike that of southern England, since units of peasant farming were characteristically larger and less constrained by communal traditions. Population densities were lighter. Yet the chronology of change was much the same as in southern England. Agricultural output reached a peak in the late thirteenth century and then contracted dramatically during the fourteenth.[48] It takes some credulity to suppose that balance between population and resources in Ireland and in England just happened to reach a critical relationship at the same time. Explanations other than the population-resource balance are needed to explain

[47] I have adopted this as a descriptive term for Postan's basic model of economic development in preference to 'Malthusian' or 'Neo-Malthusian'. For further analysis, see Hatcher and Bailey, *Modelling the Middle Ages*, pp. 21–65.

[48] Down, 'Colonial Society and Economy', p. 472.

the Irish case — notably warfare and the fall off in external demand. Recent studies of northern England similarly demonstrate clearly that the population-resource balance was not everywhere the same. In County Durham in 1300, there was more available uncultivated land than Postan's model implies, but growth there was interrupted in the second decade of the fourteenth century by famines and Scottish incursions.[49] Either we need to emphasize local conditions other than population and resources (such as weather, warfare, and disease) as the primary cause of arrested development, or we need to postulate some interdependence between Ireland, northern England, and Scotland, so that a change in one would induce changes in the others.

John Munro's argument that the downturn of European economies in the early fourteenth century was precipitated by war cuts across these deficiencies in Postan's argument, striking it at a point where it was always least defensible.[50] It both supplies an argument for commercial contraction in the fourteenth century and accounts for problems of the early fourteenth century in regions like northern England where population pressure was probably not a problem.[51] It may be interpreted to imply that only an international commercial crisis, or an international ecological disaster, can generate a universal agrarian crisis. A universal population crisis brought about along the lines of the population-resources model is inherently improbable. In some cases it is easy enough to show that the effects of war were locally destructive of the basis for local subsistence farming, as in northern England after 1314,[52] but more significantly the impact of warfare was transmitted through its effects upon cities and their trade. The weakening of urban economies through rising transaction costs and lower profits directly affected their demand for raw materials and foodstuffs. This argument will again help to explain why regions as diverse as Ireland, northern England, Flanders, the Paris region, and Tuscany went through the same sort of crisis at the same time. A weaker version relating to urban demand, that urban economies were undermined by environmental problems deriving from overcrowding, pollution, and disease,[53] remains underdeveloped and intrinsically less likely to support a model with international relevance. Most

[49] Dunsford and Harris, 'Colonisation of the Wasteland'; Dodds, *Peasants and Production*, pp. 45–70.

[50] Munro, 'Industrial Transformation', pp. 120–30.

[51] Dodds, *Peasants and Production*, pp. 36–37, 43–44, 70.

[52] Kershaw, *Bolton Priory*, pp. 14–17, 123–24.

[53] Grantham, 'Espaces privilégés', pp. 723–34.

medieval towns were no more than overgrown villages, and it is difficult to accept that they were generally suffering from problems that were not magnified many times in the larger towns of the sixteenth and seventeenth centuries. These arguments are nevertheless more than minor qualifications to Postan's interpretation. They imply that the motor force of his model as a source of fourteenth-century contraction is wrongly conceived. Checks on the demand side take over from checks on the supply side.

Besides the effective criticism that Postan's hypotheses were excessively ambitious in what they attempted to explain, a second line of attack has been to challenge the low significance he attributed to commerce, investment, and innovation and to query his emphasis on the agrarian sector as the only one relevant to dynamic analysis. Neither Postan nor Duby was oblivious of the growth of trade or commercial motivation; both wrote knowledgeably about towns, money, and markets, and their awareness is implicit in the second proposition listed earlier. Indeed, there is very little factual information at our disposal on this subject that would have surprised either historian forty years ago. Duby's caution is particularly interesting in this respect, because of the greater dynamic importance he was willing to concede to commercial development and its penetration into the countryside.[54] Recent changes in thinking about the role of commerce result more from shifts of emphasis than from the growth of factual knowledge, impressive though that has been. Nevertheless those shifts have major implications for our evaluation of twelfth- and thirteenth-century economic development. Postan did not recognize commercial growth either as a cause of growing population or as a significant source of new employment. As he saw it, the urban and commercial sector of the economy was an epiphenomenon to the central dynamic of development. He did not even deny the reality of technical progress in the medieval period, regarding it merely as severely limited by the poverty of scientific knowledge and quantitatively inadequate to maintain economic growth of a modern character.[55] In this he was arguably right, but it is not difficult to show that in developing his argument he tended to overstate the stagnant character of the thirteenth-century English economy, particularly by underestimating the long-term significance of some forms of institutional innovation. It is noteworthy, in this context, that in planning his sixteen Special Subject classes for the Michaelmas term of 1963, he left the commercial aspects of medieval agriculture to the fourteenth, the effects of

[54] Duby, *Rural Economy*, trans. by Postan, chap. 4.

[55] Postan, 'Why Was Science Backward?'.

commercialization on peasant production to the fifteenth, and town-country relations to the very last.[56] Unlike several modern analyses, most recently that of James Masschaele,[57] Postan's study considered urban demand for agrarian produce as a secondary stimulus to agrarian expansion during the twelfth and thirteenth centuries.

The counterargument owed much of its initial theoretical stimulus to Ester Boserup, who in 1965 argued that in some circumstances population growth could have beneficial implications for productivity growth.[58] The idea that excessive growth of the labour supply necessarily caused diminishing returns and falling average productivity throughout the period that population was growing has been challenged by examples of technical and institutional adaptation during the twelfth and thirteenth centuries, implying that this was a dynamic society with practical and intellectual resources able to respond to changing opportunities. Bruce Campbell, Christopher Thornton, and others have demonstrated the responsiveness of demesne agriculture all over the country to the possibilities of specialization and improved productivity.[59] Mark Bailey has illustrated the capacity of a poor-soil region to respond creatively to market opportunity and argued that Postan's concept of 'marginal soils' as a determinant of productivity possibilities is misleading.[60] David Stone has demonstrated the responsiveness of the managers of medieval demesnes to price signals in choosing what to produce and how to produce it.[61] John Langdon has demonstrated widespread technical progress in the ancillary technologies of haulage and milling.[62] The factual support for arguments along these lines is often based on extensive and nationwide data sets, so the evidence admits of little argument as to the reality of the changes in question. The extent to which they subvert or merely modify the population-resources model hinges on the

[56] Similarly, Postan, *The Medieval Economy and Society* has thirteen chapters, of which trade, markets, towns, and prices occupy the last three.

[57] Masschaele, *Peasants, Merchants and Markets*.

[58] Boserup, *The Conditions of Agricultural Growth*.

[59] Campbell, 'Land, Labour, Livestock', pp. 144–78; Thornton, 'The Determinants of Land Productivity'.

[60] Bailey, 'The Concept of the Margin'; Bailey, *A Marginal Economy?*, esp. pp. 1–24, 191–99, 319–22.

[61] Stone, 'The Productivity of Hired and Customary Labour'; Stone, 'Medieval Farm Management'; Stone, *Decision-Making in Medieval Agriculture*.

[62] Langdon, *Horses, Oxen and Technological Innovation*, pp. 254–55; Langdon, *Mills in the Medieval Economy*. But see too Langdon, 'Was England a Technological Backwater?'.

extent to which they affect Postan's argument that thirteenth-century population growth became increasingly precarious and unsustainable.

A related, perhaps more fundamental, criticism of the population-resources model, as applied to the period after 1250, is that it uses population growth not only as the primary determinant of welfare but also as an independent variable. If all that is at stake here were the need for some alternative feedback model, in which the growth of population and expansion of agrarian opportunities are jointly determined, then little harm would be done to Postan's hypotheses. Nor would the model be seriously jeopardized by a spiral version in which population and output in turn triggered growth in the other: $O^1 \rightarrow P^2 \rightarrow O^2 \rightarrow P^3 \rightarrow O^3$, and so on.[63] In such a model, the availability of agricultural land would determine a limit on population growth just as much as if population was growing entirely autonomously. If, however, enterprise and investment in the thirteenth century was independently determined by the availability of new commercial opportunities, the discovery of new resources, or the invention of new techniques, then it could have an autonomous role in stimulating employment and population growth. The study by Langdon and Masschaele of the long wave of development from the late twelfth century to the early fourteenth century strongly indicates just such an autonomous foundation for the growth of investment up to the mid-thirteenth century and its decline afterwards.[64] The extent to which this attractive analytical development replaces or merely complements the population-resources model depends upon how far the impact of the investment cycle in question on employment and population growth can take over from the questions raised by Postan concerning the availability of resources.

What Remains?

If Postan's model survives, it can only be with numerous adjustments to accommodate the various criticisms that have been made. The first necessity, since the relevance of the population-resources model to late medieval agrarian contraction is barely tenable, will be to substitute alternative models, driven by exogenous shocks, for the problems of the fourteenth and fifteenth centuries. The second necessity will be sharper awareness of regional variations in population densities and agrarian conditions and of the commercial relationships between

63 Langdon and Masschaele, 'Commercial Activity and Population Growth', pp. 41–42.

64 Langdon and Masschaele, 'Commercial Activity and Population Growth'.

different parts of Europe. The application of the Postan model to the whole of Britain or Europe results in implausible generalization about conditions outside the core areas of agrarian development. A third necessity is more sensitive awareness of the creative aspects of the medieval economy and of the ability of people to respond to the growth of population and trade. In particular, any viable model needs to assess the causal importance of commerce, investment, and innovation in making population growth possible. Quite apart from any short-term relevance, this perspective is needed for any assessment of the significance of thirteenth-century development in historical perspective.

Yet, even given the need for all these modifications, the extent to which they overthrow Postan's arguments is problematic. As we have seen, criticism of the population-resources model leaves intact much of the evidence used to construct it. Although four of the principle observations on which Postan's model was constructed have been challenged, many of the key data that he used to explain or predict declining possibilities for growth in the later thirteenth century remain valid, at least with respect to southern England, and they are sufficient to support a modified version of the overall model. Arguably the main importance of investment and innovation was to make it possible for population to grow at all, and so remove the most serious flaws in Postan's work, notably the absence of an explanation for population growth and the absence of any adequate account of how the poor could subsist. To that extent they would leave Postan's hypotheses modified rather than overthrown, unless the possibility of technical progress was sufficiently widespread to permit sustained and sustainable increases in aggregate output through the early fourteenth century. There is a valid pessimistic interpretation of thirteenth-century development that has nothing to do with the impact of taxation and war or the failure of investment opportunities.

Any valid reconstruction of what remains of Postan's argument has to be built around the proposition that the agrarian economy of England, as elsewhere in western Europe, was approaching some limit to growth around 1300, at least in core areas; without that there is nothing left of the hypothesis worth preserving. Opinions are bound to differ about whether it is worthwhile to persist with the concept of a ceiling to development of the sort Postan envisaged. To sustain this idea would now require a more elaborate concept of the barriers to growth than the original model offered, since the literature about commercialization has made serious dents in any argument to be derived from the supposition that there were absolute limits. A sceptic might argue that, for all we know, the medieval economy would have launched gradually into early capitalism and modern economic growth in the fourteenth century had it not been for the external shocks of war and plague. Maybe the notion of a ceiling to development around 1300 is a hypothesis too many, and it would be better for historians to proceed without it.

Yet there are surely legitimate doubts about the capacity of thirteenth-century institutions to change sufficiently to permit sustained growth, in the absence of new agricultural land, based on technical change and institutional reform, except over a very long period.[65] Minimal institutional adaptation to commercial opportunities is to be found in thirteenth-century English agrarian institutions, even under the pressure of high prices and land values. Peasant enterprises in Bruce Campbell's Norfolk became smaller, not larger. Manorial lords exploited serfs and insisted on the preservation of customary relationships rather than selling rural liberties. The common-field system of the midlands remained intact. Obstacles to change in the thirteenth-century economy included the smallness of most farms and the consequent small size of peasant savings and limited scope for peasant enterprise, institutional restrictions on the use of land to best advantage, the non-commercial nature of rents, a legal and cultural system in which social status was embedded in particular forms of exploitative lordship, the absence of institutions for the creation and dissemination of knowledge, and the absence of any tradition of public intervention to bring about reform. Is it credible that land reform could have sprung from new private enterprise in the context of declining investment opportunities and economic stagnation after 1300? In the event it was the catastrophes of the fourteenth and fifteenth centuries that induced the transformation of the old order of manorial lordship, not the commercial opportunities of the twelfth and thirteenth.

A more eclectic model than Postan's, benefiting from the work that has been done in recent years on commercialization, would abandon the rigidity of Malthusian theory (insofar as that implies an insuperable ceiling to pre-industrial growth) but retain a more familiar notion of emerging constraints on development, using ideas relating to long trade cycles. This follows the line proposed by Langdon and Masschaele but attributes more importance than they do to constraints upon agrarian expansion identified by Postan.

Let us suppose, with Langdon and Masschaele, that in the course of the later twelfth and earlier thirteenth centuries new production possibilities became available which were invaluable for long-term economic development. These

[65] The argument in this paragraph owes much to Bailey, 'Peasant Welfare in England', pp. 230–33; Campbell, 'The Agrarian Problem', pp. 60–70.

new developments included new knowledge (about crops, animals, and manufacturing techniques), the growth of infrastructure (such as markets, fairs, roads and bridges, educational facilities, credit instruments), and new trading patterns, such as those between Britain, Ireland, and the Continent. Population growth was at least in part stimulated by the resulting new investments and the employment opportunities they created. However, the capacity of these institutions and technologies to promote sustained growth was adversely affected in the late thirteenth and early fourteenth centuries by supply constraints (the rising costs of winning new land for cultivation, rising prices) and institutional constraints in the core economy (such as the fragmented and customary structure of land tenure, the limited diffusion of technical knowledge, the restrictiveness of urban trading institutions, and the negative and essentially extractive roles of lordship and government). At the point when agrarian economic development approached a limit, growth was further checked partly by endogenous constraints created by the waning of investment opportunities that had initiated the thirteenth-century upswing and partly by exogenous shocks deriving from government activity (war and wartime taxation), bad weather, disease, and military destruction (in the North). We could build in further elements of demographic history by supposing that the scale of warfare was encouraged by the abundance of cheap manpower and that the impact of plagues and famines was intensified by the poverty of the population and the multiplication of commercial interactions. These exogenous shocks converted the gradual retardation of growth into demographic catastrophe. This, however, created the circumstances in which some of the constraints of the thirteenth-century economy were removed, and removed more rapidly than they would have been in a stagnant economy operating about the production possibility frontier. The costs of institutional transformation were very much lower in the fifteenth and sixteenth centuries because of high mortality rates and the consequent tenurial adjustments, many of them explicable by the operation of market forces; farms became larger, livestock ratios improved, communal constraints on agriculture weakened, and the powers of lords to constrain economic activity were reduced.

When significant growth of output was resumed in the sixteenth century, with new commercial opportunities, both producers and traders benefited both from the institutions and knowledge gained during the thirteenth century and from the subsequent elimination of institutional constraints that had existed before 1300. This new upswing in the sixteenth century was not, therefore, a mere repeat of what had gone before. An interpretation along these lines preserves features of Postan's hypotheses to account for some late thirteenth-century phenomena without stretching them to explain fourteenth-century developments. It broadens the number of relevant variables in play by deploying a Ricardian model in conjunction with ideas from the alternative Marxist and commercialization models.[66] In so doing, it retains the historical reality of long-term obstacles to growth, as in Postan's model, without being committed to the impossibility of permanent gains from innovation.

[66] For the desirability of such eclecticism, see Britnell, 'Agriculture, Marketing and Rural Change', pp. 117–20.

Bibliography

Bailey, Mark, 'The Concept of the Margin in the Medieval English Economy', *Economic History Review*, 2nd ser., 42 (1989), 1–17

——, *A Marginal Economy? East Anglian Breckland in the Later Middle Ages* (Cambridge: Cambridge University Press, 1989)

——, *Medieval Suffolk: An Economic and Social History, 1200–1500* (Woodbridge: Boydell, 2007)

——, 'Peasant Welfare in England, 1290–1348', *Economic History Review*, 51 (1998), 223–51

Beveridge, William H., 'Wages in the Winchester Manors', *Economic History Review*, 7 (1936–7), 22–43

——, 'The Yield and Price of Corn in the Middle Ages', *Economic History*, 1 (1927), 155–67

Biddick, Kathleen, *The Other Economy: Pastoral Husbandry on a Medieval Estate* (Berkeley: University of California Press, 1989)

Boserup, Ester, *The Conditions of Agricultural Growth: The Economics of Agrarian Change under Population Pressure* (London: Allen and Unwin, 1965)

Bridbury, Anthony R., *The English Economy from Bede to the Reformation* (Woodbridge: Boydell, 1992)

——, *Medieval England: A Survey of Social and Economic Origins and Development* (Leicester: Troubadour, 2009)

Britnell, Richard H., 'Agriculture, Marketing and Rural Change, 1100–1500', in *A Common Agricultural Heritage? Revising French and British Rural Divergence*, ed. by John Broad, Agricultural History Review Supplement Series, 5 (Exeter: British Agricultural History Society, 2009), pp. 107–20

——, 'Commercialisation and Economic Development in England, 1000–1300', in *A Commercialising Economy: England 1086 to c. 1300*, ed. by Richard H. Britnell and Bruce M. S. Campbell (Manchester: Manchester University Press, 1995), pp. 7–26

——, *The Commercialisation of English Society, 1000–1500*, 2nd edn (Manchester: Manchester University Press, 1996)

——, 'Specialization of Work in England, 1100–1300', *Economic History Review*, 54 (2001), 1–16

——, 'The Winchester Pipe Rolls and their Historians', in *The Winchester Pipe Rolls and Medieval English Society*, ed. by Richard Britnell (Woodbridge: Boydell, 2003), pp. 1–19

Campbell, Bruce M. S., 'The Agrarian Problem of the Early Fourteenth Century', *Past and Present*, 188 (2005), 3–70

——, 'Agricultural Progress in Medieval England: Some Evidence from Norfolk', *Economic History Review*, 2nd ser., 36 (1983), 26–46

——, *English Seigniorial Agriculture, 1250–1450* (Cambridge: Cambridge University Press, 2000)

——, 'The Land', in *A Social History of England, 1200–1500*, ed. by Rosemary Horrox and W. Mark Ormrod (Cambridge: Cambridge University Press, 2006), pp. 179–237

——, 'Land, Labour, Livestock, and Productivity Trends in English Seignorial Agriculture, 1208–1450', in *Land, Labour and Livestock: Historical Studies in European

Agricultural Productivity, ed. by Bruce M. S. Campbell and Mark Overton (Manchester: Manchester University Press, 1991), pp. 144–82

——, 'Measuring the Commercialisation of Seigneurial Agriculture', in *A Commercialising Economy: England 1086 to c. 1300*, ed. by Richard H. Britnell and Bruce M. S. Campbell (Manchester: Manchester University Press, 1995), pp. 132–93

——, 'Population Pressure, Inheritance and the Land Market in a Peasant Community', in *Land, Kinship and Life-Cycle*, ed. by Richard M. Smith (Cambridge: Cambridge University Press, 1984), pp. 87–134

Campbell, Bruce M. S., and Mark Overton, 'A New Perspective on Medieval and Early Modern Agriculture: Six Centuries of Norfolk Farming, c. 1250–c. 1850', *Past and Present*, 141 (1993), 38–105

Dodds, Ben, *Peasants and Production in the Medieval North-East: The Evidence from Tithes, 1270–1536* (Woodbridge: Boydell, 2007)

Down, Kevin, 'Colonial Society and Economy in the High Middle Ages', in *A New History of Ireland*, II: *Medieval Ireland, 1169–1534*, ed. by Art Cosgrove (Oxford: Clarendon Press, 1987), pp. 439–91

Duby, Georges, *L'économie rurale et la vie des campagnes dans l'Occident Médiéval (France, Angleterre, Empire, IXe–XVe siècles): Essai de synthèse et perspectives de recherches*, 2 vols (Paris: Aubier, 1962)

——, *Rural Economy and Country Life in the Medieval West*, trans. by Cynthia Postan (Columbia: University of South Carolina Press, 1968)

Dunsford, Helen, and Simon Harris, 'Colonisation of the Wasteland in County Durham, 1100–1400', *Economic History Review*, 56 (2003), 34–56

Dyer, Christopher, *Making a Living in the Middle Ages: The People of Britain, 850–1520* (New Haven: Hambledon, 2002)

Farmer, David L., 'Prices and Wages [1000–1355]', in *The Agrarian History of England and Wales*, II: *1042–1350*, ed. by Herbert E. Hallam (Cambridge: Cambridge University Press, 1988), pp. 716–817

Grantham, George W., 'Espaces privilégés: Productivité agraire et zones d'approvisionnement des villes dans l'Europe préindustrielle', *Annales*, 52 (1997), 695–725

Hallam, Herbert E., *The New Lands of Elloe: A Study of Early Reclamation in Lincolnshire* (Leicester: Leicester University Press, 1954)

——, 'Population Density in Medieval Fenland', *Economic History Review*, 2nd ser., 14 (1961), 71–81

Hare, John, *A Prospering Society: Wiltshire in the Later Middle Ages*, Studies in Regional and Local History, 10 (Hatfield: University of Hertfordshire Press, 2011)

Hatcher, John, and Mark Bailey, eds, *Modelling the Middle Ages: The History and Theory of England's Economic Development* (Oxford: Oxford University Press, 2001)

Jordan, William Chester, *The Great Famine: Northern Europe in the Early Fourteenth Century* (Princeton: Princeton University Press, 1996)

Kershaw, Ian, *Bolton Priory: The Economy of a Northern Monastery, 1286–1325* (London: Oxford University Press, 1973)

King, Edmund, *Peterborough Abbey, 1086–1310: A Study in the Land Market* (Cambridge: Cambridge University Press, 1973)

Kitsikopoulos, Harry, 'Standards of Living and Capital Formation in Pre-Plague England: A Peasant Budget Model', *Economic History Review*, 53 (2000), 237–61

Kosminsky, Evgeny A., *Studies in the Agrarian History of England in the Thirteenth Century*, ed. by Rodney H. Hilton, trans. by Ruth Kisch (Oxford: Blackwell, 1956)

Langdon, John, *Horses, Oxen and Technological Innovation: The Use of Draught Animals in English Farming from 1066 to 1500* (Cambridge: Cambridge University Press, 1986)

——, *Mills in the Medieval Economy: England, 1300–1540* (Oxford: Oxford University Press, 2004)

——, 'Was England a Technological Backwater in the Middle Ages?', in *Medieval Farming and Technology: The Impact of Agricultural Change in Northwest Europe*, ed. by Grenville Astill and John Langdon (Leiden: Brill, 1997), pp. 275–91

Langdon, John, and James Masschaele, 'Commercial Activity and Population Growth in Medieval England', *Past and Present*, 190 (2006), 35–81

Masschaele, James, *Peasants, Merchants and Markets: Inland Trade in Medieval England, 1150–1350* (New York: St Martin's Press, 1997)

Miller, Edward, *The Abbey and Bishopric of Ely: A Social History of an Ecclesiastical Estate from the Tenth Century to the Early Fourteenth Century* (Cambridge: Cambridge University Press, 1951)

Munro, John H., 'Industrial Transformation in the North-West European Textile Trades, *c.* 1290 – *c.* 1340: Economic Progress or Economic Crisis', in *Before the Black Death: Studies in the 'Crisis' of the Early Fourteenth Century*, ed. by Bruce M. S. Campbell (Manchester: Manchester University Press, 1991), pp. 110–48

Newman, Edward I., and Paul D. A. Harvey, 'Did Soil Fertility Decline in Medieval English Farms? Evidence from Cuxham, Oxfordshire', *Agricultural History Review*, 45 (1997), 119–36

Page, Mark, 'Challenging Custom: The Auditors of the Bishopric of Winchester, *c.* 1300 – *c.* 1310', in *Thirteenth Century England*, VI, ed. by Michael Prestwich, Richard H. Britnell, and Robin Frame (Woodbridge: Boydell, 1997), pp. 39–48

Poos, Lawrence R., *A Rural Society after the Black Death: Essex 1350–1525* (Cambridge: Cambridge University Press, 1991)

Postan, Michael M., 'Medieval Agrarian Society in its Prime: England', in *The Cambridge Economic History of Europe*, I: *The Agrarian Life of the Middle Ages*, ed. by Michael M. Postan, 2nd edn (Cambridge: Cambridge University Press, 1966), pp. 549–632

——, *The Medieval Economy and Society: An Economic History of Britain 1100–1500* (London: Weidenfeld and Nicolson, 1972)

——, 'Why Was Science Backward in the Middle Ages?', in Michael Postan, *Essays on Medieval Agriculture and General Problems of the Medieval Economy* (Cambridge: Cambridge University Press, 1973), pp. 81–86

Postan, Michael M., and Jan Z. Titow, 'Heriots and Prices on Winchester Manors', *Economic History Review*, 2nd ser., 11 (1959), 383–411

Raftis, J. Ambrose, *Assart Data and Land Values: Two Studies in the East Midlands, 1200–1350*, Subsidia Mediaevalia 3 (Toronto: Pontifical Institute of Medieval Studies, 1974)

——, *The Estates of Ramsey Abbey: A Study in Economic Growth and Organization*, Studies and Texts, 3 (Toronto: Pontifical Institute of Medieval Studies, 1957)

Rush, Ian, 'The Impact of Commercialization in Early Fourteenth-Century England: Some Evidence from the Manors of Glastonbury Abbey', *Agricultural History Review*, 49 (2001), 123–39

Schofield, Phillipp R., *Peasant and Community in Medieval England, 1200–1500* (Basingstoke: Palgrave Macmillan, 2003)

Smith, Richard M., 'Demographic Developments in Rural England, 1300–48', in *Before the Black Death: Studies in the 'Crisis' of the Early Fourteenth Century*, ed. by Bruce M. S. Campbell (Manchester: Manchester University Press, 1991), pp. 25–77

——, 'Human Resources', in *The Countryside of Medieval England*, ed. by Grenville Astill and Annie Grant (Oxford: Blackwell, 1988), pp. 188–212

——, 'Plagues and Peoples: The Long Demographic Cycle, 1250–1670', in *The Peopling of Britain: The Shaping of a Human Landscape*, ed. by Paul Slack and Ryk Ward (Oxford: Oxford University Press, 2002), pp. 177–210

Stone, David J., 'The Consumption of Field Crops in Late Medieval England', in *Food in Medieval England: Diet and Nutrition*, ed. by Christopher M. Woolgar, Dale Serjeantson, and Tony Waldron (Oxford: Oxford University Press, 2006), pp. 11–26

——, *Decision-Making in Medieval Agriculture* (Oxford: Oxford University Press, 2005)

——, 'Medieval Farm Management and Technological Mentalities: Hinderclay before the Black Death', *Economic History Review*, 54 (2001), 612–38

——, 'The Productivity of Hired and Customary Labour: Evidence from Wisbech Barton in the Fourteenth Century', *Economic History Review*, 50 (1997), 640–56

Thornton, Christopher, 'The Determinants of Land Productivity on the Bishop of Winchester's Demesne of Rimpton, 1208–1403', in *Land, Labour and Livestock: Historical Studies in European Agricultural Productivity*, ed. by Bruce M. S. Campbell and Mark Overton (Manchester: Manchester University Press, 1991), pp. 183–210

Titow, Jan Z., *Land and Population on the Bishop of Winchester's Estates 1209–1350* (unpublished doctoral thesis, University of Cambridge, 1962)

——, 'Some Differences between Manors and their Effects on the Condition of the Peasantry in the Thirteenth Century', *Agricultural History Review*, 10 (1962), 1–13

——, 'Some Evidence of the Thirteenth-Century Population Increase', *Economic History Review*, 2nd ser., 14 (1961–62), 218–24

Medieval Small Towns and the Late Medieval Crisis

Christopher Dyer

Developments in Historical Writings

In the two decades after the Second World War, when Michael Postan was developing his ideas about the dynamic forces in the medieval economy, the study of English medieval urban history was moving forward rather slowly. Work on the 'borough' (a constitutional term) had reached its definitive moment with the publication of Tait's book in 1936, which made the subject seem very technical, dull, and legalistic.[1] There was not much intellectual energy in urban studies to challenge Postan's agrarian interpretation of the Middle Ages. The chapter on 'Markets, towns and gilds' in Postan's textbook of 1972 is perfunctory and is not integrated into the central thesis.[2] More satisfactory was his perceptive essay on the trade of northern Europe in the Middle Ages, published in 1952, which linked the changing commercial patterns in northern Europe to movements in population and the rural economy.[3] In France the story was rather different. There had also been a parallel concern for constitutional issues in the early twentieth century, represented by the work of such historians as Charles Petit-Dutaillis on the communes, but social and economic studies continued in the 1950s, 1960s, and 1970s with monographs on Metz, Toulouse,

[1] Tait, *The Medieval English Borough*.

[2] Postan, *The Medieval Economy and Society*, pp. 207–23.

[3] Postan, 'The Trade of Medieval Europe'.

Christopher Dyer (cd50@le.ac.uk) is emeritus professor of local and regional history at the University of Leicester.

Crisis in the Later Middle Ages: Beyond the Postan-Duby Paradigm, ed. by John Drendel, TMC 13 (Turnhout: Brepols, 2015) 35–52 BREPOLS PUBLISHERS 10.1484/M.TMC.5.103783

Reims, and many others.[4] Georges Duby was interested in towns and promoted research into them in his years at Aix-en-Provence. He conceived of the market as an important stimulus to the rural economy, so it is perhaps wrong to talk of an approach common to both Postan and Duby.[5] Many of the comments that follow are directed towards Postan's distinctive theory with its strong emphasis on population growth in the countryside and the resulting fragmentation of holdings and ecological damage both to marginal lands and to the long-cultivated field systems.

There has been a tendency in both countries to concentrate research on large towns, with work, much of it rewarding and fruitful, in England on such places as London, York, and Winchester.[6] Also a common theme has been to identify the links between the urban economy and the aristocracy: they held urban property, on occasion lived in towns, spent their surpluses in towns on the goods that townsmen made or traded, and sometimes invested in the urban economy. Duby in particular connected the early growth of towns in the post-Carolingian period with the changes in the seigneurial regime. Increased demands by lords for cash rent, and a rising flow of money into the hands of the lord, stimulated the town markets, and they in turn fed back into the rural economy to encourage more commodity production.[7]

Once we begin to focus on the relations between town and country, the small towns gain in prominence, because the numerous and widely distributed trading centres would have provided most country dwellers with readily accessible venues for sale and purchase. The countryside can be divided into territories defined by their attachment to towns as hinterlands: in practice towns were so densely spread that the rural population often had a choice of urban centres, with two or three in easy reach. The selection of destination for a country dweller setting out to buy or sell was influenced by the specialization of some towns in particular commodities or services.

Investigations of small towns have developed from a number of different directions. In France studies have been devoted to all of the towns of a particular region, such as Forez and Britanny, as well as histories of individual

[4] Petit-Dutaillis, *Les communes françaises*; Schneider, *La ville de Metz*; Wolff, *Commerce et marchands de Toulouse*; Desportes, *Reims et les Rémois*.

[5] Duby, *L'économie rurale*, I, 220–74. Duby, *Rural Economy*, trans. by Postan.

[6] Thrupp, *The Merchant Class*; Swanson, *Medieval Artisans*; Keene, *Survey of Medieval Winchester*.

[7] Duby, *The Early Growth of the European Economy*, pp. 232–56.

towns.[8] In England, Wales, and Gascony, Beresford devised a special category of new towns, or planted towns of the twelfth and thirteenth centuries, in contrast with organic towns, known to some scholars as 'primary towns'.[9] Historical geographers have developed techniques for analysing town plans, which provide insights into the initial conceptions of the founders of towns and the often-complex expansion of the urban space in stages.[10] Archaeologists have provided gazetteers of 'historic towns', county by county, or in Scotland have produced surveys of each town, using both physical and documentary evidence.[11] Sites in small towns threatened with development have been excavated, which has produced significant new evidence for the chronology of urban growth: for example, some towns according to the structures and artefacts originated before the period of the first documentary evidence for their urban status. Their material remains provide many insights into crafts, trade connections, and housing.[12] Among economic and social historians, small town studies began anew with Rodney Hilton's identification of them as a significant category in the 1970s and 1980s, and since then a dozen late medieval small towns have been the subjects of detailed investigation.[13] In the early medieval period a great stimulus to the subject has come from John Blair's revelation that in many cases the small town grew up in the vicinity of a minster church, which implies that they had deep roots in the centuries before 1100 and were not just mushroom growths in the phase of economic expansion that reached its peak in the thirteenth century.[14] The results of this surge of interest have been summarized in chapters on regions and different types of town in the *Cambridge Urban History of Britain*.[15] Work on small towns throughout continental Europe (with a bias towards the early modern period) has been explored in two volumes of essays.[16]

[8] Leguay, *Un réseau urbain au Moyen Âge*; Fournial, *Les villes et l'économie d'échange*.

[9] Beresford, *New Towns of the Middle Ages*.

[10] Slater, 'Understanding the Landscape of Towns'.

[11] For example, Astill, *Historic Towns in Berkshire*; Dennison and Coleman, *Historic Melrose*.

[12] Dyer, 'The Archaeology of Medieval Small Towns'.

[13] Hilton, *The English Peasantry*, pp. 76–94; Hilton, 'Medieval Market Towns'; for other studies examples include May, *Newmarket*; Hilton, 'Low-Level Urbanization'; Newman, *Late Medieval Northallerton*; Grieve, *The Sleepers and the Shadows*; Bailey, 'A Tale of Two Towns'.

[14] Blair, *The Church in Anglo-Saxon Society*, pp. 323–41.

[15] Palliser, *Cambridge Urban History of Britain*.

[16] Clark, *Small Towns in Early Modern Europe*; Epstein, *Town and Country in Europe*.

New Thinking on Small Towns

To sum up some of the main conclusions of this new work, small towns (defined as towns with populations below two thousand) are judged to have been numerous and to have contained large numbers of people. Towards the end of the Middle Ages there were more than six hundred in England, two thousand in France, and three thousand in the Holy Roman Empire. They varied in size between three hundred and two thousand inhabitants, which cumulatively gave them about half of the urban population as a whole, and perhaps 10 per cent of the whole population. Almost a half million English people lived in small towns in *c.* 1300; in France at that time, assuming similar proportions, the small-town population would have been about two million. In England we find that small towns would be distinguished from the countryside by the concentration of people pursuing varied occupations; about twenty different crafts and trades would have been practised in the smallest towns. There were representatives of the main branches of manufacture, using wood, metal, wool, linen, and leather. Food and drink were prepared and sold in considerable quantity. Cloth was woven, and clothing made. Different building trades were practised, and services provided, such as inn keeping. The artisans and traders catered for the needs of their fellow townspeople and the rural population within a ten kilometre radius.[17] The specialist occupations might include administrators and clergy, because the small town often had a role in local government and religious life. The small town commonly had a school. It was a cultural centre, with a higher proportion of literate people than would be found in the country. The fraternity, which lay at the centre of the social and religious life of many small towns, would often put on processions and drama.[18] The town served as a place of entertainment, with specialist musicians and such shows as bull baiting and dancing bears.

At the heart of the town was the marketplace, often stretching along the length of the main street. Although it only covered a few hectares, like larger centres the small town had closely packed houses, rising to two or three storeys, and all of the environmental problems of pollution and fire hazards which are associated with concentrated urban living. Townspeople, even in a very small town, were proud of their community and often expressed their sense of identity with civic buildings, such as a guildhall and a market cross. They paved the streets and would occasionally pipe water into the town.[19]

[17] Dyer, 'Market Towns'.

[18] Rosser, 'Going to the Fraternity Feast'.

[19] Palliser, *Cambridge Urban History of Britain*, pp. 528–34.

Here then is a new subject for investigation, which has developed during the period after the formulation of the Postan-Duby hypothesis. The network of small towns can be traced back in embryonic form to the early Middle Ages, but their period of most rapid growth belongs in the twelfth and thirteenth centuries. Their development during the expansion leading to the crisis of the fourteenth century must throw light on the whole conception of overexpansion culminating in a Malthusian or ecological disaster. Does this focus of historical investigation throw light on the broader interpretation of the period? Is the growth of the small-town sector compatible with the Postan-Duby hypothesis?

Some Negative Views of Small Towns

Various arguments have been advanced and prejudices expressed to denigrate the economic and social significance of small towns. The urban character of small towns is frequently doubted, which is a view often connected with the denial that a divide between the urban and the rural can be discerned at all. Sometimes it is said that a spectrum existed with varying degrees of urbanization, with purely agricultural villages at one end and metropoles at the other, in which small towns occupied some grey twilight zone in the middle.[20] Those who subscribe to this view will make much play with the agricultural activity which is often visible among the inhabitants of small towns. They show that many townspeople owned livestock and cultivated some land. They emphasize the close links between the town and the agrarian economy and the dependence of the urban economy on supplies of agricultural produce, which suggests that these towns are no more than a species of village. Work in small towns tended to be unspecialized, and their inhabitants often pursued a number of occupations.

When those who wish to disparage small towns consider their origins, the role of lords is given pride of place. Many small towns, set up in the shadow of a castle or monastery, were feudal artefacts. They were established partly for non-economic reasons — a town at the castle gate would be as appropriate an expression of power and status as a deer park or a small monastery. A few towns — notably Wells and Lichfield — were founded partly to provide an appropriately urban setting for a bishop's see. The inhabitants of some of these towns lived under a lord's close supervision and lacked the freedom and independence of real townsmen. The officials were appointed by the lord, and

[20] Prestwich, *Plantagenet England 1225–1360*, pp. 468–73.

the borough court was run for the lord's profit. It is said that some towns were merely adjuncts of feudal power and were primarily designed to serve the lord's household needs, and when the lord departed, the town withered.

Another view of the lord's exploitation of towns is to see them as an indirect means by which lords took an extra share of the peasants' surplus. The lord would demand that payments be made by rural tenants in cash rather than in kind or in labour. This would be convenient for him but would also force the peasants to sell produce. The tenants of the rural estates which often surrounded a seigneurial borough would then come to the market and contribute through their tolls to the revenues that the lord gained from the market, or at least helped to provide a living for grain dealers or wool mongers, who would pay rents to the lord for their burgages or market stalls.

The migration of large numbers of people into towns, it has been argued, was not a sign of a healthy exchange economy, but rather a symptom of poverty.[21] Country people, desperate for work in an overpopulated countryside, crowded into towns to make a precarious living from intermittent and part-time employment. In this respect, towns offered some short-term safety valve for the rural crisis, but as market centres they were of little help to the hard-pressed peasantry in the difficult years between *c.* 1290 and *c.* 1325. Town markets and shops are said to have been most actively used by the aristocracy, and insofar that peasants were able to take advantage of trade, they carried their produce to the small-scale village markets as much as to those in towns.

These views can all be justified by evidence, but are all in varying degrees exaggerated or mistaken, and contrary views will now be advanced, which will help to establish the economic and social significance of small towns, and to show that if we assess their importance properly, they can contribute to a critique of the Postan-Duby hypothesis.

The Contribution of Small Towns

Of course we have difficulties on occasion in separating the rural from the urban. Individual communities, with a strong agricultural dimension to their economies and containing a cluster of artisans and traders around a market-place, are sometimes impossible to classify with precision and certainty. But in a great number of cases the distinctive urban character of a place cannot be doubted. Take the example of Shipston-on-Stour (once in Worcestershire, now in south Warwickshire). This place was very small, with no more than

[21] Bridbury, 'English Provincial Towns', esp. p. 3.

three hundred to four hundred inhabitants. It was awarded the privileges of a borough grudgingly by its lord, Worcester Cathedral Priory, and although it was well established by the early fourteenth century (having been founded in 1268), some of its tenants were treated as serfs by its lord. The main source for the life of the town comes not from records kept by a municipality but from the monks' court rolls for the rural manor of Blackwell, to which Shipston was attached. Eventually, soon after 1400, its status as a borough was cancelled by the monastery, as the tenants' claim to be burgesses put dangerous ideas into their heads. Nonetheless Shipston was topographically distinct from the village near which it was sited. It had a fully formed town plan, with a marketplace, a row of shops, and a small grid of streets; the tenants occupied plots, which had the same dimensions as those in other planned towns. Its inhabitants pursued a wide range of occupations, such as those of weaver, smith, ironmonger, and butcher. They had a strong sense of common purpose, rallying round their chapel as an institution which they felt belonged to them, and mounting collective disputes with their lord.[22] Places like Shipston were differentiated from large cities by their size, but in terms of their economies, topography, and consciousness they had an urban character. A sharp and clear distinction can be drawn between many small towns and their rural neighbours.

Some small towns included along their streets houses tenanted by peasants. All small towns provided homes for rooting pigs; heaps of dung hindered the progress of travellers; and barns full of straw and hay stood behind the main streets. This was an inevitable dimension of towns in an agrarian society. Of course towns depended on the countryside for their food, raw materials, and fuel, as this was an 'organic' economy. The inhabitants of Florence and Paris were similarly involved with processing and consuming agricultural produce, and large towns had their pigs, orchards, and cornfields. In no way can this agrarian context cause us to deny the urban character of town economies, whether in the context of large or small communities. Similarly the lack of specialization in work, and especially in the household economy, was a normal feature of large and small towns alike. An artisan would, for example, deal in grain, and his wife would brew.

Lords played a vital role in the foundation of towns, and many new towns of the twelfth and thirteenth centuries were designed by lords' officials and received an initial impetus from the issue of privileges to migrants. Feudal influence and power could not sustain a small town on its own. If the town were established on an unsuitable site, like the borough on a hilltop next to the cas-

[22] Dyer, 'Small-Town Conflict'.

tle at Almondbury in west Yorkshire, it would not attract settlers and would ultimately be abandoned.[23] Much depended on the choice of a good location. The success of a new town rested on a combination of both its lord's initiatives and the response of the townspeople. Some new towns were founded on a site which was already being used for small-scale or intermittent trade, which made its success as an urban centre more assured. After foundation, lords might continue to cultivate the new growth with extra charters or additional streets, sometimes as the result of requests from the townspeople. While towns in Wales and Scotland could claim some forms of monopoly, such as a prohibition on the sale of certain goods in the countryside around the town, in England such compulsion was sometimes attempted, but rarely succeeded. The royal lawyers recommended that lords of existing markets could object if a new market was founded within ten kilometres, but they did not always do so. Lords occasionally had the right of pre-emption of goods, such as buying fish cheaply at a fishing port. A lord might attempt to force serfs to use his market, but in general seigneurial control over the market was limited. Peasants were not entirely unwilling participants in the market. They preferred money rents to labour services, and those with larger holdings saw opportunities in the sale of produce.

Often historians, who are sceptical of the 'urban' nature of these communities, whether because they were 'too small' or 'too agrarian' or because they were 'artificial' extensions of feudal power, have not taken sufficient note of the material evidence. The town plan became more complex in the decades after foundation, with the building of permanent shops and stalls in the marketplace, sometimes filling whole sections of the space originally designed for temporary booths. The plots laid out near the busiest centre of the market were subdivided into narrow strips with small shops, counters, and other points of sale facing on to the street. Both developments show that an intense market activity had fulfilled the aims of the founding lord and the traders who moved into the town. Excavation of small town sites can sometimes disappoint, because the backyards contain little more than a few rubbish pits. On the other hand, the material evidence even in an apparently small and sleepy town such as Brewood in Staffordshire shows that it had become an industrial centre, with leather-working and hemp processing even in the early stages of its growth.[24]

Towns of all kinds attracted poor migrants by the charitable handouts from institutions and at the gates of wealthy houses. Towns offered prospects

[23] Faull and Moorhouse, *West Yorkshire*, III, 737–38.

[24] Ciaraldi, Cuttler, and Dingwall, 'Medieval Tanning and Retting'.

of casual employment for the unskilled. Women and children had a chance of finding a niche in the urban economy, however precarious. Immigration by the poor was perceived by urban authorities as a problem and threat. The removal of undesirable newcomers was a constantly repeated theme in the court of the midland town of Tamworth, which was probably especially vulnerable as it lay near the main road — Watling Street — by which travellers from Wales came into England.[25] But towns were not just swollen by the surplus of indigent people from the countryside. Better-off peasants moved into towns, or at least sent their sons, and presumably they brought some capital with them, earned from the profits of the sale of produce. People moved from one town to another — they might arrive in a small town from a much larger place, even from London, and presumably could contribute to the community skills and experiences which could benefit the small town. Such people clearly believed that they could better themselves, and their move demonstrates well-informed optimism about the short-term future of the town economy.

Towns, especially small towns, were not dependent on aristocratic commercial patronage. Lords would sell their grain in local markets, as we know happened in western Wiltshire, where the market of the tiny town of Hindon received grain for sale from nearby manors of Glastonbury Abbey.[26] Lords would often arrange for their grain to be taken to more distant and larger markets, where the demand was greater and the prices higher. Wool was frequently bought by a contractor, even by the exporting merchants, which cut out the local middlemen. Aristocratic purchasers were not great supporters of small-town traders, as the wealthy magnates in particular bought their household supplies of cloth, wine, spices, and fish in bulk from the great fairs, London, larger towns, and the ports by direct negotiation with major merchants.[27] They would buy goods when they were moving from one residence to another, but the small-town traders did not benefit from a very consistent demand. Lesser households, of the gentry, small monasteries, and parish clergy, were more regular users of the local market towns, but their purchases alone would not have kept so many traders and artisans in business.

We do not need to speculate that peasants sold and bought in small towns, because we have direct evidence from pleas of debt, like those from the Worcestershire town of Pershore in the early fourteenth century, when named individuals from specific villages were brought before the court for failing to

[25] Dyer, 'The Urbanizing of Staffordshire', esp. pp. 14–16.

[26] Farmer, 'Two Wiltshire Manors and their Markets'.

[27] Lee, *Cambridge and its Economic Region*, pp. 143–52.

pay money to small-town traders.[28] Better-off peasants provided themselves with horses and vehicles which enabled them to visit markets at some distance from their villages — they were not tied to the very local village markets — and a substantial proportion of peasants, 40 per cent in some regions, produced saleable surpluses. Small-town marketplaces must have been crowded with peasants each selling a few bushels of grain, a stone or two of wool, some cheeses, poultry, eggs, fruit, and vegetables. They needed cash to pay rents and taxes, but often they had some cash to spare to buy goods.

The nature of small-town customers can be readily deduced from the range of occupations found in the towns, which might include the occasional goldsmith or spicer who supplied the upper end of the market, but mainly consisted of sellers of bread, ale, meat, fish, shoes, cloth, horseshoes, ropes, tubs and barrels, cart wheels, and other ordinary commodities used in a wide range of households and on small peasant landholdings.[29] Confirmation that peasants bought goods with an urban origin comes from excavations of village sites, where many bronze buckles, belt ends, and other dress accessories are found, often dated to the thirteenth and fourteenth centuries. These came from workshops in large towns and were sold, attached to leather or cloth belts and girdles no doubt, by small-town retailers. Similarly peasants bought hand mills, mortars, whetstones, and pottery, all originating in rural places of manufacture but distributed through urban fairs and markets. The many goods made from organic materials, especially articles of clothing and wooden implements, have not survived in the ground to be excavated.

The purpose of this section of the paper has been to show that the small towns were a symptom of economic growth in the thirteenth century. Small towns were real towns, with a life of their own that was not entirely dependent on aristocratic patronage. The small towns were enmeshed in the peasant economy: the peasants provided the migrants who made up the town population, and the small-town market was mainly a peasant market. The small town was integrated into the larger and wealthier commercial world. Peasants bought a few goods which had been imported from the Continent such as German millstones and Norwegian whetstones, and the cloth that they wore had been made and finished with the help of imported oil, alum, and dyestuffs.[30] The small town acted as a local collection and distribution point for the large town

[28] Dyer, 'Market Towns', p. 20.

[29] Dyer, 'Luxury Goods in Medieval England'.

[30] Dyer, 'Did Peasants Need Markets and Towns?'.

merchant, but some small towns themselves became specialist centres of production, supplying a wider clientele. Ropes from Bridport (Dorset) and knives from Thaxted (Essex) were known throughout the country.

If the towns were as well populated as I have indicated above, and both large and small together accounted for almost a fifth of the population, then the rural economy must be judged to have achieved a considerable surplus. According to some authorities, 20 per cent lay near to the maximum possible in pre-industrial economies. In the later Middle Ages every four workers in agriculture were capable of producing enough food to supply their own needs, and in addition to feed a fifth worker in a craft or trade who made little or no direct contribution to his or her own subsistence. This statistic becomes even more impressive if we take into account the industrial workers in the countryside, and of course we should remember the 2 or 3 per cent of the population represented by the clergy and aristocracy and their servants. The proportion of people who made most of their living from non-agricultural work was probably in excess of 20 per cent, even taking into account the part-time agricultural production of a proportion of town dwellers.

Small Towns and Crisis

The account that I have given of the small towns in the thirteenth century could be used to construct a more up-beat account of the pre-crisis economy. It suggests that some elements in rural society were prospering in the climate of rising demand for agricultural produce and enhancing their spending power in the thirteenth century. The new work on small towns does not, however, contradict the idea that expansion in population led to a growth in smallholdings, as the small town was closely related to the economic activities of the better-off peasants, who had a surplus of produce to sell and the capacity to consume manufactured and traded goods. They were the people who made the running in the village economy, lending money to their poorer neighbours and accumulating land, especially in years of poor harvests. The cottagers and smallholders were less closely connected with the towns. They earned wages and bought food, but these transactions probably took place in the village, and with wages of 1d.–2d. per day, they did not have much to spend on urban goods. They were heavily influenced by the urban economy, in the sense that they handled cash and operated in the labour and produce market, but one suspects that they visited towns only occasionally. These people felt the brunt of the crisis, as they were most vulnerable to food shortages, and died in thousands in the 1315–17 famine.

The fortunes of small towns provide us with clear evidence about the end of thirteenth-century growth. The numbers of new market foundations and development of boroughs slowed down in the fourteenth century, especially after about 1325.[31] Lords' income from the rents and tolls of small towns tended to level off or even diminish. There were episodes of high mortality from epidemic disease in small towns (Battle in Sussex, for example), and buildings were falling into decay.[32] Some towns in Wales and the Scottish borders suffered from the warfare of the period, while outside the war zones all towns were contributing to military costs through taxation. The tax lists compiled in such years as 1327 and 1332 do not suggest that towns were bearing a heavier burden of taxation than the countryside, but this may be a sign of the small towns' economic weakness. A high proportion of urban households were exempt, and payments of about 1s. to 2s. each by those who were caught in the tax net were no more than the contributions recorded in nearby villages by the peasants.

A marked episode of urban unrest, some of it expressing grievances against the royal government, can be found in the years 1312–18. Serious disputes between towns and their lords, which had their origin in the thirteenth century, increased in violence, especially in the years 1327 and the early 1340s, at such places as Cirencester, Dunstable, and Wells. At Andover in Hampshire, a self-governing royal town, the leading townspeople fell into factional struggles in 1327.[33] The small towns could be said to have been demonstrating their similarity to the larger towns, because this was a period of unrest in places such as Bristol and Bury St Edmunds. At the same time peasants were conspiring against their lords at village level, or just expressing discontent by neglecting their labour services or avoiding unpopular dues, and perhaps the small towns were participating in social conflicts which reflected the tensions and discontents of the countryside.

To prove conclusively that small towns suffered from a general ecological and demographic crisis, it would be necessary to show that individual towns went through changes very similar to those affecting their rural hinterland, and no town has been the subject of this level of detailed research. Two points need to be made, however, about the overall pattern of small-scale urbanization.

[31] Letters, *Gazetteer of Markets*, p. 34; Beresford and Finberg, *English Medieval Boroughs*, pp. 37–40.

[32] Mate, 'The Agrarian Economy', esp. p. 51.

[33] Cohn, *Popular Protest*, pp. 144–58; Gross, *The Gild Merchant*, II, 317–18.

The first is that the history of small towns does not support the notion that the worst effects of the crisis were felt in the thinly settled 'marginal' regions, where much of the land consisted of woodland and grazing, and where such evidence as tax returns suggests that the rural population had low per capita incomes. The density of small towns, and the cumulative urban population, was high in the western counties, notably Devon, Cornwall, and Staffordshire. There are many explanations for this paradox, among them the need for trading contacts among pastoralists and those active in rural industry. In addition, more difficult communications over hills and valleys made a denser urban network desirable. Sharp contrasts between different types of landscape generated trade between regions in basic commodities such as grain and fuel.

The towns of these 'marginal' regions did not collapse as cultivation 'retreated' from the poorer soils, as Postan's model of the crisis predicted. If we look at the towns of western counties, like Shropshire and Staffordshire, in the late fourteenth and fifteenth centuries we find that the majority of towns survived, though their relative position in the local urban hierarchy often changed. This supports the finding that the rural population of these regions, far from foolishly ploughing up infertile soils and then regretting their ventures, adapted their farming methods to their environment. They were able to diversify their economies after the crisis, in particular by developing the pastures and participating in rural crafts.

The second point is to raise the problem of continuity in towns of all kinds throughout England. We might expect in a catastrophic upheaval to find that the urban network would have gone through a transformation. Some small towns disappear from view, or at least lost their urban character. Any regional or county study of towns will produce a list of dubious cases, that is, places which were treated as boroughs but which do not seem to have accumulated a large population of traders and artisans, or places which seem to reflect in their plan or in their occupational structure at least a potential to be called towns. These places are difficult to categorize either in the Middle Ages or in more recent times. It would, however, be deterministic to dismiss them as failures, as they may well have served for at least a few decades as useful centres of trade or manufacture, and they might have fulfilled the modest aims of their founders and inhabitants.[34] Nor can it be said that these 'proto towns' or 'townish places' all showed potential before 1300 and failed in the early fourteenth century, as some of them showed signs of activity after 1350 and persisted at least in a low key well into the fifteenth century. However, a list from the 1320s of the towns which had an indubitably urban character, with ten or twenty in each county, bears a strong

[34] Goddard, 'Small Boroughs and the Manorial Economy'.

resemblance to those still active in the 1520s.[35] The commercial patterns, perhaps even the commercial mentality, which had developed in the period of growth were not diminished in the subsequent troubled period. Some of the greatest changes are found in the industrial regions, and the striking shift in the urban network was the emergence of new towns, or complex industrial villages on the verge of urbanization, rather than the wholesale abandonment or drastic decline of the towns that had emerged by 1300. This was happening sometimes even in the generations before the Black Death, when cloth making was ensuring the prosperity of small centres, such as Worstead and North Walsham in Norfolk.[36]

These observations strengthen our belief that the urbanization of the twelfth and thirteenth centuries, when more than four hundred towns were founded in England, had been remarkably successful. As they jostled for position in relation to existing centres, some hoped-for towns failed to survive, and there were probably casualties before 1300 as well as in subsequent years. But by the early fourteenth century, a strong network of small towns had established themselves and defined their hinterlands in the surrounding countryside, and these persisted through the subsequent changes.

The cause of the crisis is of course an intractable problem, for which there are no easy answers. The argument that much of the fourteenth century saw an exceptionally profound period of climatic instability, with its deepest trough in 1315–17, helps us to understand the mechanics of the crisis, but we still have to ask why the economy and society was so vulnerable to these adverse circumstances, and why recovery was so slow.[37]

A new development in thinking has been to connect the commercial opportunities of the thirteenth century to the growth in population.[38] The small towns provided peasants with convenient access to the market, and it became easier for them to sell produce and buy goods. Rural households with surplus children were able to contribute to the flow of migrants from country to town, and the offspring were sometimes able to gain profitable employment and marriage partners. More people could obtain in the commercial world sufficient income to form households and procreate. We have also become recently aware of the importance of credit, which enabled traders at markets to buy peasants' produce, made purchases affordable for rural households, and allowed peas-

[35] Lee, *Cambridge and its Economic Region*, pp. 33–34 ; Laughton, Jones, and Dyer, 'The Urban Hierarchy'.

[36] Palliser, *Cambridge Urban History of Britain*, p. 65.

[37] Campbell, 'Nature as Historical Protagonist'.

[38] Langdon and Masschaele, 'Commercial Activity and Population Growth'.

ants to embark on strategic expenditure, in buying land or paying for livestock and buildings, for example.[39] Peasants became involved in consumer spending and in investment for which payment could be made over a period but did not require immediate transfers of cash.

Growth slowed down at the end of the thirteenth century and halted in the 1310s. The quantity of international trade was levelling off, which presumably had repercussions lower down the hierarchy of towns. Rents were sticking at their old level, especially the entry fines paid by tenants acquiring new holdings, which were sensitive to changes in demand for land. Aristocratic incomes reached a plateau beyond which they could expand no further. New land was no longer being brought into cultivation. There may have been some recovery in the second quarter of the century, but the epidemic of 1348–49 and subsequent trends delayed a return to rising prices and rents until well after 1500. Just as country people had interacted with their local towns in the period of growth, so the downturn in the rural economy was reflected in reduced activity in the towns, which became smaller and suffered reductions in market activity measured by the tolls collected from transactions. This may have had demographic repercussions, and delayed marriage was combined with increased mortality to reduce population levels.

Through the small towns which joined peasants to the whole urban hierarchy and to the great commercial movements across Europe, we can conceive of economic changes that began in the towns of the Low Countries and eventually impacted on the English countryside. It still seems more likely that we should search for the explanation of the economic problems of the period in the fields and barns of peasantry, but our conception of the peasant world should include their intimate relationship to that part of the urban sector that was closest to them and sought to satisfy their needs.

Conclusion

The rediscovery of small towns and a proper assessment of their economic role means that that any reformulation of the Postan-Duby thesis must take into account this network of commercial centres and their influence on the countryside. No longer can the medieval economy be seen just as an elemental struggle between man and nature, without taking full account of the influence of the local flow of exchange among rural producers and consumers.

[39] Briggs, *Credit and Village Society*.

Bibliography

Astill, Grenville G., *Historic Towns in Berkshire: An Archaeological Appraisal* (Reading: Berkshire Archaeological Committee, 1978)
Bailey, Mark, 'A Tale of Two Towns: Buntingford and Standon in the Later Middle Ages', *Journal of Medieval History*, 19 (1993), 351–71
Beresford, Maurice W., *New Towns of the Middle Ages* (London: Lutterworth, 1967)
Beresford, Maurice W., and Herbert P. R. Finberg, *English Medieval Boroughs: A Handlist* (Newton Abbot: David and Charles, 1973)
Blair, John, *The Church in Anglo-Saxon Society* (Oxford: Oxford University Press, 2005)
Bridbury, Anthony R., 'English Provincial Towns in the Later Middle Ages', *Economic History Review*, 2nd ser., 34 (1981), 1–24
Briggs, Chris, *Credit and Village Society in Fourteenth-Century England* (Oxford: British Academy and Oxford University Press, 2009)
Campbell, Bruce M. S., 'Nature as Historical Protagonist: Environment and Society in Pre-Industrial England', *Economic History Review*, 63 (2010), 281–314
Ciaraldi, Marina, Richard Cuttler, and Lucie Dingwall, 'Medieval Tanning and Retting at Brewood, Staffordshire: Archaeological Excavations 1999–2000', *Staffordshire Archaeological and Historical Society Transactions*, 40 (2004), 1–57
Clark, Peter, ed., *Small Towns in Early Modern Europe* (Cambridge: Cambridge University Press, 1995)
Cohn, Samuel K., *Popular Protest in Late Medieval English Towns* (Cambridge: Cambridge University Press, 2013)
Dennison, E. Patricia, and R. Coleman, *Historic Melrose: The Archaeological Implications of Development* (Scottish Burgh Survey, 1998)
Desportes, Pierre, *Reims et les Rémois aux XIIIe et XIVe siècles* (Paris: Picard, 1979)
Duby, Georges, *The Early Growth of the European Economy: Warriors and Peasants from the Seventh to the Twelfth Century* (London, Weidenfeld and Nicolson, 1974)
——, *L'économie rurale et la vie des campagnes dans l'Occident Médiéval (France, Angleterre, Empire, IXe–XVe siècles): Essai de synthèse et perspectives de recherches*, 2 vols (Paris: Aubier, 1962)
——, *Rural Economy and Country Life in the Medieval West*, trans. by Cynthia Postan (Columbia: University of South Carolina Press, 1968)
Dyer, Christopher, 'The Archaeology of Medieval Small Towns', *Medieval Archaeology*, 47 (2003), 85–114
——, 'Did Peasants Need Markets and Towns? The Experience of Late Medieval England?', in *London and Beyond: Essays in Honour of Derek Keene*, ed. by Matthew Davies and James Galloway (London: Institute of Historical Research, 2012), pp. 25–47
——, 'Luxury Goods in Medieval England', in *Commercial Activity, Markets and Entrepreneurs in the Middle Ages: Essays in Honour of Richard Britnell*, ed. by Ben Dodds and Christian D. Liddy (Woodbridge: Boydell and Brewer, 2011), pp. 217–38
——, 'Market Towns and the Countryside in Late Medieval England', *Canadian Journal of History*, 31 (1996), 17–35

——, 'Small-Town Conflict in the Later Middle Ages: Events at Shipston- on-Stour', *Urban History*, 19 (1992), 183–210

——, 'The Urbanizing of Staffordshire: The First Phases', *Staffordshire Studies*, 14 (2002), 1–31

Epstein, Larry, ed., *Town and Country in Europe, 1300–1800* (Cambridge: Cambridge University Press, 2001)

Farmer, David L., 'Two Wiltshire Manors and their Markets', *Agricultural History Review*, 37 (1989), 1–11

Faull, Margaret, and Stephen Moorhouse, *West Yorkshire: An Archaeological Survey to AD 1500*, 4 vols (Wakefield: West Yorkshire Metropolitan County Council, 1981)

Fournial, Étienne, *Les villes et l'économie d'échange en Forez aux XIIIe et XIVe siècles* (Paris: Les Pressures du Palais Royal, 1967)

Goddard, Richard, 'Small Boroughs and the Manorial Economy: Enterprise Zones or Urban Failures?', *Past and Present*, 210 (2011), 3–31

Grieve, Hilda, *The Sleepers and the Shadows: Chelmsford, a Town, its People and its Past* (Chelmsford: Essex County Council, 1988)

Gross, Charles, *The Gild Merchant*, 2 vols (London: Oxford University Press, 1890)

Hilton, Rodney H., *The English Peasantry in the Later Middle Ages* (Oxford: Oxford University Press, 1975)

——, 'Low-Level Urbanization: The Seigneurial Borough of Thornbury in the Middle Ages', in *Medieval Society and the Manor Court*, ed. by Zvi Razi and Richard Smith (Oxford: Oxford University Press, 1996), pp. 482–517

——, 'Medieval Market Towns and Simple Commodity Production', *Past and Present*, 109 (1985), 3–23

Keene, Derek, *Survey of Medieval Winchester*, Winchester Studies, 2 (Oxford: Oxford University Press, 1985)

Langdon, John, and James Masschaele, 'Commercial Activity and Population Growth in Medieval England', *Past and Present*, 190 (2006), 35–81

Laughton, Jane, Evan Jones, and Christopher Dyer, 'The Urban Hierarchy in the East Midlands in the Later Middle Ages', *Urban History*, 28 (2001), 331–57

Lee, John, *Cambridge and its Economic Region 1450–1560* (Hatfield: Hertfordshire University Press, 2005)

Leguay, Jean-Pierre, *Un réseau urbain au Moyen Âge: Les villes du duché de Bretagne aux XIVe et XVe siècles* (Paris: Librairie Maloine, 1981)

Letters, Samantha, *Gazetteer of Markets and Fairs in England and Wales*, Special Ser. 32 and 33 (London: List and Index Society, 2003)

Mate, Mavis, 'The Agrarian Economy of South-East England before the Black Death: Depressed or Buoyant?', in *Before the Black Death: Studies in the 'Crisis' of the Early Fourteenth Century*, ed. by Bruce M. S. Campbell (Manchester: Manchester University Press, 1991), pp. 79–109

May, Peter, *Newmarket: Medieval and Tudor* (Newmarket: P. May, 1982)

Newman, Christine M., *Late Medieval Northallerton: A Small Market Town and its Hinterland, c. 1470–1540* (Stamford: Shaun Tyas, 1999)

Palliser, David, ed., *Cambridge Urban History of Britain*, I: *c. 600–c. 1540* (Cambridge: Cambridge University Press, 2000)

Petit-Dutaillis, Charles, *Les communes françaises: Caractères et évolution des origines au XVIIIe siècle* (Paris: A. Michel, 1947)

Postan, Michael, *The Medieval Economy and Society: An Economic History of Britain 1100–1500* (London: Weidenfeld and Nicolson, 1972)

——, 'The Trade of Medieval Europe: The North', in *The Cambridge Economic History of Europe*, II: *Trade and Industry in the Middle Ages*, ed. by Michael Postan and Edward Miller, 2nd edn (Cambridge: Cambridge University Press, 1987; first published 1952), pp. 191–256

Prestwich, Michael, *Plantagenet England 1225–1360* (Oxford: Oxford University Press, 2005)

Rosser, Gervase, 'Going to the Fraternity Feast: Commensality and Social Relations in Late Medieval England', *Journal of British Studies*, 33 (1994), 430–46

Schneider, Jean, *La ville de Metz aux XIIIe et XIVe siècles* (Nancy: Georges Thomas, 1950)

Slater, Terry, 'Understanding the Landscape of Towns', in *Landscape: The Richest Historical Record*, ed. by Della Hooke, Society for Landscape Studies Supplementary Series, 1 (Birmingham: Society for Landscape Studies, 2000), pp. 97–108

Swanson, Heather, *Medieval Artisans* (Oxford: Blackwell, 1989)

Tait, James, *The Medieval English Borough* (Manchester: Manchester University Press, 1936)

Thrupp, Sylvia L., *The Merchant Class of Medieval London* (Ann Arbor: University of Michigan Press, 1948)

Wolff, Philippe, *Commerce et marchands de Toulouse (vers 1350 – vers 1450)* (Paris: Plon, 1954)

The Long Thirteenth Century: An Era of Schumpeterian Growth?

John Langdon

A conference on Georges Duby and Michael Postan brings together two of the very most influential historians of the medieval economy. Each, however, told a very different story. Postan, as is well known, was heavily influenced by the precepts of Thomas Malthus and believed that, certainly by the late eleventh century, medieval society (and certainly in England) was locked into a cycle determined almost solely by the struggle between population and agricultural resources. This situation, he claimed, was further exacerbated by environmental degradation and a very weak technological response.[1] For Postan, the advent of the plague in the mid-fourteenth century simply reinforced a pattern already established from at least fifty years before.[2]

In contrast, although he was certainly mindful of the cyclical nature of population during the period, Georges Duby brought a much more activist style to his interpretation of the economic development of the Middle Ages, particularly in its growth phase to the early fourteenth century. This was particular evident in his seminal *L'économie rurale et la vie des campagnes dans l'Occident médiéval*,

[1] Postan's vision is most clearly articulated in Postan, 'Medieval Agarian Society', esp. pp. 548–59; but see also Postan, *The Medieval Economy and Society*, esp. chap. 4 ('Land Use and Technology').

[2] Postan, 'Medieval Agarian Society', pp. 569–70.

John Langdon (jlangdon@ualberta.ca) is professor of history at the University of Alberta. His most recent book is *Horses, Oxen and Technological Innovation: The Use of Draught Animals in English Farming from 1066 to 1500* (Cambridge: Cambridge University Press, 2004).

Crisis in the Later Middle Ages: Beyond the Postan-Duby Paradigm, ed. by John Drendel, TMC 13 (Turnhout: Brepols, 2015) 53–71 BREPOLS PUBLISHERS 10.1484/M.TMC.5.103784

published in 1962.[3] Rather than seeing society as being passively trapped by the biological imperative of reproducing themselves, Duby emphasized the potential that medieval people had for breaking out of Malthusian restrictions. His emphasis on technological innovations was much stronger than Postan's, and it is interesting to note that the appearance of *L'économie* coincided with the publication — in the same year — of Lynn White Jr's, *Medieval Technology and Social Change*,[4] another aggressively technophilic interpretation of the Middle Ages. Also, Duby was much more sanguine about the role of entrepreneurs in promoting growth, particularly through their engagement with the market, which markedly energized the hunt for profits.[5]

Altogether, both Postan and Duby provided powerful visions of the Middle Ages, and some way of combining the cyclical nature of the Postan vision with the more proactive view of Duby would be attractive. In this regard, it might be useful to turn to more modern economic theory. In his very useful book about the development of western technology, *The Lever of Riches*, Joel Mokyr made considerable use of modern theories to explain technological innovation as far back in time as the medieval period or even earlier. Mokyr claimed, for example, that the introduction of the horse to medieval agriculture was 'a prime example of how Schumpeterian growth fed Smithian growth'.[6] Schumpeterian theories in particular hold promise for dealing not only with that cluster of technological innovations we associate with the 'long thirteenth century' (here defined as being roughly from 1185 to 1315), but also, more importantly, with the human activity associated with it. Indeed, Schumpeter himself did not place so much emphasis upon technological innovation as upon the entrepreneurial endeavour which brought it to the fore.[7]

First, I should provide a little more about Schumpeter and his theories. Joseph Alois Schumpeter was an Austrian economist born in 1883. He moved to Harvard in 1932, where he died in 1950, so that his intellectual perspective encompassed both European and North American influences. He wrote a num-

[3] Duby, *L'économie rurale*, see esp. I, Livre II (for the English translation, see Duby, *Rural Economy*, trans. by Postan, pp. 59–165).

[4] White, *Medieval Technology and Social Change*.

[5] Duby, *L'économie rurale*, I, 261–74.

[6] Mokyr, *The Lever of Riches*, p. 38.

[7] See especially Schumpeter, *The Theory of Economic Development*, trans. by Opie. Schumpeter's crucial discussion of entrepreneurial activity occurs in chap. 4, and, in fact, he does not mention technological innovation until p. 229.

ber of books, of which the most important for our purposes are *The Theory of Economic Development* (originally published in German in 1912) and *Business Cycles* (1939). Many of Schumpeter's ideas figure prominently in the explanation of modern economic cycles, especially when dealing with technology and entrepreneurship. Essentially what Schumpeter argued was that periods of economic growth are initiated by surges of entrepreneurial activity, often invoking clusters of technological innovations or new formulations of existing technologies. Initially started by a few exceptionally farsighted and energetic individuals in a time of relative economic and technical stagnation (i.e. recession or depression in our terms), the healthy profits or revenues delivered by the new entrepreneurial investments stimulate other entrepreneurs to follow the lead of the first, thus creating a period of economic boom.[8] Eventually, however, the competitive edge that these new economic or technological formulations conferred upon these entrepreneurs lucky enough to be among the forerunners is eventually eroded by a flood of followers who want to share in the prosperity. Profit margins shrink while the economic boom subsides and perhaps even goes into reverse as enthusiasm for the new economic or technological formulations fades and investment confidence declines or even collapses. But, nonetheless, a new technological or economic equilibrium (or 'circular flow', as it was translated from the German *Kreislauf*, meaning literally 'circulation'[9]) has been reached. Future economic development must wait until a new set of innovations or economic reformulations are available to fire the enthusiasm of entrepreneurs yet again and set off a new economic surge. In many ways, this entrepreneurial cycle has many similar characteristics to the population-resources cycle originally proposed by Malthus in 1798. If we use Malthus's notion of arithmetic versus geometric increase,[10] at the start of an economic cycle, the economic and technical opportunities for entrepreneurial activity might be seen as growing in arithmetic fashion — 1, 2, 3, 4, 5, etc. On the other hand, initially at least, entrepreneurial enthusiasm, once under way, has the tendency to grow in something like geometric fashion — 1, 2, 4, 8, 16, etc. Eventually, however, such heated investment outstrips its technological and economic base. The profits from investment eventually dry up, and any new ventures become exceedingly risky. The economy as a whole enters a recession.

[8] Most of this is outlined in Schumpeter, *The Theory of Economic Development*, trans. by Opie; Schumpeter, *Business Cycles*, provides a more theoretical formulation.

[9] Schumpeter, *The Theory of Economic Development*, trans. by Opie, p. vii.

[10] Malthus, *The Works*, ed. by Wrigley and Souden, I, esp. chap. 2 (pp. 11–17 in 'An Essay on the Principle of Population').

The Long Thirteenth Century

What are the characteristics of the 'long thirteenth century' which seem to fit such Schumpeterian notions? First, it would seem clear that a number of opportunities presented themselves for 'entrepreneurs', virtually of all social ranks, from the late twelfth century onwards. Georges Duby, Lynn White Jr, and Jean Gimpel all pointed to a number of innovations and investment opportunities that were accumulating during the period leading up to the end of the twelfth century.[11] Many of these (such as the use of the heavy plough) had already been in existence for several centuries, but others — such as the windmill, increased use of water power for industry, the increased use of horses in agriculture and road transport, improvements in ship design and navigation — were all encompassed in part or even in total within the long thirteenth century. To these we could add other economic opportunities — not so obviously involving new technology — such as land clearance, the increased use of markets, developments in transport infrastructure (particularly bridges), the spread of accounting and other written procedures (the so-called 'pragmatic literacy'), new sources of bullion, and new mining opportunities generally.[12]

The timing of these developments is a crucial issue for how seriously we should take Schumpeterian economics for the long thirteenth century. But much of this often very technologically oriented activity matched the contours of the long thirteenth century remarkably well. I will give a few examples, stemming from English cases but having, I know, many parallels on the Continent. The post windmill, for instance, followed a classic Schumpeterian pattern. Initially invented somewhere around the lower North Sea around 1185, its growth in numbers was quite spectacular over the next 130 years, where it appears to have become a popular choice for investment for lords in particular all around the lower North Sea. In England alone it has been estimated that these windmills numbered around four thousand by the beginning of the four-

[11] Duby, *L'économie rurale*, I, esp. pp. 191–202; Duby, *The Early Growth of the European Economy*, esp. pp. 186–99; White, *Medieval Technology and Social Change*, esp. chaps 2 and 3; Gimpel, *The Medieval Machine*.

[12] E.g. Hallam, *The Agrarian History of England and Wales*, chap. 4; Britnell, 'The Proliferation of Markets in England'; Britnell, *The Commercialisation of English Society*, esp. chap. 4; Langdon, 'Horse Hauling'; Harrison, 'Bridges and Economic Development' (for a later and more amplified version, see also Harrison, *The Bridges of Medieval England*); Britnell, 'Pragmatic Literacy in Latin Christendom'; Spufford, *Money and its Use*, esp. part II; Gimpel, *The Medieval Machine*, pp. 59–74, 93–99.

teenth century.[13] If so, over the period 1185 to 1315, it would mean that new windmills were built in the country at an average rate of about thirty per year. Much of this growth seemingly took place around the middle of the thirteenth century,[14] so that it is not impossible to imagine over a hundred windmills being built in particular years. By the end of the century, however, growth in the number of windmills had slowed considerably, such that windmills built after 1300 were clearly risky investments.[15] Profit margins for new windmill constructions had now shrunk considerably. This is reflected by the growing complaints about competition which appear in many of the records in the early fourteenth century, as in a 1325 inquisition post-mortem for Wyberton, Lincolnshire, where it was stated that the manor's windmill was valued only at 10s. per year 'and no more because of the smallness of the soke [that is, the number of tenants who owed suit of mill to the windmill] and because there are mills on either side of the same mill'.[16] The number of windmills (and water-mills) in England seems to have been static at best from 1300 until the plague set in a more permanent drop in numbers.[17]

Markets and fairs provide another economic activity that displayed essentially the same pattern over the period. In England again, the formation of new markets escalated markedly from 1200 onwards, the peak for most regions coming somewhere between 1250 and 1275.[18] Although markets continued to be established in the early fourteenth century, these later foundations were likely to have very uncertain futures and, indeed, may often have been created for other than economic reasons.[19] As Richard Britnell commented in regards to the impact this had upon non-agricultural labour: 'It is unlikely that non-agricultural employment expanded steadily throughout the period of 150 years [1180–1330] under discussion. The founding of new towns and new markets

[13] Langdon, 'The Birth and Demise', p. 55.

[14] E.g. Holt, *The Mills of Medieval England*, pp. 21–24.

[15] E.g. Langdon, 'The Birth and Demise', pp. 54–76.

[16] Kew, National Arch., C 134/90/5, m. 4. This case is also cited in Langdon, 'Lordship and Peasant Consumerism', p. 26.

[17] Langdon, *Mills in the Medieval Economy*, esp. chap. 2.

[18] Britnell, 'The Proliferation of Markets in England', pp. 209–10.

[19] Britnell feels that lords sometimes founded markets 'more to accommodate the poor than for profit' (Britnell, 'The Proliferation of Markets in England', p. 221). If so, this would be similar to the building of the Turweston, Buckinghamshire, windmill in 1303, which I have speculated was erected primarily to boost the prestige of Westminster Abbey in a locality where the monks had just acquired a manor: Langdon, 'The Birth and Demise', pp. 68–69.

implies that the possibilities for growth were deteriorating from the third quarter of the thirteenth century'.[20]

Both markets and mills were heavily promoted by lords. An innovation with a similar timing but different social origins was the greater introduction of the horse to farm and road transport. This was an occurrence with a longer span than the long thirteenth century, starting arguably in the early twelfth century and reaching its apogee perhaps not until after the Black Death,[21] but its period of most obvious transition was probably between 1150 and 1300.[22] Although adopted across the whole social spectrum, the animal was a particular favourite of the peasantry and, perhaps because of that, harder to analyse in profit terms.[23] In previous publications I have characterized the advantages of horses in medieval agriculture primarily in terms of versatility and cost-cutting.[24] Certainly the use of horses by the peasantry might well have been part of a larger survival strategy, especially among smallholders, in effect a 'stepping down' in traction which paralleled a similar reduction in diet and housing over the long thirteenth century.[25] As a result, any contribution to entrepreneurial activity (such as quicker access to market) may have been rather unintended,[26] but certainly market activity and the increased use of horses for transport generally seemed to have had a very close correlation.[27] Other peasant-oriented innovations, such as the use of vetches,[28] are similarly very difficult to assess from a profit motive but clearly contributed to new agricultural formulations which might have favoured horses and hence improved access to markets.[29]

[20] Britnell, *The Commercialisation of English Society*, p. 127.

[21] Langdon, *Horses, Oxen and Technological Innovation*; Campbell, *English Seigniorial Agriculture, 1250–1450*, pp. 120–31.

[22] As in the case of the use of horses for hauling: Langdon, 'Horse Hauling'.

[23] Langdon, *Horses, Oxen and Technological Innovation*, chap. 4.

[24] Langdon, 'The Economics of Horses'; Langdon, *Horses, Oxen and Technological Innovation*, pp. 164–70.

[25] Especially again among smallholders: see Dyer, *Standards of Living in the Later Middle Ages*, pp. 159, 166.

[26] Langdon, 'The Use of Animal Power'.

[27] Langdon, *Horses, Oxen and Technological Innovation*, pp. 270–72, 286–87; Hatcher and Bailey, *Modelling the Middle Ages*, pp. 148–49.

[28] Campbell, 'The Diffusion of Vetches'.

[29] Campbell, *English Seigniorial Agriculture, 1250–1450*, pp. 227–29; Campbell, 'Towards an Agricultural Geography'.

There are other developments which show marked capital investment during the long thirteenth century. Some were more regional in nature. The application of water power to industrial purposes was an activity which gathered speed over the long thirteenth century, although its use was limited to those areas where the industry in question was well developed, as in the case of the cloth industry where western parts of the country in particular experienced the construction of significant numbers of fulling mills.[30] The proliferation of tide mills, particularly along the lower Thames and its estuary,[31] provides another case of a geographically limited but powerful application of capital investment, with expenditure sometimes exceeding £100 for a single mill.[32] Perhaps the most significant expression of the new mood of investment and its eventual ebb, however, was the explosion in ecclesiastical, governmental, or civic building during the long thirteenth century. For England, one of the more dramatic proofs of this is Morris's analysis of church building, where the number of major ecclesiastical building projects peaked in the 1270s or 1280s and then went into a long decline.[33] The same might be said of Crown spending on building, which continued powerfully through most of the reigns of Henry III and Edward I, particularly with the burst of Welsh castle building up to 1304, but was relatively slack from then until the advent of the plague.[34] One could also add the building up of walls and other defences around towns, which seems mostly to have been a thirteenth-century affair.[35] Also important countrywide were investments in the transportation network, particularly in bridges, which in the thirteenth century very nearly reached the number evident in the eighteenth century.[36] Although all of these instances would require future investment for upkeep, the peak for all of them in terms of initial construction would

[30] E.g. see Pelham, *Fulling Mills*, pl. 4.

[31] E.g. Carlin, *Medieval Southwark*, pp. 55–57; Keene, 'Issues of Water', p. 165.

[32] As in the case of the tide mill at Lydden (in Thanet), Kent, which was constructed in 1305–06 by the then prior of Christ Church, Canterbury, Henry de Eastry, for £143 13s.: Mate, 'Property Investment', pp. 8–9.

[33] Morris, *Cathedrals and Abbeys of England and Wales*, pp. 177–81.

[34] Brown, Colvin, and Taylor, *The History of the King's Works*, esp. pp. 113–14, 120, 155–57, 161–62. Crown building picked up again in the 1350s and 1360s under Edward III (ibid., p. 162), which might help explain why the economy remained buoyant for some decades after the arrival of the plague.

[35] Palliser, Slater, and Dennison, 'The Topography of Towns', p. 174; Schofield and Stell, 'The Built Environment', pp. 372–73.

[36] Harrison, 'Bridges and Economic Development'.

seem to have been reached sometime during the thirteenth century or, at the very latest, the first decade of the fourteenth.

As a consequence of all this activity, the workforce which developed to deal with all this investment had considerably more variety and specialization at the end of the long thirteenth century than it had at the beginning.[37] It was also a workforce which was likely much less connected with the land than it had been before and thus more ill-equipped to deal with the difficulties of the early fourteenth century.[38] With the downturn (or at least stabilization) in investment which seemingly characterized the early fourteenth century, should we see the 'crisis' of the early fourteenth century as mainly (1) of high food prices or (2) of low employment rates? At the very least, we should see welfare problems of the early fourteenth century as not only stemming from the cyclical movement of population and its precarious relationship with the food supply, but also from the cyclical nature of investment and entrepreneurial activity (à la Schumpeter). It would seem that investment peaked first, probably even before the end of the thirteenth century. As I have indicated in another publication, the wages of English craftsmen on medieval manors were falling relative to wages for agricultural workers from about the 1280s onwards, indicating a lessening of demand for their services.[39] David Farmer, noting the fact that the real wages of English carpenters and slaters were cut in half from the middle of the thirteenth to the beginning of the fourteenth century, commented: 'The real wages of the craftsmen declined, one must assume, because they were too many of them at a time when investment in new manorial developments was slackening'.[40] If these indicators have any validity, it suggests that declining entrepreneurial activity and investment was in part already creating an environment of considerable danger for a still expanding population.

How Did Entrepreneurial Activity Get Started?

Even if we were to accept that the issue of investment and entrepreneurial activity played an important role in determining the 'shape' of the long thirteenth century, it is not clear how such activity was originally initiated. For example,

[37] E.g. Britnell, *The Commercialisation of English Society*, pp. 79–81; Britnell, 'Specialization of Work in England'.

[38] Langdon, 'The Mobilization of Labour', p. 55.

[39] Langdon, 'The Mobilization of Labour', pp. 53–55.

[40] Farmer, 'Prices and Wages [1000–1355]', p. 769.

what caused investment to 'take off'? One could say that it is fine to postulate a growth in entrepreneurship, but that it could only happen in very favourable circumstances which of necessity would take precedence. Certainly the underlying conditions were favourable. The twelfth and thirteenth centuries comprised a period of relative peace (and also relatively good weather) around the lower North Sea. Much, too, has been made of the impact of the Crusades both as a stimulus and a hindrance to the medieval European economy. Peter Spufford, for instance, has suggested that the Crusades were a tremendous drain on western European monetary resources, which was only counteracted by the opening up of new silver mines in the 1160s.[41] Georges Duby, on the other hand, saw the Crusades as 'an initial springboard of overseas adventures and a justification of profit-making and accumulation of monetary capital',[42] while Edwin Hunt and James Murray, in a similar vein, saw heightened business activity as stemming out of upper-class consumer aspirations.[43]

In one sense, however, this is immaterial to our concern. Economic cycles — whether Malthusian, Schumpeterian, or whatever — can be disrupted or encouraged by any number of external events such as those above (later on, of course, the plague would cause the greatest disruption of all), but it is the internal logic of the cycle which matters.[44] The great strength of Postan's approach was that, in order to explain the cyclical nature of the medieval economy (particularly of the long thirteenth century), he applied a *cyclical* model. It is my argument here that another cyclical model — that of Schumpeter's — might well be as strong in explanatory value, particularly if it is used in conjunction with Postan's neo-Malthusian view. Also, one of the most notable features of Schumpeterian economics is its emphasis on human agency. Entrepreneurial activity has to be mediated through the minds of people willing to take the risk, and it is their perceptions of the economic opportunities which drive the cycle

[41] Spufford, *Money and its Use*, pp. 158–59; see also chap. 5 (pp. 109–31).

[42] Duby, *The Early Growth of the European Economy*, p. 264.

[43] As they state quite baldly: 'The overriding theme of this book is that medieval business was driven from beginning to end by the continuous demands of the elite. [...] The initial thrust came from the elite's dietary preferences, inherited from Mediterranean and Christian cultures, and from their insatiable desire for luxuries of food, clothing, and ornamentation. These pressures stimulated exchange and the need for business specialists to provide or procure the goods. Thus, we depart somewhat from tradition as we argue that elitist demands affected, directly or indirectly, virtually all businesses, rather than just those dealing in luxury goods': Hunt and Murray, *A History of Business*, pp. 2–3.

[44] As Schumpeter himself wrote: Schumpeter, *Business Cycles*, I, 34.

and constitute its internal logic. In contrast, Postan's model is very impersonal (as was Malthus's first proposal), essentially discounting any human decision-making beyond that of the biological imperative. Another notable feature of Schumpeter's theory is that it does have an evolutionary element to it, in that the end of each cycle is qualitatively different from the beginning: that is, a new 'circular flow' with its own distinctive economic characteristics is created. In the case of the long thirteenth century, this was reflected in an economy which was much more monetized than it had been before and very different — quantitatively and qualitatively — in its market and labour infrastructure. Looked at in Schumpeterian terms, much of this was set in train by human decision-making inspired by the profits promised and delivered by the economic opportunities of the late twelfth century. Although this may be too modern a way of looking at it, certainly some major benefits were perceived at the time, either in cash or some other form of material advantage which guaranteed improved subsistence or personal comfort, which in turn proved enticing to those willing to invest either time, labour, or financial resources. Georges Duby, I think, gives the best and certainly very broadly based view, socially, of this growing entrepreneurial spirit, where he discusses the contribution of virtually all classes to the take-off in the western European economy from the late twelfth century onwards.[45] Clearly, we need to think more about how and why particular people at the time were willing to take the plunge, an exercise that may well take us into the realm of cognitive theory — that is, how people create and apply new entrepreneurial ideas.[46]

As a consequence, current views about the expansion period of the economy from the late twelfth century to about 1250, as espoused by Duby and others, seem to me to be more or less in line with a Schumpeterian vision. What I find curious about the current state of historical opinion is that, when we get to the end of the long thirteenth century, the implications of this entrepreneurial interpretation seem to get lost. Explanations for the end of the cycle shift dramatically to the balance of population versus resources, à la Postan, with a leavening of other theories, ranging from surplus extraction models, whether by seigneurial or state expropriation, or to monetarist or even weather explanations.[47]

[45] Duby, *The Early Growth of the European Economy*, chap. 9 ('Take-off').

[46] I explore this issue in relation to the development of the technology and economy of milling during the later Middle Ages: Langdon, *Mills in the Medieval Economy*, esp. chaps 3 ('The Technology of the Late Medieval English Milling Industry') and 5 ('Entrepreneurs').

[47] Much of this is covered usefully in Hatcher and Bailey, *Modelling the Middle Ages*.

The consequences of entrepreneurial slowdown (that is, recession) are scarcely considered. In other words, from the perspective of this conference, we mostly believe Duby for the beginning of the period and Postan for the end. This, I think, has resulted in a very curious mixing of theoretical standpoints which needs further elaboration.

Two Cycles?

As a first step to a more helpful articulation of the issues, it is probably important to recognize that there are at least two cyclical patterns at work here. From the late twelfth century, increased entrepreneurial activity went hand in hand with an increase in population, as did the seeming decline of both in the early fourteenth century. In some aspects, a fairly direct connection between the two cycles seems clear, as in the clearance of woodland, where entrepreneurial activity and the accommodation for population growth were both involved, but in others, such as the introduction of the horse to agriculture or the extension of water power for industrial purposes, the connection seems less clear. In any case, it does appear likely that one cycle probably preceded the other. Did, for example, population growth create the conditions for entrepreneurial growth or vice versa? When two trends run in parallel, it is often difficult to elucidate their relationship or to prioritize them. For me, intuitively, it would seem that population growth would tend occur within an expanding economic environment fueled by a stronger entrepreneurial spirit, but it does not follow that population growth necessarily leads to increased entrepreneurial activity or, if it does, it should probably lead to a more narrowly based set of entrepreneurial activities (that is, more directed to subsistence issues) than we see in the late twelfth / early thirteenth century.

As a result, timing is critical here. When does the entrepreneurial take-off occur vis-à-vis that for population? Considering English population, only two scholars have tried to create a detailed profile of population rise from 1086 to 1348, J. C. Russell and H. E. Hallam, both using the number of holdings recorded in various manorial surveys and extents, Hundred Rolls, and inquisitions post-mortem. Hallam's treatment is so clumsy that I think it adds little to the discussion. Indeed, in the end, he portrays the rise of population from 1086 to 1348 more or less as a straight line.[48] Russell, on the other hand, does attempt to provide a stronger sense of when the bulk of population rise between 1086

[48] Hallam, 'Population Movements in England', pp. 512–13.

and 1348 occurred. In fact, he believed that most of it took place before 1240.[49] More recently, however, Christopher Dyer has tentatively suggested that the bulk of population rise probably took place after 1200.[50] This is a view with which I agree,[51] although it clearly needs more work. On the other hand, the new entrepreneurial cycle seems to have been gaining pace by at least the 1180s and might well even have its starting point as early as the opening up of the Freiberg silver mines perhaps as early as the 1160s. If so, entrepreneurial take-off might have preceded marked population acceleration by at least twenty years and perhaps thirty or more. Critically, for the growth of the economy in the long thirteenth century, there seems to have been a period of fifty to one hundred years, perhaps, at its greatest, from around 1200 to around 1300, when both entrepreneurial activity and population rise worked very much in concert. That is, entrepreneurial growth fed population growth which, in turn, provided the demand for more entrepreneurial growth. This conjuncture arguably provided the prime motor for growth during the long thirteenth century.

The timing of the cycles at the end of the long thirteenth century seems much clearer. As indicated above, entrepreneurial activity and its offshoot in monumental building was slackening well before the end of the thirteenth century. At the very least, it would suggest that problems in the early fourteenth century had a significant element of investment slowdown if not stagnation accompanied by a greater rate of unemployment or underemployment among people in general, especially among non-agricultural workers. Eventually, problems of food supply and underemployment coincided. An analysis of building investment on the bishopric of Winchester's estates, for example, shows that investment in building on the estate slowed dramatically during the famine years from 1315 to 1322, indicating that high food prices coupled with much reduced employment opportunities may have contributed considerably to the

[49] Russell, *British Medieval Population*, pp. 246–60. A large part of the reason for Russell believing this was because he set his estimate of the population at 1348, just before the advent of the Black Death, at the very low level of 3.7 million. The 1.5 or so times increase in population he postulated for the period from 1086 to 1240 thus did not leave much room for further increase to 1348.

[50] Dyer, *Making a Living in the Middle Ages*, pp. 155–56, 235; see also Dyer, *Standards of Living in the Later Middle Ages*, p. 4.

[51] For example, the number of mills on west midland estates in England seems to have stagnated for a century after 1086, perhaps because of lack of demand from population growth during that period: Langdon, 'Water-mills and Windmills', table 1 (p. 430).

severity of the crisis.[52] Perhaps most obvious is that the economy had in fact been raised to a new 'circular flow', to use Schumpeter's words, one in which the non-agricultural component of the workforce had been significantly and irreversibly altered. It was a labour force more in tune with a much more monetized economy and to a very different investment mentality than had existed in the late twelfth century, but also much more vulnerable.[53]

Conclusions

Altogether, there are some indicators that might lead one to think that there was a cycle of investment (or entrepreneurial activity generally) which preceded the cycle of population by about a generation, and if so, the former would seem to have been having a marked impact upon the latter. The truth or not of this statement can only be confirmed by future research and examination, but it is, for me, a vision as plausible as that provided by Postan in imposing a long view of economic development over medieval European history, particularly for the so-called long thirteenth century. It presupposes a certain sort of economy in place — one that is monetized and open to extensive market activity. Critically, too, it had to be one where the infrastructure was developed enough to allow rapid growth. This involved not only sufficient transport, currency, and market facilities, but also strong institutional control, that is, based within a commonly accepted legal structure and with effective policing, all of which considerably reduced transaction costs. Most crucially it was one where profit margins, however these should be expressed at the time, could be visualized — and realized — by entrepreneurs. Furthermore, the success of firstcomers had to be obvious enough to convince others to join. It was also a development which, I would argue, reached very deeply into the society of the time. Finally, in Schumpeterian terms, it was very much a lifting from one 'circular flow' to the next, where the economic structure of society — here involving a much

[52] Langdon, Walker, and Falconer, 'Boom and Bust'.

[53] Richard Britnell's recent characterization of this labour force as more differentiated than specialized is, I think, an interesting distinction which in many ways downplays the divergence between the early fourteenth-century non-agricultural labour force and that which existed earlier (Britnell, 'Specialization of Work in England', esp. p. 14). Nonetheless, a more well-defined non-agricultural labour force, the welfare of which was very much affected by periodic fluctuations in the demand for building, seems clearly to have been in existence by the beginning of the fourteenth century: e.g. Langdon, 'The Mobilization of Labour', pp. 52–55; Langdon, Walker, and Falconer, 'Boom and Bust', pp. 154–55.

more deeply monetized economy, an extensive network of markets, and a very differently structured labour force — was markedly dissimilar in quantitative and qualitative terms from the economy which had existed at the start of the cycle. In this sense, Postan's ideas are patently inadequate, because they tend to deny any fundamental change from the beginning of a cycle to its end,[54] and in fact we are much better served by Duby here, who had a vision of change or evolution from one economic state to the next.[55] Nevertheless, Postan's view has always been more elegant theoretically. We need some other theoretical line to capture that elegance and to accommodate the strengths of both Postan and Duby. This, I would argue, can be achieved along Schumpeterian lines.

Epilogue

This paper, written a decade ago, had a fundamental impact upon subsequent publications of mine. It opened up interests for me concerning the way that economic growth (or decline) was actually fashioned in pre-industrial societies, emphasizing more proactive elements of human action in the economy of the time rather than seeing these same humans as passively trapped within more impersonal Malthusian or environmental constraints (such as climate). These subsequent investigations, however, have tended to go beyond Schumpeterian principles in emphasizing group rather than individual social mechanics. Of critical relevance in this regard was the family as the locus in which individual economic and demographic initiatives took place. In an article written with James Masschaele, the idea of the two cycles ventured in the paper above was taken further by looking at the issue from the point of view of family income rather than individual real wages.[56] If family income is considered rather than real wages, the often observed virtuous cycles of strong economic growth tied

[54] See, for example, Postan's very dismissive views about the changes in agricultural technology and investment over the thirteenth century: Postan, *The Medieval Economy and Society*, pp. 45–49.

[55] As perhaps most succinctly expressed in Duby, *L'économie rurale*, I, 272–74 (Duby, *Rural Economy*, trans. by C. Postan, pp. 164–65). Where I personally differ most from Duby is in his interpretation of the end of the cycle (which he dated from 1275 to 1330). He views this period as exhibiting a split between *les petites gens des campagne* and a group of entrepreneurs who continued to go from strength to strength (Duby, *L'économie rurale*, I, 273–74). My feeling is that the investment downturn had an impact upon all levels of society, although some were clearly more able to deal with the increasing difficulties of the early fourteenth century than others.

[56] Langdon and Masschaele, 'Commercial Activity and Population Growth'.

to vigorous demographic expansion occurring in pre-industrial societies, what Jack Goldstone has memorably called 'efflorescences',[57] seem easier to explain. Accordingly, in the later Langdon/Masschaele article, Masschaele used a reworking of H. E. Hallam's data to obtain a much more realistic vision for demographic growth over the thirteenth century as a sharp acceleration that made more sense in the context of family incomes than individual real wages.[58] As argued in my paper here, this acceleration was, among other things, reflected in the building of the period, from castles and churches through to mills. Milling especially was a demand-sensitive area of building, where peasant desires for local access to water- and wind-powered grinding facilities, alongside lords' wishes to profit from the activity, have been shown to have had a particularly important impact upon the appearance of watermills and windmills in the medieval English countryside.[59] Even in the difficult circumstances following the advent of the Black Death, the milling capacity which had been established in the runup to the start of the fourteenth century remained largely in place for the next couple of centuries.[60]

Of particular interest in the area of building was how family income was likely enhanced by the appearance of women and children in what was usually a male-dominated workforce, which was likely important for bolstering cash reserves for things like new family formation.[61] The timing of this appearance of womens' and childrens' labour in building, as a result, might serve as a crude unemployment index, where the appearance of this labour indicates that adult males were fully employed to the point that reserve labour in the form of women and children was called into action. When such 'reserve' labour was not apparent it suggests that employment might have been relatively scarce. Where a building account series is substantial enough, it can thus give a rough sense of the contours of labour demand over time, as in the case of the works accounts for the palace and park at Old Woodstock, Oxfordshire.[62] Here the incidence of womens' labour was particularly evident for the latter part of the thirteenth

[57] Goldstone, 'Efflorescences and Economic Growth', esp. pp. 333–34.

[58] Langdon and Masschaele, 'Commercial Activity and Population Growth', pp. 54–68.

[59] See esp. Langdon, 'Lordship and Peasant Consumerism'.

[60] The number of mills in medieval England, even at the nadir of the economic slump during the fifteenth century, still remained at 75 per cent or so of what it had been at its peak around 1300: see especially Langdon, *Mills in the Medieval Economy*, pp. 26–31.

[61] This theme is explored in Langdon, 'Waged Building Employment'.

[62] Langdon, 'Minimum Wages and Unemployment Rates'.

century at a time when, as traditional in the literature, Malthusian forces of population versus food resources were leading to a steady erosion of individual real wages. The alternate argument advanced in the Langdon/Masschaele article is that, due to the employment opportunities still available for the entire family, as reflected in the appearance of women and probably children in building accounts, family income was still increasing and would only begin to decline around the beginning of the fourteeenth century, when these employment opportunities began to fade away.[63] In terms of explaining the much-discussed early fourteenth-century malaise, this vision introduces a much stronger sense of recession — that is, a failure in investment and employment — which can be added to the subsistence crisis also looming for the population. As a theoretical framework from which to situate the findings of future research, it is in this light that Schumpeterian ideas can probably be most fruitfully applied in adding texture to the concepts and ideas circulating around the nature of the medieval economy and society.

[63] Langdon and Masschaele, 'Commercial Activity and Population Growth', esp. pp. 41–42, 71–72.

Bibliography

Archives

Kew, The National Archives, C 134/90/5

Primary Sources

Malthus, Thomas Robert, *The Works of Thomas Robert Malthus*, ed. by E. A. Wrigley and David Souden, 8 vols (London: William Pickering, 1986)

Secondary Sources

Britnell, Richard, *The Commercialisation of English Society 1000–1500* (Cambridge: Cambridge University Press, 1993)

——, 'Pragmatic Literacy in Latin Christendom', in *Pragmatic Literacy East and West, 1200–1330*, ed. by R. H. Britnell (Woodbridge: Boydell and Brewer, 1997), pp. 3–24

——, 'The Proliferation of Markets in England, 1200–1349', *Economic History Review*, 2nd ser., 34 (1981), 209–21

——, 'Specialization of Work in England, 1100–1300', *Economic History Review*, 54 (2001), 1–16

Brown, R. A., H. M. Colvin, and A. J. Taylor, *The History of the King's Works*, I: *The Middle Ages* (London: HMSO, 1963)

Campbell, Bruce, 'The Diffusion of Vetches in Medieval England', *Economic History Review*, 2nd ser., 41 (1988), 193–208

——, *English Seigniorial Agriculture, 1250–1450*, Cambridge Studies in Historical Geography, 31 (Cambridge: Cambridge University Press, 2000)

——, 'Towards an Agricultural Geography of Medieval England', *Agricultural History Review*, 36 (1988), 87–98

Carlin, Martha, *Medieval Southwark* (London: Hambledon, 1996)

Duby, Georges, *The Early Growth of the European Economy: Warriors and Peasants from the Seventh to the Twelfth Century* (London: Weidenfeld and Nicolson, 1974)

——, *L'économie rurale et la vie des campagnes dans l'Occident Médiéval (France, Angleterre, Empire, IXe–XVe siècles): Essai de synthèse et perspectives de recherches*, 2 vols (Paris: Aubier, 1962)

——, *Rural Economy and Country Life in the Medieval West*, trans. by Cynthia Postan (Columbia: University of South Carolina Press, 1968)

Dyer, Christopher, *Making a Living in the Middle Ages: The People of Britain, 850–1520* (New Haven: Hambledon, 2002)

——, *Standards of Living in the Later Middle Ages: Social Change in England c. 1200–1520*, rev. edn (Cambridge: Cambridge University Press, 1998)

Farmer, David L., 'Prices and Wages [1000–1355]', in *The Agrarian History of England and Wales*, II: *1042–1350*, ed. by Herbert E. Hallam (Cambridge: Cambridge University Press, 1988), pp. 716–817

Gimpel, Jean, *The Medieval Machine: The Industrial Revolution of the Middle Ages* (Harmondsworth: Penguin, 1977)

Goldstone, Jack, 'Efflorescences and Economic Growth in World History: Rethinking the "Rise of the West" and the Industrial Revolution', *Journal of World History*, 13 (2002), 323–89

Hallam, Herbert E., ed., *The Agrarian History of England and Wales*, II: *1042–1350* (Cambridge: Cambridge University Press, 1988)

——, 'Population Movements in England, 1086–1350', in *The Agrarian History of England and Wales*, II: *1042–1350*, ed. by Herbert E. Hallam (Cambridge: Cambridge University Press, 1988), pp. 508–93

Harrison, David, 'Bridges and Economic Development, 1300–1800', *Economic History Review*, 2nd ser., 45 (1992), 240–61

——, *The Bridges of Medieval England: Transport and Society 400–1800* (Oxford: Oxford University Press, 2004)

Hatcher, John, and Mark Bailey, eds, *Modelling the Middle Ages: The History and Theory of England's Economic Development* (Oxford: Oxford University Press, 2001)

Holt, Richard, *The Mills of Medieval England* (Oxford: Basil Blackwell, 1988)

Hunt, Edwin, and James Murray, *A History of Business in Medieval Europe, 1200–1550* (Cambridge: Cambridge University Press, 1999)

Keene, Derek, 'Issues of Water in Medieval London to *c.* 1300', *Urban History*, 28 (2001), 161–79

Langdon, John, 'The Birth and Demise of a Medieval Windmill', *History of Technology*, 14 (1992), 54–76

——, 'The Economics of Horses and Oxen in Medieval England', *Agricultural History Review*, 30 (1982), 31–40

——, 'Horse Hauling: A Revolution in Vehicle Transport in Twelfth- and Thirteenth-Century England?', *Past and Present*, no. 103 (1984), 37–66

——, *Horses, Oxen and Technological Innovation: The Use of Draught Animals in English Farming from 1066 to 1500* (Cambridge: Cambridge University Press, 1986)

——, 'Lordship and Peasant Consumerism in the Milling Industry of Early Fourteenth-Century England', *Past and Present*, 145 (1994), 3–46

——, *Mills in the Medieval Economy: England, 1300–1540* (Oxford: Oxford University Press, 2004)

——, 'Minimum Wages and Unemployment Rates in Medieval England: The Case of Old Woodstock, Oxfordshire, 1256–1357', in *Commercial Activity, Markets and Entrepreneurs in the Middle Ages: Essays in Honour of Richard Britnell*, ed. by Ben Dodds and Christian D. Liddy (Woodbridge: Boydell and Brewer, 2011), pp. 25–44

——, 'The Mobilization of Labour in the Milling Industry of Thirteenth- and Early Fourteenth-Century England', *Canadian Journal of History*, 31 (1996), 37–58

——, 'The Use of Animal Power from 1200 to 1800', in *Economia e Energia*, ed. by Simonetta Cavaciocchi, Proceedings from the 34th Annual Conference of the Istituto Internazionale di Storia Economica 'F. Datini', Prato, 15–19 April 2002 (Firenze: Le Monnier, 2003), pp. 213–21

——, 'Waged Building Employment in Medieval England: Subsistence Safety Net or Demographic Trampoline?', in *Survival and Discord in Medieval Society: Essays in Honour of Christopher Dyer*, ed. by Richard Goddard, John Langdon, and Miriam Müller, The Medieval Countryside, 4 (Turnhout: Brepols, 2010), pp. 109–26

——, 'Water-mills and Windmills in the West Midlands, 1086–1500', *Economic History Review*, 2nd ser., 44 (1991), 424–44

Langdon, John, and James Masschaele, 'Commercial Activity and Population Growth in Medieval England', *Past and Present*, 190 (2006), 35–81

Langdon, John, Jill Walker, and John R. Falconer, 'Boom and Bust: Building Investment on the Bishop of Winchester's Estate in the Early Fourteenth Century', in *The Winchester Pipe Rolls and Medieval English Society*, ed. by Richard Britnell (Woodbridge: Boydell, 2003), pp. 139–55

Mate, Mavis, 'Property Investment by Canterbury Cathedral Priory 1250–1400', *Journal of British Studies*, 23 (1984), 1–21

Mokyr, Joel, *The Lever of Riches: Technological Creativity and Economic Progress* (New York: Oxford University Press, 1990)

Morris, Richard, *Cathedrals and Abbeys of England and Wales: The Building Church, 600–1540* (London: J. M. Dent & Sons, 1979)

Palliser, D. M., T. R. Slater, and E. Patricia Dennison, 'The Topography of Towns 600–1300', in *The Cambridge Urban History of Britain*, I: *600–1540*, ed. by D. M. Palliser (Cambridge: Cambridge University Press, 2000), pp. 153–86

Pelham, R. A., *Fulling Mills: A Study in the Application of Water Power to the Woollen Industry*, no. 5 (London: Society for the Protection of Ancient Buildings, 1958)

Postan, Michael, 'Medieval Agarian Society in its Prime: England', in *The Cambridge Economic History of Europe*, I: *The Agrarian Life of the Middle Ages*, ed. by Michael M. Postan, 2nd edn (Cambridge: Cambridge University Press, 1966), pp. 548–632

——, *The Medieval Economy and Society* (Harmondsworth: Penguin, 1975)

Russell, Josiah Cox, *British Medieval Population* (Albuquerque: University of New Mexico Press, 1948)

Schofield, John, and Geoffrey Stell, 'The Built Environment 1300–1540', in *The Cambridge Urban History of Britain*, I: *600–1540*, ed. by D. M. Palliser (Cambridge: Cambridge University Press, 2000), pp. 371–94

Schumpeter, Joseph, *Business Cycles: A Theoretical, Historical, and Statistical Analysis of the Capitalist Process*, 2 vols (New York: McGraw-Hill, 1939)

——, *The Theory of Economic Development: An Inquiry into Profits, Capital, Credit, Interest, and the Business Cycle*, trans. by Redvers Opie (New York: Oxford University Press, 1961; originally published in German in 1912)

Spufford, Peter, *Money and its Use in Medieval Europe* (Cambridge: Cambridge University Press, 1988)

White, Lynne, Jr, *Medieval Technology and Social Change* (Oxford: Oxford University Press, 1962)

M. M. Postan and the Peasant Economy

Phillipp Schofield

Introduction

There are, as Hatcher and Bailey have usefully reminded us in their survey of explanatory models of economic change in the Middle Ages, three main causative mechanisms of that change to which historians subscribe: population, class struggle, and commercialization.[1] The work of M. M. Postan, as is well known, was central to the first, building a chronology of change into the machinery of population movement. At the core of Postan's thesis is a model of population in relation to resources, with an inbuilt assumption that resources are finite but also incapable, within the institutional context of the period, of significant expansion. Thus, a process of colonization and some intensification of land use in the High Middle Ages ultimately did not solve the population's problems, but added to them. Resources per capita were reduced as yields, despite the attentions of medieval farmers, failed to keep pace with increases in population. Wages failed to match price movements in the period before plague also; as wages fell in relative terms so people's existence became even more precarious. At the same time, growing population pressure had a significant impact on landholding, with a combination of inheritance and a land market (where such existed) leading to a subdivision of holdings.

* A first version of this paper was given at the Postan-Duby conference at Montreal in October 2002. I am very grateful to John Drendel for the invitation to attend that conference and for the valuable comments of participants at that meeting

[1] Hatcher and Bailey, *Modelling the Middle Ages*.

Phillipp Schofield (prs@aber.ac.uk) is professor of medieval history in the Department of History and Welsh History at Aberystwyth University.

Crisis in the Later Middle Ages: Beyond the Postan-Duby Paradigm, ed. by John Drendel, TMC 13 (Turnhout: Brepols, 2015) 73–93 BREPOLS PUBLISHERS 10.1484/M.TMC.5.103785

Further to this, Postan acknowledged that trade and marketing opportunities provided some outlet to this population-resources pressure, but as Hatcher and Bailey in their summary of this aspect of the model remark, 'the proponents of population-resources models downplay the cumulative importance of commerce and urbanization in medieval economic development, and consequently are pessimistic about their implications for peasant welfare'.[2]

In this short chapter, an attempt will be made to explore the extent to which Postan's commitment to a particular model served to fashion his view of the English medieval peasantry, as well, of course, as shaping the research agendas and approaches of later historians.[3] In order to do this, we can begin with a brief review of Postan's work on the English medieval peasantry, setting out some key publications and their main contributions, before offering a short summary of the accumulated main themes which Postan associated with the peasantry of the Middle Ages. From there, we will both examine the degree to which Postan's agenda was absorbed by later work on the peasantry (which will also encourage some short reflection on other schools of thought with regard to the medieval peasantry) and, above all, consider the extent to which Postan's own agenda kept him from possible interpretations of that peasantry or, rather, encouraged him to grant significance to certain aspects and to reduce the likely role of others. In a concluding section, the discussion will, albeit in the most summary of fashions, touch upon recent developments in the economy of the medieval peasantry in the light of my earlier comments.

Postan and the Medieval Peasantry

While Postan's framing of his broad explanatory model of economic change dates from at least as early as the 1940s, the bulk of Postan's work on the economy of the medieval peasant is later. With the sole and very important exception of the essay on 'The Chronology of Labour Services' (1937), Postan's contribution to the historiography of the English medieval peasantry is revealed in a series of articles, chapters, and a short synthesis, published between the mid-

[2] Hatcher and Bailey, *Modelling the Middle Ages*, p. 50. Postan's main arguments on the relationship between population and the economy occupy a middle phase of his writing career, central to which was his keynote address to the IXe Congrès International des Sciences Historiques, late summer 1950, published as Postan, 'The Economic Foundations'.

[3] For that commitment and commentary upon it, see Hatcher and Bailey, *Modelling the Middle Ages*, pp. 53–54.

1950s and early 1970s.[4] In particular, in his introductory essay to the *Carte Nativorum* and in his more general discussions of the peasant economy in the *Cambridge Economic History* and in *Medieval Society and Economy*, Postan set out some significant features of the medieval economy. It is in his discussion of the medieval land market that Postan is most explicit in his description of the driving force of the medieval village economy. In his essay on 'Legal Status and Economic Conditions' (1968), Postan writes of the village land market and 'its responsiveness to demographic factors, and its lack of response to such purely economic considerations as prices of agricultural produce'.[5]

As is well known, Postan described inequalities in land market behaviour in relation to demographic variables, the 'natural sellers' and 'natural buyers' of the village economy a consequence of relativities of family size.[6] While Postan acknowledges that the individuals who purchased land in the late thirteenth and early fourteenth centuries may have been wealthy villagers, he doubted whether the relatively wealthy predominated amongst the buyers. Instead, he notes that 'among the buyers whose economic position we know, we find numerous men of humble rank, smallholders, or wholly landless persons who presumably disposed of idle hands, but were under-provided with land'.[7] Importantly, Postan weighs the relative merits of 'commercialisation' and 'family form' as explanations of the peasant land market and plumps for the latter. He accepts that 'some of the inducements were purely economic; they might even be described as commercial' but then continues to suggest that 'the balance of evidence suggests that the *main* stimulus for traffic in land was generated within the peasant community and owed more to certain abiding features of peasant life than to the higher values of the thirteenth century and their attraction for speculators'.[8] Interestingly, also, in his brief consideration of the 'commercial' impetus for a peasant land market in the thirteenth century, Postan frames his discussion in a demographically determined context, arguing that commercial pressures may have come into existence as a result of rising land prices in a period of land

[4] Postan, 'The Chronology of Labour Services'; Postan and Titow, 'Heriots and Prices'; Postan, 'Village Livestock'; Postan, 'Glastonbury Estates'; Postan, 'Legal Status and Economic Conditions'. All of the above titles are also published in Postan, *Essays on Medieval Agriculture*, from which all subsequent references are taken. But see also Postan, *The Cambridge Economic History of Europe*, I, 600–32; Postan, *Medieval Economy and Society*.

[5] Postan, 'Legal Status and Economic Conditions', p. 280.

[6] Brooke and Postan, *Carte Nativorum*, p. 115.

[7] Brooke and Postan, *Carte Nativorum*, pp. 116–17.

[8] Brooke and Postan, *Carte Nativorum*, p. 114 (my italics).

hunger. At such moments, those with a surplus of land may have chosen to hive off portions of their land to take advantage of market conditions. In this case, as in his earlier statement regarding the relative ubiquity of poorer buyers in comparison with wealthier purchasers, Postan is disinclined to provide the peasant entrepreneur with a motive force. Postan's wealthy villager of the thirteenth century responds to demographic circumstance, as does, therefore, the market environment in which he (or she) operates.[9]

These views, as outlined here, were central to Postan's essay on the *Carte Nativorum*, but they reappear in modified form in some of his later work. In his final assessment of the medieval peasant economy, published in the early 1970s, but in fact, insofar as it discusses the village economy, a close reworking of the section on England in *Cambridge Economic History* (1966),[10] Postan offered some departure from his earlier statement on the peasant land market. In *The Medieval Economy and Society* (1972), Postan retreated, in part, from his position of a decade earlier (in his introduction to the *Carte Nativorum*), suggesting in the later work that 'where evidence of villagers' transactions — mostly in court rolls — is sufficiently detailed to reveal the social condition of the parties, it invariably suggests that wealthy villagers bought more than others'.[11] Here, as elsewhere, land is described as being perceived principally as a subsistence resource but also as an indicator of status.[12] Above all, the motive force behind these relationships remains population movement: 'the transmission of land by purchase or by marriage, and the declining proportion of transmission by ordinary inheritance, was merely one of the signs of the increasing land hunger'.[13]

Further, when reflecting on the use to which the wealthier peasants put their relative advantage, Postan essentially internalizes the village economy, suggesting that where the more successful peasants chose not to establish larger family farms, they opted to sublet holdings to under-settles; what is more, in furnishing a local market with credit, an aspect discussed in a very interesting aside at the close of his chapter on the village economy (and a point to which we shall return), wealthier peasants were presenting opportunities for land purchase to

[9] Brooke and Postan, *Carte Nativorum*, p. 114.

[10] Postan, 'Medieval Agarian Society'.

[11] Postan, *Medieval Economy and Society*, pp. 150–51; see also Postan, 'Medieval Agarian Society', p. 625.

[12] Postan, *Medieval Economy and Society*, pp. 151–53; see also Postan, 'Medieval Agarian Society', pp. 627–28.

[13] Postan, *Medieval Economy and Society*, p. 37.

those who were less advantaged. Postan, therefore, limits the potential function of the peasant economy and sets its focus upon its own subsistence and consumption needs.[14] These views were also carried over into Postan's middle and later work on trade. In his essay on 'The Trade of Medieval Europe: The North' (1952), Postan, while acknowledging the potential for a market-orientated peasantry, retreated from the full implications of such a thesis.[15] In writing of the early Middle Ages, he rejected any notion of self-sufficiency and concluded that 'an unbiased student of medieval agriculture cannot avoid the conclusion that social existence in medieval villages would have been impossible without some market and some trade'.[16] Intriguingly, having arrived at such a conclusion, Postan attempts later in his essay to distance himself from it, drawing a distinction between the early and late Middle Ages and stressing the tendency for the bulk of trade to be predominantly local and 'unprofessional' but also, in the later period, for a professionalization of a mercantile elite to reflect a distinction between levels of trade with the countryside essentially isolated from direct contact with trade and with wider markets.[17] In particular, Postan stresses the extent to which a feudal countryside was, in the High Middle Ages, obliged to abandon its earlier association with trading activity, arguing that 'conditions of feudal society made it difficult for the expanding trade to remain in the hands of the rural classes and to be combined with other rural pursuits'.[18]

Of course, as Postan was all too aware, the nature of the medieval village economy varied institutionally, temporally, and spatially. Within the long thirteenth century, regional distinctions, as well as institutional differences, affected the landholding of the tenantry and their ability to alienate property, an important theme of Postan's work on the *Carte Nativorum*. Postan recognized that the condition of the peasantry of eastern England was likely to be quite distinct from, for instance, those of the Winchester estates. That said, Postan, especially in his work on village livestock, the central argument of which has been much refuted in recent years,[19] attempted to iron out regional

[14] Postan, *Medieval Economy and Society*, pp. 152–53; see also Postan, 'Medieval Agarian Society', pp. 627–28.

[15] Postan, 'The Trade of Medieval Europe' (subsequent references are taken from the reprint version).

[16] Postan, 'The Trade of Medieval Europe', p. 127.

[17] Postan, 'The Trade of Medieval Europe', pp. 140–41.

[18] Postan, 'The Trade of Medieval Europe', p. 142.

[19] See, for instance, Masschaele, *Peasants, Merchants and Markets*, pp. 42–44.

distinctiveness in the face of the juggernaut of population pressure. In discussing the livestock resources of villagers in Suffolk and Wiltshire in the thirteenth century, his conclusion that peasants held, on average, few livestock resources was, to quote, no 'more than a restatement in concrete and social terms of the economic and social "model" of the thirteenth-century economy', one in which 'land was scarce and getting scarcer, and men in search of sustenance were forced to till the lands which in other and more spacious periods would and should have been used as pasture, and in fact were to be used again from the fourteenth century onwards'.[20]

Postan and the Peasant Economy: The Dominance of a Paradigm

Having reviewed Postan's key statements on the economy of the medieval peasantry, and described ways in which his view of the peasant economy was dominated by his commitment to a model of economic change founded upon population, a commitment which predates much of his close engagement with aspects of the peasant economy, it is time to explore the extent to which that view of the peasantry, as a direct result of Postan's re-employment of his own model, inevitably overlooked other important aspects of that economy.

In order to do this we will first need to refer to research on the medieval village, some of which predates the work of Postan and some of which, the bulk in fact, follows his contributions. This will also encourage some brief comment on Postan's other work on the medieval economy in order to tease out the possible inferences which Postan may have drawn from his research, based on his exceptional knowledge of the economy of the period, but which, constrained by his own paradigm, he did not.

The Medieval Peasant Economy: Before and After Postan

R. H. Tawney's *The Agrarian Problem of the Sixteenth Century* (1912) had offered a version of the medieval peasantry quite distinct in many of its attributes from that identifiable in Postan's work. For Tawney, in his invaluable discussion of the nature of the economy of the village before and after the plague, it was the market and a drive towards acquisitiveness which, as well as exciting the indignation of Tawney, provided a significant driving force to that local economy. Tawney, in discussing the land market and the village economy before

[20] Postan, 'Village Livestock', p. 247.

the plague, speaks of the wealthy whose advantage lies in the disadvantage of their neighbours, for instance, and elsewhere describes the village moneylender as a familiar bugbear of such an economy. Tawney's was an important departure, but it was one with which Postan, in his own work on the peasantry, did not engage (judging at least by a review of Postan's references in his key and most relevant works).[21]

In fact, we might suggest that Postan diverted discussion from Tawney's early analysis, which offered what was essentially a schema of a Leninist-differentiation kind for the medieval peasant economy, and replaced it with a Chayanovian model that, for at least a generation of scholars, was broadly accepted. Thus, for instance, historians of high-status land sales and leases have been long aware of the latent effects of credit in the land market, as, for example, in their analysis of the purchase of encumbered estates by wealthier buyers in the twelfth century;[22] historians of the land market in other social contexts, especially the peasant land market, have, however, been less aware of the potential underpinning of debt and credit relationships. As Hyams has argued, in what is also a critique of Postan's introduction to the edition of the *Carte Nativorum*, an awareness of the importance of loans as a vital element of the market in land inevitably modifies our view of that market.[23] Instead of being simply a means of exchanging plots of land according to need, evidence of an aggressive employment of credit gives the impression that the inter-vivos transfer of small plots was a more truly commercial market than has always been allowed.[24] To date, however, most investigations of the inter-peasant lease market in late medieval England have overlooked the possibility of gages and, instead, have tended to see the lease as a temporary expedient intended to adjust the size of the holding.[25]

[21] Tawney, *The Agrarian Problem*; see also Hudson, 'The Prior of Norwich's Manor'.

[22] Richardson, *The English Jewry*, pp. 91–92.

[23] Hyams, 'The Origins of a Peasant Land Market', p. 20; see also Spufford, 'Peasant Inheritance Customs', pp. 162–63.

[24] Postan, 'Medieval Agarian Society', pp. 626–28.

[25] Chayanov, *The Theory of Peasant Economy*; Postan, 'The Charters of the Villeins'; see also Hilton, *The English Peasantry*, pp. 6–7; Smith, 'Some Issues Concerning Families', pp. 6–38; Dyer, 'Changes in the Size of Peasant Holdings', pp. 277–78; Harvey, 'Conclusion'. Postan felt that mortgages were not easily accommodated within this thesis, whilst 'husbandry leases', those simply intended to be cultivated by the lessee, were, but as Paul Hyams has shown, both can be happily assimilated: Hyams, 'The Origins of a Peasant Land Market', pp. 28–31. The mortgaging of peasant land is well evidenced in the early modern period: see, for example, Holderness,

In this respect, work has been much informed by Postan's discussion of the lease, a discussion central to his introductory chapter on the 'Charters of the Villeins'. In his description of the lease in the medieval countryside, Postan was careful to show, as was undoubtedly the case, that leasehold, including an inter-tenant lease market, was a significant aspect of the village land market from, he suggests, at least the twelfth century.[26] For Postan, the inter-tenant leases are best seen as 'current adjustments to the fluctuating circumstances of individuals'.[27] Villagers, according to Postan, attempted at all costs to avoid outright alienation. Postan also suggests a temporal distinction between the late Middle Ages (post-1350) when leasehold transfer gave way to outright sale and an earlier period when transfer by lease fulfilled a distinct need in a period of population pressure, when the landless or near landless saw leases as a means to supplement their meagre holdings.[28] These 'husbandry leases' are contrasted, in Postan's argument, with 'beneficiary leases' associated with mortgages of land.[29] Postan is at pains to reject any notion that the leases which can be found at the village level are in any way associated with the extension of and security for credit.[30] As already suggested, it is certainly the case that historians working within the last quarter century have been heavily influenced by Postan's model of the peasantry and, in particular, of the peasant land market. Thus, for instance, Williamson's discussion of the peasant land market in thirteenth-century Norfolk follows a strictly Postanian/Chayanovian line in her characterization of such a market. In particular, she identifies leases recorded in the manor court as 'husbandry leases' in the same way as did Postan, and there is clear indication of the influence of his work in her conclusions.[31] Other historians writing on the peasant land market through into the mid-1980s also employed

'Widows in Pre-Industrial Society', pp. 437–39; Wyndham, *Petworth Manor*, pp. 11–13, and passim. For the late Middle Ages, Harvey, *Westminster Abbey*, pp. 317–18; Dyer, *Standards of Living in the Later Middle Ages*, p. 180; Mate, 'The East Sussex Land Market', p. 60. For further discussion of these points, see also van Bavel and Schofield, 'Introduction', pp. 13, 16–17.

[26] Postan, 'The Charters of the Villeins', pp. 132–43.

[27] Postan, 'The Charters of the Villeins', p. 136.

[28] Postan, 'The Charters of the Villeins', pp. 137–38.

[29] Postan, 'The Charters of the Villeins', p. 141.

[30] Postan, 'The Charters of the Villeins', pp. 141–42.

[31] For examples of the interpretation of all leases as 'husbandry leases', see Williamson, 'Norfolk: Thirteenth Century', pp. 53–54, 59, 77.

this Chayanovian approach and made direct and largely approving reference to the work of Postan in doing so.[32]

As already noted at the outset of this chapter, Postan's view of the peasantry did not enjoy a universal hegemony in the decades during which he wrote or in the years following. The two 'alternative' models of economic change — class struggle and commercialization — have both found their proponents in discussion of the medieval peasant economy. While it is the latter which has, more than any model, come to dominate thinking on the medieval peasant since the 1980s, the former offered the most trenchant anti-Postanian position during the years that Postan was active as a researcher and writer.

Marxist historians of the English medieval peasantry came, as we shall see, to write in response to the work of Postan, but the earliest seminal contributions of Marxists were written with only passing direct reference to his views.[33] In discussing Postan's work on the medieval land market and his implicit commitment to Chayanov, Rodney Hilton notes that 'there seemed to be an element of Chayanov versus Lenin in the arguments used'.[34] The same could also be said to be true of Hilton's own characterization of the medieval village economy, which shares some essential elements with Postan's. While Hilton acknowledges and, indeed, is at pains to illustrate the potential for market exchange within the village, he is also wary of the suggestion that the medieval peasant was committed to a quasi-capitalist system; instead he argues that 'transfer of use values from household to household' remained important and rejects the prominence of 'a land market involving permanent alienation'.[35] We might, in other words, detect a consonance of views with Postan and a commitment to a Chayanovian perspective, or at the very least, a perspective which found little room for a peasant economy dominated by competitive markets and acquisitiveness. While Hilton's view of the peasant economy shared similar features to that expressed in the work of Postan, its provenance was quite different: for Hilton, a peasantry which could eschew commercial rivalry and combine in

[32] Other contributors to Harvey, *The Peasant Land Market in Medieval England* drew similar conclusions on the nature of the peasant land market: Faith, 'Berkshire', pp. 125–26; Jones, 'Bedfordshire', p. 243; Lomas, 'Durham', pp. 293–94.

[33] References to Postan's work in Hilton's own output seem to be relatively few; direct discussion of its central theses is also minimal; for examples of direct engagement, see Hilton, 'Introduction', p. 28.

[34] Hilton, *The English Peasantry*, pp. 6–7.

[35] Hilton, *The English Peasantry*, p. 47.

opposition to lordship remained a primary tenet of his thinking.[36] However, as Postan and Hatcher note in a rather gleeful response to Brenner, orthodox Soviet Marxism commentators could lump Postan and Hilton together as exponents of the 'economist view of medieval history'. They note also, as does Hatcher in a much more recent publication, that Hilton identified the central importance of demographic processes.[37]

By contrast, Brenner's work is far more explicit in its rejection of a Postanian perspective.[38] Overtly theoretical and lacking a developed empirical base, Brenner's main target was the demographic model of economic change of which Postan's work, along with that of Le Roy Ladurie, was the most significant example. As such, Brenner has less of immediate significance to say on the peasant economy but, by implication, there are a series of important inferences which can be drawn from his work and which can be compared with Postan's own view of the peasant economy. As has been noted, Brenner shares with Postan a conception of the peasant economy as, by the thirteenth century, essentially stagnated. For Brenner, however, the explanation for this stagnation lies in a lack of peasant resource which, in turn, was a consequence of 'landlords' extraction of rent and the extreme maldistribution of both land and capital, especially livestock'.[39] A crisis of productivity resulted from peasants' inability to invest in the means of production, itself a consequence of this surplus-extraction.[40] Most importantly, in the context of this discussion, Brenner reflects upon the relationship of lordship to the productivity of wealthier peasants and identifies the constraints and demands of lordship as 'a barrier to the development of productivity'. He argues that feudal rent acted against effective accumulation, that restrictions on mobility reduced market and labour opportunities, and, most pertinently, that feudal restrictions on the mobility of land tended to prevent its concentration. Unfree peasants were not allowed to convey their land to other peasants without the lord's permission. Yet it was often

[36] Hilton, *The English Peasantry*, p. 53; Hilton, 'Medieval Peasants: Any Lessons?', p. 117. Similar perspectives are identifiable in the work of Hilton's students. See, for instance, Razi, 'The Struggles Between the Abbots'; Dyer, *Lords and Peasants in a Changing Society*; Dyer, *Making a Living in the Middle Ages*, p. 168.

[37] Postan and Hatcher, 'Population and Class Relations', p. 65, n. 2, citing also Hilton, *Bond Men Made Free*, pp. 234–35. See also Hatcher and Bailey, *Modelling the Middle Ages*, p. 64.

[38] Brenner, 'Agrarian Class Structure', pp. 13–24; also Hatcher and Bailey, *Modelling the Middle Ages*, p. 65.

[39] Brenner, 'Agrarian Class Structure', p. 33.

[40] Brenner, 'Agrarian Class Structure', p. 33.

in the lord's interest to prevent large, accumulating tenants from receiving more land, because they might find it harder to collect the rent from such tenants, especially if they had free status.[41]

Here, as earlier in our discussion of the work of Hilton in relation to that of Postan, we find described a peasant economy which, although its nature is accounted for in diametrically different terms from that employed by Postan, shares many elements with Postan's own characterization. This is a peasant economy which is tied to convention, largely static, and ill-equipped to engage with the wider market. The constraints are discrete — lordship rather than family and the forces of demography — but the everyday realities are shared. If, importantly, Brenner's own characterization of the peasant economy in the High and late Middle Ages was informed by Postan's description of its nature (and having accepted it he chose to explain it in starkly different terms), there are others who have reacted against and rejected such a characterization.[42]

As Brenner notes, Postan's model of economic change was itself a response to earlier explanations of change in the medieval economy. Postan had, in his earliest work, rejected any simple association between the rise of a money economy and the commutation of labour services.[43] Instead, processes such as commutation responded to supply and demand which, in turn, were the consequences of population change. As Britnell has described, in reviewing Postan's thesis, 'within this paradigm, commercialisation, specialisation and technical change were peripheral topics for the history of the Middle Ages'.[44] In recent years, however, a reassessment of the role of the peasant within the wider economy and, separated, at least implicitly, from any close commitment to a demographic or class-based model of economic change, detailed study of the economics of the medieval village have seen significant advance in our understanding of the nature of the peasant economy.

Richard Smith, for instance, writing in the early 1980s, had already begun to question, especially in a wide-ranging introduction to *Land, Kinship and Life-Cycle* (1984), some of the Chayanovian principles which appeared to

[41] Brenner, 'Agrarian Class Structure', pp. 33–34. Here, as well as citing Raftis and Searle, Brenner refers to Postan's work on the *Carte Nativorum*. Brenner's reference is to Postan, 'The Charters of the Villeins', pp. 112–22 (i.e. pp. xxxi–xxxiiff in the original pagination).

[42] Brenner clearly draws upon Postan's work in establishing a view of the peasant economy: Brenner, 'Agrarian Class Structure', pp. 26 (n. 33), 31 (nn. 41, 42), 33 (n. 46), 34 (nn. 49, 50).

[43] Postan, 'The Chronology of Labour Services', p. 90.

[44] Britnell, 'Commercialisation and Economic Development', p. 8.

buttress Postan's discussion of the peasant economy. Smith, engaging directly with Postan's employment of a Chayanovian model of land transfer, argued that a Leninist model of acquisitiveness could be as effectively applied to the thirteenth-century peasant land market in eastern England. He is largely dismissive of an anti-economic view of land transfer with regard to the medieval peasantry.[45] Urban historians had also commenced explorations of the relationship between town and hinterland, which challenged some of the tenets of a Postanian characterization of the village economy.[46] Britnell's later broad study of commercialization and the work of Masschaele, Raftis, and others have also stressed the capitalization and potential market orientation of the medieval peasantry, from at least the thirteenth century.[47]

In all of this work, and in explicit contrast to the views of Postan (as well, of course, as Marxists such as Brenner), is the recognition that peasants, especially peasant elites, were capable of generating a usable surplus. Masschaele's estimates of peasant output, employing taxation data in particular, has illustrated the vital role that peasant surplus played in the national economy, while Raftis also argued that it was the capitalization of the peasant, and the need to protect and nourish that capitalization, that most informed lord–tenant relations.[48] This surplus was both the product and cause of engagement with local and more distant markets. Research upon this engagement has generated an increasingly detailed understanding of the processes of accumulation and the mechanisms, including the use of law and the employment of credit, which facilitated it.[49] This development both accords with and stands in significant

[45] Smith, 'Some Issues Concerning Families', p. 31. See also the discussion in Schofield, 'Peasants and Contract'.

[46] Hilton, 'Small Town Society'; Dyer, 'The Consumer and the Market'; Kowaleski, *Local Markets and Regional Trade*; Campbell and others, *A Medieval Capital and its Grain Supply*.

[47] Britnell, 'Commercialisation and Economic Development'; Masschaele, *Peasants, Merchants and Markets*; Raftis, *Peasant Economic Development*.

[48] Masschaele, *Peasants, Merchants and Markets*, second chapter; Raftis, *Peasant Economic Development*.

[49] Clark, 'Debt Litigation'; Schofield, 'Dearth, Debt and the Local Land Market'; Schofield, 'L'endettement et le crédit'; Schofield, 'Access to Credit'; Briggs, 'Manor Court Procedures'; Beckerman, 'Procedural Innovation'; Bonfield, 'The Nature of Customary Law'; Bonfield, 'What Did Edwardian Villagers Mean by "Customary Law"?'; Beckerman, 'Toward a Theory of Medieval Manorial Adjudication'; Hyams, 'What Did Edwardian Villagers Mean by "Law"?'; Schofield, 'Peasants and the Manor Court'; Smith, 'Some Thoughts on "Hereditary" and "Proprietary" Rights'.

contrast to Postan's approach to the medieval peasant. As we shall discuss in a little more detail below, Postan was aware of the potential significance of credit and the use of law in the Middle Ages and was also not ignorant of the likely presence of creditors and debtors within the medieval village. As we have also already noted, Postan was not keen to associate leasehold with security linked to credit arrangements and was quite probably correct in considering such associations as rare at the level of manor and village.[50] Neither was Postan especially desirous of elevating the role of unsecured credit in the medieval village. In his fullest statement on rural credit at the village level he notes the existence of rural/peasant creditors and debtors. In pondering the question of how peasant buyers entered into a land market, and rejecting the possibility that creditors external to the village had a significant role to play, Postan suggests instead that some villagers, the most substantial, must have extended credit to their neighbours. In doing so, Postan argues, these creditor-peasants added one more level of authority to those they enjoyed over their neighbours and which, allied to their undoubted roles as lessors of their neighbours' lands and employers of their labour, separated them greatly 'from the ideal type of medieval peasant'.[51]

Medieval historians writing in the last two decades or so, and especially those examining rural credit and the nature of transactions at the local level, would not necessarily reject the notion that the wealthier creditors of the medieval village were atypical. However, what might distinguish their approach from that of Postan would be their tendency, in the first instance, to 'foreground' such interaction and, secondly, to set out more fully the nature of these transactions as well as the standing of the parties involved. Thus, most obviously, Briggs has discussed in detail the nature of credit in village society and, as he is keen to stress, promotes the use of low-level rural credit beyond that of a device generated by distress and crises into an everyday mechanism for exchange, and one illustrative of the potential for investment-credit rather than purely subsistence-credit in village society.[52] In setting out this view of rural credit, Briggs distinguishes his approach from an earlier view of village-level credit agreements which had, as he rightly notes, tended to locate credit — or at least its study — in the decades either side of 1300 and especially in the crisis years of the early fourteenth century.[53] Briggs sees such an emphasis as, in itself,

[50] See also Schofield, 'Peasants and Contract', pp. 144–45.

[51] Postan, 'Medieval Agarian Society', pp. 627–28.

[52] Briggs, *Credit and Village Society*.

[53] Briggs, *Credit and Village Society*, pp. 8–10. A notable exception to this is Clark, 'Debt

dependent upon the persistent attachment to Postan's thesis of 'agrarian crisis, over-population and [...] declining rural living standards' in the decades before the arrival of plague.[54] Briggs is undoubtedly correct to identify a Postanian emphasis in some elements of this analysis, notably a tendency for historians to use evidence of debt litigation in manorial courts as an index of impoverishment and crisis.[55] It is also evident that, by the time work on rural credit was underway in any systematic manner, that is, in the mid-1990s, it was set within a context of aggressive and dynamic exchange which, in eastern England at least, appeared to be encouraged by an active and seemingly increasingly volatile land market, themes that would not have sat so comfortably with a Postanian orthodoxy.[56] In other words, work by medievalists writing since the late 1970s and early 1980s had begun to lay new theoretical foundations upon which a good deal of subsequent work was laid; in fact, even in the most difficult and crisis-ridden years of the thirteenth and early fourteenth centuries, decades that sat at the heart of the Postan thesis of population outstripping resources, historians had begun to identify active land markets driven by peasant entrepreneurs, small-scale trade in goods other than staples, and interaction between town and countryside which included the exchange of relatively high-status goods. This has been most fully and forcefully discussed by Christopher Dyer who, in one of the most recent and significant discussions of these developments, places great emphasis upon the complexity of the high and later medieval economy.[57] He also notes, for instance, how polarized wealth, even in the thirteenth century, permitted investment by wealthier peasants and encouraged significant trading within and between rural communities.[58]

Postan and the Medieval Economy

If a later generation of historians appears to have generally thrown off the shackles of Postan's view of the operation of the high and late medieval rural economy, it was, of course, not possible for Postan himself to do the same. Postan's

Litigation', whose work illustrates the involved credit networks established in fifteenth-century Writtle.

[54] Briggs, *Credit and Village Society*, p. 8.

[55] On this, see also the comments in Schofield, 'Dearth, Debt and the Local Land Market', p. 1.

[56] See, for instance, Schofield, 'Dearth, Debt and the Local Land Market'.

[57] Dyer, *An Age of Transition?*, pp. 21–33.

[58] Dyer, *An Age of Transition?*, pp. 25–29.

model of population and resources was partially, but only partially, ill equipped to accommodate this view of a market-orientated peasantry. It was, as has been observed, the emphasis which Postan placed upon land availability relative to 'other resources, such as the acquired knowledge of technical and institutional practices' which may have almost prevented him from admitting this aspect of peasant economy into his narrative of the Middle Ages.[59] In Postan's work what we see, we might suggest, is the tyranny of his own paradigm, and what makes this especially ironic is that there was no better historian than Postan to have considered some of the issues that now confront and interest historians of the medieval peasantry: credit and debt; the relationship between the local economy and wider trade networks; the marketability of produce; and so on. These were issues, as is well known, that were central to his first phase of research and publication in medieval English economic history.[60] His work on credit in medieval trade remains a first point of departure for discussion of credit and indebtedness to the present day. Postan's discussion of credit in trade, first presented in his 1928 article on the same, has remained a valuable tour-de-force, a review of the potential for examining the ways in which medieval credit was employed as well as a discussion of the mechanisms involved in credit and its use.[61] Similarly, his invaluable discussions of private financial instruments and of partnership in medieval trade are founded upon consideration of mercantile trade and large-scale dealing at the national and, especially, the international level.[62] There is, as we might expect when we consider Postan's view of high and late medieval trade as activity dominated by dedicated professionals, little or no examination of low-level exchange or the movement of capital and credit within the lower reaches of rural society. However, as we have seen when we read about credit at the village level or avenues into exploration of credit, in Postan's later work it is as an unwelcome aside, crowded out by his major hypothesis.[63] Postan's wholesale commitment to a population-resources model and his reduction of the significance of low-level trade almost certainly encouraged him to underplay the importance of a commercial economy within peasant society in the High and late Middle Ages.

[59] Britnell, 'Commercialisation and Economic Development', p. 8.

[60] Postan, 'Credit in Medieval Trade' (subsequent references are taken from the reprint version); Postan, 'Private Financial Instruments'.

[61] Postan, 'Credit in Medieval Trade'.

[62] Postan, 'Private Financial Instruments'.

[63] Postan never sailed on the 'uncharted sea of the [...] various local court rolls'; Postan, 'Credit in Medieval Trade', p. 3.

In this respect, there is an irony. As more than one commentator in the last decade or so has come to observe, historians of the rural economy in the High Middle Ages do not necessarily reject a demographic model of economic change by embracing a view of a commercialized peasantry.[64] In fact, the expansion of trade and the economy may have increased the demographic penalty for sections of society, separating them from the means of production and leaving them exposed to an imperfect market, which was itself subject to the vagaries of both endogenous and exogenous shocks.[65] The important distinction, however, remains one between mobility and stagnation, a distinction which is writ large in the central tenets of, respectively, a commercialization and a population-resources model of economic change. Population became the exogenous component which, in historiographical terms, moulded the lives of Postan's peasantry and greatly influenced a generation and more of historians who followed him, including those who considered themselves fundamentally at odds with his own conception of process in the medieval economy.

[64] Hatcher and Bailey, *Modelling the Middle Ages*.

[65] Britnell, 'Commercialisation and Economic Development', pp. 22–23; Bailey, 'Peasant Welfare in England'; Campbell, 'The Agrarian Problem'.

Bibliography

Bailey, Mark, 'Peasant Welfare in England, 1290–1348', *Economic History Review*, 51 (1998), 223–51

Beckerman, John S., 'Procedural Innovation and Institutional Change in Medieval English Manorial Courts', *Law and History Review*, 10 (1992), 198–252

——, 'Toward a Theory of Medieval Manorial Adjudication: The Nature of Communal Judgements in a System of Customary Law', *Law and History Review*, 8 (1995), 1–22

Bonfield, Lloyd, 'The Nature of Customary Law in the Manor Courts of Medieval England', *Comparative Studies in Society and History*, 31 (1989), 515–34

——, 'What Did Edwardian Villagers Mean by "Customary Law"?', in *Medieval Society and the Manor Court*, ed. by Zvi Razi and Richard Smith (Oxford: Oxford University Press, 1996), pp. 103–16

Brenner, Robert, 'Agrarian Class Structure and Economic Development in Pre-Industrial Europe', *Past and Present*, 70 (1976), 30–75; reprinted in *The Brenner Debate: Agrarian Class Structure and Economic Development in Pre-Industrial Europe*, ed. by Trevor H. Aston and C. H. E. Philpin (Cambridge: Cambridge University Press, 1985), pp. 10–63

Briggs, Chris D., *Credit and Village Society in Fourteenth-Century England* (Oxford: Oxford University Press 2009)

——, 'Manor Court Procedures, Debt Litigation Levels, and Rural Credit Provision in England, *c.* 1290–*c.* 1380', *Law and History Review*, 24 (2006), 519–58

Britnell, Richard H., 'Commercialisation and Economic Development in England, 1000–1300', in *A Commercialising Economy: England 1086 to c. 1300*, ed. by Richard H. Britnell and Bruce M. S. Campbell (Manchester: Manchester University Press, 1995), pp. 7–26

Brooke, Christopher N. L., and Michael M. Postan, *Carte Nativorum, a Peterborough Abbey Cartulary of the Fourteenth Century* (Oxford: Oxford University Press, 1960)

Campbell, Bruce M. S., 'The Agrarian Problem of the Early Fourteenth Century', *Past and Present*, 188 (2005), 3–70

Campbell, Bruce M. S., and others, *A Medieval Capital and its Grain Supply: Agrarian Production and Distribution in the London Region, c. 1300*, Historical Geography Research Series, 30 (London: Institute of British Geographers, 1993)

Chayanov, Alexander V., *The Theory of Peasant Economy*, ed. by Daniel Thorner, Basile Kerblay, and R. E. F. Smith (Homewood: Irwin, 1966)

Clark, Elaine, 'Debt Litigation in a Late Medieval English Vill', in *Pathways to Medieval Peasants*, ed. by James Ambrose Raftis (Toronto: Pontifical Institute of Mediaeval Studies, 1981), pp. 247–79

Dyer, Christopher, *An Age of Transition? Economy and Society in the Later Middle Ages* (Oxford: Oxford University Press, 2005)

——, 'Changes in the Size of Peasant Holdings in Some West Midland Villages, 1400–1540', in *Land, Kinship and Life-Cycle*, ed. by Richard M. Smith (Cambridge: Cambridge University Press, 1984), pp. 277–94

——, 'The Consumer and the Market in the Later Middle Ages', *Economic History Review*, 2nd ser., 42 (1989), 305–27; reprinted in Christopher Dyer, *Everyday Life in Medieval England* (London: Hambledon, 1994), pp. 257–81

——, *Lords and Peasants in a Changing Society: The Estates of the Bishopric of Worcester, 680–1540* (Cambridge: Cambridge University Press, 1980)

——, *Making a Living in the Middle Ages: The People of Britain, 850–1520* (London: Penguin, 2003).

——, *Standards of Living in the Later Middle Ages: Social Change in England c. 1200–1520*, rev. edn (Cambridge: Cambridge University Press, 1998)

Faith, Rosamond, 'Berkshire: Fourteenth and Fifteenth Centuries', in *The Peasant Land Market in Medieval England*, ed. by Paul D. A. Harvey (Oxford: Clarendon Press, 1984), pp. 106–77

Harvey, Barbara F., *Westminster Abbey and its Estates in the Middle Ages* (Oxford: Oxford University Press, 1977)

Harvey, Paul D. A., 'Conclusion', in *The Peasant Land Market in Medieval England*, ed. by Paul D. A. Harvey (Oxford: Clarendon Press, 1984), pp. 349–53

——, ed., *The Peasant Land Market in Medieval England* (Oxford: Clarendon Press, 1984)

Hatcher, John, and Mark Bailey, eds, *Modelling the Middle Ages: The History and Theory of England's Economic Development* (Oxford: Oxford University Press, 2001)

Hilton, Rodney H., *Bond Men Made Free: Medieval Peasant Movements and the English Rising of 1381* (London: Methuen, 1973)

——, *The English Peasantry in the Later Middle Ages* (Oxford: Oxford University Press, 1975)

——, 'Introduction', in *The Transition From Feudalism to Capitalism*, ed. by Paul M. Sweezy (London: Verso, 1976), pp. 9–30

——, 'Medieval Peasants: Any Lessons?', *Journal of Peasant Studies*, 1 (1974), 207–19; reprinted in *Class Conflict and the Crisis of Feudalism: Essays in Medieval Social History*, ed. by Rodney Howard Hilton (London: Hambledon, 1985), pp. 114–21

——, 'Small Town Society in England before the Black Death', *Past and Present*, 105 (1984), 53–78

Holderness, B. A., 'Widows in Pre-Industrial Society: An Essay upon their Economic Functions', in *Land, Kinship and Life-Cycle*, ed. by Richard M. Smith (Cambridge: Cambridge University Press, 1984), pp. 423–42

Hudson, William, 'The Prior of Norwich's Manor of Hindolveston: Its Early Organisation and Rights of the Customary Tenants to Alienate their Strips of Land', *Norfolk Archaeology*, 20 (1921), 179–214

Hyams, Paul R., 'The Origins of a Peasant Land Market in England', *Economic History Review*, 23 (1970), 18–31

——, 'What Did Edwardian Villagers Mean by "Law"?', in *Medieval Society and the Manor Court*, ed. by Zvi Razi and Richard Smith (Oxford: Oxford University Press, 1996), pp. 69–102

Jones, Andrew C., 'Bedfordshire: Fifteenth Century', in *The Peasant Land Market in Medieval England*, ed. by Paul D. A. Harvey (Oxford: Clarendon Press, 1984), pp. 178–251

Kowaleski, Maryanne, *Local Markets and Regional Trade in Medieval Exeter* (Cambridge: Cambridge University Press, 1995)

Lomas, Tim, 'Durham: Late Fourteenth and Fifteenth Centuries', in *The Peasant Land Market in Medieval England*, ed. by Paul D. A. Harvey (Oxford: Clarendon Press, 1984), pp. 252–327

Masschaele, James, *Peasants, Merchants and Markets: Inland Trade in Medieval England, 1150–1350* (New York: St Martin's Press, 1997)

Mate, Mavis E., 'The East Sussex Land Market and the Agrarian Class Structure in the Late Middle Ages', *Past and Present*, 139 (1993), 46–65

Postan, Michael M., *The Cambridge Economic History of Europe*, I: *The Agrarian Life of the Middle Ages*, 2nd edn (Cambridge: Cambridge University Press, 1966)

——, 'The Charters of the Villeins', in Christopher Nugent Lawrence Brooke and Michael M. Postan, *Carte Nativorum, a Peterborough Abbey Cartulary of the Fourteenth Century* (Oxford: Oxford University Press, 1960), pp. xxviii–lxv; reprinted in Michael M. Postan, *Essays on Medieval Agriculture and General Problems of the Medieval Economy* (Cambridge: Cambridge University Press, 1973), pp. 107–49

——, 'The Chronology of Labour Services', *Transactions of the Royal Historical Society*, 4th ser., 20 (1937), pp. 169–93; reprinted in Michael M. Postan, *Essays on Medieval Agriculture and General Problems of the Medieval Economy* (Cambridge: Cambridge University Press, 1973), pp. 89–106

——, 'Credit in Medieval Trade', *Economic History Review*, 1st ser., 1 (1928), 234–61; reprinted in Michael M. Postan, *Medieval Trade and Finance* (Cambridge: Cambridge University Press, 1973), pp. 1–27

——, 'The Economic Foundations of Medieval Society', in Michael Postan, *Essays on Medieval Agriculture and General Problems of the Medieval Economy* (Cambridge: Cambridge University Press, 1973), pp. 3–27, a translation of 'Die wirtschaftlichen Grundlagen der mittelalterlichen Gesellschaft', *Jahrbücher für Nationalökonomie*, 161 (1951), 180–284 (both texts are revised versions of his contribution in Carlo Cipolla, Jan Dhondt, Michael Postan, and Philippe Wolff, 'Rapports collectif', in *IX*[e] *Congrès international des sciences historiques: Congrès international des sciences historiques. Rapports, colloque de Paris, 28 août – 3 septembre 1950* (Paris: Colin, 1950), pp. 225–41)

——, *Essays on Medieval Agriculture and General Problems of the Medieval Economy* (Cambridge: Cambridge University Press, 1973)

——, 'Glastonbury Estates in the Twelfth Century', *Economic History Review*, 2nd ser., 5 (1953), 358–67; reprinted in Michael M. Postan, *Essays on Medieval Agriculture and General Problems of the Medieval Economy* (Cambridge: Cambridge University Press, 1973), pp. 249–77

——, 'Legal Status and Economic Conditions in Medieval Villages', in *Modernization and Industrialization* (Tokyo: Ichijo Shoten, 1968), pp. 278–90; reprinted in Michael M. Postan, *Essays on Medieval Agriculture and General Problems of the Medieval Economy* (Cambridge: Cambridge University Press, 1973), pp. 278–89

——, 'Medieval Agarian Society in its Prime: England', in *The Cambridge Economic History of Europe*, I: *The Agrarian Life of the Middle Ages*, ed. by Michael M. Postan, 2nd edn (Cambridge: Cambridge University Press, 1966), pp. 548–632

——, *Medieval Economy and Society* (London: Pelican, 1972)

——, 'Private Financial Instruments in Medieval England', *Vierteljahrschrift für Sozial und Wirtschaftsgeschichte*, 22 (1930), pp. 26–75; reprinted in Michael M. Postan, *Medieval Trade and Finance* (Cambridge: Cambridge University Press, 1973), pp. 28–64

——, 'The Trade of Medieval Europe: The North', in *The Cambridge Economic History of Europe*, II: *Trade and Industry in the Middle Ages*, ed. by Michael M. Postan and Edwin Ernest Rich (Cambridge: Cambridge University Press, 1952), pp. 191–256; reprinted in Michael M. Postan, *Medieval Trade and Finance* (Cambridge: Cambridge University Press, 1973), pp. 92–231

——, 'Village Livestock in the Thirteenth Century', *Economic History Review*, 2nd ser., 15 (1962), 219–49; reprinted in Michael M. Postan, *Essays on Medieval Agriculture and General Problems of the Medieval Economy* (Cambridge: Cambridge University Press, 1973), pp. 214–48

Postan, Michael M., and John Hatcher, 'Population and Class Relations in Feudal Society', *Past and Present*, 78 (1978), 24–37; reprinted in *The Brenner Debate: Agrarian Class Structure and Economic Development in Pre-Industrial Europe*, ed. by Trevor H. Aston and C. H. E. Philpin (Cambridge: Cambridge University Press, 1985), pp. 64–78

Postan, Michael M., and Jan Zbigniew Titow, 'Heriots and Prices on Winchester Manors', *Economic History Review*, 2nd ser., 11 (1959), 383–411; reprinted in Michael M. Postan, *Essays on Medieval Agriculture and General Problems of the Medieval Economy* (Cambridge: Cambridge University Press, 1973), pp. 150–85

Raftis, J. Ambrose, *Peasant Economic Development within the English Manorial System* (Montreal: Mcgill-Queens, 1996)

Razi, Zvi, 'The Struggles Between the Abbots of Halesowen and their Tenants in the Thirteenth and Fourteenth Centuries', in *Social Relations and their Ideas: Essays in Honour of R. H. Hilton*, ed. by Trevor H. Aston, Peter R. Coss, Christopher Dyer, and Joan Thirsk (Cambridge: Cambridge University Press, 1983), pp. 151–67

Richardson, Henry Gerald, *The English Jewry under Angevin Kings* (London: Greenwood, 1960)

Schofield, Phillipp R., 'Access to Credit in the Early Fourteenth-Century English Countryside', in *Credit and Debt in Medieval England, c. 1180 – c. 1350*, ed. by Phillipp R. Schofield and Nicholas J. Mayhew (Oxford: Oxbow, 2002), pp. 106–26

——, 'Dearth, Debt and the Local Land Market in a Late Thirteenth-Century Suffolk Community', *Agricultural History Review*, 45 (1997), 1–17

——, 'L'endettement et le crédit dans la campagne anglaise au Moyen Âge', in *Endettement paysan et crédit rural dans l'Europe médiévale et moderne: Actes des XVII*[e]*s journées internationales d'histoire de l'Abbaye de Flaran, Septembre 1995*, ed. by Maurice Berthe (Toulouse: Flaran, 1998), pp. 69–97

——, 'Peasants and Contract in the Thirteenth Century: Village Elites and the Land Market in Eastern England', in Phillipp R. Schofield and Thijs Lambrecht, *Credit and the Rural Economy in North-western Europe, c. 1200-c.1800* (Turnhout: Brepols, 2009), pp. 129–52

——, 'Peasants and the Manor Court: Gossip and Litigation in a Suffolk Village at the Close of the Thirteenth Century', *Past and Present*, 159 (1998), 3–42

Smith, Richard M., 'Some Issues Concerning Families and their Property in Rural England 1250–1800', in *Land, Kinship and Life-Cycle*, ed. by Richard M. Smith (Cambridge: Cambridge University Press, 1984), pp. 1–86

——, 'Some Thoughts on "Hereditary" and "Proprietary" Rights in Land under Customary Law in Thirteenth- and Early Fourteenth-Century England', *Law and History Review*, 1 (1983), 95–128

Spufford, Margaret, 'Peasant Inheritance Customs and Land Distribution in Cambridgeshire from the Sixteenth to the Eighteenth Centuries', in *Family and Inheritance: Rural Society in Western Europe, 1200–1800*, ed. by Jack Goody, Joan Thirsk, and Edward P. Thompson (Cambridge: Cambridge University Press, 1976), pp. 157–76

Tawney, Richard Henry, *The Agrarian Problem in the Sixteenth Century* (London: Longmans, Green, 1912)

van Bavel, Bas J. P., and Phillipp R. Schofield, 'Introduction. The Emergence of Lease and Leasehold in a Comparative Perspective: Definitions, Causes and Consequences', in *The Development of Leasehold in Northwestern Europe, c. 1200–1600*, ed. by Bas J. P. van Bavel and Phillipp R. Schofield (Turnhout: Brepols, 2008), pp. 11–30

Williamson, Janet, 'Norfolk: Thirteenth Century', in *The Peasant Land Market in Medieval England*, ed. by Paul D. A. Harvey (Oxford: Clarendon Press, 1984), pp. 30–105

Wyndham, Lord Leconfield, *Petworth Manor in the Seventeenth Century* (Oxford: Oxford University Press, 1954)

Historians and Peasant Agency: Studies of Late Medieval English Peasants

Anne DeWindt

Michael Postan's conclusions regarding the complex connections linking population levels, agrarian productivity, the fiscal demands of Church and State, and standard of living were controversial and thought provoking. As a result, his students and colleagues trawled even deeper into various estate records in order to either defend or challenge the 'Postan thesis'. The resulting focus on individual villages and towns across England brought the issue of peasant agency into the conversation, revealing some of the strategies employed by rich and poor, free and unfree, men and women. Few historians would now argue with the proposition that medieval peasants were capable of defining their own goals, of reasoning about appropriate strategies for achieving these goals, and of freely choosing one strategy or another after calculating their relative merits as effective means to the desired end.[1] But crit-

* I want to thank the participants at the Postan-Duby conference for their helpful and stimulating comments.

[1] 'An agent performs activity that is directed at a goal, and commonly it is a goal the agent has adopted on the basis of an overall practical assessment of his options and opportunities'; even more useful is that idea that peasant agency involves the peasant's 'acting on a desire with which the agent identifies': Wilson and Shpall, 'The Nature of Action and Agency'. Robert Goheen states the case for peasant agency most blatantly: 'If it is possible to maintain that the most extreme forms of domination [citing a study of Auschwitz] are unable absolutely to

Anne DeWindt (adewindt@yahoo.com) teaches history at the University of Detroit, Mercy. Her most recent book, a collaboration with Edwin DeWindt, is *Ramsey: The Lives of an English Fenland Town* (Washington, DC: Catholic University of America Press, 2006).

Crisis in the Later Middle Ages: Beyond the Postan-Duby Paradigm, ed. by John Drendel, TMC 13 (Turnhout: Brepols, 2015) 95–125 BREPOLS PUBLISHERS 10.1484/M.TMC.5.103786

ics of this approach, which is known as 'rational choice theory', challenge it as simplistic.[2] This paper will discuss a sample of research on the subject of medieval English peasants in order to explore efforts to place peasant agency within a social and cultural context and to consider the complexities resulting from the interactions between peasants and the personal and impersonal forces affecting, and affected by, their decisions.[3] This discussion concludes with a sample of the archival data associated with the Ramsey Abbey manor of Warboys, revealing some of the possibilities available to historians seeking evidence of the exercise, and nature, of peasant agency.

Most historians have moved beyond a historiography committed to the study of 'mere' peasants 'bound to the soil', and seen as victims of a social order destined to failure. As a result, peasants' opportunities for decision making have been examined within three distinct contexts.

First, some historians have looked at the powerful forces, both personal and impersonal, that shaped the options available to peasants. In this case, historians are looking at those forces 'from the bottom up' in order to identify forms of resistance or peasant strategies designed to limit losses or minimize risk. This approach can be seen as an examination of the 'constraints' within which peasants exercised their freedom of choice.[4]

deprive men and women of all ability to choose, how much stronger is the case for extending the concept of agency to the political discourse between medieval English peasants and the crown' (Goheen, 'Peasant Politics?', p. 62).

[2] For two examples, see Emirbayer and Goodwin, 'Network Analysis'; Nee, 'Review of *Rational Choice Theory*'.

[3] Important contributions have been made to the discussion of peasant agency since this essay was first written. They include Beattie, *Medieval Single Women*; Bennett, 'Compulsory Service'; Briggs, '"Seigniorial Control of Villagers"'; Britnell, 'Land and Lordship'; Campbell, 'The Agrarian Problem'; Cassidy-Welch and Sherlock, *Practices of Gender*; Dodds, *Peasants and Production*; Dyer, 'A Suffolk Farmer'; Dyer, 'Were Late Medieval English Villages "Self-Contained"?'; Dyer, Coss, and Wickham, *Rodney Hilton's Middle Ages*; Goldberg, *Medieval England*; McIntosh, *Working Women*; Langdon and Masschaele, 'Commercial Activity and Population Growth'; Masschaele, *Jury, State, and Society*; Masschaele, 'Town, Country and Law'; Schofield, *Peasant and Community*; Stone, *Decision Making*; Vergunst, 'Social Integration'; Whittle, 'Housewives and Servants'; Whittle, 'Population Mobility'; van Zanden, 'In Good Company'.

[4] Indeed, two insightful sociologists have even suggested that cultural constraints actually assist and enable freedom of choice because they clarify a finite set of options within what would otherwise be a chaotic universe. Culture is seen, thus, as a 'reduction of complexity': Emirbayer and Goodwin, 'Network Analysis', p. 1441.

Second, other studies have focused primarily on the options themselves and upon evidence of the variety of choices that were available to the peasantry. Peasants' decisions can thus be seen as the creative power behind some of those impersonal forces or institutions which the first set of historians examined. For example, decisions about when or whether to marry had profound effects on demographic shifts over time. Market forces or the institution of the manor can be seen as the end products of numerous individual decisions. Indeed, 'Social outcomes can be the sum of individual inputs without reflecting anyone's intentions'.[5] In these articles, individual choices often produced economic and demographic results completely unforeseen and unintended by any of the decision makers.

Finally, decision making for all of us — and certainly for the medieval peasant — took place within a social context. It is therefore not easy to determine which decisions were made by groups or by individuals. Much work on the local parish or village community has encouraged us to delve deeper into local peasant society, with its own micro social and economic hierarchies, to discover how and where decisions were made. The goal is to describe how rational agents managed to 'negotiate and renegotiate conventions, while remaining subject to the normative demands of the games of social life'.[6]

To begin with the powerful personal and impersonal influences on peasant decision making, lordship and manorial institutions are key factors. Indeed, Whittle has discussed peasants' decisions as evidence of their ability to adapt to 'harsh financial and legal restraints'.[7] Recent work demonstrates the variety of responses exercised by peasants towards their lords' orders and exactions. A spectrum of reactions has been described from violent rebellion and negotiated compromise to a simple lack of compliance. Muller notices the peasants of Winslow manor in Buckinghamshire refusing to pay marriage fines over the course of the late fourteenth century.[8] Hargreaves sees the lord–tenant relationship as one of a 'protracted struggle' for control over land, labour, and capital and describes fleeing peasants who took their *principalia* with them, while others stayed on the manor but resisted orders to build new houses or repair their tenements. Here is a vision of determined recalcitrance and of peasants 'prepared to risk financial ruin before submitting to the lord's will'.[9]

[5] Hollis, *The Philosophy of Social Science*, p. 111.

[6] Hollis, *The Philosophy of Social Science*, p. 164. Relevant here is Goheen's comment: 'The village, as moral community, conquered the jury' (Goheen, 'Peasant Politics?', p. 54).

[7] Whittle, 'Individualism and the Family-Land Bond', p. 63.

[8] Muller, 'The Function and Evasion of Marriage Fines'.

[9] Hargreaves, 'Seignorial Reaction', p. 73.

Whittle and Yates analyse manorial administrations in Berkshire and East Anglia and describe administrations as either 'tight' or 'loose', with each type inspiring different peasant responses. 'Discriminating tenants were exerting their power of choice and taking the more attractive tenancies to the detriment of other landlords'.[10] Whittle and Langdon associate greater freedom of choice with improvement in the peasants' legal status and the decline of direct demesne cultivation by lords. Family ties to the land loosen, and technological progress is enabled by these processes.[11] Bruce Campbell has long argued that loose manorial organization in East Anglia and a 'relatively free and enterprising rural population' encouraged peasant economic development in that region.[12]

Peasants were actively involved in the mid-thirteenth-century English barons' revolt, as they tended to rebel against particular lords rather than against lordship in general.[13] Studying the later rebellions of 1381, Eiden describes violent resistance to carefully chosen targets beyond the manor, against men exercising power at the county and national level at a time when the very institution of lordship may have been under attack.[14] If the institution of lordship was, in fact, weakened by political resistance to particular lords, we may well wonder whether results were rather different from what was intended by individual actors. An article by Sylvia Federico acknowledges the various motives for the violence perpetrated by both men and women in 1381 — targets being specific seigniorial officers or representatives of 'local or royal governance'.[15]

Fourteenth-century parliaments also passed legislation aimed at aiding the poor and at controlling individual behaviour in order to promote moral reform. An individual's choice of clothing, food, and recreation was presumably a matter for state intervention. The relationship between state control and individual freedom may well have impinged significantly on the pre-eminence of landlord–tenant relations by the end of the fifteenth century.[16]

In some cases, peasants wanted predictable, well-defined dues and taxes, and Chris Dyer cites examples of negotiations towards that end that reminded him

[10] Whittle and Yates, '"Pays Réel or Pays Légal"', p. 15.

[11] Whittle, 'Individualism and the Family-Land Bond'; Langdon, 'Was England a Technological Backwater?'.

[12] Campbell, 'Economic Rent', p. 244.

[13] Carpenter, 'English Peasants in Politics'.

[14] Eiden, 'Joint Action'.

[15] Federico, 'The Imaginary Society', p. 161.

[16] Given-Wilson, 'Service, Serfdom and English Labour'.

of the achievements of the barons of Magna Carta.[17] Raftis and Bisson suggest the possibility that lordship as a cultural phenomenon may even have represented a positive choice on the part of a lord's followers, while they acknowledge that sympathizing with such hierarchical social arrangements is not easy in the twenty-first century.[18] Decisions were made that would surprise moderns. Indeed, in one case a villein brought a case jointly with his lord against a third party, even though this third party attempted to prove that the villein was a free man. The case was recorded in Common Pleas in 1355 and arose when the prior of the Hospitallers in England claimed to be the villein's legal employer. But this particular peasant apparently preferred his lord, even though this required acceptance of villein status.[19]

There is one area where the relationship between choice and constraint was recognized as an important one not only by modern historians but also by medieval authorities — the question of the lord's right to control the marriage of serfs. Sheehan and Miller discuss marriage and choice, emphasizing that consent was required for a valid Christian marriage and demonstrating the relevance of decisions about when to marry and whether or not to control fertility.[20]

Within marriage, a patriarchal culture certainly shaped options for peasant women. Building on the work of Judith Bennett and Maryanne Kowaleski, Helena Graham has argued that adolescent women and widows exhibited behaviours closer to those of males than to married females. She thus found that behaviours and choices made by women in Alrewas, Staffordshire, were profoundly affected by both their marital status and the size of their families' tenements.[21]

Lords and spouses certainly influenced a peasant's choices, just as a peasant's lord and spouse were influenced in turn by the choices made by that peas-

[17] Dyer, 'Memories of Freedom'.

[18] Raftis, 'Peasants and the Collapse of the Manorial Economy', p. 205; Bisson, 'Medieval Lordship'.

[19] Cited by Given-Wilson, 'Service, Serfdom and English Labour', pp. 22–23.

[20] Sheehan, 'Theory and Practice'; Miller, 'People'. Also Berkhofer, 'Marriage, Lordship and the "Greater Unfree"', reminds us that in the midst of debates over the origins of merchet and formariage 'we must work out their [the unfree] perspectives before we can work out our own'. In an illustration of the essential association between agency and the oath he cites a twelfth-century woman who swore 'that she would never marry another man' without the permission of her lord. (p. 24.) So here a woman chooses to give her consent to a lord's authority to give *his* consent to a marriage which she, in turn, must consent to in order for it to be valid. Here indeed, the concept 'agency' leads into a veritable maze of intersecting decisions.

[21] Graham, '"A Woman's Work"'.

ant, but numerous impersonal forces were also at work. Raftis, Miller, King, and Hallam emphasize the importance of economic and ecological factors in shaping the options available to peasants. Raftis wonders why peasants left Ramsey Abbey villages in great numbers after the demesne had been farmed and suggests that declining economic opportunities transcended local manorial policies as a driving force.[22] Miller and King discuss the cost of labour, the availability of land, and the market for grain and wool as important influences on peasant decision-making. Opportunities to rent meadow, take up demesne land, or invest in sheep and cattle provided richer peasants with a variety of choices.[23] Peasants could also 'vote with their feet', and villages and towns had long attracted immigrants.

Hallam emphasizes the power of demographic forces in shaping decision making, but he acknowledges that population pressure 'could spur creativity', so he does not see demographic forces as simple restraints on freedom of choice.[24] Patricia Hogan, Dyer, and Yates show how important the quality of local soils, the climate, and native flora and fauna were to choices about settlement patterns, field systems, and cropping patterns.[25]

Several historians have made the important point that poverty — seen, understandably, as a force often beyond the control of any individual peasant — was a major factor limiting, but never eliminating, an individual's choices. Britnell warns of the negative effects on the poor of the 'unpredictable vagaries of the market'.[26] Schofield describes opportunities available to the richer peasant to exploit his poor neighbours.[27] Kitsikopolous describes a major dichotomy between rich and poor in his reconstruction of a peasant budget, and Mark Bailey sees a growing polarization between rich and poor by the beginning of the fourteenth century and urges us to 'disaggregate' the peasantry when assessing their commercial strategies.[28] Walter and Desai discuss subsistence strategies and describe some of the difficult choices that had to be made by both rich

[22] Raftis, 'Peasants and the Collapse of the Manorial Economy', p. 205.

[23] Miller, 'Introduction'; King, 'Occupation of the Land'.

[24] Hallam, 'Rural England and Wales', p. 976.

[25] Hogan, 'Clays, *Culturae*, and the Cultivator's Wisdom'; Dyer, 'Medieval Farming'; Yates, 'Change and Continuities'. A review article about modern Rwanda illustrates the dangers of ignoring local peasant expertise in these areas: Newbury and Newbury, 'Bringing the Peasants', p. 856.

[26] Britnell, 'Specialization of Work in England', p. 8.

[27] Schofield, 'Dearth, Debt and the Local Land Market'.

[28] Kitsikopolous, 'Standards of Living'; Bailey, 'Peasant Welfare in England', p. 237.

and poor during famine years when the weather and disease were perhaps the key 'material agents' affecting peasant decision-making.[29]

Just as these historians have described the impersonal and personal forces to which the peasant responded, many writers, including many of those already cited, want us to be aware that peasants were, in their turn, shaping those very forces by means of the decisions they were making. This observation encourages discussion of an even wider variety of peasant choices.

As agriculturalists, peasants made decisions about cropping and livestock investments. Karakacili, Mate, and Campbell argue that peasants could have been more productive than lords, that they made critical decisions about extra labour inputs, and that the pastoral sector was largely a peasant enterprise.[30] Dyer and Langdon point to innovations in technology including the development of fish ponds, rabbit warrens, and the use of the horse and attribute them to the peasantry.[31] Martin and Martin and Fox describe capital investment in peasant housing and family decisions about hiring practices and the deployment of the labour of adolescent sons.[32] Households needed to decide whether to hire out their labour or apply that labour to their own tenements. Commutations of labour services further increased flexibility. For example, in Warboys, Huntingdonshire, in 1342, 46 per cent of all labour rents were commuted for cash. This meant that only about forty-six days a year were spent on demesne jobs by each virgator.[33]

Peasants sometimes resisted pressure to accept commutation to money rents, indicating that occasionally labour rents were preferred. Smaller tenants may have found it difficult to come up with the cash, and many would have had sufficient family labour to maintain both a small tenement and labour for the demesne. Manor court rolls from the village of Elton, Huntingdonshire, contain a complaint against a reeve. Among the reeve's derelictions was the fact that he had 'taken gifts from the rich tenants that they should not become tenants at a money rent, and [had] put the poor tenants at a money rent'.[34]

[29] Walter, 'Subsistence Strategies'; Desai, 'The Agrarian Crisis'.

[30] Karakacili, 'Peasants, Productivity and Profit'; Mate, 'Agricultural Technology', p. 273; Campbell, 'Economic Rent', pp. 227, 244.

[31] Dyer, 'Medieval Farming', p. 310; Langdon, *Horses, Oxen and Technological Innovation*.

[32] Martin and Martin, 'Adapting Houses to Changing Needs'; Fox, 'Exploitation of the Landless'; Karakacili, 'Peasants, Productivity and Profit', p. 79.

[33] Karakacili, 'Peasants, Productivity and Profit', p. 97.

[34] Bland and others, *English Economic History*, p. 85.

As important as agrarian and pastoral production and management of family labour were to the peasant, the cultivation of what McIntosh has called 'social capital' was also critical.[35] In making comparisons with contemporary Nigeria, she depicts a range of decisions regarding how much time and capital should be invested in social networks. For example, peasants had to decide how much capital to lend and to whom. These decisions would affect the level of 'social insurance' available in times of trouble. These choices would be influenced in part by the number and personalities of the other people in one's village or local town. Other scholars also point to the myriad of debt relationships among English peasants that reflect a series of what could have been very difficult decisions.[36]

Richer male peasants made decisions regarding local office holding. Serving as court juror, or taster, or manorial bailiff or reeve could be time consuming and could expose an individual to considerable resentment. Schofield has also pondered the nature of local decisions that resulted in the decline of the tithing and frankpledge system.[37] Davidson Cragoe and Johnston turn our attention to decisions in the religious and cultural sphere, describing investments in the production of plays and in improvements to a local parish church, where the widening of chancel arches was undertaken to make the elevation of the host more visible to parishioners. Much of the expense for these projects depended on local contributions and local tastes.[38]

But the peasants' horizons extended beyond the village, of course, and their access to local and royal courts posed further opportunities that required choices. Should a lawsuit be pursued, and if so where and in which court?[39] Punishments differed in ecclesiastical courts from those in secular courts, and a plaintiff might decide where to raise his or her complaint on that basis. Peasants also appeared on juries of presentment for quarter sessions, assizes, and inquisitions post-mortem, as well as at the Eyre.[40] Some were in a position to choose which juries to participate in after local politics had determined who would be

[35] McIntosh, 'The Diversity of Social Capital'.

[36] For example, Schofield, 'Peasants and the Manor Court'; Clark, 'Social Welfare and Mutual Aid'.

[37] Schofield, 'The Late Medieval View'.

[38] Davidson Cragoe, 'Making Tradition'; Johnston, 'Parish Playmaking'.

[39] Schofield, 'Peasants and the Manor Court'.

[40] Goheen, 'Peasant Politics?', p. 46; DeWindt and DeWindt, *Royal Justice*.

eligible to represent their neighbours outside the village.[41] As members of the anonymous 'public' at shaming rituals, peasants made other choices regarding the nature of their participation in that process.[42] Here was one arena where women as well as men certainly played a role — unlike the more formal roles of juror which remained a male domain.[43]

The further down the social hierarchy we descend and the further we penetrate the countryside to identify decision makers and their various opportunities to make decisions, the greater the temptation becomes to attribute major long-term changes to this particular accumulation of individual choices. Many authors have noted the role of peasant choice in transforming tenurial contracts over the course of the fourteenth century, for example. Regarding the lord's manorial institutions, Raftis also suggests that decisions by customary tenants played a role in the decline of the demesne.[44]

Building on that theme, Masschaele and Karakacili emphasize the importance of peasant choices as the driving force behind thirteenth-century commercialization and economic development. Masschaele argues that production decisions were made by peasants who decided where and how to dispose of their surplus. He thus argues that commercialization rather than demography should now be seen as the more important engine for change.[45] Karakacili argues that the amount of labour inputs was 'primarily determined by the commercial interests of peasants rather than population pressures'.[46] And David Stone argues that manorial reeves made their decisions with the market in mind.[47] Campbell also credits peasants with increasing production and thus enabling the feeding of an expanding population.[48]

Efforts to locate the origins of agrarian capitalism have inevitably focused on peasant decisions to engross holdings and to make investments with an eye to the market in both produce and labour.[49] Reaching beyond the peasants'

[41] Goheen, 'Peasant Politics?', pp. 48–49; 'the jurors became, willy-nilly, members of the expanding universe of consensual politics' (p. 50).

[42] Masschaele, 'The Public Space'.

[43] Bennett, 'Public Power and Authority'.

[44] Raftis, 'Peasants and the Collapse of the Manorial Economy', p. 193.

[45] Masschaele, 'The Public Space', p. 383.

[46] Karakacili, 'Peasants, Productivity and Profit', p. 126.

[47] Stone, 'Medieval Farm Management', p. 634.

[48] Campbell, 'Economic Rent', p. 245.

[49] Whittle, *The Development of Agrarian Capitalism*, pp. 306–10.

abilities to shape broad economic trends, their 'determination to become free' has even been credited with the formation of nuclear families.[50] Goheen has noted their influence on the changing nature of national common law and on Crown policies. He points out that the common law declared that a peasant was either a freeman or a serf. But countrymen used their own markers to distinguish status. 'In the confrontation, muted but real, between the two incompatible political definitions of agrarian community, peasant perceptions and practices gradually prevailed against the crown's novelties'.[51]

In what might be seen as early versions of government 'spin' and public relations, Masschaele notes that English monarchs acknowledged the significance of peasant decision-making by taking the effort to send announcements to local marketplaces declaring and justifying royal policies.[52] Also, as the state extended its influence over labourers and 'the poor' during the course of the fourteenth and fifteenth centuries by means of labour legislation, the enforcement of that legislation depended heavily on the cooperation of those villagers who not only worked for wages but hired wage earners as well. Parliament was well aware of the need to provide incentives to encourage peasants to present their neighbours for infringements of the labour laws. The solution was to enable reductions in villagers' contributions to the lay subsidies, if they cooperated.[53] So the state's attempt to limit choices — by controlling wages and limiting mobility — was undermined by its dependence on the cooperation of many of those very people they were attempting to control.

Finally, before taking a look at a peasant family from the Ramsey Abbey village of Warboys, we need to consider the role of the local community in this process of decision making. It is not necessary to apply a modern concept of individualism in order to uncover opportunities for decision making. Many critical decisions were certainly made by small groups rather than by individuals, and it is not always clear what counts as an 'individual' or 'unit' in a social

[50] Razi, 'The Myth of the Immutable English Family', p. 42.

[51] Goheen, 'Peasant Politics?', p. 58; Goheen adds that 'No one has ever doubted that peasants acted as jurors — or as taxpayers or soldiers. The issue is one of their responsibility for what they did, one of agency' (p. 62). Goheen points out that as action of trespass became an alternative to possessory assizes for litigation over property, oath taking for those juries did not require 'freedom' (p. 59).

[52] Masschaele, 'The Public Space', pp. 392–93.

[53] Given-Wilson, 'Service, Serfdom and English Labour', p. 27. Given-Wilson cites Poos, 'The Social Context'.

system.[54] The importance of the village bylaws, stinting regulations, the joint decisions made by local presentment and inquest jurors, and the local policing institution of the hue and cry are only some examples of this phenomenon.[55] Furthermore, groups of villagers did decide to what extent they were willing to cooperate with royal tax assessors and with royal purveyors. The reeve along with the chief tenants made cropping decisions from season to season.[56] None of these decisions can be understood in terms of the lone individual.

Elaine Clark has described the intricate network of influences on marriage decisions coming from lords, local juries, and family desires to enhance or defend social status in the village.[57] Peasant agents were thus creating or affirming their own identity through their marriage choices, and these choices were obviously not made by individuals independently of forceful influences from family and neighbours, what we might call a local village culture.

Decisions to cooperate and an individual's commitment to a community shift the focus of agency from an individual to a group. Rosemary Hopcroft argues that 'the social organization of agriculture' was perhaps more important even than lordship, ecology, or demography in the shaping of decisions that would lead to improved agricultural efficiency and hence agrarian economic development. She argues that strong historical traditions of land sharing led to the regular open-field system and that this strong commitment to communal control ultimately inhibited economic growth.[58]

Bruce Campbell argues that peasants' ability to defend customary tenurial arrangements enabled them, as both free and villein tenants, to keep most rents below the 'economic rents' landlords might otherwise have received.[59] Junichi Kanzaka pointed out that strong communities could keep money rents lower than they would have been otherwise.[60]

[54] Hollis, *The Philosophy of Social Science*, p. 109.

[55] Using sources from a small town rather than for peasants per se, see DeWindt, 'Local Government'. See also Olson, 'Jurors of the Village Court'.

[56] Karakacili, 'Peasants, Productivity and Profit', p. 231.

[57] Clark, 'The Decision to Marry'. 'Sometimes free choice in marriage was to prefer to abide by the wishes of others': McSheffery, *Love and Marriage*, p. 25.

[58] Hopcroft, 'The Social Origins', p. 1562; also see Hopcroft, 'The Origins of Regular Open-Field Systems'.

[59] Campbell, 'The Agrarian Problem', pp. 7–9.

[60] 'This means that villeins paid a lower level of money rents in the vills whose communities were strong': Kanzaka, 'Villein Rents in Thirteenth-Century England', p. 615.

As scholars now debate the relationship between wealth distribution and economic growth in developing countries of the modern world, medievalists also acknowledge that group decisions were made at the local level in fifteenth-century villages regarding acceptable levels of wealth accumulation within the context of open-field village organization and communal rights to pasture. It remains to be determined how those decisions were affected by, and had an affect on, agrarian growth.[61] There also is disagreement at the moment about the timing and the degree of inequality in the distribution of wealth among late medieval English peasants, but a major factor in that process must have been local tolerance for engrossing of holdings and for other forms of capital accumulation.

Perhaps decision-making power was being concentrated over time into the hands of fewer and fewer villagers. And this may have been part of a process begun much earlier when manorial court decisions once made by *tota villata*, or the entire homage, became the responsibility of twelve selected jurors.[62] This phenomenon is surely related to the growing discrepancy between the living standards of rich and poor peasants and raises the question of whether a culture that encourages the pursuit of individual material wealth is more likely to experience significant commercialization and increased agrarian productivity. Masschaele certainly adds this factor into the equation and cites Marshall Sahlins's argument that wealth accumulation is 'the distinguishing characteristic of western societies'.[63]

Therefore, the challenge facing historians interested in peasant agency lies in sorting out the relationships between decisions that were made by lords, individual peasant tenants, 'the family', communities of tenants, their poorer

[61] For an example of such discussions, see Fields, 'Growth and Income Distribution', and Moorthy, *Economic Development and Income Distribution*. Hartmut Elsenhans argues that 'a relatively egalitarian income distribution is necessary for economic development and was actually the basis for the emergence of capitalism': Elsenhans, *Equality and Development*, p. 2. In reference to modern developing countries, R. M. Sundrum writes, 'small peasant farms may be able to compete effectively with larger farms, and [...] there may be no tendency towards concentration of ownership': Sundrum, *Income Distribution*, p. 187. Also, 'recent literature does not support a view that higher initial inequality allows a higher rate of growth. Some studies suggest no effect, and others suggest that high inequality inhibits growth'; 'A more equitable distribution of physical assets, notably land, can also help greatly': Bruno, Ravallion, and Squire, 'Equity and Growth', pp. 138–39.

[62] Beckerman, 'Procedural Innovation'.

[63] Masschaele, *Peasants, Merchants and Markets*, p. 229, n. 3.

neighbours, and their local peasant leaders.[64] Historians, for example, have sometimes assumed that local manorial jurors were acting as agents of their lords rather than pursuing agendas of their own. Furthermore, decisions made by rich peasants were surely influenced by those made by poorer peasants, and vice versa.[65] Personal status, local influence, and property were linked at all levels of the social hierarchy. But there is no doubt, as Jim Masschaele reminded us, that we need to study the decision-making process before we will ever understand any of the economic and demographic trends that have attracted so much scholarly attention lately, or before we can construct meaningful models to help us make sense of long-term changes — now recognized to be more evolutionary than revolutionary in nature.[66]

There seems no better way to illustrate in concrete terms the relevance of this discussion about peasant agency than to take a close look at the activities of one particular group of villagers — in this case a group of *c.* sixty individuals bearing the surname Berenger who were active in the fenland village of Warboys, Huntingdonshire, between 1250 and *c.* 1500. There are enough discrete references in the sources to reveal an astounding variety in their personal profiles.[67] One might assume that where there is variety, there is either a remarkably large number of determining forces at play in directing the lives of these men and women, or that there were enough opportunities for freedom of choice so that individuals managed to carve out for themselves distinctive and near-unique identities for future historians to ponder. I think we can acknowledge the latter possibility and should, as historians, attempt to locate evidence of the nature of those choices in the records available to us. Acknowledgment of the Berengers' ability to resist and respond to personal and impersonal constraints and a will-

[64] See Goheen, 'Peasant Politics?': 'At the center of these interests [of the peasant] was the family' (p. 50); '"hereditary" service in the crown's juries was, in effect, a strategy of peasant family in its quest for status and authority' (p. 52). And regarding marriage strategies, see Clark, 'The Decision to Marry'.

[65] Goheen points out that local politics tended to result in the appointment of richer men to the village jury, and, in turn, sent them beyond the village to service on regional Crown juries: Goheen, 'Peasant Politics?', p. 48. Poorer peasants played some role in this process, even if that role may be very difficult to determine.

[66] Masschaele, 'Review of John Hatcher and Mark Bailey, *Modelling the Middle Ages*'; Raftis, 'Peasants and the Collapse of the Manorial Economy', p. 206.

[67] Manorial court rolls, account rolls, and the Ramsey Abbey gersuma book. The Berengers are introduced in Raftis, *Warboys*. Manorial court roll manuscript sources, with dates, are identified in Raftis, *Peasant Economic Development*, pp. 222–23.

ingness to recognize their participation in group decisions from the level of the nuclear family to the regional level will allow us to be more sensitive to the significance of the evidence that this group of Warboys residents has left behind. (The fact that decisions were made by juries and court scribes regarding what information was recorded in the surviving records can't be considered in depth here, but should at least be acknowledged.)

Variety is best illustrated by describing the 'careers' of two quite different family groups bearing the surname Berenger. Robert was remarkable for his regular refusal to cooperate with the manorial regime and his reluctance to fulfill the social responsibilities usually associated with tenants of his level of wealth. Of the thirty-three references to Robert Berenger, a villein, between 1313 and 1347, ten are citations for failure to perform work services or, in one case, for failure to perform them properly.[68] On one occasion the court rolls indicate quite clearly that he simply 'did not care' to show up for his labour services at harvest time.[69] It was usually the wealthy tenants, and non-jurors — men like Robert — who refused work services. So when there was a larger number of resisters than usual who refused carrying services in 1320, it is possible that Robert was one of the leaders of this protest.[70] Another six references to Robert in the records are to trespasses, often with livestock, into meadow, woods, or grain of the lord. He kept a cartload of reeds that had been meant for the lord Abbot. Furthermore, he appeared on only one jury list. In a very unusual court roll entry Robert was even accused by six of his fellow jurors of 'presenting badly'.[71] Robert did serve as witness to charters and as a pledge, but not nearly as frequently as one might expect from a member of such a prominent local family.[72] Almost half of Robert's recorded activity took the form of non-involvement or non-cooperation.

[68] BL, Add. Roll 34910; BL, Add. Roll 34324; BL, Add. Roll 39757; BL, Add. Roll 34896; BL, Add. Roll 34918; BL, Add. Roll 34898; BL, Add. Roll 39597; BL, Add. Roll 39760; BL, Add. Roll 39758; BL, Add. Roll 39761; BL, Add. Roll 34777; BL, Add. Roll 39470; BL, Add. Roll 39762; BL, Add. Roll 34899; BL, Add. Roll 39853; BL, Add. Roll 39856; BL, Add. Roll 39759.

[69] BL, Add. Roll 34918: 'non curavit venire' (1320).

[70] Raftis points out that resistance to work services increased around the time of the Great Famine which represented a turning point in the frequency and pattern of such resistance: Raftis, *Peasant Economic Development*, p. 58.

[71] BL, Add. Roll 39470.

[72] Raftis cites the fact that villeins witnessed charters conveying free land as a sign of the status and respect afforded certain such individuals: Raftis, *Peasant Economic Development*, Appendix 1, p. 135.

Refusal to perform work services was thus a strategic option for some customary tenants in Warboys. The sale of works offered another option. William Berenger, a half-virgator in 1298–99, bought works for 13d.[73] Raftis found that it tended to be the larger landholders who purchased works from the lord, a system which provided flexibility with advantages to both the lord and the tenant. There are no references in Warboys to fines for refusing to purchase works, indicating a strong demand on the part of customary tenants for control over their labour supply.[74] Raftis suggests that sales of *opera* may also have been a perk offered first to those willing to undertake the responsibilities of local office holding. Indeed, unlike Robert, William had been willing to hold office. A William Berenger was elected bedel in 1294, was juror that same year, and had served as capital pledge and juror back in 1290.[75]

Robert's willingness to ignore communal and manorial restrictions on access to resources in meadow, woods, and marsh illustrates what Raftis has interpreted as a system of licensing giving major tenants access to many village resources. Trade in reeds from Ramsey marsh, for example, was a 'commercial operation'.[76]

Also in contrast to Robert, there were two John Berengers whose careers overlapped between 1347 and 1387.[77] Of the eighteen references to this two-generation family, seven entries refer to a John's service as juror, constable, taster (albeit for failure to perform), or pledge. As a tenant of at least a half virgate of land, he apparently decided to undertake the official duties usually associated with such property. Whereas the John Berengers shared with Robert the inclination to invest in sheep and other livestock, Robert was more willing to lend and borrow money from his fellow villagers and was probably more aggressively involved in a local land market.

A third example will reveal further options open to fifteenth-century branches of this prolific clan. Three generations of William Berengers took advantage of the general decline in population to acquire various plots of land in Warboys at a time when the Abbot was having a hard time finding tenants. One William appears exclusively as a man willing and perhaps eager to take up

[73] Raftis, *Peasant Economic Development*, p. 53.

[74] Raftis, *Peasant Economic Development*, pp. 52–54.

[75] BL, Add. Roll 39597; BL, Add. Roll 39754.

[76] Raftis, *Peasant Economic Development*, p. 27.

[77] BL, Add. Roll 39856; BL, Add. Roll 39764; BL, Add. Roll 39858; BL, Add. Roll 39857; BL, Add. Roll 39766; BL, Add. Roll 34306; BL, Add. Roll 39474.

land abandoned by others. He took up one plot and one virgate in 1417 'on condition that he not give up any other lands that he holds'. As a *naïf* of the Abbot he already had taken on a half virgate of servile land with one plot back in 1401.[78] As a relatively well-endowed tenant, he was also willing to serve regularly as manor court juror. There is no surviving evidence of conflict with his neighbours.[79]

Towards the middle of the fifteenth century, another William Berenger extended his investments beyond the village. He inherited a half virgate from his parents and took up another half virgate several years later. He also invested in the fen resources of the neighbouring village of Wistow, where he was fined for trespassing.[80] This particular William, however, apparently refused to serve in any local office even though the *Liber Gersumarum* identified him as William Berenger, the son of John Berenger, bailiff.[81] His single-minded concentration on arable investments is illustrated by the fact that he appears only in the *gersuma* book or account rolls and never in the village court rolls. Perhaps because his older namesake had been willing to serve regularly on the jury and his father was bailiff of Warboys, this released him from similar obligations.

Reasons for this decision to focus on his exploitation of arable and fen resources seem clear. After 1350 Warboys arable was worth more per acre than the other Ramsey villages in Huntingdonshire, and farms of over a hundred acres in the region were not uncommon.[82] Correspondingly, the yields from Warboys's fields were unusually high and its labour inputs per acre relatively low. So while other villages were turning towards pastoral investments because of lack of labour, such was not required necessarily by Warboys's investors.[83]

On the other hand, John and Richard Berenger, the sons of yet another William, abandoned all commitments to Warboys and emigrated to the county of Lincolnshire where Richard was living when he purchased his manumission in 1468.[84] We only know of these decisions because of the Abbot's determina-

[78] DeWindt, *The Liber Gersumarum of Ramsey Abbey*, pp. 129, 53.

[79] BL, Add. Roll 39769; BL, Add. Roll 39864; BL, Add. Roll 39865; BL Add. Roll 34370; BL Add. Roll 39480.

[80] DeWindt, *The Liber Gersumarum of Ramsey Abbey*, pp. 249, 278; BL Add. Roll 39867.

[81] DeWindt, *The Liber Gersumarum of Ramsey Abbey*, p. 278

[82] Karakacili, 'Peasants, Productivity and Profit', pp. 202, 231.

[83] King, 'Farming Practice and Techniques', p. 216; Karakacili, 'Peasants, Productivity and Profit', p. 232.

[84] BL Add. Roll 39729; BL Add. Roll 39774; Raftis, *Tenure and Mobility*, p. 186.

tion to keep track of his wandering *nativi* and because of the willingness of the Berengers' fellow villagers, and the jury, to reveal their locations.

One final observation will illustrate a variety of other options available to members of the Berenger clan during the course of the fifteenth century. In an effort to keep track of a rather large number of individuals sharing the forename 'John', the court rolls provide extra labels indicating a range of occupations, including carpenter, wright, and even pewterer. A John Berenger was reported in 1483 to be off to London to take up that rather specialized trade.[85] John Berenger 'carpenter' had presumably left for the nearby village of Little Stukeley, but still had enough of an investment in Warboys to be fined for trespass there during the same year he was reported to be in Little Stukeley.[86] The John Berenger 'wright' maintained an interest in agriculture, as he took up a life tenancy in 1401.[87] Decisions thus had to be made about how best to invest one's labour and capital. Some acquired more land, while others pursued a craft or perhaps worked for wages. Falling regional rents and rising wages may have provided incentives to leave Warboys.

Decisions were certainly made at the level of the nuclear family, and it is possible to discern in the Warboys records hints of family strategy as well as individual strategies. Due to the very small number of forenames assigned to Berenger offspring over the course of the fourteenth and fifteenth centuries, it is very difficult to ascertain sibling relationships. Nonetheless, it does seem highly likely, based on the frequency of Berenger appearances in the records, that younger sons were able to acquire property in the village, along with their older brothers. Raftis suggested that the younger son of John Berenger 'wright' provides an example of one of the various ways young men, denied a share of the family tenements due to primogeniture, could gain property in their native village. John Berenger junior rendered a capon as entry fine in 1412 to gain access to a mondaymanland. Later, the account roll of 1421 reveals that he took up another fifteen acres. So John junior was able to establish his own family in Warboys, which eventually included two daughters, Agnes and Joan.[88]

[85] BL. Add. Roll 39775.

[86] In 1455, BL, Add. Roll 39774.

[87] 'One "ruined plot", 1 quarter of servile land "*in arentatio*" for life': DeWindt, *The Liber Gersumarum of Ramsey Abbey*, p. 53.

[88] Raftis, *Peasant Economic Development*, pp. 81–82; DeWindt, *The Liber Gersumarum of Ramsey Abbey*, pp. 101, 268, 278.

William Berenger was John junior's older brother. As his father's heir, it appears that he did not need to acquire land of his own as soon as his younger brother did. It was not until 1425 and 1438 that he received fifteen acres from his father and, later, a house and a croft 'in partnership' with his father.[89] Berenger wives were not excluded from these partnerships, and in 1437 one couple and their son took up one plot, one croft, and one-half virgate, in *arentatio*, for life.[90]

It certainly was the case that during the early decades of the fifteenth century, Berengers managed to enable many of their relatives to gain access to tenements. In a pattern unlike many other families where there was a tendency to concentrate tenements among fewer family branches, nine Berenger males held a variety of tenements in varying combinations, including one- or two-acre plots, single sellions, or a maltmanland, a dichmanland, or fractions of virgates.[91] Raftis thus points out that the system of impartible land inheritance based on primogeniture provided flexibility. The Berengers illustrate, once again, the variety of peasant experiences.

In five Ramsey villages, including Warboys, 'Among the most common customary units, the virgate or semi-virgate, there was only a ten per cent chance that two villagers would hold properties of the same size'.[92] But furthermore, each virgate or fraction of a virgate represented in itself an investment in a variety of resources which could be exploited according to individual and family strategies. 'There was the physical homestead proper, that is the messuage with its main house, out-buildings such as granges, along with gardens and orchards'. There were also rights to common 'in fen, marsh, and meadow', and arable was spread throughout the open fields in units available for subletting.[93] Raftis thus sees customary tenants in an 'entrepreneurial role' and was able to appreciate 'their range of decision-making'.[94]

One John Berenger apparently took up enough of the demesne lands abandoned by the abbey to merit the description 'farmer' in 1483, the year he also

[89] Raftis, *Peasant Economic Development*, p. 82.

[90] John Berenger sr, Juliana wife of John Berenger sr, and William son of John Berenger sr: DeWindt, *The Liber Gersumarum of Ramsey Abbey*, p. 249.

[91] Raftis, *Warboys*, p. 179; Raftis, *Peasant Economic Development*, p. 111.

[92] Raftis, *Warboys*, p. 71; also see Raftis, *Peasant Economic Development*, p. 87.

[93] Raftis, *Peasant Economic Development*, p. 12.

[94] Raftis, *Peasant Economic Development*, p. 123.

served as local constable.[95] John's experience provides an interesting example of what some might see as upward social mobility, because his recent ancestors were serfs. He eventually became the farmer of the Abbot's demesne in Warboys and took upon himself an office derived from royal authority. Constables became more and more influential in local communities as a near avalanche of parliamentary statutes designed to deal with growing social dislocation, poverty, and unrest descended on the countryside by the early fifteenth century.[96]

In what may be considered another form of upward social mobility, the son of a Berenger died in London, having composed a will identifying himself as a chaplain. A 1440 manorial court roll from Warboys reveals that Richard, son of John Berenger, was 'outside the manor' at Ramsey where he was 'at school'. Richard was apparently able to acquire the education he needed at the abbey's almonry school and was ordained to the priesthood, in spite of the fact the he and his father were serfs.[97]

This data on the Berengers certainly clarify Raftis's observation that over the course of the fifteenth century economic conditions 'favoured more individual peasant action'.[98] One indication of this is the fact that women as well as men left Ramsey villages in large numbers. Indeed, only about 10 per cent of the Warboys emigrants during the course of the fourteenth century were women, whereas *c.* 40 per cent of Warboys emigrants from the first half of the fifteenth century were women.[99] The Warboys records reveal clues to the nature of women's choices within three broad contexts: marriage, trades, and migration. Berenger women, as serfs, were not limited in choice of marriage partner to other serfs or to Warboys residents, but the active involvement of brothers and fathers in the decision process is often evident when they paid the license fee. When Mariota Berenger married a butcher based in the nearby town of Ramsey in 1450, her brother Richard paid the fine.[100] Margaret Berenger may have acted without family approval, then, when she married an unnamed free-

[95] John Berenger 'farmer', in 1455, BL, Add. Roll 39774; John Berenger 'farmer' served as constable in 1483, BL, Add. Roll 39775.

[96] Haven Putnam, *The Enforcement of the Statutes*; Kent, *The English Village Constable*.

[97] Richard Berenger's will: Commissary Court of London, Register 5, fol. 168. LMA DL/C/B/004/MS09171/05.

[98] Raftis, 'Peasants and the Collapse of the Manorial Economy', p. 201.

[99] DeWindt, 'Leaving Warboys', pp. 100–01; Raftis, *Warboys*, pp. 145–50.

[100] DeWindt, *The Liber Gersumarum of Ramsey Abbey*, p. 350.

man back in 1360 without license, resulting in a fine of 13s. 4d.[101] Similarly, when Joan Berenger married John Weston in 1406, he paid the license fee — not Joan's father or brother.[102] Weston was an outsider, probably from Abbot's Ripton, with no Warboys property.[103] Perhaps this marriage was Joan's decision and was not encouraged by her family?

Several Berenger daughters left Warboys in the 1440s and 1460s either before or soon after they married. Joan, daughter of John Berenger Jr, apparently acted without financial help from a father or brother when she paid 20s. 'to marry whom she wishes'. Joan and her sister Cristina then both left Warboys and went to London.[104]

A different Christine, daughter of John Berenger, ended up at St Ives, having married 'without license', prior to 1448, and Agnes, daughter of John Berenger Jr, was married to a carpenter in Woodhurst by 1439.[105] Other women simply emigrated with no indication that marriage was part of the plan. Joan, daughter of John Berenger, went to 'Harowatehill', Surrey, in 1462, and Katherine, daughter of Richard Berenger, was reported to be in Potton, Bedfordshire, from 1455 to 1483.[106] She must have left her home village at a fairly young age, but apparently kept in touch with relatives back in Warboys, because they were able to report to the jurors her current 'address'.[107]

Berenger access to major tenements in Warboys was also certainly a factor in the complex decision-making process that preceded marriage alliances. In 1408 Richard Smith paid 13s. 4d. for license to marry Katherine, daughter of Richard Berenger, *naïf* of the lord.[108] The Smith surname only appeared in Warboys after the Black Death and had only one representative until after this fortuitous marriage.[109] A couple of years after this Berenger-Smith union,

[101] BL, Add. Roll 39764. A relative also married a freeman. Katherine, daughter of Richard Berenger, married John Attewode, freeman, in 1405. He was tenant of a medium-sized holding back in 1393–94. Raftis, *Warboys*, p. 179.

[102] DeWindt, *The Liber Gersumarum of Ramsey Abbey*, p. 69.

[103] Raftis, *Peasant Economic Development*, pp. 111–13 ; Raftis, *Warboys*, pp. 62, 191.

[104] DeWindt, *The Liber Gersumarum of Ramsey Abbey*, p. 278; BL, Add. Roll 39771.

[105] BL, Add. Roll 39773; DeWindt, *The Liber Gersumarum of Ramsey Abbey*, p. 268.

[106] BL, Add. Roll 39729; Raftis, *Warboys*, p. 147.

[107] Indeed, Rodney Hilton demonstrated that a significant number of the immigrants to the small town of Halesowen were women: Hilton, 'Women Traders'.

[108] DeWindt, *The Liber Gersumarum of Ramsey Abbey*, p. 81.

[109] Raftis, *Warboys*, pp. 51, 61.

Katherine's father stood as surety for his son-in-law when he acquired one and a half virgates in the Warboys open fields. The investment Richard Smith made in the marriage fine thus paid off. (In what must have been some sort of family arrangement, the land went back to Richard Berenger five years later.)[110]

In 1420, William London, member of an old Warboys family, paid 6s. 8d. for license to marry Agnes, daughter of John Berenger, '*naïf* of the lord'. In the same court book entry he also gained access to one messuage and a half virgate 'recently John Berenger's'. When he acquired another half virgate in 1426, he must thereby have proven himself a worthy suitor.[111]

Hugo Fordyngton also gained access to Warboys property through marriage to a Berenger woman, but he was a newcomer to the village and his 1415 marriage roughly coincided with the beginnings of a successful career accumulating a collection of tenements.[112] He married Emma, daughter of John Berenger sr, and his new wife's father paid the license fee of 3s. 4d.[113]

Berenger women thus had access to land primarily through their husbands and fathers, even when they do not appear in the records as tenants. There is one fascinating exception. Katherine Attewode, a relative by marriage of Katherine, daughter of Richard Berenger, was a joint tenant by 1414 of another woman — Mary Wyne.[114] What better illustration of the variety of women's experiences, even within the constraints of a patriarchal society.

Leyrwite fines for unacceptable sexual behaviour provide evidence of another option apparently chosen by some women. If these fines were meant to protect women's reputations and thus their value on the marriage market, the system was a highly effective restraint on Berenger women. In the nearly sixty cases of leyrwite recorded in Warboys court rolls prior to the Black Death, no Berenger women appear.[115]

110 DeWindt, *The Liber Gersumarum of Ramsey Abbey*, pp. 96, 129.

111 DeWindt, *The Liber Gersumarum of Ramsey Abbey*, pp. 154, 197.

112 Raftis, *Warboys*, p. 184.

113 DeWindt, *The Liber Gersumarum of Ramsey Abbey*, p. 128.

114 DeWindt, *The Liber Gersumarum of Ramsey Abbey*, p. 64; Raftis, *Warboys*, p. 179. The dichmanland in question was previously held by another woman, Juliana Pakerell: DeWindt, *The Liber Gersumarum of Ramsey Abbey*, p. 101. See Katherine Attewode and Mariota Wyne, BL, Add. Roll 39828.

115 Raftis, *Warboys*, p. 255. For discussion of the various local customs regarding leyrwite, see Olson, *A Chronicle of All That Happens*, pp. 214–16. Edward Britton found that very few women fined for leyrwite turned to male relatives for sureties, indicating, in his opinion, 'family troubles resulting from adultery': Britton, *The Community of the Vill*, p. 37.

Many peasant women chose the ale and victualling trades to supplement personal and family income. Ambrose Raftis suggested that women's labour was used in this manner primarily by smaller tenants. The larger tenancies must have required too much family labour elsewhere to allow time for brewing, baking, and selling. Indeed, only four Berenger women were fined for ale infractions in the fourteenth-century Warboys court rolls.[116] And there is no other evidence of Berenger women involving themselves in trades other than brewing.[117] This was either not an attractive option for women of their family's wealth and status, or the demands of large landed investments precluded the opportunity.

It may well have been fifteenth-century emigration that opened access to the trades for Berenger women. For example, in 1452 Mariota Berenger married a butcher at Ramsey.[118] Those Berenger women who ventured to Slepe, Cambridge, Lynn, Potton, or Surrey must have made their livings in service or in some trade, because no husbands are mentioned in the frustratingly terse acknowledgements of their departures from home.[119]

To conclude, it is with all due respect to legal and political historians that one can certainly sympathize with H. E. Hallam's frustration when he wrote: 'A peasant diary from the thirteenth century or a peasant family's correspondence from the twelfth century would be worth all the Pipe Rolls and Curia Regis Rolls in the Public Record Office'.[120] Given the absence of such personal documents, I can also appreciate Hilton's offering us the following quotation from

[116] Raftis, *Warboys*, pp. 236–40. In contrast, Judith M. Bennett found that in Iver, Buckinghamshire, 'men whose wives brewed were twice as likely as other men to hold local office'. Many brewsters in Brigstock were of 'middling socioeconomic status', but she concludes that 'the trade was not restricted in any sense to women of particular circumstances': Bennett, *Ale, Beer, and Brewsters in England*, pp. 32–35.

[117] BL, Add. Roll 39858.

[118] DeWindt, *The Liber Gersumarum of Ramsey Abbey*, p. 350.

[119] Katherine daughter of Richard to Potton, Bedfordshire, by 1455 (BL, Add. Roll 39774). Joan daughter of William went to Slepe with Thomas Belleman, in 1405 (BL, Add. Roll 39862). Thomas Belleman had a booth at St Ives, but he was dead by 1407. Perhaps Joan returned home to marry John Weston by 1407? There is a later connection between the Berenger and Belleman surnames when, in 1440, John Berenger sr of Warboys and William Berenger of Warboys pledged for property once belonging to John Belman in St Ives (DeWindt, *The Liber Gersumarum of Ramsey Abbey*, pp. 68–59, 273). Joan daughter of William Berenger was at Cambridge in 1421 and at Lynn in 1424 (BL, Add. Roll 39770, BL, Add. Roll 39865). Joan daughter of John Berenger was in Surrey by 1462 (BL, Add. Roll 39729).

[120] Hallam, 'The Life of the People', p. 845.

Marc Bloch: 'In social life is there any more elusive notion than the free will of a small man?'[121]

But in spite of these epistemological difficulties, one powerful message our sources do manage to broadcast is variety. Should we really be surprised, therefore, that D. A. Carpenter was able to write: 'Here then we find, at the peasant level, the same diversity of conduct characteristic of other sections of society'?[122] Writers in the past, whether ridiculing, romanticizing, or paying homage to 'the peasant', would rarely attribute a greater array of choices to this presumably humble country-dweller than to the knight. Indeed, it was his or her relative lack of choice and decision-making power that defined the category 'peasant' in the popular imagination.

But, in fact, historians are now incapable, and rightly so, of even talking about a peasant who does not make choices. Hence our fascination with resistance to lordship because we assume that lordship, qua lordship, is somehow incompatible with peasant agency. Choosing to create for oneself an identity that grows out of loyalty to a particular lord is a concept difficult for inhabitants of the modern West.

This realization, along with criticism by sociologists of the relevance and utility of rational choice theory, can heighten a historian's sensitivity to the complexity of the issues raised by any investigation of peasant agency. Agents coexist within particular physical environments and within particular cultural and social contexts. Their decision-making process was, indeed, a process that emerged over time as the result of constant interactions with that culture, social structure, or environment. The non-human, material 'agents' in the peasant's universe influenced and were influenced by those decisions.[123] A peasant with a tenement on heavy clay soil within an open-field system owing labour rents to a manorial lord of high social status would certainly have made decisions distinct from those made by peasants in heavily forested regions with quite different environmental and social contexts.

As decisions were made, those very elements of the social, environmental, and cultural contexts also changed, of course, in response to those decisions. The more sensitivity historians exhibit to this constant 'give and take', the better their work will be. But human agents themselves are complex bundles of

[121] Hilton, 'Individualism', pp. 110–11.

[122] Carpenter, 'English Peasants in Politics', p. 15.

[123] Ben Sandford Cullen even granted ideas the status of 'agents' in Sandford Cullen, *Contagious Ideas*. I want to thank John Langdon for this reference.

attributes with evolving combinations of perceptions, goals, values, and identities. A half virgator with several sons might place higher value on grain production than on religious pilgrimage at one stage in his life, just as his assessment of the honesty and judgment-making abilities of the manorial reeve would certainly change from one regime to another and would influence his willingness to cooperate with communal cropping decisions. His various identities as father, neighbour, tenant, parishioner, or tithing head would compete over the course of time for the role of prime motivator.

What this insight provides for the historian is the opportunity to examine any or all of these complex interactions: the agent's perceptions, goals, values, or identity as they affect and are affected by his/her physical environment and economic forces; the agent's perceptions, goals, values, or identity as they affect and are affected by his or her social and/or cultural environment.[124]

Perhaps in the end, we have to admit that we are simply facing an old dilemma that dates back to the very origins of scholarly interest in the social sciences: 'Since science must generalize, individuals are relevant only if they are typical'.[125] But how can we, as historians, pursue this quest for choices and insist on peasant agency if we search for and study only 'typical individuals'? A 'typical individual' is a contradiction in terms.

John Hatcher and Mark Bailey have expressed their own concerns about the difficulty of relying on any one 'supermodel' to explain economic development, and they recommend closer study of the particular before valid generalizations can be made. Peter Coss's tribute to Professor Hilton comes to mind: 'His concern was not with impersonal forces but with real people: with their enterprises and their ideas, with their struggles and their ambitions'.[126] To conclude with a tribute to Postan's ability to motivate and inspire economic and social historians, it was one of his own students who insisted that 'from the late thirteenth century, the active agents on the economic scene would not be the landlords'.[127]

[124] For a very useful discussion of these issues, see Emirbayer and Goodwin, 'Network Analysis'.

[125] Hollis, *The Philosophy of Social Science*, p. 177.

[126] Coss, 'Rodney Hilton', p. 8.

[127] Raftis, *Peasant Economic Development*, p. 10; Bruce M. S. Campbell claims that 'Peasant farmers were probably responsible for between two-thirds and three-quarters of total agricultural production': Campbell, 'Ecology Versus Economics', p. 90.

Bibliography

Manuscripts and Archival Sources

London, British Library, Add. Roll 34306
London, British Library, Add. Roll 34324
London, British Library, Add. Roll 34370
London, British Library, Add. Roll 34777
London, British Library, Add. Roll 34814
London, British Library, Add. Roll 34815
London, British Library, Add. Roll 34817
London, British Library, Add. Roll 34896
London, British Library, Add. Roll 34898
London, British Library, Add. Roll 34899
London, British Library, Add. Roll 34910
London, British Library, Add. Roll 34918
London, British Library, Add. Roll 39470
London, British Library, Add. Roll 39474
London, British Library, Add. Roll 39480
London, British Library, Add. Roll 39597
London, British Library, Add. Roll 39729
London, British Library, Add. Roll 39754
London, British Library, Add. Roll 39757
London, British Library, Add. Roll 39758
London, British Library, Add. Roll 39759
London, British Library, Add. Roll 39760
London, British Library, Add. Roll 39761
London, British Library, Add. Roll 39762
London, British Library, Add. Roll 39764
London, British Library, Add. Roll 39766
London, British Library, Add. Roll 39768
London, British Library, Add. Roll 39769
London, British Library, Add. Roll 39770
London, British Library, Add. Roll 39771
London, British Library, Add. Roll 39772
London, British Library, Add. Roll 39773
London, British Library, Add. Roll 39774
London, British Library, Add. Roll 39775
London, British Library, Add. Roll 39828
London, British Library, Add. Roll 39853
London, British Library, Add. Roll 39856
London, British Library, Add. Roll 39857
London, British Library, Add. Roll 39858
London, British Library, Add. Roll 39862
London, British Library, Add. Roll 39864
London, British Library, Add. Roll 39865
London, British Library, Add. Roll 39867
London, Commissary Court of London, Register 5, fol. 168, LMA DL/C/B/004/MS09171/05 (Richard Berenger's will)

Primary Sources

DeWindt, Edwin Brezette, *The Liber Gersumarum of Ramsey Abbey: A Calendar and Index of BL. Harley ms. 445* (Toronto: Pontifical Institute of Mediaeval Studies, 1976)

Secondary Sources

Bailey, Mark, 'Peasant Welfare in England, 1290–1348', *Economic History Review*, 51 (1998), 223–51

Beattie, Cordelia, *Medieval Single Women: The Politics of Social Classification in Late Medieval England* (Oxford: Oxford University Press, 2007)

Beckerman, John S., 'Procedural Innovation and Institutional Change in Medieval English Manorial Courts', *Law and History Review*, 10 (1992), 198–252

Bennett, Judith M., *Ale, Beer, and Brewsters in England: Women's Work in a Changing World, 1300–1600* (New York: Oxford University Press, 1996)

——, 'Compulsory Service in Late Medieval England', *Past and Present*, 209 (2010), 7–51

——, 'Public Power and Authority in the Medieval English Countryside', in *Women and Power in the Middle Ages*, ed. by Mary Erler and Maryanne Kowaleski (Athens: University of Georgia Press, 1988), pp. 18–36

Berkhofer, Robert, 'Marriage, Lordship and the "Greater Unfree" in Twelfth-Century France', *Past and Present*, 173 (2001), 3–27

Bisson, Thomas N., 'Medieval Lordship', *Speculum*, 70 (1995), 743–59

Bland, Alfred E., and others, *English Economic History Select Documents* (London: G. Bell and Sons, 1914)

Briggs, Chris, '"Seigniorial Control of Villagers" Litigation beyond the Manor in Later Medieval England', *Historical Research*, 81 (2008), 399–422

Britnell, Richard, 'Land and Lordship: Common Themes and Regional Variations', in *Agriculture and Rural Society after the Black Death*, ed. by Ben Dodds and Richard Britnell (Hatfield: University of Hertfordshire Press, 2008), pp. 3–19

——, 'Specialization of Work in England, 1100–1300', *Economic History Review*, 54 (2001), 1–16

Britton, Edward, *The Community of the Vill: A Study in the History of the Family and Village Life in Fourteenth-Century England* (Toronto: Pontifical Institute of Mediaeval Studies, 1977)

Bruno, Michael, Martin Ravallion, and Lyn Squire, 'Equity and Growth in Developing Countries: Old and New Perspectives on the Policy Issues', in *Income Distribution and High-Quality Growth*, ed. by Vito Tanzi and Ke-young Chu (Cambridge: Cambridge University Press, 1998), pp. 117–46

Campbell, Bruce M. S., 'The Agrarian Problem of the Early Fourteenth Century', *Past and Present*, 188 (2005), 3–70

——, 'Ecology Versus Economics in Late Thirteenth- and Early Fourteenth-Century English Agriculture', in *Agriculture in the Middle Ages: Technology, Practice, and Representation,* ed. by Del Sweeney (Philadelphia: University of Pennsylvania Press, 1995), 76–108

——, 'Economic Rent and the Intensification of English Agriculture, 1086–1350', in *Medieval Farming and Technology: The Impact of Agricultural Change in Northwest Europe*, ed. by Grenville Astill and John Langdon (Leiden: Brill, 1997), pp. 225–50

Carpenter, David A., 'English Peasants in Politics 1258–1267', *Past and Present*, 136 (1992), 3–42

Cassidy-Welch, Megan, and Peter Sherlock, eds, *Practices of Gender in Late Medieval and Early Modern Europe* (Turnhout: Brepols, 2008)

Clark, Elaine, 'The Decision to Marry in Thirteenth- and Early Fourteenth-Century Norfolk', *Medieval Studies*, 49 (1987), 496–516

——, 'Social Welfare and Mutual Aid in the Medieval Countryside', *Journal of British Studies*, 33 (1994), 381–406

Coss, Peter, 'Rodney Hilton', *Past and Present*, 176 (2002), pp. 7–10

Davidson Cragoe, Carol, 'Making Tradition: Architecture and Liturgy in Parish Churches', paper presented at 'The Late Medieval English Parish', Harlaxton Symposium, 23–26 July 2002

Desai, Meghnad, 'The Agrarian Crisis in Medieval England: A Malthusian Tragedy or a Failure of Entitlements?', *Bulletin of Economic Research*, 43 (1991), 223–58

DeWindt, Anne, 'Leaving Warboys: Emigration from a Fifteenth-Century English Village', in *Writing Medieval Women's Lives*, ed. by Amy Livingstone and Charlotte Goldy (New York: Palgrave-Macmillan, 2012), pp. 85–111

——, 'Local Government in a Small Town: A Medieval Leet Jury and its Constituents', *Albion*, 23 (1991), 627–54

DeWindt, Anne Reiber, and Edwin Brezette DeWindt, *Royal Justice and the Medieval English Countryside* (Toronto: Pontifical Institute of Mediaeval Studies, 1981)

Dodds, Ben, *Peasants and Production in the Medieval North-East: The Evidence from Tithes, 1270–1536* (Woodbridge: Boydell, 2007)

Dyer, Christopher, 'Medieval Farming and Technology: Conclusion', in *Medieval Farming and Technology: The Impact of Agricultural Change in Northwest Europe*, ed. by Grenville Astill and John Langdon (Leiden: Brill, 1997), pp. 293–312

——, 'Memories of Freedom: Attitudes towards Serfdom in England, 1200–1350', in *Serfdom and Slavery: Studies in Legal Bondage*, ed. by Michael L. Bush (London: Longman,1996), p. 277–95

——, 'A Suffolk Farmer in the Fifteenth Century', *Agricultural History Review*, 55 (2007), 1–22

——, 'Were Late Medieval English Villages "Self-Contained"?', in *The Self-Contained Village? The Social History of Rural Communities, 1250–1900*, ed. by Christopher Dyer (Hatfield: University of Hertfordshire Press, 2007), pp. 6–27

Dyer, Christopher, Peter R. Coss, and Chris Wickham, eds, *Rodney Hilton's Middle Ages: An Exploration of Historical Themes* (Oxford: Oxford University Press, 2008)

Eiden, Herbert, 'Joint Action against "Bad" Lordship: The Peasants' Revolt in Essex and Norfolk', *History*, 83 (1998), 5–30

Elsenhans, Hartmut, *Equality and Development* (Dhaka: Dana, 1992)

Emirbayer, Mustafa, and Jeff Goodwin, 'Network Analysis, Culture, and the Problem of Agency', *American Journal of Sociology*, 99 (1994), 1411–54

Farmer, David L., 'Prices and Wages [1000–1355]', in *The Agrarian History of England and Wales*, II: *1042–1350*, ed. by Herbert E. Hallam (Cambridge: Cambridge University Press, 1988), pp. 716–817

Federico, Sylvia, 'The Imaginary Society: Women in 1381', *Journal of British Studies*, 40 (2001), 159–83

Fields, Gary S., 'Growth and Income Distribution', in *Essays on Poverty, Equity and Growth*, ed. by George Psacharopoulos (Oxford: Pergamon, 1991), pp. 1–52

Fox, H. S. A., 'Exploitation of the Landless by Lords and Tenants in Early Medieval England', in *Medieval Society and the Manor Court*, ed. by Zvi Razi and Richard Smith (Oxford: Oxford University Press, 1996), pp. 518–68

Given-Wilson, Chris, 'Service, Serfdom and English Labour Legislation, 1350–1500', in *Concepts and Patterns of Service in the Later Middle Ages*, ed. by Anne Curry and Elizabeth Matthew (Woodbridge: Ashgate, 2000), pp. 21–37

Goheen, Robert, 'Peasant Politics? Village Community and the Crown in Fifteenth-Century England', *American Historical Review*, 96 (1991), pp. 47–62

Goldberg, P. J. P., *Medieval England: A Social History 1250–1550* (London: Arnold, 2004)

Graham, Helen, '"A Woman's Work ...": Labour and Gender in the Late Medieval Countryside', in *Woman Is a Worthy Wight: Women in English Society c. 1200–1500*, ed. by P. Jeremy Goldberg (Stroud: Allen Sutton, 1992), pp. 126–48

Hallam, Herbert E., 'The Life of the People', in *The Agrarian History of England and Wales*, II: *1042–1350*, ed. by Herbert E. Hallam (Cambridge: Cambridge University Press, 1988), pp. 818–53

——, 'Rural England and Wales, 1042–1350', in *The Agrarian History of England and Wales*, II: *1042–1350*, ed. by Herbert E. Hallam (Cambridge: Cambridge University Press, 1988), pp. 966–1008

Hargreaves, Paul V., 'Seignorial Reaction and Peasant Responses: Worcester Priory and its Peasants after the Black Death', *Midland History*, 24 (1999), pp. 53–78

Haven Putnam, Bertha, *The Enforcement of the Statutes of Labourers during the First Decade after the Black Death 1349–1359* (New York: Columbia University Press, 1908)

Hilton, Rodney, 'Individualism and the English Peasantry', *New Left Review*, 120 (1980), pp. 109–12

——, 'Women Traders in Medieval England', *Women's Studies*, 11 (1984), pp. 139–55

Hogan, M. Patricia, 'Clays, *Culturae*, and the Cultivator's Wisdom: Management Efficiency at Fourteenth-Century Wistow', *Agricultural History Review*, 36 (1988), 117–31

Hollis, Martin, *The Philosophy of Social Science: An Introduction* (Cambridge: Cambridge University Press, 1994)

Hopcroft, Rosemary L., 'The Origins of Regular Open-Field Systems in Pre-Industrial Europe', *Journal of European Economic History*, 23 (1994), 563–77

——, 'The Social Origins of Agrarian Change in Late Medieval England', *American Journal of Sociology*, 99 (1994), 1559–95

Johnston, Alexandra, 'Parish Playmaking', paper presented at 'The Late Medieval English Parish', Harlaxton Symposium, 23–26 July 2002

Karakacili, Eona, 'Peasants, Productivity and Profit in the Open Fields of England: A Study of Economic and Social Development' (unpublished doctoral thesis, University of Toronto, 2001)

Kanzaka, Junichi, 'Villein Rents in Thirteenth-Century England: An Analysis of the Hundred Rolls of 1279–1280', *Economic History Review*, 55 (2002), pp. 593–618

Kent, Joan R., *The English Village Constable 1580–1642: A Social and Administrative Study* (Oxford: Clarendon Press, 1986)

King, Edmund, 'Farming Practice and Techniques, East Midlands', in *The Agrarian History of England and Wales*, III: *1348–1500*, ed. by Edward Miller (Cambridge: Cambridge University Press, 1991), pp. 210–21

——, 'Occupation of the Land: The East Midlands', in *The Agrarian History of England and Wales*, III: *1348–1500*, ed. by Edward Miller (Cambridge: Cambridge University Press, 1991), pp. 67–76

Kitsikopolous, H., 'Standards of Living and Capital Formation in Pre-Plague England: A Peasant Budget Model', *Economic History Review*, 53 (2000), 237–61

Langdon, John, *Horses, Oxen and Technological Innovation: The Use of Draught Animals in English Farming from 1066 to 1500* (Cambridge: Cambridge University Press, 1986)

——, 'Was England a Technological Backwater in the Middle Ages?', in *Medieval Farming and Technology: The Impact of Agricultural Change in Northwest Europe*, ed. by Grenville Astill and John Langdon (Leiden: Brill, 1997), pp. 275–91

Langdon, John, and James Masschaele, 'Commercial Activity and Population Growth in Medieval England', *Past and Present*, 190 (2006), 35–81

Martin, David, and Barbara Martin, 'Adapting Houses to Changing Needs: Multi-Phased Medieval and Transitional Houses in Eastern Sussex', *Sussex Archaeological Collections*, 137 (1999), 121–32

Masschaele, James, *Jury, State, and Society in Medieval England* (New York: Palgrave-Macmillan, 2008)

——, *Peasants, Merchants and Markets: Inland Trade in Medieval England, 1150–1350* (New York: St Martin's Press, 1997)

——, 'The Public Space of the Marketplace', *Speculum*, 77 (2002), 383–421

——, 'Review of John Hatcher and Mark Bailey, *Modelling the Middle Ages: The History and Theory of England's Economic Development* (Oxford, 2001)', in *Canadian Journal of History*, 38 (2003), 91–93

——, 'Town, Country and Law: Royal Courts and Regional Mobility in Medieval England, *c.* 1200–*c.* 1400', in *Survival and Discord in Medieval Society: Essays in Honour of Christopher Dyer*, ed. by Richard Goddard, John Langdon, and Miriam Müller (Turnhout: Brepols, 2010), pp. 127–44

Mate, Mavis, 'Agricultural Technology in Southeast England, 1348–1530', in *Medieval Farming and Technology: The Impact of Agricultural Change in Northwest Europe*, ed. by Grenville Astill and John Langdon (Leiden: Brill, 1997), pp. 251–74

McIntosh, Marjorie K., 'The Diversity of Social Capital in English Communities, 1300–1640 (with a Glance at Modern Nigeria)', *Journal of Interdisciplinary History*, 29 (1999), 459–90

——, *Working Women in English Society, 1300–1620* (Cambridge: Cambridge University Press, 2005)

McSheffery, Shannon, *Love and Marriage in Late Medieval London* (Kalamazoo: Medieval Institute Publications, 1995)

Miller, Edward, 'Introduction: Land and People', in *The Agrarian History of England and Wales*, III: *1348–1500*, ed. by Edward Miller (Cambridge: Cambridge University Press, 1991), pp. 1–33

——, 'People', in *The Agrarian History of England and Wales*, III: *1348–1500*, ed. by Edward Miller (Cambridge: Cambridge University Press, 1991), pp. 1–7

Moorthy, Krishna, *Economic Development and Income Distribution; An Empirical Study*, with preface by N. S. Iyengar (New Delhi: Discovery, 1992)

Muller, Miriam, 'The Function and Evasion of Marriage Fines on a Fourteenth-Century English Manor', *Continuity and Change*, 14 (1999), 169–90

Nee, Victor, 'Review of *Rational Choice Theory: Advocacy and Critique*, ed. by James S. Coleman and Thomas J. Fararo (Sage: Newbury Park, 1992)', *American Journal of Sociology*, 99 (1994), 1083–90

Newbury, David, and Catharine Newbury, 'Bringing the Peasants "Back In": Agrarian Themes in the Construction and Corrosion of Statist Historiography in Rwanda', *American Historical Review*, 105 (2000), pp. 832–77

Olson, Sherri, *A Chronicle of All That Happens: Voices from the Village Court in Medieval England* (Toronto: Pontifical Institute of Mediaeval Studies, 1996)

——, 'Jurors of the Village Court: Local Leadership Before and After the Plague in Ellington, Huntingdonshire', *Journal of British Studies*, 30 (1991), 237–56

Poos, Larry, 'The Social Context of Statute of Labourers Enforcement', *Law and History Review*, 1 (1983), 27–52

Raftis, J. Ambrose, *Peasant Economic Development within the English Manorial System* (Montreal: Mcgill-Queens, 1996)

——, 'Peasants and the Collapse of the Manorial Economy on Some Ramsey Abbey Estates', in *Progress and Problems in Medieval England: Essays in Honour of Edward Miller*, ed. Richard Britnell and John Hatcher (Cambridge: Cambridge University Press, 1996), pp. 191–206

——, *Tenure and Mobility* (Toronto: Pontifical Institute of Mediaeval Studies, 1964)

——, *Warboys: Two Hundred Years in the Life of an English Mediaeval Village* (Toronto: Pontifical Institute of Mediaeval Studies, 1974)

Razi, Zvi, 'The Myth of the Immutable English Family', *Past and Present*, 140 (1993), pp. 3–44

Sandford Cullen, Ben, *Contagious Ideas: On Evolution, Culture, Archaeology, and Cultural Virus Theory*, ed. by James Steele, Richard Cullen, and Christopher Chippindale (Oxford: Oxbow, 2000)

Schofield, Phillipp R., 'Dearth, Debt and the Local Land Market in a Late Thirteenth-Century Suffolk Community', *Agricultural History Review*, 45 (1997), 1–17

——, 'The Late Medieval View of Frankpledge and the Tithing System: An Essex Case Study', in *Medieval Society and the Manor Court*, ed. by Zvi Razi and Richard Smith (Oxford: Oxford University Press, 1996), pp. 408–49

——, *Peasant and Community in Medieval England, 1200–1500* (Basingstoke: Palgrave Macmillan, 2003)

——, 'Peasants and the Manor Court: Gossip and Litigation in a Suffolk Village at the Close of the Thirteenth Century', *Past and Present*, 159 (1998), 3–42

Sheehan, Michael M., 'Theory and Practice: Marriage of the Unfree and the Poor in Medieval Society', *Mediaeval Studies*, 50 (1988), 457–87

Stone, David, *Decision Making in Medieval Agriculture* (Oxford: Oxford University Press, 2005)

——, 'Medieval Farm Management and Technological Mentalities: Hinderclay before the Black Death', *Economic History Review*, 54 (2001), 612–38

Sundrum, R. M., *Income Distribution in Less Developed Countries* (London: Routledge, 1990)

Vergunst, Petra, 'Social Integration: Re-Socialisation and Symbolic Boundaries in Dutch Rural Neighbourhoods', *Journal of Ethnic and Migration Studies*, 34.6 (2008), 917–34

Walter, John, 'Subsistence Strategies, Social Economy and the Politics of Subsistence in Early Modern England' in *Just a Sack of Potatoes? Crisis Experiences in European Societies*, ed. by Antti Hakkinen (Helsinki: SHS, 1992), pp. 53–85

Whittle, Jane, *The Development of Agrarian Capitalism: Land and Labour in Norfolk 1440–1580* (Oxford: Oxford University Press, 2000)

——, 'Housewives and Servants in Rural England: 1440–1650', *Transactions of the Royal Historical Society*, 15 (2005), 51–74

——, 'Individualism and the Family-Land Bond: A Reassessment of Land Transfer Patterns Among the English Peasantry *c.* 1270–1580', *Past and Present*, 160 (1990), 25–63

——, 'Population Mobility in Rural Norfolk among Landholders and Others *c.* 1440–*c.* 1600', in *The Self-Contained Village? The Social History of Rural Communities, 1250–1900*, ed. by Christopher Dyer (Hatfield: University of Hertfordshire Press, 2007), pp. 28–45

Whittle, Jane, and Margaret Yates, '"Pays Réel or Pays Légal"? Contrasting Patterns of Land Tenure and Social Structure in Eastern Norfolk and Western Berkshire, 1450–1600', *Agricultural History Review*, 48 (2000), pp. 1–26

Wilson, George, and Samuel Shpall, 'The Nature of Action and Agency', *The Stanford Encyclopedia of Philosophy*, ed. by Edward N. Zalta, Summer 2012 edn, <http://plato.stanford.edu/entries/action/> [accessed 5 June 2014]

Yates, Margaret, 'Change and Continuities in Rural Society from the Later Middle Ages to the Sixteenth Century: The Contribution of West Berkshire', *Economic History Review*, 52 (1999), 617–37

van Zanden, Jan Luiten, 'In Good Company: About Agency and Economic Development in Global Perspective', *Economic History of Developing Regions*, 27(Supplement 1) (2012), 16–27

'Money Matters': A Critique of the Postan Thesis on Medieval Population, Prices, and Wages

John Munro

Postan and the Medieval Population Question

For the English-speaking world, no historian has had a more profound influence, in the past half century, upon our conception of the later medieval economy and society than has the late Michael Moïssey Postan (1899–1981) of Cambridge University. His greatest fame lies in his analyses of the relationships between demographic, economic, and social changes in medieval England, though more generally also in medieval Europe. For their respective areas of medieval Europe, a very similar claim may be made for the equally eminent Georges Duby (for France), Wilhelm Abel (for Germany and Central Europe), and B. H. Slicher-Van Bath (for the Low Countries).[1] Though none of these four historians ever claimed that population was in itself the ultimate 'prime mover', they certainly portrayed demographic factors to be the primary agency for explaining the economic and social changes in medieval Europe. Postan's most profound influence on English economic history began with two papers on population change, published in 1950 and 1951. His last major work on this theme was a textbook survey, largely devoted to demography and agricul-

[1] Duby, *L'économie rurale*, Duby, *Rural Economy*, trans. by Postan; Abel, *Agrarkrisen und Agrarkonjunktur*; Abel, *Die Wüstungen*; Slicher-Van Bath, *De agrarische geschiedenis*.

John Munro (1938–2013) was Professor Emeritus of Economics, University of Toronto, and was a renowned scholar of the medieval economy, with many publications on textile and monetary history.

Crisis in the Later Middle Ages: Beyond the Postan-Duby Paradigm, ed. by John Drendel, TMC 13 (Turnhout: Brepols, 2015) 127–194 BREPOLS PUBLISHERS 10.1484/M.TMC.5.103787

ture, published in 1972; but his final publication on English demography was a *Past and Present* article that he co-authored with John Hatcher.[2]

Consequently, any discussion of Postan's model must begin with medieval demography (up to *c.* 1520). Most historians now believe that western Europe's population at least doubled from the tenth to the early fourteenth century and, further, that the most rapid growth took place during the so-called long thirteenth century, from *c.* 1180 to *c.* 1315. But there still remains considerable dispute about when England itself reached its maximum population and at what level. While many historians continue to believe that English population continued to grow until the Black Death, few would now accept the pioneering estimate of J. C. Russell: 3.7 million.[3] Postan, while warning his readers to eschew the 'lure of aggregates', rejected Russell's views by contending, first, that it had peaked much earlier, about the time of the Great Famine (1315–22), and second, that it had peaked at a far higher level, possibly six to eight million — or even more precisely 'nearer 7 millions'.[4] Most of Postan's English and

[2] Postan, 'Some Economic Evidence'; Postan, 'The Economic Foundations'; Postan, 'The Trade of Medieval Europe'; Postan and Titow, 'Heriots and Prices'; Postan, 'Medieval Agarian Society', esp. pp. 560–70; Postan, *The Medieval Economy and Society*, pp. 27–40; Postan and Hatcher, 'Population and Class Relations'.

[3] Russell, *British Medieval Population*, pp. 280, 314. Russell had extrapolated evidence from the 1377 poll tax to contend that England's population was then 2.235 million, about 40 per cent lower than the pre-plague level of (therefore) 3.7 million.

[4] See Postan's publications in n. 2. The direct quotation is from Postan, 'Medieval Agarian Society', p. 562; the estimate of six to eight million is given subsequently in Postan, *The Medieval Economy and Society*, p. 30. Postan's critique was based on Russell's following assumptions about the 1377 poll tax: that the tax-evasion rate was only 2.5 per cent; that the proportion of those under fourteen and thus untaxed was 35 per cent; that the proper household multiplier was 3.6 persons; and that the post-plague mortality rate was about 40 per cent (so that 2.235/0.60 = 3.725 million). In rebuttal, and thus in providing reasons for estimating the early fourteenth-century peak population at six to eight million, Postan contended that, in the 1377 poll tax, tax evasion was likely ten times as much, at 25 per cent; that the untaxed (under fourteen) probably accounted for 40–45 per cent of the total; that the household multiplier was more likely 4.5 or 5.0; and that total post-plague mortality was probably 50 per cent. Subsequently, J. C. Russell defended his original views in Russell, 'The Preplague Population', reiterating his contention that England's population had reached a peak of 3.7 million in 1347 (pp. 1, 16, 19, 21) and that 'the decline came only with the plague' (p. 21). But, while stoutly defending his household multiplier of 3.5 — rather than 3.6 (p. 17) — as do many historians, and while conceding points on tax evasion and those untaxed, he presented a revised and even lower population estimate for 1377: 2,199,915 (or 2.2 million; but note that 2.2/0.60 = 3.667 million). Postan never did provide an estimate for the nadir of England's population; but in Postan, 'Medieval Agarian Society', p. 570, he stated that 'It is even doubtful whether England's rural population

especially his younger Cambridge colleagues have supported the now standard 'orthodox' view that England's population had peaked around 1300, at about six million or somewhat more.[5] More recently, however, Bruce Campbell and fellow historians engaged in the 'Feeding the City Project' have favoured an estimate that is much closer to Russell's views than those of Postan in contending that a figure of '4 million is more credible than one of 4.75 million' for England's maximum population *c.* 1300.[6]

What then happened, during and after the Great Famine (1315–22) — whose consequences, as we now know, were greatly aggravated by a cattle panzootic ('plague') — is also of considerable dispute.[7] Postan himself suggested that the Great Famine marked the great watershed, with what was evidently a full blown Malthusian crisis.[8] In partial support of that view, at least for East Anglia, Lawrence Poos has provided some strong evidence demonstrating a decline in Essex's population following the Great Famine, though with a more precipitous fall after the Black Death.[9] Bruce Campbell, on the other

came up to its thirteenth-century peak until the very eve of the industrial revolution of the eighteenth century', when (in 1750), according to current estimates, the population was 5.922 million. See Wrigley and others, *English Population History*, pp. 613–17.

[5] In chronological order of publication: Hatcher, *Plague, Population, and the English Economy*, p. 68 (that England's population in 1348, probably below that of 1300, was 'within the range of 4.5 to 6 million' and most likely closer to the latter); Miller and Hatcher, *Medieval England: Rural Society and Economic Change*, p. 29 ('between 5 and 6 million' in 1347), and p. 33 ('population probably tripled between 1086 [1.75–2.25 million] and the first half of the fourteenth century'); Hallam, 'Population Movements in England' (over seven million, by *c.* 1300); Smith, 'Demographic Developments', p. 50 (that England's population *c.* 1300 was possibly 'a million greater than in the mid-seventeenth century [when it was 5.2 million]'; Miller and Hatcher, *Medieval England: Towns, Commerce and Crafts*, p. 393 (that 'current thinking would suggest a total of 6 millions or rather more' for England's population *c.* 1300); Hatcher and Bailey, *Modelling the Middle Ages*, p. 31 ('perhaps reaching 6 million at its peak', *c.* 1300).

[6] Campbell and others, *A Medieval Capital and its Grain Supply*, pp. 44–45; Campbell, *English Seigniorial Agriculture, 1250–1450*, pp. 234, 247–48, 386–410; Nightingale, 'The Growth of London'.

[7] See Jordan, *The Great Famine*; Kershaw, 'The Great Famine'; Newfield, 'A Cattle Panzootic'; Slavin, 'The Fifth Rider of the Apocalypse'; Slavin, 'The Great Bovine Pestilence'; Campbell, 'Nature as Historical Protagonist'.

[8] Postan, 'The Economic Foundations', pp. 14–15. Virtually the same words are presented in Postan, 'Some Economic Evidence', p. 213.

[9] Poos, 'The Rural Population'; Poos, *A Rural Society after the Black Death*, pp. 89–129, esp. figs. 5.21–5.22, on pp. 96–103.

hand, while also finding evidence in Norfolk for an incipient Malthusian crisis just before the Great Famine, nevertheless concluded that Norfolk's population adjusted to that crisis and continued to grow, albeit much more slowly, to the eve of the Black Death.[10] Similar views are also held by Barbara Harvey,[11] and evidently also by Richard Smith.[12]

If Postan dismissed the view that the Black Death was the true medieval watershed, most historians still see it in that same light, in marking the peak of late medieval England's population growth and the onset of rapid demographic decline.[13] That England's population continued to fall thereafter during the later fourteenth century and continued to drift downward through the entire fifteenth century now seems likely. In all likelihood, the turning point did not occur until about the 1520s, when the population of England and Wales can be estimated with some certainty at 2.25–2.30 million.[14] That figure, one should note, is only 50 per cent of the very conservative Campbell estimate of about 4.0 to 4.5 million. Unquestionably England, along with most of western Europe, suffered a demographic catastrophe in the later Middle Ages, whether or not it began with the Black Death.

[10] Campbell, 'Population Pressure, Inheritance'. See also Bailey, 'Peasant Welfare in England'.

[11] Harvey, 'The Population Trend in England'; Harvey, 'Introduction'; Russell, *British Medieval Population*, pp. 280, 314; Russell, 'The Preplague Population'. See also Bridbury, 'Before the Black Death', suggesting that England was not overpopulated on the eve of the Black Death, thus contradicting his earlier views put forth in Bridbury, 'The Black Death'.

[12] Smith, 'Demographic Developments', pp. 25–77: with no definitive conclusion on whether England had suffered a net loss of population between the Great Famine and the Black Death. See also Hatcher, *Plague, Population, and the English Economy*, pp. 11–20.

[13] See Postan's publications cited above in note 2.

[14] For English population estimates in the early 1520s, see Cornwall, 'English Population'; Blanchard, 'Population Change'; Campbell, 'The Population of Early Tudor England'; Hatcher, *Plague, Population, and the English Economy*, p. 69 (range of 2.25 to 2.75 million); Rigby, 'Urban Population' (with some critical comments on these earlier population estimates). For studies on English demography, indicating either demographic stagnation or further decline to the early sixteenth century, see the sources cited notes 9–12, and also Hatcher, 'Mortality in the Fifteenth Century'; Hatcher, 'England in the Aftermath'; Hatcher, Piper, and Stone, 'Monastic Mortality'; Nightingale, 'Some New Evidence'; Poos, 'The Historical Demography'; Hinde, *England's Population*.

The Postan Demographic Model on Late Medieval Prices and Wages: The Ricardian and Malthusian Foundations

What, according to Postan and his followers, were the economic and social consequences of such drastic depopulation? Their model, essentially based on the economic principles of the English classical economist David Ricardo (1772–1823), assumes that falling population in medieval and early modern Europe had the following economic consequences (*ceteris paribus*): (1) a fall in grain prices, (2) a consequent decline in rents, both landowners' rents and pure economic rent, and (3) a rise in real wages, as defined later in this study.[15] Most modern economic historians have also been deeply influenced in their pessimistic views by those of another English classical economist, Thomas Malthus (1776–1834), who contended that population growth, if left unchecked by 'providential' and 'prudential' constraints, would tend to grow exponentially, while the food supply, at best, could increase only by arithmetical, incremental additions.[16] The inevitable result would thus be falling real incomes, increasing impoverishment for the masses, a rising death toll from malnutrition and disease, and then a falling population, until a new equilibrium was established. Malthus himself, however, believed that, in a developed society, 'prudential' constraints — what we would now call the European marriage pattern — would check the growth in population before the drastic 'providential' forces of famine, disease, and war became necessary.[17] Subsequently, in the late nineteenth century, the Marginal Utility School combined these concepts into the law of diminishing returns. It specifies that if increased units of labour are applied to a fixed stock of land and capital, with an unvarying technology, the extra or marginal output from each added unit of labour will increase to a maximum point of efficiency, beyond which any extra labour units will produce smaller and smaller additional or 'marginal' outputs.

[15] See Ricardo, *Principles of Political Economy and Taxation*. Ricardo was the first classical economist to demonstrate that agricultural prices determine land rents, and not the other way around.

[16] Malthus, *An Essay on the Principles of Population*; Malthus, *Principles of Political Economy*. For very good modern analyses of the Ricardo-Malthusian demographic model, especially in relation to the Postan thesis, see Rigby, *English Society in the Later Middle Ages*, pp. 104–27; Smith, 'Demographic Developments', pp. 24–37; Hatcher and Bailey, *Modelling the Middle Ages*, pp. 21–30, 52–65, 175–79 (with some criticisms of the Postan thesis).

[17] See especially Hajnal, 'European Marriage Patterns'; De Moor and Luiten Van Zanden, 'Girl Power'; Foreman-Peck, 'The Western European Marriage Pattern'.

In the light of all these considerations, therefore, the Postan model stipulates that the drastic late medieval fall in population, in radically altering the land:labour ratio, led to a steep rise in the marginal productivity of labour. In a fundamentally agrarian economy, such changes would have taken place fairly quickly, with the abandonment of many high-cost marginal lands which, because of extensive prior population growth, had been subject to severely diminishing returns. Thus arable husbandry would subsequently — after some delays in adjustments — have become concentrated on much better quality, higher-yielding lands that produced much more grain and livestock products with proportionately less labour, at much lower cost.[18]

The Postan model then stipulates that grain prices would have fallen, relative to other prices, for three Ricardian-based reasons. First, the marginal cost of producing a bushel of grain would have decreased, for the reasons just stated. Second, the lower-cost lands on which that grain was now being produced were presumably closer to markets, so that average transportation costs would also have fallen. Third, the reduction in the quantity of grain supplied to the market probably would have been less than the decline in population, if only because some redundant but still good lands would have remained in production, so that per capita supplies on the market would have increased.

The Postan model further assumes that, as a consequence of these changes, real wages of agricultural labourers would have risen, again for basically three reasons. First, according to classical economics, the real wage is determined by the marginal productivity of labour; and as previously contended, the Postan model assumes that the marginal productivity of labour rose after the Black Death (or even after the Great Famine). Second, we may assume that, over time, the supply of available labour to work lands in production became even scarcer, as former itinerant labourers either took up vacated tenancies or sought employment at higher wages in the towns or in the now expanding rural cloth industry.[19] Third, these agrarian changes themselves would have led to a rise in real wages by reducing the prices of foodstuffs and the cost of living in general, including housing costs, with so much more available land. The term 'real wage' means, after all, the quantity of goods and services that can be purchased with

[18] On the abandonment of land in so much of medieval western Europe, see the sources cited above in note 1.

[19] On this point, see Postan, 'Some Economic Evidence', p. 211, and other publications cited in note 2. But, while accepting the impact of a twofold depletion, as former labourers took up depleted holdings, Postan rejected the view that the expanding cloth industry, still so small in scale, affected the supply of agricultural labour.

the daily, weekly, or annual money wage (plus any additional material benefits supplied by the employer).

Classical economic theory further assumes that any such rise in real wages in the agrarian sector would necessarily have been transmitted to other sectors, especially the towns, lest the latter lose labour to the agrarian sector. The tables in this study do indicate that English rural and urban wages followed basically the same trends. Such a process would presumably have been facilitated by the increased labour mobility that ensued from the later fourteenth century, with the breakdown of the manorial demesne economies, the consequent leasing of demesne lands to peasant tenants, and the decay of villeinage (serfdom).[20]

These changes would in turn have led to further changes in *relative* commodity prices, producing a widening divergence between falling grain prices and rising prices for livestock products and industrial goods. Thus labourers and artisans, in both rural and urban areas, on finding that they were enjoying greater disposable real incomes, after meeting the basic necessities of life, probably would have chosen to increase their spending on meat, dairy products, industrial goods, and semi-luxuries, thus driving up the relative prices of such goods. Prices for manufactured goods should have risen even more, because the continued rise in industrial wages would have accounted for an even greater share of total production costs than did the wages spent in producing grain and livestock products.

Such is the classic demographic model for the late medieval English and indeed west European economy, one that certainly seems both credible and reasonable in its delineation of expected changes in relative prices, including that of labour (i.e. in the form of real wages).

Postan on Money and Prices in the Late Medieval Economy

As already indicated, Postan's Ricardo-based demographic model does not permit any role for monetary factors. Contending that the fall in prices was almost entirely confined to grains, so that grain prices diverged from other prices, Postan argued that 'monetary factors could not have been the sole or the main cause of the price changes, for the pure logic of the monetary explanation demands that the effects of changes in the circulating medium should

[20] See Hilton, *The Decline of Serfdom*; Raftis, *Tenure and Mobility*, pp. 129–204; Raftis, 'Peasants and the Collapse'; Farmer, 'The *Famuli* in the Later Middle Ages'; Hatcher, 'England in the Aftermath'; Munro, 'The Late-Medieval Decline'.

be felt throughout the economy'; in other words, the role of money had to be 'neutral'. In like fashion, he also argued that a 'fall in population would also have, so to speak, a selective effect on prices, in that it would tend to lower the prices of agricultural products, which were previously being produced at high and ever rising cost under steeply diminishing returns'; but falling population would have had 'little effect on commodities not greatly subject to diminishing returns, i.e., most industrial products'.[21]

Postan's primary contention, that all prices had to move together in unison during periods of inflation or deflation, is simply a fallacy, which will be refuted by all the price tables in this study.[22] His view neglects the historical reality that, during long periods of major monetary fluctuations, involving inflation or deflation, a combination of changes in various *real* factors — population, technology, capital investments, etc. — were always acting to alter the *relative* prices of many or most individual commodities. Second, monetary changes are in themselves never 'neutral'. For example, distributions of increased stocks of money, with regional variations, would have benefited some economic sectors more than others, thus allowing some groups or socio-economic strata to achieve relatively greater increases in their money incomes. The consequent changes in their savings and expenditure patterns would also have altered the relative prices of a wide variety of individual goods and services through their impact on the price- and income-elasticities of demand for various commodities and also their elasticities of supply. Furthermore, to the extent that such increases in money supplies produced inflation, those with relatively fixed incomes would have faced budget constraints, forcing them to spend proportionately more on necessities (foodstuffs and fuels) and thus less on luxuries (most industrial goods), with a similar impact on relative prices. For monetary contractions, we may simply reverse the roles of the economic variables in this model.

[21] The first quotation is from Postan, *The Medieval Economy and Society*, p. 239; the others are from Postan, 'The Trade of Medieval Europe', pp. 213, 209–10, respectively. See also the Appendix. Postan's hostility to monetary explanations of late medieval price and economic changes is largely though not totally endorsed in Hatcher, *Plague, Population, and the English Economy*, pp. 52–54, and Hatcher and Bailey, *Modelling the Middle Ages*, pp. 186–92. While they do concede the 'rightful role of monetary factors alongside all the other influences' (p. 192) they fail to demonstrate how 'money matters' and certainly ascribe far greater importance to demographic factors.

[22] See this specific criticism in Schwartz, 'Review of Frank Spooner, *International Economy*'.

The Evidence on Late Medieval Prices and Wages in England

To test the validity of Postan's economic model, and its rejection of monetary factors, we need statistical evidence to substantiate the three aforementioned propositions for the post-plague era: (1) that grain prices fell, relative to other commodity prices; (2) that the marginal productivity of agricultural labour rose; and (3) that the real wages and total incomes of agricultural and other labourers and craftsmen also rose. In brief, the now available statistical evidence does not support Postan's model on prices and wages, either before or after the Black Death. In fairness to Postan, however, we must note that very few continuous series of medieval prices and wages were available in the early 1950s, when his principal publications appeared. In 1956, the team of Sir Henry Phelps Brown and Sheila Hopkins published a now famous 'Basket of Consumables Price Index', running from 1264 to 1954.[23] The present author has revised these prices and index numbers in using their data sheets, including the prices for all commodities in their 'Basket of Consumables', now deposited in the Archives of the British Library of Political and Economic Science, and the results are presented in the following tables.[24]

Some important differences, other than numerous corrections of the data entries, must be noted. First, while the published Phelps Brown and Hopkins data were published only in the form of index numbers, and with fixed-weight components for each commodity set, my revised series are based on the actual prices, and the commodity weights are fluctuating, not fixed, varying with changes in relative prices. Thus, when grain prices rose, relative to other commodity prices, the weight of the grain price index in the basket rose correspondingly, thereby reducing the weights of the livestock/fish and industrial goods indexes. Third, this revised price-based series thereby allowed me to compute a new real-wage index: one based on the number of commodity baskets that could have been purchased with the annual money wage of building craftsmen, computed in current silver pence sterling.[25]

[23] Phelps Brown and Hopkins, 'Seven Centuries of the Prices of Consumables' (with price indexes not in the original). A recent alternative set of agricultural prices (not used in this study) is presented in Clark, 'The Price History', but it contains only agricultural prices.

[24] The work sheets are contained in Phelps Brown Papers. Some of these data were previously published in Munro, 'Wage-Stickiness, Monetary Changes'; Munro, 'Builders' Wages in Southern England'; Munro, 'Before and After the Black Death'; Munro, 'The Late-Medieval Decline'.

[25] This estimate of the employment year in the medieval building trades consists of

The Behaviour of Prices in Late Medieval England

The statistical results for late medieval commodity prices in England are presented, though only in quinquennial means, in Tables 6.1–6.2. All the tables, for both commodity prices and wages (Tables 6.3–6.7), have the same common index base: the mean values of 1451–75 = 100, the one that Phelps Brown and Hopkins established: 'chosen because it lies within a long period of stability'.[26] Thus the price and wage indexes in all these tables are really percentages of the values for that base period. These tables, along with Figure 6.1, clearly demonstrate an oscillating series of inflations and deflations, from the late thirteenth to the early sixteenth century: that is, inflation from the 1270s to the 1320s (including the Great Famine); deflation from the mid-1320s to the late 1340s, to the eve of the Black Death; a severe inflation following the Black Death, lasting to the 1370s in England (but to the late 1380s in Flanders); then very severe deflation in both countries until the 1420s; then inflation for both during the next twenty years, until the early 1440s; then more severe deflation lasting until the 1470s, followed by inflation until the 1490s, in turn followed by deflation until just after 1510, to the eve of the sixteenth-century price revolution (*c.* 1520 – *c.* 1650, which lies beyond the scope of this study).

The most striking feature of these tables is the very severe inflation that followed the Black Death. The quarter century preceding the plague had been one of deflation, during which the consumer price index (CPI) had fallen from a quinquennial mean of 130.704 in 1321–25 to a nadir of 85.533 in 1341–45: a stark decline of 34.56 per cent.[27] Thereafter, the CPI rose to a peak of 137.976 in 1361–65, an even more dramatic increase of 61.31 per cent. The CPI remained at virtually that high level in 1366–70 (136.460), and in 1371–75 it was still elevated well beyond this era's long-term trend, at 127.345. See Figure 6.1.

As Tables 6.1–6.2 also indicate, the prices of all commodities in these price 'baskets' all rose together (and later, all fell together): and that is the proper measure of inflation. These component price indices did not, however, rise together exactly in tandem, and the differences, reflecting the operation of real forces on relative commodity prices, are themselves very instructive in evaluat-

210 days. For an explanation and justification of this employment year, see Munro, 'Wage-Stickiness, Monetary Changes', pp. 201–02, and n. 40 (p. 274); Munro, 'Builders' Wages in Southern England', pp. 1028–29 and nn. 41–45.

[26] Phelps Brown and Hopkins, 'Seven Centuries of the Prices of Consumables', p. 305.

[27] Because of the fortuitous supply shocks of the preceding Great Famine era, measuring the decline from the peak CPI of 154.560 in 1316–20 would be very inappropriate.

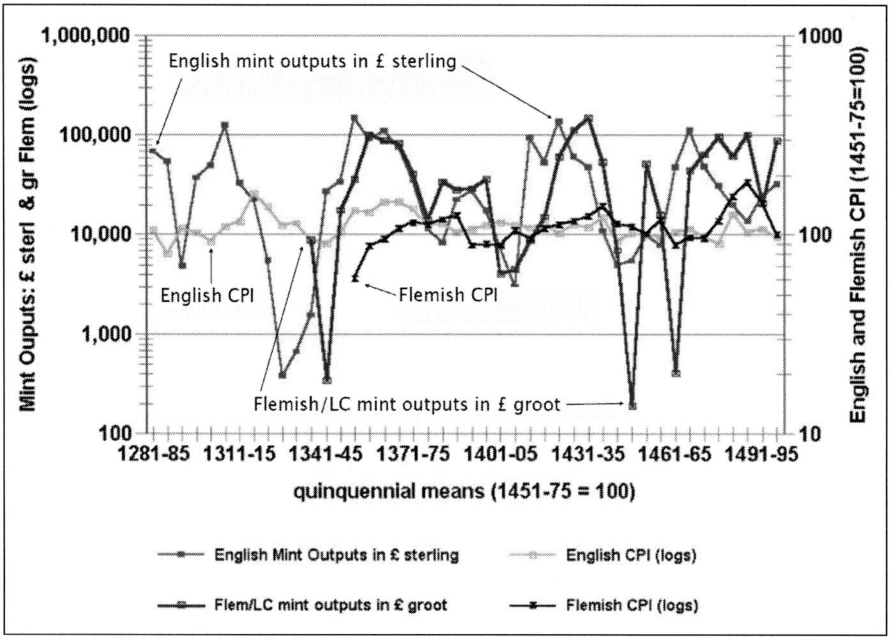

Figure 6.1. Mint Outputs and Prices, 1281–1500, England, Flanders, Low Countries.

ing the Postan thesis.[28] Thus, for the twenty years of inflation that followed the Black Death in England, the increase in grain prices (wheat, rye, barley, peas, malt) well exceeded the price increases for the meat-fish-dairy products and industrial products (textiles, fuels) categories. From 1341–45 to 1371–75, prices for grains (wheat, rye, barley, peas) rose by 43.20 per cent, for meat-fish-dairy products by 28.60 per cent, and for industrial products by 35.05 per cent. The late medieval English experience fits well the classic budget-constraint model, indicating that most lower-class wage-earning families were forced to spend proportionately more of their limited money incomes on bread grains, and thus proportionately less on meat, fish, dairy products, and industrial goods (except fuels). Such an expenditure shift can be seen in Table 6.1 (columns 7–9), and that shift would have limited the increases in non-grain commodity prices during this inflationary era.

The most important observations to be derived from these price tables are that, in stark contrast to the Postan model, grain prices in both nominal and

[28] Foodstuffs collectively accounted for 80 per cent of the commodity price-weights in the English commodity-price baskets. See Table 6.2.

real terms rose — not fell — after the Black Death, and furthermore, that the demographic factors can hardly have been responsible for these sets of price changes. Subsequently, from the later 1370s, English grain prices did indeed fall, but so did other commodity prices, though again not in tandem. To contend that the Black Death and depopulation took more than a quarter of a century to bring about this fall in prices strains one's credulity. The explanation for those subsequent changes in commodity prices, continuing into the fifteenth century, must again await the final section of this study.

The Evidence on Late Medieval English Wages: Nominal and Real

The importance of these changes in commodity prices for real wages is clearly evident from the very formula so widely used to measure changes in real wages: RWI = NWI/CPI, necessarily using index numbers. Thus dividing the nominal or money wage index (in silver pence) for English building craftsmen (Oxford-Cambridge region) by the consumer price index produces the real wage index (RWI), and as just indicated, we now have an alternative method based on the number of commodity baskets purchased with the annual money wages in silver pence.[29] When converted into index numbers, the results are identical.

Though Postan and his followers have long contended that real wages experienced a sustained rise in the fourteenth century — from the Great Famine, according to Postan, and from at least the Black Death, according to most of his followers — the evidence contradicts that view, even in the evidence published long before Postan's initial articles. First, as Lord William Beveridge had noted (in 1936), nominal wages on many Winchester manors, having begun to rise from 1362–63, though well after the Black Death, were forced down in 1367–68, evidently at the behest of the new Bishop William of Wykeham; but then the higher money rates were restored between 1370 and 1375. Only thereafter — almost thirty years after the Black Death — did their real wages enjoy a sustained rise (as indicated by Table 6.3).[30] The manorial records of Taunton (Somerset) provide the most striking if admittedly unusual deviation from the presumed norm in the behaviour of labourer's wages in the later fourteenth century. To be sure, after the onslaught of the Black Death, casual farm-labourers on the Taunton manor had experienced a doubling in their money wages, with a substantial increase as well in their real wage, from 1349 to 1356.

[29] See above, note 25.

[30] Beveridge, 'Wages in the Winchester Manors'. See also Beveridge, 'Westminster Wages'.

Thereafter, however, both their money and real wages fell, and from 1362–63 (i.e. before the election of Bishop William) they fell sharply to pre-plague levels. Their real wages fell even more steeply below such levels, recovering only from 1378, but their money wages did not recover before 1412–13.[31]

As Beveridge has also shown, however, piece-work money wages for seasonal harvest workers on eight Winchester manors did rise substantially over the thirty-year period from 1340–49 to 1360–69, especially for threshers and winnowers: by an average of 21.27 per cent (in decennial means).[32] But, as already shown, the English CPI, with the previously highlighted post-plague inflation, rose by 48.14 per cent over these three decades, so that their 'real wages' had correspondingly fallen very substantially — not risen, as so commonly and wrongly assumed — after the Black Death.[33]

A far more comprehensive set of supposedly 'national' agricultural wages was published by the late David Farmer, between 1983 and 1991.[34] There are, however, many serious problems with his statistics. Obviously, for a country as regionally diverse as medieval England, the concept of 'national' wages is an absurdity. Furthermore, calculations of these annual wages suffer from two 'compositional' errors that distort their values, in producing spurious annual fluctuations. The first is the periodic absence of wage data from higher and/or lower wage regions; and second is the periodic absence of higher and lower

[31] See Munro, 'Wage-Stickiness, Monetary Changes', table 7, pp. 245–48. I have not found, however, any other comparable examples in manorial accounts whose data are preserved in Beveridge Price and Wage History Collection. Beveridge, 'Wages in the Winchester Manors', p. 30, commented that wages in the Taunton manor 'are affected by the greater importance there of customary services and the best method of presenting the [wage] series has not been determined'. But that does not satisfactorily explain why building wages at Taunton were generally higher before the Black Death than elsewhere. Yet if Beveridge was correct, then wages on many late medieval English manors would have been — to a greater or lesser degree — affected by the relative supplies of servile labour, before and after the Black Death.

[32] Beveridge, 'Wages in the Winchester Manors', pp. 22–43: from a mean of 5.03d. per quarter of grain (= eight bushels) to one of 6.10d. per quarter. See the next note.

[33] This calculation is based on combining the quinquennial means for the 1340s and the 1370s, in Tables 6.1–6.2 (for prices), to produce decennial means. The rate of inflation from the quinquennium 1341–45 to 1366–70 was even greater: 59.54 per cent. The comparisons are not fully accurate, since Beveridge used decennial means commencing in year zero (or ten) and ending in year nine (1340–49), while these tables commence the decade in year one and end them in year ten (1341–50).

[34] Farmer, 'Crop Yields, Prices and Wages'; Farmer, 'Prices and Wages [1000–1355]', pp. 760–78, 811–17; Farmer, 'Prices and Wages [1350–1500]', pp. 467–90, 516–24.

Table 6.1. Values in Pence of the Main Commodity Groups in the English Basket of Consumables Price Index: The Phelps Brown and Hopkins Index Revised by John Munro. Commodity values in pence sterling and their percentage shares of the total consumption basket in quinquennial means, 1266–70 to 1516–20 with index numbers for the total basket: mean of 1451–75=100.

Year (five-year means)	Grains & Drink (barley & hops) (in d. sterling)	Meat, Fish, Dairy (in d. sterling)	Industrial: Fuel, Light, Textiles (in d. sterling)	Total value of the basket (in d. sterling)	Index number (1451–75 = 100) Munro 112.801d. sterling	Grains & Drink (barley & hops) (as percent total)	Meat, Fish, Dairy (as percent total)	Industrial: Fuel, Light, Textiles (as percent total)
1266–70	45.693	30.945	19.073	95.711	84.850	47.74%	32.33%	19.93%
1271–75	60.300	40.026	18.942	119.267	105.733	50.56%	33.56%	15.88%
1276–80	51.566	41.440	19.822	112.827	100.023	45.70%	36.73%	17.57%
1281–85	61.669	40.321	16.658	118.648	105.184	51.98%	33.98%	14.04%
1286–90	41.581	36.477	14.386	92.444	81.953	44.98%	39.46%	15.56%
1291–95	68.542	35.681	14.640	118.863	105.375	57.66%	30.02%	12.32%
1296–1300	57.257	39.703	16.162	113.122	100.285	50.62%	35.10%	14.29%
1301–05	49.163	37.105	17.146	103.414	91.679	47.54%	35.88%	16.58%
1306–10	58.224	43.141	15.641	117.006	103.728	49.76%	36.87%	13.37%
1311–15	56.096	50.895	17.588	124.580	110.443	45.03%	40.85%	14.12%
1316–20	100.359	54.667	19.318	174.344	154.560	57.56%	31.36%	11.08%
1321–25	78.288	50.301	18.846	147.434	130.704	53.10%	34.12%	12.78%
1326–30	54.550	44.100	19.467	118.116	104.712	46.18%	37.34%	16.48%
1331–35	60.016	44.551	18.507	123.074	109.108	48.76%	36.20%	15.04%
1336–40	41.997	41.660	17.025	100.682	89.256	41.71%	41.38%	16.91%
1341–45	41.585	38.899	15.999	96.482	85.533	43.10%	40.32%	16.58%
1346–50	51.221	41.597	20.055	112.873	100.064	45.38%	36.85%	17.77%
1351–55	68.656	48.430	25.575	142.661	126.472	48.13%	33.95%	17.93%
1356–60	59.555	48.017	25.636	133.209	118.092	44.71%	36.05%	19.25%
1361–65	77.057	53.063	25.518	155.637	137.976	49.51%	34.09%	16.40%
1366–70	73.347	53.496	27.085	153.928	136.460	47.65%	34.75%	17.60%
1371–75	60.083	56.820	26.743	143.646	127.345	41.83%	39.56%	18.62%
1376–80	48.326	50.545	25.087	123.958	109.891	38.99%	40.78%	20.24%
1381–85	52.673	48.493	26.513	127.679	113.190	41.25%	37.98%	20.77%

1391–95	51.005	44.093	22.161	117.259	103.953	43.50%	37.60%	18.90%
1396–1400	53.816	49.719	21.277	124.812	110.648	43.12%	39.83%	17.05%
1401–05	58.498	47.457	21.118	127.073	112.653	46.04%	37.35%	16.62%
1406–10	52.646	49.584	21.768	123.998	109.927	42.46%	39.99%	17.55%
1411–15	48.726	50.018	23.375	122.119	108.261	39.90%	40.96%	19.14%
1416–20	55.549	50.041	22.548	128.139	113.598	43.35%	39.05%	17.60%
1421–25	49.284	44.618	23.118	117.020	103.740	42.12%	38.13%	19.76%
1426–30	55.745	47.861	23.419	127.025	112.610	43.89%	37.68%	18.44%
1431–35	53.252	47.420	22.418	123.090	109.122	43.26%	38.52%	18.21%
1436–40	66.745	51.010	22.363	140.118	124.218	47.63%	36.40%	15.96%
1441–45	36.681	45.505	22.238	104.424	92.574	35.13%	43.58%	21.30%
1446–50	44.519	48.482	21.199	114.200	101.241	38.98%	42.45%	18.56%
1451–55	47.534	46.528	20.712	114.774	101.750	41.42%	40.54%	18.05%
1456–60	42.531	47.008	20.961	110.500	97.961	38.49%	42.54%	18.97%
1461–65	48.251	46.781	19.457	114.489	101.497	42.14%	40.86%	16.99%
1466–70	46.067	48.073	21.729	115.869	102.720	39.76%	41.49%	18.75%
1471–75	45.745	42.228	20.397	108.370	96.072	42.21%	38.97%	18.82%
1476–80	43.615	38.688	22.227	104.529	92.667	41.72%	37.01%	21.26%
1481–85	67.062	48.205	21.653	136.921	121.383	48.98%	35.21%	15.81%
1486–90	45.334	47.027	21.871	114.232	101.269	39.69%	41.17%	19.15%
1491–95	45.836	48.417	21.418	115.671	102.545	39.63%	41.86%	18.52%
1496–1500	44.531	45.161	21.460	111.152	98.538	40.06%	40.63%	19.31%
1501–05	53.526	44.578	21.901	120.005	106.386	44.60%	37.15%	18.25%
1506–10	44.637	52.336	21.526	118.499	105.052	37.67%	44.17%	18.17%
1511–15	49.015	48.157	22.413	119.584	106.014	40.99%	40.27%	18.74%
1516–20	54.594	61.580	23.504	139.678	123.827	39.09%	44.09%	16.83%

See Table 6.2 below, for the index numbers for each of the seven major components in the basket.

Sources: Phelps Brown Papers, BOX Ia: 324.

This significantly revised version should be compared with the price indexes in the original version presented in Phelps Brown and Hopkins, 'Seven Centuries of the Prices of Consumables'. That comparison may be seen in the fnal two columns (nos. 9 and 10) of the following Table 6.2.

Table 6.2. Phelps Brown and Hopkins Composite Price Index for Southern England (Revised by Munro). In quinquennial means: 1266–70 to 1516–20; mean of 1451–75 = 100; index numbers for each commodity component of the basket and for the total basket.

Years (five-year means)	Grains: wheat, rye, barley, peas (base value in d. 21.799)	Meat: pigs, mutton, beef (base value in d. 23.950)	Fish: herring, cod (base value in d. 6.595)	Dairy Products: butter, cheese (base value in d. 15.579)	Drink: malt, hops (base value in d. 24.227)	Fuel/Light: charcoal, candles, lamp oil (base value in d. 8.153)	Textiles: woollens, canvas, linen (base value in d. 12.499)	Total Basket: Munro Revised Index (base value in d. 112.801)	Phelps Brown & Hopkins Original Index numbers
1266–70	93.495	69.780	26.764	80.027	104.481	137.304	63.040	84.850	78.667
1271–75	129.148	106.889	25.766	81.694	132.691	129.628	66.995	105.733	104.200
1276–80	105.241	107.620	34.043	86.140	118.151	120.480	80.002	100.023	96.800
1281–85	111.528	103.705	46.023	79.908	154.197	101.642	66.978	105.184	102.200
1286–90	79.081	91.023	33.411	80.065	100.476	92.576	54.718	81.953	80.600
1291–95	139.541	85.490	36.166	82.300	157.360	92.038	57.099	105.375	107.200
1296–1300	108.480	101.148	45.871	79.936	138.728	97.346	65.813	100.285	102.400
1301–05	93.544	94.467	34.119	78.503	118.760	114.210	62.685	91.679	92.400
1306–10	117.048	109.551	44.633	89.608	135.013	116.569	49.105	103.728	110.600
1311–15	116.607	123.486	56.592	112.898	126.625	125.881	58.613	110.443	115.200
1316–20	194.864	132.724	65.478	119.145	238.913	127.026	71.704	154.560	162.000
1321–25	164.702	111.064	57.876	127.634	174.948	131.758	64.843	130.704	138.200
1326–30	101.931	105.950	43.723	101.686	133.446	128.719	71.789	104.712	111.000
1331–35	110.302	110.021	50.913	95.281	148.479	123.733	67.359	109.108	114.200
1336–40	84.730	96.346	58.293	94.622	97.109	115.110	61.129	89.256	94.400
1341–45	81.356	89.666	55.033	88.547	98.444	106.893	58.279	85.533	90.000
1346–50	101.499	94.572	57.459	97.299	120.095	118.731	83.008	100.064	102.400
1351–55	131.100	113.987	77.273	102.921	165.428	131.392	118.918	126.472	132.800
1356–60	115.863	108.455	67.796	112.790	141.572	131.870	119.097	118.092	130.800
1361–65	130.413	131.419	79.927	104.738	200.720	127.247	121.164	137.976	146.600
1366–70	150.487	131.607	80.875	106.830	167.344	143.980	122.784	136.460	146.200
1371–75	133.638	143.653	86.182	107.403	127.757	153.580	113.786	127.345	135.400
1376–80	96.219	118.580	87.597	105.066	112.898	139.896	109.466	109.891	110.600

1386–90	83.336	108.055	98.061	96.590	108.486	129.251	94.497	101.233	102.400
1391–95	96.639	106.471	109.181	73.130	123.578	131.190	91.735	103.953	106.200
1396–1400	105.084	111.064	112.214	100.898	127.583	122.933	90.044	110.648	110.600
1401–05	117.530	110.071	77.058	102.790	135.709	111.724	96.083	112.653	114.800
1406–10	108.229	106.555	112.425	106.878	119.921	109.523	102.721	109.927	111.200
1411–15	91.411	105.599	114.787	110.132	118.876	120.772	108.239	108.261	108.000
1416–20	114.066	103.055	129.702	107.879	126.654	123.370	99.931	113.598	112.800
1421–25	94.999	93.213	122.294	91.331	117.948	131.817	98.984	103.740	102.000
1426–30	107.222	99.581	116.106	104.979	133.620	122.182	107.674	112.610	112.600
1431–35	110.106	106.078	81.498	106.810	120.734	120.031	101.071	109.122	108.600
1436–40	148.525	109.585	114.857	110.342	141.862	118.457	101.656	124.218	122.000
1441–45	75.504	96.624	109.282	97.290	83.469	116.799	101.740	92.574	92.800
1446–50	97.399	106.245	96.604	106.978	96.123	108.833	98.617	101.241	101.000
1451–55	102.327	100.600	100.898	101.294	104.133	103.918	97.930	101.750	100.400
1456–60	94.082	101.948	100.070	102.652	90.899	101.898	101.243	97.961	97.000
1461–65	103.681	101.972	96.494	102.675	105.874	92.172	95.549	101.497	102.800
1466–70	100.888	105.161	96.911	105.886	99.373	104.869	105.447	102.720	106.400
1471–75	99.022	90.320	105.628	87.492	99.721	97.143	99.832	96.072	97.800
1476–80	107.053	83.116	100.299	78.102	83.701	93.890	116.589	92.667	91.000
1481–85	148.173	110.420	84.839	103.760	143.487	101.428	107.085	121.383	129.800
1486–90	109.393	106.973	87.146	100.521	88.693	93.340	114.103	101.269	102.800
1491–95	100.342	111.863	79.611	105.115	98.909	81.642	118.110	102.545	103.400
1496–1500	103.260	102.599	84.438	96.411	90.899	86.299	115.406	98.538	96.800
1501–05	128.266	100.137	90.008	94.097	105.526	93.464	114.259	106.386	110.600
1506–10	104.004	119.888	92.077	112.656	90.666	88.070	114.780	105.052	99.800
1511–15	121.826	108.781	93.701	102.219	92.698	95.511	117.022	106.014	108.600
1516–20	116.520	148.352	84.375	131.498	120.502	99.745	122.987	123.827	120.600

Sources: Phelps Brown Papers, File 204: folders I–IV, VI–X, XIV–XVI.
Commodity weights: see Munro, 'The Late-Medieval Decline', table 27, p. 338.

Table 6.3. National Means of Manorial Agricultural Wages in England. In quinquennial means: 1266–70 to 1496–1500; in pence and in index numbers, for nominal and real wages; Index: Mean of 1451–75 = 100.

		Reaping and Binding Grains (per acre of grains)			Threshing and Winnowing Grains (piece rates per razed quarter (8 bushels))		
Year, Michaelmas (five-year period)	**Phelps Brown& Hopkins CPI (Munro revised version)**	**Reaping & Binding (per acre of grains d.)**	**Reaping & Binding (per acre of grains) Index: 1451–75 = 100; 9.966d**	**Real Wage Index RWI=NWI/CPI harmonic means 1451–75=100**	**Threshing & Winnowing (razed quarter of grains d.)**	**Threshing & Winnowing (razed quarter of grains) Index: 1451–75 = 100; 10.366d**	**Real Wage Index RWI=NWI/CPI harmonic means 1451–75=100**
1266–70	84.850	4.681	46.970	55.367	3.502	33.787	39.707
1271–75	105.733	4.349	43.636	41.228	3.648	35.188	33.315
1276–80	100.023	4.784	48.000	47.142	3.802	36.676	35.575
1281–85	105.184	5.158	51.758	49.043	3.909	37.714	34.224
1286–90	81.953	4.530	45.455	55.327	4.057	39.132	47.621
1291–95	105.375	4.844	48.606	45.995	4.595	44.322	41.587
1296–1300	100.285	4.941	49.576	49.445	4.519	43.596	43.269
1301–05	91.679	5.243	52.606	57.296	4.982	48.059	51.808
1306–10	103.728	5.641	56.606	54.342	4.508	43.492	41.802
1311–15	110.443	6.390	64.121	58.012	4.648	44.841	40.427
1316–20	154.560	6.644	66.667	42.366	5.025	48.474	30.356
1321–25	130.704	6.245	62.667	47.913	5.488	52.938	40.421
1326–30	104.712	6.535	65.576	62.282	5.111	49.305	46.875
1331–35	109.108	6.402	64.242	58.730	5.358	51.692	46.586
1336–40	89.256	5.919	59.394	66.710	5.358	51.692	57.893
1341–45	85.533	6.076	60.970	71.277	5.402	52.107	60.912
1346–50	100.064	7.055	70.788	66.331	5.832	56.259	55.738
1351–55	126.472	7.876	79.030	62.273	6.262	60.411	46.468
1356–60	118.092	6.572	65.939	55.741	5.746	55.429	46.704
1361–65	137.976	8.033	80.606	58.291	6.252	60.307	43.542
1366–70	136.460	8.299	83.273	60.776	6.671	64.355	46.566

1376–80	109.891	9.954	99.879	90.925	7.704	74.320	67.418
1381–85	113.190	9.072	91.030	78.986	8.038	77.538	68.007
1386–90	101.233	9.205	92.364	91.244	7.500	72.348	71.425
1391–95	103.953	8.734	87.636	83.473	7.414	71.518	68.700
1396–1400	110.648	8.734	87.636	77.934	7.962	76.811	69.165
1401–05	112.653	9.241	92.727	82.430	8.436	81.378	69.795
1406–10	109.927	9.918	99.515	90.550	8.726	84.181	76.101
1411–15	108.261	10.038	100.727	93.009	7.812	75.358	69.618
1416–20	113.598	9.857	98.909	86.918	8.920	86.049	74.925
1421–25	103.740	9.362	93.939	90.009	8.317	80.237	77.243
1426–30	112.610	9.048	90.788	79.884	8.221	79.302	70.570
1431–35	109.122	9.386	94.182	86.265	8.070	77.849	71.231
1436–40	124.218	9.561	95.939	77.596	10.254	98.920	77.342
1441–45	92.574	10.981	110.182	118.832	9.415	90.824	97.297
1446–50	101.241	9.942	99.758	98.561	8.920	86.049	84.038
1451–55	101.750	9.821	98.545	96.827	9.447	91.136	88.540
1456–60	97.961	10.268	103.030	105.470	10.448	100.789	102.479
1461–65	101.497	10.026	100.606	114.032	10.674	102.969	101.542
1466–70	102.720				10.340	99.751	96.804
1471–75	96.072				10.921	105.355	109.663
1476–80	92.667						
1481–85	121.383	10.026	100.606	82.833*			
1486–90	101.269						
1491–95	102.545						
1496–1500	98.538						

* arithmetic means based on nominal wages for 1480–81 only.

Sources: Farmer, 'Crop Yields, Prices and Wages'; Farmer, 'Prices and Wages [1000–1355]', pp. 760–78, 811–17; Farmer, 'Prices and Wages [1350–1500]', pp. 467–90, 516–24.

Note that Farmer's wage data do not go beyond 1500, and there are few agricultural wages available from manorial sources after *c.* 1450.

Table 6.4. National Means of Manorial Industrial Wages in England. Part A: for Carpenters and Masons (Masters): In quinquennial means, 1266–70 to 1496–1500; in pence per day and in index numbers, for nominal and real wages; Index: Mean of 1451–75 = 100.

		Carpenters: Manorial (in d. per day)			Masons: Manorial (in d. per day)		
Year, Michaelmas (five-year period)	**Phelps Brown & Hopkins CPI (Munro revised version)**	**Carpenter, solo (per day in d.)**	**Carpenter, solo (per day Index: 1451–75 = 100; 5.508d)**	**Real Wage Index RWI=NWI/CPI harmonic means**	**Mason, solo (per day in d.)**	**Mason, solo (per day Index: 1451–75 = 100; 5.695d)**	**Real Wage Index RWI=NWI/CPI harmonic means**
1266–70	84.850	2.836	51.489	58.407			
1271–75	105.733	3.205	58.195	54.083			
1276–80	100.023	2.379	43.192	44.665			
1281–85	105.184	2.398	43.533	41.241			
1286–90	81.953	2.529	45.920	54.590			
1291–95	105.375	2.704	49.102	46.535			
1296–1300	100.285	3.092	56.149	55.482			
1301–05	91.679	2.742	49.784	53.739			
1306–10	103.728	2.886	52.398	50.588			
1311–15	110.443	2.861	51.944	47.006			
1316–20	154.560	3.337	60.582	38.920			
1321–25	130.704	3.249	58.991	45.063			
1326–30	104.712	2.999	54.444	52.063			
1331–35	109.108	3.243	58.877	54.050			
1336–40	89.256	3.136	56.945	63.373			
1341–45	85.533	2.999	54.444	63.364			
1346–50	100.064	3.293	59.786	59.090			
1351–55	126.472	3.524	63.992	50.181	3.901	68.495	54.123
1356–60	118.092	3.956	71.835	60.774	4.031	70.770	59.784
1361–65	137.976	4.188	76.040	55.102	4.331	76.039	55.057
1366–70	136.460	4.332	78.654	57.697	4.215	74.003	53.838

1376–80	109.891	4.194	[illegible]	[illegible]	[illegible]	[illegible]	[illegible]
1381–85	113.190	4.319	78.427	69.095	4.788	84.062	73.735
1386–90	101.233	4.207	76.381	75.388	4.269	74.961	73.418
1391–95	103.953	4.269	77.518	74.465	4.528	79.511	75.455
1396–1400	110.648	4.276	77.631	70.193	4.324	75.919	68.453
1401–05	112.653	4.639	84.224	74.644	4.651	81.667	71.885
1406–10	109.927	4.733	85.929	77.377	5.054	88.732	80.270
1411–15	108.261	4.344	78.882	72.716	4.849	85.140	77.680
1416–20	113.598	4.582	83.201	73.118	5.296	92.983	80.323
1421–25	103.740	4.657	84.565	81.328	5.429	95.318	91.175
1426–30	112.610	4.970	90.248	80.267	5.313	93.282	82.142
1431–35	109.122	4.826	87.634	79.953	4.979	87.415	78.991
1436–40	124.218	5.396	97.977	79.105	5.569	97.773	77.873
1441–45	92.574	5.064	91.953	99.365	5.224	91.726	98.609
1446–50	101.241	5.283	95.931	94.597	5.531	97.114	95.690
1451–55	101.750	5.321	96.613	94.979	5.592	98.192	96.412
1456–60	97.961	5.590	101.500	103.403	5.490	96.396	98.141
1461–65	101.497	5.390	97.863	96.414	5.487	96.336	94.422
1466–70	102.720	5.446	98.886	96.013	5.954	104.538	101.697
1471–75	96.072	5.791	105.138	109.609	5.954	104.538	108.307
1476–80	92.667	5.878	106.729	114.305	5.886	103.341	111.453
1481–85	121.383	5.584	101.387	83.131	5.333	93.641	76.871
1486–90	101.269	5.834	105.933	104.362	5.647	99.150	97.402
1491–95	102.545	5.872	106.615	103.621	5.797	101.784	99.217
1496–1500	98.538	5.647	102.523	103.518	5.575	97.892	99.135

Sources: Farmer, 'Crop Yields, Prices and Wages'; Farmer, 'Prices and Wages [1000–1355]', pp. 760–78, 811–17; Farmer, 'Prices and Wages [1350–1500]', pp. 467–90, 516–24.

Note that Farmer's wage data do not go beyond 1500.

Table 6.5. National Means of Manorial Industrial Wages in England. Part B: For Thatchers and Slaters (Masters and Servants); In quinquennial means, 1266–70 to 1496–1500; in pence per day and in index numbers, for nominal and real wages; Index: Mean of 1451–75 = 100.

		Thatcher & Mates: Manorial (in d. per day)			Slater/Tilers & Mates: Manorial (in d. per day)		
Year, Michaelmas (five-year period)	Phelps Brown & Hopkins CPI (Munro revised version)	Thatcher & mate (per day d.)	Thatcher & mate (per day Index: 1451–75 = 100, 9.108d)	Real Wage Index RWI=NWI/CPI harmonic means	Slater/Tiler & mate (per day d.)	Slater/Tiler & mate (per day Index: 1451–75 = 100, 9.698d)	Real Wage Index RWI=NWI/CPI harmonic means
1266–70	84.850	2.715	29.813	34.266	5.788	59.680	68.969
1271–75	105.733	3.258	35.767	33.259	5.740	59.187	54.330
1276–80	100.023	3.093	33.960	33.793	7.129	73.505	n.a.
1281–85	105.184	4.002	43.939	46.619	5.310	54.753	48.292
1286–90	81.953	3.433	37.697	45.543	5.767	59.461	71.162
1291–95	105.375	3.620	39.750	37.145	5.071	52.289	n.a.
1296–1300	100.285	3.531	38.765	38.410	5.615	57.901	n.a.
1301–05	91.679	3.613	39.668	43.006	5.299	54.643	57.687
1306–10	103.728	3.523	38.683	37.242	5.055	52.124	49.494
1311–15	110.443	3.987	43.775	39.686	5.979	61.651	55.768
1316–20	154.560	4.107	45.089	29.503	5.650	58.257	37.338
1321–25	130.704	3.882	42.625	32.672	5.066	52.234	38.460
1326–30	104.712	3.531	38.765	36.901	5.023	51.796	49.556
1331–35	109.108	3.792	41.639	38.030	5.565	57.381	52.569
1336–40	89.256	3.882	42.625	47.834	5.135	52.946	59.428
1341–45	85.533	3.553	39.011	45.560	5.246	54.095	63.104
1346–50	100.064	4.204	46.156	45.180	5.172	53.329	52.674
1351–55	126.472	4.682	51.413	40.626	6.011	61.980	49.061
1356–60	118.092	4.608	50.591	42.687	6.117	63.075	53.339
1361–65	137.976	5.333	58.558	42.389	6.499	67.017	48.544
1366–70	136.460	5.685	62.418	45.798	7.041	72.602	53.385

1381–85	113.190	6.171	67.756	59.676	7.519	77.530	68.059
1386–90	101.233	6.119	67.181	66.293	7.492	77.256	76.249
1391–95	103.953	6.313	69.317	66.240	7.190	74.135	71.409
1396–1400	110.648	6.253	68.660	62.010	7.381	76.106	68.835
1401–05	112.653	6.567	72.109	63.613	8.050	83.005	73.674
1406–10	109.927	6.829	74.984	67.938	7.848	80.924	73.568
1411–15	108.261	6.552	71.945	66.124	7.816	80.596	73.867
1416–20	113.598	6.882	75.558	66.445	8.326	85.852	75.202
1421–25	103.740	6.171	67.756	65.038	8.358	86.180	83.027
1426–30	112.610	7.667	84.182	74.515	8.167	84.209	74.237
1431–35	109.122	7.443	81.718	74.736	8.454	87.166	79.566
1436–40	124.218	8.774	96.337	77.113	9.006	92.860	74.641
1441–45	92.574	8.767	96.255	102.614	9.091	93.736	101.119
1446–50	101.241	8.804	96.666	95.316	9.154	94.393	92.497
1451–55	101.750	9.260	101.675	99.135	9.547	98.445	96.740
1456–60	97.961	9.544	104.796	106.531	9.696	99.978	101.526
1461–65	101.497	9.013	98.965	97.505	9.462	97.569	95.970
1466–70	102.720	9.013	98.965	96.344	10.025	103.373	100.246
1471–75	96.072	8.707	95.598	99.170	9.760	100.635	104.876
1476–80	92.667	9.500	104.304	103.620	9.919	102.278	109.830
1481–85	121.383				9.186	94.722	77.814
1486–90	101.269	9.986	109.642	105.206	8.974	92.532	88.788
1491–95	102.545	9.874	108.410	104.366	9.016	92.970	87.332
1496–1500	98.538	9.175	100.745	100.799	8.990	92.696	96.476

Sources: Farmer, 'Crop Yields, Prices and Wages'; Farmer, 'Prices and Wages [1000–1355]', pp. 760–78, 811–17; Farmer, 'Prices and Wages [1350–1500]', pp. 467–90, 516–24.

Note that Farmer's wage data do not go beyond 1500.

Table 6.6. Nominal and Real Wages for Master Building Craftsmen in Small Towns of SE England:in pence sterling and in index numbers in quinquennial means: 1266–70 to 1516–20. Mean of 1451—75 = 100; RWI = NWI/CPI.

Year (five-year means)	Total Value of PBH Basket in d. ster. (arithmetic mean)	PBH Prices Consumer Price Index Munro version1451–75 = 100 (arithmetic mean)	Master: Nominal Day Wage in d. (arithmetic mean)	Master Mason: Nominal Wage Index, 1451–75 = 100 (= 6d. daily) (arithmetic mean)	Master Mason: Real Wage Index (Munro), 1451–75 = 100 (harmonic mean)	Master RWI no. of Baskets consumed in one year; 1451–75 = 100 (harmonic mean)	Master RWI no. of Baskets Consumed in one year (210 days) (harmonic mean)
1266–70	95.711	84.850	3.000	50.000	58.928	58.928	6.582
1271–75	119.267	105.733	3.000	50.000	47.289	47.289	5.282
1275–80	112.827	100.023	3.000	50.000	49.988	49.988	5.584
1281–85	118.648	105.184	3.000	50.000	47.536	47.536	5.310
1286–90	92.444	81.953	3.000	50.000	61.010	61.010	6.815
1291–95	118.863	105.375	3.000	50.000	47.450	47.450	5.300
1296–1300	113.122	100.285	3.000	50.000	49.858	49.858	5.569
1301–05	103.414	91.679	3.300	55.000	59.714	59.714	6.670
1306–10	117.006	103.728	3.600	60.000	57.971	57.971	6.475
1311–15	124.580	110.443	4.000	66.667	60.363	60.363	6.743
1316–20	174.344	154.560	4.000	66.667	43.133	43.133	4.818
1321–25	147.434	130.704	4.000	66.667	51.006	51.006	5.697
1326–30	118.116	104.712	4.000	66.667	63.666	63.666	7.112
1331–35	123.074	109.108	4.000	66.667	61.102	61.102	6.825
1336–40	100.682	89.256	3.600	60.000	66.986	66.986	7.482
1341–45	96.482	85.533	3.000	50.000	58.457	58.457	6.530
1346–50	112.873	100.064	3.000	50.000	49.968	49.968	5.582
1351–55	142.661	126.472	3.600	60.000	46.552	46.552	5.200
1356–60	133.209	118.092	4.600	76.667	64.611	64.611	7.217
1361–65	155.637	137.976	5.000	83.333	60.397	60.397	6.746
1366–70	153.928	136.460	5.000	83.333	61.068	61.068	6.821
1371–75	143.646	127.345	5.000	83.333	65.439	65.439	7.310

1386–90	114.191	101.233	5.000	83.333	82.319	82.319	9.195
1391–95	117.259	103.953	5.000	83.333	80.165	80.165	8.955
1396–1400	124.812	110.648	5.000	83.333	75.314	75.314	8.413
1401–05	127.073	112.653	5.100	85.000	75.156	75.156	8.395
1406–10	123.998	109.927	5.800	96.667	88.115	88.115	9.843
1411–15	122.119	108.261	6.000	100.000	92.369	92.369	10.318
1416–20	128.139	113.598	6.000	100.000	88.030	88.030	9.833
1421–25	117.020	103.740	6.000	100.000	96.395	96.395	10.767
1426–30	127.025	112.610	6.000	100.000	88.802	88.802	9.919
1431–35	123.090	109.122	6.000	100.000	91.641	91.641	10.236
1436–40	140.118	124.218	6.000	100.000	80.504	80.504	8.992
1441–45	104.424	92.574	6.000	100.000	108.022	108.022	12.066
1446–50	114.200	101.241	6.000	100.000	98.774	98.774	11.033
1451–55	114.774	101.750	6.000	100.000	98.280	98.280	10.978
1456–60	110.500	97.961	6.000	100.000	102.082	102.082	11.403
1451–65	114.489	101.497	6.000	100.000	98.525	98.525	11.005
1466–70	115.869	102.720	6.000	100.000	97.352	97.352	10.874
1471–75	108.370	96.072	6.000	100.000	104.088	104.088	11.627
1476–80	104.529	92.667	6.000	100.000	107.913	107.913	12.054
1481–85	136.921	121.383	6.000	100.000	82.384	82.384	9.202
1486–90	114.232	101.269	6.000	100.000	98.747	98.747	11.030
1491–95	115.671	102.545	6.000	100.000	97.518	97.518	10.893
1496–1500	111.152	98.538	6.000	100.000	101.483	101.483	11.336
1501–05	120.005	106.386	6.000	100.000	93.997	93.997	10.500
1506–10	118.499	105.052	6.000	100.000	95.191	95.191	10.633
1511–15	119.584	106.014	6.000	100.000	94.327	94.327	10.537
1516–20	139.678	123.827	6.000	100.000	80.758	80.758	9.021

Sources: (1) Prices: Phelps Brown Papers, File 204. (2) Wages: Phelps Brown and Hopkins, 'Seven Centuries of Building Wages'.

Table 6.7. Nominal and Real Wages of Building Labourers (Journeymen) in the Small Towns of SE England.
In pence and index numbers: in quinquennial means, 1266–70 to 1516–20: mean of 1451–75 = 100.

Years (five-year means)	Labourer: Nominal Day Wage in d. (arithmetic mean)	Labourer's Wage as Percent of Master (arithmetic mean)	Mason Labourer: Nominal Wage Index, 1451–75 = 100 (= 4d. daily) (arithmetic mean)	Mason Labourer: Real Wage Index (Munro), 1451–75 = 100 (harmonic mean)	Master RWI: no. of Baskets consumed in one year (210 days) (harmonic mean)	Labourer RWI: no. of Baskets consumed in one year (210 days) (harmonic mean)
1266–70	1.500	50.00%	37.500	44.196	6.582	3.291
1271–75	1.500	50.00%	37.500	35.467	5.282	2.641
1276–80	1.500	50.00%	37.500	37.491	5.584	2.792
1281–85	1.500	50.00%	37.500	35.652	5.310	2.655
1286–90	1.500	50.00%	37.500	45.758	6.815	3.407
1291–95	1.500	50.00%	37.500	35.587	5.300	2.650
1296–1300	1.500	50.00%	37.500	37.393	5.569	2.785
1301–05	1.650	50.00%	41.250	44.786	6.670	3.335
1306–10	1.800	50.00%	45.000	43.478	6.475	3.238
1311–15	2.000	50.00%	50.000	45.272	6.743	3.371
1316–20	2.000	50.00%	50.000	32.350	4.818	2.409
1321–25	2.000	50.00%	50.000	38.254	5.697	2.849
1326–30	2.000	50.00%	50.000	47.750	7.112	3.556
1331–35	2.000	50.00%	50.000	45.826	6.825	3.413
1336–40	1.800	50.00%	45.000	51.019	7.482	3.741
1341–45	1.500	50.00%	37.500	43.843	6.530	3.265
1346–50	1.500	50.00%	37.500	37.476	5.582	2.791
1351–55	1.800	50.00%	45.000	34.914	5.200	2.600
1356–60	2.600	56.22%	65.000	54.039	7.217	4.024
1361–65	3.000	60.00%	75.000	54.357	6.746	4.048
1366–70	3.000	60.00%	75.000	54.961	6.821	4.093
1371–75	3.000	60.00%	75.000	58.895	7.310	4.386

1386–90	3.000	60.00%	75.000	74.087	9.195	5.517
1391–95	3.000	60.00%	75.000	72.148	8.955	5.373
1396–1400	3.000	60.00%	75.000	67.782	8.413	5.048
1401–05	3.200	62.70%	80.000	70.065	8.395	5.218
1406–10	3.800	65.50%	95.000	86.562	9.843	6.446
1411–15	4.000	66.70%	100.000	92.369	10.318	6.879
1416–20	4.000	66.70%	100.000	88.030	9.833	6.555
1421–25	4.000	66.70%	100.000	96.395	10.767	7.178
1426–30	4.000	66.70%	100.000	88.802	9.919	6.613
1431–35	4.000	66.70%	100.000	91.801	10.236	6.824
1436–40	4.000	66.70%	100.000	80.504	8.992	5.995
1441–45	4.000	66.70%	100.000	108.022	12.066	8.044
1446–50	4.000	66.70%	100.000	98.774	11.033	7.356
1451–55	4.000	66.70%	100.000	98.280	10.978	7.319
1456–60	4.000	66.70%	100.000	102.082	11.403	7.602
1461–65	4.000	66.70%	100.000	98.525	11.005	7.337
1466–70	4.000	66.70%	100.000	97.352	10.874	7.250
1471–75	4.000	66.70%	100.000	104.088	11.627	7.751
1476–80	4.000	66.70%	100.000	107.913	12.054	8.036
1481–85	4.000	66.70%	100.000	82.384	9.202	6.135
1486–90	4.000	66.70%	100.000	98.747	11.030	7.353
1491–95	4.000	66.70%	100.000	97.518	10.893	7.262
1496–1500	4.000	66.70%	100.000	101.483	11.336	7.557
1501–05	4.000	66.70%	100.000	93.997	10.500	7.000
1506–10	4.000	66.70%	100.000	95.191	10.633	7.089
1511–15	4.000	66.70%	100.000	94.327	10.537	7.024
1516–20	4.000	66.70%	100.000	80.758	9.021	6.014

Sources: (1) Prices: Phelps Brown Papers, File 204.(2) Wages: Phelps Brown and Hopkins, 'Seven Centuries of Building Wages'.

Table 6.8. English Mint Outputs of Silver and Gold Coinage, in kilogrammes of pure silver and gold and in current pound sterling values in quinquennial means, 1266–70 to 1516–20.

Years (five-year means)	Silver Outputs in kg fine metal	Value of Silver in £ sterling	Gold Outputs in kg fine metal	Value of Gold in £ sterling	Total Value in £ sterling
1266–70	8,550.489	26,637.383			26,637.383
1271–75	3,559.688	11,089.515			11,089.515
1276–80	22,194.388	69,353.587			69,353.587
1281–85	21,913.309	68,548.734			68,548.734
1286–90	17,280.596	54,056.784			54,056.784
1291–95	1,552.352	4,856.034			4,856.034
1296–1300	12,071.417	37,761.545			37,761.545
1301–05	16,017.465	50,105.484			50,105.484
1306–10	40,226.553	125,835.827			125,835.827
1311–15	10,706.712	33,492.502			33,492.502
1316–20	7,275.676	22,759.610			22,759.610
1321–25	1,780.107	5,568.492			5,568.492
1326–30	121.857	381.190			381.190
1331–35	209.056	665.131			665.131
1336–40	429.488	1,551.599			1,551.599
1341–45	5,077.456	17,710.473	240.011	9,859.484	27,569.958
1346–50	1,991.051	7,090.874	675.837	27,123.297	34,214.171
1351–55	17,442.905	67,245.275	1,939.777	83,567.731	150,813.007
1356–60	4,423.016	17,081.461	1,726.695	74,406.844	91,488.305
1361–65	1,630.811	6,298.107	2,415.242	104,077.756	110,375.864
1366–70	293.822	1,134.727	1,729.027	74,507.352	75,642.079
1371–75	316.966	1,224.108	802.608	34,586.019	35,810.127
1376–80	356.898	1,378.322	235.330	10,140.847	11,519.169
[illegible]	[illegible]	[illegible]	[illegible]	[illegible]	8,199.633

1391–95	193.489	747.245	626.546	26,999.152	27,746.397
1396–1400	175.596	678.143	391.143	16,855.142	17,533.285
1401–05	66.344	256.216	168.671	7,268.390	7,524.606
1406–10	10.592	40.907	69.005	2,973.568	3,014.475
1411–15	967.484	4,483.340	1,870.669	89,519.896	94,003.236
1416–20	837.763	3,882.476	1,035.150	49,563.076	53,445.552
1421–25	3,186.020	14,765.093	2,557.314	122,444.369	137,209.462
1426–30	6,858.608	31,785.107	599.478	28,703.069	60,488.176
1431–35	8,059.545	37,350.656	220.785	10,571.183	47,921.839
1436–40	977.025	4,527.863	132.274	6,333.298	10,861.161
1441–45	130.700	605.707	90.778	4,346.467	4,952.174
1446–50	517.373	2,397.681	64.336	3,080.422	5,478.103
1451–55	1,460.637	6,769.085	63.526	3,041.629	9,810.714
1456–60	1,415.094	6,558.024	26.719	1,279.288	7,837.312
1461–65	3,432.915	18,067.349	488.118	29,731.331	47,798.679
1466–70	5,168.090	29,938.348	1,288.157	83,263.992	113,202.339
1471–75	2,422.654	14,034.247	538.669	34,818.552	48,852.799
1476–80	834.683	4,835.252	404.477	26,144.624	30,979.875
1481–85	995.231	5,765.296	219.449	14,184.753	19,950.049
1486–90	926.785	5,368.794	129.749	8,386.730	13,755.524
1491–95	1,270.840	7,361.876	268.983	17,386.525	24,748.402
1496–1500	2,490.940	14,429.823	278.926	18,029.238	32,459.060
1501–05	4,313.544	24,988.026	516.604	33,392.271	58,380.297
1506–10	3,633.212	21,046.916	1,523.115	98,451.267	119,498.183
1511–15	1,089.012	6,308.562	694.599	44,897.564	51,206.126
1516–20	79.145	458.481	743.656	48,068.530	48,527.011

Sources: Challis, 'Appendix 1: Mint Output, 1220–1985'; Munro, *Wool, Cloth, and Gold*; Munro, 'Mint Policies, Ratios, and Outputs'; Munro, 'Bullion Flows'; Munro, 'Wage Stickiness, Monetary Changes'.

paid wage-earners in each occupation (agricultural and industrial) recorded, for each manorial location.[35] These problems become especially acute from the 1420s, when, after four decades of leasing, very few manorial demesne accounts remain — possibly only those for the most profitable demesnes, with (possibly) the highest wages.[36] Furthermore, the purely agricultural wages are for piece-work tasks, for seasonal workers, so that we have no way of estimating their annual money-wage incomes. We also cannot be absolutely certain that the payments for these tasks were in money (silver pence) alone, without supplementary payments in kind.

With these important caveats in mind, we may examine the wage data presented in Tables 6.3–6.7, in which Farmer's annual data have been converted from his index numbers into silver pence. I have also computed quinquennial means of those wages, and means (both arithmetic and harmonic) of the nominal and real wage indexes, adding as well my revised version of the Phelps Brown and Hopkins CPI (from Tables 6.1–6.2).[37] For threshers and winnowers, during this same period, Table 6.3 also shows a very similar increase in nominal money wages: of 23.51 per cent, from 1341–45 to 1366–70, but a much sharper rise of 36.58 per cent for reapers and mowers. Once again, however, these data also demonstrate that the post-plague inflation inflicted a dismal loss in real wages: a decline of 23.56 per cent for threshers and winnowers and a lesser one of 14.73 per cent for reapers and mowers. The changes were fundamentally if not totally the same for the manorial wages of industrial workers in Farmer's 'national' series, as tabulated in Tables 6.4–6.5. The nominal money wages for carpenters rose, over these three decades, by 44.47 per cent; those for tilers and slaters, by almost the same, 45.30 per cent; those for thatchers, by even more, 60.00 per cent. But similarly, over this period, the inflation-ravaged real wages for manorial carpenters fell by 5.67 per cent; those for slaters and tilers, by much more, 15.40 per cent; but those for thatchers remained virtually the same (a minuscule gain of 0.52 per cent), perhaps reflecting their very large gain in nominal wages.

[35] A more detailed analysis of such compositional errors is presented in Munro, 'Wage-Stickiness, Monetary Changes', pp. 196–97.

[36] See Munro, 'The Late-Medieval Decline'.

[37] For the use of harmonic rather than arithmetic means, see Mills, *Introduction to Statistics*, pp. 108–12, 401; Munro, 'Wage-Stickiness, Monetary Changes', p. 278, n. 83; and especially Munro, 'Builders' Wages in Southern England', p. 1028 and n. 40.

While our focus is on agrarian society, we may still usefully compare these results with those that Henry Phelps Brown and Sheila Hopkins had earlier produced for urban industrial craftsmen — carpenters and masons.[38] Their wage series, presented in Tables 6.6 (for masters) and 6.7 (for journeymen labourers) are more useful than those of Farmer, because Phelps Brown and Hopkins had carefully avoided the previously discussed 'compositional' problems. First, they selected just the prevalent or predominant daily wages, in money alone (excluding all payments in kind), without computing mean wages for those employed on each work site. Second, they drew their evidence from one common regional source: chiefly the building accounts of Oxford, Cambridge, and some other small towns in south-east England (but excluding London).[39] As noted earlier, these tables provide, in addition to the standard index-number format, the additional method of presenting real wages in the number of 'baskets of consumables' that master craftsmen and their labourers could have bought with their annual money wage income.[40] The aggregate annual mean values of those baskets, in pence sterling, are also presented in Table 6.1 (column 5).[41]

From the much longer perspective, beginning in the 1260s, we find that nominal money wages for master building craftsmen remained perfectly stable until the beginning of the fourteenth century (at 3d. per day), and then rose by a third to peak in the mid-1330s (at 4d. per day), and then fell back to the late thirteenth-century level (3d.), remaining there until the eve of the Black Death. Real wages also experienced a rise in the early fourteenth century, except obviously during the Great Famine era, and peaked during the deflationary era from *c.* 1325 to *c.* 1345, despite the fall in nominal wages (reflecting that deflation). From its peak in 1336–40, the RWI of 66.986 fell sharply in the aftermath of the Black Death: by 30.51 per cent, from 66.986 to 46.552 in 1351–55 (from

[38] See also Clark, 'The Long March of History'; Clark, 'Work, Wages and Living Conditions'; Clark, 'The Condition of the Working Class'. I found his 'national' wage series to be unusable for this study, for reasons set forth in Munro, 'The Late-Medieval Decline', p. 311, n. 17: especially his use of regression analysis to convert piece-work rates into daily wages.

[39] See Phelps Brown and Hopkins, 'Seven Centuries of Building Wages'. Their primary published source was Rogers, *A History of Agriculture and Prices in England*, in which the raw price and wage data are presented in volumes I: *1259–1400* (1866) and IV: *1401–1582* (1887).

[40] See above, note 25.

[41] Table 6.2 repeats the aggregate 'basket' index numbers in column 9, while column 10 presents, for comparison, Phelps Brown and Hopkins's original index numbers.

7.482 commodity baskets to 5.200 baskets). Real wages then recovered, but even as late as 1371–75 (RWI = 65.439), they were still slightly below that earlier peak. Only from the late 1370s — again three decades after the Black Death — did these urban craftsmen experience a sustained rise in their real wages, for reasons to be seen later in this study.

Tables 6.3–6.5 demonstrate a similar pattern of real-wage changes in the English countryside. Thus, according to Farmer's data on 'national' manorial wages for reapers and binders, their RWI similarly fell from their pre-plague peak of 71.277 in 1341–45 to a post-plague low of 55.741 in 1356–60, after which they began to recover and finally to enjoy a sustained rise (as will also be seen later). The RWI for threshers and winnowers also fell from the pre-plague peak of 60.912 in 1341–45 to a nadir of 43.542 in 1361–65, thereafter enjoying a rather less impressive recovery. The experience of manorial craftsmen in Farmer's series (Tables 6.4–6.5) lay between those of the urban craftsmen (Table 6.6) and the manorial agricultural labourers (Table 6.3). The manorial carpenters similarly suffered a decline in real wages: falling from the pre-plague peak RWI of 63.364 in 1341–45 to a low of 50.181 in 1351–55, thereafter recovering but not exceeding the pre-plague peak until 1376–80. Somewhat, if not fundamentally, different was the experience of the slaters and tilers. Their RWI, falling from the pre-plague peak of 59.248 in 1336–40 to a post-plague nadir of 48.544 as late as 1361–65, similarly surpassed the pre-plague peak only in the late 1370s (Table 6.5).

An Alternate Method of Estimating Real Wages: Computing the Marginal Productivity of Labour

Before we can pursue this analysis further, we must next consider an alternative method of reckoning real wages, for a proper evaluation of the Postan thesis. For most economists, the only proper way to reckon and explain changes in real wages is by calculating changes in the marginal productivity of labour — as explained earlier in this study. As was also stressed earlier, the Postan model stipulates that the marginal productivity of labour necessarily rose with population decline and the consequent shift in the land:labour ratio to favour labour.

What then is the evidence for changes in agricultural labour productivity after the Black Death and into the fifteenth century? Labour productivity did indeed rise in pastoral farming on many manors: for proportionally fewer men were required to manage larger flocks on an increased acreage.[42] On arable lands, however, labour productivity generally fell over the seven decades from 1341 to 1421, as indicated by manorial records in the Winchester, Glastonbury, Ramsey, and other ecclesiastical estates.[43]

Bruce Campbell has provided the best resolution of this seeming paradox, and a demographic one. He had first demonstrated that, during the later thirteenth and early fourteenth centuries, growing population pressures had provided the necessary incentives for fruitful agricultural innovations, especially in the form of very labour-intensive multiple-crop rotations and related techniques to reduce the fallow; but those new methods became impractical with the labour scarcities that followed the Black Death. He thus concludes that 'it was consequently when labour was cheapest and most abundant that the most intensive arable farming systems attained their peak of productivity'.[44]

His recent publications have amply demonstrated a significant decline in arable productivity (for land, labour, and capital combined) for much of England over the century that followed the Black Death.[45] In Norfolk, the most advanced agricultural county of medieval England, weighted average grain yields per harvested acre fell from a mean of 119.0 in 1325–49 to one of just 82.0 in 1350–74, partially recovered to a mean of 97.0 in 1375–99, but

[42] On various Winchester manors, the number of sheep under the care of a single shepherd rose from 231 in 1341 to 342 in 1421, a 48.1 per cent increase. See Farmer, 'The *Famuli* in the Later Middle Ages', esp. table 11.4, pp. 214–20; Dyer, *Lords and Peasants in a Changing Society*, pp. 150–51, noting that on the Worcester manors in the late 1380s, one shepherd managed a flock of 250–300 sheep, but that by 1450 one shepherd was managing a flock of 400–500 sheep. See also Stone, 'The Productivity and Management of Sheep'; Stone, *Decision Making*, and sources cited in the next note.

[43] According to Farmer, 'The *Famuli* in the Later Middle Ages', esp. table 11.4, pp. 214–20, labour productivity on arable lands of these Winchester manors fell from 34.3 acres per famuli ploughman in 1305 to 32.3 acres in 1382, thus only a marginal decline; but thereafter it fell much more precipitously, to 27.9 acres per ploughman in 1421, a 15.8 per cent decline. For some corroborative evidence on the Glastonbury and Ramsey manors, see also Raftis, 'Peasants and the Collapse'; Stone, 'The Productivity of Hired and Customary Labour'; Stone, 'Medieval Farm Management'. See also further if unexplained evidence in Clark, 'Labour Productivity', table 8.7, p. 225; table 8.10, p. 235.

[44] Campbell, 'Land, Labour, Livestock' (quotation on p. 182). This view is further elaborated in Campbell, 'Grain Yields', pp. 157–58. See also Stone, 'The Productivity of Hired and Customary Labour'.

[45] See the sources in the previous note, and also Campbell, 'Agricultural Progress'; Campbell, 'Arable Productivity'; Campbell and Overton, 'A New Perspective on Medieval and Early Modern Agriculture'; Campbell, 'Matching Supply to Demand', tables 6.4–5, pp. 837, 840; Campbell, *English Seigniorial Agriculture, 1250–1450*, pp. 306–85, 411–40.

then fell again to a mean of just 79.0 in 1400–24.[46] On the once progressive demesnes of Battle Abbey's Alciston manor (Sussex), grain yields per acre fell from a mean index of 147.0 in 1340–49 to 100.0 in 1360–69, briefly recovered to a mean of 123.0 in 1370–79, but then progressively fell to a dismal nadir of 71.0 in 1420–29. That index remained below 90.0 for the rest of the fifteenth century.[47]

In any event, the Ricardo-based Postan model can be relevant only for agricultural labour. Certainly this model fails to demonstrate why late medieval population decline should have led to any rise in industrial productivity. In woollen-textile manufacturing, for example, productivity in fact remained quite unchanged from the early fourteenth to the late eighteenth centuries.[48] Some medieval industries did benefit, to be sure, from applications of more complex forms of water-powered machinery, but in the leading industries — textiles, mining, and metallurgy — most were instituted either long before or a full century after the Black Death.[49] For late medieval industries in general, evidence is lacking to indicate that the direct aftermath of the Black Death led to any other positive changes in labour productivity.

[46] Campbell, *English Seigniorial Agriculture, 1250–1450*, table 7.13, p. 374. The index for these means is 1275–99 = 100.

[47] Campbell, 'Grain Yields', table 8, p. 136. For these Alciston grain data, the base period is 1360–69 = 100. In this same study, Campbell also analyses changes in weighted grain yields per seed: the decennial mean seed:yield ratios for all of England (mean of 1300–49 = 100) fell from a peak of 106.80 in 1331–40 to 90.20 in 1351–60, and then rose sharply in the 1370s to reach a new peak of 110.80 in 1381–90, thereafter declining to a fifteenth-century nadir of 95.50, again in 1421–30: for an overall decline of 13.80 per cent. See his Appendix I, pp. 163–68. The differences from the actual yield per acre and the overall decline are explained by a complex set of factors, of which the most important may have been climatic changes: an onset of global cooling, interrupted in the immediate post-plague years by three decades of temporary warming. See pp. 137–62 for an analysis of these factors (including labour shortages).

[48] Fulling had been mechanized in England (waterwheels) from the thirteenth century and remained the only manufacturing process in textiles to be so mechanized before the modern Industrial Revolution. For evidence that textile productivity remained unchanged from the fourteenth to eighteenth centuries, see Munro, 'Medieval Woollens'; Endrei, 'La productivité et la technique'.

[49] See Reynolds, *Stronger Than a Hundred Men*; Langdon, *Mills in the Medieval Economy*; Munro, 'Industrial Energy from Water-Mills'.

Determining Real Wages from the Marginal Revenue Product of Labour

The proper and certainly more accurate method of reckoning real wages also involves the market values of the output of labour, and the correct formula for doing so is therefore: RW = MRP_L (the marginal revenue product of labour). By this formula, the real wage equals the market value of that extra unit of output produced by that extra unit of labour applied to the production processes, as added to a fixed stock of land, capital, and technology. The Postan model does not explicitly recognize the inherent problem for agricultural labour, since it necessarily insists that relative grain prices fell with depopulation. Hence any rise in the marginal productivity of agricultural labour may well have been offset by a fall in its revenue product, that is, with the fall in real grain and related food prices, as did happen, from the later 1370s. For industrial labourers, however, a fall in food prices would certainly have contributed to their rise in real wages or, specifically, the wages of any urban industrial labourers who produced no foodstuffs but purchased them from the urban market. If, therefore, as economic theory contends, rises in real wages in the agrarian sector were necessarily translated to other sectors, the employment of urban industrial labour should have been restricted to those crafts in which, after adjustments, RW = MRP_L. Thus, any rise in relative industrial prices should have increased the employer's marginal revenue product, thereby leading to a rise in real wages, independently of any fall in the cost of living. Obviously, therefore, this standard definition of real wages, based on the marginal revenue product of labour, necessarily also involves the crucial role of commodity prices, as does our earlier definition of real wages (with index numbers): RWI = NWI/CPI.

The Monetary Approach to Late Medieval Economic History: The Quantity Theories of Money

Our final task in evaluating Postan's model is to compare the role of demographic and monetary factors in those commodity price changes. That does not mean that any such evaluations involve so-called 'monetarist' ideology, for most modern economists agree that long-term trends in prices, those described as inflationary and deflationary, were and are today fundamentally, though not exclusively, monetary in origin. The necessary role of 'real factors' (including demographic) can be clearly seen in the modernized version of the equation of exchange (the so-called Fisher identity): M·V = P·y. In this equation, 'M' stands for the national stock of high-powered money; 'V', for the income velocity of that money; 'P', for the CPI; and 'y' for real net national product (i.e. NNP = GNP less depreciation), which necessarily equals real net national income, or current-valued NNI (P·y) deflated by the CPI. Note in particular that historically an increase in the stock of money (M) has almost always led to some decrease in V, since V reflects society's desire to economize on scarce stocks of money.[50]

Most economists, however, prefer a variant known as the Cambridge Cash Balances approach, in which V is replaced by the much more predictable variable 'k': that proportion of national income that society chooses to hold in active cash balances — those that do not earn investment income. Thus k is a measure of society's 'liquidity preference', determined by the collective demand for money for three reasons: to transact goods and services (current expenditures); to take advantage of current speculative opportunities (potentially profitable but risky investments); and to provide financial security for any future adversities (insurance, risk aversion). Mathematically, k is the reciprocal of V: that is, $k = 1/V$; $V = 1/k$.

The modernized Cambridge Cash Balances equation is $M = k \cdot P \cdot y$. We should note in particular the changing relationships between the variables M, k, and y: for an increase in M will likely result in a lower rate of interest (if liquidity preference remains unchanged); and a lower rate of interest will in turn, along with expansion in monetized aggregate demand, stimulate economic growth and thus lead to an increase in y. A lower rate of interest will also increase the incentive to hold larger cash balances (with no investment earnings). Thus in both equations, an increase in M may lead to some inflation, whose degree will be tempered by an increase in k (reflecting a decrease in V) and by some increase in y. At the same time, other independent 'real' forces (population growth, technological changes, expanded trade and colonization, etc.) may stimulate an increase in y, which may in turn call forth an accommodating increase in M (itself produced by financing increased investments). Thus, no supposedly 'monetarist' interpretations can ignore concurrent changes in real factors; similarly, no 'real' explanation can ignore related monetary changes.

[50] The price revolution era provides the only historical exception when both M and V expanded at the same time. See Mayhew, 'Population, Money Supply'; Munro, 'Money, Prices, Wages'; Munro, 'The Price Revolution'.

The Role of Monetary Factors in Medieval Price Trends ('Long Waves'): Before the Black Death

While most economists today would concur with this analysis, many historians will not, especially those still wedded to the Postan thesis, with a corresponding prejudice against 'monetarism'. A recent and very prominent example of such views is David Hackett Fischer's widely praised *The Great Wave*, which seeks to explain all historical 'long waves' of inflation and deflation exclusively in demographic terms, while explicitly rejecting monetary explanations.[51] One cannot, however, dispute Fischer's contention that the first European inflationary 'long wave' began in the 1180s, representing the apogee of the medieval Commercial Revolution era. While this period, commonly called the long thirteenth century (1180–1320), was certainly also an era of pronounced population growth, it was, in fact, preceded by a silver-mining boom in England (Cumberland-Northumberland), followed by an even greater silver-mining boom in the Harz Mountains region of Saxony, which poured out vast quantities of silver until the early fourteenth century.[52] We must also consider the contemporary accompanying 'financial revolution', also evident from the 1180s, in Genoa and Lombardy. Certainly the institutional innovations in both domestic deposit banking and international foreign-exchange banking increased not only the supply of credit but also the volume of monetary flows, contributing to the economic expansion of this first 'long wave'.[53]

In Fischer's view, this 'long wave' came to an end with the demographic catastrophe of the Black Death (1347–52). In my view, the end of that 'long wave' came about much earlier, and it was due to an entirely different set of 'real' forces, but combined with monetary factors.[54] From the 1290s up to and

[51] Fischer, *The Great Wave*. See my critical review in Munro, 'Review of David Hackett Fischer, *The Great Wave*'.

[52] Blanchard, 'Lothian and Beyond'; Blanchard, *Mining, Metallurgy and Minting*, II, 583–685 (English silver production), 687–710 (European production), 711–61 (silver flows, 1125–1225). See also Allen, 'Silver Production', for a critique of Blanchard's English mining output estimates.

[53] Such financial instruments may have had more impact on the income velocity of money (flows) than on the supply of money (stocks). See De Roover, 'The Organization of Trade'; Van der Wee, 'European Banking in the Middle Ages'; notes 58, 87 below.

[54] Fischer, *The Great Wave*, pp. 11–34: section entitled 'The First Wave, the Medieval Price Revolution, 1180–1350'; but in fairness to Fischer, he also discusses, on pp. 35–45, 'The Crisis of the Fourteenth Century', beginning with the Great Famines, while also referring to the wars from the 1290s.

continuing into the Hundred Years War era (1337–1453), in both the eastern and western Mediterranean basins, and in north-west Europe, an ever spreading stain of widespread, chronic, and often devastating warfare, combined with related piracy and brigandage, seriously disrupted or dislocated traditional patterns of regional and international trade and related monetary flows, certainly reducing the aggregate level of both by the 1330s.[55] Far more harmful than the actual military conflicts were the war-related fiscal, monetary, and commercial policies (trade bans). Especially pernicious were the monetary policies of coinage debasements, to help finance wars from seigniorage profits, which, also beginning in the 1290s, invited retaliatory measures from victimized neighbouring states, further reducing trade and bullion flows.[56]

The monetary structure of the early fourteenth-century European economy has yet to be fully explored, but some other forces promoting monetary contraction may be cited for this era. First, the output of European silver mines had begun to decline by the 1320s or 1330s, partly because of inevitable diminishing returns in mining, possibly also because of war-related disruptions.[57] Postan had countered this particular argument by contending that, after centuries of continuous silver mining, the current precious-metal stocks must have been so large that any decline in mined outputs would not have seriously affected the aggregate money supply.[58] But in opposing this argument, Nicholas Mayhew has argued that the stock of medieval coined silver, far from being immutable, was perishable to some considerable degree: from wear, tear, and normal loss in circulation, from shipwrecks, unrecovered hoards, conversion into jewellery and plate, etc. Thus, unless European mints continually replenished the current

[55] Munro, 'Bullionism and the Bill of Exchange'; Munro, 'Industrial Transformations'; Munro, 'The Origins of the English "New Draperies"'; Munro, 'The "Industrial Crisis"'; Munro, 'The Low Countries' Export Trade'; Munro, 'The "New Institutional Economics"'. See also Miller, 'War, Taxation, and the English Economy', whose negative views are disputed in Bridbury, 'Before the Black Death'.

[56] See Munro, 'The Technology and Economics'; Girard, 'La guerre des monnaies'; Graus, 'La crise monétaire du XIVe siècles'; Grunzweig, 'Les incidences internationales'; Cazelles, 'Quelques reflexions'; Lane, 'The First Infidelities'; Spufford, *Money and its Use*, pp. 289–318 ('The Scourge of Debasement').

[57] See Blanchard, *Mining, Metallurgy and Minting*, III, 971, dating the onset of aggregate European decline from the 1330s; see also the graph on p. 925, and the text on pp. 927–70; Braunstein, 'Innovations in Mining'; Nef, 'Mining and Metallurgy'; Kovacevic, 'Les mines d'or et d'argent'; Paulinyi, 'The Crown Monopoly', pp. 27–39, 41–69.

[58] Postan, '"Note"'; Postan, 'The Trade of Medieval Europe', pp. 211–12.

coinage, medieval Europe's aggregate coined money supply would have necessarily contracted over time.[59]

Two other contemporary monetary factors were likely peculiar to England. First, some historians have also contended that England's foreign military expenditures, under Edward II and III, in the 1320s and 1330s, had led to major outflows of bullion, though the fall in mint outputs and the onset of deflation seem to precede any evidence for any such drastic bullion outflows.[60] Second, since England was then minting only silver — and no gold before December 1343 — the very dramatic rise in the bimetallic ratio, from about 12.0:1.0 in the 1290s to 14.2:1.0 in the late 1320s, may have instigated a large outflow of silver coinage to acquire the higher-valued gold. Such bullion movements may have been necessary to permit England's inauguration of an effective gold coinage in the period 1344–52, though with a then falling bimetallic ratio.[61]

Firm statistical evidence for monetary contraction during the early fourteenth century, in terms of both deflation and falling mint outputs, is clearly available for England. The severe deflation — a fall of 35 per cent in the CPI from the quinquennium 1321–25 to that of 1341–45 — has already been discussed and is clearly evident in both Tables 6.1–6.2 and Figure 6.1. As Table 6.8 also clearly demonstrates, England's silver mint outputs, having achieved their highest ever volume in 1306–10 (mean of £125,835.83 sterling), following Edward I's successful full-scale recoinage, still remained high until the eve of the Great Famine; but mint outputs then plunged dramatically, with by far the steepest decline in English monetary history, reaching an abysmal nadir of just £381.19 in 1326–30, recovering to a mean of only £7,090.87 in 1346–50 (just 5.6 per cent of the 1306–10 peak), at the outbreak of the Black Death.[62]

[59] Mayhew, 'Numismatic Evidence'; Mayhew, 'Money and Prices'. See also Patterson, 'Silver Stocks and Losses'; Munro, 'Bullion Flows'; and note 55 above.

[60] Ames, 'The Sterling Crisis'; Feavearyear, *The Pound Sterling*, pp. 13–18; Mate, 'High Prices'; Mayhew, 'Numismatic Evidence'; Mayhew, 'Money and Prices'; Prestwich, 'Currency and the Economy'.

[61] See Lane, 'The First Infidelities', pp. 52–59; Spufford, *Handbook of Medieval Exchange*, graph 3 and table II, pp. lxi–lxiii; Spufford, *Money and its Use*, pp. 267–88, 340–42 (adjusting his dates by those from Lane); Mate, 'The Role of Gold Coinage'. The fall in the bimetallic ratio may have been due to both declining silver outputs from Bohemian mines and increasing supplies of West African (Sudanese) and Hungarian gold. See especially Blanchard, *Mining, Metallurgy and Minting*, III, 950–70.

[62] For Edward I's recoinage of 1299–1300 and its aftermath, see Feavearyear, *The Pound Sterling*, pp. 12–13; Mayhew, 'From Regional to Central Minting', pp. 137–40; and other sources in notes 60–61 above.

Mint accounts provide, however, only a very general, tenuous guide to current money supplies, especially because so often, with either debasements or recoinages, they reflect a recycling of current stocks, and thus mint outputs reflect a combination of both stocks and flows. Low mint outputs may mean only that neighbouring mints were offering higher prices for bullion; certainly they do not necessarily mean any corresponding contraction in the money supplies. Recently, however, two historians have used a combination of mint accounts and coin hoards to show that the English money supply contracted by over one half during the early to mid-fourteenth century.[63] Even more enlightening is Figure 6.1, which compares the aggregate values of English mint outputs with the index numbers for the Phelps Brown and Hopkins CPI (both in quinquennial means). One can clearly see the lagged relationships, with changes in the price level following, within a few years, changes in mint outputs. Especially striking is the severe deflation from the later 1320s to the 1340s. One can hardly deny the obvious: that 'money matters'.

What is especially striking and peculiar about this deflation, and further evidence of genuine deflation, was the marked decline in the nominal wages of most English agricultural workers and building craftsmen, both rural (manorial) and urban, from 1331–35 to 1341–45, as shown in Tables 6.3–6.7. The best evidence is in Tables 6.6–6.7, because these urban wage data do not suffer from the aforesaid 'compositional errors' that afflict Tables 6.3–6.5 (based on Farmer's data).[64] From 1337 to 1340, the mean money wage (nominal wage) of master building craftsmen of various small towns in south-east England fell from 4d. per day to 3d. per day: a decline of 25 per cent.[65] That very low wage-

[63] See Mayhew, 'Money and Prices', table I, p. 125: indicating that the coined money supply contracted from about £1,100,000 sterling in 1311–24 to just £500,000 in the 1340s. For a more recent estimate, see Allen, 'The Volume of the English Currency', table 1, p. 603, indicating a larger estimated coined silver stock of £1,900,000 to £2,300,000 in 1319, falling to about £700,000 to £900,000 in 1351; table 2, p. 607, providing, for 1470, an estimate of just £350,000 to £450,000 in silver, £400,000 to £500,000 in gold, and thus a total of no more than £750,000 to £950,000. See also Allen, 'Silver Production'; Allen, *Mints and Money*, chap. 10: 'The Changing Size of the Currency', pp. 317–45, esp. table 10.12, p. 344.

[64] As Table 6.3 indicates, nominal wages for threshers and winnowers, unlike those for reapers and binders, having modestly declined in the 1320s, did not decline further in the 1330s, though such data are again afflicted by these compositional errors. Similarly, the nominal wages for thatchers, having fallen earlier, in the 1320s, then recovered and did not fall until the early 1340s; those for slaters fell in the 1320s, but not later. See Table 6.5.

[65] Wages for carpenters and masons in the college accounts of Oxford and Cambridge are more stable in this period, but with evidence of decline (from 4d. to 3d.) in the early 1340s. See

rate was maintained until 1352, several years after the Black Death (Tables 6.6–6.7).[66] Despite this fall in nominal wages, masons' real wages actually rose, if only briefly, in the late 1330s (peaking at RWI = 66.986 in 1336–40), simply because consumer prices had fallen even further.

The Role of Monetary Factors in the Post-Plague Inflations

With the Black Death, and indeed with the increased tempo of the Hundred Years War (1337–1453), the monetary structures of western Europe soon became radically transformed. First and foremost, as David Herlihy so aptly commented, 'men were dying, but coins were not'.[67] Thus, whatever the current status of western European precious-metal mining, the effect of such drastic depopulations, perhaps as much as 40–50 per cent of the total inhabitants, was undoubtedly to augment dramatically the per capita supplies of coined money. Second, the fiscal consequences of warfare in western Europe, with increased taxes and other levies, probably induced considerable dishoarding; while at the same time the French, Flemish, Germans, and many Italian town governments sought to finance and facilitate the necessary cash flows for warfare by engaging in horrendous coinage debasements. Third, as some historians have suggested, citing evidence from contemporary Italian literature, paintings, adornments in dress, and housing, the socio-psychological consequences of the horrors from both plague and warfare were to foster fatalistic yet hedonistic spending sprees, all the more facilitated by suddenly inherited cash balances: that is, to increase the income velocity of money.[68]

The overall consequences, as demonstrated in Table 6.8 and Figure 6.1, was a truly momentous increase in English coinage outputs, and consequently,

Rogers, *A History of Agriculture and Prices in England*, I, table III, p. 317, but again this table has compositional errors; see also the following note.

[66] As Tables 6.3–6.7 indicate, however, wages for manorial workers, both agricultural and industrial, did experience fluctuations not seen in the urban industrial wages, and those fluctuations included brief periodic declines. Those fluctuations may reflect compositional errors rather than any decline in money payments per artisan or labourer.

[67] Herlihy, *Medieval and Renaissance Pistoia*, p. 125. If the aggregate supply of European coins did diminish, it certainly did not do so to the extent of the immediate post-plague population decline.

[68] The most frequently cited is Boccaccio's famous *Decameron*. See Cassell, 'Boccaccio, Giovanni'. See also Lopez, 'Hard Times'; Miskimin, *The Economy of Early Renaissance Europe*, pp. 132–40; Stuard, 'Gravitas and Consumption'; Stuard, *Gilding the Market*.

from both increased stocks and increased flows, drastic inflations. That inflation, unaffected by any English coinage debasements after 1351, persisted until the late 1370s.[69] Figure 6.1 again demonstrates a clear if lagged relationship between increases in mint outputs and the ensuing inflation.

The Role of Monetary Factors in the Later Medieval Deflations of c. 1375–1415 and c. 1440–1480: Their Impact on Real Wages

Thereafter, during the final quarter of the fourteenth century, north-western Europe experienced an equally dramatic deflation that continued into the fifteenth century, until the resumption of the Hundred Years War in France. Once again Figure 6.1 demonstrates that same lagged relationship between falling mint outputs and the ensuing and indeed dramatic fall in consumer prices, during the later fourteenth and early fifteenth centuries. Since most consumer prices fell rapidly, while money wages largely remained stable, their purchasing power finally did rise substantially — thirty years or more after the Black Death — as can be clearly seen in the English real-wage indices in Tables 6.3–6.7.

For the small towns of south-eastern England, the quinquennial mean real wages of master building craftsmen (Table 6.6) rose by 52.93 per cent: from the previous trough in 1361–65 (near the end of the inflationary cycle) to the new peak of 1411–15: thus from an RWI of 60.397 (= 6.746 baskets) to one of 92.369 (= 10.318 baskets). For manorial carpenters, according to Farmer's less reliable 'national' wage data (Table 6.4), mean real wages rose by 40.45 per cent from trough to peak: from a RWI of 55.102 in 1361–65 to the peak of 77.377 in 1406–10; for manorial masons, by somewhat more, by 45.79 per cent (Table 6.4), over the same period; for manorial thatchers, by much more, 60.27 per cent; and for tilers, by 51.55 per cent, over the period 1361–65 to 1406–10 (Table 6.5). Experiencing many more fluctuations were the real-wage gains of manorial reapers (Table 6.3), whose RWI rose overall 66.85 per cent: from the low of 55.741 in 1356–60 to (ultimately) 93.009 in 1411–15. Over these same years, the threshers and winnowers (Table 6.3) experienced an increase of only 49.06 per cent, but by 1421–25 their RWI had risen to 77.243 (an overall gain of 65.39 per cent).

[69] For coinage debasements (from 1351) and inflations in England (and the Low Countries), see Munro, *Wool, Cloth, and Gold*, pp. 43–63; Munro, 'Mint Policies, Ratios, and Outputs'; Munro, 'Bullion Flows'; Munro, 'Deflation and the Petty Coinage'; Munro, 'Wage-Stickiness, Monetary Changes'; Munro, 'Before and After the Black Death'; Munro, 'The Late-Medieval Decline'.

Those positive real-wage trends were quickly reversed, after the Battle of Agincourt in 1415 and the ensuing final phases of the Hundred Years War, when much of north-western Europe was again ravaged by an inflation that lasted until about 1440. But, while the Low Countries and France in this era suffered from particularly severe coinage debasements during this war-torn period, England experienced only one debasement, a purely defensive one, in 1411–12, and England's first in over sixty years, reducing the silver content by 16.67 per cent.[70] England, although then spared wars on home soil and the drastic debasements experienced on the Continent, did experience some inflation (if to a lesser extent than did France and Flanders): a 14.74 per cent rise in the CPI, from 108.261 in 1411–15 to 124.218 in 1436–40. Consequently, urban industrial building craftsmen in south-east England, with static nominal daily wages (at 6d.), experienced a 12.85 per cent decline in real wages (Tables 6.6–6.7) during this same period: with a fall in the quinquennial mean RWI, from 92.369 (10.318 baskets) to one of 80.504 (8.992 baskets) over this same period. The English rural scene was, however, more complex, with fluctuating wage rates, possibly reflecting the aforesaid compositional errors, as indicated for Tables 6.3–6.5.[71] Thus, while manorial reapers and binders also experienced a decline in real wages in this same period, by 16.57 per cent, manorial threshers experienced a gain of 11.09 per cent (Table 6.3). Among manorial building craftsmen, the thatchers experienced a gain of 16.62 per cent, the carpenters, a smaller gain of 8.79 per cent, while real wages for masons and slaters remained virtually unchanged (Tables 6.4–6.5).

With the end of the Hundred Years War in 1453 — though followed in England by the domestic Wars of the Roses (1455–87) — that war-induced inflationary era was succeeded by yet another era of prolonged deflation, actually commencing in the 1440s, and as severe as that of the later fourteenth century (Tables 6.1–6.5). In England, from peak to trough, from 1436–40 to 1476–80, the CPI fell by 25.40 per cent: from 124.218 to 92.667. Despite a brief rise in consumer prices during the 1480s, prices fell again in the 1490s,

[70] See Munro, *Wool, Cloth, and Gold*, pp. 60–103; tables C–G, pp. 198–204; Munro, 'The Technology and Economics', pp. 24–32; Feavearyear, *The Pound Sterling*, pp. 37–39; Mayhew, 'From Regional to Central Minting', pp. 171–75.

[71] For other problems in utilizing English manorial wage rates in the fifteenth century, contending that they were not indicative of real incomes in rural societies, especially wage rates for seasonal workers, see Hatcher, 'Unreal Wages'.

and that deflationary trend continued until the onset of the price revolution in 1516–20 (a persistent inflation lasting until *c*. 1650).[72]

This mid- to later fifteenth-century era in turn also consequently produced the most substantial real-wage gains for later medieval England (and also for Flanders);[73] but such gains must be seen in the perspective of the previous fifteenth-century era of falling real wages, at least for urban industrial artisans, from *c*. 1415 to *c*. 1440. From 1436–40 to the peak of real wages in 1476–80, the mean real wages for urban building craftsmen in the towns of south-eastern England rose 34.05 per cent (Tables 6.3–6.5): from a RWI of 80.504 (8.992 baskets, for masters) to one of 107.913 (12.054 baskets) (Table 6.6).[74] Similar increases in real wages can also be found for manorial wage earners, though the validity of the data in Tables 6.6–6.8 is further undermined by the paucity of manorial accounts from this era. For the same period, from 1436–40 to the peak of 1476–80, the RWI for carpenters rose by 44.50 per cent; that for masons, by 43.12 per cent (Table 6.4); for slaters and tilers, by 47.14 per cent; and for thatchers, by 34.37 per cent (Table 6.5). For agricultural workers (Table 6.3) the data are even sparser and terminate earlier. The RWI for manorial threshers rose by 41.79 per cent over the shorter period, from 1436–40 to 1471–75; and that for reapers, for the even shorter period from 1436–40 to 1461–65, rose by 46.96 per cent.

Forces for Monetary Contraction: The Debate about Late Medieval 'Bullion Famines'

While the periodic late medieval eras of inflation can be readily explained by a combination of war-induced fiscal and monetary policies, especially by coinage debasements, and by wartime 'supply shocks', more difficult to explain are the post-plague deflations, though less so than the earlier, pre-plague deflation.

[72] In 1481–85, the CPI rose to 129.8, but fell to 103.4 by 1491–95, and was 99.8 in 1506–10. See Table 6.2, and Munro, 'The Monetary Origins'; Munro, 'Money, Prices, Wages'.

[73] For fifteenth-century Flanders and Brabant, see sources cited in note 69 above.

[74] In London, in the building accounts for Westminster Abbey and the London guild houses, the nominal daily wage rate for master craftsmen (carpenters, mason, tilers) had risen from 7.0–7.5d. to a standard 8.0d. by the 1420s, remaining at this level for the rest of the century: one third higher than the standard 6d. rate in the smaller towns of south-east England. But without a London-based cost-of-living index, we cannot properly estimate their real wages. For London wages, see Munro, 'Wage-Stickiness, Monetary Changes', pp. 196–98, 202, 211, and 232 (table 2).

Currently the favoured explanations concern the two so-called 'bullion famines': from the 1370s to the 1410s; and from the 1440s to the 1470s. But the published analyses are often contradictory. The predominant theories focus upon a net reduction in the supply of precious metals, from three possible causes. The first suggested cause, one examined earlier for the pre-plague bullion famine, was simply a continuation and severe worsening of Europe's late medieval mining slump, with a veritable cessation of silver mining in some regions, so that even the subsequent post-plague opening of new mines in Serbia and Sardinia failed to compensate for the sharp decline in outputs elsewhere.

The much more important cause, for most historians, was western Europe's supposedly worsening of balance-of-payments deficit with Asia, with consequent bullion outflows via the Levant and the eastern Baltic.[75] A third, if lesser cause, aggravating that balance-of-payments deficit, was a severe diminution in imports of 'Sudanese' west African gold, in Italian trade with the north Africa ports. That decline became even more severe from the 1370s, after the collapse of the once mighty Mali Empire and the inability of its successor, the Songhai Empire, to guarantee security along the trans-Saharan trade routes from Timbuktu to Mediterranean ports.[76]

The problem with this 'balance of payments' explanation, however, is that western Europe had chronically sustained a deficit in payments with the East from ancient Roman times. Despite Ashtor's impressive evidence for Venice's large silver exports to the Levant in the later fifteenth century, there is little evidence to demonstrate that an overall European balance-of-payments deficit had been worsening from a full century earlier.[77] Indeed, a major factor that helped to end the so-called bullion-famine era in the later fifteenth century was the Central European silver-copper mining boom, which began during the very nadir of deflation in the 1460s, when the consequently high value of silver (i.e.

[75] For problems in mining, see note 57 above, especially Blanchard, *Mining, Metallurgy and Minting*, III, 974–77; Nef, 'Silver Production in Central Europe'; Nef, 'Mining and Metallurgy'. For balance-of-payments deficits, see Miskimin, 'Monetary Movements'; Miskimin, 'Money and Money Movements'; Miskimin, *The Economy of Early Renaissance Europe*, pp. 25–72, 132–57; Lopez, Miskimin, and Udovitch, 'England to Egypt'; Day, 'The Great Bullion Famine'; Day, 'The Question of Monetary Contraction'; Spufford, *Money and its Use*, pp. 267–88, 340–42.

[76] See Day, 'The Great Bullion Famine', pp. 36–39; Bovill, *The Golden Trade*, pp. 13–44, 79–131; and Blanchard, *Mining, Metallurgy and Minting*, III, 1111–1339, esp. pp. 1165–1210. For a contrary view about African gold inflows, see MacKay, *Money, Prices and Politics*.

[77] Ashtor, *Les métaux précieux*; Ashtor, *A Social and Economic History*, pp. 319–31; Ashtor, *The Levant Trade*. But see also Munro, 'South German Silver'.

its high purchasing power) promoted the application of previous innovations in both civil and chemical engineering, for mining and metallurgy. That mining boom augmented European silver production by over fivefold by the 1530s, and without such large increases in its silver stocks, Venice would never have been able to conduct such an increased volume and value of trade with the Levant in the 1490s.[78] Furthermore, the success of mints in England, France, and the Low Countries in reviving their coinage outputs in the 1420s and 1430s, well before this mining boom commenced, indicates the absence of a clear linear trend for any augmented bullion outflows to the East.[79] A greater problem with all of the theses concerning a steadily worsening diminution in Europe's physical stocks of precious metals is the failure to prove that, by the mid-fifteenth century, those stocks had declined more than had Europe's population, that is, by about 40–50 per cent. As noted earlier, the initial impact of the Black Death was to create a per capita surplus of precious metals.

An alternative explanation for the late medieval monetary contractions may be found in examining not stocks but flows: that is, adverse changes in the income velocity of money or in the increased demand for idle cash balances, which may have been related to the pernicious effects of warfare and plagues, from the 1370s. Chronic, devastating warfare throughout so much of Europe, combined with more plagues and depopulation, produced even more severe dislocations to established trade patterns, while sharply raising transaction costs, thus reducing even more flows of both commodities and bullion. Worse, the aforementioned responses to political and military conflicts, in terms of commercial blockades, confiscations, and especially coinage debasements that were the most severe ever encountered in medieval Europe, curtailed bullion flows even more drastically, through policies known as 'bullionism'. Most rulers, in defending themselves against aggressive debasements by their neighbours, necessarily banned the domestic circulation of most foreign coins, especially silver coins (all the more subject to surreptitious debasements); such bans also forced

[78] The first set of innovations involved adits and mechanical pumps to permit much deeper, well-drained mining shafts; the second is known as the Saigerhütten process, for smelting argentiferous-cupric ores with lead to separate the two metals. See Westermann, 'Die Bedeutung des Thüringer Saigerhandels'; Westermann, 'Zur Silber- und Kupferproduktion Mitteleuropas'; Nef, 'Silver Production in Central Europe'; Nef, 'Mining and Metallurgy'; Braunstein, 'Innovations in Mining'; Spufford, *Money and its Use*, pp. 363–77; Munro, 'The Central European Mining Boom'; Munro, 'The Monetary Origins'. See also Blanchard, *Mining, Metallurgy and Minting*, III, 973–74: dating the European adoption of the Saigerhüttenprozess to the 1390s.

[79] See sources cited in notes 69–70 and 78.

most merchants to surrender non-legal tender foreign coin as bullion to their local mints. More important, in seeking to attract more bullion to their own mints, to increase coinage outputs and their seigniorage revenues, virtually all rulers banned its export (while only England also banned coin exports). Even when enforcement of those bans failed to prevent international exchanges of precious metals, they still depressed monetary and trade flows by raising commercial transaction costs.[80]

Finally, the noxious combination of warfare, famines, plagues, depopulation, and consequent commercial disruptions led to periodic but often severe economic depressions, aggravated by these self-serving monetary policies and higher taxes. Commencing by the late 1370s and 1380s, the worst of all these cyclical depressions (in northern Europe) took place in the mid-fifteenth century.[81] Such conditions also bred a more general climate of insecurity and widespread pessimism that further discouraged spending and investment and also increased hoarding, which together further deepened those depressions.[82] Such hoarding — that is, an increase in the demand for idle cash balances — is itself a self-justifying deflationary phenomena, for as prices fell, the rational response was to save rather than to spend, in anticipation of even lower future prices, and thus of the increased value of hoarded coins. As Figure 6.1 and Tables 6.1, 6.2, and 6.8 clearly demonstrate, monetary contraction and deflation were together the predominant overall trend from the 1370s to about 1510, though interrupted by the inflationary final phases of the Hundred Years War (and in Flanders, by the civil wars of the 1480s).[83]

[80] See sources in notes 69–70 above; also Munro, *Wool, Cloth, and Gold*, pp. 11–41, and the various studies in Munro, *Bullion Flows*.

[81] See in particular Hatcher, 'The Great Slump'; Nightingale, 'England and the European Depression'; Munro, 'Economic Depression'.

[82] See Spufford, *Money and its Use*, pp. 346–47, citing the views of many contemporary European observers who believed that 'thesaurisation [hoarding, the accumulation of plate] was the main cause of the bullion famines' during the later fourteenth and early fifteenth centuries. Disagreeing, he comments that, 'In retrospect it appears that it was itself in part a response to the famine. Nevertheless it made that shortage worse, although the export of precious metals from Europe now seems more important, combined with the failures of the mines to make good the losses'. For increased coin hoards in this era, see Thompson, *Inventory of British Coin Hoards*; for increased consumption of precious metals in dress and art, as a form of hoarding, see Stuard, 'Gravitas and Consumption', and Stuard, *Gilding the Market*; for evident reductions in the income velocity of money, see Mayhew, 'Population, Money Supply'. See also Munro, 'Bullion Flows', pp. 97–122.

[83] See Nightingale, 'Gold, Credit, and Mortality', esp. pp. 1100–02, which contends that another cause of England's deflation from the 1380s was its pro-gold monetary policies, with a

Those military conflicts produced drastic coinage debasements and vast increases in taxes and military expenditures, which in turn all promoted temporary dishoarding. But when peace resumed, so did deflation.

The Role of Credit and Banking Institutions: Did they Remedy Late Medieval Bullion Scarcities?

Nevertheless, according to many historians, a supposed growth in the use of credit during the later Middle Ages offset or counteracted those deflationary forces, particularly through the agency of deposit-and-transfer banking, bills-of-exchange banking, and letters obligatory (promissory notes). Yet none was an innovation in this era, and they had seen their most rapid initial diffusion during the later thirteenth and early fourteenth centuries. Why credit instruments largely failed to provide a sufficient remedy for periodic monetary contractions in late medieval Europe is very complex but may be briefly summarized here. First, late medieval Europe experienced very few additional innovations, and most credit instruments were still far from being effective substitutes for coined money, with the possible exception of some commerce conducted by Italian merchant-bankers. Second, much more widespread and more powerful forces, economic and political, involving increased hostility from both Church and State, seriously impeded the employment or circulation of credit, with a multitude of examples to be cited in England, France, the Low Countries, and many Hanse towns, if not so much in Italy itself. Indeed, in both England and the Low Countries, late medieval nationalist monetary policies effectively prevented the emergence of deposit banking in the former, and virtually closed down such banks in the latter, following the Burgundian unification of the Low Countries, in a series of ever more severe ordinances (1433–35, 1467, 1480, and 1489).[84]

consequent predominance of high-valued gold coins having a very low income velocity; that policy took place at the expense of minting much lower-valued silver coins, with a far higher income velocity of circulation. But this argument overlooks the fact that English minting had become predominantly gold from as early as the 1360s (98.50 per cent gold in 1366–70), a decade before inflation had peaked, and that during the severely deflationary trough of the mid-fifteenth century, the proportion of mint outputs in silver had recovered (from the mid-1420s) to levels as high as 83.68 per cent in 1456–60 (44.46 per cent in 1496–1500). Furthermore, deflationary pressures were just as severe in Flanders, from the 1380s, which usually maintained more pro-silver monetary policies. See Mayhew, 'Population, Money Supply'; Munro, 'The Monetary Origins', pp. 21–24, table 1.6 (pp. 22–23); Mate, 'The Role of Gold Coinage'; and other sources cited in notes 69–70 and 78 above. For Flanders in the 1480s, see Spufford, 'The Debasement of the Coinage'.

[84] For the most recent views on the positive role of credit, but only in England, see Bolton,

Third, because of those increasingly hostile attitudes from state-dominated legal institutions, despite the growth of a more international law merchant, the enforcement of debt repayments, especially those involving holograph documents, became even more costly and ineffective, thus restricting credit instruments to a small circle of merchants who knew and trusted each other. Fourth, therefore, most European states and principalities, even in Italy, failed to provide the legal institutions to protect the rights of debt assignees and thus to guarantee negotiability, while the universal usury prohibitions severely hindered the ability of merchants to discount bills (thereby revealing the implicit interest) in transferring them before maturity.[85] Such a conversion of credit instruments into cash or goods is the fundamentally necessary condition in allowing them to augment the effective money supply. Fifth, credit instruments were far from being divorced from the use of coined money. As Spufford, Nightingale, Spooner, Mueller, Mayhew and others have effectively demonstrated, credit either expanded or contracted with the coined money supply in the late medieval and early modern economies, usually in a non-proportional fashion.[86] As Mayhew has so aptly commented: 'credit reflected the supply of coin rather than compensated for it'.[87]

'Was There a "Crisis of Credit"?'; Bolton, *Money in the Medieval English Economy*, pp. 258–303. His views have been challenged in Nightingale, 'A Crisis of Credit', and also in Munro, 'EH. Net Review of Jim Bolton'. See also, for deposit banking, Munro, 'English "Backwardness"', esp. pp. 142–44. See also the older views of Michael Postan, as published in Postan 'Credit in Medieval Trade', and Postan, 'Private Financial Instruments'. For the Low Countries, see De Roover, *Money, Banking and Credit*, pp. 130, 236–46, 331–57, esp. pp. 339–42; De Roover, 'The Organization of Trade'; Van der Wee, *Growth of the Antwerp Market*, II, 85–86, 333–40, 355–58; Van der Wee, 'Monetary, Credit, and Banking Systems', pp. 302, 312, 323–24, 361–62; Van der Wee, 'European Banking in the Middle Ages', pp. 87–112, 125–33.

[85] The European usury ban was first modified in the Habsburg Netherlands by an imperial decree of October 1540, permitting interest on commercial loans up to 12 per cent; in England, a parliamentary statute of 1547, revoked 1552, but restored in 1571, permitted interest up to 10 per cent (on all loans). See Munro, 'The Medieval Origins'; Munro, 'The International Law Merchant'; Munro, 'Usury, Calvinism and Credit in Protestant England'; Munro, 'Bullionism and the Bill of Exchange'; Munro, 'English "Backwardness"'.

[86] See Spooner, *International Economy*, pp. 3, 53–71; Mueller, '"Chome l'ucciello di passegio"'; Nightingale, 'Monetary Contraction'; Nightingale, 'Money and Credit'; Nightingale, 'Gold, Credit, and Mortality', esp. pp. 1100–02, for the period from the 1380s; Spufford, *Money and its Use*, pp. 345–48; Briggs, *Credit and Village Society*; and especially Briggs, 'The Availability of Credit'. See also note 84 above and the next note.

[87] Mayhew, 'Money and Prices', p. 121: 'Lending does not contract in time of glut of coin or expand in times of scarcity'. See also Mayhew, 'Population, Money Supply', pp. 238–57.

Finally, we may call upon the evidence for the stark deflations that accompanied the two late medieval bullion famines (Figure 6.1) as further proof that the use of credit instruments did not compensate for periodic scarcities of coined money in the late medieval English economy. The only valid explanation for those deflations (of *c.* 1375–1425 and *c.* 1440–80) is monetary contraction — and not demographic decline.

Conclusions on the Postan Paradigm: The Importance of Money for Late Medieval Prices and Wages

The chief conclusions therefore are, first, that the Postan paradigm does not hold true in asserting that demographic factors were the predominant determinants of change in prices, including wages, during the medieval era. Furthermore, there is very little if any evidence to indicate that demographically induced improvements in labour productivity (from changes in the land:labour ratio) had anything to do with the increases in real wages recorded in this study, except possibly in pastoral agriculture (for which wage data are largely missing). Nevertheless, the rise in both nominal and real wages for building craftsmen, in England (Tables 6.4–6.7) in the early fifteenth century cannot be adequately explained by other models used in this study. They may reflect productivity gains not yet explained: possibly changes in Total Factor Productivity rather than just in labour productivity.[88]

The second major conclusion is that monetary factors deserve far more consideration for their role in influencing changes in both commodity prices and real wages than Postan and his followers were willing to admit.[89] Demographic factors were not, however, irrelevant and indeed were linked to monetary factors. In terms of the modernized equation of exchange (M·V = P·y), population decline was often important in influencing changes in the income velocity of money and always crucial in determining independent changes in y (i.e. the deflated NNI or NNP), if only by influencing changes in relative prices. Furthermore, per capita money supplies were obviously influenced by a falling population.

[88] See Munro, 'Builders' Wages in Southern England', pp. 1046–47: from changes in land, labour, and capital inputs.

[89] For example, see Hatcher, *Plague, Population, and the English Economy*, pp. 47–54, placing primary emphasis on demographic factors, while admitting that monetary forces may have had some influence on declining prices. For a more nuanced view, giving a greater role to monetary forces, see Hatcher, 'The Great Slump'.

The Problem of Wage Stickiness

For the post–Black Death era, real wages were generally determined by what is called 'wage stickiness': that is, the downward rigidity of nominal wages during periods of deflation. During times of inflation, nominal wages were usually not so sticky; but clearly, from all the historical evidence, they generally rose to a much lesser extent than did the CPI. Consequently, insofar as monetary factors were chiefly responsible for long-term trends of deflation and inflation, they also played a strong role in determining real wages under such conditions of stickiness. Thus, real wages necessarily rose during periods of falling consumer prices and usually fell during periods of rising consumer prices — and did so in the ensuing early modern era of the price revolution.[90] That, as we have seen, is self-evident from the first equation used in this study to examine the patterns of real wage changes: RWI = NWI/CPI.

But that is only half the story, for obviously monetary factors could not possibly have determined the nature of wage stickiness itself. By standard economic theory, monetary contraction ought to have led to a fall in nominal wages, as the price for labour. Indeed, we saw that in England during the severe deflation from the late 1320s to the eve of the Black Death, money wages for industrial craftsmen (and some agricultural workers) did fall, but because they did not fall as much as did commodity prices, real wages did rise, if only briefly. Thereafter, however, (nominal) money wages for industrial craftsmen and labourers in England did not fall for seven centuries: not until the 1920s.[91] Such wage stickiness is therefore largely a post-plague phenomenon — so evident in Tables 6.3–6.7 (and also in the southern Low Countries); but John Langdon has recently found some instances of sticky wages in England before the Black Death.[92]

This very complex subject has been examined in a number of recent studies, so that a detailed analysis is not required in this current study.[93] Suffice it to say

[90] Munro, 'The Monetary Origins', pp. 1–34; Munro, 'Money, Prices, Wages', pp. 13–71; Munro, 'The Price Revolution', pp. 631–34.

[91] Phelps Brown and Hopkins, 'Seven Centuries of Building Wages'.

[92] Langdon, 'Waged Building Employment'; Langdon, 'Minimum Wages and Unemployment Rates'. For Flanders and Brabant, see Munro, 'Wage-Stickiness, Monetary Changes', pp. 219–27, tables 10–15 (pp. 252–63), and figs 5–6 (pp. 268–69).

[93] See Munro, 'Wage-Stickiness, Monetary Changes'; Munro, 'Builders' Wages in Southern England'; Munro, 'Before and After the Black Death'; Munro, 'The Late-Medieval Decline'; and the previous note. These studies, which use only silver money wages, also examine the

that wage stickiness became essentially socio-institutional in nature, especially when wage earners were better able to organize and resist arbitrary reductions in their daily pay. Few would now doubt the proposition that the bargaining power of labour increased substantially in the aftermath of the Black Death. Wage stickiness tended to be much more prevalent in industrial occupations: not just in the building trades (carpenters, masons, pavers, etc.), but also in textiles and services, in both villages and towns, in both England and the Low Countries.[94] Wage stickiness was also much less evident in purely agricultural occupations (with piece-work wages), but the apparent wage fluctuations in Tables 6.3–6.5 (but not in Tables 6.6–6.7) may again simply reflect the previously discussed 'compositional errors'.

Real Wages and Real Incomes

Three more intractable problems concerning wages remain. First, our evidence concerns only daily wages, not annual incomes, and we cannot begin to measure such incomes without better knowledge of the average number of days worked each year. Other recent publications provide some justifications for an estimate of 210 days per year for the building trades in the fifteenth century (an estimate lower than most).[95] Second, we do not know the extent to which male wage earners practised more than one craft and/or gained supplementary incomes from other sources, in agriculture or commerce; nor do we know the contributions to total household incomes from wives and other family members.

Third, we must remember that wage earners were still a minority in society, though an important one. According to Penn and Dyer, 'at least one-third of the population of late-medieval England gained all or a part of their livelihood' from cash wages.[96] If, however, a fall in the cost of foodstuffs (about 80 per cent of the consumer basket: Table 6.2) was the major factor in the rise in their real wages from the late 1370s, then possibly their gains were offset by a fall in real incomes for a much greater proportion of society: that is, those who

extent to which wages were paid partially in kind, noting that the proportion (in value) fell from about one-half in kind before the Black Death to about one-third by the late fourteenth century.

[94] For both England and the southern Low Countries, see Munro, 'Wage-Stickiness, Monetary Changes'; Munro, 'Builders' Wages in Southern England'.

[95] See my publications cited in note 25 above.

[96] Penn and Dyer, 'Wages and Earnings', p. 356.

produced agricultural products for the market and those who traded in such goods. That situation, however, was far more true of fifteenth-century England than of the more urbanized and industrialized Flanders (more dependent on imported foodstuffs). Furthermore, as John Hatcher has recently pointed out, the apogee of the so-called Golden Age of the Labourer, in the mid-fifteenth century was also an era of deep depression in England (as it was also in the southern Low Countries).[97]

The behaviour of late medieval prices and wages is a very complex issue, for which the Postan demographic model provides the least satisfactory explanation. Those who still think that late medieval prosperity depended on demographic factors should ponder the wise words of the late Ralph Davis: 'The economy of modern Europe would never have come into existence on the basis of population decline'.[98]

[97] See Hatcher, 'Unreal Wages', with other strong arguments to oppose the 'Golden Age' thesis. See also sources cited in notes 92–93 above. For the mid-fifteenth-century depression in both England and the southern Low Countries, see the sources cited above in note 81, and also Munro 'The Symbiosis of Towns and Textiles', esp. pp. 44–70.

[98] Davis, *The Rise of the Atlantic Economies*, p. 16.

Appendix

Postan on Money and Prices in Chronological Order of Publication

(1) Postan, 'The Economic Foundations', pp. 188–89 (repr. in Postan, *Essays on Medieval Agriculture*, p. 9)

> Yet even silver cannot be easily made to account for the economic trend. If changes in the supply of silver were responsible for the rise in prices, we would expect the rise to be 'general'; i.e. to affect more or less the entire range of medieval commodities entering into local trade. But most recent writers have pointed out that the movements of agricultural and industrial prices did not synchronize; that in the twelfth and thirteenth centuries industrial prices did not rise as high and as fast as the prices of wheat and did not fall or stagnate in the later Middle Ages.

(2) Postan, 'The Trade of Medieval Europe', pp. 208–14

> (a) On the whole the evidence [...] will not support the hypothesis of prices as the main, and still less as the sole, cause of the slump. Our knowledge of medieval prices is largely confined to grain, but in so far as other series are available they suggest that the fall in prices was highly compartmentalized. Thus it does not appear that prices for cloth or for iron, or indeed those for other commodities, fell at all, or fell in the same proportion as prices for agricultural products. (p. 208)

> (b) Thus the prices for separate commodities did not move together [...]. The prices for animal products in current coinage actually rose and were considerably higher in the period of 1401 to 1425 than in that of 1351 to 1375 [...]. Indeed, expressed in current prices, the series after 1351 continues the rising trend of the previous two centuries for at least another 125 years. (p. 208)

> (c) Trade in butter may appear to the uninitiated too slight a foundation for any argument [...]. Yet in spite of being cast on a small scale, it has turned out to be an important index of wider movements. For butter was a merchandise circulating over great distances and commanding an international price; and what is even more important is that it happened to be a semi-luxury entering into popular consumption [...]. It is not necessary to know what Alfred Marshall said about the elasticity of the demand for bread to conclude that agricultural labourers were now better able to indulge in a little butter, however expensive. The price of butter was therefore highly responsive to changes in demand and supply, and was more sensitive as a barometer of markets than prices of more indispensable foods. It is therefore very significant that the price of butter and the price of grain diverged more widely than the prices of any other commodities. In the fourteenth and fifteenth centuries the butter prices rose very steeply, in both current coinage and in silver. (pp. 209–10)

(d) Thus price movements there were, and from most of them important consequences followed; but they could not be entirely ascribed to monetary causes, and moreover they were not general. And price changes which are not 'general' but are mainly confined to grain, point to a factor which has already been shown to have operated in the direction in the early centuries of the Middle Ages, i.e. population. (p. 213)

(e) A fall in population would also have, so to speak, a selective effect on prices, in that it would tend to lower the prices of agricultural products, which were previously being produced at high and ever rising cost — or, to use the economist's terminology, under steeply diminishing returns — but would have little effect on commodities not greatly subject to diminishing returns, i.e. most industrial products. (p. 214)

(3) Postan, *The Medieval Economy and Society*, pp. 238–39

(a) Most historians rightly assume that the use of various instruments of credit was more widespread and more sophisticated in the fifteenth century than it had been in the thirteenth. (p. 238)

(b) The pure logic of the monetary explanation demands that the effects of changes in the circulating medium should be felt throughout the economy, i.e. in the prices of all the goods sold and bought, since changes in money must be, so to speak, 'neutral' as between different commodities. It therefore follows that, if the price movement for different commodities diverged, monetary factors could not have been the sole or the main cause of price changes. (p. 239)

(c) So much for the purely theoretical reasons why the currency could not be accepted as the sole or even the main factor behind the rise of prices in the thirteenth century and their decline in the fifteenth. (p. 238)

(d) An alternative 'real' hypothesis has in fact been suggested. The rising secular trend of grain prices could be accounted for by concomitant demographic trends. Population was increasing, or in other words the number of mouths was getting even greater. The output of agriculture, though expanding, could not keep pace with the increasing numbers to be fed. (p. 239)

Bibliography

Archives

The Beveridge Price and Wage History Collection, Boxes A: 31–32, Archives of the British Library of Political and Economic Science (London School of Economics)

The Phelps Brown Papers, File 204: folders I-XVI, Archives of the British Library of Political and Economic Science (London School of Economics)

Primary Sources

Rogers, James E. Thorold, *A History of Agriculture and Prices in England from the Year after the Oxford Parliament (1259) to the Commencement of the Continental War (1793)*, 7 vols (Oxford: Clarendon Press, 1866–1902)

Spufford, Peter, *Handbook of Medieval Exchange*, Royal Historical Society Guides and Handbooks, 13 (London: Offices of the Royal Historical Society, 1986)

Thompson, J. D. A., *Inventory of British Coin Hoards, AD 600–1500* (Oxford: Royal Numismatic Society Publications, 1956)

Secondary Sources

Abel, Wilhelm, *Agrarkrisen und Agrarkonjunktur: Geschichte des Land- und Ernährungswirtschaft Mitteleuropas seit dem hohen Mittlealter*, 3rd edn (Berlin: Parey, 1978); trans. by Olive Ordish as *Agricultural Fluctuations in Europe from the Thirteenth to the Twentieth Centuries*, with a forward by Joan Thirsk (London: Methuen, 1980)

——, *Die Wüstungen des ausgehenden Mittelalters*, Quellen und Forschungen zur Agrargeschichte, 1 (Stuttgart: G. Fischer, 1976)

Allen, Martin, *Mints and Money in Medieval England* (Cambridge: Cambridge University Press, 2012)

——, 'Silver Production and the Money Supply in England and Wales, 1086–*c.* 1500', *Economic History Review*, 64 (2011), 114–31

——, 'The Volume of the English Currency, 1158–1470', *Economic History Review*, 54 (2001), 595–611

Ames, Edward, 'The Sterling Crisis of 1337–1339', *Journal of Economic History*, 25 (1965), 496–552

Ashtor, Eliyahu, *The Levant Trade in the Later Middle Ages* (Princeton: Princeton University Press, 1983)

——, *Les métaux précieux et la balance des payements du Proche-Orient à la basse époque* (Paris: S.E.V.P.E.N, 1971)

——, *A Social and Economic History of the Near East in the Middle Ages* (London: Collins, 1976)

Bailey, Mark, 'Peasant Welfare in England, 1290–1348', *Economic History Review*, 51 (1998), 223–51

Beveridge, William H., 'Wages in the Winchester Manors', *Economic History Review*, 7 (1936–7), 22–43

——, 'Westminster Wages in the Manorial Era', *Economic History Review*, 8 (1955), 18–35

Blanchard, Ian, 'Lothian and Beyond: The Economy of the "English Empire" of David I', in *Progress and Problems in Medieval England: Essays in Honour of Edward Miller*, ed. Richard Britnell and John Hatcher (Cambridge: Cambridge University Press, 1996), pp. 23–45

——, *Mining, Metallurgy and Minting in the Middle Ages*, II: *Afro-European Supremacy, 1125–1225 (African Gold Production and the First European Silver Production Long Cycle)*, 4 vols (Stuttgart: Franz Steiner Verlag, 2001)

——, *Mining, Metallurgy and Minting in the Middle Ages*, III: *Continuing Afro-European Supremacy, 1250–1450*, 4 vols (Stuttgart: Franz Steiner Verlag, 2005)

——, 'Population Change, Enclosure, and the Early Tudor Economy', *Economic History Review*, 23(1970), 427–45

Bolton, James L., *Money in the Medieval English Economy: 973–1489* (Manchester: Manchester University Press, 2012)

——, 'Was There a "Crisis of Credit" in Fifteenth-Century England?', *British Numismatic Journal*, 81 (2011), 146–64

Bovill, E. W., *The Golden Trade of the Moors*, 2nd edn (Oxford: Oxford University Press, 1968)

Braunstein, Philippe, 'Innovations in Mining and Metal Production in Europe in the Late Middle Ages', *Journal of European Economic History*, 12 (1983), 573–79

Bridbury, Anthony R., 'Before the Black Death', *Economic History Review*, 30 (1977), 393–410

——, 'The Black Death', *Economic History Review*, 26 (1973), 577–92

Briggs, Chris D., 'The Availability of Credit in the English Countryside, 1400–1480', *Agricultural History Review*, 56 (2008), 1–24

——, *Credit and Village Society in Fourteenth-Century England* (Oxford: Oxford University Press, 2009)

Campbell, Bruce M. S., 'Agricultural Progress in Medieval England: Some Evidence from Norfolk', *Economic History Review*, 2nd ser., 36 (1983), 26–46

——, 'Arable Productivity in Medieval England: Some Evidence from Norfolk', *Journal of Economic History*, 43 (1983), 379–404

——, *English Seigniorial Agriculture, 1250–1450*, Cambridge Studies in Historical Geography, 31 (Cambridge: Cambridge University Press, 2000)

——, 'Grain Yields on English Demesnes after the Black Death', in *Town and Countryside in the Age of the Black Death: Essays in Honour of John Hatcher*, ed. by Mark Bailey and Stephen Rigby, The Medieval Countryside, 12 (Turnhout: Brepols, 2012), pp. 121–74

——, 'Land, Labour, Livestock, and Productivity Trends in English Seignorial Agriculture, 1208–1450', in *Land, Labour and Livestock: Historical Studies in European Agricultural Productivity*, ed. by Bruce M. S. Campbell and Mark Overton (Manchester: Manchester University Press, 1991), pp. 144–82

——, 'Matching Supply to Demand: Crop Production and Disposal by English Demesnes in the Century of the Black Death', *Journal of Economic History*, 57 (1997), 827–58

——, 'Nature as Historical Protagonist: Environment and Society in Pre-Industrial England', *Economic History Review*, 63 (2010), 281–314

——, 'The Population of Early Tudor England: A Re-evaluation of the 1522 Muster Returns and the 1524 and 1525 Lay Subsidies', *Journal of Historical Geography*, 7 (1981), 145–54

——, 'Population Pressure, Inheritance, and the Land Market in a Fourteenth-Century Peasant Community', in *Land, Kinship and Life-Cycle*, ed. by Richard M. Smith (Cambridge: Cambridge University Press, 1984), pp. 87–134

Campbell, Bruce M. S., and Mark Overton, 'A New Perspective on Medieval and Early Modern Agriculture: Six Centuries of Norfolk Farming, *c.* 1250–*c.* 1850', *Past and Present*, 141 (1993), 38–105

Campbell, Bruce M. S., and others, *A Medieval Capital and its Grain Supply: Agrarian Production and Distribution in the London Region, c. 1300*, Historical Geography Research Series, 30 (London: Institute of British Geographers, 1993)

Cassell, Anthony, 'Boccaccio, Giovanni', in *Dictionary of the Middle Ages*, ed. Joseph Strayer and others, 13 vols (New York: Macmillan, 1983), II, 277–90

Cazelles, R., 'Quelques reflexions à propos des mutations monétaires de la monnaie royale française (1295–1360)', *Le Moyen Âge*, 72 (1966), 83–105 and 251–78

Challis, Christopher, 'Appendix 1: Mint Output, 1220–1985', in *A New History of the Royal Mint*, ed. by Christopher Challis (Cambridge: Cambridge University Press, 1992), pp. 673–98

Clark, Gregory, 'The Condition of the Working Class in England, 1209–2004', *Journal of Political Economy*, 113 (2005), 1307–40

——, 'Labour Productivity in English Agriculture, 1300–1860', in *Land, Labour and Livestock: Historical Studies in European Agricultural Productivity*, ed. by Bruce M. S. Campbell and Mark Overton (Manchester: Manchester University Press, 1991), pp. 211–35

——, 'The Long March of History: Farm Wages, Population, and Economic Growth: England, 1209–1869', *Economic History Review*, 60 (2007), 97–135

——, 'The Price History of English Agriculture, 1209–1914', *Research in Economic History*, 22 (2004), 125–81

——, 'Work, Wages and Living Conditions: Building Workers in England from Magna Carta to Tony Blair', in *L'Edilizia prima della rivoluzione industriale, secc.* XIII–XVIII, ed. by Simonetta Caviocochi, Atti delle 'Settimana di Studi' e altri convegni, 36, Istituto Internazionale di Storia Economica 'F. Datini' (Firenze: Le Monnier, 2005), pp. 889–932

Cornwall, Julian, 'English Population in the Early Sixteenth Century', *Economic History Review*, 23 (1970), 32–44

Davis, Ralph, *The Rise of the Atlantic Economies* (Ithaca: Cornell University Press, 1973)

Day, John, 'The Great Bullion Famine of the Fifteenth Century', *Past and Present*, 79 (1978), 1–54

——, 'The Question of Monetary Contraction in Late Medieval Europe', in *Nordisk Numismatisk Arsskrift: Nordic Numismatic Journal, 1981: Coinage and Monetary Circulation in the Baltic Area, c. 1350 – c. 1500*, ed. by Jørgen Steen Jensen (Copenhagen:

Nordisk Numismatisk Unions Medlemsblad, 1981), pp. 12–29; reprinted in John Day, *The Medieval Market Economy* (Oxford: Basil Blackwell, 1987), pp. 55–71

De Moor, Tine, and Jan Luiten Van Zanden, 'Girl Power: The European Marriage Pattern and Labour Markets in the North Sea Region in the Late Medieval and Early Modern Period', *Economic History Review*, 63 (2010), 1–33

De Roover, Raymond, *Money, Banking and Credit in Mediaeval Bruges: Italian Merchant-Bankers, Lombards, and Money Changers: A Study in the Origins of Banking* (Cambridge, MA: Mediaeval Academy of America, 1948)

——, 'The Organization of Trade', in *The Cambridge Economic History of Europe*, III: *Economic Organization and Policies in the Middle Ages*, ed. M. M. Postan and E. E. Rich (Cambridge: Cambridge University Press, 1963), pp. 42–118

Duby, Georges, *L'économie rurale et la vie des campagnes dans l'Occident Médiéval (France, Angleterre, Empire, IXe–XVe siècles): Essai de synthèse et perspectives de recherches*, 2 vols (Paris: Aubier, 1962)

Dyer, Christopher, *Lords and Peasants in a Changing Society: The Estates of the Bishopric of Worcester, 680–1540* (Cambridge: Cambridge University Press, 1980)

Endrei, Walter, 'La productivité et la technique dans l'industrie textile du XIIIe au XVIIe siècle', in *Produttività e tecnologia nei secoli XII–XVII*, ed. by Sara Mariotti, Atti delle 'Settimana di Studi' e altri convegni, 3, Istituto Internazionale di Storia Economica 'F. Datini' (Firenze: Le Monnier, 1981), pp. 253–62

Farmer, David L., 'Crop Yields, Prices and Wages in Medieval England', *Studies in Medieval and Renaissance History*, o.s., 6 (1983), 117–55

——, 'The *Famuli* in the Later Middle Ages', in *Progress and Problems in Medieval England: Essays in Honour of Edward Miller*, ed. by Richard Britnell and John Hatcher (Cambridge: Cambridge University Press, 1996), pp. 207–366

——, 'Prices and Wages [1000–1355]', in *The Agrarian History of England and Wales*, II: *1042–1350*, ed. by Herbert E. Hallam (Cambridge: Cambridge University Press, 1988), pp. 716–817

——, 'Prices and Wages [1350–1500]', in *The Agrarian History of England and Wales*, III: *1348–1500*, ed. by Edward Miller (Cambridge: Cambridge University Press, 1991), pp. 467–524

Feavearyear, Albert, *The Pound Sterling: A History of English Money*, rev. by E. V. Morgan, 2nd edn (Oxford: Clarendon Press, 1963)

Fischer, David Hackett, *The Great Wave: Price Revolutions and the Rhythm of History* (Oxford: Oxford University Press, 1996)

Foreman-Peck, James, 'The Western European Marriage Pattern and Economic Development', *Explorations in Economic History*, 48 (2011), 292–309

Girard, Albert, 'La guerre des monnaies', *Revue de synthèse*, 19 (1940–45), 83–101

Graus, F., 'La crise monétaire du XIVe siècles', *Revue belge de philologie et d'histoire*, 29 (1951), 445–54

Grunzweig, A., 'Les incidences internationales des mutations monétaires de Philippe le Bel', *Le Moyen Âge*, 59 (1953), 117–72

Hajnal, John, 'European Marriage Patterns in Perspective', in *Population in History: Essays in Historical Demography*, ed. by David V. Glass and D. E. C. Eversley (London: E. Arnold, 1965), pp. 101–46

Hallam, Henry E., 'Population Movements in England, 1086–1350', in *The Agrarian History of England and Wales*, II: *1042–1350*, ed. by Herbert E. Hallam (Cambridge: Cambridge University Press, 1988), pp. 508–93

Harvey, Barbara, 'Introduction: The "Crisis" of the Early Fourteenth Century', in *Before the Black Death: Studies in the 'Crisis' of the Early Fourteenth Century*, ed. by Bruce M. S. Campbell (Manchester: Manchester University Press, 1991), pp. 1–24

——, 'The Population Trend in England Between 1300 and 1348', *Transactions of the Royal Historical Society*, 5th ser., 16 (1966), 23–42

Hatcher, John, 'England in the Aftermath of the Black Death', *Past and Present*, 144 (1994), 3–35

——, 'The Great Slump of the Mid-Fifteenth Century,' in *Progress and Problems in Medieval England: Essays in Honour of Edward Miller*, ed. Richard Britnell and John Hatcher (Cambridge: Cambridge University Press, 1996), pp. 237–72

——, 'Mortality in the Fifteenth Century: Some New Evidence', *Economic History Review*, 39 (1986), 19–38

——, *Plague, Population, and the English Economy, 1348–1530* (London: MacMillan, 1977)

——, 'Unreal Wages: Long-Run Living Standards and the "Golden Age" of the Fifteenth Century', in *Commercial Activity, Markets and Entrepreneurs in the Middle Ages: Essays in Honour of Richard Britnell*, ed. by Ben Dodds and Christian D. Liddy (Woodbridge: Boydell and Brewer, 2011), pp. 1–24

Hatcher, John, A. J. Piper, and David Stone, 'Monastic Mortality: Durham Priory, 1395—1539', *Economic History Review*, 59 (2006), 667–87

Hatcher, John, and Mark Bailey, eds, *Modelling the Middle Ages: The History and Theory of England's Economic Development* (Oxford: Oxford University Press, 2001)

Herlihy, David, *Medieval and Renaissance Pistoia: The Social History of an Italian Town, 1200–1430* (New Haven: Yale University Press, 1967)

Hilton, Rodney H., *The Decline of Serfdom in Medieval England*, Studies in Economic History, 2nd rev. edn (London: MacMillan, 1983)

Hinde, Andrew, *England's Population: A History Since the Domesday Survey* (London: Hodder Arnold, 2003)

Jordan, William Chester, *The Great Famine: Northern Europe in the Early Fourteenth Century* (Princeton: Princeton University Press, 1996)

Kershaw, Ian, 'The Great Famine and Agrarian Crisis in England, 1315–1322', *Past and Present*, 59 (1973), 3–50

Kovacevic, D., 'Les mines d'or et d'argent en Serbie et en Bosnie médiévales', *Annales: Économies, Sociétés, Civilisations*, 15 (1960), 248–58

Lane, Frederic C., 'The First Infidelities of the Venetian Lire', in *The Medieval City*, ed. H. A. Miskimin, David Herlihy, and A. L. Udovitch (New Haven: Yale University Press, 1977), pp. 43–64

Langdon, John, *Mills in the Medieval Economy: England, 1300–1540* (Oxford: Oxford University Press, 2004)

——, 'Minimum Wages and Unemployment Rates in Medieval England: The Case of Old Woodstock, Oxfordshire, 1256–1357', in *Commercial Activity, Markets and Entrepreneurs in the Middle Ages: Essays in Honour of Richard Britnell*, ed. by Ben Dodds and Christian D. Liddy (Woodbridge: Boydell and Brewer, 2011), pp. 25–44

——, 'Waged Building Employment in Medieval England: Subsistence Safety Net or Demographic Trampoline?', in *Survival and Discord in Medieval Society: Essays in Honour of Christopher Dyer*, ed. by Richard Goddard, John Langdon, and Miriam Müller, The Medieval Countryside, 4 (Turnhout: Brepols, 2010), pp. 109–26

Lopez, Robert S., 'Hard Times and Investment in Culture', in *The Renaissance: Six Essays*, ed. by Wallace Ferguson, Metropolitan Museum of New York (New York: Harper and Row, 1962), pp. 29–52

Lopez, Robert S., Harry A. Miskimin, and A. L. Udovitch, 'England to Egypt, 1350–1500: Long Term Trends and Long Distance Trade', in *Studies in the Economic History of the Middle East: From the Rise of Islam to the Present Day*, ed. by M. A. Cook (Oxford: Oxford University Press, 1970), pp. 93–128

MacKay, Angus, *Money, Prices and Politics in Fifteenth-Century Castile* (London: Royal Historical Society, 1981)

Malthus, Robert Thomas, *An Essay on the Principles of Population*, 1st edn (Oxford: Oxford University Press, 1993)

——, *Principles of Political Economy: Considered with a View to their Practical Application*, 2nd edn (New York: A. M. Kelly, 1968)

Mate, Mavis, 'High Prices in Early Fourteenth-Century England: Causes and Consequences', *Economic History Review*, 28 (1975), 1–16

——, 'The Role of Gold Coinage in the English Economy, 1338–1400', *Numismatic Chronicle*, 7th ser., 18 (1978), 126–41

Mayhew, Nicholas J., 'From Regional to Central Minting, 1158–1464', in *A New History of the Royal Mint*, ed. by Christopher Challis (Cambridge: Cambridge University Press, 1992), pp. 83–178

——, 'Money and Prices in England from Henry II to Edward III', *Agricultural History Review*, 35 (1987), 121–32

——, 'Numismatic Evidence and Falling Prices in the Fourteenth Century', *Economic History Review*, 27 (1974), 1–15

——, 'Population, Money Supply, and the Velocity of Circulation in England, 1300–1700', *Economic History Review*, 48 (1995), 238–57

Miller, Edward, 'War, Taxation, and the English Economy in the Late Thirteenth and Early Fourteenth Centuries', in *War and Economic Development: Essays in Memory of David Joslin*, ed. by J. M. Winter (Cambridge: Cambridge University Press, 1975), pp. 11–32

Miller, Edward, and John Hatcher, *Medieval England: Rural Society and Economic Change, 1086–1348*, Social and Economic History of England (London: Longman, 1978)

——, *Medieval England: Towns, Commerce and Crafts, 1086–1348* (London: Longman, 1995)

Mills, F. C., *Introduction to Statistics* (New York: Henry Holt, 1956)

Miskimin, Harry A., *The Economy of Early Renaissance Europe, 1300–1460* (Cambridge: Cambridge University Press, 1975)

——, 'Monetary Movements and Market Structures: Forces for Contraction in 14th and 15th Century England', *Journal of Economic History*, 24 (1964), 470–90

——, 'Money and Money Movements in France and England at the End of the Middle Ages', in *Precious Metals in the Later Medieval and Early Modern Worlds*, ed. by John F. Richards (Durham: Carolina Academic Press, 1983), pp. 79–96

Mueller, Reinhold, '"Chome l'ucciello di passegio": La demande saisonnière des espèces et le marché des changes à Venise au Moyen Âge', in *Études d'histoire monétaire, XIIe–XIXe siècles*, ed. by John Day (Lille: Presses universitaires de Lille, 1984), pp. 195–220

Munro, John H., 'Before and After the Black Death: Money, Prices, and Wages in Fourteenth-Century England', in *New Approaches to the History of Late Medieval and Early Modern Europe: Selected Proceedings of Two International Conferences at the Royal Danish Academy of Sciences and Letters in Copenhagen in 1997 and 1999*, ed. by Troels Dahlerup and Per Ingesman (Copenhagen: Royal Danish Academy of Sciences and Letters, 2009), pp. 335–64

——, 'Builders' Wages in Southern England and the Southern Low Countries, 1346–1500: A Comparative Study of Trends in and Levels of Real Incomes', in *L'Edilizia prima della rivoluzione industriale, secc. XIII–XVIII*, ed. by Simonetta Caviocdébchi, Atti delle 'Settimana di Studi' e altri convegni, 36, Istituto Internazionale di Storia Economica 'F. Datini' (Firenze: Le Monnier, 2005), pp. 1013–76

——, 'Bullion Flows and Monetary Contraction in Late-Medieval England and the Low Countries', in *Precious Metals in the Later Medieval and Early Modern Worlds*, ed. by John F. Richards (Durham: Carolina Academic Press, 1983), pp. 97–158

——, *Bullion Flows and Monetary Policies in England and the Low Countries, 1350–1500* (Aldershot: Variorum Ashgate, 1992)

——, 'Bullionism and the Bill of Exchange in England, 1272–1663: A Study in Monetary Management and Popular Prejudice', in *The Dawn of Modern Banking*, ed. by Center for Medieval and Renaissance Studies, UCLA (New Haven: Yale University Press, 1979), pp. 169–239

——, 'The Central European Mining Boom, Mint Outputs, and Prices in the Low Countries and England, 1450–1550', in *Money, Coins, and Commerce: Essays in the Monetary History of Asia and Europe (From Antiquity to Modern Times)*, ed. by Eddy H. G. Van Cauwenberghe (Leuven: Leuven University Press, 1991), pp. 119–83

——, 'Deflation and the Petty Coinage Problem in the Late-Medieval Economy: The Case of Flanders, 1334–1484', *Explorations in Economic History*, 25 (1988), 387–423

——, 'Economic Depression and the Arts in the Fifteenth-Century Low Countries', *Renaissance and Reformation*, 19 (1983), 235–50

——, 'EH.Net Review of Jim Bolton, *Money in the Medieval Economy*', <http://eh.net/book_reviews/money-medieval-english-economy-973–1489> [accessed 17 June 2013]

——, 'English "Backwardness" and Financial Innovations in Commerce with the Low Countries, 14th to 16th Centuries', in *International Trade in the Low Countries (14th–16th Centuries): Merchants, Organisation, Infrastructure*, ed. by Peter Stabel, Bruno Blondé, and Anke Greve, Studies in Urban, Social, Economic, and Political History of the Medieval and Early Modern Low Countries, 10 (Leuven-Apeldoorn: Garant, 2000), pp. 105–67

——, 'The "Industrial Crisis" of the English Textile Towns, 1290–1330', in *Thirteenth-Century England*, VII, ed. by Michael Prestwich, Richard Britnell, and Robin Frame (Woodbridge: Boydell Academic Press, 1999), pp. 103–41

——, 'Industrial Energy from Water-Mills in the European Economy, 5th to 18th Centuries: The Limitations of Power', in *Economia ed energia, secoli XIII–XVIII*, ed. by Simonetta Cavaciocchi, Atti delle 'Settimane di Studi' e altrie Convegni, Istituto Internazionale di Storia Economica, 'Francesco Datini', 34 (Firenze: Le Monnier, 2003), pp. 223–69

——, 'Industrial Transformations in the North-West European Textile Trades, *c.* 1290-*c.* 1340: Economic Progress or Economic Crisis?', in *Before the Black Death: Studies in the 'Crisis' of the Early Fourteenth Century*, ed. by Bruce M. S. Campbell (Manchester: Manchester University Press, 1991), pp. 110–48

——, 'The International Law Merchant and the Evolution of Negotiable Credit in Late-Medieval England and the Low Countries', in *Banchi pubblici, banchi privati e monti di pietà nell'Europa preindustriale: amministrazione, tecniche operative e ruoli economici*, ed. by Dino Puncuh, Atti della Società Ligure di Storia Patria, Nouva Serie, 31 (Genoa: Società Ligure di Storia Patria, 1991), pp. 49–80; reprinted in John Munro, *Textiles, Towns, and Trade: Essays in the Economic History of Late-Medieval England and the Low Countries*, Variorum Collected Studies series, 442 (Aldershot: Ashgate Publishing, 1994)

——, 'The Late-Medieval Decline of English Demesne Agriculture: Demographic, Monetary, and Political-Fiscal Factors', in *Town and Countryside in the Age of the Black Death: Essays in Honour of John Hatcher*, ed. by Mark Bailey and Stephen Rigby, The Medieval Countryside, 12 (Turnhout: Brepols, 2012), pp. 299–348

——, 'The Low Countries' Export Trade in Textiles with the Mediterranean Basin, 1200–1600: A Cost-Benefit Analysis of Comparative Advantages in Overland and Maritime Trade Routes', *International Journal of Maritime History*, 11 (1999), 1–30

——, 'The Medieval Origins of the Financial Revolution: Usury, *Rentes*, and Negotiability', *International History Review*, 25 (2003), 505–62

——, 'Medieval Woollens: Textiles, Textile Technology, and Industrial Organisation, *c.* 800–1500', in *The Cambridge History of Western Textiles*, ed. by David Jenkins, 2 vols (Cambridge: Cambridge University Press, 2003), I, 181–227

——, 'Mint Policies, Ratios, and Outputs in England and the Low Countries, 1335–1420: Some Reflections on New Data', *Numismatic Chronicle*, 141 (1981), 71–116

——, 'The Monetary Origins of the "Price Revolution": South German Silver Mining, Merchant-Banking, and Venetian Commerce, 1470–1540', in *Global Connections and Monetary History, 1470–1800*, ed. by Dennis Flynn, Arturo Giráldez, and Richard von Glahn (Aldershot: Ashgate Publishing, 2003), pp. 1–34

——, 'Money, Prices, Wages, and "Profit Inflation" in Spain, the Southern Netherlands, and England during the Price Revolution era, *c.* 1520 – *c.* 1650', *História e Economia: Revista Interdisciplinar*, 4 (2008), 13–71

——, 'The "New Institutional Economics" and the Changing Fortunes of Fairs in Medieval and Early Modern Europe: The Textile Trades, Warfare, and Transaction Costs', *Vierteljahrschrift für Sozial- und Wirtschaftsgeschichte*, 88 (2001), 1–47

——, 'The Origins of the English "New Draperies": The Resurrection of an Old Flemish Industry, 1270–1570,' in *The New Draperies in the Low Countries and England, 1300–1800*, ed. by Negley B. Harte, Pasold Studies in Textile History, 10 (Oxford: Oxford University Press, 1997), pp. 35–127

——, 'The Price Revolution', in *The New Palgrave Dictionary of Economics*, ed. by Steven N. Durlauf and Lawrence E. Blume, 2nd edn, 8 vols (London: Palgrave Macmillan, 2008), VI, 631–34

——, 'Review of David Hackett Fischer, *The Great Wave: Price Revolutions and the Rhythm of History* (Oxford, 1996)', in *EH.Net Review*, <http://eh.net/book_reviews/great-wave-price-revolutions-and-rhythm-history> [accessed 24 February 1999]

——, 'South German Silver, European Textiles, and Venetian Trade with the Levant and Ottoman Empire, *c.* 1370 to *c.* 1720: A Non-Mercantilist Approach to the Balance of Payments Problem', in *Relazioni economiche tra Europa e mondo islamico, secoli XIII–XVIII / Europe's Economic Relations with the Islamic World, 13th–18th Centuries*, ed. by Simonetta Cavaciocchi, Atti delle 'Settimana di Studi' e altri convegni, 38 (Firenze: Le Monnier, 2007), pp. 907–62

——, 'The Symbiosis of Towns and Textiles: Urban Institutions and the Changing Fortunes of Cloth Manufacturing in the Low Countries and England, 1270–1570', *Journal of Early Modern History: Contacts, Comparisons, Contrasts*, 3 (1999), 1–74

——, 'The Technology and Economics of Coinage Debasements in Medieval and Early Modern Europe: With Special Reference to the Low Countries and England', in *Money in the Pre-Industrial World: Bullion, Debasements and Coin Substitutes*, ed. by John Munro, Financial History Series, 20 (London: Pickering & Chatto, 2012), pp. 15–32, 185–89

——, 'Usury, Calvinism and Credit in Protestant England: From the Sixteenth Century to the Industrial Revolution', in *Religione e istituzioni religiose nell'economia europea, 1000–1800 / Religion and Religious Institutions in the European Economy, 1000–1800*, ed. by Francesco Ammannati, Fondazione Istituto Internazionale di Storia Economica F. Datini, Prato, Serie II: Atti delle Settimane de Studi e altri Convegni, 43 (Firenze: Firenze University Press, 2012), pp. 155–84

——, 'Wage-Stickiness, Monetary Changes, and Real Incomes in Late-Medieval England and the Low Countries, 1300–1500: Did Money Matter?', *Research in Economic History*, 21 (2003), 185–297

——, *Wool, Cloth, and Gold: The Struggle for Bullion in Anglo-Burgundian Trade, c. 1340–1478* (Brussels: Editions de l'Université de Bruxelles, 1973)

Nef, John U., 'Mining and Metallurgy in Medieval Civilization', in *Cambridge Economic History of Europe*, II: *Trade and Industry in the Middle Ages*, ed. by M. M. Postan and Edward Miller, rev. edn. (Cambridge: Cambridge University Press, 1987), pp. 696–734

——, 'Silver Production in Central Europe, 1450–1618', *Journal of Political Economy*, 49 (1941), 575–91

Newfield, Timothy P., 'A Cattle Panzootic in Early Fourteenth-Century Europe', *British Agricultural History Review*, 57.2 (2009), 155–90

Nightingale, Pamela, 'A Crisis of Credit in the Fifteenth Century — Or of Historical Interpretation?', *British Numismatic Journal*, 83 (2013), 148–63

——, 'England and the European Depression of the Mid-Fifteenth Century', *Journal of European Economic History*, 26.3 (1997), 631–56

——, 'Gold, Credit, and Mortality: Distinguishing Deflationary Pressures on the Late Medieval English Economy', *Economic History Review*, 63.4 (2010), 1081–1104

——, 'The Growth of London in the Medieval English Economy', in *Progress and Problems in Medieval England: Essays in Honour of Edward Miller*, ed. Richard Britnell and John Hatcher (Cambridge: Cambridge University Press, 1996), pp. 89–106

——, 'Monetary Contraction and Mercantile Credit in Later Medieval England', *Economic History Review*, 43.4 (1990), 560–75

——, 'Money and Credit in the Economy of Late Medieval England', in *Medieval Money Matters*, ed. by Diana Wood (Oxford: Oxbow Books, 2004), pp. 51–71

——, 'Some New Evidence of Crises and Trends of Mortality in Late Medieval England', *Past and Present*, 187 (2005), 33–68

Patterson, C. C., 'Silver Stocks and Losses in Ancient and Medieval Times', *Economic History Review*, 25.2 (1972), 205–35

Paulinyi, Oszkar, 'The Crown Monopoly of the Refining Metallurgy of Precious Metals and the Technology of the Cameral Refineries in Hungary and Transylvania, 1325–1700, with Data and Output', in *Precious Metals in the Age of Expansion*, ed. by Hermann Kellenbenz (Stuttgart: Klett-Cotta, 1981), pp. 27–39

Penn, Simon, and Christopher Dyer, 'Wages and Earnings in Late Medieval England: Evidence from the Enforcement of the Labour Laws', *Economic History Review*, 43.3 (1990), 356–76

Phelps Brown, E. Henry, and Sheila V. Hopkins, 'Seven Centuries of Building Wages', *Economica*, 22.87 (1955), 195–206; reprinted in Henry Phelps Brown and Sheila Hopkins, *A Perspective of Wages and Prices* (London: Methuen, 1981), pp. 1–12

——, 'Seven Centuries of the Prices of Consumables, Compared with Builders' Wage Rates', *Economica*, 23.92 (1956), 296–314; reprinted in Henry Phelps Brown and Sheila Hopkins, *A Perspective of Wages and Prices* (London: Methuen, 1981), pp. 13–39

Poos, Lawrence, 'The Historical Demography of Northern Europe, 1400–1650', in *New Approaches to the History of Late Medieval and Early Modern Europe: Selected Proceedings of Two International Conferences at The Royal Danish Academy of Sciences and Letters in Copenhagen in 1997 and 1999*, ed. by Troels Dahlerup and Per Ingesman (Copenhagen: Royal Danish Academy of Sciences and Letters, 2009), pp. 365–96

——, 'The Rural Population of Essex in the Later Middle Ages', *Economic History Review*, 38.4 (1985), 515–30

——, *A Rural Society after the Black Death: Essex 1350–1525* (Cambridge: Cambridge University Press, 1991)

Postan, Michael M., 'Credit in Medieval Trade', *Economic History Review*, 1 (1928), 234–61; reprinted in Michael Postan, *Medieval Trade and Finance* (Cambridge: Cambridge University Press, 1973), pp. 1–27

——, 'The Economic Foundations of Medieval Society', in Michael Postan, *Essays on Medieval Agriculture and General Problems of the Medieval Economy* (Cambridge: Cambridge University Press, 1973), pp. 3–27, a translation of 'Die wirtschaftlichen Grundlagen der mittelalterlichen Gesellschaft', *Jahrbücher für Nationalökonomie*, 161 (1951), 180–284 (both texts are revised versions of his contribution in Carlo Cipolla, Jan Dhondt, Michael Postan, and Philippe Wolff, 'Rapports collectif', in *IXe Congrès international des sciences historiques: Congrès international des sciences historiques. Rapports, colloque de Paris, 28 août – 3 septembre 1950* (Paris: Colin, 1950), pp. 225–41)

——, 'Medieval Agarian Society in its Prime: England', in *The Cambridge Economic History of Europe*, I: *The Agrarian Life of the Middle Ages*, ed. by Michael M. Postan, 2nd edn (Cambridge: Cambridge University Press, 1966), pp. 548–632

——, *The Medieval Economy and Society: An Economic History of Britain 1100–1500* (London: Weidenfeld and Nicolson, 1972)

——, '"Note" in Response to W. C. Robinson, "Money, Population, and Economic Change in Late Medieval Europe"', *Economic History Review*, 12.1 (1959), 63–76, 77–82

——, 'Private Financial Instruments in Medieval England', *Vierteljahrschrift für Sozial- und Wirtschaftsgeschichte*, 22.1 (1930), 26–75; reprinted in Michael Postan, *Medieval Trade and Finance* (Cambridge: Cambridge University Press, 1973), pp. 28–64

——, 'Some Economic Evidence of Declining Population in the Later Middle Ages,' *Economic History Review*, 2.1(1950), 130–67; reprinted as 'Some Agrarian Evidence of Declining Population in the Later Middle Ages', in Michael Postan, *Essays on Medieval Agriculture and General Problems of the Medieval Economy* (Cambridge: Cambridge University Press, 1973), pp. 186–213

——, 'The Trade of Medieval Europe: The North', in *Cambridge Economic History of Europe*, II: *Trade and Industry in the Middle Ages*, ed. by Michael Postan and E. E. Rich (Cambridge: Cambridge University Press, 1952), pp. 119–256; reprinted in *Cambridge Economic History of Europe*, II: *Trade and Industry in the Middle Ages*, ed. by M. M. Postan and Edward Miller, rev. edn (Cambridge: Cambridge University Press, 1987), pp. 168–305, and in Michael Postan, *Medieval Trade and Finance* (Cambridge: Cambridge University Press, 1973), pp. 92–31 (with bibliography)

Postan, Michael M., and John Hatcher, 'Population and Class Relations in Feudal Society', *Past and Present*, 78 (1978), 24–37; reprinted in *The Brenner Debate: Agrarian Class Structure and Economic Development in Pre-Industrial Europe*, ed. by Trevor H. Aston and C. H. E. Philpin (Cambridge: Cambridge University Press, 1985), pp. 64–78

Postan, Michael M., and Jan Zbigniew Titow, 'Heriots and Prices on Winchester Manors', *Economic History Review*, 2nd ser., 11 (1959), 383–411; reprinted in Michael M. Postan, *Essays on Medieval Agriculture and General Problems of the Medieval Economy* (Cambridge: Cambridge University Press, 1973), pp. 150–85

Prestwich, Michael, 'Currency and the Economy of Early Fourteenth-Century England', in *Edwardian Monetary Affairs, 1279–1344*, ed. by Nicholas Mayhew, BAR International Series, 36 (Oxford: British Archeological Reports, 1977), pp. 45–58

Raftis, J. Ambrose, 'Peasants and the Collapse of the Manorial Economy on Some Ramsey Abbey Estates', in *Progress and Problems in Medieval England: Essays in Honour of Edward Miller*, ed. by Richard Britnell and John Hatcher (Cambridge: Cambridge University Press, 1996), pp. 191–206

——, *Tenure and Mobility: Studies in the Social History of the Medieval English Village* (Toronto: Pontifical Institute of Mediaeval Studies, 1964)

Reynolds, Terry, *Stronger Than a Hundred Men: A History of the Vertical Water Wheel*, Johns Hopkins Studies in the History of Technology, n.s. 7 (Baltimore: Johns Hopkins University Press, 1983)

Ricardo, David, *Principles of Political Economy and Taxation*, with an introduction by Donald Wench (London: Dent, 1982)

Rigby, Stephen H., *English Society in the Later Middle Ages: Class, Status, Gender* (London: Macmillan, 1995)

——, 'Urban Population in Late Medieval England: The Evidence of the Lay Subsidies', *Economic History Review*, 63.2 (2010), 393–417

Russell, Josiah Cox, *British Medieval Population* (Albuquerque: University of New Mexico Press, 1948)

——, 'The Preplague Population of England', *Journal of British Studies*, 5.2 (1966), 1–21

Schwartz, Anna Jacobson, 'Review of Frank Spooner, *International Economy and Monetary Movements in France, 1493–1725* (Cambridge, Mass.: Harvard University Press, 1972)', *Journal of European Economic History*, 3.1 (1974), 252–55

Slavin, Philip, 'The Fifth Rider of the Apocalypse: The Great Cattle Plague in England and Wales and its Economic Consequences, 1319–1350', in *Le Interazioni fra economia e ambiente biologico nell'Europa preindustrielle seccoli XIII–XVIII*, ed. by Simonetta Cavaciocchi, Atti delle 'Settimana di Studi' e altri convegni, 40, Istituto Internazionale di Storia Economica 'F. Datini' (Firenze: Firenze University Press, 2010), pp. 165–79

——, 'The Great Bovine Pestilence and its Economic and Environmental Consequences in England and Wales, 1318–50', *Economic History Review*, 65.4 (2012), 1239–66

Slicher-Van Bath, B. H., *De agrarische geschiedenis van West Europa, 500–1850*, trans. by Olive Ordish as *The Agrarian History of Western Europe, A.D. 500–1850* (London: E. Arnold, 1963)

Smith, Richard M., 'Demographic Developments in Rural England, 1300–48', in *Before the Black Death: Studies in the 'Crisis' of the Early Fourteenth Century*, ed. by Bruce M. S. Campbell (Manchester: Manchester University Press, 1991), pp. 25–77

Spooner, Frank, *International Economy and Monetary Movements in France, 1493–1725* (Cambridge, MA: Harvard University Press, 1972)

Spufford, Peter, 'The Debasement of the Coinage and its Effects on Exchange Rates and the Economy in England in the 1540s, and in the Burgundian-Habsburg Netherlands in the 1480s', in *Money in the Pre-Industrial World: Bullion, Debasements and Coin Substitutes*, ed. by John Munro, Financial History Series, 20 (London: Pickering & Chatto, 2012), pp. 68–85

——, *Money and its Use in Medieval Europe* (Cambridge: Cambridge University Press, 1988)

Stone, David, *Decision Making in Medieval Agriculture* (Oxford: Oxford University Press, 2005)

——, 'Medieval Farm Management and Technological Mentalities: Hinderclay before the Black Death', *Economic History Review*, 54 (2001), 612–38

——, 'The Productivity and Management of Sheep in Late Medieval England', *Agricultural History Review*, 51 (2003), 1–22

——, 'The Productivity of Hired and Customary Labour: Evidence from Wisbech Barton in the Fourteenth Century', *Economic History Review*, 50 (1997), 640–56

Stuard, Susan M., *Gilding the Market: Luxury and Fashion in Fourteenth-Century Italy* (Philadelphia: University of Pennsylvania Press, 2006)

——, 'Gravitas and Consumption', in *Conflicted Identities and Multiple Masculinities: Men in the Medieval West*, ed. by Jacqueline Murray, Garland Medieval Casebooks, 25 (New York: Garland, 1999), pp. 215–42

Van der Wee, Herman, 'European Banking in the Middle Ages and Early Modern Period (476–1789)', in *A History of European Banking*, ed. by Herman Van der Wee and G. Kurgan-Van Hentenrijk, 2nd edn (Antwerp: Mercator Fonds, 2000), pp. 71–266

——, *Growth of the Antwerp Market and the European Economy, 14th–16th Centuries*, 3 vols (The Hague: Nijhoff, 1963)

——, 'Monetary, Credit, and Banking Systems', in *Cambridge Economic History of Europe*, v: *The Economic Organization of Early Modern Europe*, ed. by E. E. Rich and C. H. Wilson (Cambridge: Cambridge University Press, 1977), pp. 290–392

Westermann, Ekkehard, 'Die Bedeutung des Thüringer Saigerhandels für den mitteleuropäischen Handel an der Wende vom 15. zum 16. Jahrhundert', *Jahrbuch für die Geschichte Mittel- und Ostdeutschlands*, 21 (1972), 68–92

——, 'Zur Silber- und Kupferproduktion Mitteleuropas vom 15. bis zum frühen 17. Jahrhundert: über Bedeutung und Rangfolge der Reviere von Schwaz, Mansfeld und Neusohl', *Der Anschnitt: Zeitschrift für Kunst und Kultur im Bergbau*, 38 (1986), 187–211

Wrigley, Edward Anthony, R. S. Davies, J. E. Oeppen, and R. S. Schofield, *English Population History from Family Reconstitution*, Cambridge Studies in Population, Economy and Society in Past Time, 32 (Cambridge: Cambridge University Press, 1997)

The Family or the Farm: A Sophie's Choice? The Late Medieval Crisis in Flanders

Erik Thoen and Tim Soens

Flanders as a Test Case of the Malthusian Explanation for the Crisis of the Late Middle Ages

The county of Flanders provides an interesting test case with which to verify the neo-Malthusian Duby-Postan thesis about the so-called late medieval crisis. The reason is that, on the eve of this period, this county was one of the most densely populated areas of Europe. Malthusian theory would therefore lead us to expect a bottleneck between food supply and demand, creating population losses and other crises. Yet few historians believe that Flanders as a whole experienced a profound crisis. Even the Black Death could not disrupt the economy. A plausible and consistent explanation of the gap between theory and history has never been attempted. Did Malthusian checks fail to materialize because of the area's local characteristics? Or does the Flemish experience deny the applicability of the Malthusian model? For a long time Flemish historians could only speculate about these questions. We will show that historians have underestimated the dimensions of crisis in parts of Flanders. Our results demonstrate the need to get past older generalizations in order to formulate better explanations. There was a crisis in Flanders, a crisis that must be explained within the structure of the larger medieval rural economy.

Erik Thoen (erik.thoen@UGent.be) is professor of rural and environmental history and chairman of the History Department of Ghent University.

Tim Soens (tim.soens@uantwerpen.be) is associate professor of medieval and environmental history at the University of Antwerp.

Crisis in the Later Middle Ages: Beyond the Postan-Duby Paradigm, ed. by John Drendel, TMC 13 (Turnhout: Brepols, 2015) 195–224 BREPOLS PUBLISHERS 10.1484/M.TMC.5.103788

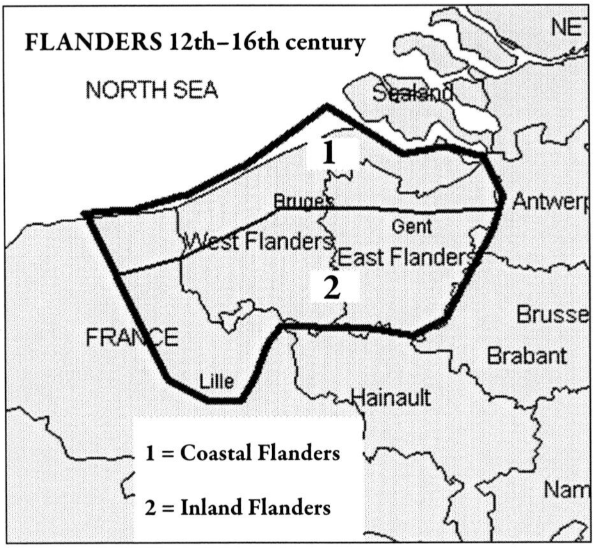

Map 7.1.
The Former County of Flanders on a Current Map.

Although Flanders is not large, within it different regions experienced the classical elements of crisis in different ways, so a regional explanation is necessary. We will explain how regions of Flanders differed and why distinct areas grew and declined in varied ways. This diversity requires a definition of local economic and social structures, a theoretical framework we call 'social agro-systemic' areas.

The Regional 'Social Agro-Systemic' Approach

We define a 'social agro-system' as a system of rural production based upon region-specific social relations involved in the economic reproduction of a given geographical area. Social agro-systems in this particular sense were not stable and underwent structural changes. Social agro-systems consisted of many qualifying and mutually influencing factors. They were determined by the different social relations and structures of local society, such as the soil and the environment, the social relations influenced by property rights, property relations, and power structure, labour relations and income policies (and possibilities) of peasants, agricultural techniques, and the relations with other agro-systemic areas. In the later Middle Ages, possibilities for economic growth as well as vulnerabilities to economic decline resulted from an interplay among all these elements; differences in their features reflect regional differences in social agro-systems.[1]

[1] The theoretical framework of agro-systems is developed in Thoen, 'Social Agro-systems as an Economic Concept'. This text was last revised in 2010.

Further on, we will show that the effects of the crisis were different in two regions: sandy inland Flanders and the coastal area, two areas which were evolving towards different social agro-systems during the Middle Ages (see Map 7.1). However, before trying to link the economic crisis of the later Middle Ages in Flanders with the differentiating features of these regional agro-systems, we need to describe the regional impact of the crisis phenomena in these areas.

The Late Medieval Crisis in Flanders: Data and Regional Difference

Direct demographic information is very poor for medieval Flanders. Series of demographic parameters such as hearth censuses are missing.[2] Most data are indirect, based on mortality censuses, sources about family composition, archaeological data, and so on. Within the limited context of this paper, we cannot elaborate on demography, but it is nevertheless clear that the number of inhabitants declined in the late Middle Ages in both coastal and inland Flanders.

It is likely that a demographic peak in inland Flanders came at the end of the thirteenth century. Nevertheless, most signs of demographic decline manifest themselves later, between about 1370 and 1410, as the result of high mortality rates.[3] The influence of the mid-fourteenth-century shocks of the Black Death was thus not immediately apparent; on the other hand, real demographic and economic recovery came quite late, after the civil war against Maximilian of Austria ended in 1492.[4]

As far as we know from research, the demographic decline did not bring about either abandoned fields or the disappearance of settlements. If we look at the size of landholdings, only a limited process of concentration took place. As Figure 7.1 shows, the majority of very small holdings, created in the twelfth and thirteenth centuries, survived the crisis. Often some of the smaller holdings even became smaller since part of the available land was integrated within newly created estates owned by townspeople who emulated the clergy and nobility.

[2] Thoen, 'Historical Demography'.

[3] Thoen, 'Historical Demography', pp. 577–80.

[4] Due to this late recovery and the relative light effects, Gérard Sivéry labeled the crisis in the Southern Netherlands 'the Burgundian crisis model': Sivéry, *Structures agraires*.

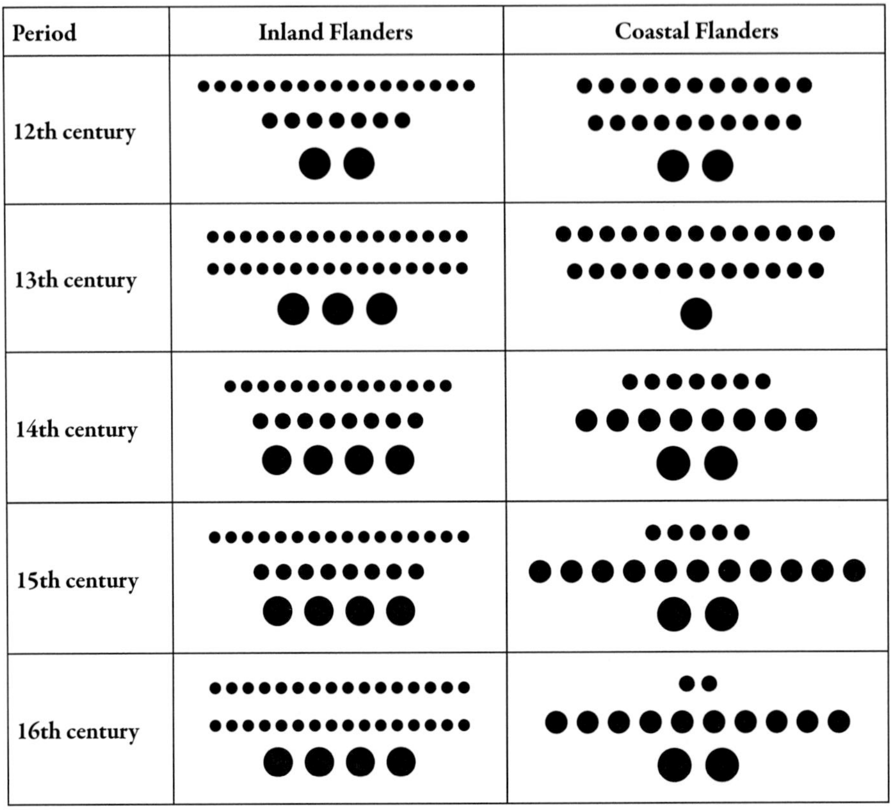

Figure 7.1. Diagram showing the evolution of the size of the holdings in both inland and coastal Flanders (● represents the size and relative number of the holdings). Of course, the diagram is partly based on conjectures and can probably still be refined in the future. See note 5.

Production did not change in any fundamental way as a result of this decline; Flanders retained a fundamentally mixed-farming economy, focused on the production of cereals, combined with significant production for the market.[5]

In coastal Flanders, signs of crisis emerge at the end of the thirteenth century. Here, structural changes were occurring since the thirteenth century. It appears

[5] Data for Inland Flanders in Thoen, *Landbouwekonomie en bevolking in Vlaanderen*, II, 845–77, and Scholliers, *De Conjunctuur van een Domein*; Meyhuys and Daelemans, *De oudste domeinrekeningen van Herzele 1386–1394*; Van Maelzake, 'De financieel-economische politiek'. For Coastal Flanders, see Verstockt, 'Conjunctuurstudie van een domein in de late middeleeuwen'. The results of this study about the evolution of the size of the holdings are published in Soens and Thoen, 'The Origin of Leaseholding'. Other unpublished data are used as well.

that the smaller holdings gradually disappeared during the later Middle Ages. In some areas this tendency accelerated during the later fourteenth century, near Oostburg, for example, an area which is well documented.[6] Here many farmsteads went bankrupt and disappeared, their land absorbed into larger holdings. Many larger settlements and villages with churches fell victim to storm surges; some resurrected, others never recovered.[7] The majority of farms became larger mid-sized concerns. More than before, they turned to breeding cattle, a tendency reflected in growing consumption of dairy products and meat in this area.[8] Nevertheless, grain production also remained important. The end of the crisis is difficult to detect: it seems that the evolution which had begun before the late Middle Ages continued well into the sixteenth century.[9] The process of concentration and demographic regression can be traced in the written sources which mention many 'lost villages' as well as 'lost farms'. Archaeology and aerial photography have also uncovered numerous *Wüstungen*, and recent research provides much new evidence of desertion of habitat.

We have been able to trace prices and wages back much earlier in time than the series known until now. They allow us to measure the influence of the crisis much more clearly on a local basis.[10] In our opinion, wages of unskilled workers give particularly useful indications about the changes in the supply of labour.[11] In Figure 7.2 we compare the wages, expressed in values of wheat, of unskilled labourers and skilled carpenters working in both areas. The results are eloquent. Although data are scarcer for inland Flanders, they show that around 1300, wages in the coastal area were lower than in inland Flanders. In the course of

[6] St Peters Abbey of Ghent and the hospital of St John in Bruges had numerous estates in this area. Also the water board called *Oude Yevene*, north of Oostburg, left abundant cadastral archives, records analysed by Vanslembrouck, Lehouck, and Thoen, 'Past Landscapes and Present-day Techniques'.

[7] The North Sea engulfed a large part of the territory of Flanders near the coast in the fourteenth to fifteenth centuries. Kuipers, *Sluimerend in slik* provides an overview of the actual state of research about lost villages in this area.

[8] Dehaeck, 'Voedselconsumptie in het Brugse Sint-Janshospitaal'.

[9] The concentration process continued in the seventeenth century: Thoen, 'De twee gezichten van de Vlaamse landbouw'.

[10] For a long time, wages and prices for Flanders were only available from the second half of the fourteenth century, but data for the earlier period can be now be found in Thoen, *Landbouwekonomie en bevolking in Vlaanderen*. Newer unpublished data for the coastal area in Vandenborre, 'Prijzen, lonen en levensstandaard'.

[11] Wages are also influenced by other elements, as we will see below.

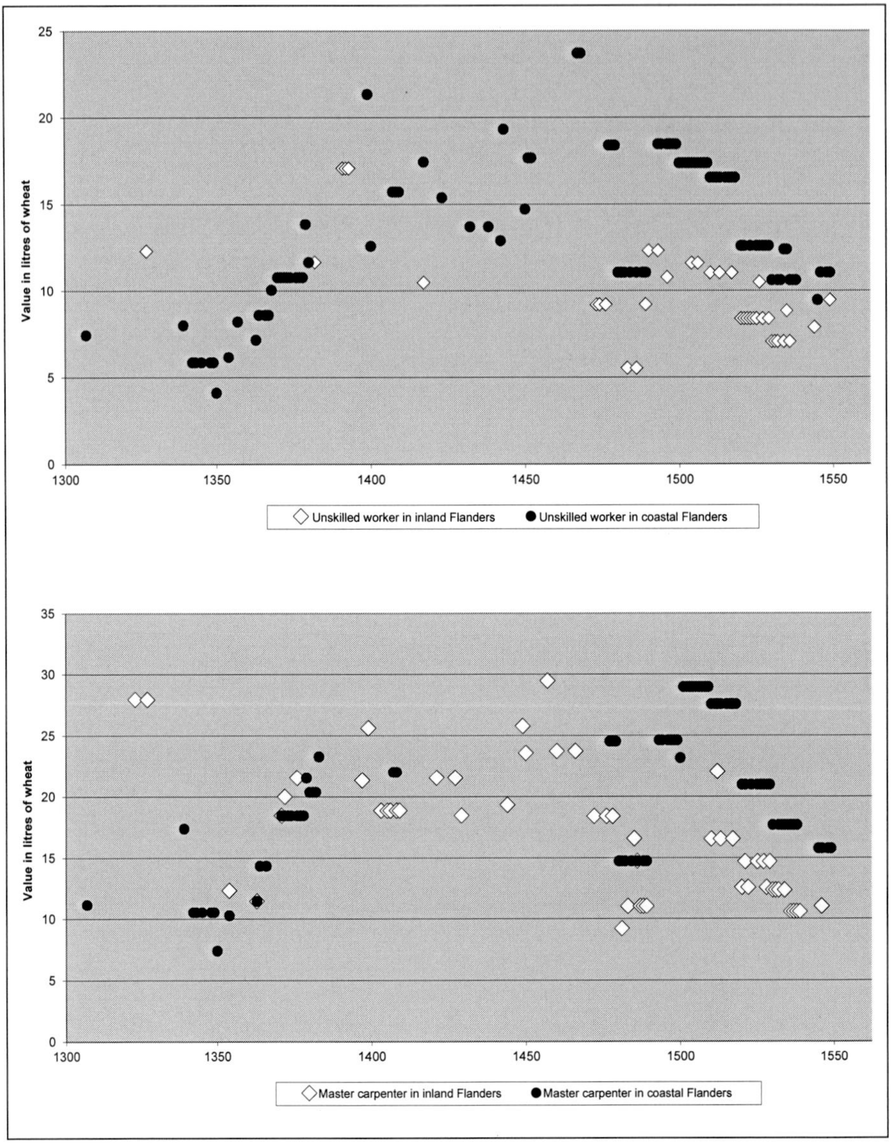

Figure 7.2. Value of wages in rural Flanders (in litres of wheat).

the fourteenth century regional differences narrowed: workers in inland and coastal Flanders seemed to have earned about the same daily wage. This suggests that wages rose more in the coastal area than in inland Flanders. In comparison with the period around 1300, wages of unskilled labourers near the littoral more than doubled by 1400. No increase of that magnitude occurred in inland Flanders, where wages stagnated. The differences between both areas became even more pronounced in the course of the fifteenth and sixteenth centuries: in the fifteenth century real wages in inland Flanders were between 20 and 40 per cent cheaper than along the coast. This striking difference is partly due to the fact that the labour supply became tighter in coastal Flanders than in inland Flanders. This evidence of the unequal impact of the later medieval crises begs for an explanation.

Some historians categorically reject the evidence for a price scissors in the southern Netherlands on the whole, when discussing prices of cereals and industrial products.[12] Nevertheless, it is clear that if we start our price series around 1300, industrial products show more upward movement than commodities such as cereals in the later Middle Ages.[13] Moreover, new data show that a relative decline of grain prices had already begun in the 1270s.[14]

Land leases provided another classic index of economic development. In Figure 7.3 we compared leases of parcels in inland and coastal Flanders. The cost of leases was heavy in both areas around the beginning of the fifteenth century. Although for inland Flanders, this graph does not cover the period before 1430, it shows that, during course of the fifteenth century, a divergent movement widened with the upward pressure on leasing costs higher in inland Flanders than in the coastal area.[15] Although we cannot explore in the context of this article the full dimension of this split, we can dispose of data which suggest that this divergent evolution started much earlier than the figures show. Indeed, around 1270–1300, leasing prices in the coastal area were already much higher than in inland Flanders. Moreover, the scissors between prices and wages opened with different intensity depending upon the area.

[12] Genicot, *La crise agricole*. Price scissors are unequal long-term evolutions of prices such as cereals, meat, industrial products, and wages. In this respect, the works of Wilhelm Abel are still valuable.

[13] Thoen, *Landbouwekonomie en bevolking in Vlaanderen*, I, 234–99.

[14] This will be elaborated in a later study.

[15] The data in Figure 7.3 are based on Verstockt, 'Conjunctuurstudie van een domein in de late middeleeuwen' and Van Maelzake, 'De financieel-economische politiek'.

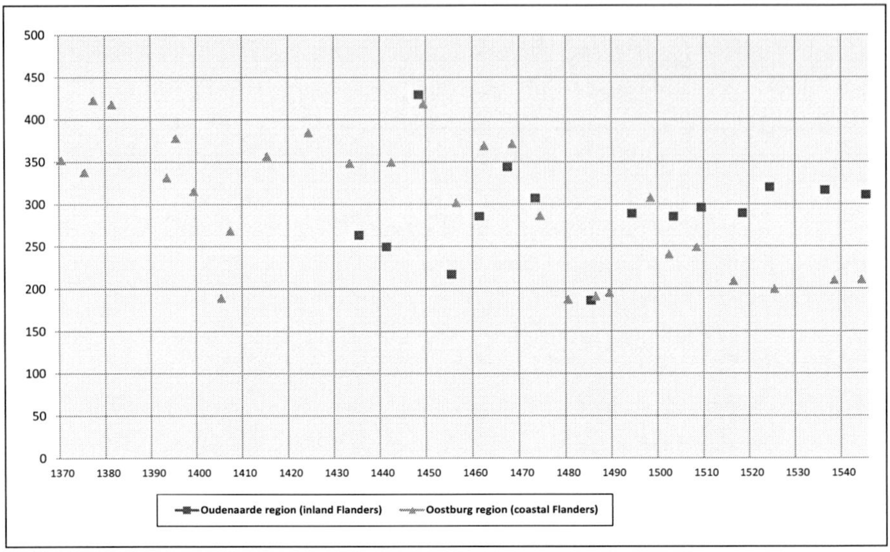

Figure 7.3. Prices of leases in Inland and Coastal Flanders (1375–1545, in litres of wheat).

Some historians have argued that a late medieval crisis resulted from a crisis in feudal relations. In this model, lords, in the broad sense of the word, reacted against the structural changes of the twelfth to thirteenth centuries by increasing their incomes, with negative effects for society as a consequence.[16] In some areas, the aristocracy increased its income in the late thirteenth century; in western Europe this was mainly a reaction to financial difficulties confronting lords. In Flanders, we have shown that between about 1250 and 1300 the falling rate of feudal levy per head brought difficulties to many lords who could no longer expand their demesne incomes through land reclamation. Nor could they profit from the population increase, which they had often stimulated in the twelfth and thirteenth centuries.[17] Near the end of the thirteenth century, various seigniorial groups maximized their opportunities to extract surplus in order to maintain their income. But the struggle between different seigneurial classes had affected seigneurial revenues, albeit differently depending upon the group and the area, and especially depending on their ability to adapt income strategies to changing circumstances.

[16] See e.g. Kosminsky, 'The Evolution of Feudal Rent'; Hilton, 'A Crisis of Feudalism'; Bois, *Crise du féodalisme*.

[17] As clearly shown for Normandy by Bois, *Crise du féodalisme*.

Although we cannot elaborate this here, an increasing number of foreign studies confirms our view that one of the typical characteristics of the classic feudal period before the later Middle Ages was not arbitrary rent collecting, but rather fixed customary charges, often laid down in perpetuity, and originating from pressures which peasants themselves brought to bear. As the decline in value of the feudal levy per head gradually lowered the incomes of large landowners, they tried to adapt their extraction of surplus through various means at their disposal. Many wanted to change the fixed rents and taxes into variable levies. But this was not easily accomplished and could happen only in areas where seigniorial property and power structures would allow it. It was much easier for lords to change fixed rents in the coastal area than in inland Flanders.

'Long Live the Family': The Rise of a 'Commercial Survival Economy' (CSE) in Inland Flanders

In the rural area of inland Flanders, a specific model of economic and social behaviour emerged before the late Middle Ages. It underwent some changes during the late Middle Ages, but fundamentally it dates back to the period before the crisis, the central Middle Ages (1100–1300).

Inland Flanders consists of lighter sandy and sandy-loamy soils whose formation was not influenced by the sea. Reclamation of land began in the early Middle Ages and earlier. This resulted in a less than rational infrastructure. Aside from the growing shortage of firewood, largely overcome through the creation of a hedgerow landscape, the physical environment in inland Flanders did not burden peasants.[18] Smallholdings were by far in the majority, and their size gradually decreased. Many things contributed to the fragmentation of the countryside into a mosaic of smallholdings. Already a common phenomenon in many areas on the Continent, fragmentation in inland Flanders reached a level unusual in Europe for a range of reasons. We cannot go into all the details, but these are the basic reasons.

Firstly, peasants in this area slowly obtained access to most of the property rights of their cultivated lands in the course of the twelfth to thirteenth centuries. Existing customary rents were low and even decreasing in value, and rents were often symbolic for newly reclaimed lands. Earlier than elsewhere, lords allowed many of the rents in kind to convert into rents in money which were prone to depreciation. Lords in this area manifested a precocious interest

[18] Thoen and Soens, 'Energy: Tension between Ecology and Economy'.

in earning cash money because of the influence of the developing monetary economy in this intensively urbanized area. Moreover, a structural competition between different groups of lords in this area weakened their possibilities for extracting peasant income.

So, from a very early stage, most peasants were de facto owners of farmsteads for which they still paid depreciated seigneurial dues. Especially in the first stage of the Middle Ages, these peasants did not compete with one other; on the contrary, during the eleventh and twelfth centuries, communities cooperated in the management of infield-outfield rotations systems.[19] They also frequently lived together in hamlets, called greens, generally situated next to the infield. Peasant solidarity dissolved during the thirteenth century as common fields and common practices lost importance and disappeared.

Many peasants depended upon revenues from part-time work on larger holdings, especially during the slack periods of the agricultural season. Every village had one or a few larger holdings owned by large landlords. Some of them dated back to the early or classic Middle Ages and were former demesne centres, *curtes*. The institutional links between the smaller holdings and the larger manors through services were traditionally limited. These large estates not only delivered additional incomes to the smallholders through wages, they also gave peasants the means to share capital like horses or ploughing in exchange for work on the farm.[20] The first concern of these peasants was to assure the survival of their families.

Because of this attitude of family survival — typical for a pre-capitalist society — the peasants were not interested in large holdings.[21] During the demographic boom of the twelfth to thirteenth centuries, they divided their holdings.[22] But there were additional, typically Flemish reasons which stimulated the extreme fragmentation of the holdings in this social agro-system. First of all, the low rents encouraged Flemish peasants to invest as much as possible in their own land, leading to intensive husbandry. But beyond this, it became increasingly easy after 1250 for peasants to borrow through the sale annuities, again because of the abundance of cash money in this highly commercialized region, which encouraged children to obtain their own holdings. After marriage, children got their own share of the family estates, which they could then

[19] Thoen with Lambrecht, 'Le paysage flamand'.

[20] Lambrecht, *Een grote hoeve in een klein dorp*.

[21] Brenner, 'The Low Countries'.

[22] Simple acquisition of property rights encouraged peasants: Brenner, 'The Low Countries'.

use as collateral for the sale of an annuity. Since customary rents were low, they could borrow quite a lot using their land as collateral.[23] Land *and* credit markets grew very dynamic because of the widespread peasant ownership of land and ready access to capital.

In sum, in inland Flanders there were extra stimuli for an extreme fragmentation of holdings. This could provide explanations for questions we have yet to formulate; for example, why so many of the common fields dating back to the High Middle Ages were eliminated so early in Flanders compared with many other regions.[24] They may have played a key function in this economy. Perhaps the abundance of cash and persistently low rents for newly reclaimed land limited the resistance of peasants to their disappearance. Moreover, the precocious fragmentation of holdings and the consequent disappearance of a middle class may have weakened the ability of very small peasants to resist their disappearance. The structure of the village community became too weak. It is also not unlikely that during the thirteenth century, the private appropriation of these commons was not seen as a negative practice by other peasants, if it curbed the tendency of holdings to diminish in size. During the thirteenth century, the struggle for land became the basis of survival. Agrarian individualism became the standard. Unlike the first stage of the classic Middle Ages when infield-outfield and communal practices were common and common fields still functional, the survival economy of inland Flanders was no longer an agro-system based upon community solidarity. The hunt for land raised prices.

Seigniorial power influenced the social relations within an agro-system as well. The word 'seigniorial' is used here in the broad sense of the word: it refers to all non-peasant individuals and institutions owning substantial amounts of land which exercised some form of extra-economic or political power over the peasant population. It is easy to imagine how any changes in the type of lordship affected property relations and thus the social agro-system of inland Flanders. We think that at least two features already mentioned — peasant property rights and the decreasing peasant solidarity — were both affected by seigniorial structures.

Since the second half of the eleventh century and especially since the twelfth century, lords exercised extremely scattered power in inland Flanders. A tactical power struggle took place among the count, numerous secular and ecclesiastical local lords, and of course, given the level of urbanization, increasing numbers

[23] Thoen and Soens, 'Appauvrissement et endettement'.

[24] Research on this topic for the Middle Ages in the Southern Netherlands is still very scarce.

of bourgeois investors after the second half of the thirteenth century.[25] This struggle prevented a harmonious coexistence between large landownership and the possession of jurisdictional rights. The counts used the towns to eliminate the judicial power of local lords while the larger towns, from the twelfth century onwards, became a judicial threat for the count, which led to many disputes and resulted in civil wars in the later Middle Ages. Judicial power lost its influence over property rights, and this eventually advanced peasant property rights. The result was that the peasant holdings, which were almost free given the restrained customary rents, could survive more easily and much longer here than along the coast.

This competition between different elites gave birth to another institution which undermined village solidarity in inland Flanders. This institution was called the *bourgeoisie foraine* or *buitenpoorterij* (literally 'external burghership'). Since about 1250 it was possible for village people to acquire the status of townsman, and many peasants seized the opportunity.[26] In some areas up to 40 and 50 per cent of all villagers were *buitenpoorters* in the later Middle Ages. This institution could only thrive under the protection of the count whose alliance with the Flemish towns created it in order to increase the influence of the towns in the hinterland. The count fostered *buitenpoorterij*, of course, in order to curb the power of local lords in the countryside in favour of the town's and the count's own judicial representatives. Only in a later period, when large towns such as Ghent, Bruges, and Ypres threatened comital power, did the counts put brakes upon this privilege, but they nonetheless continued to encourage *buitenpoorterij* in smaller towns, in an attempt to use them as counterbalances to the power of the large urban centers. *Buitenpoorterij* lost some of its importance in the later Middle Ages, although it survived until the end of the Ancien Régime. It probably undermined the political coherence and internal solidarity of village communities since local inhabitants were split up into people who were *buitenpoorters* and people who were not. Thus we believe that this institution was responsible for, *inter alii*, the early disappearance of peasant solidarity reflected in the loss of the commons. Here as in coastal Flanders, village communities gradually based social relations upon purely economical ties loosely connected to a small administrative backbone.

[25] Thoen, 'A "Commercial Survival Economy" in Evolution', pp. 107–10. The idea that power competition or collaboration had great infuence on local economic development has been put forward by Brenner, 'Agrarian Class Structure', pp. 30–75.

[26] The influence of the *buitenpoorterij* on power structures has been described in Thoen, 'Rechten en plichten'.

In both the coastal area and inland Flanders the contrast between unfree and free labour lost its influence upon the organization of work. Since the High Middle Ages, free labour was predominant, and the ties between large and small holdings determined the organization of labour. Since the distribution of large and small holdings was different in each region, labour relations diverged as well. In inland Flanders most workers were non-residents working part time. If they lived in large farms, it was temporarily, during a limited stage of their family life cycle. Generally speaking, wage labour in inland Flanders provided only a part of the peasants' income, because it was combined with the very intensive cultivation of a smallholding, as well as with proto-industrial activity. The latter, mostly wool and later also linen processing, can be traced back to the thirteenth century.[27] In later periods there is proof that the large holdings even provided organizational support for proto-industrial activity; this may already have been the case earlier.[28] But the interdependence between large farms and smallholdings in the same area was influenced as well by the distribution of capital; it is likely that, in exchange for labour, larger holdings lent horses for ploughing and other goods to the smaller ones.[29]

This kind of economic and social structure affected labour productivity. Small peasant holdings, which the majority of the holdings were or became in the course of the twelfth to thirteenth centuries, probably had very low productivity with a tendency to fall. The cultivation of flax and the processing of linen used labour inefficiently, as did the spade with which a large part of the arable land was turned.[30] However, was not this tendency of labour productivity to fall countered by increasing physical productivity?

To a certain extent it was. Recently, historians have concluded that a major intensification of agriculture using mixed farming methods became common in Flanders before the late Middle Ages. Yields per hectare were high from at least 1300: 1500 to 2000 litres for rye and 2500 to 3000 litres for the widely cultivated oats were not uncommon. Since the thirteenth century, smaller farms in particular applied large inputs of labour in order to reduce the fallow in crop

[27] Linen became much more important after 1500 as a proto-industrial activity and this until the nineteenth century.

[28] Thoen, *Landbouwekonomie en bevolking in Vlaanderen*, II, 1004–05; Lambrecht, *Een grote hoeve in een klein dorp*, pp. 101–07.

[29] As later in the eighteenth century, see Lambrecht, *Een grote hoeve in een klein dorp*, pp. 113–33.

[30] For calculations about the unproductivity of linen processing, see Thoen, *Landbouwekonomie en bevolking in Vlaanderen*, II, 997–99. For the use of the spade in Flemish agriculture, see ibid., pp. 781–83.

rotations and cultivated fodder crops and industrial crops such as dyes, flax, and hemp.[31] Thus an increasing physical productivity per unit of surface was made possible only through the expenditure of enormous amounts of human labour. This increased labour input was way out of proportion to the increased physical output which a shortage of fertilizer limited until the modern period.[32] In sum, it is likely that, despite the increasing physical productivity per surface unit, labour productivity had declined in the course of the twelfth and thirteenth centuries.[33]

The survival economy of inland Flanders was not a survival economy isolated from markets. We have called this a 'commercial survival economy' or CSE.[34] Since the size of peasant holdings gradually declined as holdings split up in times of demographic growth, survival of family members was the prime concern of peasants. They developed different strategies to ensure this survival: intensive cultivation of the land resulting in a high physical output per acre, a constant search for additional sources of income such as wage labour leading to symbiotic labour relations with large farms, and production for the market through proto-industrial activities such as the cropping of vegetable dyes, flax, and so on. The first concern was not investment or profit making which might increase a holding, but rather the survival of family members.[35]

Further Evolution of the Inland-Flemish Agro-system in the Later Middle Ages after 1250

How did this agro-system react to the crises of the late Middle Ages? In fact, it did not change much at all. The majority of minor farms were preserved. The average size of these smallholdings in some cases increased a little, but most of them still did not exceed five hectares in area. Some peasants lost their land to holders of larger farms. Indeed the number of large farms increased between *c.* 1250 and 1450 because of purchases of small plots of land by townspeople

[31] Verhulst, 'L'intensification et la commercialisation'; Thoen, 'The Birth of the "Flemish Husbandry"'.

[32] Despite the high labour input, Flemish agriculture could only produce about 1500–2500 litres of rye and wheat per hectare until the late nineteenth century.

[33] Proof of this bipartite evolution from data in the nineteenth century can be found in Thoen, 'A "Commercial Survival Economy" in Evolution'.

[34] Thoen, 'A "Commercial Survival Economy" in Evolution'.

[35] See Brenner, 'The Low Countries'.

who wanted to create large farms. These larger farms in this period were all leaseholds, created in emulation of the nobility and to assure the personal provisioning of the richer townspeople in periods of grain shortage or high prices. So, the number of *coqs de village* increased, although their farms were not in general larger than twenty-sixty hectares. These large farms dominated the economies of rural communities through the work they provided and through the offices their holders occupied.

Some big farms worked land with resident servants, but this was not a major trend. From about the fifteenth century until the sixteenth century, the number of larger farms remained more or less the same in the villages; every village had between one and five, with a maximum of about ten, cultivating a large percentage of the total area under plough (between 25 and 50 per cent).[36] During this period many large farms decreased in size and giant farms disappeared. This trend nevertheless favoured the bond between large and small holdings, providing smaller holdings with a survival strategy based upon wage earning. The peasant economy became an economy based upon this collaboration between smaller peasants and larger farms.

Since about 1250, leaseholding became common for these larger farms, while small peasants generally held light customary rents.[37] As larger giant farms lost land, the detached plots were occasionally leased as well. In inland Flanders leaseholding became common during this period for most of the smaller plots of land as well. Because it was especially the large farms which were taken in lease, the inland market for land to lease was completely different from that on the coast and so too were the relations between large landowners and leaseholders. Indeed, contrary to the coastal area, in inland Flanders there was not yet a competitive market for land since there were candidates for renting a large farm. In general, farms were leased for many generations by the same families, so long as they paid their rents and maintained a good relationship with the owner.[38] Large farmers had few occasions to compete for leased land, since that kind of land was not available to increase their land significantly.[39] Therefore

[36] Between 25 and 60 per cent of the cultivated area.

[37] In our opinion, in the Ancien Régime, larger farms could only survive in the long term with large financial backers since the risks of destruction were so high. Only in the course of the eighteenth century did risks (e.g. from war) decline, allowing larger farms to come into the hands of country people.

[38] This has been noticed by Tits-Dieuaide, 'Peasants Dues in Brabant', although she did not give an explanation for this phenomenon.

[39] For smaller plots of land competition occurred as much as in the coastal area, but the

these large inland farmers in the CSE system, although they produced for the market, did share the same competitive capitalist mentality which prevailed on the coast. For many of them, the principal concern also was the survival of family members. They competed in the market for the purchasing of land, not for the leasing of it. Except for the oldest son of the farmer, all other members of the family had to begin their independent careers as a small peasant, like other members of the village community.

As was the case before 1250, most peasants in the area kept the largest part of their land and the buildings on their farmsteads in a form of customary tenure akin to full property. Proto-industrialization remained an important additional income for many peasants. The rural flax and linen industry had two periods of expansion: 1370–1420 and after 1470.[40] As before, inland Flanders was influenced by towns as the power of local lords declined, with the consequence that judicial property rights and the rights over estates were often in different hands.

This made a seigniorial reaction much more difficult. The shift from fixed and stable nominal rents of decreasing real value to adaptable rents like leases was, as we have seen before, not so easily accomplished in the inland area. Secondly, it curbed, for a long time, capital extraction by the count's taxation. Direct taxes collected by the comital state became common in the 1360s. But only from the late sixteenth century onwards did this new financial levy become a pressing burden upon Flemish peasant society. Until then, these taxes remained relatively low. Because the count negotiated the taxes (*beden*) with representative groups of which the large towns had the most influence, these taxes rose only for brief periods, for example, before and after insurrections, unlike in other countries. Historians have overlooked this for a long time.[41] In short, local power structures hindered a seigniorial reaction in Flanders. 'State feudalism', which replaced lordly feudalism in many areas of Europe, could not fully develop.[42] Thus the CSE system, which originated in the classic Middle Ages, survived and was responsible for the limited symptoms of crisis in Flanders.

supply of land which was leased was much too small to influence the agro-system fundamentally (see the high leases in Figure 7.3).

[40] Thoen, *Landbouwekonomie en bevolking in Vlaanderen*, II, 980–1020.

[41] Thoen, *Landbouwekonomie en bevolking in Vlaanderen*, I, 613–36, and the graph in Thoen, 'A "Commercial Survival Economy" in Evolution', p. 136.

[42] Kosminsky, 'The Evolution of Feudal Rent'.

Crisis and the CSE Agro-system in Inland Flanders

The CSE agro-system was less vulnerable to crisis: although small peasants were market oriented, they were not dependent upon the market or market prices of cereals. They produced a 'survival basket' of products for their own consumption which also stabilized their incomes: in addition to cereals, most had one or a few cows, some bees, and produced some textiles. This was all part of a survival strategy. Many peasants purchased some grain, at least when prices were cheap, and the price evolution favoured their income more than it damaged it. In short periods of crisis when grain prices rose dramatically, peasants appealed to larger farmers for help. Some industrial and semi-industrial products such as dyes could be sold for better prices during a short-term crisis. Moreover, it is likely that their employment rate was going up as the number of larger farms who needed part-time wage labourers increased. Their market sales allowed peasants to profit from changes in urban industry like the new orientation towards fashionable textiles.[43] It is well known that these changes in the Flemish textile industry relied in part upon 'putting out' work to the countryside.[44] Proto-industrial activities were flexible, well suited to the needs of a majority of the inhabitants of smallholdings, and were fully employed on their own land. Larger farms, in which wages were important to the incomes of smallholders, took advantage of this situation as well. The wages became lower in inland Flanders than in coastal Flanders.[45] This was almost certainly caused by the fact that wage earning was, for most of the labourers, only a part-time activity; after all, the number of resident labourers was small. The income of these part-time labourers was not solely dependent on employment because they were peasants, and during the months that most labourers were needed on the larger farms, the supply of labour was very high since most members of peasant families hired themselves out in the labour market. These are additional causes which help explain how the CSE of inland Flanders was structurally responsible for the lack of crises.

[43] Kosminsky, 'The Evolution of Feudal Rent'.

[44] Holbach, *Frühformen von Verlag und Grossbetrieb*.

[45] See Figure 7.2. Other mechanisms probably also helped the larger farms to survive in this CSE system, e.g. the fact that they often worked in proto-industrial crafts (with family members, with wage earners, and even as brokers), the fact that they had good relations with the owners of the farms (who needed these farms for their own survival during the crisis), and the fact that they could often pay part of the rent in kind to religious landowners who did not have to pay undirect taxes when they imported foodstuffs into towns.

Features and Origin of the Coastal Agro-system before about 1250: First Signs of Change

The most important environmental feature distinguishing the agrarian system of the coast from that of the inland is, of course, the North Sea. The sea could be a positive force, but usually it was a threat. In the High Middle Ages, and especially between the tenth and the thirteenth centuries, the soils composed of embanked and re-embanked heavy marine clays and sands gradually replaced salt marshes and peat bogs. This was the result of both human intervention and natural changes to the environment: peat bogs settled, partly in response to human drainage systems; storm surges and overexploitation by humans of the natural dune barrier gave the tidal outlets of the sea more occasions to flood and depose sediment. Historians have made various attempts to distinguish successive waves in the influence of the sea from the Carolingian period onwards, but there is no agreement about the exact chronology. It is, however, undeniable that the cost of protecting the area against the sea steadily rose in the twelfth, thirteenth, and fourteenth centuries, although these costs were not yet rationally used in favour of the environment. Ecology aside, underinvestment in infrastructure by large landowners with short-term profits in mind — and their influence was increasing in the central Middle Ages — increased the cost of maintaining vulnerable coastal infrastructures like dikes. The consequences for the peasants were considerable. Yet peasants invested in significant infrastructure, rationally developed. They were responsible for an extensive and ever expanding network of canals, necessary for draining the area, as well as for transport over water to regional markets.

We still do not know enough about the structures of the rural society in the coastal area before 1300, but it is likely that until about 1250–1300, differences in social structures between inland and coastal Flanders were probably less pronounced than they became in later centuries. In 1300, peasant smallholders were in the majority, or they were at least very common both inland and on the coast. However, in the coastal area there must have been more large holdings (including some giant ones) in the eleventh to thirteenth centuries than in inland Flanders, since flocks of sheep (especially until the twelfth century, often on salt marshes) and stockbreeding (especially since the twelfth century?) were common. A social relation between smaller peasants and larger landowners must have been common too, just as was the case in inland Flanders. Although concrete data about the size of the smallholdings are scarce, many of the small peasants (as in inland Flanders) needed an additional income via various proto-industrial activities such as wool processing, fishing, and especially peat digging and salt making, activities which were practised on a very large scale in this area.[46] Peat became an essential product for the increasing town economies.

In many areas in coastal Flanders in the tenth to twelfth centuries, the smallholders were freeholders of much of their land. According to recent research, in this period, and maybe even earlier, these peasant landowners played a major part in the occupation of the salt marshes and peat bogs.[47]

This kind of society, like that of inland Flanders, could, despite some structural differences which were surely present, be labeled as a commerical survival economy (CSE). However, in contrast to inland Flanders, it would not endure. Although the major changes in our description seem to have taken place after 1250, the cornerstones for a new kind of society were gradually laid from about 1200, although its beginnings are hard to measure.

It is likely that this new society was caused by a different seigniorial structure in combination with ecological changes. Indeed, the increasing influence of the count in combination with a growing influence of large landowners (see below) was affecting this picture since about the twelfth century, since the classic Middle Ages seigniorial structures in this area were not based on competition, like in inland Flanders.[48] The old seigniorial power of lay lords was restrained, and the count as an overlord had and kept much more judicial power here from the beginning of the emergence of the county in the twelfth century.[49] The count was able to keep the early medieval system of officials representing committal power on a local level (the *schout*) intact. This was one of the main reasons that the power of the rare local lordships, which came into existence in this area during the High Middle Ages, was limited. So, as we have mentioned, many peasants enjoyed a completely free status.

Due to the same sustained local power of the counts, the large strips of wasteland in this area, especially the vast tracts of initially common peat land, could from the twelfth and thirteenth centuries onwards smoothly become full property of the count.[50] These lands were subsequently sold to private institutions (monasteries, hospitals, alms houses, and the like) and rich townspeople. In this way the buyers could reinforce their position of power in the redistribu-

[46] Soens, 'Les tourbières disparues de Flandre'.

[47] Tys, 'Landschap als materiële cultuur'.

[48] Thoen, 'Social Agro-systems as an Economic Concept', pp. 54–57.

[49] Partly because the Count of Flanders was originally a local lord from the coastal area in the neighbourhood of Bruges: Tys, 'Domeinvorming in de "wildernis"'.

[50] Tys, 'Domeinvorming in de "wildernis"'.

tion of income between a new category of lords, whose power was especially based on rural estate, and peasants. Next to this, it also provided an easy way to increase their income, because there was no pressing power of traditional local lords whose power was based on rights of justice which could oppose them or nibble at their income. The interests of local administrative and judicial power went along with the interests of the large private landlords. The seigneurial pressure on the peasants became clearer.

This contrasting evolution of property structures in coastal Flanders was certainly intensified by the above-mentioned growing ecological pressure on the coastal area from about the period 1100–1300 onwards, with heavy financial consequences for its population — mischief from which inland Flanders was spared. Although it is difficult to measure in this early period, it is likely that many peasants in the coastal area could not afford the increased maintenance costs for the infrastructure, let alone the costs for re-diking after storm surges. For many peasants living in the belt between the sea and the River Scheldt the increased number or increased effects of storm surges made it impossible to contribute sufficiently to new embankments. This resulted in numerous evictions of impoverished peasants. The application of the so-called 'right of abandon', which was only possible due to the important committal power, automatically transferred the private property rights of insolvent peasants to those who could bear these costs, that is, the larger landowners like abbeys, hospitals, and the urban bourgeoisie.[51]

So, near the sea, the lordly collaboration model between the count and the upper classes favoured new structures of large landownership. Its corollary was the beginning of the loss of property rights of numerous peasants who, until that time, had virtually, if not always nominally, owned their land. In this period many lost part of their rights by becoming peasant fief holders either of the count or of a religious institution. In this case their loss was only partial because fiefs were hereditary and entrance fees were low. Much more dramatic was the effect of the 'right of abandon', which was applied in the area since at least the twelfth century. To get their land back, the peasants had to pay high customary rents. As we will see below, since about 1250 many peasants not only lost their properties, they also had to become leaseholders if they wanted to continue their agricultural activities. This was clear proof of the effectiveness of the collaboration between the judicial power of the count and local lordly power based on the possession of land and capital.

[51] Soens and Thoen, 'The Origin of Leaseholding'.

'Long Live the Farm': The New Social Agro-system or 'Commercial Business Economy' (CBE) after 1250–1300

Although the structures of the society were already clearly under pressure before the second half of the thirteenth century, the CSE system was quickly decaying during the later Middle Ages. During the later Middle Ages the more well-to-do farmers could overcome their problems in the longer term; a large part of the peasant smallholders disappeared and were integrated in larger holdings. As we have noticed already at the beginning of this article, the economy became gradually more and more based on a majority of larger more commercially oriented farms. The number of small peasants was gradually going down.[52] In some places this evolution is noticeable in the sources as early as the late thirteenth century; elsewhere it took place after 1400 in particular.

The social polarization created a growing class of full-time and resident farm labourers, who, for most of their lives, worked on a large farm. Proto-industrial activities or non-agricultural income strategies such as fishing, peat digging, and perhaps also salt making, which were still very popular in the twelfth to fourteenth centuries, gradually lost importance in the course of the later Middle Ages. Peat, the basic product of most of the proto-industrial activity, became scarce. Many peat layers had become less accessible because they were covered with sediments from the sea. Moreover, around the middle of the sixteenth century most of the peat at surface level, the easiest to be cut, was gone. But as farms grew larger and became more commercially oriented, they were also less interested in non-agrarian subsidiary business.

Contrary to what occurred in inland Flanders, the accelerated decrease of peasant property rights to land almost completely changed the property structures of this society.[53] In the coastal area since about 1250 there was an unmistakable evolution towards a rural society in which leaseholding dominated. At the eve of the early modern period most peasants had been forced into leasing. As if this was not enough, many of the families, if they were very unlucky, were evicted from their farmsteads, which were gradually absorbed by larger farms in the course of the fourteenth and fifteenth centuries and even later on in the sixteenth century.

Indeed, the ecological pressure on the coastal area increased in the later Middle Ages. The costs for maintaining the infrastructure were high and fur-

[52] Soens and Thoen, 'The Origin of Leaseholding', p. 38.

[53] Soens and Thoen, 'The Origin of Leaseholding'.

ther impoverished the peasants. Large environmental disasters are known to have permanent consequences, such as the cascade of storms in the late fourteenth century, especially in 1375, 1389, 1404, and 1424.[54]

We have already mentioned that, as far as we can see, even in the coastal area and despite the institutional arrangements via water boards, durable investments by large landowners provoking ecological stability were limited; their profits exceeded their reinvestments by a lot. In the coastal area the failing of large landowners to think on a long-term basis was to a large extent responsible for the disastrous impact of storm surges between the thirteenth and the sixteenth centuries.[55] Durable investments in the environment via a well-maintained infrastructure were indeed absent, although the necessity to invest in a sustainable environmental policy became pressing as a consequence of changes in the physical environment. Let us not forget that this was a medieval feudal system in which money was only put into the short-term maintenance of dikes and locks. Undoubtedly this was partly due to the fact that the water boards were more and more dominated by the large landowners, most of whom did not live in threatened areas themselves. What's even more, in the long run they could actually even profit from the floodings, since they were the only ones able to finance new embankments, and this situation offered them opportunities for the enlargement of their estates and consequently for their power in the area. It is only from the second half of the seventeenth century that regular taxes for a durable sustainable environmental policy became common, under the influence of a more centralized government and a new class of more capitalist-oriented towns, people, and investors. It is likely that the influence of central government also increased, but further investigation is needed. At any rate, after 1600 damage from storm surges decreased.

The aforementioned ecological changes and ecological disasters freighted many peasants with difficulties. This impoverishment of peasants was causing losses of peasant property. Many peasants obtained credit by the selling of annuities. This practice became very common, but many peasants could not pay the annuities and lost their land to large landowners from whom they took it back in lease.[56]

The more common application of the so-called 'right of abandon' accelerated this process of impoverishment and expropriation. The implementation

[54] Gottschalk, *Stormvloeden en rivieroverstromingen*.

[55] Thoen and Soens, 'Van landschapsgeschiedenis'.

[56] This does not exclude other reasons (see above, note 5).

of this legal device transferred the private property rights of insolvent peasants to those who could carry the freight, that is, the larger landowners. Indeed, this practice furthered the development of short-lease arrangements benefiting the latter group since peasants who lost their land in property had no other choice than to take this land back in lease. As we mentioned before, the application of this legal system was only possible thanks to the described seigniorial relations based on collaboration between the large landowners, mostly religious institutions, and the centralized judicial power in the hands of the count.

Thus increased ecological pressure, combined with the specific seigniorial power relations and the increased needs of lords for variable rents, caused and accelerated changing property structures in the coastal area on a much larger scale than in inland Flanders. Leaseholding became the typical form of landholding during the late Middle Ages.

The process of impoverishment wiped out the smallest peasants. The prevailing leasing system hindered the division of holdings. Those who survived through leaseholding were forced to compete for land. This stimulated further engrossment and innovation.[57] It opened the way towards a 'commercial business economy' (CBE). This agro-system consisted of a majority of larger, but not giant, farms. They produced for the markets, and their goal was not survival of the family, but survival of the commercial farm. In coastal Flanders many larger farms emerged out of peasant smallholdings, worked with resident servants who were much cheaper. The number of smallholders who needed an additional income was low, which made wage earners expensive. As some scarce data from later periods such as the seventeenth and eighteenth centuries seem to reveal, there was a constant migration from the coastal area towards inland Flanders, where many sons of farmers tried to buy land to start their own holding. Vice versa, it is likely that the coastal area was attracting multitudes of seasonal workers from inland Flanders, who were needed during harvest time. In this way, both agro-systems supported each other's existence and evolution.

In sum, while in inland Flanders, the CSE survived despite shocks in the later Middle Ages, in the coastal area, the peasant economy which was already under pressure was replaced by a new kind of social relation based on a majority of larger and middle-sized, to a large extend commercially oriented, farms (CBE).

This CBE system affected labour productivity in a different way than in inland Flanders. While difficult to measure, it is likely that labour productivity was higher on commercially oriented farms of middle and large size. This

[57] See the very clear study of Brenner, 'The Low Countries'.

implies that, from the later medieval period onwards, labour productivity must have been increasing in the coastal area, while simultaneously going down in inland Flanders. Compared to inland Flanders, cash crops in the coastal area, such as wheat, and fodder crops, such as vetches, which were often consumed on the spot, clearly demanded less labour, as did cattle breeding, which was gaining importance.[58] That was probably also the main reason that, with the increasing size of farms, the production of madder (a dye product requiring a lot of labour input) declined in coastal Flanders.[59]

Typically for this area, increasing labour productivity was supported by high physical productivity. A combination of intensive techniques of arable farming, which mostly date back to the period during which the area still had features of a peasant society (CSE), and the switch to more valuable and labour-reducing cash crops such as wheat suggests that labour productivity was growing. In inland Flanders, productivity was probably already declining on the eve of the late Middle Ages and remained low, as the survival economy stood firm.

Until the later Middle Ages, village solidarity within these coastal communities was important. Nevertheless, contrary to what has often been written, the change from a CSE towards a CBE brought about a decline in solidarity.[60] Here, a parallel can be seen with inland Flanders, where village solidarity eroded within the CSE itself. This evolution manifested itself in the fact that the rural inhabitants of coastal Flanders gradually lost influence in local public administration. Initially, they exercised a certain measure of coercive power via the water boards (Dutch: *wateringen*, *waterschappen*, or *wateringues*), since all local landowners (in the thirteenth century still a majority of peasants) were represented in these boards according to the amount of land they possessed. After the beginning of the fifteenth century they gradually lost this type of influence and power over their own community to the advantage of non-peasant large landowners.[61] This was due to the fact that the new class of large farmers were leaseholders who did not have property rights of the land they cultivated. One should realize that these *wateringen* probably had become more important as channels of local power than other local institutions such as parishes, seigneuries, *schoutheetdommen*, or bailiwicks. Therefore, the increasing dominance of non-resident large landowners in the water boards probably

[58] Thoen, 'A "Commercial Survival Economy" in Evolution'; Brenner, 'The Low Countries'.

[59] See Mertens, 'De meekrapteelt'.

[60] Soens, 'Het waterschap en de mythe van de democratie'.

[61] Soens, 'Het waterschap en de mythe van de democratie'.

did contribute much to the diminishing solidarity of the village communities, which were still so very prominent in the well-known insurrection of coastal Flanders of 1323–28.[62] So, village community solidarity eroded and probably not in a lesser degree than was the case in inland Flanders.

The CBE Agro-system and Crisis

The late medieval crisis was much more perceptible in coastal Flanders than it was in inland Flanders. It is likely that the described agro-system (CBE) was more vulnerable to shocks. We have shown it evolving between 1100 and 1700 from a CSE to a CBE system. More and more of these peasants were becoming farmers dependent upon market prices for cereals and cattle they sold. The described expropriation process had driven them into a competitive leasing system. The late medieval price scissors did not favour the farms: as pure wage labourers became more expensive farmers switched as much as possible to resident labourers. Their only way to react against this changing agro-system and the changing economic development was engrossment. The price evolution favoured the bigger commercial farms over smaller semi-commercial farms.[63] Proto-industry could not counter this evolution as it declined together with the number of smallholdings. What was left was a very polarized society: many dispossessed poor people living alongside large and middle-sized farms. It is likely that the death rate was highest within the layer of peasants without landed property. Many of them probably moved to inland Flanders, trying to buy a small property there, or else to the towns to find work. A greater scarcity of labour, as well as the fact that many of the wage labourers had to live from their wages to sustain their families, meant that they could not build up their income with revenues from smallholdings or proto-industrial activities. This was responsible for the higher wages in coastal Flanders. It is clear that these high wages also contributed to an increased vulnerability of the CBE system, since bankruptcy was never far for a large number of the farmers.

The economy became commercial, but more vulnerable for another reason as well. Contrary to inland Flanders, this economic system could not profit from a structure of low taxes and other forms of surplus extraction. As we mentioned, the large majority of the holdings became leaseholdings. These leases

[62] There is evidence that the peasant revolt was a reaction against new property and power structures; this will be developed in another paper.

[63] Cruyningen, *Behoudend maar buigzaam*.

were much higher than the customary rents paid by the smaller peasants still prevailing in inland Flanders. Moreover the costs which had to be paid to maintain the perilous ecological balance were often high, notwithstanding the fact that a structure for sustainable development was not yet established, as we explained earlier in this paper. The result was that major environmental problems such as storm surges caused a lot of damage in the late Middle Ages. In sum, because of the described specific seigniorial relations the farmers of coastal Flanders could not avoid a high burden of taxes and levies. Here, the efforts by the possessing classes to switch from stable to flexible levies largely succeeded, with a resulting concentration process and the disappearance through bankruptcy of small farms. The decreasing numbers of farmers eventually drove down the price of leases in the fifteenth and sixteenth centuries (Figure 7.3).

'Long live the farm', the motto of farms in the CBE system created in the late Middle Ages, came at the expense of the CSE motto 'long live the family'.

Concluding Remarks

In the past, many models have been put forward to explain the late medieval crisis in Flanders. Often these models also tried to explain the relatively limited effects of this crisis. A new set of data based on regional studies gives us a clearer picture of this crisis and provides for better explanations. Most researchers have written that, in Flanders, the Malthusian check was partly overcome by special conditions in supply and demand, such as better nutrition.[64] The regional differences shown in this article make that argument less likely. Others supposed that in Flanders peasants raised production during the crisis through higher physical productivity and new techniques.[65] Nowadays we know that the most progress in physical productivity occurred in the thirteenth century in both agro-systems, so this explanation is not satisfactory either. Others attributed the light effects of the crisis to the nearness of a dense town network or suggested accidental or monetary explanations.[66]

[64] Van Werveke, *De zwarte dood*.

[65] Slicher van Bath, 'The Rise of Intensive Husbandry'.

[66] The role of the towns has been underlined by Van Der Wee, 'Typologie des crises et changements'; Blockmans, 'The Social and Economic Effects'; Blockmans, 'Die Niederlande vor und nach 1400'. Monetary explanations can be found in Aerts and Van Cauwenberghe, 'Die Grafschaft Flandern'.

This paper has shown that an in-depth study of the structures of production and social relations on a regional basis, the so called social agro-systemic approach, can help put forward nuanced explanations of the late medieval crisis. Because the former county of Flanders evolved towards different agro-systems, the effects of the crisis diverged from region to region. In the area where the CSE (Flemish commercial survival economy) agro-system survived, the effects were more restrained than in those areas which evolved towards a more commercially organized system, the CBE (Flemish commercial business economy) system.

Bibliography

Aerts, Erik, and Eddy Van Cauwenberghe, 'Die Grafschaft Flandern und die sogenannte spätmittelalterliche Depression', in *Europa 1400 : Die Krise des Spätmittelalters*, ed. by Ferdinand Seibt and Winfried Eberhard (Stuttgart: Klette-Cotta, 1984), pp. 95–116

Blockmans, Willem, 'Die Niederlande vor und nach 1400: eine Geselleschaft in der Krise?', in *Europa 1400 : Die Krise des Spätmittelalters*, ed. by Ferdinand Seibt and Winfried Eberhard (Stuttgart: Klette-Cotta, 1984), pp. 117–32

——, 'The Social and Economic Effects of Plague in the Low Countries 1349–1500', *Belgisch Tijdschrift voor Filologie en Geschiedenis*, 58, (1980), 833–63

Bois, Guy, *Crise du féodalisme: Économie rurale et démographie en Normandie orientale du début du 14e siècle au milieu du 16e siècle* (Paris: Presses de la Fondation Nationale des Sciences Politiques, 1976)

Brenner, Robert, 'Agrarian Class Structure and Economic Development in Pre-Industrial Europe', *Past and Present*, 70 (1976), 30–75; reprinted in *The Brenner Debate: Agrarian Class Structure and Economic Development in Pre-Industrial Europe*, ed. by Trevor H. Aston and C. H. E. Philpin (Cambridge: Cambridge University Press, 1985), pp. 10–63

——, 'The Low Countries in the Transition to Capitalism', in *Peasants into Farmers? The Transformation of Rural Economy and Society in the Low Countries (Middle Ages–19th Century) in Light of the Brenner Debate*, ed. by Peter C. M. Hoppenbrouwers and others, CORN-Publication Series, 4 (Turnhout: Brepols, 2001), pp. 275–338

Cruyningen, Piet van, *Behoudend maar buigzaam: boeren in West-Zeeuws-Vlaanderen 1650–1850*, AAG Bijdragen, 40 (Wageningen: Afdeling Agrarische Geschiedenis, Wageningen Universiteit, 2000)

Dehaeck, Sigrid, 'Voedselconsumptie in het Brugse Sint-Janshospitaal tijdens de Middeleeuwen (1280–1440)', *Handelingen van het Genootschap voor Geschiedenis 'Société d'Emulation' te Brugge*, 141 (2004), 3–4, 332–64

Genicot, Leopold, *La crise agricole du bas Moyen-Âge dans le Namurois*, (Louvain: Centre belge d'histoire rurale, 1970)

Gottschalk, Maria, *Stormvloeden en rivieroverstromingen*, 3 vols (Assen: Van Gorcum, 1971–73)

Hilton, Rodney H., 'A Crisis of Feudalism', *Past and Present*, 97 (1982), 3–15

Holbach, Rudolf, *Frühformen von Verlag und Grossbetrieb in der gewerblichen Production (13.–16. Jahrhundert)*, Vierteljahrschrift für Sozial-und Wirtschaftsgeschichte, Beihefte, 110 (Stuttgart: F. Steiner, 1994)

Kosminsky, Evgeny G., 'The Evolution of Feudal Rent in England from the XIth to the XVth Centuries', *Past and Present*, 7 (1955), 12–36

Kuipers, Jan J. B., ed., *Sluimerend in slik: Verdronken dorpen en verdronken land in zuidwest Nederland* (Middelburg: Stichting Cultureel Erfgoed Zeeland, 2004)

Lambrecht, Thijs, *Een grote hoeve in een klein dorp: relaties van arbeid en pacht op het Vlaamse platteland tijdens de 18de eeuw*, Historische Economie en Ecologie (Ghent: Academia Press, 2002)

Mertens, Jacques, 'De meekrapteelt in de omgeving van Brugge vooral in de 14de en 15de eeuw', *Het Brugs Ommeland*, 21 (1981), 259–82

Meyhuys, Vera, and Frank Daelemans, *De oudste domeinrekeningen van Herzele 1386–1394*, Herzele-Dossier, 7, Centrum Sociale Structuren en Economische Conjunctuur (Brussels: VUB, 1979)

Scholliers, Etienne, with the collaboration of Frank Daelemans, *De Conjunctuur van een Domein: Herzele 1444–1752*, Herzele- Dossier, 8, Centrum Sociale Structuren en Economische Conjunctuur (Brussels: VUB, 1981)

Sivéry, Gérard, *Structures agraires et vie rurale dans le Hainaut à la fin du Moyen Âge*, 2 vols (Lille: Université de Lille, 1977–80)

Slicher van Bath, Bernard H., 'The Rise of Intensive Husbandry in the Low Countries', in *Britain and the Netherlands*, ed. by J. S. Bromley and E. H. Kossman (London: Chatto, 1960), pp. 130–53

Soens, Tim, 'Les tourbières disparues de Flandre: Histoire d'un milieu humide d'une grande richesse', in *Aux rives de l'incertain: Histoire et représentation des marais occidentaux du Moyen Âge à nos jours*, ed. by Philippe Bata (Paris: Somogy, 2002), pp. 32–38

——, 'Het waterschap en de mythe van de democratie in het Ancien Régime: Het voorbeeld van de Vlaamse Kustvlakte in de Late Middeleeuwen', *Jaarboek voor Ecologische Geschiedenis*, 4 (2001), 39–56

——, *De spade in de dijk? Waterbeheer en rurale samenleving in de Vlaams kustvlakte (1280–1580)* (Ghent: Academia Press, 2009)

Soens, Tim, and Erik Thoen, 'The Origin of Leaseholding in the Former County of Flanders', in *The Development of Leasehold in Northwestern Europe, c. 1200–1600*, ed. by Bas J. P. van Bavel and Phillipp R. Schofield, CORN-Publication Series, 10 (Turnhout: Brepols, 2008), pp. 31–56

Thoen, Erik, 'The Birth of the "Flemish Husbandry": Agricultural Technology in Medieval Flanders', in *Medieval Farming and Technology: The Impact of Agricultural Change in Northwest Europe*, ed. by Grenville Astill and John Langdon (Leiden: Brill, 1997), pp. 69–88

——, 'A "Commercial Survival Economy" in Evolution: The Flemish Countryside and the Transformation to Capitalism (Middle Ages – Nineteenth Century)', in *Peasants into Farmers? The Transformation of Rural Economy and Society in the Low Countries (Middle Ages – 19th Century) in Light of the Brenner Debate*, ed. by Peter C. M. Hoppenbrouwers and Jan Luiten van Zanden, CORN-Publication Series, 4 (Turnhout: Brepols, 2001), pp. 102–58

——, 'Historical Demography in Medieval Rural Flanders: Recent Results and Possibilities', in *Peasants and Townsmen in Medieval Europe: Studia in honorem Adriaan Verhulst*, ed. by Jean-Marie Duvosquel and Erik Thoen (Ghent: Snoeck-Ducaju & Zoon, 1995), pp. 573–82

——, *Landbouwekonomie en bevolking in Vlaanderen gedurende de late Middeleeuwen en het begin van de Moderne Tijden. Testregio: de kasselrijen van Oudenaarde en Aalst*, Belgisch Centrum voor Landelijke Geschiedenis, 90 (Ghent: Belgisch Centrum voor Landelijke Geschiedenis, 1988)

——, 'Rechten en plichten van plattelanders als instrumenten van machtspolitieke strijd tussen adel, stedelijke burgerij en grafelijk gezag in het laat-middeleeuwse Vlaanderen: Buitenpoorterij en mortemain-rechten ten persoonlijke titel in de kasselrijen van Aalst en Oudenaarde, vooral toegepast op de periode rond 1400', in *Les structures du pouvoir en Belgique et dans les pays limitrophes (XIIe–XIXe siècle): Actes du 13e Colloque International Spa 3–5 sept. 1986*, Crédit Communal, Collection Histoire, série in-8°, 77 (Brussels: Crédit Commercial,1988), pp. 469–90

——, 'Social Agro-systems as an Economic Concept: An Essay Taking the Former County of Flanders as an Example (Middle Ages – Nineteenth Century)', in *Landholding and Land Transfer in the North Sea Area*, ed. by Bas P. J. van Bavel and others, CORN Pubication Series, 5 (Turnhout: Brepols 2004), pp. 47–66

——, 'De twee gezichten van de Vlaamse landbouw en het probleem der 'Wüstungen': Middeleeuwen-Moderne Tijden', in *Docendo discimus: Liber Amicorum Romain Van Eenoo*, ed. by Jan Art and Luc Francois (Ghent: Academia Press, 1999), pp. 75–84

Thoen, Erik, with Thijs Lambrecht, 'Le paysage flamand et la structure de la société médiévale: Nouvelles hypothèses sur l'origine et la fonction des kouters', in *Autour du 'village': Établissements humains, finages et communautés rurales entre Seine et Rhin (IVe–XIIIe siècles). Actes du colloque international de Louvain-la-Neuve, 16–17 mai 2003*, ed. by Jean-Marie Yante and Anne-Marie Bultot-Verleysen (Louvain: Institut d'Études Médiévales de l'Université Catholique de Louvain, 2010), pp. 379–400

Thoen, Erik, and Tim Soens, 'Appauvrissement et endettement dans le monde rural: Étude comparative du crédit dans les différents systèmes agraires en Flandre au bas Moyen Âge et au début de l'Époque Moderne', in *Il Mercato della Terra: Secc. XIII–XVIII*, ed. by Simonetta Cavaciocchi (Firenze: Le Monnier, 2004), pp. 703–820

——, 'Energy: Tension beteween Ecology and Economy in Flanders before 1800', paper presented at the International Conference, European Society for Environmental History, Prague, 2003

——, 'Van landschapsgeschiedenis naar ecologische geschiedenis: Waterbeheer in de Vlaamse kustvlakte in de Late Middeleeuwen en het Ancien Régime', *Jaarboek voor Ecologische Geschiedenis*, 4 (2001), 1–24

Thoen, Erik, and others, *Landscapes or Seascapes? The History of the Coastal Environment in the North Sea Area Reconsidered*, CORN Publication Series, 13 (Turnhout: Brepols, 2013)

Tits-Dieuaide, Marie-Jeanne, 'Peasants Dues in Brabant: The Example of the Meldert Farm near Tirlemont, 1380–1797', in *Productivity of Land and Agricultural Innovation in the Low Countries (1250–1800)*, ed. by Herman Van Der Wee and others (Leuven: Leuven University Press, 1978), pp. 109–22

Tys, Dries, 'Domeinvorming in de "wildernis" 'en de ontwikkeling van vorstelijke macht: Het voorbeeld van het bezit van de graven van Vlaanderen in het IJserestuarium tussen 900 en 1200', *Jaarboek voor Middeleeuwse Geschiedenis*, 7 (2004), 31–83

——, 'Landschap als materiële cultuur: De interactie tussen macht en ruimte in een kustgebied en de wording van een laatmiddeleeuws tot vroegmodern landschap. Kamerlings Ambacht, 500–1200/1600' (unpublished doctoral thesis, Free University of Brussels, 2003)

Vandenborre, Chris, 'Prijzen, lonen en levensstandaard in Brugge en omgeving tijdens de 14de en het begin van de 15de eeuw' (unpublished doctoral thesis, Ghent University, 1999)

Van Der Wee, Herman, 'Typologie des crises et changements de structures aux Pays-Bas (xve–xvie siècles)', *Annales: Économies, Sociétés, Civilisations*, 18 (1963), 209–25

Van Maelzake, Bart, 'De financieel-economische politiek van het Onze-Lieve-Vrouwhospitaal van Oudenaarde in de 15de en 16de eeuw', *Handelingen van de Geschied- en Oudheidkundige Kring van Oudenaarde*, 39 (2002), 261–92

Vanslembrouck, Nele, Alexander Lehouck, and Erik Thoen, 'Past Landscapes and Present-day Techniques: Reconstructing Submerged Medieval Landscapes in the Western Part of Sealand Flanders', *Landscape History*, 27 (2005), 51–64

Van Werveke, Hans, *De zwarte dood in de Zuidelijke Nederlanden (1349–1351)* (Brussels: Paleis der Academiën, 1950)

Verhulst, Adriaan, 'L'intensification et la commercialisation de l'agriculture dans les Pays-Bas méridionaux au XIIIe siècle', in *La Belgique rurale du Moyen-Âge à nos jours: Mélanges offerts à Jean-Jacques Hoebanx* (Brussels: Editions de l'Université de Bruxelles, 1984), pp. 89–100

Verstockt, Anne, 'Conjunctuurstudie van een domein in de late middeleeuwen: Het West-Zeeuws-Vlaams domein van de Gentse Sint-Pietersabdij in Oostburg Ambacht aan de hand van pachtprijzen' (unpublished masters' thesis, Ghent University 1998)

Le destin heuristique d'une histoire de la panique. La Crise en Provence au Moyen Âge finissant : Jalons historiographiques pour le XIVe siècle

Thierry Pécout

La notion de crise comme élément de périodisation historique ne laisse pas de poser problème. Le terme suppose la conception d'un temps cyclique, procédant lui-même d'une vision anthropomorphique ou organiciste des sociétés, et sous-tend les théories des cycles économiques et des fluctuations, ainsi que l'idée de processus de régulation. On en connaît certes l'origine médicale, depuis les traités hippocratiques et galéniques, le *Krisis/Krinein* qui suggère le moment crucial, le tri et l'idée de dénouement, transmis dans le vocabulaire technique médical du bas latin pour désigner la phase décisive d'une maladie.[1] Mais ce n'est qu'au XIXe siècle, à la suite d'une lente évolution sémantique entamée au XVIIe siècle, qu'il revêt un sens politique, lorsque la crise

[1] Je précise que le texte de cette intervention est daté de plusieurs années, du fait des délais pris par la publication du présent recueil: je n'en reprends pas la bibliographie et la laisse telle qu'elle était au moment de sa rédaction, en 2005. Depuis, un certain renouveau a marqué l'histoire économique, dont témoignent notamment les récents axes de recherche du laboratoire de Paris I, l'UMR LAMOP, sur le salariat, la mesure ou les techniques de construction. Je renvoie pour la période antérieure à 2005 aux remarques lexicographiques proposées par Morsel, « Crise? Quelle crise? ». Un premier bilan historiographique: Graus, *Das Spätmittelalter als Krisenzeit*, pp. 8–34.

Thierry Pécout (pecout@univ-st-etienne-fr) est professeur des universités à l'université Jean Monnet à St-Étienne. Il est directeur de l'édition de l'Enquête de Leopard da Foligno en Provence dont huit tomes ont été publiés aux Éditions du Comité des travaux historiques et scientifiques.

Crisis in the Later Middle Ages: Beyond the Postan-Duby Paradigm, ed. by John Drendel, TMC 13 (Turnhout: Brepols, 2015) 225–249 BREPOLS PUBLISHERS 10.1484/M.TMC.5.103789

devient révolutionnaire et qu'elle s'attache ainsi à la problématique du changement social. Dans la deuxième moitié du siècle, par le détour de la finance et du commerce, la crise prend une dimension économique, principalement à la faveur de la dépression de 1873 et de ses conséquences. Dans cette acception, elle reste désormais pleinement associée à une appréhension cyclique du temps. Joseph Schumpeter acheva de mettre en perspective la notion de cycle économique au milieu du XXe siècle, en articulant le propos d'un Clément Juglar (d. 1905), au sujet des contractions décennales du grand commerce, à la mise en évidence de cycles conjoncturels plus longs par Nicolas Kondratieff (d. 1938).[2] Du reste, au regard du moment historique qui nous préoccupe ici, l'enjeu principal n'est plus tellement aujourd'hui de savoir si crise il y eut, mais d'évaluer si cette notion apporte encore quelque chose à la compréhension de l'Europe du XIVe siècle, et si elle reste pertinente pour penser le processus de changement historique.

La genèse du terme comme outil d'interprétation des évolutions historiques est également bien connue. Aussi nous bornerons-nous à poser quelques jalons. Elle résulte de la conjonction de deux démarches intellectuelles qui marquèrent la pensée historique, tandis que l'érudition mettait désormais à sa disposition une plus abondante documentation comptable susceptible d'éclairer les phénomènes de conjoncture. En premier lieu, la notion émerge d'une réflexion portant sur les causes du déclin économique, de l'instabilité des monnaies et de la contraction des échanges, en particulier à l'issue des dépressions de 1920–21 et de 1929. Ainsi de John Maynard Keynes (d. 1946), dans sa *Théorie générale de l'emploi, de l'intérêt et de la monnaie* parue en 1936, partant d'une réflexion sur les problèmes récents de l'inflation, de l'endettement et de leur rôle économique, tout en articulant ce dernier avec celui de la monnaie et de sa circulation, celui du niveau des prix, indicateurs de phénomènes sociaux plus profonds.[3] De son côté, François Simiand (d. 1935), et son ouvrage sur *Les fluctuations économiques à longue période et la crise économique* paru en 1932, partait d'un examen des fluctuations des prix, pour en induire celles de l'économie et de ses rythmes, dans une démarche leur associant une évaluation du comportement des groupes sociaux.[4] Ce climat intellectuel définit les repères d'une réflexion historique qui, portée à l'examen des conjonctures, donna à l'histoire écono-

[2] Juglar, *Les crises commerciales*; Kondratieff, *Les grands cycles de la conjoncture*; Schumpeter, *Business Cycles*; Schumpeter, *The Theory of Economic Development*, trans. by Opie.

[3] Keynes, *The General Theory of Employment*.

[4] Simiand, *Les salaires*, puis Simiand, *Les fluctuations économiques*.

mique naissante son vocabulaire et ses outils, mais aussi ses premiers travers: « L'histoire économique reste une histoire dramatique, perverse, fébrile, histoire de la panique », pouvait déclarer Pierre Chaunu.[5]

Cette démarche fut sous-tendue par l'élaboration de méthodes statistiques et quantitatives, sous l'influence d'un François Simiand qui avait posé le prix comme baromètre essentiel de la vie économique. Il s'agissait alors de dépasser l'histoire déjà vieillissante des conversions et mutations monétaires, pour aborder celle de l'identification d'une conjoncture. La réflexion sur l'histoire des prix s'avère déjà nourrie autour des années 1930, témoin le *Money, Prices and Wages in Valencia, Aragon and Navarre* d'Hamilton, en 1936, ou encore l'article de Marc Bloch paru dans les *Annales* en 1939.[6] Elle débouche après guerre sur l'analyse de l'essor économique et des phénomènes de croissance, du décollage des économies et des inégalités de développement, avec en particulier Walt Rostow et ses *Étapes de la croissance* de 1960, connu en français en 1963.[7]

Au demeurant, cette fermentation a tout d'abord touché l'histoire moderne et contemporaine, avant de s'étendre à la période du Moyen Âge finissant. Le modèle historiographique élaboré par Ernest Labrousse, qui propose un processus historique composé de phénomènes étagés et de cycles imbriqués, détermina la vision d'un XVIIIe siècle en proie à une crise multiforme, posant l'économique comme élément central du changement social et politique. Avec son *Esquisse du mouvement des prix et des revenus en France au XVIIIe siècle* de 1932, puis sa *Crise de l'économie française à la fin de l'Ancien Régime*, parue en 1943, il s'agissait d'induire du mouvement des prix et des revenus une histoire de l'évolution sociale, ces derniers permettant d'isoler et de caractériser les classes sociales.[8] Le modèle de la crise dite d'Ancien Régime, propre aux sociétés préindustrielles, en émergeait.

Se trouvait ainsi posé un cadre explicatif applicable à la fin du Moyen Âge, du moins pour les régions les mieux documentées dans ce domaine. L'apport de l'historiographie allemande et anglaise marqua en outre profondément les méthodes de réflexion, en particulier pour l'histoire rurale, en inscrivant le problème dans une dimension spatiale, avec le thème de la désertion de l'habitat et des finages. Wilhelm Abel, dans son *Agrarkrisen und Agrarkonjunktur in Mitteleuropa* (1935), puis Michael Postan mettaient en relation nécessaire les

[5] Chaunu, « L'histoire sérielle ».

[6] Un premier jalon avait été posé par Vivier, « Une crise économique ». Hamilton, *Money, Prices and Wages*. Bloch, « L'histoire des prix ».

[7] Rostow, *Les étapes de la croissance*.

[8] Labrousse, *Esquisse du mouvement*, puis Labrousse, *Crise de l'économie française*.

capacités de production et le niveau démographique, dans un contexte technique donné. L'ajustement malthusien — notamment sous la forme des « obstacles positifs » isolés par le pasteur anglais — de la population aux ressources, caractérisait les crises frumentaires du XIVe siècle.[9] Ces dernières se manifestaient principalement à travers deux phénomènes, les *Wüstungen* au regard de l'espace habité et cultivé, et la *Preisshere* à propos des revenus et des prix.

Il appartint à la génération suivante d'affiner en France ou en Flandre l'usage de la crise et d'en déployer les potentialités. Robert Boutruche en décrivait les composantes sociales et politiques à propos de la classe nobiliaire, pour laquelle il isolait « une terrible crise », dans « Aux origines d'une crise nobiliaire: Donations pieuses et pratiques successorales en Bordelais du XIIIe au XVIe siècle » (1939), en articulant effets des guerres, morcellement des héritages et des patrimoines, disparition des vieilles familles.[10] Édouard Perroy proposait quant à lui un modèle d'histoire rurale, avec « À l'origine d'une économie contractée: Les crises du XIVe siècle », paru dans les *Annales* en 1949, tout en soulignant que la notion de crise s'avérait ambivalente, puisqu'elle désignait à la fois une rupture brutale et des transformations s'inscrivant dans la longue durée. Pour sa part, Léopold Génicot en s'attachant à la *Crise agricole du bas Moyen Âge dans le Namurois*, insistait aussi sur les mutations spatiales, en étudiant à partir du dernier quart du XIVe siècle la désertion de l'habitat et l'abandon des finages, en stigmatisant la baisse des prix céréaliers (terres agricoles et grains) et la hausse des coûts du travail et de la main d'œuvre. Il proposait ainsi de nuancer fortement l'impact de ces phénomènes de crise selon les groupes sociaux.[11] Un modèle achevé de ce type d'interprétation figurait en 1966 sous la plume à nouveau de Génicot, dans un chapitre intitulé « Crisis:

[9] Abel, *Agrarkrisen und Agrarkonjunktur in Mitteleuropa*. Et les mises au point plus récentes, Abel, *Agrarkrisen und Agrarkonjunktur*; Abel, *Strukturen und Krisen*; Postan, « The Fifteenth Century »; Postan, « Some Social Consequences »; Postan, « Some Economic Evidence ». Sur l'interprétation des diverses manifestations de la crise du XIVe siècle, et la discussion des thèses de Postan, voir l'intéressante petite synthèse de Herlihy, *La peste noire et la mutation*; sur l'épidémie de peste comme facteur exogène de déblocage d'un développement occidental figé, Campbell, *Before the Black Death*; Lucas, « The Great European Famine ». Pour le modèle malthusien formulé en 1798, puis par des rééditions successives jusqu'en 1826: Malthus, *An Essay on the Principle of Population*, qui distingue « obstacles positifs », comme les crises épidémiques ou frumentaires, et « obstacles préventifs », telles les pratiques matrimoniales et testamentaires induites par les coûts de la vie ou de la terre.

[10] Boutruche, « Aux origines d'une crise nobiliaire »; Boutruche, *La crise d'une société*.

[11] Perroy, « La crise économique »; Perroy, « A l'origine d'une économie contractée »; Génicot, *La crise agricole du bas Moyen Âge*.

From the Middle Ages to Modern Times », de la *Cambridge Economic History of Europe*.[12] L'ensemble de ces courants historiographiques complexes marque encore les travaux de Marie Jeanne Tits-Dieuaide, avec *La formation des prix céréaliers en Brabant et en Flandre au XV*e *siècle* (1975), et les *Prix et salaires à Florence au XIV*e *siècle (1280–1380)* de Charles de La Roncière (1982).[13] Enfin, dans un contexte idéologique proche du marxisme, la réflexion aboutissait en 1976 avec Guy Bois à propos de la Normandie orientale au XIVe siècle, à la mise en évidence d'un modèle où la crise résultait des hiérarchies et inégalités sociales, d'un déséquilibre de l'économie agraire provenant de la ponction seigneuriale conçue alors comme un sur-prélèvement, sans toutefois que la perspective ne se départe de certains présupposés néo-malthusiens.[14]

Dans le cas de la Provence, les efforts pour élaborer une histoire de la conjoncture économique se sont heurtés aux difficultés pour constituer un *corpus* documentaire ample, suffisamment pour dépasser l'étude des structures seigneuriales. En cela, on notera le rôle déterminant, mais tardif, de la découverte et de l'exploitation des sources notariales qui ont ouvert de larges perspectives, y compris très récemment pour l'histoire des représentations, des conflits et de leurs modes de régulation.[15]

Dans l'historiographie provençale, longtemps la conjoncture économique parut tributaire à l'envi de la trame événementielle mise en place par l'histoire politique. À une période de construction dynastique et d'essor territorial, sous les maisons comtales catalane et angevine, succède ainsi une ère de troubles politiques à partir du milieu du XIVe siècle, au premier chef sous le règne de Jeanne de Naples.[16] Cette trame et ses conséquences socio-économiques se trouvent sans doute marquées par Henri Denifle et sa *Guerre de Cent ans et la désolation des églises de France*, comme le suggère la perspective d'un Victor-Louis Bourrilly dans son article sur Du Guesclin paru dans la *Revue historique* en 1926.[17]

[12] Génicot, « Crisis: From the Middle Ages ».

[13] Tits-Dieuaide, *La formation des prix céréaliers*, et De la Roncière, *Prix et salaires à Florence*.

[14] Bois, *Crise du féodalisme*.

[15] Nous pensons pour le monde urbain aux travaux de Smail, « Common Violence »; Smail, « Démanteler le patrimoine »; Smail, « Notaries, Courts and the Legal Culture »; Smail, « The General Taille of Marseille »; Smail, *Imaginary Cartographies*; Smail, « La topographie socio-professionnelle »; Smail, *The Consumption of Justice*.

[16] Le monumental travail, très touffu mais demeuré inachevé, d'Émile-G. Léonard, mettait à la disposition des chercheurs une trame événementielle tragique: Léonard, *La jeunesse de Jeanne I*, et du même, Léonard, *Histoire de Jeanne reine de Naples*, III.

[17] Denifle, *La guerre de Cent*. Cette perspective marque encore le premier Coulet, « La

La meilleure histoire synthétique de la Provence médiévale demeure l'œuvre de Raoul Busquet et de Victor-Louis Bourrilly. Elle date de 1924. Le chapitre consacré à la vie économique et sociale y occupe une place secondaire, en fin de volume. L'attention des auteurs s'y porte en particulier sur l'évocation des structures seigneuriales. Aucune recherche ne permettant alors de retracer la moindre évolution de conjoncture, l'essentiel reste la description du prélèvement et de la composition de la rente seigneuriale. S'y adjoint une évocation des activités de production et d'échange. Elle s'articule autour de grands secteurs économiques, division sans doute on ne peut plus discutable pour le Moyen Âge. L'agriculture connaît un développement limité, marqué par le repli sur soi et de faibles rendements entre les XIe et XIIIe siècles. Son évolution, tout comme celle de la démographie, reste tributaire de la situation politique et de l'insécurité des campagnes: la guerre est particulièrement mise en avant comme facteur de déséquilibre. Ainsi, « minée, écrasée de tailles, la population diminua dans des proportions qu'il est impossible de chiffrer, mais qui furent certainement considérables »; puis, « c'est seulement à partir du milieu du XVe siècle, avec le rétablissement de la tranquillité et de l'ordre, que s'amorça une sorte de renaissance ».[18] L'explication par la peste et le facteur démographique n'avaient pas encore trouvé droit de cité avant les travaux d'Édouard Baratier. L'industrie est pour sa part marquée par la misère, la raréfaction de la main d'œuvre et l'augmentation des prix. Si elle connaît une « crise » grave, elle s'avère moins profonde que dans le secteur précédent. Quant au commerce, essentiellement tributaire des études de l'archiviste Louis Blancard sur le port de Marseille, son évolution reste largement liée à l'expansion politique angevine en Méditerranée à la fin du XIIIe siècle, puis à ses difficultés militaires au XIVe siècle.[19]

La génération suivante a mené des recherches beaucoup plus fines, sans se départir toutefois pleinement de ce cadre. La synthèse d'Édouard Baratier parue en 1971, dans un chapitre sur « Splendeur d'Avignon et malheurs des temps », explore la notion de crise et intègre cette trame politique dans une perspective beaucoup plus large.[20] Elle part cependant d'un postulat très général, selon lequel « dans toute l'Europe occidentale, le XIVe siècle apparaît comme une période où tout est remis en question: la hiérarchie sociale, l'équilibre politique

désolation des églises de Provence ». Victor-Bourrilly, « Du Guesclin ».

[18] Bourrilly et Busquet, *La Provence au Moyen Âge*, p. 426. Il s'agit d'une édition de leurs contributions respectives à l'ouvrage Masson, *Les Bouches-du-Rhône*, II.

[19] Blancard, *Documents inédits sur le commerce*; Blancard, « Note sur la lettre de change ».

[20] Baratier, *Histoire de la Provence*, 186–207.

des nations, les croyances philosophiques et religieuses ». L'historien y insère une « crise générale » en Provence, comme une illustration locale d'un phénomène total. Elle se caractérise désormais par l'épidémie de peste, dès 1347; des famines, dont Édouard Baratier peut dresser les rythmes et proposer la chronologie, en particulier grâce aux travaux de Louis Stouff: en 1323, 1329, 1332, 1357 et 1368–75; et enfin des troubles politiques durant le règne de la reine Jeanne de Naples, dès 1355 avec le brigandage des routiers, entre 1382 et 1388 avec la guerre de l'Union d'Aix, puis en 1392–99 avec la mise en coupe réglée du pays par les bandes de Raymond de Turenne. Et le Grand Schisme ajoute encore à l'instabilité de la période.

L'historiographie provençale a donc posé depuis longtemps comme une évidence l'existence d'une crise polymorphe, durant tout le XIVe siècle: d'abord larvée et se manifestant dans la stagnation de l'activité et de la démographie, puis beaucoup plus brutale avec la guerre et la peste. Cette piste s'est avérée féconde, et elle a marqué l'esprit de toute une école de pensée locale qui déborde les cadres érudits et universitaires.

L'ombre tutélaire de Georges Duby plane indéniablement sur cette dernière, qui a su lui donner une formulation synthétique dans les pages de son *Économie rurale* évoquant la Provence.[21] Ce sont tout d'abord les formes de la crise, et notamment ses éléments démographiques, qui ont bénéficié les premiers d'un travail fondateur et pionnier, la *Démographie provençale* d'Édouard Baratier, parue en 1961.[22] Il s'agit en fait d'un recueil de données statistiques et de précieuses mises au point sur la fiscalité comtale, détour obligé de toute réflexion d'ordre démographique pour cette période. Localement, l'ouvrage inspire l'étude menée sur le recours de feu de Puget-Théniers en 1343, qui met en évidence la crise démographique marquant alors la haute Provence, et il inspire encore en partie le travail universitaire de Guillaume de Jerphanion sur *Population et peuplement dans la baillie de Barjols au XIVe siècle*.[23] Tous mettent en évidence les signes d'une crise démographique affectant la Provence dans

[21] Duby, *L'économie rurale*. Nous n'insisterons pas ici sur le modèle proposé par G. Duby, déjà traité dans l'introduction.

[22] Baratier, *La démographie provençale*. L'étude s'enrichit en outre de l'édition des Baratier, *Enquêtes sur les droits et revenus de Charles Ier*.

[23] Jonas, « Note sur un recours ». Voir aussi, pour la fin du siècle précédent: Baratier, « Entraunes et Saint-Martin d'Entraunes ». Laure Verdon a complété cette approche sous l'angle de l'économie et des pouvoirs seigneuriaux dans Verdon, « La seigneurie en Provence au XIIIe siècle »; de Jerphanion, « L'évolution démographique dans la baillie de Barjols du XIVe au XVe siècle », qui synthetise les resultats de son travail universitaire.

les vingt années précédant la peste. En revanche, sur cette dernière, les travaux, comme les sources, demeurent rares: aussi a-t-elle été surtout envisagée indirectement, à travers certaines formes de violence collective, notamment anti-judaïques.[24]

Toutefois, Louis Stouff relevait en 1976, dans un article des *Annales de démographie historique*, le manque de finesse des données démographiques disponibles, qui ne permettent au mieux que d'identifier de grandes tendances, tels la désertion de l'habitat, la répartition de la population entre haute et basse Provence et les principaux flux migratoires.[25] La recherche concernant les problèmes de subsistance et l'économie céréalière restait encore à faire.[26] Mais ces questions débouchèrent sur la mise au point d'outils inestimables, tel le travail cartographique considérable proposé par les auteurs de l'*Atlas historique* paru en 1969, ou encore sur des recherches monographiques fondées sur les sources cadastrales et mettant à profit les premières générations de l'informatique, comme l'illustrent les publications de Monique Zerner.[27] Sans doute fécondèrent-elles aussi en partie les premières grandes prospections archéologiques, dominées par la question du peuplement, de la désertion et du perchement de l'habitat, de ses relations avec les lieux de culte ou de pouvoir, comme en témoigne la présentation de Gabrielle Démians d'Archimbaud et Michel Fixot en 1977.[28]

C'est que la problématique de l'habitat castral constitue un deuxième type d'approfondissement de la question de la crise et de ses formes. La perspective était déjà placée dans la longue durée, avec la parution en 1964 de l'ouvrage de Paul-Albert Février sur *Le développement urbain en Provence*.[29] Le déplacement de l'habitat, qu'il soit d'ailleurs urbain ou villageois, la réflexion sur le lexique, la toponymie et le binôme *villa-castrum*, le perchement et les phénomènes d'*incastellamento*, ont bénéficié de l'apport de l'archéologie, avec la singulière

[24] Shatzmiller, « Les Juifs de Provence ».

[25] Stouff, « Alimentation et démographie ». Voir cependant, à partir des testaments, Michaud, « La peste, la peur et l'espoir ».

[26] Lesage, « Les difficultés de ravitaillement »; Stouff, « Le ravitaillement ».

[27] Baratier et autres, *Atlas Historique*; Zerner, *Le cadastre, le pouvoir et la terre*; Zerner, « Recherche d'une méthode d'interprétation démographique »; Zerner, « Une crise de mortalité »; Zerner, « Les trois états du Comtat Venaissin »; Coulet, « À propos d'un cadastre provençal ».

[28] Démians d'Archimbaud et Fixot, « L'organisation de la campagne ».

[29] Février, *Le développement urbain en Provence*.

et exhaustive monographie sur le village de Rougiers et les prospections de la région de Pélissanne ou du centre Var, même si dans ces deux derniers cas, c'est essentiellement le premier *incastellamento* qui s'est trouvé mis en évidence.[30] Le déperchement et la désertion de l'habitat étaient, dès 1965, l'objet d'une mise au point de Gabrielle Démians d'Archimbaud, tandis que Noël Coulet en brossait un cas d'école avec la localité du Sambuc, dans l'arrière-pays aixois, en 1977.[31] Les nouveaux phénomènes de dispersion de l'habitat aux derniers siècles du Moyen Âge, centrés sur le thème des bastides, donnent enfin des travaux comme ceux de Louis Stouff et de Noël Coulet en 1980.[32] En 1987, la synthèse publiée par les mêmes à propos du *Village de Provence au bas Moyen Âge*, rend compte en partie de ces diverses perspectives, tout en insistant toutefois sur les problèmes de structure.[33]

La démographie historique posait la question des équilibres, induisant par-là une interrogation sur les méthodes de gestion et de financement de l'économie seigneuriale ou paysanne. Or, la réflexion sur les causes de la crise et les facteurs de ruptures a bénéficié de l'ouverture de nouveaux champs historiques. L'exploitation de fonds d'archives, jusqu'ici restés peu étudiés, celui des Hospitaliers du grand prieuré de Saint-Gilles, puis les sources notariales, ont fourni aux recherches des aliments de choix.[34] La question des ressources économiques et des niveaux de population a paru d'abord nourrir des travaux portant sur la haute Provence montagneuse. Cette perspective néo-malthusienne typique s'est appliquée à l'écosystème fragile des vallées alpines ou basses alpines. C'est en particulier le thème du surpâturage qui a alimenté la réflexion, depuis les *Cultures en Haute-Provence* de Thérèse Sclafert parues en 1959, débouchant ensuite sur de nombreux travaux aux perspectives nouvelles, portant sur les pratiques de l'élevage, sa signification au regard des contractions démographiques, du développement des marchés urbains, du recul des

[30] Démians d'Archimbaud, *Rougiers, village médiéval*; Fixot, « La construction de châteaux »; Fixot, « À la recherche des formes les plus anciennes ».

[31] Démians d'Archimbaud, « Archéologie des villages désertés »; Coulet, « La survie des communautés »; Coulet, « Encore les villages disparus »; Coulet, « Un village éphémère ».

[32] Coulet, « La naissance de la bastide provençale »; Coulet, « La bastide provençale »; Stouff, « Le mas arlésien ».

[33] Coulet et Stouff, *Le village de Provence*.

[34] De grandes réorganisations archivistiques et la mise au point de guides critiques en facilitent l'accès. Baratier et autres, *Répertoire de la série H. 56 H*. Bautier et Sornay, *Les sources de l'histoire économique et sociale du Moyen Âge*, I; Bautier et autres, *Les sources de l'histoire économique et sociale du Moyen Âge*, II.

cultures.[35] La réflexion sur les équilibres économiques pose aussi le problème de la dette et de l'investissement. Ce dernier s'est vu abordé sous un angle sociologique, à travers l'étude des hiérarchies et valeurs sociales. La recherche sur l'endettement paysan doit en effet se relier à un mode d'approche privilégiant l'idée de paupérisation, mais s'interrogeant aussi bien sur sa dimension économique qu'idéologique. En 1973, Rodrigue Lavoie développe ainsi une réflexion féconde sur l'endettement, à partir des listes de la justice comtale des XIVe et XVe siècles, et s'interroge sur la signification sociale de la pauvreté,[36] thèmes qui se prolongent chez Andrée Courtemanche et aujourd'hui chez John Drendel.[37]

La question des facteurs de la crise agraire a très vite amené les chercheurs à s'interroger sur la rentabilité de l'économie seigneuriale. C'est Georges Duby qui a su tirer parti du fonds exceptionnel des Hospitaliers du grand prieuré de Saint-Gilles et de ses dépendances provençales, singulièrement de l'enquête générale menée en 1338 dans leurs possessions, éditée en 1982, et celle de 1373.[38] Se trouvent dès lors exploitées les questions des techniques, des rendements, du recours au salariat, du passage à un mode de faire-valoir indirect, avec facherie et mègerie. Elles génèrent à leur tour de nouveaux repères, au regard de l'évolution des coûts du travail, des formes de redistribution de la rente seigneuriale, et des difficultés de sa gestion. Benoît Beaucage caractérise ainsi le déficit chronique des commanderies de la vallée du Rhône.[39] En revanche, la guerre et les troubles politiques, sans doute surévalués dans un premier temps, ont connu par la suite une longue éclipse. Fred Menkès, à propos de Trets, en minimise l'impact.[40] Plus récemment, dans le sillage de Noël Coulet, qui l'a appréhendée en termes de fiscalité urbaine et de financement de la mise en défense des villes provençales, la guerre connaît un regain d'intérêt comme objet historique, avec ses implications fiscales et politiques, et l'émergence des assemblées représentatives, aussi bien

[35] Sclafert, *Cultures en Haute-Provence*. Par la suite, les travaux sur l'élevage et les transhumances ont connu un très fort développement: Coste, « La vie pastorale »; Coste, « L'origine de la transhumance en Provence »; Coulet, « Sources et aspects de l'histoire »; Coste, « Du XIIIe au XVe siècle »; Coste, « Notes sur l'élevage ».

[36] Lavoie, « Endettement et pauvreté »; Lavoie, « Processus de marginalisation en milieu rural ».

[37] Courtemanche, « Les femmes juives »; Drendel, « Gens d'Église et crédit ».

[38] Duby, « Techniques et rendements agricoles »; Duby, « Note sur les corvées »; Duby, « La seigneurie et l'économie paysanne »; Beaucage, *Visites générales des commanderies*.

[39] Beaucage, « Une énigme des Hospitaliers »; Beaucage, « L'effondrement de la gestion du patrimoine ».

[40] Menkès, « Une communauté juive en Provence ».

chez un Régis Veydarier à propos des déprédations de Raymond de Turenne, que chez un Germain Butaud dans le Comtat Venaissin entre 1355 et 1451.[41]

Enfin, certain scepticisme affiché devant le caractère généralisé d'une crise en Provence, précocement formulé par Louis Stouff en 1964, devait conduire à affiner considérablement la recherche sur la conjoncture économique et agraire. Il s'agissait d'abord de mener à bien une réflexion sur le mouvement des prix, en exploitant des sources très riches, comme les informations ponctuelles de la chambre des comptes, en particulier pour le milieu du XIVe siècle.[42] Puis c'est l'économie céréalière, et le problème des crises de subsistance, qui sont abordés avant 1970, et en 1976 avec la parution de l'enquête de Louis Stouff sur l'alimentation et la démographie en Provence, qui s'interroge sur la fréquence des disettes à partir de 1315.[43] De fait, la terminologie les caractérisant reste des plus floues et le chercheur remarque notre incapacité à donner une évaluation précise de leur impact sur la mortalité. Elles provoquent indéniablement des phénomènes migratoires, des carences alimentaires probables que permettent d'induire un examen des sources comptables de certains établissements, telles les petites écoles urbaines que la papauté d'Avignon tente d'installer en Provence.[44] Actuellement, les travaux de John Drendel donnent à ce domaine de nouveaux outils chronologiques et méthodologiques.[45]

La réflexion menée jusqu'alors a permis de mettre en valeur de nouvelles pistes et d'exploiter des fonds d'archives restés peu sollicités. C'est ainsi l'apport des sources notariales, des délibérations communales et des enquêtes comtales qui a suscité un véritable bouleversement des perspectives.[46] Leur angle

[41] Coulet, *Aix en Provence*; Michel Hébert avait montré la voie: Hébert, « Guerre, finance et administration »; Hébert, « Aux origines des États de Provence ». Veydarier, « Raymond de Turenne »; Butaud, « Guerre et vie publique »; Butaud, « Villages et villageois ».

[42] Ainsi du registre Archives départementales des Bouches-du-Rhône, B 1143, exploité par Stouff, « Une enquête économique », aussi bien au regard de l'évolution des prix que des poids et mesures.

[43] Stouff, *Ravitaillement et alimentation*; Stouff, « Alimentation et démographie ».

[44] Stouff, « Une création d'Urbain V ».

[45] En témoignent les contributions de John Drendel au groupe de recherche portant sur « La conjoncture de 1300 en Méditerranée occidentale », qui fédère les efforts de chercheurs de l'UMR LAMOP (Paris I), de l'Université du Québec à Montréal et de l'École Normale Supérieure: Bourin, Drendel, and Menant, *Les disettes dans la conjoncture de 1300.* En particulier celle portant sur la Provence, au séminaire tenu à l'École française de Rome en février 2004, Bourin et Menant, « Les disettes dans la conjoncture de 1300 ».

[46] En cela, occupe une place pionnière l'étude de Malaussena, *La vie en Provence orientale.*

de vue local a nécessité l'abandon de considérations générales et a suscité une série de travaux monographiques, seuls aptes à cerner les contours de l'économie agraire et de sa conjoncture. La moisson a été considérable, depuis l'étude de Louis Stouff sur les pays de la montagne de Lure, aux confins du Vaucluse et des Alpes-de-Haute-Provence actuels, jusqu'aux monographies urbaines portant sur Aix, Arles, Tarascon, qui posent le problème des relations complexes avec un territoire rural et ses réseaux; en passant par des localités plus modestes, mais à l'apport d'autant plus significatif pour l'histoire rurale, comme Berre, où Jean Birrel montrait, dès 1968, l'insuffisance des sources pour isoler des phénomènes de conjoncture et signalait néanmoins des « signes de dépression », ou bien Manosque, Reillanne, Draguignan, Pourrières, Trets, et encore Brignoles.[47] La haute Provence n'est pas en reste, avec sa structure économique spécifique combinant élevage et exploitation forestière.[48]

En outre, la réflexion autour du crédit rural a permis de montrer les grandes capacités d'adaptation du monde agraire aux aléas de la conjoncture et à la pression démographique, le rôle déterminant joué par le notariat, et la présence de modes d'investissement locaux, tandis que s'est affinée la réflexion sur l'impact des prélèvements comtaux sur la société paysanne.[49] Très récemment enfin, on assiste à un renouveau des recherches portant sur la conjoncture du XIVe siècle, en particulier à propos du problème de la crise frumentaire.[50] Quant à la vie économique de Marseille, après une attention soutenue sur ses activités com-

[47] Stouff, « Un aspect de la Haute-Provence »; Coulet, *Aix en Provence*; Stouff, *Arles à la fin du Moyen Âge*; Hébert, « La ville de Tarascon »; Roux, « Tarascon au XVe siècle »; Shatzmiller, *Recherches sur la communauté juive*; Rutkowska-Płachcińska, *Salon-de-Provence*; Birrel, « Berre à la fin du Moyen-Âge ». Poppe, *Economie et société d'un bourg provençal*, et Poppe, « Saint-Christol à l'époque médiévale », qui exploite cependant d'autres fonds que les documents notariés et achève ses investigations à la fin du XIIIe siècle, prodrome d'une crise postulée; Coulet, « Population et société à Pourrières ». Saint-Pierre, « Le corpus notarial de Brignoles », qui s'attache essentiellement aux pratiques notariales. Drendel, « Society and Economy »; Trets est éclairé par les plus anciens registres notariés de la Provence rurale.

[48] Boyer, *La Vésubie*; Boyer, « Pour une histoire des forêts de Haute-Provence ».

[49] Bourin, Drendel, and Menant, *Les disettes dans la conjoncture de 1300*, voir note *supra*; Drendel, « Notarial Practice Rural Provence »; Drendel, « Gens d'Église et crédit ». Pour le notariat à Toulon: Barnel, « Une ville provençale »; Zerner, « La question du crédit dans les campagnes »; Shatzmiller, *Shylock revu et corrigé*, qui, à propos du Juif marseillais Bondavin de Draguignan, amène à reconsidérer les relations entre le créancier et sa clientèle, au moins en milieu urbain; Drendel, « Jews, Villagers and the Count ».

[50] Voir *supra* à propos de Bourin, Drendel, and Menant, *Les disettes dans la conjoncture de 1300*.

merciales, les recherches se sont déplacées vers l'espace urbain et portuaire, à la suite de fructueuses prospections archéologiques.[51] Mais les activités artisanales et les métiers restèrent un domaine peu fréquenté par la recherche, jusqu'à une date récente.[52] Les milieux professionnels marseillais, la question des salaires et des prix, du marché de l'emploi, de l'apprentissage et de l'essor de familles drapières, ont connu ainsi de notables avancées, en particulier grâce aux travaux de Francine Michaud.[53] Dans le sillage des recherches de Mathieu Arnoux, et à travers celles de Philippe Bernardi, l'existence d'une activité industrielle propre à la période médiévale est aussi posée.[54]

Enfin, la dernière génération de recherches monographiques a connu sensiblement un déplacement de ses centres d'intérêts, davantage marqués par l'histoire sociale. Elle se caractérise par une réflexion portée vers les groupes sociaux dominants, leur cohésion et leur capacité à perpétuer leur rang, leur patrimoine et leur statut. Francine Michaud étudia les structures familiales à Marseille, en un travail très original et pionnier qui s'attache au problème de la transmission des patrimoines, entre les années 1270 et 1320, et qui bénéficie indirectement de l'apport lointain des études classiques de juristes tels Roger Aubenas ou Charles de Ribbe.[55] Cette démarche peut se comparer à celle de Monique Wernham à propos de la communauté juive de Salon-de-Provence.[56] Le thème

[51] André-Sayous, « L'activité de deux capitalistes commerçants marseillais »; Pernoud, « Essai sur l'histoire du port de Marseille ». Jusqu'à la synthèse proposée par Busquet et Pernoud, *Histoire du commerce de Marseille*; Baratier et Reynaud, *Histoire du commerce de Marseille*, un renouveau stimulé par le dépouillement des plus anciennes sources notariales; Pryor, *Business Contracts of Medieval Provence*; Pryor, « Commenda: The Operation of the Contract ». Ce sont aujourd'hui le port et son environnement qui sont l'objet des recherches les plus actives, Bouiron, « Marseille, du Lacydon au faubourg Sainte-Catherine »; Bouiron et autres, *Marseille*.

[52] Dupanloup, « La corporation des cuiratiers »; Murat, « Navires et navigations »; Bernardi, *Métiers du bâtiment et techniques de construction*; Bernardi, « Apprentissage et transmission »; Bernardi, « Statuts inédits de la confrérie ».

[53] Maurel, « Grands marchands »; Michaud, « Apprentissage et salariat »; Michaud, « Exploités ou profiteurs? »; Michaud, « Travail et mouvements »; Michaud, « Serviteurs et domestiques »; Barnel, « Une famille de drapiers »; Barnel, « La boutique des frères Favas »; Grava, « Marchands, pêcheurs ».

[54] Arnoux, *Mines, férons et maîtres de forge*; Coulet, « Prospections minières ».

[55] Michaud, *Un signe des temps*. À rapprocher de Courtemanche, *La richesse des femmes* et Courtemanche, « Femmes et accès au patrimoine »; Ribbe, *La société provençale*; Aubenas, « La famille en Provence »; Aubenas, « Le servage à Castellane »; Aubenas, « Tendances archaïsantes ».

[56] Wernham, *La communauté juive*.

des stratégies familiales autour du pouvoir et de la notabilité, la question de la survie des familles dominantes en milieu urbain, et celle aussi de la fabrication puis de la pérennité des élites, sous-tendent les travaux de Christian Maurel à propos des Forbin,[57] ou encore de Lucie Larochelle sur la notabilité aixoise.[58]

Ce questionnement répond en écho à celui qui est mené à propos du groupe nobiliaire, et de la « crise de la noblesse », autrement dit de son adaptation. Déjà se trouvait posée la question du renouvellement des élites seigneuriales, à travers les transferts de patrimoines seigneuriaux examinés par Michel Hébert en 1987.[59] Ce sont les études monographiques, portant sur des groupes précisément localisés qui, à la suite du travail novateur de Martin Aurell sur la famille arlésienne des Porcelet, ont permis de souligner les plus ou moins grandes facultés d'adaptation des vieilles familles aristocratiques, aussi bien en basse Provence, avec les Baux, les Agoult-Simiane et les vicomtes de Marseille, qu'en haute Provence, avec les Blacas, les Moustiers, les Pontevès, les Augier-Spada et les Castellane, ou bien dans les Baronnies des Mévouillon, des Montauban et des Mison, ou encore en Comtat Venaissin.[60] Il reste cependant à préciser beaucoup de points, en particulier à propos de la frange inférieure de l'aristocratie, de ses contours mouvants et de la diversité de ses revenus.[61] Autant de perspectives qui ont pour la plupart abandonné le thème d'une crise globale de la noblesse, pour souligner ses recompositions internes et la complexité de ses relations avec le pouvoir princier.

Ce bref survol est loin d'avoir épuisé le sujet. Au moins aura-t-il fourni le prétexte d'un inventaire des investigations économiques qui ont marqué l'historiographie de la Provence des derniers siècles du Moyen Âge. On aura remarqué à quel point la démarche strictement économique semble avoir aujourd'hui déserté les préoccupations des chercheurs. Sans doute s'est-elle déplacée vers l'histoire des techniques, des mutations patrimoniales et des structures de l'espace et de l'habitat ruraux. Il reste que l'idée d'une crise dans la Provence du

[57] Maurel, « Structures familiales ».

[58] Larochelle, « Boni, probi et sufficientes ».

[59] Hébert, « Les ordonnances de 1289–1294 »; Hébert, « Les mutations foncières ».

[60] Aurell, *Une famille de la noblesse provençale*; Mazel, « La noblesse et l'Église en Provence »; Pécout, « Une société rurale »; Estienne, « Les réseaux castraux et l'évolution »; Butaud, « Guerre et vie publique ».

[61] C'est en grande partie le propos de la recherche menée au sein de l'UMR CÉPAM de l'université de Nice-Sophia Antipolis, qui, à l'initiative de Germain Butaud, a pris pour objet d'étude la coseigneurie depuis 2004. Voir aussi les quelques pistes que j'avais proposées: Pécout, « Les mutations du pouvoir seigneurial »; Pécout, « Noblesse provençale et pouvoir comtal ».

XIVe siècle a généré une profonde refonte des outils intellectuels et des méthodes d'analyse, conduisant les chercheurs à exploiter de nouveaux fonds d'archives et à valoriser la démarche monographique. Est-ce à dire que la perspective macro-économique, que postule *a priori* pareille notion, ne nous apprend jamais grand chose sur le fonctionnement d'une société? Ou bien qu'elle n'est tout simplement que l'autre face de l'historicité? Indéniablement discutable dans ses présupposés, la notion de crise a sans doute suggéré une approche tragique de l'histoire provençale, toujours susceptible d'éveiller curiosités, questionnements et vocations de chercheurs. Du destin heuristique d'une histoire de la panique, en quelque sorte.

Bibliographie

Sources primaires imprimées

Baratier, Édouard, éd., *Enquêtes sur les droits et revenus de Charles Ier d'Anjou en Provence (1252 et 1278)* (Paris: Bibliothèque Nationale, 1969)

Beaucage, Benoît, éd., *Visites générales des commanderies dépendantes du grand prieuré de Saint-Gilles, 1338* (Aix-en-Provence: Université de Provence,1982)

Sources secondaires

Abel, Wilhelm, *Agrarkrisen und Agrarkonjunktur in Mitteleuropa vom 13. bis 19. Jahrhundert* (Berlin: Parey, 1933)

——, *Agrarkrisen und Agrarkonjunktur: Geschichte des Land- und Ernährungswirtschaft Mitteleuropas seit den hohen Mittlealter*, 3rd édn (Berlin: Parey, 1978)

——, *Strukturen und Krisen der spätmittelalterlichen Wirtschaft* (Stuttgart: Fischer, 1980)

André-Sayous, Emile, « L'activité de deux capitalistes commerçants marseillais du XIIIe siècle: Bernard de Manduel (1227–1237) et Jean de Manduel (1233–1263) », *Revue d'histoire économique et sociale*, 17 (1929), 137–55

Arnoux, Matthieu, *Mines, férons et maîtres de forge: Études sur la production du fer dans la Normandie du Moyen Âge, XIe–XVe siècles* (Paris: CTHS, 1993)

Aubenas, Roger, « La famille en Provence », *Annales d'histoire économique et sociale*, 8 (1936), 526–41

——, « Le servage à Castellane au XIVe siècle », *Revue Historique de droit français et étranger*, 16 (1937), 77–93

——, « Tendances archaïsantes et famille artificielle en pays de droit écrit au Moyen Âge », *Annales du Midi*, 53 (1941), 113–41

Aurell, Martin, *Une famille de la noblesse provençale au Moyen Âge, les Porcelet* (Avignon: Aubanel, 1986)

Baratier, Édouard, *La démographie provençale du XIIIe au XVIe siècle avec chiffres de comparaison pour le XVIIIe siècle* (Paris: SEVPEN, 1961)

——, éd., *Enquêtes sur les droits et revenus de Charles I d'Anjou en Provence (1252 et 1278)* (Paris: Bibliothèque Nationale, 1969)

——, « Entraunes et Saint-Martin d'Entraunes au XIIIe siècle », dans *Actes du 90e Congrès des Sociétés Savantes, Bulletin philologique et historique*, tenu à Nice en 1965 (Paris: CTHS, 1968), pp. 13–36

——, éd., *Histoire de la Provence* (Toulouse: Privat, 1971)

Baratier, Édouard, et Félix Reynaud, *Histoire du commerce de Marseille*, II: *de 1291 à 1481* (Paris: Plon, 1951)

Baratier, Édouard, et autres, éds, *Atlas Historique: Provence, Comtat Venaissin, Principauté d'Orange, Comté de Nice* (Paris: Colin, 1969)

——, éds, *Répertoire de la série H. 56 H: grand prieuré de Saint-Gilles des Hospitaliers de Saint-Jean de Jérusalem* (Marseille: Archives départementales des Bouches du Rhône, 1966)

Barnel, Christine, « La boutique des frères Favas: Drapiers et draperie à Marseille au XIVe siècle », *Provence historique*, 49 (1999), 61–78

——, « Une famille de drapiers dans la Marseille angevine, 1302–1473 », *Provence historique*, 39 (1989), 367–83

——, « Une ville provençale et sa clientèle au XIVe siècle: Toulon, les notaires et leur clientèle », dans *La ville au Moyen Âge*, I: *Villes et espace*, éd. par Noël Coulet et autres (Paris: CTHS, 1998), pp. 233–46

Bautier, Robert-Henri, et Janine Sornay, *Les sources de l'histoire économique et sociale du Moyen Âge*, I: *Provence, Comtat Venaissin, Dauphiné, Savoie* (Paris: CNRS, 1968)

Bautier, Robert-Henri, et autres, *Les sources de l'histoire économique et sociale du Moyen Âge*, II: *Archives ecclésiastiques, communales et notariales. Archives des marchands et des particuliers* (Paris: CNRS, 1971)

Beaucage, Benoît, « L'effondrement de la gestion du patrimoine de l'Hôpital en France du Sud-Est (1373–1429) », dans *Les commanderies des Hospitaliers de Saint-Jean de Jérusalem, de Rhodes et de Malte, dépendantes du Grand Prieuré de Saint-Gilles du XIIe au XVIIe siècle*, colloque d'Aix-en-Provence, mai 1994, *Provence historique*, 45 (1995), 119–42

——, « Une énigme des Hospitaliers de Saint-Jean-de-Jérusalem: Le déficit chronique des Commanderies du moyen Rhône, au Prieuré de Provence, en 1338 », *Provence Historique*, 30 (1980), 137–64

Bernardi, Philippe, « Apprentissage et transmission du savoir dans les métiers du bâtiment à Aix-en-Provence à la fin du Moyen Âge (1400–1550) », dans *Actes du 1 colloque du CRISIMA: Apprentissages, éducation, initiation, éducation au Moyen Âge, Montpellier 1991*, *Les cahiers du CRISIMA*, 1 (1993), 69–79

——, *Métiers du bâtiment et techniques de construction à Aix-en-Provence à la fin de l'époque gothique (1400–1550)* (Aix-en-Provence: Université de Provence, 1995)

——, « Statuts inédits de la confrérie des maçons, plâtriers et charpentiers d'Aix-en-Provence (1450–1463) », *Provence historique*, 49, (1999), 93–104

Birrel, Jean, « Berre à la fin du Moyen-Âge », *Cahiers du Centre d'études des sociétés méditerranéennes*, 2 (1968), 109–68

Blancard, Louis, *Documents inédits sur le commerce de Marseille au Moyen Âge*, I et II, *Contrats commerciaux du XIIIe siècle*; III, *Les commandites commerciales des Béguines de Roubaud, congréganistes marseillaises du XIIIe siècle*; IV, *Pièces commerciales diverses* (Marseille: Barlatier-Feissant, 1884–85 ; repr. 1978)

——, « Note sur la lettre de change à Marseille au XIIIe siècle », *Bibliothèque de l'École des Chartes*, 39 (1878), 110–28

Bloch, Marc, « L'histoire des prix: Remarques critiques », *Annales d'histoire sociale*, 11 (1939), 141–51

Bois, Guy, *Crise du féodalisme: économie rurale et démographie en Normandie orientale, du début du XIVe s. au milieu du XVIe s.* (Paris: Presses de la fondation nationale des sciences politique, 1981)

Bouiron, Marc, « Marseille, du Lacydon au faubourg Sainte-Catherine (Ve s. av. J.-C.–XVIIIe s.) », dans *Les fouilles de la place du Général de Gaulle*, éd. par M. Bouiron (Paris: Documents d'archéologie française, 2001), pp. 312–21

Bouiron, M, et autres, éds, *Marseille, trames et paysages urbains de Gyptis au roi René. Actes du colloque international d'archéologie, Marseille, 3–5 novembre 1999*, Études massaliètes, 7 (Aix-en-Provence: Edisud, 2001)

Bourin, Monique, John Drendel, and François Menant, éds, *Les disettes dans la conjoncture de 1300 en Méditerranée occidentale: La conjoncture de 1300 en Méditerranée occidentale*, Collection de l'École française de Rome, 450 (Roma: École française de Rome, 2012)

Bourin, Monique, et François Menant, « Les disettes dans la conjoncture de 1300 en méditerranée occidentale », <http://www.histoire.ens.fr/IMG/file/Menant/02%20-%20Bourin%20-%20Menant.pdf>

Bourrilly, Victor-L., et Raoul Busquet, *La Provence au Moyen Âge: Histoire politique; l'Église; les Institutions (1112–1481)* (Marseille: Archives départmentales des Bouches-du-Rhône, 1924)

Boutruche, Robert, « Aux origines d'une crise nobiliaire: Donations pieuses et pratiques successorales en Bordelais du XIIIe au XVIe siècle », *Annales d'histoire sociale*, 11 (1939), 161–77 et 257–77

——, *La crise d'une société: seigneurs et paysans du Bordelais pendant la guerre de Cent ans* (Paris: Belles Lettres, 1947)

Boyer, Paul-Paul, *La Vésubie: Hommes et communautés du Haut Pays niçois médiéval, XIIIe–XVe siècles* (Nice: Centre d'études médiévale de Nice, 1990)

——, « Pour une histoire des forêts de Haute-Provence (XIIIe–XVe siècles) », *Provence historique*, 40 (1990), 267–90

Busquet, Raoul, et Régine Pernoud, *Histoire du commerce de Marseille*, I: *Antiquité et Moyen Âge jusqu'en 1291* (Paris: Plon,1949)

Butaud, Germain, *Guerre et vie publique en Comtat Venaissin et à Avignon (vers 1350 – vers 1450)* (thèse de doctorat d'histoire médiévale inédite, Université de Nice-Sophia Antipolis, 2001)

——, « Villages et villageois du Comtat Venaissin en temps de guerre (milieu XIVe siècle – début XVe siècle) », dans *Les villageois face à la guerre (XIVe–XVIIIe siècles): Actes des XXIIes Journées Internationales d'Histoire de l'Abbaye de Flaran, 8, 9 et 10 septembre 2000*, éd. par Christian Desplat (Toulouse: Presses de l'Université du Mirail, 2002), pp. 53–64

Campbell, Bruce M. S., éd., *Before the Black Death: Studies in the 'Crisis' of the Early Fourteenth Century* (Manchester: Manchester University Press, 1991)

Chaunu, Pierre, « L'histoire sérielle: Bilans et perspectives », *Revue historique*, 243 (1970), 297–320

Coste, Pierre, « Du XIIIe au XVe siècle, mise en place d'un système: Histoire et actualité de la transhumance en Provence », *Les Alpes de lumière*, 95–96 (1986), 50–55

——, « Notes sur l'élevage en Haute-Provence, XIVe–XVe siècles », *Provence historique*, 40 (1990), 257–66

——, « L'origine de la transhumance en Provence », dans *L'élevage en Méditerranée occidentale*, Colloque du CNRS (Paris: CNRS, 1977), pp. 113–19

——, « La vie pastorale en Provence au milieu du XIVe siècle », *Études Rurales*, 46 (1972), 61–75

Coulet, Noël, « À propos d'un cadastre provençal du XIVe siècle: Note d'histoire démographique », dans *Économies et sociétés au Moyen Âge: Mélanges offerts à É. Perroy* (Paris: Publications de la Sorbonne, 1973), pp. 161–70

——, *Aix en Provence: Espace et relations d'une capitale (milieu XIVe – milieu XVe s.)* (Aix-en-Provence: Université de Provence, 1988)

——, « La bastide provençale au bas Moyen Âge, contribution à une histoire de l'habitat rural dispersé en Provence », *Archeologia Medievale*, 7 (1980), 55–72

——, « La désolation des églises de Provence », *Provence historique*, 6 (1956), 34–52 et 123–41

——, « Encore les villages disparus: Dépeuplement et repeuplement autour Aix-en-Provence XIVe–XVIe », *Annales: Économies, Sociétés, Civilisations*, 28.6 (1973), 1463–83

——, « La naissance de la bastide provençale », dans *Géographie historique du village et de la maison rurale*, éd. par Charles Higounet, colloque de Bazas, octobre 1978 (Paris: CNRS, 1979), pp. 145–59

——, « Population et société à Pourrières, 1368–1430, premier bilan d'une enquête », *Études Rurales*, (1976), 84–111

——, « Prospections minières en Provence à la fin du Moyen Âge », dans *Actes du 98e congrès national des sociétés savantes, Saint-Étienne, 1973*, I: *Mines et métallurgie, XIIe–XVIe s.* (Paris: CTHS, 1975), pp. 159–68

——, « Sources et aspects de l'histoire de la transhumance des ovins en Provence au Bas Moyen Âge », *Le Monde alpin et rhodanien*, 6 (1978), 213–47

——, « La survie des communautés d'habitants des villages disparus: L'exemple d'Aix et du pays d'Aix aux XIVe et XVe siècles », *Annales de la faculté des lettres et sciences humaines de l'Université de Nice*, 9 (1969), 81–91

——, « Un village éphémère du pays d'Aix au XIIIe siècle: Le Sambuc », *Provence historique*, 27 (1977), 39–57

Coulet, Noël, et Louis Stouff, *Le village de Provence au bas Moyen Âge*, Cahiers du Centre d'études des sociétés méditerranéennes, 2e série (Aix-en-Provence: Centre d'études des sociétés méditerranéennes, 1987)

Courtemanche, Andrée, « Femmes et accès au patrimoine en Provence: Manosque au XIVe siècle », *Le Moyen Âge*, 96 (1990), 3–4, 479–501

——, « Les femmes juives et le crédit à Manosque au tournant du XIVe siècle », *Provence historique*, 37 (1987), 545–58

——, *La richesse des femmes: Patrimoines et gestion à Manosque au XIVe siècle* (Montréal: Bellarmin-Vrin, 1993)

De Jerphanion, Guillaume, « L'évolution démographique dans la baillie de Barjols du XIVe au XVe siècle: Le cas de Pontevès » (diplôme d'études approfondies d'histoire inédit, Université d'Aix-Marseille I, 1975)

De la Roncière, Charles, *Prix et salaires à Florence au XIVe siècle (1280–1380)* (Roma: École Française de Rome, 1982)

Démians d'Archimbaud, Gabrielle, « Archéologie des villages désertés en Provence: Résultats de fouilles », dans *Villages désertés et histoire économique (XIe–XVIIIe siècles)*, éd. par Jean-Marie Pesez et Emmanuel Le Roy Ladurie (Paris: 1965), pp. 287–301

——, *Rougiers, village médiéval: Approche archéologique d'une société méditerranéenne* (Paris: CNRS, 1982)

Démians d'Archimbaud, Gabrielle, et Michel Fixot, « L'organisation de la campagne en Provence occidentale: Indices archéologiques et aspects démographiques (XIe–XVe) », *Provence Historique*, 27 (1977), 3–23

Denifle, Henri, *La guerre de Cent ans et la désolation des églises de France* (Paris: Picard, 1897–99)

Drendel, John, « Gens d'Église et crédit dans la vallée de Trets au XIVe siècle », *Provence historique*, 54 (1994), 77–88

——, « Jews,Villagers and the Count in *Haute Provence*: Marginality and Mediation », *Provence historique*, 49 (1999), 217–31

——, « Notarial Practice Rural Provence in the Early Fourteenth Century », dans *Urban and Rural Communities in Medieval France, Provence and Languedoc, 1000–1500*, éd. par Kathryn Reyerson et autres (Leiden: Brill, 1998), pp. 209–38

——, « Society and Economy in a Medieval Provençal Town: Trets, 1296–1347 » (thèse de doctorat d'histoire inédite, University of Toronto, 1991)

Duby, Georges, *L'économie rurale et la vie des campagnes dans l'Occident Médiéval (France, Angleterre, Empire, IXe–XVe siècles): Essai de synthèse et perspectives de recherches*, 2 vols (Paris: Aubier, 1962)

——, « Note sur les corvées dans les Alpes du sud en 1338 », dans *Études d'histoire du droit privé offertes à Pierre Petot* (Paris: Montchrestien, 1959), pp. 141–46

——, « La seigneurie et l'économie paysanne, Alpes du Sud, 1338 », *Etudes Rurales*, 2 (1961), 5–36

——, « Techniques et rendements agricoles dans les Alpes du sid en 1338 », *Annales du Midi*, 70 (1958), 403–13

Dupanloup, Marc, « La corporation des cuiratiers à Marseille dans la première moitié du XIVe siècle », *Provence historique*, 19 (1969), 189–213

Estienne, Marie-Pierre, « Les réseaux castraux et l'évolution de l'architecture castrale dans les baronnies de Mévouillon et de Montauban, de la fin du Xe au début du XIVe siècle » (thèse de doctorat d'archéologie médiévale inédite, Université d'Aix-Marseille I, 1999); paru sous *Châteaux, villages, terroirs en Baronnies, X^e^–XVe siècle* (Aix-en-Provence: Université de Provence, 2004)

Février, Paul-Albert, *Le développement urbain en Provence, de l'époque romaine à la fin du XIVe siècle (Archéologie et histoire urbaine)* (Paris: Boccard, 1964)

Fixot, Michel, « À la recherche des formes les plus anciennes de la fortification privée en Provence: L'enceinte du domaine de Cadrix (Saint-Maximin, Var) », dans *Château-Gaillard, études de castellologie médiévale*, IX– X: *Actes du colloque international de Bâle 1978, et de Durham 1980* (Caen: Université de Caen, 1982), pp. 389–406

——, « La construction de châteaux dans la campagne d'Apt et de Pélissanne du XIe au XIIIe siècle », *Archéologie médiévale*, 4 (1973–74), 245–96

Génicot, Léopold, *La crise agricole du bas Moyen Âge dans le Namurois* (Louvain: Bibliothèque de l'Université, 1970)

——, « Crisis: From the Middle Ages to Modern Times », dans *The Cambridge Economic History of Europe*, I: *The Agrarian Life of the Middle Ages*, éd. par Michael M. Postan, 2e édn (Cambridge: Cambridge University Press, 1966), pp. 660–741

Graus, Frantisek, *Das Spätmittelalter als Krisenzeit: Ein Literaturbericht als Zwischenbilanz* (Praha: CSAV, 1969)

Grava, Yves, « Marchands, pêcheurs et gens de mer sur les bords de l'étang de Berre à la fin du Moyen Âge », dans *Navigation et gens de mer en Méditerranée de la Préhistoire à nos jours: Actes de la table ronde du groupement d'intérêt scientifique sciences humaines sur l'aire méditerranéenne. Cahier 3. Collioure, septembre 1979* (Paris: CNRS,1980), pp. 48–58

Hamilton, Earl J., *Money, Prices and Wages in Valencia, Aragon and Navarre* (Cambridge, MA: Harvard University Press, 1936)

Hébert, Michel, « Aux origines des États de Provence: la cavalcade générale », dans *Actes du 110e congrès national des sociétés savantes, Montpellier 1985* (Montpellier: CTHS, 1987), pp. 53–68

——, « Guerre, finance et administration: Les États de Provence de novembre 1359 », *Le Moyen Âge*, 83 (1977), 103–30

——, « Les mutations foncières et l'évolution sociale en Haute-Provence au XIVe siècle », *Provence historique*, 37 (1987), 421–37

——, « Les ordonnances de 1289–1294 et les origines de l'enquête domaniale de Charles II », *Provence historique*, 36 (1986), 45–57

——, « La ville de Tarascon à la fin du XIVe siècle (v. 1370–1400): Structures et transformation d'une communauté urbaine » (thèse de troisième cycle inédite, Université d'Aix-Marseille I, 1975), publié sous le titre *Tarascon au XIVe siècle* (Aix-en-Provence: Edisud, 1979)

Herlihy, David, *La peste noire et la mutation de l'Occident* (Paris: Montfort, 1999)

Jonas, Ilona, « Note sur un recours de feux dans la baillie de Puget-Théniers en 1343 », *Provence historique*, 27 (1977), 59–80

Juglar, Clément, *Les crises commerciales et leur retour périodique en France, Angleterre et Etats-Unis* (Paris: [n.pub.], 1862)

Keynes, John M., *The General Theory of Employment, Interest and Money* (London: McMillan, 1936; traduction française en 1942)

Kondratieff, Nicolas, *Les grands cycles de la conjoncture* (Paris: Economica,1992; pour l'édition anglaise, New York: Richardson & Snyder, 1984)

Labrousse, Ernest, *Crise de l'économie française à la fin de l'Ancien Régime* (Paris: Presses Universitaires de France, 1944)

——, *Esquisse du mouvement des prix et des revenus en France au XVIIIe siècle* (Paris: Dalloz, 1932)

Larochelle, Lucie, « Boni, probi et sufficientes: Pouvoir et notabilité à Aix-en-Provence entre 1400 et 1535 » (thèse de doctorat d'histoire médiévale inédite, Université d'Aix-Marseille I, 2002)

Lavoie, Rodrigue, « Endettement et pauvreté en Provence d'après les listes de la justice comtale, XIVe–XVe siècles », *Provence Historique*, 23 (1973), 201–16

——, « Processus de marginalisation en milieu rural: Castellane au début du XIVe siècle », dans *Exclus et systèmes d'exclusion dans la littérature et la civilisation médiévales*, Sénéfiance, 5 (Aix-en-Provence: CERMA, 1978), 313–29

Léonard, Émile-G., *Histoire de Jeanne reine de Naples, comtesse de Provence (1343–1382)*, 3 vols (Monaco: Imprimerie de Monaco, 1936), III: *Le règne de Louis de Tarente*

——, *La jeunesse de Jeanne Ire, reine de Naples et comtesse de Provence*, 2 vols dans 1 (Monaco-Paris: Picard, 1932)

Lesage, Gustave, « Les difficultés de ravitaillement de Marseille en blé au XIVe siècle », *Bulletin officiel du musée du vieux Marseille*, 56 (1938–40), 3–7

Lucas, Henry S., « The Great European Famine of 1315–1316–1317 », *Speculum*, 5 (1930), 341–77

Malaussena, Louis-Paul, *La vie en Provence orientale aux XIVe et XVe siècles. Un exemple: Grasse à travers les actes notariés* (Paris: Librairie générale de droit et de jurisprudence, 1969)

Malthus, Thomas, *An Essay on the Principle of Population* (Harmondsworth: Penguin, 1970)

Masson, Paul, éd., *Les Bouches-du-Rhône, Encyclopédie départementale*, II: *Antiquité et Moyen Âge* (Paris: Archives départmentales des Bouches-du-Rhône, 1924)

Maurel, Christian, « Grands marchands et "petites et moyennes industries" à Marseille au Bas Moyen Âge (1350–1480) », in *Le marchand au Moyen Âge: XIXe Congrès de la S.H.M.E.S. (Reims, juin 1988)* (Paris: CTHS, 1992), pp. 105–12

——, « Structures familiales et solidarités lignagères à Marseille au XVe siècle: Autour de l'ascension sociale des Forbin », *Annales: Économies, Sociétés, Civilisations*, 41 (1986), 657–81

Mazel, Florian, « La noblesse et l'Église en Provence (XIe–XIVe s.): L'exemple des familles d'Agoult-Simiane, de Baux et de Marseille » (doctorat d'histoire inédite, Univerisité d'Aix-Marseille I, 2000); paru sous *La noblesse et l'Église en Provence, fin X^e^ – début XIVe siècle* (Paris: CTHS, 2002)

Menkès, Fred, « Une communauté juive en Provence au XIVe siècle: Étude d'un groupe social », *Le Moyen Âge*, 77 (1971), 278–303 et 417–50

Michaud, Francine, « Apprentissage et salariat à Marseille avant la peste noire », *Revue historique*, 291 (1994), 3–36

——, « Exploités ou profiteurs? Les apprentis marseillais avant la peste noire », *Médiévales*, 30 (1996), 83–96

——, « La peste, la peur et l'espoir: Le pèlerinage jubilaire de romeux marseillais en 1350 », *Le Moyen Âge*, 104 (1998), 399–434

——, « Serviteurs et domestiques à Marseille au XIVe siècle », dans *Actes du Congrès International 'Le petit peuple dans la société de l'Occident médiéval: Terminologies, perceptions, réalités', Université de Montréal, 18–23 octobre 1999*, éd. par Pietro Boglioni et autres (Paris: Publications de la Sorbonne 2002), pp. 395–605

——, « Travail et mouvements migratoires avant et après la peste noire à Marseille », *Provence historique*, 49 (1999), 367–83

——, *Un signe des temps: Accroissement des crises familiales autour du patrimoine à Marseille à la fin du XIIIe siècle* (Toronto: Pontifical Institute of Mediaeval Studies, 1994)

Morsel, Joseph, « Crise? Quelle crise? Remarques à propos de la prétendue crise de la noblesse allemande à la fin du Moyen Âge », *Sources. Travaux historiques*, 14 (1988), 17–42

Murat, Josée-Valérie, « Navires et navigations à Marseille au XIVe siècle » (doctorat d'histoire inédit, Université d'Aix-Marseille I, 2001)

Pécout, Thierry, « Les mutations du pouvoir seigneurial en haute Provence sous les premiers comtes angevins, vers 1260 – début du XIVe siècle », dans *La noblesse dans les territoires angevins à la fin du Moyen Âge*, éd. par Noël Coulet et autres, Colloque international d'Angers-Saumur, juin 1998 (Roma: École Française de Rome, 2000), pp. 71–87

——, « Noblesse provençale et pouvoir comtal: L'exemple du pays de Riez (Alpes-de-Haute-Provence), XIIe–XIVe siècle », dans *Aspects du pouvoir seigneurial de la Catalogne à l'Italie (IXe–XIVe s.)*, *Rives nord-Méditerranéennes*, 7 (2001), 37–56, <http://rives.revues.org/document79.html>

——, « Une société rurale du XIIe au XIVe siècle en haute Provence: Les hommes, la terre et le pouvoir dans le pays de Riez » (doctorat d'Histoire inédit, Université d'Aix-Marseille I, 1998)

Pernoud, Régine, « Essai sur l'histoire du port de Marseille, des origines à la fin du XIIIe siècle » (thèse de doctorat inédit, Université de Paris, 1935)

Perroy, Édouard, « À l'origine d'une économie contractée: Les crises du XIVe siècle », *Annales: Économies, Sociétés, Civilisations*, 4 (1949), 167–82

——, « La crise économique du XIVe siècle d'après les terriers foréziens », *Bulletin de la Diana*, 29 (1945), 67–80

Poppe, Danuta, *Economie et société d'un bourg provençal au XIVe siècle: Reillanne en haute Provence* (Wrocław: Instytut Historii Kultury Materialnej Polska Akademia Nauk, 1980)

——, « Saint-Christol à l'époque médiévale », *Cahiers du Centre d'études des sociétés méditerranéennes*, 1 (1966), 7–33

Postan, Michael, « The Fifteenth Century », *Economic History Review*, 9 (1939), 160–67

——, « Some Economic Evidence of Declining Population in the Later Middle Ages », *Economic History Review*, 2 (1950), 221–46

——, « Some Social Consequences of the Hundred Years War », *Economic History Review*, 12 (1942), 1–12; repris dans Michael Postan, *Essays on Medieval Agriculture and General Problems of the Medieval Economy* (Cambridge: Cambridge University Press, 1973), pp. 49–62

Pryor, John, *Business Contracts of Medieval Provence: Selected Notulae from the Cartulary of Giraud Amalric of Marseilles, 1248* (Toronto: Pontifical Institute of Mediaeval Studies, 1981)

——, « Commenda: The Operation of the Contract in Long Distance Commerce at Marseilles during the Thirteenth Century », *Journal of Economic European History*, 13 (1984), 397–440

Ribbe, Charles de, *La société provençale à la fin du Moyen Âge d'après des documents inédits* (Paris: Perrin, 1898)

Rostow, Walt, *Les étapes de la croissance* (Paris: Seuil, 1963)

Roux, Claude, « Tarascon au XVe siècle: Espace et société au temps des derniers Angevins de Provence (1400–1481) » (thèse de doctorat d'histoire médiévale inédite, Université d'Aix-Marseille I, 2004)

Rutkowska-Płachcińska, Anna, *Salon-de-Provence, une société urbaine du bas Moyen Âge* (Wrocław: Instytut Historii Kultury Materialnej Polska Akademia Nauk, 1982)

Saint-Pierre, Benoît, « Le corpus notarial de Brignoles (XIVe–XVe s.): Critique et histoire sociale », dans *Sources of Social History: Private Acts of the Late Middle Ages*, éd. par Paolo Brezzi et Egmont Lee (Toronto: Pontifical Institute of Mediaeval Studies, 1984), pp. 23–48

Schumpeter, Joseph, *Business Cycles: A Theoretical, Historical, and Statistical Analysis of the Capitalist Process*, 2 vols (New York: McGraw-Hill, 1939)

——, *The Theory of Economic Development: An Inquiry into Profits, Capital, Credit, Interest, and the Business Cycle*, trad. par Redvers Opie (New York: Oxford University Press, 1961)

Sclafert, Thérèse, *Cultures en Haute-Provence, déboisements et pâturages au Moyen Âge* (Paris: SEVPEN, 1959)

Shatzmiller, Joseph, « Les Juifs de Provence pendant la peste noire », *Revue des études juives*, 133 (1974), 457–80

——, *Recherches sur la communauté juive de Manosque au Moyen Âge, 1241–1329* (Paris: Mouton, 1973)

——, *Shylock revu et corrigé: Les Juifs, les Chrétiens et le prêt d'argent dans la société médiévale* (Paris: Les Belles Lettres, 2000)

Simiand, François, *Les fluctuations économiques à longue période et la crise économique* (Paris: Alret, 1932)

——, *Les salaires, l'évolution sociale et la monnaie* (Paris: Alret, 1931)

Smail, Daniel, « Common Violence: Vengeance and Inquisition in Fourteenth-Century Marseille », *Past and Present*, 151 (1996), 28–59

——, *The Consumption of Justice: Emotions, Publicity and Legal Culture in Marseille, 1264–1423* (Ithaca: Cornell University Press, 2003)

——, « Démanteler le patrimoine: Les femmes et les biens dans la Marseille médiévale », *Annales: Histoire, sciences sociales*, 52 (1997), 343–68

——, « The General Taille of Marseille, 1360–1361: A Social and Demographic Study », *Provence historique*, 49 (1999), 473–85

——, *Imaginary Cartographies: Possession and Identity in Late Medieval Marseille* (Ithaca: Cornell University Press, 2000)

——, « Notaries, Courts and the Legal Culture of Late Medieval Marseille », dans *Urban and Rural Communities in Medieval France, Provence and Languedoc, 1000–1500*, éd. par Kathryn Reyerson et autres (Leiden: Brill, 1998), pp. 23–50

——, « La topographie socio-professionnelle de Marseille au XIVe siècle », dans *Marseille, trames et paysages urbains de Gyptis au roi René: Actes du colloque international d'archéologie, Marseille, 3–5 novembre 1999*, éd. par M. Bouiron et H. Tréziny, Études massaliètes, 7 (Aix-en-Provence: Edisud, 2001), pp. 307–16

Stouff, Louis, « Alimentation et démographie en Provence aux XIVe et XVe siècles », *Annales de démographie historique*, 1976, 61–69

——, *Arles à la fin du Moyen Âge* (Aix-en-Provence: Université de Provence, 1986)

——, « Le mas arlésien aux XIVe et XVe siècles: À propos de l'habitat dispersé dans la Provence du bas Moyen Âge », dans *Cadres de vie et société dans le Midi médiéval, Hommage à Charles Higounet*, dir. par Pierre Bonnassie et autres (Toulouse: Privat, 1990), pp. 161–71

——, « Le ravitaillement des villes de Provence au bas Moyen Âge », *Acta historica et archeologica mediævalia*, 19 (1998), 57–74

——, *Ravitaillement et alimentation en Provence aux XIVe et XVe siècles* (Paris: Mouton, 1970)

——, « Un aspect de la Haute-Provence à la fin de la période médiévale: Peuplement, économie et société de quelques villages de la montagne de Lure, 1250–1450 », *Cahiers du Centre d'études des sociétés méditerranéennes*, 1 (1966), 35–109

——, « Une création d'Urbain V: Le studium papal de Trets, 1364–1365 », *Provence historique*, 16 (1966), 528–39

——, « Une enquête économique en Provence au XIVe siècle », *Le Moyen Âge*, 23 (1968), 507–42

Tits-Dieuaide, Marie Jeanne, *La formation des prix céréaliers en Brabant et en Flandre au XVe siècle* (Brussels: Unversité de Bruxelles, 1975)

Verdon, Laure, « La seigneurie en Provence au XIIIe siècle: Entraunes et Saint-Martin d'Entraunes d'après l'enquête de 1285 », *Rives*, 7 (2001), 57–79

Veydarier, Roger, « Raymond de Turenne, la deuxième maison d'Anjou et la Provence: Étude d'une rébellion nobiliaire à la fin du XIVe siècle (1386–1400) » (thèse de doctorat d'histoire inédite, Université du Québec à Montréal, 1994)

Victor-Bourrilly, L., « Du Guesclin et le duc d'Anjou en Provence, 1368 », *Revue historique*, 51 (1926), 161–80

Vivier, Robert, « Une crise économique au milieu du XIVe siècle. La première grande intervention de la royauté dans le domaine économique: ses causes », *Revue d'histoire économique et sociale*, 8 (1920), 199–230

Wernham, Monique, *La communauté juive de Salon-de-Provence d'après les actes notariés 1391–1435* (Toronto: Pontifical Institute of Mediaeval Studies, 1988)

Zerner, Monique, *Le cadastre, le pouvoir et la terre: Le Comtat Venaissin pontifical au début du XVe siècle* (Roma: École Française de Rome, 1993)

——, « La question du crédit dans les campagnes du Comtat Venaissin au début du XVe siècle: Enquête dans les registres », dans *Endettement paysan et crédit rural dans l'Europe médiévale et moderne: Actes des XVIIe s journées internationales d'histoire de l'Abbaye de Flaran, Septembre 1995*, éd. par Maurice Berthe (Toulouse: Flaran, 1998), pp. 199–216

——, « Recherche d'une méthode d'interprétation démographique des cadastres du Comtat Venaissin (1414): Le cas de Ménerbes », *Provence historique*, 23 (1973), 243–60

——, « Les trois états du Comtat Venaissin dans la première moitié du XVe siècle: Une crise significative », *Journal des savants*, (1990), 125–54

——, « Une crise de mortalité au XVe siècle à travers les testaments et les rôles d'imposition », *Annales: Économies, Sociétés, Civilisations*, 34 (1979), 566–89

De nouveaux chemins de développement dans le Languedoc d'avant la peste

Monique Bourin

C*um status hodiernus cuiuscumque sit multoplus sic altior in moribus et portamentis temporibus retroactis*: ces quelques mots qui affirment avec force l'amélioration récente de l'état de la région sont extraits de l'un des documents conservés où les consuls de Béziers présentent leurs arguments contre le projet de supprimer l'interdiction royale d'exporter les draps hors de la sénéchaussée de Carcassonne et Béziers en 1330.[1] Quels que soit les intérêts qui s'affrontent autour de cette affaire, ce témoignage comporte, présentée par les consuls, une analyse en quelques points de la situation du Languedoc dans ces premières années du XIVe siècle:

- La population s'est considérablement accrue dans le siècle qui a précédé;
- L'expansion des cultures dans des zones, notamment montagneuses, jusqu' alors vouées au pacage des moutons rend la laine chère;
- Le prix des draps s'élève à la fois parce que les gens sont plus nombreux, les revenus que les gens de toute condition en tirent sont plus élevés et le *status hodiernus* est meilleur que dans le passé.

[1] Ce texte est publié et présenté par Romestan, « Les consuls de Béziers ». Le texte est connu par sa copie dans le fonds Doat de la BnF, Tome 157, fols 58–72.

Monique Bourin (monique.bourin@univ-paris1.fr) est professeur émérite à l'université de Paris 1 Panthéon-Sorbonne. Elle est l'auteur des plusieurs études sur la société rurale en Languedoc au XIIe et XIIIe siècles et elle a collaboré à la direction du projet « La conjoncture de 1300 en Méditerranée occidentale ».

Crisis in the Later Middle Ages: Beyond the Postan-Duby Paradigm, ed. by John Drendel, TMC 13 (Turnhout: Brepols, 2015) 251–272 BREPOLS PUBLISHERS 10.1484/M.TMC.5.103790

En somme c'est une sorte de spirale vertueuse d'une hausse des prix enrichissante pour tous, fondée principalement sur le travail textile et notamment le parage des draps, que les consuls de Béziers décrivent.

Qu'ils défendent leurs intérêts est une évidence. Et que bien de points ne soient pas envisagés dans cette présentation de la conjoncture économique aussi. Reste à voir à travers les textes disponibles, notamment de rares registres de notaire et quelques comptes de l'archevêque de Narbonne, si cette image florissante se confirme et si ce Languedoc drapant constitue en effet une région de prospérité, alors que la mention de famines a jusqu'à présent conduit à l'impression d'un épuisement du pays et de ses ressources.

La situation languedocienne telle qu'elle est présentée au roi par les consuls de Béziers diffère évidemment de l'image historiographique classique, qui dérive en Languedoc directement du paradigme malthusien tels que l'ont développé Michael Postan, puis Georges Duby. Je n'en prendrai qu'un exemple: dans le même volume où est présentée par Guy Romestan la plaidoirie des consuls de Béziers, Jean Combes, à propos de l'histoire de Béziers au XVe siècle, résume l'opinion générale: « les ressources alimentaires en raison de l'insuffisance des techniques agricoles ne s'étaient pas accrues au même rythme et il avait suffi de quelques mauvaises récoltes, en liaison sans doute avec les premières atteintes du refroidissement du climat pour détruire un équilibre fragile ».[2] Dans les années 70 du XXe siècle, le Languedoc est vu, à l'instar du reste de l'Europe, à travers le prisme décrit par Postan et Duby: dès la fin du XIIIe siècle, une économie essentiellement céréalière et une population qui croît sans rapport avec les ressources potentielles et sans modernisation technique, instaurent tout à la fois une crise de l'économie seigneuriale, dont les revenus ne cessent de baisser au fur et à mesure que s'arrêtent les défrichements et que ne sont plus mises en culture que des terres épuisées ou « marginales » et ingrates et une paupérisation générale à laquelle n'échapperaient que quelques créanciers avides.

Qu'en penser aujourd'hui?[3] Que retenir de cet ancien modèle historiographique?

[2] Romestan, « Les consuls de Béziers », p. 221.

[3] En une dizaine d'années, l'historiographie de cette période a bien changé. Les travaux sur la commercialisation qui sont partis d'Angleterre, notamment à la suite de Richard Britnell ont reçu un écho pour les régions méditerranéennes, dans un programme pluriannuel porté par l'École Française de Rome, la Casa de Velázquez, l'ENS et le LAMOP (Université de Paris 1-CNRS). Ce programme a donné lieu à plusieurs réunions dont les actes sont parus dans la collection de l'Ecole Française de Rome (la publication n'a pas suivi l'ordre des réunions): no. 450, Bourin, Drendel, et Menant, *Les disettes dans la conjoncture de 1300*; no. 490, Bourin,

Croissance démographique ou surpopulation?

Les consuls de Béziers le disent eux-mêmes: le nombre de gens augmente, parce qu'il en naît plus qu'il n'en meurt; il y a plus de monde qu'il y a vingt ans, plus encore qu'il y a cinquante et plus encore qu'il y a cent ans. Mais pour eux, à la différence des historiens actuels, le phénomène est universel: *in regno Francie et in aliis regnis*.

Les études ont confirmé la croissance démographique languedocienne. On ne peut pas faire confiance dans le détail aux évaluations du nombre des feux, mais les dénombrements quasi-exhaustifs de la population que permettent certains documents, comme les très nombreux terriers ou des enquêtes locales, dans les seigneuries montpelliéraines des Nogaret comme dans les villages ariégeois d'Axat et Caramany[4] révèlent une forte densité et un croît persistant dans les premières décennies du XIVe siècle.

Surpopulation? Les années 1329–33 sont difficiles. Mais on sait aussi aujourd'hui combien les disettes sont liées au problème de distribution au moins autant qu'à ceux de la production dans le passage de la mauvaise récolte à la famine.

Doit-on admettre que la population subit cette croissance non contrôlée?

Les consuls de Béziers ne signalent pas clairement les risques de faim et de disette et n'évoquent pas une cherté dangereuse du blé dans le tableau; mais il est vrai qu'ils ont une vision très textile et surtout urbaine des choses. Le risque qu'ils évoquent si le travail manque, c'est l'émigration, ou la mendicité.[5]

Ils disent aussi qu'il faut défricher les montagnes pour faire du blé, sans lequel on ne peut vivre. Pierre de Brenac avait, de son côté, visiblement insisté sur la réduction du bétail. Les consuls n'y voient pas un péril: de ce fait, disent-ils, le prix des produits animaux augmentent, laines, fromages et autres revenus, notamment les pâtures, et tout le monde en profite: « emolumenta quae homines cuiuscumque conditionis et status [...] percipiunt ».[6]

Menant, et To Figueras, *Dynamiques du monde rural*; no. 436, Carocci, *La mobilitá sociale nel medioevo*. On y trouvera une bibliographie prenant en compte les récentes publications sur ce champ de recherches. La conception de ce programme consacré à la conjoncture de 1300 dans la Méditerranée occidental a pris corps pour une grande part lors du colloque de Montréal.

[4] Thomas, « La population du Bas Languedoc »; Maillard et Bautier, « Un dénombrement des feux ».

[5] Article IX: « multae personae regnicolae quae vivunt de factione dictorum pannorum aut exirent regnum et se transportarent ad loca alia ubi dictae lanae extraherentur operarentur aut mendicarent » (Romestan, « Les consuls de Béziers », p. 316).

[6] Romestan, « Les consuls de Béziers », p. 217.

De fait les terres vacantes sont rares dans les documents du premier XIVe siècle.

Le terrier dressé dans la seigneurie royale de Ventajou sur les rebords de la Montagne Noire en 1316, comme les reconnaissances à l'abbaye de Fontcaude en Minervois en 1331 et 1339, celles des seigneurs de Thézan autour de Bédarieux, ou celles des Hospitaliers près de Limoux en 1338, sont toutes concordantes sur ce point.[7] Curieusement si l'ensemble des terriers de la plaine biterroise aboutit à un pourcentage de terres incultes, les erms, inégal, mais à peine supérieur au total à 1 pour cent, les zones plus élevées n'en comptent presque aucun.

Les zones boisées ou en garrigues sont l'objet d'une pression déjà étudiée ailleurs, mais c'est le manque de bois d'œuvre et de chauffe qui est évoqué, pas l'insuffisance de l'espace de pâture. D'autres indices cependant montrent bien que toute terre est précieuse et convoitée.

Un océan de très jeunes vignes?

Cet espace très cultivé est majoritairement céréalier, avec une intensivité différente de la culture, une céréaliculture assez intensive pour un peu moins de la moitié des terres emblavées et une céréaliculture extensive elle-même majoritaire.

Mais les jardins sont presque 10 pour cent des parcelles cultivées; beaucoup moins en superficie, mais d'un énorme rapport nourricier.

Quant aux vignes, fortement présentes, elles constituent 22 pour cent des 4000 parcelles et plus dont les reconnaissances sont conservées pour l'année 1338 dans la région:

- jusqu'à 36 pour cent dans la plaine de l'Hérault, au Nord de Béziers;
- mais seulement 12,5 pour cent sur les rebords de la Montagne Noire au Nord-Ouest de Carcassonne en 1316;
- 8 pour cent autour de Bédarieux en 1332;
- de 11 à 3 pour cent suivant les seigneuries en Minervois entre 1330 et 1335.

Mais la conversion est galopante, comme le montre la proportion de « mailleuls »: une vigne nouvellement plantée est un mailleul, qui donne peu ou pas de récolte, pendant plusieurs années, sachant qu'une vigne vit une grosse quar-

[7] Paris, Arch. Nat., Q 1, fols 62–63; Inventaire de ces fonds dans Pasquier et Olive, *Le fonds Thézan*.

antaine d'années.[8] Au total, 6 pour cent de mailleuls au moment où les vignes constituent 22 pour cent. À ce rythme, il suffit d'une vingtaine d'années pour doubler la superficie encépagée. Il faut donc être très attentif à une chronologie fine: à la vitesse où se plantent les vignes, le paysage se modifie vite. En 1308 autour de Pézenas, il y avait déjà 29 pour cent de vignes et 6 pour cent de mailleuls. Mais on voit encore des terroirs entiers se couvrir de mailleuls: ils constituent 58 pour cent de la centaine de terres reconnues en une seigneurie des Hospitaliers de cette région en 1338, 45 pour cent des 250 parcelles du terrier des Hospitaliers à Capestang à la même date.

Le Minervois est en retard: au total 7,5 pour cent de vignes et 11,5 de mailleuls, mais la plantation est rapide:

- En 1312 à Minerve, 5 pour cent de vignes et 12 de mailleuls;
- En 1331 à Olonzac, 11 pour cent de vignes et 8,5 de mailleuls;
- En 1338 autour d'Homps, 3 pour cent de vignes et 15 de mailleuls (sur plus de 500 parcelles);
- Sur le rebord de la Montagne Noire en 1316, 12,5 pour cent de vignes et 16 de mailleuls;
- Plus loin des concentrations urbaines, dans des zones climatiquement un peu moins favorables à la vigne, autour de Bédarieux ou au-dessus de Limoux, on avoisine en 1338 les 10 pour cent de vignes.

Les incidences du mouvement de plantation en quantité de travail par unité de surface ne sont pas négligeables; la productivité du sol et du travail humain s'accroît, dans une mesure malheureusement inestimable à partir de nos sources. Mais, en comparaison d'un système céréalier biennal, la plantation représente un investissement: le sol et le travail ne rendront qu'après plusieurs années. Peut-on imaginer un tel mouvement dans une atmosphère de disette menaçante? Ce serait alors l'énergie du désespoir.

Pour qui, pour quoi tout ce vin? Les gens des villes? L'exportation? En tous cas, on produit bien au-delà de la consommation domestique. Reste à interpréter le calcul qui est derrière ce mouvement de plantation et à en évaluer le bien-fondé. Mais pour ce faire, il nous manque les pièces essentielles, c'est-à-dire à la

[8] Un *maliolus*, devenu mailleul dans le français méridional. La vigne commence à produire dans sa troisième année, mais n'est pas adulte avec cinq ans.

fois des éléments des rendements des vignes et les traces du commerce du vin, ses chemins tout aussi bien que les cours auxquels ils sont achetés.[9]

Le phénomène est en tous cas le propre des moyens et des petits propriétaires. La grande propriété reste fidèle au blé et aux moutons. Calcul prenant en compte le coût élevé du travail viticole ou conservatisme peu sensible aux sollicitations du marché ?

Le marché de la terre : propriété et mutations

Dans les études classiques, la croissance démographique et plus encore le manque de terres et la surpopulation ont une incidence sur le marché foncier qui s'accélère. La plantation massive de vignes introduit ici une variante particulière à une incontestable hausse de la densité.

Les sources ne permettent pas une vision évolutive du marché foncier. Mais par les comptes de l'archevêque de Narbonne partiellement conservés pour l'année 1334 on peut le voir fonctionner au moment même décrit par les consuls : la baylie de Canet a conservé la liste des mutations.[10] Canet et les villages qui l'environnent sont situés dans la riche plaine de l'Aude, juste en amont du point où l'Aude est en train de difluer ; seul le terroir de Cruscades comporte une plus grande part de relief aride. Narbonne, à une quinzaine de kilomètres, est alors au sommet de sa puissance, avec ses sept mille feux. Canet est en outre sur la route chérie de la papauté d'Avignon, et l'on y voit tout au long de l'année passer les proches de l'archevêque, entre le Bordelais et le Comtat.

Les transactions sont enregistrées une par une, avec le nom de l'acheteur et celui du vendeur, la nature du bien cédé, son prix et le montant du droit de mutation (*foriscape*) d'environ 1/6 du prix de la vente. Manquent les superficies. Les vignes et les mailleuls y occupent-ils une place de choix ?[11]

Au total une centaine de transactions pour un montant total de 270 livres tournois ont associé soixante-sept vendeurs et soixante-deux acheteurs. Un certain nombre d'acteurs de ce marché est donc mentionné plusieurs fois : deux-

[9] Kathryn Reyerson a montré en tous cas à quel point cette évolution mettait entre les mains des marchands montpellierains les petits viticulteurs des environs touchés par la disette et la cherté des prix des grains : Reyerson, « Urban/Rural Exchange » ; Reyerson, « Montpellier et le trafic ».

[10] Stato della Città del Vaticano, Arch. du Vatican, Reg. Aven. 122, fols 491–496v.

[11] Onze transactions sont enregistrées à part, sans le nom du vendeur, ni la nature du bien. La valeur n'en paraît pas sensiblement différente. Elles représentent environ 20 pour cent du total des autres transactions.

tiers des vendeurs n'apparaissent qu'une fois et un peu moins de la moitié des acheteurs. La moyenne de chaque transaction est de £2,5. Au même moment, une journée de maître artisan se paye jusqu'à 2s., un sergent non nourri reçoit 18d., une journée de manœuvre vaut entre 8 et 12d., 5d. pour celle d'une femme. Une poule s'achète 1s., le *companagium* fourni à un salarié coûte 5d. aussi. L'impression est d'une valeur très modérée des biens fonciers qui s'échangent: la valeur moyenne des transactions se situe à vingt-cinq journées de maître artisan, à cinquante de manœuvre, soit deux mois de travail plein. A condition que le prix déclaré soit celui qui est effectivement payé et qu'une dette non remboursée ne soit pas cachée.

Evidemment la valeur moyenne cache des disparités: le prix le plus élevé est de £10 pour un champ et même plus encore puisqu'une transaction comporte outre un échange de champs un solde de £20. Mais beaucoup de biens sont vendus entre £4 et £1,5.[12] La comparaison avec les loyers est surprenante: la même année, dans divers villages du Minervois, l'archevêque loue des bâtiments (*hospicia*) pour caser le produit de ses dîmes, on ne sait pour combien de temps: les loyers varient entre £2 et 1s.[13] La valeur moyenne des ventes d'*hospicium* à Canet et à l'entour est à peine supérieure: un peu plus de £4.

Le marché porte assez peu sur les vignes et les mailleuls, un dixième des transactions, sans doute moins que la proportion de parcelles encépagées. Et le prix des vignes et des mailleuls est bas, en moyenne la moitié de celui des champs et des maisons. Il est vrai qu'en règle générale les parcelles encépagées sont beaucoup plus petites que les céréalières. Certes on voit investir dans la vigne: Jean Mathei, qui est actif à sept reprises au cours de l'année (le plus actif), avec £10 d'acquets, qui le placent à la 3ème place des investisseurs de Canet, achète trois mailleuls.[14] Il acquiert ainsi la moitié des mailleuls qui ont été mis sur le marché cette année-là à Canet. On verra plus loin qu'il est fustier (menuisier). On voit aussi sans doute des échecs retentissants: c'est du moins ainsi que j'interprète l'histoire de Jean Vesiani, de Cruscades, qui doit vendre ses biens sous la pression des créanciers, une maison, trois champs et un mailleul. Mais le mailleul vaut à lui-seul plus que la maison et presque autant que les trois champs. Comme rien n'indique par ailleurs une pression sur le prix des mailleuls, n'a-t-il pas risqué un investissement aventureux qui a mal tourné? Mais ces deux

[12] C'est le même ordre de grandeur que les biens fonciers vendus par Jean de Furno notaire à Clermont l'Hérault en 1346, Montpellier, Arch. Départ. de l'Hérault, II E 39/528.

[13] Stato della Città del Vaticano, Arch. du Vatican, Reg. Aven. 122, fol. 517v.

[14] Et vend une faïsse de terre (parcelle de forme allongée) pour £9.

exemples sont extrêmes: la plupart du temps, la plantation se fait sans achat ni vente, notamment en sollicitant l'autorisation de planter, qui est considérée comme un acapt (droit d'entrée sur une tenure) à Canet.[15]

Un vrai marché foncier

Il y a bien dans la baylie de Canet un vrai marché foncier. Certes, une partie des transactions se fait au sein de la famille, sans doute en règlement d'héritage: au total 7 pour cent des transactions.[16] C'est très secondaire: même en ajoutant à ce chiffre quelques transactions entre frère et soeur mariée, dont le lien de parenté nous échappe, les prix se situent exactement dans la moyenne.[17] Un certain nombre de transactions se font en fratrie: certaines agissent ensemble à plusieurs reprises et sont sans doute des frérèches, peut-être temporaires; dans d'autres cas, un frère s'adjoint tel frère pour une opération, tel pour une autre.[18] Le nombre des fratries venderesses n'est pas supérieur à celui des fratries qui achètent: deux contre trois. Se confirme donc l'image de fratries conquérantes et durables, souvent parmi les notables, et non pas fratrie contrainte de demeurer ensemble, par faiblesse de l'héritage et pour des « économies d'échelle ».

Cependant ce marché est pour une part « chaïanovien »: les veuves sont venderesses; elles n'achètent pas. L'exemple du couple de Pierre Raimond Rosselli et de sa femme va sans doute dans le même sens: successivement, le couple vend un pré pour £2; puis, Pierre Raimond se défait seul d'un mailleul pour un peu plus de £2; enfin, devenue veuve, elle se sépare d'un jardin pour £1.[19]

[15] Les trois acapts de Canet en 1334 sont trois autorisations de planter, données à des habitants L'un d'entre eux se défait d'une ferragine, parcelle de culture intensive produisant du fourrage, pour une modique somme de 8 sous.

[16] Aucune ne concerne une maison; une seule un mailleul.

[17] On ne note pas le phénomène signalé par Giovanni Levi d'un sur-prix dans les relations internes à la famille, mais on ne compte que sept cas.

[18] Pons Grassi achète une fois seul une pièce de terre, mais avec Raimond une demi-aire et une maison. Guillaume Rosselli achète une fois seul une pièce de terre, une autre fois un pré avec Raimond et un champ avec Etienne. Ce n'est apparemment pas le poids financier de l'opération qui l'oblige à s'associer.

[19] Dans le même temps, des Rosselli achètent: Guillaume, Guillaume et Raimond, Guillaume et Etienne et Raimond seul deux fois. Sont-ils les enfants de Pierre Raimond? Il en va de même pour le couple de Pierre Raimond Durand et de sa femme, qui vendent un champ ensemble, la femme vend seule une maison et un champ et le mari seul un champ, le tout pour des sommes considérables.

Mais ce marché est surtout celui où « ceux qui perdent » et « ceux qui gagnent » échangent leurs biens. Bien peu sont actifs comme acheteurs et vendeurs à la fois: cinq seulement.

Il y a d'abord les trois cas de vente forcée par les créanciers. Pour Jean Vesiani de Cruscades, on a imaginé une aventure viticole qui tourne mal. Pour Guillaume Fortis, qui se défait d'un patu de 12s., l'acquéreur est le boucher de Canet: est-il le créancier? Pour Guillaume Recoversi, quatre parcelles vendues, dont trois par l'action des créanciers: le jardin va à un habitant de Canet, la pièce de terre à un habitant de Narbonne; le clos d'oliviers conjointement à un pareur et un couturier de Narbonne. Peu d'exemples certes, mais le crédit urbain n'en est pas moins présent et pesant.[20]

Quelles relations entre vendeurs et acheteurs ? Certaines sont peut-être un crédit qui ne s'avoue pas: Bernard Buxi achète deux des trois terres acquises à Jean Bartholomei et Agnès, femme de Jean Guitfredi vend trois pièces de terre au même Jean Agelli, le fabre de Saint-Marcel, pour la somme rondelette de £14.[21] Mais ce n'est pas l'habitude: les vendeurs qui dispersent des biens le font entre des acheteurs différents et les acheteurs de même acquièrent des terres de provenance diverse. L'impression est celle d'un marché peu contraint, mais il reste que les transactions se font entre habitants du même village, qui se connaissent bien, comme on le verra mieux plus loin.[22]

La prospérité des artisans

Les acteurs de ce marché sont pour la plupart sans mention distinctive qui permette de caractériser leur activité principale. Mais les comptes complètent ces maigres informations en faisant référence à quelques-uns uns d'entre eux.

Lorsqu'un détail est ajouté au nom, le vendeur est artisan, boucher, barbier ou fabre, notaire ou prêtre. Aucun ne vend et tous achètent. Parmi les acheteurs qui investissent plus que la moyenne, la palme revient au prêtre, Dom Stefanus Dominici qui achète pour plus de £30, quand la moyenne est à £6, ou au forgeron de Saint Marcel. L'autre prêtre de Canet, Etienne Mancipii fait aussi partie des acheteurs pour presque £10 livres. Un certain Me R. Predigonis, le deu-

[20] Son métier n'est pas connu; les Rosergue ont compté parmi eux des tisserands.

[21] Même chose à Villedaigne pour les deux frères Salas qui achètent ensemble les deux champs vendus par Ermengarde, la veuve de Raimond Bonelli.

[22] Un habitant de Canet investit peut-être aussi à Villedaigne, village voisin, mais ce peut être un homonyme, bien que le nom ne soit pas spécialement fréquent.

xième acheteur de Canet (£22) est cité à plusieurs reprises dans les comptes du bayle: il achète les revenus de l'archevêque à Villedaigne et surtout il est chargé des transports de fonds à destination de Narbonne.[23] Quant aux deux maîtres fustiers que le bayle emploie à longueur d'année, pour le cellier, pour la « domus » où il faut faire des portes ou des étagères, pour la prison dont il faut refaire les portes, pour le bac qu'il faut réparer, nous les retrouvons en bonne place parmi les acheteurs: l'un est le Jean Mathei, évoqué plus haut, et l'autre est Raymond Rosselli. L'un investit £20 en cinq biens différents; l'autre une somme équivalente en trois achats dont une maison. Il achète d'ailleurs une faïsse à son collègue Jean Mathei pour £9.[24] Parmi les acheteurs encore, p. Druade que l'on voit vendre des dizaines de quintaux de bois au bayle. Mais tous les marchands de bois ne sont pas des investisseurs fonciers: Jean Tolsa, qui a la même activité que Pierre Druade, est vendeur à deux reprises, précisément au même Pierre Druade. Quant à Michel Pelati, le seul des manœuvres employés par le bayle que nous connaissions parmi les acteurs du marché foncier, il est à la fois vendeur et acheteur, les deux fois avec sa femme, vendant un champ pour acheter une faïsse avec un solde acheteur d'environ £2.[25]

Il est, en revanche, d'autres relations d'affaires du bayle qui ne sont pas actifs sur le marché foncier, notamment ceux qui afferment les revenus seigneuriaux: ni le fermier du four, ni celui du bateau, ni celui du vêt du vin n'ont payé de *foriscape*. Ni le notaire de Canet, ce qui est exceptionnel pour un notaire; mais à Cruscades, village qui appartient aussi à la baylie de Canet, le notaire est parmi les acheteurs, modestes il est vrai.

Les artisans actifs sur le marché foncier investissent des sommes moyennes pour des parcelles à des prix moyens, sans manifester une stratégie foncière originale.

Parmi les acteurs du marché foncier, il en est aussi qu'on retrouve en justice, payant une amende. Vendeurs: la femme de Jean Guitfredi qui, chargée d'une amende de £1, vend plusieurs biens au forgeron, et, Barthélémy Milhani qui a ouvert dans sa maison une porte fermée par le bayle, et a dû payer une amende de 10s. Pourtant la corrélation n'est pas parfaite; le villageois soumis à une amende, n'est pas toujours contraint de vendre un bien. Les Rotberti pour avoir injurié le bayle, sont punis de £5, vendent certes un bien, mais ils le cèdent

[23] Ainsi, il y est envoyé les 14 et le 19 septembre, le 3 novembre, le 19 décembre (Stato della Città del Vaticano, Arch. du Vatican, Reg. Aven. 122, fol 539^{v}).

[24] Parcelle caractérisée par sa forme allongée, dans un parcellaire à dominante compacte.

[25] La plupart ne sont pas nommée.

à leur frère et rien ne prouve que c'est sous l'empire de la nécessité. Quant à ce frère, il est puni de £5 pour adultère, sa femme de £1 pour avoir méprisé un ordre du bayle. Or les deux amendes ne le ruinent pas; il n'est pas parmi les vendeurs, mais parmi les acquéreurs. Ni Jean Gautier pour avoir choisi un autre notaire que celui de Canet, ni Laurent Salas pour avoir frappé un certain Vinas.

Autant une activité de maître artisan, ou mieux encore de prêtre ou de notaire assure d'être du bon côté, autant avoir maille avec la justice n'assure pas la décadence. Pourtant en moyenne l'amende vaut 2 livres, à peine moins qu'un bien échangé.

Le marché concentre les biens: soixante-sept vendeurs et soixante-deux acheteurs. La différence est sensible. Elle n'est pas écrasante. Mais, même si les biens échangés ne constituent pas un gros capital, on sent le poids de l'artisanat dans l'évolution de la hiérarchie des fortunes. Il est peu de « gros » acheteurs qui ne soient ni artisans ni clercs. En revanche on ne voit pas d'acheteurs explicitement portés par le succès de leur activité viticole.

Un marché plus actif à la bourgade

Entre Canet et les villages voisins, les différences sont sensibles. D'abord dans le prix des biens et les investissements: la valeur moyenne des biens échangés est de £3 à Canet et £2 dans les villages voisins. L'investissement moyen des acheteurs est de £6 à Canet, £2 dans les villages voisins. Le plus gros investisseur a acquis des biens pour £31 à Canet et le forgeron de Saint-Marcel £14. Dans les villages, aucun acheteur forain, aucun narbonnais. Un marché où les veuves venderesses sont plus nombreuses, alors qu'à Canet les vendeurs sont principalement des couples: la moitié à Canet et seulement sept pour cent dans les villages voisins. Les artisans jouent à Canet un rôle plus important.[26]

Ainsi, le centre de la baylie apparaît comme le lieu où artisans et clercs créent une richesse, que l'on sent moins ailleurs. On peut lire les nuances du marché foncier comme une différenciation et une hiérarchisation des lieux habités.

On peut aussi lire la concentration amorcée des terres entre les mains de quelques-uns uns comme un déséquilibre nouveau. Pourtant l'évolution semble lente. Le marché est très vif: soixante-quatre transactions foncières dans l'année pour 155 feux à Canet, soit en moyenne une transaction pour plus d'un feu sur trois. Un peu moins dans les villages: trente-huit transactions pour 102 feux.

[26] Même en tenant compte du fait que les comptes du bayle nous font mieux connaître les artisans de Canet que ceux des villages voisins.

Mais la « koulakisation » n'est pas très perceptible. D'ailleurs les koulaks sont, pour une large part, ceux qui ont des revenus autres qu'agricoles.

L'agriculture n'est pourtant pas pour rien dans la richesse de la région. Si les artisans que l'on voit prospérer à Canet sont pour une part soutenus par les commandes de la seigneurie, il faut bien qu'ils aient aussi des clients parmi les paysans. Paysans consommateurs, sur le marché local et sans doute en ville, et vendeurs de leurs produits, disposant éventuellement d'un appoint de salaire.

Une commercialisation en profondeur

Car la circulation monétaire et le commerce sont partout. Il serait faux de penser que c'est dans le prélèvement seigneurial qu'est le principal moteur de la circulation monétaire. Les redevances foncières sont encore pour l'essentiel en nature: les cens en argent ne constituent que 20 à 40 pour cent des tenures, selon les lieux. Le marché des denrées agricoles dépend fortement des surplus seigneuriaux, dans la main du seigneur ou affermés. Certes les tailles pèsent plus lourd, mais c'est aussi parce que les paysans détiennent de l'argent qu'ils peuvent être ponctionnés par les seigneurs et la nouvelle fiscalité royale.

Les salaires sont tous exprimés en argent, et rarement est spécifié qu'ils comprennent la nourriture du salarié.[27] Du haut en bas de la société et dans les divers domaines d'activité l'argent semble d'usage commun.

Dès le XIIIe siècle, les formidables frappes de monnaie de Melgueil, étudiées par Marc Bompaire, correspondent, au moins pour une part, à ce besoin local, à quoi s'ajoute, dans la première moitié du XIVe siècle, un crédit très répandu. Les minutes du notaire de Ganges, Pierre Marcial, en 1320 montrent que les clients habituels du notaire sont à la fois et suivant les circonstances débiteurs et créanciers.[28]

L'activité d'échanges se fait au quotidien et sur place: ainsi le bayle de Canet achète ce qu'il lui faut pour tenir table ouverte aux hôtes de passage. Mais aussi aux temps forts des foires qui constituent désormais un cycle très dense et où Montagnac et Pézenas ne constituent que les plus brillants des pôles, mais deux

[27] Ainsi les salaires qui sont mentionnés pour les opérations de traitement des laines et le parage des draps ne prévoient que très rarement le *victum* à côté de la somme en argent. Sur les treize opérations présentées, seul les hommes qui tondent les toisons et les femmes qui lavent les laines reçoivent le *victum*.

[28] Bompaire, « La circulation monétaire »; Pascal, « Notariat ».

parmi bien d'autres.[29] D'ailleurs les consuls de Caux ont fait l'observation que le nombre croissant des foires fait croître l'activité commerciale, car les marchands savent pouvoir vendre à l'une ce qu'ils n'ont pas écoulé à l'autre.[30] Et cet accroissement qui se fait sans nul doute dans un contexte de concurrence n'empêche pas la progression du mouvement des marchandises. En 1310, la foire de la Saint Martin d'hiver à Pézenas était affermée pour 70 livres; pour 80 en 1320, puis 90 et 100 livres en 1324.[31] La société languedocienne mérite d'être qualifiée de société commerçante.[32]

Ainsi en est-il à Canet où la part de l'activité textile paraît faible, et où l'économie locale ne paraît pas sous domination urbaine, hormis par la présence de deux créanciers narbonnais. Ainsi en est-il a fortiori dans les zones drapantes: c'est sur l'activité textile et la richesse qu'elle crée qu'insistent certains documents.

La richesse de la région: laines, draps et toiles

Pour revenir sur ce terrain, je voudrais repasser brièvement par la plaidoirie des consuls de Béziers. Même s'ils poursuivent un objectif précis, le maintien des impositions sur les draps fabriqués dans la sénéchaussée de Carcassonne, et si l'essentiel de l'argumentation concerne l'imposition elle-même, les conditions dans lesquelles elle est levée, les conséquences prévisibles de sa suppression, et plus largement le contexte de la conjoncture économique sont toujours présents, tout particulièrement dans l'un des deux mémoires, la réponse à Pierre de Brenac.[33]

Le discours bien informé des élites

L'ampleur et la précision du tableau de la situation régionale dressé par les consuls biterrois constitue la caractéristique première du document. Ils situent leur Languedoc dans un espace qui va de l'Angleterre, avec ses laines, aux terres

[29] Combes, « Les foires en Languedoc ».

[30] Pézenas, Arch. Mun., A/5/7.

[31] Pézenas, Arch. Mun., A/5/7.

[32] Le concept issu de l'historiographie anglaise s'adapte parfaitement à bien des régions méditerranéennes.

[33] Pierre de Brenac est alors procureur des pareurs de Béziers, mais il avait aussi auparavant conduit, comme commissaire du roi, une enquête sur ce sujet.

ultramarines dont les marchands apportent de nombreuses marchandises; ils viennent notamment avec les produits nécessaires à la teinture et remportent des draps afin, disent les consuls, de ne pas repartir à vide. Dans ce vaste espace, l'attention des consuls est particulièrement vive pour la Catalogne.

L'ampleur de l'espace considéré n'empêche pas la précision des informations sur les terres voisines de Béziers: la distinction est soigneusement faite entre la sénéchaussée de Toulouse et celle de Carcassonne, à laquelle les auteurs du mémoire appartiennent. Divers centres drapants sont mentionnés pour leur position dans le conflit, mais Carcassonne et Narbonne sont évidemment les partenaires distingués des consuls de Béziers. La précision concerne aussi la désignation des draps, non pas dans le détail des fabrications, mais dans le genre: laines, fils, draps (*panni*) de laine et de lin, toiles (*telae*) de laine.

Les consuls connaissent bien les raisons des marchands étrangers, savent qu'ils n'ont pas d'autre guide que les prix et leurs bénéfices, et ils sont attentifs aux risques que représenterait une présence amoindrie de ces marchands aussi bien *extranei* que *regnicolae*.

Ils ont une conscience aiguë de l'importance des mesures fiscales et de leur incidence sur la situation économique du pays.

Ils s'essayent aussi au raisonnement économique remarquant notamment que fabriquer un produit de forte valeur ajoutée est créateur de plus de richesse que fabriquer un produit brut et plus encore une matière première telle que la laine. Ils dénoncent les effets des ententes illicites sur les prix. Certes toutes les données fournies ne sont pas parfaitement cohérentes: à la fois l'article VIII affirme que les taxes à l'exportation accroissent la marchandise disponible sur place et permettent au plus grand nombre, notamment les pauvres qui sont salariés, de se vêtir pour des prix moindres (donc semble impliquer des prix à la baisse) et l'article XIII note que les draps et les produits nécessaires à leur fabrication sont plus chers qu'auparavant. Ils sont évidemment très peu libéraux: favorables notamment, outre aux gabelles et taxes à l'exportation, au renforcement du monopole d'exportation de la ville d'Aigues-Mortes et aux contrôles divers.

La logique marchande n'est pas leur seule considération: ils indiquent clairement qu'il faut prendre en compte l'intérêt du plus grand nombre (*utilitas generalis, communis, et publica*) et pas seulement celui de quelques riches peu nombreux, vendeurs de laine ou fabricants de draps crus. Ils sont très conscients des disparités sociales et de la nécessité d'assurer du travail à tous ceux qui vivent de la fabrication (*factio*) des draps. C'est d'ailleurs un argument présent dans nombre d'autres documents contemporains, notamment les ordonnances de 1318 et 1320.

De ce premier commentaire, je retiendrai deux points:

- la présence d'une foule de travailleurs du textile, *Leitmotif* de l'argumentaire des consuls de Béziers que l'on retrouve dans d'autres rapports contemporains;
- la qualité de la plaidoirie qui renvoie à celle des élites qui dirigent le pays, à leur prise en compte des contraintes économiques, et des nécessités sociales dans la santé d'une région.

Les articles de Pierre de Brenac, sur lequel nous reviendrons plus loin, ne sont pas connus directement, mais seulement à travers la réponse des consuls de Béziers. Ils semblent se limiter un peu plus étroitement aux problèmes fiscaux et aux revenus que le roi peut attendre. De même l'autre mémoire des consuls de Béziers. En revanche la même qualité d'information caractérise les arguments que les consuls de Narbonne présentent au roi.[34] En vingt ans, les progrès de la réflexion économique et de sa présentation sont considérables. Tout le dossier de la ténébreuse affaire de la gabelle des draps révèle chez les consuls et leurs conseillers une perception constructive de l'économie languedocienne.

La majeure partie de la sénéchaussée vit de la draperie

« Ex operagio lanagii vivit magna pars gentium senescallie vel ex pannis parandis vel ex eis que ad hec necessaria existunt », écrivent les consuls de Narbonne en 1329.

Tout l'Ouest du Languedoc vit de la draperie. A elle seule, la sénéchaussée de Toulouse produirait deux fois plus que celle de Carcassonne. Les chiffres avancés par les consuls de Narbonne sont impressionnants: trois mille personnes vivent directement du drap dans la sénéchaussée de Carcassonne. La draperie crée huit cent mille journées de travail par an. Le raisonnement se poursuit: la terre est stérile, ou du moins peu fertile. C'est *l'operagium lanarum et pannorum* qui la rend *satis fertilis* et les pauvres, hommes et femmes, se nourrissent très bien grâce à l'*operagium*.[35] On remarquera donc que c'est aux pauvres, ceux qui ne possèdent pas de terre, que l'ouvrage des laines et des draps permet de vivre. De fait, les consuls évaluent au tiers de la valeur du drap le coût des matières premières, l'essentiel du prix de revient étant la valeur ajoutée

[34] Blanc, *Le livre de comptes*, II, pièces justificatives XCIV, p. 845.

[35] « Optime ex operagio pauperes homines et mulieres sustentantur »: Blanc, *Le livre de comptes*, II, pièces justificatives XCIV, p. 851.

du travail. Pour le travail des laines et draps, elle est analysée en deux groupes d'opérations, le premier en comptant treize et le second, dix. Les treize opérations de l'ouvrage des laines créent une valeur de 63s. 10d. pour un drap double, dont 20s. (le tiers) pour la femme *qui lanam predictam fecit operari* et huit pour le tissage. Les dix opérations pour le parage des draps coûtent une cinquantaine de sous, dont trente pour la seule teinture. Au total chaque drap fournit du travail pour plus de 100s.[36]

Mais par toutes les activités qu'elle induit, les consuls comptant jusqu'à l'hébergement des marchands étrangers, la draperie crée 60 pour cent de la richesse locale.

L'ampleur des affaires est considérable. Les consuls de Béziers citent une société de pareurs de Carcassonne qui a fait venir 38,000 toisons du Berry, sans compter les laines venues d'Angleterre, de Bourgogne et d'ailleurs. Il se peut que nous voyions là une transformation repérée en Flandre qui conduit les pareurs à devenir de grands opérateurs industriels et que les contradictions apparentes entre les opinions des pareurs qui à Béziers sont contre la gabelle et ailleurs lui sont favorables puissent s'expliquer par cette évolution.

En tous cas, tous les textes le montrent, la question est bien celle du parage des draps. Le roi doit-il favoriser la libre circulation des draps écrus et leur exportation vers l'étranger, notamment la Catalogne? Ou bien doit-il faire en sorte que les draps écrus soient parés sur place. C'est ce point de vue que défendent les consuls des grandes villes de la sénéchaussée, Narbonne, Carcassonne et Béziers et de quelques autres centres importants.

Il est bien probable, comme l'a montré Dominique Cardon, que c'est dans ces premières années du XIVe siècle que se fait un gain technique très sensible dans une évolution qui conduit à traiter de plus en plus les laines courtes et fines.[37] Le Languedoc carde en effet: les consuls de Narbonne disent qu'il en coûte 3s. pour carder et filer la laine Mais plus encore, la chaîne du travail complète le cardage par l'arçonnage. Attesté dans la région dès le début du XIIIe

[36] À dire vrai, le calcul ne se reconstitue pas de manière simple. L'évaluation globale ne correspond pas parfaitement aux détails des opérations. Elle se monte, selon l'affirmation des consuls, exactement à 111s. 6d.

[37] Cardon, *La draperie au Moyen Âge*, passim. La présence de laine de mouton merinos ne remonte pas, comme on le pensait sur la foi de documents étudiés par Lopez, 'El origén de la oveja merina', au début du XIVe siècle puisque déjà les vêtements du « comte de l'an mil » à Toulouse attestent le travail de cette laine. Crubézy et Dieulafait, *Le comte de l'an mil*, pp. 155–85.

siècle, il est sans doute largement présent dans le premier XIVe siècle. Il faudrait en chercher les chemins et les formes de diffusion.[38]

Car ces « nouveaux » procédés font des draps moins chers. C'est là d'ailleurs un des éléments de la concurrence qui s'est installée entre la Catalogne ou le royaume de Majorque et le Languedoc.

La situation de la draperie est, de manière récurrente, présentée en concurrence avec la Catalogne et le Roussillon, concurrence que les documents placent de fait au premier rang des soucis. Elle semble apparaître dans le contexte politique des expéditions de Philippe III en Catalogne. Si l'on croit l'histoire telle que la racontent les consuls de Béziers et de Narbonne, la politique fiscale du roi en est l'élément essentiel. Il se peut aussi qu'interviennent des facteurs techniques qui nous échappent. En effet, en 1306 un mémoire catalan prétend que les draps catalans sont moins chers que les draps languedociens.[39] La concurrence s'exerce notamment pour le parage des draps écrus.

Or il semblerait que l'ordonnance de Philippe le Bel de 1305, interdisant la sortie des draps écrus et des laines ait ruiné les pareurs de Perpignan. Les consuls rapportent que de huit parayries il n'en reste plus qu'une après l'instauration de la gabelle sur les draps, qui vient, pour le roi compenser la perte des droits de douane que les draps écrus payaient à l'exportation. Néanmoins la concurrence demeure très forte; l'émigration de travailleurs de la draperie est attestée en direction du royaume de Valence où leurs techniques, moins coûteuses que les techniques locales de facture castillane rencontrent à la fois le succès et l'hostilité des populations locales dans les années 1330–40.

Outre la perception très vive de la concurrence qu'ont les élites et sans doute les populations de part et d'autre de la frontière, la volatilité de ces activités est étonnante: à quelle vitesse les pareurs de Perpignan disparaissent-ils! Et la mobilité de la population artisanale: dans un sens et dans l'autre, les divers rapports insistent sur cette caractéristique.

Ainsi se construit une image du Languedoc de la « crise », en crise certes au sens où la transformation du pays est réelle et rapide, mais d'où la prospérité semble loin d'avoir disparu. Et les transformations que la région connaît sont perçues au moins par les élites. Il se peut bien qu'elles s'opèrent sous une sorte de contrainte démographique. Que le pays ne soit pas une riche terre à blé est

[38] L'une des grandes familles narbonnaises de cette époque porte le nom d'Arquejayre: Larguier, *Le drap et le grain en Languedoc*, p. 38.

[39] Publié par H. Finke, *Acta Aragoniensia*, pp. 155–62, et cité par Romestan, « Draperie roussillonnaise ».

Tableau 9.1. Les transactions foncières dans la baylie de Canet d'après les comptabilités de l'archevêché de Narbonne en 1334.

	CANET	AUTRES	TOTAL
feux	155	60+47+40+27 = 174	
Transactions: nombre, Dont échanges	64 4	38 1	102
Valeur totale	46488 (£200)	18176 (£76)	64664 (£269)
Nombre de vendeurs	43	24	67
Nombre d'acheteurs	32	31	63
Valeur moyenne des biens	726 (£3)	491 (£2)	634
Maxi – mini	£10 – 5s.	£10 – 10s.	
Invest moyen des acheteurs	1453 d. = £6	568 (£2)	1043 (£4)
Maxi – mini acheteur	7320 = £31 (prêtre) – 180	3360 (£14 fabre) – 72	
Produit moyen par vendeur	1081 (£5)	757 (£3)	965 (£4)
Mini – maxi par vendeur		72 – 3360 (£14 femme) (4452 pour J. Vesiani)	
veuves	1 (+1)	6	7 (+1)
Mari et femmes vendeurs Total couple	23 mari et femme 6 femme et mari 29	4 mari et femme 2 femme et mari 6	27 8 35 (moitié)
Femmes seules	3	6	9
Mari et femme acheteurs	3	1	4 = (6%)
Femmes seules	1	2	3
Transactions interfamiliales	6		7%
Fratrie vendeuse	6		6
Fratrie acheteuse	5	2	7
Achats par artisans, notaires, prêtres locaux	2, 4, 5	4 – 1	
Urbains acheteurs	2	0	2
Transactions: nombre, Dont échanges	64 4	38 1	102 5
Valeur totale des transactions en dn	46488 (£200)	18176 (£76)	64664 (£270)
Hospicia: nombre Valeur totale en dn Valeur moyenne Mini – maxi	6 7140 (£30) 1428 (£6) 720 – 2540	2 1/4 1068+ échange	8 1/4 8208 (+) (13%)
Champs: nombre Valeur totale en dn Valeur moyenne Mini – maxi	9 12436 (+ 2 échanges) (£5) 360 – + 4800	7 (dt 6) 2856 476 312 – 732	16 15292 (24%)

une évidence un peu douloureuse. Mais la vigne est sans nul doute une solution et le vin s'exporte: c'est la deuxième denrée énumérée lorsqu'il s'agit de fixer un tarif de douane, après les draps.[40] Le marché foncier profite aux artisans; il est rapide, mais rien ne prouve qu'il s'emballe, même si l'accroissement de la valeur des biens immobiliers et fonciers fait partie des éléments de la conjoncture perçus par les contemporains. Mais les échanges ne concernent pas que la terre: toute la région baigne dans une commercialisation de tous les biens. Et l'appoint fondamental à la richesse vient de la draperie. Peut-être cet appoint, incontestable, est-il un peu exagérément présenté par les élites urbaines, qui vivent au contact d'une population pauvre dont la survie — et le calme — en dépend et qui sont eux-mêmes proches des milieux du négoce. Le Languedoc est actif et riche d'une abondante activité secondaire et tertiaire.

Reste que cette image, assez cohérente et nullement idyllique, présentée par la région d'entre Carcassonne, Narbonne et Béziers, entre 1320 et 1340, ne doit être pas inconsidérément étendue à tout le Languedoc et aux régions voisines.[41] Kathryn Reyerson a souligné la dure réadaptation que vit Montpellier à cette époque: la teinture des draps flamands qui avait été l'une des spécialités de la ville au siècle précédent, décline, mais l'activité artisanale est relayée par le développement très rapide du commerce de draps fabriqués par la partie occidentale de la province. De l'autre côté du Languedoc, en Lauragais, c'est une image plus noire encore que révèle l'étude de Maurice Berthe sur le marché de la terre: à Caignac: entre 1283 et 1325, en 42 ans, 922 biens ont changé de mains, avec une année d'apogée à ce mouvement, 1311 et trois phases intenses: 1283–92 (128 actes); 1296–1303 (185 actes) 1308–16 (371 actes). Maurice Berthe lie cette volatilité à « la détérioration de la situation agraire et (à) l'irruption des premières famines graves (qui) fournissent des éléments d'explication plausible ».[42] Ce sont les plus riches qui profitent du mouvement: 7 pour cent des paysans connus par la documentation ont acquis 50 pour cent des terres mises en vente. Ils sont aussi les plus fréquemment cités dans les confronts et ils appartiennent pour l'essentiel à des familles notables de vieille date. Dans le même temps, les prélèvements s'alourdissent jusqu'à une redevance d'agrier de la moitié, taux encore jamais atteint. Et c'est sans doute à la faim de terres qu'il faut associer l'interdiction d'en vendre à des étrangers. Pourtant le mou-

[40] Blanc, *Le livre de comptes*, II, document XCIII, p. 841.

[41] Elle est tout à fait conforme à celle que développe Larguier, *Le drap et le grain en Languedoc*, à propos de Narbonne et de son commerce dont le déclin avait été auparavant très surestimé.

[42] Berthe, « Marché de la terre et hiérarchie paysanne », p. 301.

vement ralentit « bien qu'on conçoive mal que les tensions sur les transactions foncières s'apaisent alors que les troubles de subsistance continuent ». Carence de la source? Quant aux disettes qui se font jour, elles renvoient à la dureté des temps, mais pas nécessairement à l'épuisement des terres; peut-être autant à des formes de spéculation nouvelles.[43]

Le Roussillon offre au même moment l'image d'un havre de prospérité, comme d'ailleurs plus au Sud le royaume de Valence.[44] En Roussillon, ce sont sans doute en grande partie les formes d'intensification agricole qui expliquent la résistance régionale au phénomène de cherté des grains. Mais ici aussi les aléas du textile rythment la prospérité, bonne dans l'ensemble, de la région. L'impression est donc d'un puzzle à échelle régionale où coexistent des zones, les plus nombreuses, emmenées par l'urbanisation, qui ont intensifié l'agriculture, développé l'artisanat et multiplié les échanges et connaissent une modernisation, peut-être douloureuse pour certains, mais rapide et d'autres qui ne semblent pas avoir surmonté cette réorientation et subissent la conjoncture.

[43] Sur ce point, Bourin, Drendel, et Menant, *Les disettes dans la conjoncture de 1300.*

[44] Puig, « Les campagnes roussillonnaises ».

Bibliographie

Archives

Montpellier, Archives Départementales de l'Hérault, II E 39/528
Paris, Archives Nationales, Q 1, 62 et 63
Paris, Bibliothèque nationale de France, Fonds Doat, Tome 157
Pézenas, Archives Municipales de Pézenas, liasse A/5/7
Stato della Città del Vaticano, Archives du Vatican, Reg. Aven. 122

Sources imprimées

Blanc, Alphonse, *Le livre de comptes de jacme Olivier, marchand de Narbonne* (Paris: Picard, 1892)

Pasquier, Félix, et Siméon Olive, *Le fonds Thézan aux archives du château de Léran* (Montpellier: Lauriol, 1913)

Sources secondaires

Berthe, Maurice, « Marché de la terre et hiérarchie paysanne dans le Lauragais toulousain vers 1270–1320 », dans *Campagnes médiévales: L'homme et son espace, Mélanges offerts à Robert Fossier*, éd. par Elisabeth Mornet (Paris: Publications de la Sorbonne, 1995), pp. 297–311

Bompaire, Marc, « La circulation monétaire en Languedoc: X^e^–XIIIe siècles » (thèse de doctorat non publiée, Université de Paris IV, 2002)

Cardon, Dominique, *La draperie au Moyen Âge: Essor d'une grande industrie européenne* (Paris: CNRS, 1999)

Crubézy, Eric, et Christine Dieulafait, éds, *Le comte de l'an mil*, Aquitania, supplément 8 (Talence: Fédération Aquitania, 1996)

Combes, Jean, « Les foires en Languedoc au Moyen Âge », *Annales: Économies, Sociétés, Civilisations*, 13 (1958), 231–59

Bourin, Monique, John Drendel, et François Menant, éds, *Les disettes dans la conjoncture de 1300 en Méditerranée occidentale: La conjoncture de 1300 en Méditerranée occidentale*, Collection de l'Ecole Française de Rome, 450 (Roma: École Française de Rome, 2012)

Bourin, Monique, François Menant, et Luis To Figueras, éds, *Dynamiques du monde rural dans la conjoncture de 1300* (Roma: École Française de Rome, 2014)

Carocci, Sandro, éd., *La mobilitá sociale nel medioevo*, Collection de l'Ecole Française de Rome, 436 (Roma: École Française de Rome, 2011)

Larguier, Gilbert, *Le drap et le grain en Languedoc: Narbonne et le Narbonnais 1300–1789* (Perpignan: Presses universitaires de Perpignan, 1996)

Levi, Giovanni, *Le Pouvoir au village: Histoire d'un exorciste dans le Piémont du XVIIe siècle* (Paris: Gallimard, 1989)

Lopez, R. S., 'El origén de la oveja merina', *Estudios de historia moderna*, 4 (1954), 3–11

Maillard, François, et Robert-Henri Bautier, « Un dénombrement des feux, des individus et des fortunes dans deux villages des Fenouillèdes en 1306 », *Bulletin philologique et historique*, 1965, 309–28

Pascal, Alice, « Notariat, économie et société à Ganges en 1320 » (mémoire de maîtrise, Université de Paris I, 1996)

Puig, Carole, « Les campagnes roussillonnaises au Moyen Âge: Dynamiques agricoles et paysagère entre le XIIe et la première moitié du XIVe s. » (thèse de doctorat inédite, Université de Toulouse, 2003)

Reyerson, Kathryn, « Montpellier et le trafic des grains en méditerranée avant 1350 », dans *Actes du XIIe Congrès de la couronne d'Aragon* (Montpellier: Société archéologique de Montpellier ,1985), pp. 142–62; repris dans *Society, Law and Trade in Medieval Montpellier*, Variorum Collected Studies (Ashgate: Aldershot, 1995), no. XII

——, « Urban/Rural Exchange: Reflections on the Economic Relations of Town and Country in the Region of Montpellier before 1350 », dans *Urban and Rural Communities in Medieval France, Provence and Languedoc, 1000–1500*, éd. par Kathryn Reyerson et autres (Leiden: Brill, 1998), pp. 253–73

Romestan, Guy, « Les consuls de Béziers et l'abolition de la gabelle des draps (1330) », dans *Béziers et le Biterrois, XLIIIe congrès de la Fédération Historique du Languedoc Méditerranéen, Béziers, 30–31 mai 1970* (Montpellier: Fédération Historique du Languedoc Méditerranéen, 1971), pp. 191–219

——, « Draperie roussillonnaise et draperie languedocienne dans la première moitié du XIVe siècle », dans *XLIIe congrès de la Fédération Historique de Languedoc Roussillon* (Montpellier: Fédération Historique de Languedoc méditerranéen, 1969), pp. 31–59

Thomas, Louis J., « La population du Bas Languedoc à la fin du XIIIe siècle et au commencement du XIVe siècle », *Annales du Midi*, 20 (1908), 469–88

Quand le bâtiment va …
Une facette des rapports ville-campagne : Le marché des matériaux

Philippe Bernardi

Introduisant, dans *The Medieval Economy and Society*, son chapitre sur « Trade and Industry », Michael M. Postan eut soin de rappeler que ces activités prenaient place dans une société anglaise médiévale « aux revenus principalement agricoles ». Leur importance n'est, en outre, reconnue que sous forme d'une litote, venant nuancer l'évidence selon laquelle,

> The numbers occupied in trade and industry formed a relatively small proportion of the total; and even those so occupied often combined their industrial and commercial occupations with some agricultural pursuits. This does not, however, mean that industrial and commercial activities were wholly insignificant and played little part in shaping the economic geography of the country or in directing the course of its economic development.[1]

Il n'est pas dans mon propos de revenir sur la part prise par chacune de ces occupations dans la société médiévale, ni de tenter d'apprécier le rôle tenu par un artisanat rural souvent considéré comme négligeable et, de fait, négligé. Il semble important, toutefois, abordant la situation économique et sociale de la fin du Moyen Âge par le biais de l'étude de la population et des échanges liés au domaine de la construction, de relever que le discours de Michael M. Postan

[1] Postan, *The Medieval Economy and Society*, p. 183.

Philippe Bernardi (bernardi.philippe@wanadoo.fr) est directeur de recherche au CNRS et attaché au Laboratoire de Médiévistique Occidentale de Paris (UMR 8589, CNRS-Université Paris 1, Panthéon-Sorbonne).

Crisis in the Later Middle Ages: Beyond the Postan-Duby Paradigm, ed. by John Drendel, TMC 13 (Turnhout: Brepols, 2015) 273–296 BREPOLS PUBLISHERS 10.1484/M.TMC.5.103791

repose implicitement, malgré le constat de « combinaisons » possibles, sur une classification préalable séparant nettement les occupations. On peut, en effet, s'interroger sur la possibilité d'application à l'économie médiévale d'une stricte « sectorisation » empruntée au langage administratif des années 1930.

La pluriactivité, largement attestée, paraît estomper encore les contours de telles catégories, et la multiplicité des revenus ruraux (ou urbains) rend bien souvent inutilisable une distinction entre « activités principale et secondaire(s) », corollaire de la sectorisation. Ces classifications butent, en outre, sur les liens fondamentaux unissant l'industrie à une agriculture qui regroupe les activités de production des denrées alimentaires et de certaines matières premières. Au sein de ces dernières, de quel poids pesa le marché des matériaux de construction dans une période (le milieu du XIVe siècle) où: « les travaux de fortification engloutirent des sommes énormes, et ceci en dépit de toutes les difficultés économiques et de la crise démographique provoquée par la Peste noire et ses récurrences » ?[2] Si, comme le note François Menant pour les vallées lombardes, une économie rurale diversifiée peut compenser la faiblesse des ressources céréalières, la question se pose d'un élargissement possible de la notion d'« excédents négociables » évoquée par Georges Duby en matière de rendements agricoles aux différentes sources de revenus potentielles du monde rural, dont les matériaux de construction.[3]

Le propos est vaste et ne saurait sans doute s'accommoder d'une réponse globale. La présente étude n'entend que contribuer à un débat à partir d'un cas particulier, celui de la Provence comtale et du Comtat Venaissin. Il a paru nécessaire, pour cela, de partir d'un panorama général de la production des matériaux de construction et de l'approvisionnement des chantiers provençaux à la fin du Moyen Âge (du XIIIe siècle au début du XVIe siècle), pour se concentrer, ensuite, sur le Comtat Venaissin et les années 1340–60 qui, outre les mouvements généraux déjà évoqués, virent, à Avignon, l'édification du Palais Neuf de Clément VI. C'est à partir des chiffres fournis par les comptes de la Chambre apostolique pour ces deux décennies que sera abordée l'éventualité d'un effet compensatoire, en milieu rural, de la production de matières premières « industrielles ».

Enfin, revenant à une séquence chronologique plus large, je tenterai d'examiner si (en certains lieux, pour certaines ressources ...) ne se fait pas jour, dans le

[2] Contamine, « Les fortifications urbaines », p. 36.

[3] Menant, « Aspects de l'économie », pp. 12–14 ; voir également l'illustration de cette diversité apportée par Zacchigna, *Sistemi d'acqua e mulini*; Duby, *L'économie rurale*, II, 200.

cadre de cette économie rurale diversifiée, une relative transformation du paysage; en essayant d'échapper, autant que possible, à ces vues de l'esprit d'« économistes en chambre » dénoncées par Edouard Perroy il y après de cinquante ans.[4]

La production des matériaux de construction : Une activité rurale

L'image forte d'un approvisionnement strictement local des chantiers médiévaux a eu tendance à minimiser l'importance du marché des matériaux ordinaires: la construction en milieu rural a — comme l'a souligné J.-M. Pesez — « peu retenu l'attention du médiéviste ».[5] C'est par analogie avec les observations ethnographiques qu'ont été dégagées quatre règles sensées être à l'œuvre dans le choix des matériaux:

- le recours à des matériaux achetés est, autant que possible, évité;
- de ce fait, le choix est dicté par les ressources locales;
- quand c'est possible, c'est le terrain à bâtir lui-même qui procure le matériau;
- c'est la pierre que l'on choisit de préférence à tout autre matériau, quand elle est accessible.[6]

Ces principes — dont la lettre, soulignons-le, est assez souple — souffrent des exceptions notables mais se trouvent figés dans une conception individualiste de l'autoconsommation ou de l'autoproduction rurale qui ne laisse que peu de place à un phénomène désigné par les économistes comme « intraconsommation » c'est-à-dire « la consommation du produit par un agent appartenant au même secteur d'activité ». Si les échanges plus ou moins gracieux entre membres d'une communauté sont probables, ceux-ci demeurent difficiles à mettre en évidence et c'est à partir des centres urbains que se saisit le mieux l'activité productrice de certains villages.

Un rapide survol des données rassemblées pour les plus grandes villes provençales montre, par exemple, que Marseille s'approvisionne en plâtre et en chaux à Allauch, en pierres à la Couronne et en bois d'œuvre des Alpes ou de localités plus proches comme le Castellet, mentionné dans un acte de 1292.[7]

[4] « Or loin de s'étendre la production lainière anglaise ne cessa de décroître, plus peut-être que la culture des céréales — et la transformation du paysage rural, imaginée par des économistes en chambre, reste une vue de l'esprit »: Perroy, « À l'origine d'une économie contractée », p. 180.

[5] Pesez, « La construction rustique en pierre », p. 63.

[6] Pesez, « La construction rustique en pierre », p. 64.

[7] Voir Baratier et Reynaud, *Histoire du commerce de Marseille*, II, 821–24.

À Aix-en-Provence, le gypse était d'extraction locale mais au tournant du XVIe siècle un moulin à plâtre fonctionnait au pied de la Sainte-Victoire, sur le terroir du village de Saint-Antonin-sur-Bayon.[8] La chaux venait, elle, de divers lieux disséminés dans la campagne aixoise et la pierre de taille était tirée des carrières du Tholonet. Le bois d'œuvre, enfin, provenait des Alpes ou du massif de l'Etoile. C'est également des Alpes, via la Durance, l'Isère, et le Rhône, que les pièces de bois arrivaient dans la ville d'Arles qui tirait, comme Tarascon ou Nîmes, une partie des pierres dont elle était dépourvue des carrières de Fontvieille et faisait parfois venir du sable de Maillane.[9] À Sisteron, le bois provenait des environs de Luz-la-Croix-Haute; à Carpentras, les travaux engagés par la ville au XIVe siècle drainaient vers la ville, par exemple, des saules de Cairanne ou des pierres de Saint-Didier, Caromb et Saint-Pierre-de-Vassols.[10] Il est inutile de multiplier les exemples, les mentions sont légions de matériaux achetés par les grands centres urbains dans les campagnes où ils puisent des ressources que leurs environs immédiats ou la récupération ne peuvent pas leur offrir. Les divers tarifs de péages conservés pour la Provence attestent amplement, par ailleurs, de la circulation de ces produits. Le phénomène n'a, bien sûr, rien de spécifiquement provençal.

Toutefois, si la localisation en milieu rural de certaines productions ne fait pas de doute, on peut s'interroger sur la qualité des producteurs. Dans certains cas les habitants des villes peuvent simplement aller « se servir » sur le territoire de telle ou telle localité. Mais même dans le cas d'une fourniture faite par les habitants des villages, s'agissait-il de paysans ou de bûcherons, de carriers, de chaufourniers, de plâtriers? La question est délicate car la frontière est bien ténue entre un cultivateur ou éleveur coupant occasionnellement (de manière saisonnière ?) et un bûcheron travaillant aussi la terre.[11] Nous retrouvons là la question, sous un autre angle, de l'artisanat rural. De nombreux historiens ont insisté — avec Postan — sur la pratique conjointe ou combinée en milieu rural (mais aussi urbain) d'une occupation artisanale et de l'agriculture. Agriculteurs-artisans ou artisans-agriculteurs? Tout est affaire de nuance et nous ne dispo-

[8] Bernardi, *Métiers du bâtiment et techniques de construction*, pp. 125–96.

[9] Stouff, « Les matériaux de construction ».

[10] AC Carpentras, CC 151, fol. 19, le 15 janvier 1361; AC Carpentras, CC157, fol. 5 (1357); AC Carpentras, CC 161, fol. 178 (1381); voir aussi Butaud, « Guerre et vie publique ».

[11] Pour le Haut-Dauphiné voisin, Thérèse Sclafert souligne ce caractère saisonnier du travail d'abattage: « Bûcherons en hiver, les manants du Bochaine redevenaient laboureurs dès que s'annonçait la bonne saison » (Sclafert, *Le Haut-Dauphiné au Moyen Âge*, p. 317).

sons pas d'éléments bien précis sur une question dont on peut se demander si elle mérite d'être tranchée. Les qualificatifs donnés par les scribes, fort rares en milieu rural, sont pour leur part difficiles à apprécier: rendent-ils compte d'une spécialisation, d'une aptitude particulière, d'une occupation ponctuelle?[12]

Des *fustiers*, *peyriers*, *gipiers* apparaissent dans les actes notariés comme habitants de divers villages, mais ne sont-ils pas également agriculteurs? Si l'on se fie à ces qualificatifs, notons que l'habitant du Castellet et son associé marseillais vendant, en 1292 des poutres à Marseille ne portent aucun qualificatif, contrairement à l'acheteur, désigné, lui, comme charpentier (*fusterius*).[13] A Digne même, les vendeurs de bois, habitants des villages voisins de Prads ou Marcoux, ne sont également pas qualifiés.[14] L'absence de qualificatif peut toutefois être considérée comme un indice bien faible. Il en va autrement de la mention, en 1514, 1520 ou 1528 — alors que les textes gagnent en précision — de vendeurs de bois désignés comme *laboratores* de Prads ou de Peyrolles.[15] Et que dire de ces trois *laboratores* d'Aix qui s'engagent, en 1526, à livrer à la veuve d'un charpentier pour 33 florins de planches et de poutrelles de pin?[16]

C'est sous le même qualificatif de *laboratores* que sont présentées, à Aix, la plupart des personnes vendant de la chaux ou possédant des plâtrières.[17] La fabrication de la chaux est, du reste, classée par Diderot et d'Alembert dans la partie de leur *Encyclopédie* consacrée à l' « Économie rustique ». Plus proche chronologiquement et géographiquement du propos de cette intervention, Olivier de Serres, dans son *Théâtre d'agriculture*, atteste également de la part prise par ce type de produits chez le « bon mesnager » qui « se servira des minéraux qui se pourront treuver chez lui: sans laisser en arrière les plastres, marnes charbons, et autres matières dont la terre est riche par ses diverses propriétés, qu'il fera fouiller avec peu de hazard, et apparente espérance de gain ».[18]

12 Coulet et Stouff, *Le village de Provence*, p. 53.

13 Marseille, Arch. Comm., 1 II 12, fol. 90v.

14 Voir par exemple, AD4, 2 E 14222, fol. 24v, 11 février 1492; AD4, 2 E 14223, fol. 2v, le 5 janvier 1487; fol. 11, 26 mars 1487; AD4, 2 E 16301, fol. 14, 19 janvier 1450; AD4, 2 E 16354, fol. 18v, 16 janvier 1525.

15 AD13, 309 E 779, fol. 737, 17 août 1514; AD13, 309 E 776, fol. 601v, 27 mars 1520; AD13, 308 E 943, fol. 10v, 6 janvier 1528. Notons que la relative rareté de ces mentions est probablement due au fait que dans les villes de basse Provence, le producteur disparaît souvent derrière le marchand-transporteur.

16 AD13, 308 E 813, fol. 69, 10 novembre 1526.

17 Bernardi, *Métiers du bâtiment et techniques de construction*, pp. 173 et 185–86.

18 de Serres, *Le Théâtre d'agriculture*, p. 1049.

S'agissant des pierrescelles que nous désignons comme les moellons ou pierres non équarries peuvent être issu d'un simple épierrage des champs, d'un ramassage de surface. L'extraction et l'équarrissage des blocs, plus délicat, requièrent, en revanche, un savoir-faire plus complexe dont on peut, *a priori*, douter qu'il fasse partie du bagage courant des agriculteurs (ce que paraît confirmer la rareté de l'emploi de la pierre de taille dans l'habitat rural médiéval). Là encore il me semble que nous sommes confrontés à une question de nuance, de niveau d'intervention des ruraux dans la chaîne opératoire conduisant de la matière première au produit fini. À nouveau s'interpose le schéma du couple agriculteur-producteur et artisan-transformateur. Le milieu rural ne fournirait-il que des matières premières brutes?

Depuis le XIIIe siècle au moins des villes comme Marseille disposent en ce qui concerne la pierre de taille d'une réglementation très précise normalisant en quelque sorte les dimensions des divers types de blocs commercialisables. Le même phénomène s'observe pour les pièces de bois, vendues bien souvent sous des formes standards, ou pour la chaux et le plâtre, produits dont la mesure et la nature font l'objet de prescriptions de plus en plus précises de la part des autorités urbaines. Normalisation des échanges et rationalisation de l'architecture mènent conjointement à l'élaboration, sur les lieux d'abattage ou d'extraction, de produits finis ou semi-finis. Les pierres de taille sont vendues sous les formes ébauchées de blocs de parement (*cairon*, *ursonus* ...), de dalles de couverture ou de pavement (*bard*, *graza* ou *lausa*), de claveaux (*ogiva*), d'éléments de voûtains (*crotencha*) ... réductibles de manière comptable en un certain nombre de *cairon*-étalon. Il en va de même pour le bois, commercialisé sous forme de bardeaux (*essandole*), de poutres équarries (*cayrat*) ou non (*redon*), de poutrelles (*biga*, *jazina*) ... aux dimensions si peu variables que les tarifs du péage de Tarascon, au XIIIe siècle, donnent pour chaque type un équivalent en « *travata de fusta* » taxée à 12 d. 1 ob.[19]

On imagine mal l'existence de lieux intermédiaires, entre la carrière et le chantier, où les blocs seraient en quelque sorte profilés pour la vente, et si une scie hydraulique est attestée à Meyrargues, en 1308–09, au point de débarquement des radeaux flottés sur la Durance, nombre de ces installations sont notées à proximité immédiate des lieux de coupe, comme on le constate, par exemple, à Colmars (Alpes-de-Haute-Provence), où, au XIIIe siècle, la Cour de Provence en vient à ordonner la destruction de ces machines.[20]

[19] Voir Baratier, *Enquêtes sur les droits et revenus de Charles I*, p. 386.

[20] Sclafert, *Cultures en Haute-Provence*, p. 40.

Le texte faisant état de cette décision est intéressant à plus d'un titre car il précise que: « postquam serrarum destructionem [...] homines pauperes et nihil habentes, cum serris ad brachis in centuplum quam antea consumptionem fecerunt ». Il n'est, on le voit, pas question alors d'artisans, d'entrepreneurs, mais d'*homines pauperes et nihil habentes*. C'est, de fait, pour l'ensemble des habitants d'un lieu que les diverses coutumes conservées concèdent (ou limitent) le droit de couper des arbres (Saint-Christol, 1271, Loriol, 1264 ...), de ramasser des pierres (Mazan, 1301, Mormoiron, 1356 ...) ou de faire des chaufours et des fours à plâtre (Le Barroux, 1335, Mormoiron, 1479 ...). Si l'on ne raisonne plus à un niveau individuel (celui de l'agriculteur) mais communautaire (celui du village), l'intervention d'artisans spécialisés tels que les chaufourniers peut prendre la forme d'une initiative collective, d'un *candol*,[21] et s'insérer dans le cadre de la politique économique d'une communauté rurale. Ainsi en va-t-il, à mon sens, du contrat passé par l'*Universitas* de Cucuron le 25 mai 1474 avec une personne chargée de prospecter son territoire à la recherche d'un éventuel gisement de gypse.[22] Des entreprises coopératives de ce type sont également attestées pour la chaux, et il dut en être de la gestion de certaines scies hydrauliques comme de celles d'autres moulins voire des tuileries ou des forges communales. Quant aux carrières de pierres de taille, nous ne pouvons que constater l'attention portée à leur fonctionnement par les autorités aixoises et arlésiennes, ou les exemptions d'impositions prévues pour les carriers à Saint-Rémy en 1429,[23] et supposer que les communautés de moindre taille montrèrent également de l'intérêt pour cette source de revenus (en 1492, par exemple, celles de Caromb vendent un vingtain portant, notamment sur les gains des carriers du lieu).[24]

Il me semble, en effet, important de ne pas cloisonner trop fortement une société rurale qui, d'une manière directe ou indirecte, peut bénéficier des retombées liées au commerce des richesses de son terroir. Comme l'a noté E. Baratier à propos du bois d'œuvre taxé à Blégiers et La Javie au XIIIe siècle: « Il s'agit là avec l'élevage de la principale richesse de ces villages de montagnes et, sous le nom de péage ou de leyde, les impositions comtales ou seigneuriales

21 Voir Coulet et Stouff, *Le village de Provence*, pp. 54 et 76: « Cando ou candol désigne l'accord par lequel une communauté retient les services d'un artisan. Le terme s'applique également à la somme d'argent qui lui est promise en retour. »

22 AD84, 3 E 36/19, fol. 29^{v}.

23 Saint-Rémy, Arch. Comm., CC 11, 20 avril 1429.

24 Avignon, Bib. Mun., MS 5933, fols 79^{r}–92^{r}.

n'ont garde d'oublier cette profitable activité ».[25] Cette notion de profit est clairement exprimée par plusieurs communautés du Dauphiné dont la situation paraît comparable à celle de leurs voisines provençales, et qui expliquent, au milieu du XVe siècle que « de eodem nemore faciebant postes ex quibus magnum reportabant emolumentum » (Sarcenas) ou « magnum hemolumentum recipiunt de dicto nemore tam in postibus quam in fusta » (Quaix et Proveysieux).[26]

J'ai, au cours de cette première partie de mon exposé, insisté sur le caractère rural de la production des principaux matériaux de construction et sur la relative dépendance des villes à l'égard de la campagne en ce domaine. Les sources disponibles privilégient un point de vue urbain qui ne représente toutefois qu'une part, difficile à évaluer et probablement variable selon le matériau considéré, d'une « consommation » médiévale qu'il conviendrait d'envisager également sous un angle rural.

Ces produits finis ou semi-finis — dont l'élaboration me semble devoir être considérée au-delà d'un affrontement stérile ou inapproprié des notions d'artisanat et d'agriculture — apparaissent comme des sources de profits individuels ou collectifs, voire seigneuriaux et comtaux. Ce ne sont là que des traits fort généraux qui apparaissent aussi bien en Lombardie que dans les campagnes bordelaises,[27] pour ne citer que ces deux exemples. Voyons à présent quel fut le comportement de ces ressources au milieu du XIVe siècle, à Avignon.

Avignon, 1340–1360: Le commerce des matériaux de construction au cœur de la crise

Il convient, tout d'abord de souligner que les travaux menés à Avignon s'inscrivent, malgré les moyens mis en œuvre, dans un contexte régional. Les grandes pièces de bois nécessaires aux charpentes proviennent, là encore, des Alpes (Seyssel, Sassenage) mais aussi des forêts plus proches de Bédarrides ou de Bourg-Saint-Andéol. La pierre de taille est tirée des carrières de Villeneuve, d'Orgon ou de Caromb, et celles qui forment la fourrure des murs sont pour

[25] Baratier, *Enquêtes sur les droits et revenus de Charles I*, p. 89.

[26] Cités par Sclafert, *Le Haut-Dauphiné au Moyen Âge*, p. 198.

[27] Menant, « Aspects de l'économie »; Robert Boutruche évoque, par exemple, au sein du paragraphe qu'il consacre aux techniques agraires : « les métiers artisanaux inséparables de toute vie rurale — fabrique des toiles, tissage du chanvre, tanneries, tuileries, briqueteries, poteries, — enfin l'exploitation des carrières », dans Boutruche, *La crise d'une société*, p. 31.

partie ramassées dans la garrigue. La chaux arrive de Sorgues et de Châteauneuf-du-Pape, tandis que le plâtre est tiré des environs de l'Isle-sur-la-Sorgue; le trafic engendré par les chantiers pontificaux faisant vivre une multitude de producteurs et de transporteurs, souvent dissimulés derrière un fournisseur, interlocuteur exclusif des comptables de la Curie.

En 1342 Clément VI succéda à Benoît XII à la tête de l'église et, tout en achevant les travaux engagés par son prédécesseur, entreprit d'ajouter au sud du palais pontifical existant — bientôt désigné comme le « palais de Benoît » ou « Palais Vieux » — un « Palais Neuf » dont les travaux débutèrent en 1344 et furent achevés par son successeur vers 1355 avec l'érection des deux dernières tours prévues pour cet ensemble (Tours de la Gâche et Saint-Laurent). C'est également en 1355, le 9 janvier, que les comptes de la Chambre apostolique font pour la première fois état de paiements « pro certis clausuris et reparationibus portalium Avinionis faciendis »; les travaux, qui devaient durer près d'une quinzaine d'années, débouchant sur la création d'une nouvelle enceinte. Jusque là épargnées par le conflit franco-anglais, les villes du Comtat et avec elles Avignon, commencèrent alors à subir les contrecoups de la guerre: « se fortifier fut dès lors un impératif qui toucha tant les villes que les villages, mobilisa le pouvoir pontifical comme les communautés ».[28]

Nous disposons, pour les chantiers pontificaux avignonnais, de l'abondante comptabilité de la Chambre apostolique qui permet de tenter une restitution de l'évolution subie, en ce lieu, par les prix et les salaires au milieu du XIVe siècle. Une telle approche ne va pas, on s'en doute, sans déconvenues et difficultés d'ordre méthodologique. Je ne ferai état que de celles — au nombre de trois — qui ont déterminé la forme finale de ce travail. La première tient au manque d'homogénéité des données relevées pour divers produits, notamment en ce qui concerne « l'unité de type et de qualité ». J'ai dû renoncer pour cela à traiter du bois et ne m'en tenir qu'à certains types de pierres ou d'aliments. Les mesures employées pour la chaux et le plâtre ne sont, elles-mêmes, pas toujours faciles à identifier et j'ai opté pour un seul type d'unité par produit: le *scandal* pour la chaux et la charretée de dix sacs pour le plâtre; en tablant sur une stabilité de l'unité pendant la période considérée.

La seconde difficulté rencontrée est relative au manque de continuité de mes séries qui m'a obligé à restreindre mon propos aux seules années 1340–60 pour lesquelles mes dépouillements me permettaient de disposer de données suffi-

[28] André-Michel, « La construction des remparts »; Butaud, « Guerre et vie publique », p. 346 and p. 425.

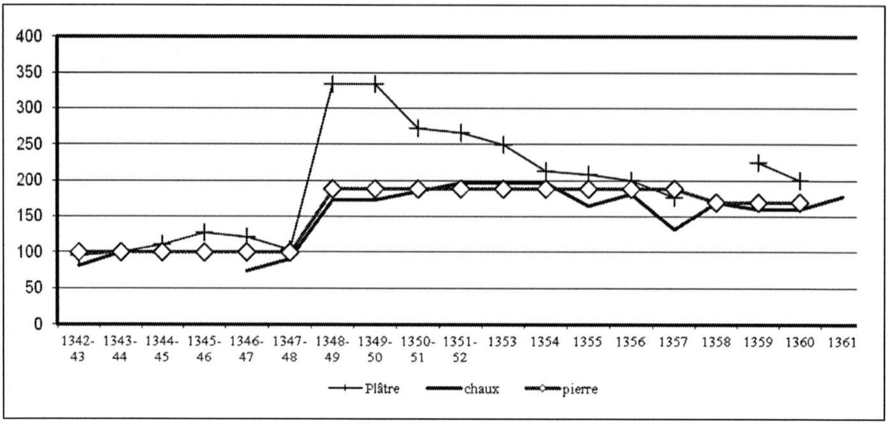

Figure 10.1. Évolution proportionnelle du prix de quelques matériaux.

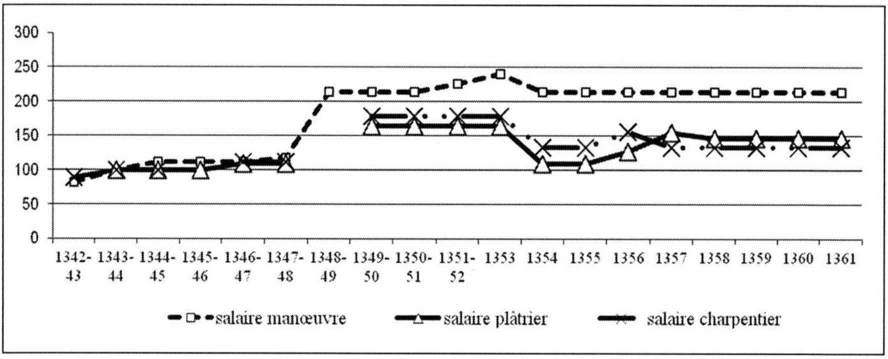

Figure 10.2. Évolution proportionnelle de quelques salaires.

samment précises. J'ai, de même, dû abandonner le pointage mensuel prévu en raison de quelques hiatus mais également du manque de lisibilité des graphiques qui en résultaient. J'ai utilisé, dans un premier temps, un prix moyen, par an ou par semestre. Le recours à des valeurs quelque peu artificielles ne m'a pas paru gêner un propos qui était de dégager des tendances, et non de suivre par le menu l'évolution d'un prix ou d'un salaire. En revanche, ces données absolues posaient un problème de comparaison et j'ai choisi de recourir à des proportions l'année 1343–44 (deuxième année du pontificat de Clément VI) me servant arbitrairement de référence.

Enfin, je me suis basé sur des prix unitaires exprimés en monnaie de compte, issus dans de rares cas de conversions quand l'équivalence était clairement exprimée. Le propos comparatiste des courbes obtenues m'a paru pouvoir s'accommoder des seuls prix et salaires nominaux.[29]

Les choix opérés ont eu pour effet de « lisser » quelque peu des courbes nettement plus chaotiques au vu du détail des prix payés. De nombreuses observations de détail ont ainsi été gommées pour concentrer l'analyse sur des mouvements que l'on peut qualifier de plus généraux.

La série de courbes réalisée (Figures 10.1 à 10.5) rend compte d'une évolution proportionnelle des prix et salaires choisis sur une période de vingt ans marquée par la peste noire et interrompue, faute d'avoir pu réunir les données nécessaires, avant la seconde grande épidémie de 1361. La première série de courbes proposée (Figure 10.1) présente l'évolution proportionnelle des prix du *scandal* de chaux, de la charretée de plâtre et du millier de *cadasta* (bloc de moyen appareil).

Le phénomène le plus marquant est la formidable augmentation que subissent les prix de ces matériaux entre le premier et le second semestre de 1348, en réaction immédiate à la peste noire. Mais alors que chaux et pierre passent d'un indice 90 à 172,5, pour le premier, et de 100 à 188,8, pour le second, le plâtre, lui, fait plus que tripler (de 103,5 à 333,5). Plus réactif, car, peut-être, d'origine plus lointaine et, de ce fait, plus affecté par la désorganisation des transports, le prix du plâtre rejoint ensuite progressivement l'évolution de celui des autres matériaux, avec une hausse nominale, vers 1354–56, avoisinant les 100 pour cent.[30] Il est à noter que l'entrée dans la guerre du Comtat (vers 1355), comme la mise en chantier de la nouvelle enceinte d'Avignon, ne semblent pas, pour leur part, avoir affecté sensiblement les prix des matériaux, ni enrayé une baisse relative. Il est vrai que les entreprises pontificales marquèrent alors le pas et que la faiblesse des quantités nécessaires aux seuls travaux de réfection et d'aménagement menés après 1355 ne les fit pas entrer en concurrence avec le chantier de la nouvelle muraille.

Les courbes des salaires (Figure 10.2) marquent, elles aussi, un accroissement net après 1348, plus sensible, à Avignon comme ailleurs, pour les travailleurs non qualifiés.[31] Notons cependant, sans pouvoir l'expliquer, que l'augmenta-

[29] J'ai bénéficié, pour les prix des denrées, de l'ouvrage récent de Weiß, *Die Versorgung*, et de l'énorme travail de collation que cet auteur présente dans une série de tableaux chronologiques.

[30] Cette hausse apparaît plus importante, pour une raison qui m'échappe, que celle constatée dans les mêmes années à Florence pour la chaux (environ 30 pour cent) : De la Roncière, *Prix et salaires à Florence*, p. 233.

[31] Voir De la Roncière, *Prix et salaires à Florence*, pp. 367–71, et Bois, *La crise du féodalisme*, p. 96.

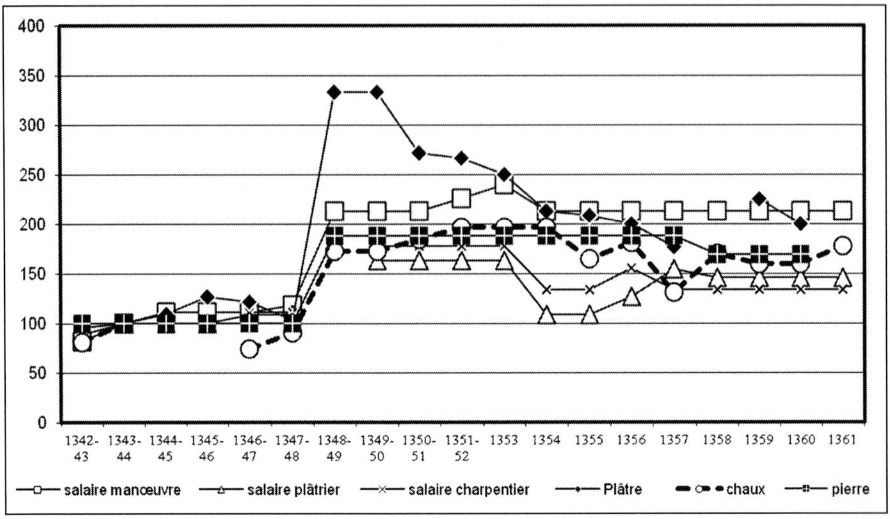

Figure 10.3. Évolution proportionnelle (en %) de prix et salaires du bâtiment.

tion est alors proportionnellement bien moindre à Avignon qu'à Florence, par exemple. Les courbes avignonnaises font état d'un accident entre 1353 et 1354 et d'une baisse conséquente (différemment vécue selon les professions), suivie d'un relèvement, pour les métiers qualifiés, peut-être due à une conjoncture favorisée par la relance des activités due à la guerre.

Si l'on compare à présent prix et salaires du bâtiment (Figure 10.3), on constate, après le sursaut simultané de 1349–50, une baisse générale et une stabilisation autour d'une hausse (par rapport à la période 1342–48) d'environ 50 pour cent, pour la plupart, et d'environ 100 pour cent pour le plâtre et le salaire des manœuvres. L'ascension des salaires et des produits « industriels » paraît ainsi progresser par pallier.[32] Il n'en va pas de même de tous les autres prix (Figure 10.4). L'impact de la peste noire n'est sensible, parmi les prix des denrées notées, que pour le bois de chauffage et le charbon — il est vrai, fort proches des matériaux de construction en ce qui concerne leur mode de production.[33] Les vivres suivent une autre progression, plus nerveuse, surtout pour le froment, qui, en prix nominaux, se résume à une stagnation.

[32] Cette différence avec la « lente et régulière ascension » évoquée par Fourquin, *Les campagnes de la région parisienne*, p. 192, tient probablement à la différence d'échelle de temps employée.

[33] Cette augmentation ne paraît pas justifier pleinement celle de la chaux et du plâtre dans

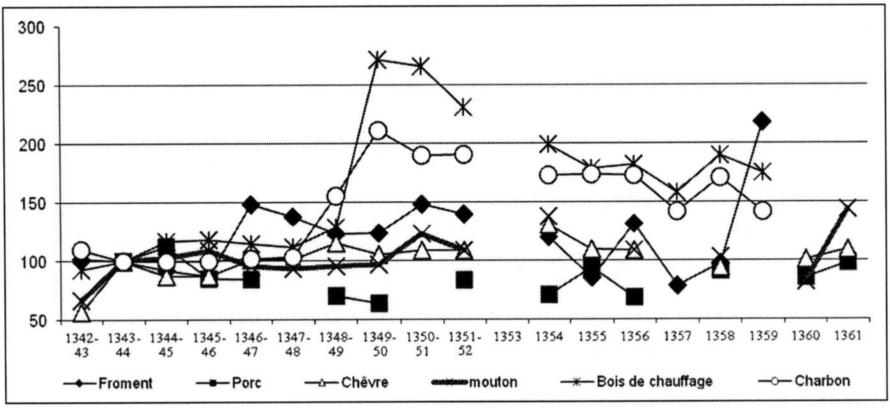

Figure 10.4. Évolution proportionnelle du prix de quelques denrées.

La comparaison des différentes courbes obtenues (Figure 10.5) met en évidence des évolutions globalement divergentes (bien que marquées, entre 1354 et 1358, par une oscillation synchrone) et une « succession de ciseaux » ou des distorsions très largement attestées par ailleurs.

Opposant l'évolution des prix « industriels » et des salaires à celle des prix « agricoles », divers auteurs ont conclu à une baisse des revenus et à une augmentation des frais du « producteur agricole ».[34] La question est de savoir à qui profita la croissance du prix des produits dits « industriels » et, parmi ceux-ci, des matériaux de construction?

Prenons l'exemple, tout d'abord, du plâtre. Sans doute extrait des terroirs de Velleron et de la Roque-sur-Pernes où se trouvent d'importants gisements de gypse exploités encore de nos jours, le plâtre est vendu à la Chambre apostolique par des marchands pour la plupart originaires de l'Isle-sur-la-Sorgue. Nous ignorons si ces derniers le produisaient ou le faisaient produire eux-mêmes, ou s'ils l'achetaient à des producteurs indépendants, mais ils se chargeaient manifestement de son transport par voie d'eau jusqu'à Avignon (situé à une quinzaine de kilomètres). Le prix versé dans cette dernière ville se compose donc en partie des frais de production (main-d'œuvre, matières premières et taxes) auxquels s'ajoutent une éventuelle commission d'intermédiaire et le coût du transport. Si l'on admet que la cuisson ait été faite sur les lieux d'extraction

la mesure où la chaux, nécessitant pour sa fabrication, beaucoup plus de combustible que le plâtre augmente proportionnellement moins.

[34] Fourquin, *Les campagnes de la région parisienne*, p. 192.

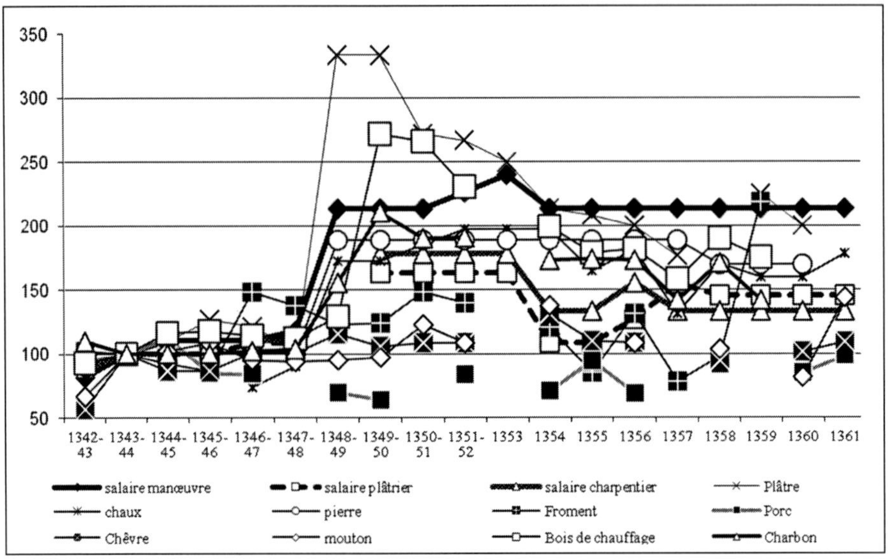

Figure 10.5. Évolution proportionnelle de tous les prix et salaires notés.

(comme on le constate à Aix, Digne, ou Allauch), il faut admettre que ces opérations étaient menées sinon par des agriculteurs, du moins par des ruraux.

En 1370, le transport paraît intervenir pour près de 45 pour cent du tarif relevé pour Avignon.[35] Qui étaient ces transporteurs? Les textes ne le précisent pas mais le fait que le prix soit toujours fixé transport compris montre qu'il était organisé par les marchands, qui disposaient, vu l'importance de la pêche à l'Isle-sur-la-Sorgue, des barques et des bras disponibles sur place. Ce point de rencontre possible entre le domaine de l'alimentation et celui du bâtiment n'est pas sans rappeler la situation aixoise décrite par une enquête de 1785 constatant l'impossibilité de se procurer du plâtre pendant les moissons ou les vendanges car: « les plâtriers ont des tombereaux pour le transport de leur plâtre, mais comme lors de la moisson et des vendanges ils louent bien chèrement leurs tombereaux et leurs attelages ils préfèrent ce salaire à faire la fourniture du plâtre nécessaire dans la ville ».[36]

La part du transport s'avère importante mais augmente-t-elle plus que celle de la production? Nos sources ne permettent pas de répondre précisément mais il est possible de constater que le roulage du Rhône au Palais, payé à part, repré-

[35] En 1374 le prix de ce matériau est de 360d. par charretée à Avignon, contre 192 à 204d. à l'Isle-sur-la-Sorgue.

[36] Aix, Arch. Comm., HH 8.

sente en 1347 et jusqu'en avril 1348, de 11 à 23 pour cent (le plus souvent de 13 à 14 pour cent) du prix d sac de plâtre livré au port, contre 6,5 à 16 pour cent (le plus souvent 11 à 13 pour cent), de 1349 à 1352. Les transporteurs suivirent la hausse mais n'en portèrent pas l'entière responsabilité. Les bénéficiaires de l'augmentation furent, on le voit, multiples, et une partie au moins d'entre eux se trouvait liée au monde rural. Ces observations s'appliquent, en outre, à un marché urbain et rien n'indique que pour leur approvisionnement en matériaux les paysans ont eu à passer par l'intermédiaire de marchands et de transporteurs.

Le gros bourg de l'Isle-sur-la-Sorgue peut apparaître à certains comme une petite ville; c'est pourquoi j'envisagerai, à présent, l'exemple plus modeste du village de Caromb et de sa production de pierres de taille.

L'emploi de la pierre de Caromb est repérable dans diverses parties du Palais des Papes datables des règnes successifs de Benoît XII (1334–42) et Clément VI (1342–52). Les comptes en attestent, pour leur part, l'achat entre 1343 et 1372 au moins. Alors que les carrières produisaient différents types de pierres, vends dans divers lieux du Comtat, les comptes avignonnais ne font, eux, mention que de dalles (bards) achetés à l'unité ou, le plus souvent, à la canne carrée (environ 4 m^2); ce mode d'évaluation soulignant encore le caractère fini du produit fourni. Les chiffres notés pour Avignon montrent que le prix de ces dalles connut, entre 1348 et 1352 (nous ne disposons pas de tarif intermédiaire), une augmentation de 130 pour cent environ; cette hausse se réduisant, vers 1357–58 à environ 80 pour cent, selon un phénomène déjà observé.

Plusieurs paiements, en 1349, 1351, et 1369, mentionnent l'envoi à Caromb par la Chambre apostolique de personnes « pro emendis bardis », ce qui atteste de la présence d'un marché local dont le rayonnement est attesté par le fait que ce produit fut utilisé en quasi-exclusivité pour les parements des remparts de Carpentras (de 1358 à 1382 au moins), ou pour la construction de l'église de Mazan, en 1377.[37] Ce marché produisait, pour Carpentras, des *cairons* au format standardisé de deux pans et demi de long sur un pan de large et un pan de haut, à un rythme soutenu. Pour le seul mois d'avril 1371, ce sont ainsi 7500 *cairons* que onze producteurs différents promettent de fournir soit environ 302,4 m^3 de pierre ou 7050 m^2 permettant de construire une longueur de 352,5 m d'un mur à double parement de dix m de

[37] Aix, Arch. Comm., HH 8; Stato della Città del Vaticano, Arch. Secrètes Vat., Coll. 462, fol. 147^v, le 6 novembre 1349; fol. 266^v, le 7 décembre 1351; Stato della Città del Vaticano, Arch. Secrètes Vat., Coll. 452, le 25 octobre 1369; Butaud, « Guerre et vie publique », p. 472.

haut.[38] Un seul de ces fournisseurs (Pierre Malvinhon) passa contrat successivement le 2 avril, le 25 avril, le 13 juin, le 4 juillet, le 18 juillet, et le 14 août de la même année (soit tous les quinze-vingt jours) pour un total des 3000 *cairons* et d'un nombre indéterminé de pierres dont le coût total équivaut au prix de 1000 autres *cairons*. L'importance de ces livraisons montre que les noms dont nous disposons sont ceux de chefs d'équipes, ou d'entreprise, ayant sous leurs ordres une main d'œuvre conséquente: or entre 1354 et 1381, nous ne rencontrons pas moins de vingt-sept carriers taillant et vendant de la pierre de Caromb, dont dix-neuf sont dits « de Caromb ». Avec Pierre et Syffrein Malvinhon, Guillaume et Isnard Albin, Gilles et Rican Raybaud, Jacques, Pierre, Pons et Raymond Pellisson, se dessine de véritables affaires de familles impliquant assez largement la communauté de Caromb dans une activité qui se poursuivit jusqu'au XIXe siècle.

Source d'un profit individuel, l'extraction de la pierre participa également aux revenus de l'*Universitas* par la perception de droits tels que le vingtain portant, entre autres, sur les gains des carriers.[39] Il est inutile de revenir sur la question du transport qui représente pour la pierre un poste plus important encore que pour le plâtre; la contraction des échanges n'affectant manifestement pas ces trafics régionaux.

Chaque village ne disposait évidemment pas des mêmes atouts. Une certaine concurrence s'exerça qui vit par exemple la production de pierres d'Orgon supplantée par celle de Caromb, parfois de manière physique dans la mesure où l'on répara les terrasses du Palais des Papes en dalles d'Orgon, avec des bards de Caromb. Mais l'histoire de cette économie reste à faire.

Une transformation du paysage rural?

La diversité des situations, soulignée par de nombreux auteurs, est encore accentuée, dans le cas qui nous occupe, par une répartition inégale des ressources naturelles, et l'angle d'approche adopté ne saurait — fut-ce pour cette seule raison — apporter de réponse tranchée à la question posée. Le fait de se concentrer sur le domaine du bâtiment ne doit pas, en outre, fausser notre vision et faire oublier ce que, de manière générale, on peut désigner comme le « poids hégémonique de l'économie agricole », c'est-à-dire de la produc-

[38] AC Carpentras, CC 156, fol. 95[v].

[39] Avignon, Bib. Mun., MS 5966, fols 79[r]–92[r].

tion des denrées alimentaires.[40] Toutefois, s'il convient d'envisager les effets des crises qui secouent la seconde moitié du XIVe siècle « à petite échelle », force est de constater que, pour certaines communautés, le dynamisme du bâtiment a pu représenter une aubaine et compenser au moins en partie les difficultés liées au marasme des prix « agricoles ». S'est-il alors agi d'une réponse ponctuelle ou d'une modification plus durable?

L'exploitation des matériaux de construction par les communautés rurales n'est, en soi, pas spécifique à la seconde moitié du XIVe siècle. Je n'en prendrai pour exemple que l'acte d'emphytéose passé entre la communauté de Pertuis et le seigneur d'Ansouis, en 1246, énumérant parmi les profits à tirer des bois cédés, « pro scindendo ad opus edificandi, et ad aliud quodlibet faciendi et exercendi, capolando, scayrando, serrando, deportando, vendendoque ubique ad beneplacitum ruscam arborum faciendo boterias sive carbonum, furnos calcencos, teuleriam et etiam giperiam si contingat ibidem infra dictos confines invenire ».[41] Le catalogue, on le voit, est large; seules y manquent les pierres de taille. Franchises et coutumes vont dans le même sens, attestant, de l'intérêt porté aux matériaux de construction par la plupart des villes et villages, bien au-delà de la Provence.

L'étude de ce type de sources permet cependant de constater ce qu'il faut bien appeler une évolution dans l'attitude des communautés vis-à-vis de ces matériaux.[42] Il n'est pas sans intérêt pour notre propos de souligner, par exemple, que le XIVe siècle vit la réglementation concernant les matériaux se développer et, surtout, se diversifier pour aborder la fabrication et la commercialisation de la chaux et du plâtre. Les autorités communales cherchèrent, au cours des XIVe et XVe siècles, à peser de plus en plus sur le marché et la production. Si nombre de décisions prises ont un caractère limitatif, la volonté de préserver un « patrimoine » qu'elles dénotent va de pair, à mon sens, avec une forme d'affirmation du droit d'exploitation par celui qui l'accorde ou le refuse.

Les coutumes du Barroux, datées de 1432 et en usage jusqu'au XVIIIe siècle, sont exemplaires à plus d'un titre. L'article concernant le plâtre se présente ainsi: « Item statuerunt et ordinaverunt quod habitatores dicti loci non possint nec valeant facere gipperias et gippum causa vendendi extra locum sine licentia domini seu ejus curie sub pena 25 s. pro vice qualibet et persona nisi tamen pro

[40] Bois, « Sur la monnaie », p. 323.

[41] AD13, B 1412, fol. 23r.

[42] Bernardi, « Construction et politique en Provence ».

eorum provisione ».[43] Nous pouvons constater tout d'abord que ce texte admet l'autoproduction et l'autoconsommation du plâtre par les « habitants » du Barroux. Ensuite, s'il y a restriction, celle-ci ne porte que sur l'exportation sur laquelle le seigneur se réserve un droit de regard et, vraisemblablement, la possibilité de percevoir quelque taxe, soulignant au passage que le plâtre au Barroux est en 1432, mais sans doute déjà avant, un objet d'exportation. Cette limitation intervient dans une réforme de 1432 qui ajoute quelques articles (dont celui-ci) aux statuts en vigueur depuis1400–01 au moins.

Rapprochée d'un litige qui opposa la communauté du Barroux à sa voisine de Malaucène en 1334 et aboutit à la décision selon laquelle « homines de Malaucena furnos calcis vel gipi facere non possint infra territorium Albaruffi sine licentia domini sive curie dicti loci », elle montre l'ancienneté du droit des habitants du Barroux, l'objet de convoitise qu'il pouvait représenter, mais aussi la main mise progressive sur les ressources du terroir du Barroux par ses habitants.[44] Une fois la concurrence exercée par les habitants de Malaucène entravée par l'obligation d'obtenir une licence de la part du seigneur du Barroux, les habitants du Barroux se posèrent, en effet, comme des producteurs privilégiés; leur production demeurant libre et pouvant se développer pour répondre aux besoins des personnes soumises, elles, à l'obtention d'une licence. À travers des tractations du type de celle de 1334 se profile la recherche d'une définition « pour le commun profit » d'un espace public englobant les lieux de production des matériaux de construction.

Le texte de 1432 montre que, conscient des profits dégagés par le commerce du plâtre, le seigneur chercha à en avoir sa part. Reprenant ici la proposition de Georges Duby selon laquelle, « l'alourdissement des tailles, en aiguisant dans les ménages paysans le besoin du numéraire, hâta sans doute également l'essor de l'artisanat rural », ne peut-on voir dans cet intérêt porté aux exportations de plâtre (ou de chaux, de pierre) la prise en compte d'une modification de sources de revenus ruraux?[45] Les gabelles et autres charges qui pèsent lourdement sur les produits alimentaires n'affectent, en effet, pas de la même manière les matériaux de construction et « l'essor de l'artisanat rural » peut correspondre aussi, pour les ruraux, à la volonté de soustraire une partie de leurs gains à certains types de prélèvements.[46] Il faudrait, par une enquête générale menée à partir

[43] AD84, 3 E 5/52.

[44] AD84, 4 E, communes, Malaucène.

[45] Duby, *L'économie rurale*, II, 251.

[46] Bernardi, « Construction et politique en Provence ».

des multiples sources réglementaires et fiscales conservées, pouvoir apprécier la manière dont les droits sur les matériaux évoluèrent au cours des derniers siècles du Moyen Âge.

On ne peut, de même, qu'appeler de nos vœux un développement des travaux sur un artisanat rural qu'il conviendrait d'étendre au-delà du seul domaine du textile. Les forêts de Haute-Provence, intensivement exploitées, ont été, comme le souligne Jean-Paul Boyer, « assaillies par les convoitises extérieures » dès 1300, phénomène qui ne se démentit pas dans les périodes postérieures.[47] On peut supposer que le développement de ce commerce n'ait pas été sans conséquences sur la vie des montagnards, mais ces dernières nous sont encore mal connues.

De même, si, de manière générale, se constate un passage progressif de la construction de bois à celle de pierre dans les campagnes médiévales autour du XIIIe siècle, les effets du développement de l'usage de la chaux — qui dans bien des cas l'accompagne — sur la production « industrielle » des campagnes n'ont pas été étudiés. Le recours exclusif à un liant à chaux et sable, d'origine locale, dès la fin du XIIe siècle à Rougiers souligne la précocité de cet emploi dans la Provence rurale.[48] Et les variations dans la qualité de la chaux, observées sur ce site, mériteraient sans doute d'être envisagées dans le cadre plus large d'une évolution du marché de ce matériau.

Les recherches menées par Alain Belmont ont montré qu'en Dauphiné la dégradation de la condition paysanne s'est accompagnée, à l'époque moderne, d'un développement de l'artisanat rural « salutaire ».[49] Faute d'estimations précises, nous ne pouvons, pour le Moyen Âge, qu'émettre l'hypothèse d'un mouvement analogue dans la seconde moitié du XIVe siècle. La question de la spécialisation progressive de certaines personnes ou de certaines communautés reste difficile à apprécier pour la période médiévale, faute de disposer d'indications comparables à celles fournies par les rôles de capitation. Nous avons vu, cependant, que des cas comme celui des habitants de Caromb se posent dans ces termes dès le milieu du XIVe siècle.

Le terme de « transformation » implique sans doute un changement trop radical pour pouvoir s'appliquer à la portée des observations ponctuelles faites ici pour le domaine provençal. Si évolution il y eut, elle est peut-être à rechercher dans la part prise, en milieu rural, par les occupations « industrielles ou

47 Boyer, « Pour une histoire des forêts de Haute-Provence », p. 287.

48 Demians d'Archimbaud, *Rougiers, village médiéval.*

49 Belmont, *Des ateliers au village.*

artisanales ». Le XIVe siècle avec ce « vaste reclassement qui affecta à la fois les conditions de l'emploi et la mise en valeur de la terre » offre des conditions favorables à un développement de ce type d'activités.[50] Il faut, en effet, compter avec l'augmentation sensible des salaires et des prix des matériaux, mais aussi avec le « repli de l'espace arable » qui libéra éventuellement certains gisements de gypse ou de chaux.[51]

La présente étude ne peut que s'achever sur une série d'interrogations et de pistes de recherches. Le bâtiment n'est qu'un exemple dont on peut discuter la pertinence. Porté, à la fin du Moyen Âge, par une conjoncture particulièrement favorable, il apparaît comme un domaine privilégié du salariat et se trouve, au moins pour la fin du Moyen Âge, fortement lié à la ville. Son « ancrage » rural est cependant indéniable et, à travers la production du bois d'œuvre, de la chaux, du plâtre et de la pierre de taille, une source de profit non négligeable se fait nettement jour pour les communautés villageoises. Il conviendrait, bien sûr, d'affiner l'approche par une distinction entre ces différents produits, la chronologie de la réglementation les concernant et l'évolution quantitative de leur production. Mais au-delà de ces activités, le problème majeur, maintes fois croisé au cours de l'enquête, s'avère être celui posé par la place de l'artisanat dans l'économie rurale. Il me semble intéressant, ici, de reprendre le terme d'« occupation » utilisé par Michael M. Postan, car il rend assez bien compte, à la fois, du caractère mouvant de telles activités et des combinaisons possibles. La séparation stricte entre produits « industriels » et agricoles ne paraît pas adaptée à une bonne appréhension des revenus ruraux. L'étude d'une période de crises peut être révélatrice dans le sens où elle pose la question du revenu lié à la production des denrées alimentaires et dévoile, par l'affaiblissement de l'image dominante de cette activité, un arrière-plan plus complexe. Ces activités secondaires, complémentaires ou compensatoires ne sont toutefois pas nées aux XIVe siècle. Le point de vue adopté permet de constater qu'elles ont pu, à la « faveur » des crises, connaître une brusque valorisation dont l'incidence réelle demanderait à être envisagée sur une durée plus longue.

Je suis volontairement resté, au cours de cet exposé, en deçà des questions de rendement ou de productivité, de prix ou de salaires réels, de salariat ou de fiscalité, dont je reconnais volontiers l'intérêt majeur mais qu'il me semble nécessaire d'asseoir sur le socle le plus large possible. Le dynamisme des recherches

[50] Duby, *L'économie rurale*, II, 196–97.

[51] Duby, *L'économie rurale*, rapproche précisément ce reclassement du cantonnement des bois « dont la valeur ne cessait de croître ».

menées sur la sidérurgie a contribué, ces dernières années, à faire éclater le cadre étroit d'un « secteur primaire » dans lequel Philippe Wolff rangeait ce type d'activité.[52] La frontière entre ville et campagne se trouve elle-même malmenée par des travaux sur le village médiéval qui n'hésitent pas à conclure à l'existence d'un « urbanisme rural ».[53] Ces ouvertures et le dépassement d'un affrontement entre rural et urbain ou agricole et industriel, qu'elles impliquent, sont le fruit de ces études à petite échelle préconisées par Georges Duby. Il convient à présent d'en intégrer les apports à une approche de l'économie rurale médiévale dans laquelle le bâtiment, avec d'autres, a son rôle à tenir.

[52] Wolff et Mauro, 'L'âge de l'artisanat', II.

[53] Bresc, « À Corleone et en quelques autres lieux », p. 106.

Bibliographie

Archives

Aix, Archives Communales, HH 8
Aix, Archives départementales de Bouches-du-Rhône (AD13), B 1412
Aix, Archives départementales de Bouches-du-Rhône (AD13), 308 E 813
Aix, Archives départementales de Bouches-du-Rhône (AD13), 308 E 943
Aix, Archives départementales de Bouches-du-Rhône (AD13), 309 E 776
Aix, Archives départementales de Bouches-du-Rhône (AD13), 309 E 779
Avignon, Archives départementales de Vaucluse (AD84), 3 E 5/52
Avignon, Archives départementales de Vaucluse (AD84), 3 E 36/19
Avignon, Archives départementales de Vaucluse (AD84), 4 E, communes, Malaucène
Avignon, Bibliothèque municipale, MS 5933
Avignon, Bibliothèque municipale, MS 5966
Carpentras, Archives communales de Carpentras (AC Carpentras), CC 151
Carpentras, Archives communales de Carpentras (AC Carpentras), CC 156
Carpentras, Archives communales de Carpentras (AC Carpentras), CC157
Carpentras, Archives communales de Carpentras (AC Carpentras), CC 161
Digne-les-Bains, Archives départementales des Alpes-de-Haute-Provence (AD4), 2 E 14222
Digne-les-Bains, Archives départementales des Alpes-de-Haute-Provence (AD4), 2 E 14223
Digne-les-Bains, Archives départementales des Alpes-de-Haute-Provence (AD4), 2 E 16301
Digne-les-Bains, Archives départementales des Alpes-de-Haute-Provence (AD4), 2 E 16354
Marseille, Archives Communales, 1 II 12
Saint-Rémy, Archive Communales, CC 11
Stato della Città del Vaticano, Archives Secrètes Vaticanes, Collectoriae 452
Stato della Città del Vaticano, Archives Secrètes Vaticanes, Collectoriae 462

Sources primaires imprimées

Baratier, Édouard, éd., *Enquêtes sur les droits et revenus de Charles I d'Anjou en Provence (1252 et 1278)* (Paris: Bibliothèque Nationale, 1969)

de Serres, Olivier, *Le Théâtre d'agriculture et mesnage des champs* (Paris, 1600; rééd. Arles: Actes Sud, 1996, d'après l'édition de 1804–05)

Weiß, Stephan, *Die Versorgung des päpstlichen Hofes in Avignon mit Lebensmitteln (1316–1378)* (Berlin: Akademie Verlag, 2002)

Sources secondaires

André-Michel, Robert, « La construction des remparts d'Avignon au XIVe siècle », *Congrès archéologique de France*, 76 (1910), 341–60

Baratier, Édouard, et Félix Reynaud, *Histoire du commerce de Marseille*, II: *De 1291 à 1481* (Paris: Plon, 1951)

Belmont, Alain, *Des ateliers au village: Les artisans ruraux en Dauphiné sous l'Ancien Régime* (Grenoble: Presses universitaires de Grenoble, 1998)

Bernardi, Philippe, « Construction et politique en Provence: L'approvisionnement en matériaux, une affaire publique? », dans *La ville au Moyen Âge*, II: *Sociétés et pouvoirs dans la ville*, éd. par Noël Coulet et Olivier Guyotjeannin (Paris: CTHS, 1998), pp. 9–20

——, *Métiers du bâtiment et techniques de construction à Aix-en-Provence à la fin de l'époque gothique (1400–1550)* (Aix-en-Provence: Université de Provence, 1995)

Bois, Guy, *La crise du féodalisme, économie rurale et féodalisme en Normandie orientale du début du XIVe siècle* (Paris: Presses de Sciences Po, 1976)

——, « Sur la monnaie et les prix à la fin du Moyen Âge: Réponse à John Day », *Annales: Économies, Sociétés, Civilisations*, 34 (1979), 323–24

Boutruche, Robert, *La crise d'une société: Seigneurs et paysans du Bordelais pendant la guerre de Cent ans* (Paris: Belles Lettres, 1947)

Boyer, Jean-Paul, « Pour une histoire des forêts de Haute-Provence (XIIIe–XVe siècles) », *Provence historique*, 40 (1990), 267–90

Bresc, Henri, « À Corleone et en quelques autres lieux: La maison sicilienne des "terres" et des casaux (XIIIe–XVe siècle) », dans *Castrum 6: Maisons et espaces domestiques dans le monde méditerranéen au Moyen Âge*, sous la direction d'André Bazzana et Etienne Hubert, Collection de l'École française de Rome, 105/106, Collection de la Casa de Velázquez, 72 (Roma: Casa de Velázquez, 2000), pp. 105–15

Butaud, Germain, « Guerre et vie publique en Comtat Venaissin et à Avignon (vers 1350 – vers 1450) » (thèse d'histoire non-édité, Université de Nice-Sophia Antipolis, 2001)

Contamine, Philippe, « Les fortifications urbaines en France à la fin du Moyen Âge: Aspects financiers et économiques », *Revue Historique*, 260 (1978), 23–47

Coulet, Noël, et Louis Stouff, *Le village de Provence au Bas Moyen Âge*, Cahiers du Centre d'études des sociétés méditerranéennes, 2e série (Aix-en-Provence: Université de Provence, 1987)

De la Roncière, Charles, *Prix et salaires à Florence au XIVe siècle (1280–1380)* (Roma: École Française de Rome, 1982)

Demians d'Archimbaud, Gabrielle, *Rougiers, village médiéval: Approche d'une société rurale méditerranéenne* (Paris: CNRS, 1981)

Duby, Georges, *L'économie rurale et la vie des campagnes dans l'Occident Médiéval (France, Angleterre, Empire, IXe–XVe siècles): Essai de synthèse et perspectives de recherches*, 2 vols (Paris: Aubier, 1962)

Fourquin, Guy, *Les campagnes de la région parisienne à la fin du Moyen Âge* (Paris: Presses Universitaires de France, 1964)

Menant, François, « Aspects de l'économie et de la société dans les vallées lombardes aux derniers siècles du Moyen Âge », dans *La sidérurgie alpine en Italie (XIIe–XVIIe siècle)*, éd. par Philippe Braunstein, Collection de l'École française de Rome, 290 (Roma: École Française de Rome), pp. 3–30

Perroy, Édouard, « À l'origine d'une économie contractée: Les crises du XIVe siècle », *Annales: Économies, Sociétés, Civilisations*, 4 (1949), 167–82

Pesez, Jean-Marie, « La construction rustique en pierre », dans *Cent maisons médiévales en France (du XIIe au milieu du XVIe siècle): Un corpus et une esquisse*, éd. par Yves Esquieu et Jean-Marie Pesez (Paris: CNRS 1998), pp. 63–66

Postan, Michael M., *The Medieval Economy and Society: An Economic History of Britain 1100–1500* (London: Weidenfeld and Nicolson, 1972)

Sclafert, Thérèse, *Cultures en Haute-Provence, déboisements et pâturages au Moyen Âge* (Paris: SEVPEN, 1959)

——, *Le Haut-Dauphiné au Moyen Âge* (Paris: Société anonyme du recueil Sirey, 1926)

Stouff, Louis, « Les matériaux de construction à Arles au XVe siècle », dans *Histoire des techniques et sources documentaires*, Cahiers du GIS, 7 (Aix-en-Provence: CNRS Maison de la Méditerranée, 1982), pp. 83–85

Wolff, Philippe, et Frédéric Mauro, « L'âge de l'artisanat, Ve–XVIIIe siècle », dans *Histoire générale du travail*, éd. par Louis-Henri Parias (Paris: Nouvelle Librairie de France, 1960)

Zacchigna, Michele, *Sistemi d'acqua e mulini in Friuli fra i secoli XIV e XV: Contributo alla storia dell'economia friulana nel bassomedioevo* (Venezia: Istituto veneto di scienze, lettere ed arti, 1996)

Réflexions sur la condition des travailleurs au cours du XIVe siècle à Marseille

Francine Michaud

Dans la mesure où la situation de la main-d'œuvre s'avère un moyen légitime de saisir le pouls de l'économie à un moment donné de son histoire, la présente étude a pour ambition de soulever quelques questions concernant l'approche des sources notariales propres à révéler, du moins en partie, la condition des travailleurs à Marseille au Bas Moyen Âge. J'examinerai ici les contrats d'embauche relevés dans tous les registres notariés connus, dont les séries débutent à la fin du XIIIe siècle, jusqu'au tournant du XVe siècle. Malgré leur ancienneté et leur abondance relative, le quantitativiste convaincu n'y trouvera pas son compte. Il faut en effet se satisfaire de ces témoignages parcellaires et frustrants en l'absence de listes de prix et de sources fiscales sérielles pour la période envisagée. Comme ailleurs dans le Midi français, la Provence d'alors traverse une période économique difficile qui s'aggrave à mesure que l'on avance dans le second versant du XIVe siècle, secoué par les épidémies, les guerres et le brigandage. Dans ce contexte, plus d'un serait tenté de parler de décroissance structurelle dont les effets exponentiels auraient acculé le grand nombre à la misère. Bien entendu, cette vision misérabiliste de l'histoire provençale échappe aux modèles courants, dont celui de Georges Duby:

> Ce fut pendant cette période (1350–1380) que le nombre des prolétaires se réduisit de manière décisive dans les campagnes. Les pauvres disparurent en partie par

Francine Michaud (michaud@ucalgary.ca) est professeur émérite à l'université de Calgary. Elle vient de finir une monographie sur le travail à Marseille à la fin du Moyen Âge.

Crisis in the Later Middle Ages: Beyond the Postan-Duby Paradigm, ed. by John Drendel, TMC 13 (Turnhout: Brepols, 2015) 297–322 BREPOLS PUBLISHERS 10.1484/M.TMC.5.103792

> élimination physique: l'épidémie les frappa plus durement que les autres. En tout cas, les survivants trouvèrent l'occasion de s'établir dans les exploitations que la mortalité avait rendues vacantes.[54]

Comme l'exprime tout aussi éloquemment Noël Coulet, il serait réducteur d'opiner en faveur « d'un temps du malheur » devant la volonté humaine de lutter avec acharnement, « de reconstruire et de revivre à chaque répit », à la ville comme à la campagne.[55] Cela dit, dans les pages qui suivent, notre position sera précautionneuse, voire moins optimiste à la lueur des sources marseillaises qui invitent à relativiser l'idée d'un « âge d'or des travailleurs » au lendemain de la grande peste, comme l'a fait avec beaucoup de discernement le regretté John Munro.[56]

Par conséquent, nous nous donnerons ici deux objectifs. D'abord, esquisser les tendances générales, sans pour autant négliger les particularités discordantes: on ne saurait passer sous silence les catégories de travailleurs qui souffrent ou profitent davantage que les autres. Ensuite, faire une place au travail juvénile (apprentis et employés) comme le souhaite depuis longtemps Charles de la Roncière, non seulement parce qu'il représente un apport non négligeable dans l'économie domestique, mais aussi parce qu'en signalant les mutations de l'économie en général, il pourrait servir d'indicateur des tendances du marché de l'emploi.[57]

Les sources

Parlons d'abord de la documentation à l'étude: celle-ci recoupe 1139 travailleurs répertoriés au gré du dépouillement de 1069 contrats d'embauche marseillais entre 1248 et 1400, y compris les mises en apprentissage (333). Ainsi toutes les formes possibles de prestation de labeur, salarié ou non, dans le cadre

[54] Duby, *L'économie rurale*, II, 196.

[55] Coulet, « Le malheur des temps », p. 315.

[56] Munro, « Wage-Stickiness, Monetary Changes », p. 227. Il est tout aussi instructif de se tourner vers les travaux récents de William Caferro qui démontrent, en outre, la difficulté d'apprécier valablement la diversité des salaires florentins dans les années qui suivirent la peste noire: Caferro, « Petrach's War ».

[57] De La Roncière, « La condition des salariés », p. 22. Cet appel n'est cependant pas resté lettre morte. À telle enseigne, Franco Franceschi s'est penché sur l'apport à l'économie domestique des jeunes salariés dans l'industrie lainière à Florence à partir de la seconde moitié du XIVe siècle jusqu'au XVe siècle: Franceschi, « Les enfants au travail ».

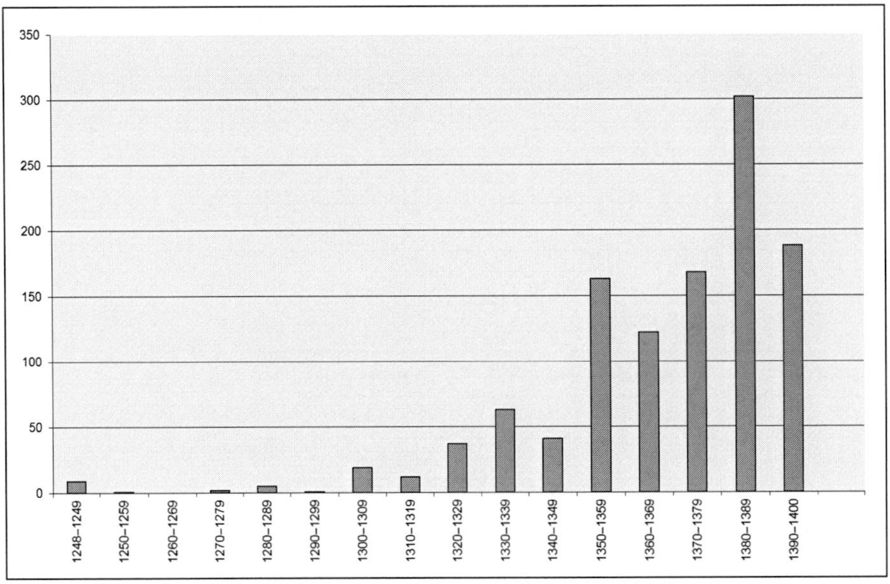

Figure 11.1. Distribution décennale du nombre de travailleurs, 1248–1400.

d'engagements entre personnes libres ont été considérées.[58] Pour les besoins de cette étude le travail des esclaves à proprement parler n'a pas été retenu bien que des individus nommément identifiés à titre de *sclavus* ou *sclava* apparaissent exceptionnellement dans la documentation.[59]

Les contrats d'apprentissage et de travail qui forment l'essentiel de mon corpus sont, il fallait s'y attendre, bien inégalement répartis en amont et en aval de la peste noire. De fait, seulement 16 pour cent de ces accords notariés appartiennent à la période précédant la grande catastrophe de 1348 (Figure 11.1). Les années antérieures à l'épidémie sont, comme on le sait trop bien, médiocrement éclairées par les sources sérielles, même dans les régions où règne le droit écrit; à Marseille, la production notariale et judiciaire n'apparaît sans discontinuité qu'à partir du dernier quart du XIIIe siècle. Il faut dire que la conservation de ces archives n'est pas sans rapport avec les premiers signes d'épanouis-

[58] La notion contemporaine du salaire s'avère en elle-même complexe, dans la mesure où elle peut exclure le déboursement d'espèces: ainsi dans près de 10 pour cent des contrats de travail passés à Marseille aux XIIIe et XIVe siècles, le *loquerium* — terme communément usité pour signifier à la fois la location de bras et sa rémunération — se limite à l'octroi du gîte, de la nourriture et du vêtement.

[59] Sur cette question, on consultera avec profit l'article de Bernardi, « Esclavage et artisanat ».

Tableau 11.1. Nombre et proportion des travailleurs étrangers au sein de la main-d'œuvre marseillaise avant et après la peste noire.

Travailleurs	Avant la peste (%)	Après la peste (%)
Étrangers	58 (32%)	555 (58%)
Locaux	122 (68%)	404 (42%)
Total	**180 (100%)**	**959 (100%)**

Tableau 11.2. Distribution des travailleurs selon le secteur d'embauche avant et après la peste noire.

Secteur	Avant la peste (%)	Après la peste (%)
Mer	41 (23%)	327 (34%)
Affaires	34 (19%)	54 (6%)
Textile	20 (11%)	32 (3%)
Cuir	16 (9%)	46 (5%)
Santé	14 (8%)	31 (3%)
Métal	12 (7%)	35 (4%)
Construction	11 (6%)	59 (6%)
Domesticité	9 (5%)	162 (17%)
Alimentation	7 (4%)	43 (4%)
Terre	2 (1%)	101 (11%)
Autres	14 (8%)*	69 (7%)
Total	**180 (100%)**	**959 (100%)**

* Les pourcentages ont été arrondis.

sement de la culture juridique qui se manifeste alors dans le Midi.[60] Elles ne se prêtent toutefois pas aisément aux manipulations statistiques, tant s'en faut. Le chambardement démographique qu'occasionne la grande crise pestilentielle de 1348 vient mettre en relief les carences des premiers contrats de travail, non seulement au plan quantitatif, mais aussi au plan de la représentation professionnelle. Dans la foulée de ce que les contemporains qualifient de *generalis mortalitas*, lorsque notaires et autres notables réfugiés à la campagne viennent

[60] Aubenas, *Étude sur le notariat provençal*. De fait, les actes de la pratique attestent d'une large représentation sociale dans les officines notariales et les cours de justice communale et comtale, Michaud, *Un signe des temps*. Pour une discussion approfondie des formes culturelles du recours à la justice, voir Smail, *The Consumption of Justice*.

reprendre leurs activités urbaines à l'aube des années 1350, on observe ainsi de saisissants développements.[61]

Le flux migratoire

On assiste d'abord à un véritable déblocage documentaire. En l'espace de cinquante ans, malgré l'hécatombe humaine, les sources ont plus que quintuplé: mille actes s'étendent alors plus ou moins uniformément entre 1350 et 1400. Tout se passe comme si la boutique du notaire s'ouvrait soudainement au flot continu de la main-d'œuvre « étrangère » attirée par les occasions d'embauche (et de débauchage) dans la grande cité portuaire. Ne composant autrefois que le tiers de la population besogneuse, les immigrants se retrouvent dorénavant dans près de 60 pour cent des ententes contractuelles (tableau 11.1).[62] Par ailleurs, chose nouvelle, trois pôles de l'économie locale semblent alors prédominer dans le marché de l'emploi ou du moins tel que les enregistrements notariés permettent de le reconstituer. Il y a d'abord et avant tout les activités maritimes — qui s'imposent alors en bien plus forte proportion —, ainsi que les domaines jadis pratiquement absents des engagements notariés, c'est-à-dire le service domestique et les travaux agricoles. Ces secteurs, qui ne comptaient avant la peste noire que 29 pour cent de tous les travailleurs à contrat, les absorbent maintenant dans une proportion de 62 pour cent (tableau 11.2).[63]

Des facteurs d'ordre démographique et économique expliquent bien évidemment cette transformation sensible du marché de l'emploi. Mais celle-ci dissimule également de profonds bouleversements au sein de l'unité de production dont la structure, de nature familiale et communautaire, fut sans l'ombre d'un doute fortement ébranlée au lendemain de la grande peste. L'embauche

[61] Devant l'affaissement brutal des revenus fiscaux, les autorités municipales pressent dès le printemps de 1349 les survivants qui avaient fui à la campagne de regagner la ville avec leurs familles: ACM, BB 20, 3 mai 1349, fols 130v–131r.

[62] Michaud, « Travail et mouvements ». Précisons toutefois que la base documentaire a augmenté depuis la parution de cet article, notamment grâce à la consultation du fonds Mortreuil (actes originaux et transcriptions) conservé au Cabinet des manuscrits de la Bibliothèque nationale de France à Paris et par conséquent, les pourcentages ont subi une légère révision.

[63] Afin de simplifier les calculs, la période de l'« après peste » inclue les six contrats d'embauche rédigés entre le 12 août et le 16 octobre 1348, soit au lendemain du passage de la maladie pesteuse dans la cité. L'étude des séries testamentaires démontre en effet que la chronologie de la *magna mortalitas* à Marseille s'étend de la fin de l'hiver au printemps de 1348, Michaud, « La peste, la peur et l'espoir », pp. 403–19.

Tableau 11.3a. Distribution des apprentis et des employés avant et après la peste noire.

Main-d'œuvre	Avant la peste (%)	Après la peste (%)
Apprentis	104 (58%)	227 (24%)
Employés	76 (42%)	732 (76%)
Total	**180 (100%)**	**959 (100%)**

Tableau 11.3b. Distribution des apprentis et des employés avant et après la peste noire, dans les arts et les métiers artisanaux seulement.*

Main-d'œuvre	Avant la peste (%)	Après la peste (%)
Apprentis	93 (73%)	208 (56%)
Employés	35 (27%)	161 (44%)
Total	**128 (100%)**	**369 (100%)**

*À l'exclusion des secteurs de la mer, de la terre et du service domestique

informelle suffisait vraisemblablement naguère à sceller les rapports entre employés et employeurs dans la mesure où elle se concluait entre « familiers »: parentèle, amis, confrères et voisins. La parole donnée, engageant l'honneur des parties, garantissait l'entente. En revanche, dans les arts nécessitant une formation technique d'une certaine durée (en moyenne de cinq ans, mais elle pouvait s'étendre bien au-delà jusqu'à vingt ans!), l'acte notarié offrait l'avantage d'une protection mutuelle supplémentaire apte à renforcer l'autorité du maître tout en assurant les besoins vitaux de l'enfant. L'imposante représentation des apprentis au sein de la main-d'œuvre artisanale avant 1348 ne peut se comprendre autrement (tableaux 11.3a et 11.3b). C'est pourquoi l'embauche maritime, agricole et domestique se trouve moins bien représentée dans la documentation d'avant 1348,[64] l'apprentissage de type institutionnel n'étant pas de rigueur dans les deux derniers secteurs d'emploi. En fait, si l'on exclut ces activités de l'ensemble des actes recensés, la proportion d'apprentis grimpe jusqu'à 73 pour cent du nombre total de travailleurs contractuels. Or après le passage de la peste, ce rapport s'inverse brusquement dans l'ensemble des

[64] Ces contrats ont été exclusivement établis par des gens de mer, ou presque, et représentent le quart des ententes. Les deux seules occurrences d'agriculteurs qui prennent à leur charge la formation de jeunes (*pro legali dicipulo / ipsum instruere*) dans les arts de la terre (*in arte ruralia*) et du jardinage (*in arte ortolaria*) datent de la seconde moitié du XIVe siècle, AD13, 381 E 79, 3 avril 1353, fol. 7^{r-v} et 24 juillet 1380, AD13, 351 E 50, fol. 148^{r-v}.

métiers. Comme on le verra, l'incidence de la mortalité infantile sur le renversement des données ne peut évidemment être niée, mais très certainement aussi l'affluence des loueurs de bras étrangers dans la cité portuaire apte à inciter plus d'un maître qui, par méfiance ou prudence, se munira désormais de l'instrument notarial.

Apprentissage et emploi

Un autre ordre d'explication mérite d'être exploré afin de comprendre globalement le rapport inversement proportionnel entre apprentis et employés dans le corpus documentaire au cours du XIVe siècle. La mortalité de 1348, à laquelle succéda une douzaine d'années plus tard une seconde vague épidémique, souvent qualifiée de peste des enfants, aura vraisemblablement contribué à l'affaissement du nombre des apprentis dans les ouvroirs marseillais, du moins dans les années 1350.[65] Ainsi, prise dans son ensemble, la main-d'œuvre juvénile (y compris les enfants et adolescents engagés comme employés et non comme apprentis) qui constituait au moins 64 pour cent de tous les travailleurs à contrats

[65] À Marseille, le premier retour de peste survint en 1361, comme l'atteste un acte tiré des archives judiciaires de la ville le 8 juillet 1362, dans lequel une femme révèle qu'une année entière s'était écoulée depuis la disparition de son époux emporté par l'épidémie (« quod annus est elapsus vel circa dum in Massilia vigebat pestifera mortalitas »), ACM, FF 537, fol. 50r. La question épineuse de la mortalité infantile durant les épidémies pesteuses ne fait pas consensus parmi les chercheurs: voir à cet égard Carmichael, *Plague and the Poor*, pp. 90–99. D'autre part, les opinions varient selon les lieux et les époques. À Halesowen, Razi, *Life, Marriage and Death*, p. 143, suggère que la réduction brutale de la taille des familles dès 1349 « is probably the result of the heavy infant and child mortality », alors qu'à Florence au XVe siècle, les adolescents semblent davantage vulnérables à la maladie que les tout petits: Herlihy et Klapisch-Zuber, *Les Toscans et leurs familles*, p. 463. Horrox, *The Black Death*, p. 12, souligne en revanche que la majorité des historiens anglais s'entendent maintenant pour attribuer la difficile reprise démographique — observable qu'à partir du XVe siècle — au caractère particulièrement meurtrier des récurrences de peste auprès des enfants dans les décennies suivant 1348. À l'appui de sa thèse sur l'immunité des survivants, Cohn, *The Black Death Transformed*, p. 131, opine dans le même sens pour l'ensemble de l'Europe, «children as the plague's chief victims continued to mount disproportionately through the second half of the fourteenth century ». À Marseille, certains indices laissent croire à un taux de mortalité juvénile assez lourd tout au long de la seconde moitié du XIVe siècle. L'importance des gages offerts à des enfants à peine pubères pourrait suggérer cette possibilité certes, encore qu'elle doit être mise en rapport avec la crise démographique dans son ensemble, mais plus encore la réduction marquée du nombre d'apprentis dans les actes de la pratique notariale. Ces points ont été ont été soumis à une analyse plus détaillée dans Michaud, « Serviteurs et domestiques ».

Tableau 11.4. Distribution de la main-d'œuvre juvénile avant et après la peste noire.

Main-d'œuvre	**Avant la peste (%)**	**Après la peste (%)**
Apprentis	63 (54%)	159 (51%)
Apprentis rémunérés	41 (35%)	70 (22%)
Employés juvéniles	12 (10%)	85 (27%)
Total	**116 (100%)**	**314 (100%)**

avant 1348, décline par la suite à 33 pour cent. Si la tendance démographique se manifeste déjà dans les années immédiatement antérieures à 1348, la crise épidémique se chargera de profondément l'aggraver.[66] Face à la catastrophe, les maîtres furent d'abord placés devant l'urgente nécessité de recruter des bras à tout prix, à se faire moins exigeants sur la qualité et l'expérience des tâcherons. Ce faisant, ils ouvrirent plus largement la porte aux enfants et aux adolescents en marge du processus de l'apprentissage. Les jeunes que l'on embauchait autrefois comme simples engagés ne comptaient que pour 10 pour cent de l'ensemble des jeunes recrues; après 1348, cette proportion s'élève à 27 pour cent. Fait intéressant, leur moyenne d'âge s'est abaissée de seize à treize ans; malgré cela, leurs émoluments rivalisent avec ceux des apprentis rémunérés, alors qu'avant ils n'en représentaient qu'une fraction. Aussi n'est-ce pas tout à fait un hasard si la proportion d'apprentis salariés a décliné par rapport à la période antérieure (tableau 11.4).

Paradoxalement, ce n'est pas comme si les maîtres-artisans, devant leur quête désespérée de bras, avaient dû alléger le joug de l'apprentissage institutionnel. Bien au contraire. Si la proportion d'apprentis simples dans la masse documentaire assemblée est restée globalement la même tout au cours de la

[66] Il est en effet pertinent de souligner que dans les années 1340, la proportion des mises en apprentissage s'affaisse soudain par rapport aux contrats d'embauche et ainsi quatre-cinquième des actes datés entre 1340 et 1348 se rapportent aux locations de travail rémunéré (38/42). De même, un seul parmi les maîtres qui s'engagent à former la main-d'œuvre à leur art impose des frais à sa jeune recrue, une apprentie-corailleuse, et encore bien modérément, à raison d'un peu plus de 3s. annuellement : BnF, nouv. acq. lat., 1321, 3 septembre 1340, p. 226. Ces données corroborent les affirmations d'Édouard Baratier sur le fléchissement démographique dans le port phocéen à la veille de la grande mortalité, Baratier, *La démographie provençale*, p. 120: « Dans l'ensemble, la progression démographique semble régulière à la fin du XIIIe siècle et dans les dix premières années du XIVe siècle, puis le peuplement reste stationnaire, manifestant encore quelque avance dans certaines régions, tandis que d'autres telles que Marseille ou la haute vallée du Var connaissent déjà les premiers signes d'une récession avant la peste».

Tableau 11.5. Distribution décennale des apprentis simples par rapport à l'ensemble de la main-d'œuvre juvénile dans les arts et métiers urbains après la peste noire.*

	1348–59	1360–69	1370–79	1380–89	1390–1400
Nombre d'individus	35/60	21/39	23/33	44/63	36/52
Proportion	58%	54%	70%	70%	69%

*À l'exclusion des secteurs de la mer, de la terre et domestique

période à l'étude, en y regardant de plus près, elle a progressé dans les arts et métiers urbains (tableau 11.5). C'est que, d'une part, la main-d'œuvre juvénile dans son ensemble s'est rajeunie et ce, à tous les niveaux, l'augmentation du nombre d'orphelins accélérant une prise en charge précoce. De toute évidence, les cadres de l'apprentissage ne sont pas demeurés insensibles aux fluctuations soudaines de l'offre et de la demande d'emploi. Il n'est guère aisé de savoir dans quelle mesure les apprentis formés dans un art donné intégrèrent plus tôt le marché du travail et, posons-nous la question, s'ils le firent dans leur domaine d'expertise. Il est toutefois clair que les secteurs moins exigeants sur le plan technique attirent des salariés de plus en plus jeunes. Ne négligeons pas, d'autre part, les effets probables de la transformation du monde du travail. De fait, l'augmentation marquée de la proportion d'apprentis simples dans les métiers artisanaux au cours des trois dernières décennies du siècle coïncide alors avec la stabilisation du mouvement des salaires.

Les salaires: hausse ou baisse?

Dans leur ouvrage sur l'économie française, Elisabeth Carpentier et Michel Le Mené ont évoqué plusieurs exemples régionaux pour souligner le trend haussier des prix et des salaires du XIVᵉ siècle. La cité phocéenne étant du nombre, les auteurs notent que « de même, à Marseille, le salaire nominal des vignerons tripla entre la décennie des années trente et celle de 1350 ».[67] La source (non-citée) de cette affirmation est sans aucun doute tirée des travaux d'Édouard Baratier sur le vin marseillais: or les chiffres avancés par l'archiviste expriment des gages journaliers, et ne reposent que sur quelques documents pour donner, de son aveu, « une appréciation générale ».[68] Tout est là. Malgré les compilations les

[67] Carpentier et Le Mené, *La France du XIᵉ au XVᵉ siècle*, p. 401.

[68] Baratier, « Production et exportation », p. 243. Duby, *L'économie rurale*, II, 191. Il faut noter que les salaires relevés par Édouard Baratier se maintiennent entre 1363 et 1409.

plus patientes des salaires nominaux glanés au fil d'innombrables registres notariés, on ne saurait se fier aveuglément à l'approche quantitative, surtout pour la période de l'avant peste, puisqu'une cinquantaine d'actes à peine se prête à l'exercice pour l'ensemble des métiers alors recensés (tableaux 11.6a et 11.6b).[69]

Si l'on dirige plus précisément l'objectif sur certaines catégories professionnelles pour lesquelles existe une base statistique relativement satisfaisante, on se résout à comprendre que l'allure des salaires nominaux varie sensiblement selon les métiers, et qu'une simple distribution d'ensemble risque de sévèrement miner la valeur de toute tentative d'interprétation historique. Bien que la monnaie locale, le menu marseillais ou le royal — *minutum massiliensis seu regalium* — ait connu de nombreuses fluctuations au cours de la première moitié du XIVe siècle,[70] c'est néanmoins l'avènement de la peste noire qui semble avoir précipité la tendance inflationniste en Provence en accélérant le processus général de la hausse des gages.[71] En 1349, Aycard Balbi, sans profession reconnue, offrait son labeur comme tâcheron en échange de son entretien et de 20s.

[69] Remarquons néanmoins la corrélation qui existe entre l'importante augmentation du nombre des contrats de travail rémunéré à l'encontre des accords d'apprentissage simple au cours des années 1340, et l'accroissement des gages journaliers versés pendant la même période aux ouvriers agricoles marseillais, suivant l'étude d'Édouard Baratier (voir supra note 68). C'est peut-être là le signe d'une conjoncture démographique déclinante dans les années immédiatement antérieures à la grande débâcle de 1348 dans la cité portuaire. Mais il faut également compter avec une probable reprise — aussi fébrile qu'éphémère dans la même décennie — des activités portuaires: voir sur ce point Bresc, *Un monde méditerranéen*, p. 332 et passim.

[70] Dans la deuxième moitié du XIVe siècle, les salaires sont cependant calculés en florins bien que la monnaie locale continue d'avoir cours, Mabilly, « La monnaie de menus marseillais », p. 3. À l'instar de nombreuses monnaies européennes, le royal marseillais subit plusieurs dévaluations au courant du XIVe siècle: entre 1319 et 1400, il s'affaiblit de 32 pour cent par rapport au florin. Or cette dépréciation s'opéra surtout dans les premières décennies du siècle, dès avant les années 1340, Rolland, *Monnaies des comtes de Provence*, p. 85; Drendel, « La monnaie dans les campagnes ». Les actes notariés en fournissent la preuve: entre 1319 et 1350, la valeur du sous royal passa de 24s. et 4d. à 30s. le florin; en 1365, elle était estimée à 32s. le florin, un taux qui demeura stable jusqu'en 1400: Michaud, *Un signe des temps*, pp. 117–18, n. 3; AD13, 355 E 2, 27 janvier 1350, fols 160r–161v; AD13, 355 E 14, 7 mai 1365, fol. 26r; BnF, nouv. .acq. lat., 1351, 5 février 1400, fol. 43v. Pour une approche comparative des monnaies européennes au XIVe siècle, voir Fournial, *Histoire monétaire de l'Occident*, pp. 97–126, de même que Spufford, *Money and its Use*, pp. 289–318.

[71] Il n'existe aucune liste de prix qui autorise l'étude précise du taux d'inflation en Provence au XIVe siècle; il est néanmoins utile de consulter à ce propos l'ouvrage de Noël Coulet sur les tendances inflationnistes dans les années subséquentes à la grande peste, Coulet, *Aix en Provence*, I, 57–107, et p. 136.

Tableau 11.6a. Distribution des salaires mensuels moyens gagnés par les employés selon le secteur d'embauche avant la peste noire (en *solidi*).*

Secteur	Moyenne	Valeurs extrêmes	Nombre d'employés
Mer	32.7	1.7 – 135	27
Affaires	38.4	26.7 – 50	2
Textile	31.7	16.7 – 50	3
Cuir	27.3	–	1
Alimentation	13.3	7.1 – 19.5	2
Métal	10	–	1
Domesticité	9.2	2.1 – 23.3	9
Bâtiment	7	–	1
Agriculture	6.3	1.7 – 10.8	2
Total	**25.7**	**1.7 – 126.1**	**48**

*À l'exclusion des apprentis salariés.

Tableau 11.6b. Distribution des salaires mensuels moyens gagnés par les employés selon le secteur d'embauche après la peste noire (en *solidi*).*

Secteur	Moyenne	Valeurs extrêmes	Nombre d'employés
Mer	103	0.5 – 480	299
Affaires	90.9	13.3 – 533	25
Métal	48.1	10.67 – 160	19
Cuir	38.9	4.2 – 120	21
Agriculture	38.3	1.7 – 128	97
Alimentation	36	4.6 – 69.3	32
Bâtiment	34.5	3.3 – 86.17	14
Services	33	13.3 – 128	9
Santé	32.2	10.7 – 66.7	9
Domesticité	29.3	1.1 – 66.7	150
Textile	26.9	7.5 – 53.3	9
Autres	44.2	15 – 136.7	8
Total	**66.4**	**1 – 533**	**692**

*À l'exclusion des apprentis salariés.

par mois;[72] or en 1357, ses gages s'élevaient à 65s.[73] En 1355, les émoluments du laboureur Guillaume Durand étaient fixés à 30s.; en 1369, il parvenait à négocier un salaire à hauteur de 53.3s.[74] Ces cas ne sont pas isolés: tout comme ce domestique et cet agriculteur, nombreux sont en effet les travailleurs — spécialisés ou non — qui connurent pareille félicité aux lendemains de la grande saignée démographique de 1348.

Tableau 11.7. Distribution décennale des salaires mensuels moyens, 1320–1400 (en *solidi*).

Métiers	**1320**	**1330**	**1340**	**1350**	**1360**	**1370**	**1380**	**1390**
Corailleurs	-	126 (3)*	-	360 (2)	-	109 (26)	165 (71)	183 (58)
Marins	-	-	28 (6)	30 (6)	37 (4)	37 (9)	43 (50)	34 (14)
Pêcheurs	13 (3)	24 (9)	68 (1)	55 (5)	24 (17)	30 (13)	35 (20)	9 (4)
Marchands	-	38 (2)	-	153 (10)	83 (1)	82 (2)	42 (11)	33 (1)
Laboureurs	-	6 (2)	-	36 (22)	40 (9)	35 (30)	35 (14)	47 (22)
Bouchers	-	7 (1)	-	17 (4)	29 (7)	38 (7)	-	43 (4)
Domestiques	-	14 (2)	8 (2)	30 (33)	24 (23)	37 (27)	29 (49)	25 (18)
Autres	15 (3)	39 (2)	-	37 (19)	32 (21)	39 (18)	47 (19)	38 (21)
Moyenne décennale	**14 (6)**	**38 (21)**	**28 (9)**	**52 (101)**	**30 (82)**	**51 (132)**	**76 (234)**	**96 (142)**

*Les chiffres entre parenthèses renvoient au nombre d'employés

Pris dans leur ensemble, les salaires nominaux s'accroissent de façon continue de 1348 à 1400. Cependant, à y regarder de plus près, on constate aisément la place disproportionnée que prennent dans le corpus les gens de mer qui s'adonnent à la pêche du corail dans le dernier tiers du siècle (tableau 11.7). Cette activité, qui se déroule le plus souvent dans les mers de Sardaigne, près du port d'Alghero, mobilise un grand renfort d'hommes et, surtout, de capitaux. Ce sont, naturellement, des spécialistes qui louent leur labeur, avec ou sans barque, à des investisseurs locaux, la plupart issus de la meilleure société marseillaise, bien que quelques mariniers fortunés s'illustrent parmi eux. L'équipage se limite normalement à quatre hommes par barque; la rémunération, qui oscille en fonction des prix du corail sur les marchés méditerranéens, se trouve

[72] Tous les salaires seront par la suite exprimés au taux mensuel.

[73] AD13, 355 E 2, 27 août 1349, fol. 78v; AD13, 355 E 35, 2 avril 1357, fol. 4v.

[74] AD13, 355 E 8, 11 octobre 1355, fol. 29r; AD13, 355 E 18, 1er décembre 1369, fol. 210v.

rigoureusement hiérarchisée suivant l'importance de la tâche assignée à chacun, patron, trehlier, prouier, mégier et poupier.[75]

On aurait cependant tort de croire, comme Géraud Lavergne l'a suggéré dans son article sur la pêche et le commerce de corail à Marseille, que ces matelots spécialisés se recrutent « dans tous les coins de Provence ».[76] Contrairement à la tendance générale, cette activité — aussi lucrative que dangereuse — demeure le quasi-monopole des fils de Marseille (tableau 11.8).[77] Les équipes de corailleurs forment en effet une véritable aristocratie au sein de la main-d'œuvre marseillaise.[78] Des réseaux familiaux (on pense aux de La Font, Fabre, Pourrières, Segnier, Thoesco, Vincent), certains remontant à plusieurs générations (les de La Font étaient déjà très actifs dans le dernier tiers du XIIIe siècle), se taillent semble-t-il la part du lion.[79] Prenons l'exemple de la famille Fabre. Au printemps de 1384, le chef, Henri, s'engageait en compagnie de ses trois fils, Henri, Jacques et Nicholas, pour une année auprès du très riche négociant Julien de Casaulx.[80] De leur retour de Sardaigne, ils avaient à leur quatre empoché 388 florins (à raison de 1034.7s. par mois), soit quatorze fois le salaire moyen de l'engagé marseillais à cette époque.[81] Il arrive que des migrants parviennent à se hisser au rang de ces seigneurs de la mer, tel Guillaume de l'Étoile, originaire d'Italie, qui débarquait à Marseille en 1393 pour se mettre au service d'un

[75] Géraud Lavergne donne un bref aperçu des cours du prix du corail à Marseille à l'époque dans Lavergne, « La pêche et le commerce », p. 203. Plus récemment, Josée Valérie Murat s'est penchée sur les activités des mariniers pendant la même période dans le port phocéen: Murat, « Navires et navigations ». Sur la rémunération différentielle des gens de mer en Méditerranée, se référer à l'étude de Dufourcq, *La vie quotidienne*, pp. 72–73. Voir également la contribution de Christian Maurel sur le rôle des investisseurs marseillais dans la pêche du corail: Maurel, « Grands marchands ».

[76] Lavergne, « La pêche et le commerce », p. 201.

[77] Le corail trouve alors de profitables débouchés en pays « infidèles », notamment sur les côtes syriennes, Baratier, *Histoire de Marseille*, pp. 110–11.

[78] Plusieurs membres de ces équipages agissent par ailleurs à leur propre compte (voir les exemples cités plus bas), ou en société, comme en témoigne un acte relevé par Lavergne, « La pêche et le commerce », pp. 200–01.

[79] Sur les de La Font, Michaud, *Un signe des temps*, pp. 66–67, et p. 99.

[80] 16 avril 1384, BnF, nouv. .acq. lat., 1342, fols 121v–123v. Au moins deux des membres de la famille Fabre, Henri père et Henri fils, reviennent à bon port de cette expédition puisqu'ils sont cités dans un acte d'apprentissage daté du 10 février 1399, AD13, 351 E 74, fols 51r–52r.

[81] Comme l'indique le tableau 11.7, le salaire mensuel dans les années 1380 est en moyenne de 76s.

pêcheur local au salaire mensuel de 21s. pendant une période de deux ans.[82] Quatre ans plus tard, il réussissait à attirer l'attention du riche marin investisseur Antoine Sénéquier qui l'embaucha comme propier moyennant 106s. par mois.[83] Il s'agit là, toutefois, d'une exception notable.

Tableau 11.8. Proportion de travailleurs étrangers parmi les gens de mer marseillais avant et après la peste noire.

Salariés	**Avant la peste**	**Après la peste**
Corailleurs	25%	29%
Simples mariniers	42%	75%
Autres salariés	33%	67%

Car pour la très grande majorité des simples matelots et pêcheurs, aux trois quarts d'origine étrangère, l'aventure sarde reste un distant mirage, et ils doivent, par conséquent, se contenter de modestes gages. Il n'est pas rare de voir ces mariniers se louer auprès des spécialistes de la pêche du corail. L'un de ces derniers, Geoffroi de la Roque, employait localement entre 1378 et 1393 des mousses au maigre salaire de 8s. par mois.[84] Au cours de cette même période, le maître se mit lui-même profitablement à la solde du négociant Antoine Gratien et, en compagnie de trois autres corailleurs, s'embarquait pour la Sardaigne, assuré de percevoir mensuellement 280s.![85] Également spécialisé dans la pêche du corail, Jean de Silva, allié à la famille Fabre, versait 8s. pour tout salaire à son jeune disciple, alors que lui-même acceptait 240s. en gages du marchand Jean Calverne au début du printemps 1399.[86] Ce qui était vrai pour l'Angleterre de la fin du XIIIe siècle, pourrait bien s'appliquer à la Provence de la fin du XIVe siècle: « town streets were not paved with gold and many who migrated there simply exchanged one form of poverty for another ».[87]

[82] AD13, 351 E 66, 24 septembre 1393, fol. 75^r–v^.

[83] BnF, nouv. .acq. lat., 1344, 18 mars 1397, fols 224^v^–225^v^.

[84] AD13, 355 E 25, 18 octobre 1378, fol. 46^v^; AD13, 351 E 36, 3 janvier 1380, fol. 197^r–v^; BnF, nouv. .acq. lat., 1344, 11 août 1393, fol. 18^r–v^.

[85] AD13, 351 E 74, 10 février 1390, fols 51^r^–52^r^.

[86] Jean apparaît comme témoin instrumentaire dans l'acte d'apprentissage de son neveu Louis Fabre, petit-fils de Henri Fabre l'aîné: AD13, 351 E 80, 7 juillet 1399, fol. 29^v^; AD13, 351 E 38, 7 août 1381, fol. 72^v–r^; AD13, 351 E 80, 31 mars 1399, fols 4^r^–6^r^.

[87] Hatcher et Bailey, *Modelling the Middle Ages*, p. 50.

En fait, la main-d'œuvre à bon marché devient dans les dernières années du siècle une denrée de moins en moins rare. Globalement, marins et pêcheurs, à l'instar des domestiques de tout acabit, subissent une baisse relative des salaires comme l'indique le tableau 11.7. En 1357, Raymond Fabre prit à son service un marin pendant une année au salaire de 35s. mensuels; en 1380, il engageait un adolescent, cette fois pendant une période de deux ans au piètre salaire de 10s.[88] Le marinier Louis Geoffroi offrait 53s. par mois à son employé en 1382; douze ans plus tard, on le voit engager un autre matelot, mais à moindre frais, c'est-à-dire 42s.[89] Geoffroi Rolland embauchait en 1379 un garçon de quatorze ans au taux mensuels de 42s.; en 1386, il n'offre plus à un employé adulte que 34s., moins ce que lui coûteront les chaussures de mer.[90] En 1381, Pierrot Audibert, alors âgé de douze ans, se louait comme moussaillon aux gages de 26s. mensuels; deux ans plus tard, cette fois en compagnie de son père, un bâtier de Martigues (Étang de Berre), il obtenait 42s.[91] Or en 1386, à l'âge de dix-sept ans, il besogne toujours comme mousse, mais cette fois à moindre salaire, soit 32s.[92] Pour sa part, le pêcheur Jean Raynaud réussit à maintenir ses émoluments entre 1387 et 1399, soit autour de 40s. mensuels: dans le contexte inflationniste, il s'agit en fait d'une réduction salariale alors qu'il dut doubler, en 1399, la durée de son engagement de deux ans.[93] On pourrait multiplier ces cas de figure à l'envi.

Les gens de mer ne sont pas les seules victimes de cette tendance à la baisse. Olivier Giraud, laboureur de Marseille, vit également ses gages chuter de moitié entre 1377 et 1395.[94] De même, le marchand Guillaume Mathieu offrait-il moins à ses laboureurs entre 1372 et 1390.[95] En 1366, le meunier Jean Tourraine donnait à son engagé 45s. mensuels pour une période de dix mois de labeur; en 1385, il ne remet que 33s. à un meunier d'Aix pour ses services d'une durée de deux ans.[96]

88 AD13, 381 E 81, 2 mai 1357, fol. 14r–v; AD13, 351 E 48, 7 janvier 1380, fol. 100v.

89 AD13, 355 E 28, 6 juin 1382, fol. 19r–v; AD13, 351 E 67, 8 juillet 1394, fols 79v–80r.

90 AD13, 351 E 36, 30 octobre 1379, fol. 16 r–v; AD13, 351 E 39, 22 mars 1386, fol. 259r–v.

91 AD13, 351 E 52, 20 avril 1381, fol. 25v; AD13, 351 E 54, 26 juin 1383, fol. 31r.

92 AD13, 351 E 41, 30 novembre 1386, fol. 65r.

93 AD13, 351 E 55, 31 décembre 1387, fol. 71r; AD13, 351 E 80, 15 juin 1399, fol. 22r.

94 AD13, 355 E 19, 4 novembre 1377, fols 125v–126r; AD13, 351 E 95, 6 octobre 1395, fol. 56v.

95 AD13, 355 E 19, 17 mai 1372, fol. 42r; AD13, 355 E 33, 1er novembre 1390, fol. 19r.

96 AD13, 351 E 28, 19 novembre 1366, fol. 233r–v; AD13, 351 E 39, 13 mars 1385, fol. 248r.

Il faut dire que celui-ci s'était endetté auprès de Jean pour payer une rançon de guerre, thème récurrent dans les actes de l'époque.[97]

La dureté des temps atteint particulièrement la main-d'œuvre non qualifiée, première victime du déclin continu des gages. Dans une étude antérieure, il fut démontré qu'un accès plus libéral au crédit dans les années subséquentes à la peste noire avait, à terme, aggravé l'endettement de nombreux loueurs de bras et compromis, par conséquent, leurs conditions de travail dans le dernier quart du XIVe siècle.[98] Nombreux sont ceux qui durent se placer auprès de leurs bailleurs de fonds en guise de remboursement. En 1392, un valet de quinze ans, Rostagnet Isnard, vit ainsi sa rémunération réduite pour près de la moitié afin de satisfaire son créancier au service duquel il fut contraint de se mettre pendant une période de deux ans.[99]

Signification du travail juvénile

De fait, la domesticité offre depuis 1348 de plus amples occasions d'emploi aux jeunes en quête soit de protection personnelle, soit de gages en monnaie sonnante et trébuchante. Notons au même moment la soudaine présence féminine sous contrat au sein du personnel de maison, alors qu'elle décroît corollairement dans les métiers artisanaux. Les salaires gagnés par les adultes auprès des maîtres de métiers urbains se maintiennent sans doute dans la deuxième moitié du

[97] Guerre et brigandage s'intensifient depuis les années 1350, non sans laisser de nombreuses traces dans la documentation; en outre, les clauses de captivité et de rançonnement se retrouvent parfois au cœur des négociations entre maîtres et engagés. Ainsi, noble Bertrand de Roquefort refusa-t-il de verser une quelconque indemnité en faveur du corailleur qu'il s'apprêtait à embaucher en cas de capture ou de décès en cours de contrat (*si caperetur vel decederet*), BnF, nouv. .acq. lat., 1342, 1 mars 1384, fol. 188^r–v^; le marchand-drapier Guillaume de Favas, qui avait réglé la rançon d'un employé en 1379, déclina de s'y engager de nouveau lorsqu'il prit à son service un garçon de seize ans en 1381: AD13, 351 E 48, 23 novembre 1379, fols 172^v^–173^v^; AD13, 351 E 52, 22 avril 1381, fol. 25^v^. En 1387, une épouse se louait comme *socia* (assitante plutôt qu'associée dans ce contexte) auprès d'un marchand de la ville afin de pouvoir racheter la liberté de son mari fait prisonnier à Meyrargues, AD13, 391 E 32, fol. 42^r^. Captif des gens d'armes de Raymond de Turenne (*per gentes armorum domini Raymundi Turena*), le laboureur Olivier Giraud réussit à racheter sa personne (*pro recaptando personam suam*) grâce au prêt de 25 florins que lui consentit le boucher Guillaume François, en échange de quoi Olivier lui promit sa force de travail à titre gratuit pour une durée d'un an: AD13, 352 E 95, 6 octobre 1395, fol. 56^v^.

[98] Michaud, « Serviteurs et domestiques ».

[99] « Pro restitutione aliorum trium florinorum per ipsum Rostagnetum habitorum ab ipso Duranto »: 26 mars 1392, AD 13, 351 E 62, fol. 117^r^.

siècle, bien qu'il sied davantage de parler plus sobrement de stagnation compte tenu du phénomène d'inflation. En outre, les employeurs recourent plus fréquemment aux bras « gratuits » si l'on en croit le nombre croissant d'apprentis qu'ils recueillent sous leur toit à partir des années 1370 (tableau 11.5). Certes, après la peste noire, il fallut abaisser et même parfois abandonner les frais de formation dans les arts traditionnellement coûteux (marchandise, change, herboristerie) pour attirer la main-d'œuvre, voire engager purement et simplement de jeunes adolescents en marge du processus de l'apprentissage.[100] Nombreuses se trouvent alors les familles placées devant la nécessité de louer leur progéniture, les soulageant ainsi d'une bouche supplémentaire à nourrir tout en leur procurant un revenu d'appoint, si modeste fût-il. Ainsi le 11 septembre 1350, une veuve nouvellement remariée, Jeannette Guillaume, remettait son fils de treize ans au maître plâtrier d'origine française Thomas de Fontaynelle qu'elle logeait dans l'une de ses maisons, en échange de l'entretien du garçon ainsi que de six florins annuels à elle dûment remis.[101] Il est intéressant de noter que le plâtrier avait pris à son service quelques jours auparavant deux Français, satisfaits de se partager entre eux sept florins pour six mois de labeur, de même qu'un jeune immigrant des Pouilles âgé de quatorze ans.[102] Celui-ci, privé de tout protecteur dans la grande cité (« nullum habet curatorem vel alium legitimum deffensorem »), avait cherché refuge auprès du maître en raison de ses besoins pressants (« propter suam magnam necessitatem »).[103]

Or passées les deux vagues de mortalité de 1348 et de 1361, les artisans se sont mis à recruter plus fortement le labeur des jeunes, gratuitement, sous le couvert de l'apprentissage. De même en est-il dans la boucherie, art où l'on observe une hausse des salaires jusqu'à la fin du siècle, phénomène qui doit être rapproché du dynamisme des activités maritimes déjà observé, les viandes salées composant le régime alimentaire des gens de mer.[104] Vaquant à une occupation

[100] Cet aspect du problème a été discuté dans Michaud, « From Apprentices to Wage-Earners ».

[101] « Precio sex florinorum auri solvendorum dicte Johannete Guillelme in operibus gippi et aliis operibus per dictum Thomacium infra domum ejusdem Johannete faciendis »: AD13, 355 E 3, fols 90r–91r.

[102] AD13, 355 E 3, 24 août 1350, fol. 85r–v.

[103] Le document, inachevé, ne recèle pas de clause salariale: AD13, 355 E 3, 2 septembre 1350, fol. 86v.

[104] L'étude de Yves Grava sur l'étang de Berre a bien démontré la prospérité au XIVe siècle des bouchers martégaux participant au ravitaillement des mariniers qui s'embarquaient au port de Bouc, Grava, « Marchands, pêcheurs », p. 52.

rigoureusement familiale, d'où la forte présence de femmes dans l'art de la triperie, les bouchers et les tripières marseillais ont dû ouvrir leur étal bon an mal an aux éléments exogènes après 1348, à commencer par de jeunes impétrants. Le tiers des actes d'embauche (11/31) concerne des enfants et adolescents qui reçoivent en moyenne 11s. par mois, soit le tiers du salaire des adultes salariés. Cela dit, notons bien qu'après 1379, le travail juvénile n'est plus rémunéré.

Il nous semble certain qu'à partir de cette époque, des signes indubitables de la dégradation des conditions de travail se multiplient dans les contrats étudiés. On l'a vu, les émoluments des jeunes matelots baissent sensiblement dans les deux dernières décennies du siècle: au tout début des années 1380, un garçon de douze ans pouvait gagner environ 10 florins par an; vers 1385, les gages annuels s'affaissent de l'ordre de 1 à 5 florins. Les versements salariaux, coutumièrement réglés par tranche de trois paiements (en début, au milieu et en fin de contrat), se font tarder, voire reportés à la toute fin du service. L'insuffisance de garantie motive même les retenues salariales.[105] Les parents doivent également partager les frais de soins de santé de leur enfant, responsabilité qui jadis incombait seule au maître.[106] L'entretien vestimentaire n'est plus, comme il l'était souvent autrefois, assuré par l'employeur; ainsi un homme promit-il de chausser et de vêtir son jeune frère placé en 1385 comme *famulus* chez un patron de navire, en sus de subvenir à ses besoins immédiats en monnaie courante, les 5 florins promis en gages ne devant être débités qu'au terme du contrat, au bout de cinq années de service. De même, une peine de dix florins pesait sur le garçon s'il était trouvé coupable de négligence dans l'exercice de ses fonctions.[107] Enfin, l'endettement en force plus d'un à s'embaucher auprès de patrons moins généreux; en outre, dans les trente dernières années du XIVe siècle, de très nombreux

[105] Olivier Jean, du village de Notre-Dame-du-Puy, aurait dû recevoir 12 florins annuellement de son employeur, Jacques de La Font, mais en l'absence de caution personnelle (fidéjussion), le maître ne s'engagea à régler la moitié du montant qu'au terme de chaque année, le reste n'étant acquitté qu'à la toute fin du contrat (« in fine cuiuslibet anni alia vero medietas retenta penes ipsum Jacobum, propter carentiam dicti Olivarii fidejussionis donec quousque ipse Olivarius complevit totum tempus predictum ipsorum tres annorum et non alia nec alio modo »), AD13, 351 E 54, 18 février 1385, fols 79^{v}–80^{r}.

[106] Bertrand et Bermonde Raynaud devaient ainsi assurer les soins de santé de leur fils Antoine âgé de douze ans placé chez le marin Jean Arvey, tant et aussi longtemps que le garçon s'activerait en terre ferme; en mer, le maître s'engageait à couvrir ces dépenses: AD13, 351 E 62, 11 novembre 1390, fol. 13^{r-v}.

[107] AD13, 391 E 31, 4 novembre 1385, fol. 26^{v}.

contrats de travail se concluent dans l'enceinte des cours de justice ou de la prison royale.[108] Il l'a été dit, les enfants eux-mêmes n'y échappent pas.

La nécessité n'est pas l'apanage exclusif des seuls orphelins et miséreux. Dans les années qui suivent la peste noire, des artisans mettent aussi leurs fillettes impubères au service domestique des plus nantis. Qu'ils soient ou non réduits à placer leurs rejetons en quasi-servitude dans la maison de particuliers, les parents marseillais du XIVe siècle ont à cœur d'assurer leur avenir à l'abri des besoins de première nécessité. Or dans cette culture urbaine, c'est la formation artisanale qui confère cette assurance, pour qu'ainsi l'enfant, « avec l'aide de Dieu, puisse gagner décemment sa vie grâce au travail honnête » comme en est persuadé Robert Roch, orfèvre anglais, lors de la mise en apprentissage de son fils chez un confrère marseillais en 1362.[109] Des mères moins fortunées n'hésitent pas à troquer le travail domestique de leurs enfants, ou le leur, contre la promesse d'une formation littéraire ou artisanale. En décembre 1386, une pauvre veuve d'Aix-en-Provence se rendit dans la cité portuaire pour faire de son fils, à peine âgé de huit ans, le valet d'un frère mendiant, assurée que celui-ci s'engagerait en retour à lui enseigner les lettres consciencieusement, comme s'il s'agissait de son fils ou de son frère.[110] En 1387, une autre veuve, Rostagne Durand, devenait la servante d'un fabricant de bât à la condition que ce dernier accepte de transmettre les secrets de son art à son fils.[111]

En ces temps troublés, les mariniers paraissent également préférer pour leurs rejetons l'enceinte sécuritaire de l'atelier artisanal à l'aventure du grand large. Certes, les profits substantiels que peuvent procurer les tréfonds marins commandent qu'on y destine un ou deux fils. Mais les dangers de la mer, et particulièrement les expéditions périlleuses dans les récifs du corail sarde, nourrissent, au fil du quotidien, de profondes angoisses.[112] Ainsi le révèlent si éloquemment les inquiétudes d'une mère marseillaise, de surcroît femme de marin, qui interdit

[108] Dix-huit engagements domestiques passés dans un lieu judiciaire datent de cette époque, de même que dix des quatorze contrats conclus par des travailleurs agricoles.

[109] « Cupiens ipsum [Antonietum] arte instruere ut possit vitam in opere deffendere et Deo dante honeste vivere in hoc mundo »: AD13, 351 E 25, 9 juillet 1362, fol. 73r–v.

[110] « Cum pacto quod ipsum doceat literas pro posse velut filium aut fratrem suum »: AD13, 351 E 41, 6 décembre 1386, fol. 121v.

[111] AD13, 351 E 41, 14 janvier 1387, fol. 77r–v.

[112] Il faut consulter à cet égard la déposition émouvante des marins et des pêcheurs marseillais venus instruire le procès de canonisation de Urbain V, sans l'intercession duquel, assurent-ils, ils auraient péri dans les mers déchaînées de Provence et de Sardaigne ou aux mains de pirates tant chrétiens que barbaresques: Amargier, « Gens de mer en Méditerranée ».

formellement au maître de son jeune fils de quinze ans de l'emmener corailler dans les eaux de Sardaigne.[113] Ne faut-il donc point non plus s'étonner que les parents désirent diversifier le parcours professionnel de leurs enfants. Ainsi, ce sont les plus fortunés des gens de mer, à savoir les corailleurs (Senequier, Fabre, Auger, Gautier, Raynaud, etc.), qui plus fréquemment destinent leurs fils, ou certains d'entre eux, vers les métiers artisanaux exécutés en terre ferme, cependant liés de très près aux activités maritimes. Les chefs de maisons dirigent ainsi énergiquement leurs fils vers les métiers de ramier, de charpentier, et surtout, de tonnelier. Loin d'être des débouchés de fortune assignés à de pauvres orphelins, ces métiers ont été choisis stratégiquement par les pères, toujours présents dans les actes d'apprentissage.[114]

Baromètre de la difficulté des temps, le bilan de l'évolution des stratégies professionnelles par le biais de l'apprentissage reste cependant difficile à esquisser pour la période étudiée. Le ratissage de toutes les bribes d'information contenues dans le corpus rassemblé ne peut donner hélas que des impressions d'ensemble. Il appert néanmoins que lorsqu'elle se manifeste, la mobilité socio-professionnelle glisse vers le bas dans le deuxième versant du XIVe siècle. Quelques éléments permettent sans doute de formuler cette hypothèse: tout d'abord, les gens de métiers modestes (laboureurs, savetiers, calfats, pêcheurs) parviennent jusqu'au milieu du siècle à se glisser dans les arts prestigieux et de fort bon rapport, tels que la draperie, le change, le négoce, l'herboristerie, l'orfèvrerie, la cuiraterie[115] et ce, malgré les frais de scolarité et d'entretien parfois élevés. Tel est le cas de Jean l'Écuyer de l'île Saint-Geniès, fils de pêcheur, qui entre en apprentissage chez un savetier marseillais en 1324; or en 1364, on le découvre courroyeur au moment où, dans le jardin de sa résidence, il s'entend avec une veuve pour former dans son art — *arte conresarie* — le fils de treize ans de cette

En outre, plusieurs de ces rescapés appartiennent aux familles de corailleurs mentionnées dans notre corpus: Fabre, de la Font, Sabatier, Viguier, Raymond, Calverie et Gassini.

[113] « Excepto tamen modo in insula Sardinie et partibus coralhandi »: AD13, 351 E 62, 28 octobre 1392, fol. 127 $^{r-v}$.

[114] En 1398, un corailleur plaçait son enfant de sept ans chez son propre frère, fabriquant de rames: AD13, 351 E 79, 12 décembre 1398, fols 132^{v}–133^{r}; AD13, 351 E 52, 12 novembre 1381, fols 226^{v}–227^{r}; AD13, 355 E 11, 8 septembre 1361, fol. 65^{v}; AD13, 351 E 54, 13 mars 1383, fol. 15^{v}; AD13, 351 E 55, 11 mai 1388, fol. 88^{r}; BnF, nouv. .acq. lat., 1344, 12 mai 1395, fol. 153^{v}; AD13, 351 E 80, 7 juillet 1399, fol. 29^{v}.

[115] ACM, I II 8, 22 février 1324, fol. 8^{r-v}; AD13, 351 E 27, 8 mai 1364, fols 32^{v}–33^{r}. En 1310, un fils de calfat âgé de dix ans devenait le disciple de l'orfèvre Hugues Foulques: AD13, 381 E 25, 21 mars 1310, fol. 49^{r}.

dernière.[116] Dans la seconde moitié du siècle, les individus d'humble extraction ne s'immiscent plus aussi souvent dans les professions supérieures (draperie et marchandise) dont les coûts d'instruction sont devenus franchement prohibitifs. Pour le prix de leur enseignement et des nécessités de la vie dispensés à leurs recrues, drapiers, marchands et apothicaires réclamaient en moyenne, avant la peste noire, près de 110s. annuellement. Dans les autres métiers, en revanche, on prélevait beaucoup moins communément des frais d'apprentissage. Les orfèvres de la ville illustrent bien le phénomène: sur les neuf contrats d'apprentissage repérés entre 1303 et 1390 dans les archives marseillaises, seulement trois, tous rédigés avant le deuxième quart du siècle, mentionnent une compensation versée au maître, dont une prestation en nature. Dans les deux derniers cas, datés de 1320 et 1324, les charges imposées furent respectivement fixées à 50s. et 60s. par an. Les frais d'entretien et d'instruction exigés des marchands et drapiers doublent et même quadruplent entre les deux périodes. Si bien que les fils des humbles, tel que celui du savetier Pierre de Reymaco, d'Aix-en-Provence, qui amorçait son apprentissage auprès du négociant Hugues Nieilli en 1338 pendant deux ans contre le déboursement de 4,5 livres par an, ne peuvent plus désormais embrasser ce dessein à raison d'une dépense annuelle moyenne de près de 12 livres, soit l'équivalent du salaire annuel d'un laboureur professionnel.[117] Ils se dispersent alors davantage dans les métiers artisanaux moins lucratifs ou moins prestigieux. Les fils de laboureurs empruntent pareille trajectoire pour devenir tisserands, tailleurs, broquiers, plâtriers, peintres, etc.[118] Notons tout de même qu'il s'agit ici plutôt de stratégies activement déployées par les chefs de famille encore vivants.[119] À l'inverse, le décès prématuré du père n'est pas sans risquer de compromettre l'avenir professionnel d'un jeune, dont tel

[116] AD13, 381 E 31, fols 3^{v}–4^{r}; AD13, III B 18, fols 101^{v}–102^{r}.

[117] AD13, 391 E 12, 6 mars 1338, fol. 113^{r}.

[118] Ces destins tranchent avec certains des parcours que dessinaient pour leurs fils les spécialistes de la terre au début du siècle. De fait, à l'époque, les affaires et plus particulièrement le commerce des épices représentaient une profession de choix, AD13, 381 E 48, 6 décembre 1306, fol. 45^{v}; AD13, 381 E 65, 21 novembre 1320, fol. 36^{r-v}; ACM, 1 II 8, 30 septembre 1324, fol. 59^{r-v}; AD13, 355 E 35, 17 avril 1357, fol. 13^{r}; AD13, 381 E 44, 24 juin 1375, fol. 3^{r-v}; AD13, 351 E 40, 11 février 1386, fol. 203^{r-v}; AD13, 351 E 33, 2 octobre 1375, fol. 68^{r}; AD13, 355 E 78, 17 novembre 1394, fol. 92^{r}; AD13, 351 E 62, 30 novembre 1395, fols 213^{v}–214^{v}; AD13, 355 E 16, 3 octobre 1367, fol. 60^{v}.

[119] En comparaison, les orphelins de laboureurs sont plus fréquemment destinés à la pêche et au service domestique: AD13, 355 E 2, 6 décembre 1349, fol. 134^{r-v}; AD13, 351 E 77, 22 juillet 1395, fol. 43^{r-v}; AD13, 355 E 5, 6 août 1352, fol. 42^{r-v}.

fils de notaire obligé de s'éloigner des écritures juridiques pour s'accommoder d'un métier manuel.[120] Dans leur ensemble, les nobles, les notables et les gens d'affaires de la ville réussissent à éviter à leur descendance ce genre de déconvenue, malgré quelques exceptions.[121] En 1357, le fils d'un drapier local, Jean de Nivers, se mit en apprentissage chez un fustier, alors qu'en 1379, se trouvant dans la gêne, Huguette Boniface, veuve et dame de la bonne bourgeoisie, dut compromettre le rang de son fils Pierrot en le plaçant chez le boucher Raymond Finaud.[122] Des revenus honnêtes et assurés valaient sans doute ce déclassement.

Conclusion

Rappelons, en conclusion, quelques observations que l'analyse des contrats d'embauche à Marseille au XIVe siècle permet de formuler. Brièvement, on voit se former dans la deuxième moitié du siècle, pour reprendre un cliché moderne, une société à deux vitesses. Au-delà des catégories sociales traditionnelles, travailleurs, bourgeois et nobles, se creuse un fossé qui polarise la population salariée.

Dans le contexte des profonds bouleversements démographiques qui secouent la cité portuaire au milieu du XIVe siècle, les salaires nominaux des travailleurs s'accroissent à première vue jusqu'à la fin du siècle. Ces gains relatifs demeurent toutefois fragiles pour le grand nombre, compte tenu du climat inflationniste de la période; en outre, ils dissimulent de fortes disparités selon les catégories d'emploi. Les spécialistes de la pêche du corail retirent de substantiels profits, suivis de loin par les marchands, les artisans et les laboureurs

[120] Avant la peste, les fils de notaires qui ne reprenaient pas la relève de leur père -décédé ou non- se formaient aux secrets de la marchandise, AD13, 381 E 56, 6 juillet 1328, fol. 20[r–v]; AD13, 391 E 7, 8 avril 1334, fol. 11[r]; et du commerce des épices, AD13, 381 E 12, 21 décembre 1314, fol. 26[v]; ACM 1 II 8, 29 octobre 1324, fol. 99[r]. Dans la seconde moitié du siècle, on les retrouve ici chez un tonnelier, BnF, nouv. .acq. lat., 1344, 24 novembre 1394, fol. 76[r]; là, chez un boucher AD13, 355 E 73, 5 avril 1389, fols 6[v]–7[r]. En 1359, Jean Bermundi, notaire de Marseille, n'hésite pas à remettre son neveu de quatorze ans, orphelin de son frère également notaire, aux bons soins du pêcheur Guillaume Aubert et ce, pour une période de dix ans à raison 2s. de gages par mois, AD13, 355 E 10, 28 avril 1359, fols 11[v]–12[r].

[121] Qu'ils répugnent ou non à manipuler les espèces pour gagner leur vie, les orphelins de l'élite locale doivent parfois se diriger vers la marchandise: voir le cas de Bertrandet Mayni (AD13, 351 E 28, 10 septembre 1366, fol. 131[r–v]), Guillaume Fournier (AD13, 351 E 55, 28 juillet 1388, fols 105[v]–106[v]) et Jeannot Langueri (AD13, 351 E 58, 11 août 1388, fol. 55[v]).

[122] AD13, 351 E 647, 1er juillet 1357, fol. 156[r–v]; AD13, 351 E 36, 31 mars 1379, fols 14[v]–15[v].

salariés. Au bas de l'échelle, la main-d'œuvre peu ou prou qualifiée n'arrive pas, dans le dernier quart du siècle, à maintenir les gages perçus aux lendemains de la peste noire, époque où des conditions de travail avantageuses, tout comme l'ouverture du salariat aux jeunes bras, bonifient sans doute la situation matérielle des familles besogneuses. En ce sens, la grande mortalité de 1348 aura favorisé dans cette communauté urbaine « la réduction du nombre des prolétaires » comme l'observait Georges Duby pour les campagnes. Seulement, cette embellie aura été de courte durée. À partir des années 1370, l'équation de l'offre et de la demande penche, cette fois, en faveur des maîtres-artisans qui recourent plus aisément à une main-d'œuvre à bon marché par le biais de l'apprentissage simple. Certes, pour les contemporains, la formation professionnelle garantit l'avenir économique, social et moral de leurs enfants, voire même, la fortune aidant, une vie meilleure. Les marins-corailleurs l'ont bien compris. Cependant, l'apprentissage ne favorise plus autant qu'autrefois dans les couches modestes les desseins d'élévation sociale; garder sa place dans la hiérarchie des métiers devient le lot du commun, sinon un véritable défi.

Bibliographie

Archives

Marseille, Archives Communales de Marseille (ACM), délibérations municipales, série BB; fonds des notaires, série II

Marseille, Archives Départementales des Bouches-du-Rhône (AD13), fonds du Tribunal du Palais de Marseille, série 3 B

Marseille, Archives Départementales des Bouches-du-Rhône (AD13), fonds des notaires, série E

Paris, Bibliothèque nationale de France, Cabinet des manuscrits, nouvelles acquisitions latines, Fonds Mortreuil (actes originaux et transcriptions), vol. 1304–1334

Sources secondaires

Amargier, Paul, « Gens de mer en Méditerranée dans les années 1375–1390 », dans *Navigation et gens de mer en Méditerranée de la Préhistoire à nos jours: Actes de la table ronde du groupement d'intérêt scientifique 'Sciences humaines sur l'aire méditerranéenne'. Cahier 3. Collioure, septembre 1979* (Paris: CNRS,1980), pp. 77–83

Aubenas, Roger, *Étude sur le notariat provençal au Moyen Âge et sous l'Ancien Régime* (Aix-en-Provence: Édition du feu, 1931)

Baratier, Édouard, *La démographie provençale du XIIIe au XVIe siècle avec chiffres de comparaison pour le XVIIIe siècle* (Paris: SEVPEN, 1961)

——, *Histoire de Marseille* (Toulouse: Privat, 1973; 2e édn, 1990)

——, « Production et exportation du vin du terroir marseillais du XIIIe au XVIe siècle », *Bulletin philologique et historique (jusqu'à 1610)*, 1 (1959), 239–49

Béghin, Cécile, « Donneuses d'ouvrages, apprenties et salariées aux XIVe et XVe siècles dans les sociétés urbaines languedociennes », *Clio*, 3 (1996), 2–16

Bernardi, Philippe, « Esclavages et artisanat: Une main d'œuvre étrangère dans la Provence des XIIIe–XVe siècles », dans *XXXe Congrès de la Société des Historiens Médiévistes de l'Enseignement Supérieur Public (Göttingen, 1999)* (Paris: CTHS, 2000), pp. 79–94

Bresc, Henri, *Un monde méditerranéen: Économie et société en Sicile, 1300–1450*, 2 vols (Roma: École française de Rome, 1986)

Caferro, William, « Petrach's War: Florentine Wages and the Black Death », *Speculum*, 88 (2013), 144–65

Carmichael, Ann G., *Plague and the Poor* (Cambridge: Cambridge University Press, 1986)

Carpentier, Élisabeth, et Michel Le Mené, *La France du XIe au XVe siècle: Population, société, économie* (Paris: Presses Universitaires de France, 1996)

Cohn, Samuel, Jr, *The Black Death Transformed: Disease and Culture in Early Renaissance Europe* (London: Arnold, 2002)

Coulet, Noël, *Aix en Provence: Espace et relations d'une capitale (milieu XIVe – milieu XVe s.)* (Aix-en-Provence: Université de Provence, 1988)

——, « Le malheur des temps », dans *Histoire de la France des origines à nos jours*, éd. par Georges Duby, mise à jour de Jean-Michel Gaillard (Paris: Larousse, 1970–71; 2e édn, 1999), pp. 315–42

De La Roncière, Charles, « La condition des salariés à Florence au XIVe siècle », dans *Il tumulto dei Ciompi: Un momento di storia fiorentina ed europea* (Firenze: Leo S. Olschki, 1981), pp. 13–40

Drendel, John, « La monnaie dans les campagnes provençales pendant la première moitié du XIVe siècle », dans *Dynamiques du monde rural dans la conjoncture de 1300*, éd. par François Menant, Monique Bourin et Lluis To Figueras (Roma: École Française de Rome, 2013), pp. 437–51

Duby, Georges, *L'économie rurale et la vie des campagnes dans l'Occident Médiéval (France, Angleterre, Empire, IXe–XVe siècles): Essai de synthèse et perspectives de recherches*, 2 vols (Paris: Aubier, 1962)

Dufourcq, Charles-Emmanuel, *La vie quotidienne dans les ports méditerranéens au Moyen Âge: Provence, Languedoc, Catalogne* (Paris: Hachette, 1975)

Fournial, Étienne, *Histoire monétaire de l'Occident* (Paris: Fernand Nathan, 1970)

Franceschi, Franco, « Les enfants au travail dans l'industrie textile florentine des XIVe et XVe siècles », *Médiévales*, 30 (1996), 69–82

Grava, Yves, « Marchands, pêcheurs et gens de mer sur les bords de l'étang de Berre à la fin du Moyen Âge », dans *Navigation et gens de mer en Méditerranée de la Préhistoire à nos jours: Actes de la table ronde du groupement d'intérêt scientifique 'Sciences humaines sur l'aire méditerranéenne'. Cahier 3. Collioure, septembre 1979* (Paris: CNRS,1980), pp. 48–58

Hatcher, John, et Mark Bailey, éds, *Modelling the Middle Ages: The History and Theory of England's Economic Development* (Oxford: Oxford University Press, 2001)

Herlihy, David, et Christiane Klapisch-Zuber, *Les Toscans et leurs familles* (Paris: Éditions de l'École des Hautes Études en Sciences Sociales, 1978)

Horrox, Rosemary, *The Black Death* (Manchester: Manchester University Press, 1994)

Lavergne, Géraud, « La pêche et le commerce de corail à Marseille aux XIVe et XVe siècles », *Annales du Midi*, 1 (1952), 199–211

Mabilly, Philippe, « La monnaie de menus marseillais et le marc d'argent (1282–1301) », *Annales de Provence*, A6 (1909), 3–8

Maurel, Christian, « Grands marchands et "petites et moyennes industries" à Marseille au Bas Moyen Âge (1350–1480) », dans *Le marchand au Moyen Âge: XIXe Congrès de la S.H.M.E.S. (Reims, juin 1988)* (Paris: CTHS, 1992), pp. 105–12

Michaud, Francine, « From Apprentices to Wage-Earners: Child Labour Before and After the Black Death », dans *Essays on Medieval Childhood: Responses to Recent Debates*, éd. par Joel Rosenthal (Donington: Paul Watkins Publishing, 2007), pp. 75–92

——, « La peste, la peur et l'espoir: Le pèlerinage jubilaire de romeux marseillais en 1350 », *Le Moyen Âge*, 104 (1998), 399–434

——, « Serviteurs et domestiques à Marseille au XIVe siècle », dans *Actes du Congrès International 'Le petit peuple dans la société de l'Occident médiéval: Terminologies, perceptions, réalités', Université de Montréal, 18–23 octobre 1999*, éd. par Pietro Boglioni et autres (Paris: Publications de la Sorbonne 2002), pp. 395–405

——, « Travail et mouvements migratoires avant et après la peste noire à Marseille », *Provence historique*, 49 (1999), 367–83

——, *Un signe des temps: Accroissement des crises familiales autour du patrimoine à Marseille à la fin du* XIII*e siècle* (Toronto: Pontifical Institute of Mediaeval Studies, 1994)

Munro, John, « Wage-Stickiness, Monetary Changes, and Real Incomes in Late-Medieval England and the Low Countries, 1300–1500: Did Money Matter? », *Research in Economic History*, 21 (2003), 185–297

Murat, Josée-Valérie, « Navires et navigations à Marseille au XIVe siècle » (thèse de doctorat non publiée, Université d'Aix-Marseille I, 2001)

Razi, S., *Life, Marriage and Death in a Medieval Parish: Economy, Society and Demography in Halesowen 1270–1400* (Cambridge: Cambridge University Press, 1980)

Rolland, Henri, *Monnaies des comtes de Provence,* XII*e–*XV*e siècles: Histoire monétaire, économique et corporative, description raisonnée* (Paris: A. J. Picard & Cie et E. Bourgey, 1956)

Smail, Daniel, *The Consumption of Justice: Emotions, Publicity and Legal Culture in Marseille, 1264–1423* (Ithaca: Cornell University Press, 2003)

Spufford, Peter, *Money and its Use in Medieval Europe* (Cambridge: Cambridge University Press, 1988)

Les *Capbreus* royaux roussillonnais et la crise malthusienne

Laure Verdon

En 1962, Georges Duby fait paraître un ouvrage majeur sur l'histoire rurale médiévale européenne: *L'économie rurale et la vie des campagnes dans l'Occident médiéval.*[1] Reflet tout à la fois d'une sensibilité d'historien et d'une certaine vision de l'histoire, cet ouvrage se voulait être avant tout un état des lieux de la recherche dans le champ de l'histoire des sociétés rurales ainsi qu'un appel à poursuivre les investigations en ce domaine.[2] La place première y est accordée à l'organisation volontariste des campagnes, sous l'effet de la mise en place de la seigneurie, du rapport de force établi entre les communautés et le pouvoir et de la conjoncture. Le village apparaît fortement fixé dès l'époque carolingienne et ses structures-clés pérennisées: ce sont le finage, le terroir et les terres. Avec les crises de la fin du Moyen Âge, ce sont les parties périphériques de ce territoire qui se trouvent abandonnées. Georges Duby développe ici une vision organique de la société villageoise intimement inscrite dans

[1] Il convient de mettre en rapport cette publication avec la fondation en 1961, par Georges Duby associé à l'anthropologue Isac Chiva et au géographe Daniel Faucher, de la revue *Etudes rurales.*

[2] Le début des années 1960 représentait une période faste en ce domaine, au rebours d'un constat général de crise des études sur la société rurale médiévale dressé à l'aube du XXIe siècle dans Alfonso, *The Rural History of Medieval European Societies.*

Laure Verdon (verdon@mmsh.univ-aix.fr) est maître de conférences à l'université d'Aix-Marseille et une spécialiste des sociétés rurales de la Méditerranée occidentale au Moyen Âge. Son dernier livre est *La voix des dominés : communautés et seigneurie en Provence au bas Moyen Âge*, paru aux Presses Universitaires de Rennes en 2012.

Crisis in the Later Middle Ages: Beyond the Postan-Duby Paradigm, ed. by John Drendel, TMC 13 (Turnhout: Brepols, 2015) 323–338 BREPOLS PUBLISHERS 10.1484/M.TMC.5.103793

le cadre de son finage: la condition des personnes et les structures de la société sont encore perçues à l'aune d'une culture juridique qui tient pour acquise la perte de sens du droit romain et de ses concepts durant le haut Moyen Âge et d'une lecture marxiste qui assimile, dans les termes employés, la condition des non-libres à l'esclavage au moins jusqu'à la fin du XIIe siècle.[3] La domestication de l'espace villageois s'opère en trois phases, qui déterminent autant de périodes d'essor ou de crise; la troisième est celle des tenures périphériques créées en lisière des communaux entre XIIIe et XIVe siècle, signe d'un « monde plein » qui peine à trouver un équilibre entre essor démographique qui se poursuit et possibilités vivrières offertes par les terroirs. Le finage villageois évolue comme un corps vivant, par adjonction ou abandons aux marges.

Depuis les années 1990, des sources de nature différente sont venues contribuer à renouveler l'approche des communautés rurales médiévales, en croisant l'analyse juridique, économique et politique.[4] Enquêtes et aveux de tenures sont ainsi aujourd'hui considérés par les historiens comme le produit de l'intervention directe des communautés sur leur environnement social et politique, en un jeu de « dialogue » avec l'autorité dont elles dépendent qui permet de sortir d'une logique d'analyse strictement conjoncturelle. La période de la seconde moitié du XIIIe siècle en particulier, qui voit l'usage de ce type de documentation se diffuser en Europe, apparaît sous un jour nouveau. Ces sources permettent d'étudier un contexte souvent complexe, où se mêlent des impératifs économiques de mise en valeur de terres, jusque alors dédiées aux pâtures ou incultes, pour répondre à la pression démographique mais aussi des enjeux plus politiques liés à la possession et à la règlementation commune sur ces territoires ou encore à la nécessaire délimitation des territoires marginaux aux finages entre communautés voisines.[5] Le moteur de ces entreprises semble bien être, comme le soulignait Georges Duby, la position prise vis-à-vis du pouvoir local, le contrôle de l'emprise individuelle sur les communaux, et le respect

[3] Hélias, « Le vocabulaire de Georges Duby dans *l'Economie rurale et la vie des campagnes dans l'Occident médiéval* ».

[4] Sur ce renouveau, voir les contributions rassemblées dans Alfonso, *The Rural History of Medieval European Societies*: pour les régions méridionales qui concernent cet article, on se reportera notamment à Cursente, « Recent Trends in the Rural History of Medieval France », pp. 57–92; de Cortàzar, Angel, et Martinez Sopena, « The Historiography of Medieval Society in Rural Spain », pp. 93–140; Provero, « Forty Years of Rural History for the Italian Middle Ages », pp. 141–72.

[5] Voir sur ce point notamment Verdon, « Le territoire avoué »; Verdon, *La voix des dominés*, pp. 136–79, et Bourin et Challet, « Temps, lieux et supplices ».

du bien-être collectif. Ces préoccupations sont précisément ce qui définit une communauté et sa conscience politique, mue tout autant par les contraintes liées à la conjoncture — telles celles d'un monde plein — que par le contexte institutionnel ouvert par l'enquête — ou toute forme de « dialogue » — qui permet aux communautés de négocier avec le pouvoir. Ainsi, les enjeux de ce demi-siècle qui précède les crises, et les annonces d'une certaine manière, sont-ils mis en lumière et permettent-ils de nuancer les effets perçus de celles-ci par l'accent mis sur les stratégies individuelles de possession de terres, les structures familiales et sociales qui reconfigurent les groupes de parenté dès avant le XIVe siècle, ou encore la place non négligeable attribuée aux femmes.

Le Roussillon, partie septentrionale de la Catalogne constitué d'un regroupement de comtés, présente également dans ses archives des exemples d'enquêtes et de terriers — qui conservent les aveux de tenures — autorisant une réflexion en prise avec le renouveau historiographique sur l'état des terroirs, notamment démographique, à l'aube du XIVe siècle. Le fonds de la Procuration royale des archives départementales des Pyrénées orientales conserve, en effet, tous les actes relatifs aux seigneuries possédées en Roussillon par les rois de Majorque aux XIIIe et XIVe siècles. On y trouve, en particulier, une série de sept terriers ou *capbreus* rédigés à la demande du roi Jacques Ier entre 1292 et 1294.[6] Un *capbreu*, *caput breve* en latin, est l'équivalent d'un terrier: il s'agit d'un inventaire de rentes et de biens immeubles dressé sous la forme d'une enquête au cours de laquelle les tenanciers du seigneur concerné viennent déclarer leur tenure et leurs taxes. Ce type d'acte apparaît en Vieille Catalogne dans la seconde moitié du XIIe siècle, faisant suite à d'autres types d'inventaires, et se généralise au XIVe siècle où il prend une forme exclusivement notariale. On trouve des *capbreus* encore à l'époque moderne, période pour laquelle il n'existe pas, en Roussillon, de cadastres.[7]

Les *capbreus* du roi de Majorque sont un modèle du genre. Entreprise pionnière pour le Midi de l'Europe, ils ont sans doute contribué à fixer les formes de ce type d'inventaire. Il s'agit d'une entreprise d'importance à replacer dans un contexte politique particulier, celui du royaume de Majorque dans les années 1290 et du conflit qui oppose alors Jacques Ier et son allié capétien Philippe IV au roi d'Aragon Alphonse III. Le conflit soldé par la paix proposée au prin-

[6] L'ensemble des *capbreus* a été édité en 2011 par Rodrigue Tréton aux éditions du CTHS. Pour une analyse détaillée de la forme et du contenu de ces documents, nous renvoyons le lecteur à la riche introduction de cette publication: Tréton, Catafau, et Verdon, *Les Capbreus*.

[7] Larguier, « Capbreus de Catalogne ».

temps 1292, le souverain catalan marque alors sa volonté de reprendre en mains le contrôle des terres et des droits possédés en Roussillon. L'objectif est donc, avant tout, fiscal et s'inscrit dans une opération de consolidation du royaume.

Cependant, le soin apporté à la *capbrevacio*, les différentes étapes de sa réalisation, la procédure suivie incitent également à penser que nous avons affaire là à l'une des phases du développement de l'administration souveraine, similaire à celle qui se fait jour dans la plupart des États à la même époque.[8] Le choix du terrier répond, ainsi, à des objectifs politiques. Il s'agit, en effet, d'une enquête, d'un type particulier puisque ne portant que sur un ensemble de droits fonciers, dont on peut retracer toutes les étapes: sur ordre du roi, deux procureurs royaux (dont le précepteur de la maison templière de Perpignan, Jacques d'Ollers) se rendent dans sept localités pour y entendre des témoins venus avouer devant eux, par la prestation d'un serment, leurs tenures, un scribe prenant ne notes les dépositions. Dans cinq cas, le *capbreu* a conservé en frontispice une enluminure fixant le souvenir de cette démarche. La confection des *capbreus*, sur la base des témoignages recueillis dans un temps assez bref- entre quatre et cinq jours par localité-a été effectuée par un notaire selon un mode de classement sans doute fondé sur le regroupement par terroirs des déclarations. Le soin apporté à la réalisation des documents et au respect des normes de la diplomatique incite à penser que le revenu fiscal des droits avoués importe, au fond, sans doute moins que la reconnaissance et l'aveu de la seigneurie royale et la volonté de marquer une emprise forte aussi bien sur la terre que sur les hommes.

Le poids démographique des terroirs ruraux à la fin du XIIIe siècle

Les *capbreus* représentent une source exceptionnelle pour qui tente d'appréhender la démographie médiévale. Les seuls documents dont dispose le médiéviste, en l'absence de registres paroissiaux, sont, en effet, d'ordre fiscal et tardif. Compter les hommes, au Moyen Âge, revient à compter les foyers de contribuables, pratique devenue courante à partir du XIVe siècle. Les *capbreus* royaux, par leur nature même, permettent une sorte « d'instantané photographique », à un moment donné et sur un territoire géographique et de pouvoir précis, ce qu'aucune autre source n'autorise. Recensant des adultes, mâles le plus souvent, représentant des familles, ils offrent des données chiffrées qu'il convient de

[8] A titre d'exemple, on se réfèrera à la série des enquêtes provençales menées à l'instigation du souverain Robert Ier de Naples, dans les années 1330, par Leopardo da Foligno et éditées sous la direction de Thierry Pécout aux éditions du CTHS: Leopardo da Foligno, *L'Enquête générale*.

traiter à l'instar des chiffres fournis par les documents fiscaux: en particulier, le choix d'un coefficient multiplicateur s'impose, qui peut varier selon que l'on a affaire à un terroir rural ou à une communauté urbaine. En outre, il convient d'établir la proportion des ménages stériles ainsi que des personnes seules. Pour le Roussillon, une enquête réalisée en 1306 dans deux villages du Fenouillèdes permet d'établir d'utiles comparaisons: les villages d'Axat et Caramany, cédés au roi Philippe IV à cette date, furent, en effet l'objet d'un recensement de feux très précis dénombrant le nombre de personnes vivant par foyers. Ainsi, sur la base de ce document, on a pu établir un nombre moyen d'individus par feu, s'élevant à cing personnes, ainsi que la proportion des ménages ne comptant qu'une ou deux personnes, soit 10,5 pour cent du total des feux.

Un *capbreu* recèle, cependant aussi, un grand nombre de limites et les chiffres que l'on en retire doivent être interprétés avec d'infinies précautions.

Confectionner un *capbreu* nécessite, en effet, de faire appel à des techniciens du droit, de diligenter une enquête sur le terrain, confiée à des représentants employés du seigneur et du notaire, de percevoir la nécessité de fixer et rationaliser l'administration de sa seigneurie. Il s'agit d'une démarche qui s'inscrit pleinement dans la culture savante, et se révèle être au fondement même du pouvoir. L'entreprise du roi est la première du genre en Roussillon et le souverain se trouve suivi par bien peu de seigneurs. De fait, si le roi de Majorque semble bien être le principal maître des terres concernées, d'autres puissants apparaissent cependant, car possédant le domaine éminent sur des tenures confrontant celles du roi ou parce qu'entretenant un lien féodal avec le souverain, sans qu'aucun terrier n'ait été dressé pour leurs possessions. Le tableau exhaustif de la seigneurie de ces lieux ne peut, donc, être brossé de façon certaine. Le cas du village de Tautavel en offre un exemple éloquent: le *capbreu* du seigneur de Peyrestortes, non cité dans celui du roi pourtant antérieur d'une année seulement, permet d'ajouter à la liste des tenanciers de Jacques Ier et de leurs voisins une quinzaine de noms supplémentaires.

On a pu remarquer, également, lorsqu'un dénombrement de feux contemporain permet d'établir une comparaison, que le nombre de tenanciers cités dans les terriers était souvent supérieur à celui des feux. C'est que le *capbreu* offre une richesse onomastique qui peut s'avérer difficile à interpréter, lorsque la toponymie s'en mêle. Il n'est pas certain, ainsi, que tous les anthroponymes désignant une terre correspondent bien à une personne encore vivante au moment de la rédaction du terrier. Les données sont souvent précises, mais ne permettent pas toujours de saisir le passage du nom de personne au toponyme.

L'anthroponymie et son évolution depuis le XIe siècle fournit, cependant, quelques outils qui permettent d'affiner les données résultant d'un simple comptage. La pratique, en particulier, de faire suivre le nom complet du tenancier d'un nom de lieu permet d'écarter à coup sûr les personnes ne résidant pas sur place. Il s'agit là d'une forme d'identification des individus par le pouvoir seigneurial qui entend, dans un souci de bonne gestion, nommer clairement et précisément ses tenanciers par leur lieu de résidence. On retrouve ce même souci chez tous les seigneurs importants à la même période, comme le Temple par exemple.[9] La pratique courante ne retient, en revanche, sans doute pas cette forme de dénomination qui ne relève pas de l'identité personnelle.

Tableau 12.1. Etat démographique des villages.

Lieux	**Nombre d'actes**	**Tenanciers du roi**	**Ménages résidants estimés**
Clayra	30	29	49
Estagel	91	91	133
Millas	262	200	400
St-Laurent	160	165	238
Tautavel	84	62	97

Comme le montre le tableau ci-dessus, en chiffres bruts, les villages roussillonnais à la fin du XIIIe siècle apparaissent très densément peuplés: on compte ainsi environ 595 habitants à Estagel, 671 à Millas, 362 à Tautavel. Dans la plaine, les chiffres sont tout aussi élevés: il y aurait autour de 219 personnes à Clayra, plus de mille à Saint-Laurent. Il s'agit d'hypothèses très hautes qui trouvent cependant quelques comparaisons contemporaines: dans la plaine du bas Emporda, un peu plus au sud, les *capbreus* fournissent des chiffres, pour les années 1311–48, tout aussi impressionnants: 166 déclarants à Cruïlles, 206 à Sant Sadurni, 112 dans le Vall d'Aro.[10] En bas Languedoc, dans la Provence rhodanienne ainsi que sur les plateaux de haute Provence, il n'est pas rare, non plus, de trouver des villages comptant plus de 100 feux.[11] En Angleterre, en 1300, 251 familles vivent sur les terres dépendant du manoir de Holywell-cum-Needingworth.[12]

[9] Verdon, *La terre et les hommes en Roussillon*.

[10] Mallorqui Garcia, « Les campagnes de Gérone », p. 349.

[11] Baratier, *La démographie provençale*.

[12] Sur les archives des manoirs anglais dépendant de l'abbaye de Ramsey, voir les travaux de Raftis, *The Estate of Ramsey Abbey*, pp. 423–24.

Profil démographique des terroirs

Ces chiffres, tout relatifs soient-ils, traduisent-ils une situation de pression démographique? A-t-on affaire à des terroirs surpeuplés par rapport aux possibilités offertes par la mise en valeur des terres, selon la thèse défendue naguère par M. Postan?[13] Les *capbreus* invitent à dresser une sorte de profil démographique des terroirs concernés en donnant quelques aperçus sur les structures familiales et les mouvements migratoires, toujours grâce au recours à l'onomastique.

La taille des ménages ne peut être appréhendée de façon certaine en raison du caractère individuel des déclarations. Contrairement, en effet, aux autres types d'actes à la disposition de l'historien pour connaître une seigneurie, tels qu'actes de donations, ventes, ou baux emphytéotiques, le caractère inquisitorial de la démarche ici en oeuvre, impliquant prestation de serment et aveu, bannit toute déclaration collective, à quelques très rares exceptions près. On sait, cependant, par ailleurs qu'en Roussillon comme dans le reste de l'Europe domine au XIIIe siècle la famille nucléaire autonome, au sein de laquelle les deux époux apparaissent comme acteurs conjoints des actes d'aliénation du patrimoine.[14] Quelques actes issus des terriers présentent, cependant, des cas de « familles élargies » où plusieurs générations possèdent des biens en commun et semblent, parfois, cohabiter sous le même toit, comme le montre le tableau 12.2.

Tableau 12.2. Associations et frérèches.

Terroirs	**Nombre de déclarations**	**% des actes**
Clayra	2	6,66%
Estagel	30	32,97%
Millas	16	6,11%
St-Laurent	22	13,75%
Tautavel	10	11,90%

Ces associations peuvent grouper une belle-mère, ayant transmis un héritage immobilier à sa fille mariée, et son gendre, ou plus souvent un oncle déclar-

13 Postan, *The Medieval Economy and Society*.

14 Ainsi, 54 pour cent des actes d'aliénation d'un bien immobilier en faveur du Temple, entre XIIe et XIIIe siècle, sont le fait de couples, Verdon, *La terre et les hommes en Roussillon*.

ant tenir un bien avec son ou ses neveux dont on peut supposer qu'il a la tutelle.[15] Ces pratiques, liées aux modes successoraux qui ne distinguent pas en Roussillon, encore au XIIIe siècle, d'héritier privilégié, se rencontrent cependant principalement entre membres d'une même fratrie élargie.[16] Leur importance peut être accentuée par le poids de l'homonymie sur ces terroirs: autour de 50 pour cent des personnes portent, en effet, le même nom. Ainsi à Saint-Laurent, sur dix-sept actes concernant deux frères ayant des biens en commun, dans quatre cas, la résidence est assurément commune, dans cinq autres cas les tenures sont contiguës. Les frérèches, commautés de biens entre individus apparentés ou non, lorsqu'elles apparaissent à la fin du XIIIe siècle peuvent donc traduire une certaine pression démographique en permettant de protéger le patrimoine de l'émiettement par son maintien en indivis.[17] Les *capbreus* roussillonnais présentent, on le voit, ce type de cas où un individu va s'associer à un ou plusieurs autres pour, soit maintenir l'intégrité d'un héritage, soit garantir une cohésion territoriale à un patrimoine, en prenant en tenure des terres contiguës à celles d'un membre de sa famille. C'est le cas, notamment à Estagel (quatre cas) et Saint-Laurent (cinq cas). Dans ce dernier exemple en outre, la totalité des frérèches rencontrées dans le terrier (soit dix-sept déclarations) associe des membres d'une même fratrie.

Le remembrement lignager, dont on peut observer les prémices dès la fin du XIIIe siècle, peut également avoir pour origine une forte mortalité. Ici encore, les *capbreus* ne peuvent fournir de données précises mais quelques indices seulement quant au régime démographique. Ainsi, entre 3 pour cent et 9,3 pour cent des actes, selon les terroirs, émanent de veufs formant foyer fiscal. Les femmes déclarant tenir seules un bien sont également très présentes (entre 7 pour cent et 15 pour cent des actes). Ces données doivent être cependant nuancées: elles sont liées, elles aussi, aux pratiques successorales régionales qui permettent aux femmes d'accéder à un héritage immobilier par la voie maternelle et en cas d'absence d'héritier mâle. L'importance des biens paraphernaux explique, ainsi, la présence des femmes, même mariées, parmi les déclarants individualisés du roi.

[15] N°12 Estagel; n°152 Millas; n°57 Tautavel.

[16] Ce peuvent être des frères: n°127 Saint-Laurent, trois frères et deux sœurs déclarent conjointement une mansate héritée de leur père mort intestat, ou des cousins ; n°46 Tautavel, Thomas Padern et Pierre Padern, cousins, déclarent tenir avec Bernard Padern fils de Jean, une mansate que possédait déjà le père de Thomas. Ce type d'association, portant sur une mansate, est directement lié au régime juridique du manse qui ne permet l'héritage qu'en ligne verticale.

[17] Elles sont nommées dans les terriers associations *pro indiviso* ou parsonneries à Tautavel uniquement.

Les mouvements migratoires sont, quant à eux, encore plus difficiles à cerner. On ne peut disposer, en l'occurrence, que des seules données de l'onomastique en noms de lieu malheureusement peu attestée dans nos terriers. Néanmoins ces éléments, exposés dans le tableau ci-dessous, permettent de faire plusieurs constatations:

- il ne semble pas y avoir eu d'exode vers les villes, proches (Perpignan) ou plus lointaines (Argelès, Collioures). Les terroirs ruraux, à supposer qu'ils soient en situation de surpeuplement, ne rééquilibrent pas leur poids démographique par ce biais;
- entre 6 pour cent et 10 pour cent des résidants sur un terroir donné portent un anthroponyme en nom de lieu identifiable. Il s'agit généralement de territoires limitrophes, chaque localité semblant avoir un rayonnement maximum de 15 à 20 km. alentour, à l'exception de Millas, véritable petit bourg dont les habitants peuvent venir d'au-delà de cette limite, des Corbères, du Vallespir et surtout du Fenouillèdes. On assiste donc plutôt à une sorte de rééquilibrage de terroirs limitrophes qu'à des mouvements migratoires de grande ampleur.

Tableau 12.3. Origines géographiques des habitants des villages.

Localité	**Nombre de personnes**	**Lieux d'origine**	**% des actes**
Clayra	4	Ponteilla; St-Laurent; St-Hippolyte; Mudagons	8,3%
Estagel	10	Cassagnes; Millas; Vingrau	10,2%
Millas	26	Clayra; Néfiach; Castelnou St-Féliu; Montner; Montalban; Tautavel; St-Martin; Corneilla, Vernet; Caramany; Garrieux; Capestang; Ceret Montferrer	6,5%
St-Laurent	5	Montner; Néfiach; Toreilles	2,1%
Tautavel	6	Montner; Toreilles,Vernet; Vingrau; Oms	6,1%

Pression démographique, organisation des territoires et structures de prélèvement

Les associations *pro indiviso* rencontrées dans nos terriers ne révèlent pas toutes une stratégie liée au maintien d'un héritage. A Estagel, ainsi, on s'aperçoit que sur les vingt-six actes faisant état d'une association ne concernant pas deux membres d'une même famille, dix-neuf sont relatifs à la tenue de terres appartenant à une cabane, une borde ou une mansate. Dans tous les cas, en outre, les tenures de chacun des protagonistes sont, en partie ou en totalité, contiguës. Il s'agit donc d'associations groupant des voisins et qui n'ont pas pour objectif de permettre une entraide économique, mais bien plutôt de dégager une élite de tenanciers, ceux qui constituent les tenanciers de manses. Certains multiplient même les associations, opérant une véritable stratégie patrimoniale: ainsi de Raimond Amalric d'Estagel que l'on retrouve dans trois associations différentes, pour un total de six terres, dont deux relèvent d'une borde et trois autres d'une cabane. Ces stratégies de groupement sont également le fruit des modes particuliers de succession sur les mansates, dont on ne peut hériter qu'en ligne verticale, ce qui peut entraîner une obligation fiscale de frérèche.

Tableau 12.4. Les manses.

Terroirs	**Nombre de manses et fractions**
St-Laurent	14+8 demi + 2 tiers + 2 quarts + 2 sixièmes
Millas	17+5 demi + 4 tiers
Estagel	3+16 demi +1 tiers + 8 quarts + 7 huitièmes + 4 sixièmes
Tautavel	4 demi + 3 tiers

Les manses, mansates ou bordes de nos terriers correspondent à des structures de prélèvement fiscal, foncier et banal, et non à une forme de peuplement. Leur composition le montre clairement, associant une ou plusieurs maisons dans la *villa* à des terres pouvant se trouver dispersées sur différents territoires, tels les manses d'Estagel dont certains incluent des terres à Tautavel et surtout ceux de Saint-Laurent pour lesquels sur trente-quatres manses cités, treize comprennent des terres à Toreilles, Saint-Hippolyte, Jugnèges, et Salses.

En Vieille Catalogne, le manse apparaît tardivement: Lluis To Figueras place l'époque de sa genèse et de sa diffusion entre la fin du XIe siècle et le début du XIIIe siècle; Pierre Bonnassie fait remarquer que ce terme apparaît dans certains secteurs seulement au début du XIIe siècle.[18] Aucun élément de notre documentation ne nous permet de saisir directement la genèse du manse roussillonnais, à l'exception du mode de dénomination de ces cellules, fondé sur un nom de personne souvent identifiable, ainsi que sur leur composition, dans certains lieux, où ils apparaissent très homogènes et comprenant encore des alleux. Le régime juridique du manse implique, en effet, que toute parcelle achetée par le tenancier soit intégrée à la structure. La présence d'alleux indique, ainsi, indirectement le

[18] Joan Vilà Valenti fait, a contrario, remonter les origines du manse en Catalogne au VIe siècle, Vilà Valenti, « El mas catalan ».

dynamisme du marché de la terre dans la région. En tant que cellule seigneuriale, le manse est soumis au paiement d'un cens général. Ce cens se compose d'une combinaison de taxes, redevances en numéraire, cens en vin et céréales, oeufs, poules ou oies, fouasses, et *pernas*, c'est à dire quartiers de porc. Les combinaisons, et donc le poids du cens général, peuvent varier en fonction des mesures utilisées mais comportent toujours une grande partie de ces éléments qui viennent s'ajouter à l'albergue, aux corvées éventuelles ainsi qu'aux taxes perçues singulièrement sur chacun des bâtiments et parcelles qui composent le manse.

Comme le suggère le tableau ci-dessus, la diversité des cens, des superficies pose la question de savoir si l'on est en train d'assister, à la fin du XIIIe siècle, à un phénomène de fractionnement du manse opéré sous la pression démographique? Si l'on peut pencher pour la solution du fractionnement, force est cependant de constater que le processus n'est pas entamé de façon égale partout: A Saint-Laurent, sur les trente-quatre actes mentionnant des mansates, seuls douze portent trace de fractionnement, allant de la moitié au sixième. Sur les quarante et un manses cités dans le terrier d'Estagel, en revanche, seuls deux bordes et une cabane ne sont pas divisées. L'ensemble des autres se trouve tenu par fraction, allant de la moitié au huitième. Certains de ces manses, fractionnés, peuvent d'ailleurs être entièrement reconstitués, chaque « morceau » se trouvant tenu par un habitant d'Estagel. C'est le cas pour cinq d'entre eux. Cependant, pour la majorité, le processus est déjà plus entamé et correspond à une parcellisation : entre la huitième partie et la moitié de ce qui fut autrefois un manse entier se sont entièrement transformées en parcelles. Ainsi trente pièces de terre tenues isolément sont issues de manses, vingt-huit maisons, neuf jardins, cinq vignes.[19] Ces fractions se traduisent par un morcellement du cens général, proportionnel à la portion tenue.

À Millas, en revanche, les mentions de fractionnement de manses sont déjà plus rares: sur un total de vingt-six manses cités, on compte cinq demies mansates ou bordes et quatre tiers. Le processus y est cependant doute plus avancé, les cens perçus sur ces portions de manses n'étant pas exprimés par une fraction d'un cens général, comme à Estagel, mais par une combinaison de mesures: les fractions de manses sont en passe de devenir des structures à part entière. Enfin lorsque le manse ou la fraction a juridiquement totalement disparu, c'est à dire lorsque l'on ne prend plus la peine de le mentionner, le cens précédemment dû peut néanmoins encore subsister. C'est le cas à Tautavel, où un certain nombre de tenanciers du roi sont soumis à des combinaisons de redevances qui viennent

[19] On trouve des exemples de terres détachées de manses également dans le *Cartulaire du Mas Déu*: fols146, 228, dans D'Albon, *Cartulaire général*, XXVII, 384; XXX, 396.

s'ajouter aux taxes perçues sur les parcelles: ainsi Bernard Catalan tient pour le roi de Majorque une maison située dans le *castrum*, trois champs, quatre pièces de terre et une vigne, tous soumis à redevance. Il doit en outre s'acquitter annuellement, à titre de cens, d'un septième de quarton d'orge, une demie quartère d'orge, une puyère de froment, sept deniers, une *perna*, un quarton et demi de vin, un oeuf et une demie fouasse ou une demie poule.[20] Par ailleurs, le terrier de Tautavel comprend sept actes faisant état de fractions de manses, entre la moitié et un quart.

Le fractionnement du manse peut donner lieu à contestations et permettre, ainsi, d'avancer quelques hypothèses quant au rapport à établir entre démographie et structures de prélèvement. Prenons l'exemple du manse dit de Malleolus Cucumer à Malloles: au début du XIIIe siècle les tenures constituant ce manse furent données au Temple lequel en céda à accapte une partie au descendant de Malleolus Cucumer, Guillaume.[21] Le reste du manse fit l'objet d'une contestation en justice en 1209, le tenancier, Pierre Guolas, prétendant que les sept vignes et le jardin qu'il tenait n'appartenaient pas au manse de Malleolus Cucumer qui, disait-il, possédait un autre manse dans la *villa* de Malloles. Le Temple, affirmait-t-il, ne pouvait, de ce fait, percevoir de droits sur ces terres.[22] Cet exemple nous permet de souligner un fait important: le manse, encore au début du XIIIe siècle, est perçu comme un district dont les limites ne sont pas concrètes mais fixées par la mémoire collective. Le Temple produit ainsi huit témoins qui affirment que les terres en litige « essent ex tenedoribus dicti mansi qui mansus erat Estefanie Cucumere set ideo Malleoli vocabatur quod Malleolus ibi moraretur ».[23] Pierre Guolas en produit trois autres pour affirmer que Malleolus Cucumer possédait un autre manse. Les raisons du fractionnement des manses peuvent donc, en partie, être liées à la délimitation des territoires juridictionnels opérée dans le courant du XIIIe siècle. On trouve ainsi trace, dans la documentation roussillonnaise, de conflits portant sur la délimitation des territoires castraux à la fin du XIIIe siècle, de la restructuration du territoire de certains villages, comme à Tautavel où la *cellera* située au pied du château s'est déplacée dans le courant du XIIIe siècle, ou encore à Néfiach dont le territoire apparaît véritablement structuré au XVe siècle mais en voie de constitution seulement au début du XIIIe siècle. Il faut lier ici ce fait à un phénomène relativement courant dans nos terriers qui consiste à déclarer tenir pour le roi

[20] Tautavel n° 38.

[21] *Cartulaire du Mas Déu*, fol. 2[r] (fol. 235[r]).

[22] *Cartulaire du Mas Déu*, fol. 218[r].

[23] *Cartulaire du Mas Déu*, fol. 218[r].

une terre relevant d'un autre terroir: c'est le cas, notamment à Estagel où cinquante-neuf déclarants tiennent à Tautavel et à Millas et seize autres à Néfiach. À Millas toujours, neuf déclarants habitent à Néfiach, huit à Montner, cinq à Saint-Féliu, cinq à Corneilla, sept à Caladroer et deux à Ille sur Têt; à Saint-Laurent, si cinq déclarants tiennent des terres à Toreilles, six autres relèvent de cette communauté, cinq sont de Saint-Hippolyte et deux de Perpignan; enfin à Tautavel, aucun déclarant ne tient de terre en dehors du territoire, mais dix-huit habitent à Vingrau et cinq à Paziols. Les tenures relevant d'un autre territoire peuvent être des terres récemment défrichées aux marges, gagnées sur la garrigue, comme à Estagel, ou sur l'étang à Saint-Laurent par exemple. Elles traduisent également la définition plus précise des juridictions seigneuriales, comme à Saint-Laurent, où les terres appartenant à des mansates et situées en dehors du territoire sont soit des achats récents soit relèvent d'un autre seigneur. On perçoit également la mise en place des paroisses: à Saint-Laurent, toujours, les terres situées à Jugnèges sont sises dans la paroisse Sainte-Marie.

Surtout, l'évolution des structures fiscales des manses s'accompagne d'une utilisation par leurs tenanciers de toutes les ressources juridiques offertes par le bail emphythéotique. En Catalogne, l'acapte permet en effet, de façon implicite le plus souvent, la sous-location de la tenure. Par ce biais, les éléments constituant une mansate peuvent se trouver disjoints, même si officiellement un seul tenancier apparaît en tant que déclarant. C'est le cas, notamment à Saint-Laurent, où huit mansates se trouvent ainsi en partie sous-louées. Or, les éléments concernés sont des maisons, en très grande majorité et des jardins.[24] Nous tenons sans doute là le seul indice fiable de pression démographique.

Les chiffres fournis par les *capbreus* sont, incontestablement, à manier avec précaution, et ne peuvent à eux seuls fonder avec certitude une situation de plein démographique. Ce que révèlent, cependant, les terriers ce sont les stratégies déployées par les tenanciers et les seigneurs pour y remédier et s'adapter à la conjoncture, par défrichements de terres aux limites du territoire, fractionnement des structures de prélèvement et adaptation des cadres juridictionnels de la seigneurie. L'utilisation faite des possibilités juridiques offertes par l'accapte, notamment la sous-location et l'association *pro indiviso*, ne doit donc pas être uniquement interprétée en termes de difficultés économiques mais révèle, bien plus, la mise en place d'une élite sociale constituée par les tenanciers de manses, souvent proches du seigneur par ailleurs.[25]

[24] Vingt-sept au total, cens entre 2s. 8d. et 1d.; en moyenne 12d.

[25] Verdon, *La terre et les hommes en Roussillon.*

Bibliographie

Archives

Cartulaire du Masdéu: Archives Départementales des Pyrénées Orientales, série 1B, Fonds de la Procuration royale

Capbreus du roi de Majorque: Archives Départementales des Pyrénées Orientales, série 1B

Sources imprimées

D'Albon, André, *Cartulaire général de l'ordre du Temple* (Paris: Champion, 1913)

Leopardo da Foligno, *L'Enquête générale de Leopardo da Foligno en Provence orientale (avril–juin 1333)*, dir. par Thierry Pécout, éd. par Germain Butaud, Marc Bouiron, Philippe Jansen, et Alain Venturini, Editions du CTHS, 45 (Paris: CTHS, 2008)

Tréton, Rodrigue, « Recueil des chartes de la maison du Temple du Masdéu en Roussillon (1001–1329): Etude et édition », 5 vols (thèse de doctorat inédite, Université de Paris I Panthéon-Sorbonne, 2007)

Tréton, Rodrigue, Aymat Catafau, et Laure Verdon, *Les capbreus du roi Jacques II de Majorque (1292–1294)*, 2 vols (Paris: CTHS, 2011)

Sources secondaires

Alfonso, Isabel, éd., *The Rural History of Medieval European Societies: Trends and Perspectives* (Turnhout: Brepols, 2007)

Baratier, Édouard, *La démographie provençale du XIIIe au XVIe siècle avec chiffres de comparaison pour le XVIIIe siècle* (Paris: SEVPEN, 1961)

Baraut, Cébrià, « Béns i censos dels Templers al Rossello, Vallespir, Conflent i Fenolledès segons un capbreu de l'any 1264 », dans *Etudes roussillonnaises offertes à Pierre Ponsich*, réunis et édités par Marie Grau et Olivier Poisson (Perpignan : Le Publicateur, 1987), pp. 175–80

Bourin, Monique, et Vincent Challet, « Temps, lieux et supplices: Les mémoires paysannes à l'épreuve de l'enquête (Vendres, fin du XIIIe siècle) », *Annales du Midi*, 282 (2013), 239–62

Brunel, Ghislain, et autres, éds, *Terriers et plans-terriers du XIIIe au XVIIIe siècle: Actes du colloque de Paris 23–25 septembre 1998*, Mémoires et Documents de l'École des Chartes, 62 (Paris: Association d'Histoire des Etudes Rurales, École Nationale des Chartes, 2002)

Catafau, Aymat, *Les celleres et la naissance du village en Roussillon (X^e–XVe siècles)* (Perpignan: Trabucaïre, 1998)

Comalada, Michèle, « Tautavel au XIIIe siècle d'après le capbreu de 1292 » (Diplôme d'Etudes Supérieures inédit, Faculté des Lettres d'Aix en provence, 1965)

Cursente, Benoît, « Recent Trends in the Rural History of Medieval France », dans *The Rural History of Medieval European Societies: Trends and Perspectives*, éd. par Isabel Alfonso (Turnhout: Brepols, 2007), pp. 57–92

Cursente, Benoît, et Mireille Mousnier, éds, *Les territoires du médiéviste* (Rennes: Presses Universitaires de Rennes, 2006)

de Cortàzar, Garcia, José Angel, et Pascual Martinez Sopena, « The Historiography of Medieval Society in Rural Spain », dans *The Rural History of Medieval European Societies: Trends and Perspectives*, éd. par Isabel Alfonso (Turnhout: Brepols, 2007), pp. 93–140

Falques, Marie-Ange, « La société rurale roussillonnaise au XIVe siècle d'après l'exemple de Clayra » (mémoire de maîtrise inédit, Université de Toulouse le Mirail, 1972)

Freedman, Paul, « Servitude in Roussillon », *Mélanges de l'Ecole française de Rome*, 112 (2000), 867–82

Galian, Marie-Blanche, « Saint-Laurent de la Salanque, un domaine des rois de Majorque au XIIIe siècle » (mémoire de maîtrise inédit, Université de Montpellier, 1973)

Gigot, Jean-Gabriel, « Le capbreu d'Argelès sur mer (1292) et ses enseignements », *CERCA*, 3 (1959), 32–63

——, « Le capbreu de Collioure (1292) et ses enseignements », *CERCA*, 5 (1959), 206–33

Hélias, Jean-Claude, « Le vocabulaire de Georges Duby dans *l'Economie rurale et la vie des campagnes dans l'Occident médiéval* », dans *Les territoires du médiéviste* éd. par Benoît Cursente et Mireille Mousnier (Rennes: Presses Universitaires de Rennes, 2006), pp. 45–70

Juventin, Guy, « Millas et le capbreu royal de 1294 » (mémoire de maîtrise inédit, Université de Montpellier, 1969)

Larguier, Gilbert, « Capbreus de Catalogne du nord (province du Roussillon) aux XVe–XVIIIe siècles », dans *Terriers et plans-terriers du XIIIe au XVIIIe siècle: Actes du colloque de Paris 23–25 septembre 1998*, éd. par Ghislain Brunel et others, Mémoires et Documents de l'École des Chartes, 62 (Paris: Association d'Histoire des Etudes Rurales, École Nationale des Chartes, 2002), pp. 67–78

Maillard, François, et Robert-Henri Bautier, « Un dénombrement des feux, des individus et des fortunes dans deux villages des Fenouillèdes en 1306 », *Bulletin philologique et historique du CTH, Congrès 1965*, 1965, 309–28

Mallorqui Garcia, Elvis, « Les campagnes de Gérone au travers des capbreus de la première moitié du XIVe siècle », dans *Terriers et plans-terriers du XIIIe au XVIIIe siècle: Actes du colloque de Paris 23–25 septembre 1998*, éd. par Ghislain Brunel et autres, Mémoires et Documents de l'École des Chartes, 62 (Paris: Association d'Histoire des Etudes Rurales, École Nationale des Chartes, 2002), pp. 346–49

Menant, François, et Jean-Pierre Jessenne, éds, *Les élites rurales dans l'Europe médiévale et moderne: Actes des XXVIIe journées internationales d'histoire de l'abbaye de Flaran* (Toulouse: Presses universitaires de Toulouse-le-Mirail, 2007)

Postan, Michael M., *The Medieval Economy and Society: An Economic History of Britain 1100–1500* (London: Weidenfeld and Nicolson, 1972)

Provero, Luigi, « Forty Years of Rural History for the Italian Middle Ages », dans *The Rural History of Medieval European Societies: Trends and Perspectives*, éd. par Isabel Alfonso (Turnhout: Brepols, 2007), pp. 141–72

Puig, Carole, « Les capbreus du roi de Majorque, 1292–1294 », dans *De l'estime au cadastre en Europe: Le Moyen Âge*, éd. par Albert Rigaudière (Paris: Comité pour l'histoire économique et financière, 2007), pp. 437–56

Raftis, J. Ambrose, *The Estate of Ramsey Abbey: A Study in Economic Growth and Organization* (Toronto: Pontifical Institute of Mediaeval Studies, 1957)

Reynal, Jean, « Le capbreu de Millars » (thèse de 3° cycle inédite, EHESS et Université de Paris I, 1980)

Sanchez Martinez, Manuel, *Estudios sobre rentas, fiscalidad y finanzas en la Cataluna bajomedieval* (Barcelona: Consejo Superior de Investigationes Cientificas, 1993)

To Figueras, Lluis, « Le mas catalan du XIIe siècle: Genèse et évolution d'une structure d'encadrement et d'asservissement de la paysannerie », *Cahiers de civilisation médiévale*, 36 (1993), 151–77

Verdon, Laure, *La terre et les hommes en Roussillon aux XIIe et XIIIe siècles: Structures seigneuriales, rente et société d'après les sources templières* (Aix en Provence: Université de Provence, 2001)

——, « Le territoire avoué: Usages et implcations de l'enquête dans la définition et la délimitation du territoire seigneurial en Catalogne et en Provence au XIIIe siècle », dans *Les territoires du médiéviste*, éd. par Benoît Cursente et Mireille Mousnier (Rennes: Presses Universitaires de Rennes, 2005), pp. 207–21

——, *La voix des dominés: Communautés et seigneurie en Provence au bas Moyen Âge* (Rennes: Presses Universitaires de Rennes, 2012)

Vilà Valenti, Joan, « El mas catalan; una creacion prepirenaica », dans *Acta del Tercer Congreso Internacional de Estudios Pirenaicos* (Sarragosse: Consejo Superior de Investigaciones Científicas, 1962), pp. 57–58

Cistercian Agriculture in Female Houses of Northern France, 1200–1300

Constance H. Berman*

The description by Michael Postan and Georges Duby of economic crisis in the later Middle Ages is flawed by the use of standard narrative sources from that past which privilege the viewpoints of the 'establishment': monks, abbots, bishops, nobles, and kings.[1] Their complaints about hard economic times dominate the narrative and have led historians to assume that all of society was in crisis. Postan and Duby and those who followed them confirmed the validity of these complaints using fiscal and administrative accounts even though these sources tended to be those produced by that very same clerical and royal establishment.[2] Recent studies suggest that such sources may not tell the whole story and that the tale of woes coming from that clerical establishment may not be the only possible evidence for the late medieval economy. We should add information from other sources, including those created by religious women. The alternative sources produced fewer narrative records, but

* This work received support from the National Endowment for the Humanities and the University of Iowa.

[1] Duby, *Rural Economy*, trans. by Postan; Duby, *The Early Growth of the European Economy*; Postan, *The Medieval Economy and Society*.

[2] Bois, *Crise du féodalisme*; on narratives constructed for noble self-preservation, see Spiegel, *Romancing the Past*, esp. chap. 5. On the administrative sources consulted by Duby for *Rural Economy*, see, for example, p. 151 which does cite the very unusual accounts for Maubuisson, discussed in note 24 below, but as evidence of record-keeping by the Cistercian Order, not as evidence of women's or nuns' record-keeping.

Constance H. Berman (constance-berman@uiowa.edu) is professor of medieval history at the University of Iowa and an authority on the history of the Cistercian Order.

Crisis in the Later Middle Ages: Beyond the Postan-Duby Paradigm, ed. by John Drendel, TMC 13 (Turnhout: Brepols, 2015) 339–363 BREPOLS PUBLISHERS 10.1484/M.TMC.5.103794

their charters and accounts suggest a different reality. Historians neglected the records of nuns in particular because these women left us few narrative records about their acquisition of wealth. None, for instance, produced a series of biographies or *vitae* of successive abbesses.

Sources produced by religious houses for women established in the late twelfth and thirteenth centuries suggest that complaints about poor yields, high prices, rebellious tenants, and crowds of the poor showing up at the gates of monastic houses may reflect more the concerns of a particular segment of society — which was indeed suffering an unsettling readjustment in economic realities — than the experiences of all parts of the late medieval world. We need not doubt that these older groups were under the considerable stress of an increased gap between income and expenditures. But need we allow the discourse of embattled elites to influence unduly our picture of their times? Is it possible that complaints of sagging returns and declining revenues document a decline specific to their particular economic sector, indeed all the more galling because they are not part of a total decline in the economy?

Until recently, the voices of religious women of the Middle Ages remained unheard in any discussion of the trends of medieval economic history. Historians assumed that communities of religious women declined constantly because they were small, poor, ill managed, and unlikely to produce records. Thus the relatively abundant archives those women produced have rarely been looked at or published.[3] There were many new houses of religious women in the later Middle Ages; not just beguinages (as the *Frauenfrage* question would have us believe), but houses of cloistered nuns as well, many of them belonging to the Cistercian Order.[4] A systematic survey of such records reveals that wealth

[3] Such tendencies to see religious women as peripheral are rife; see, for example, Lawrence, *Medieval Monasticism* where women are still marginalized. Recent correctives include Johnson, *Equal in Monastic Profession*; Oliva, *The Convent and the Community*; Venarde, *Women's Monasticism*; Berman, 'Abbeys for Cistercian Nuns'.

[4] On the *Frauenfrage*, see Grundmann, *Religious Movements in the Middle Ages*. A discourse within Cistercian history which denied the presence or the importance of these women's houses, along with the very real denial of women's needs by many mendicant leaders, has contributed to assumptions that there were few women's houses in the later Middle Ages; see Leclercq, 'Monachesimo femminile', pp. 63–99, which stresses how few houses of mendicant nuns there were. On how women fit into the Cistercian movement, see Berman, *The Cistercian Evolution*; Berman, *Women and Monasticism in Medieval Europe*; Evergates, 'Aristocratic Women', pp. 84–85 and pp. 104–05 where he discusses the numbers of religious women in thirteenth-century Champagne; Barrière and others, *Cîteaux et les femmes*; Jordan, 'Patronage, Prayers and Polders'.

was being conveyed to religious women.[5] Some houses of religious women, such as that at Coyroux, may have embraced the life of poverty avidly and fulfilled their duties of Christian charity so well that they remained poor.[6] But the wealth of many houses of religious women increased in the later Middle Ages, including all three houses for Cistercian nuns founded in the vicinity of Paris that I discuss here.

These Cistercian sisters not only benefitted from the largess of early thirteenth-century founders and patrons, but also actively managed their wealth themselves. They created their own endowments by consolidating land into manageable estates, and through huge investments they acquired already established fields and *villas*. Some land also came to the nuns through the hands of an increasingly powerful bourgeoisie that was building up estates in the countryside.[7] A fraction of the wealth in lands and revenues coming to those nuns in the thirteenth century also came to them as a result of clearance and reclamation, carried out either under their own direction or by the immediately preceding owners, who, as both donors and vendors, transferred new land or rents in Normandy to them.[8] The record for northern France in the later Middle Ages does not suggest an overall decline in wealth, despite the destruction of buildings and vineyards and the flight of peasants during the Hundred Years War, but rather dramatic shifts in who owned that wealth.[9]

The wealth of these nuns contradicts conclusions about an economic crisis in the late Middle Ages. Evidence from their archives confirms the presence of an economic crisis among the feudal nobility and the transfer of property

[5] Early work based on assumptions of nuns' poverty, including my own, attributed the good record-keeping by nuns to their need to keep track of every shilling, but many houses were quite wealthy as it turns out, so some of the generalizations are wrong in Berman, 'The Economic Practices'.

[6] Barrière, 'The Cistercian Monastery'; Oliva, *The Convent and the Community*, passim.

[7] See for instance, Paris, Arch. Nat., S*4376, fols 22^v seq., for acquisitions by Saint-Antoine at Montreuil, south-east of the city.

[8] Dutilleux and Depoin, *L'abbaye de Maubuisson*, where no. 167 (1239) refers to it as 'Abbacie quam karissima domina nostra Blancha, Francorum regina illustris, juxta Pontisaram edificare incepit', and no. 244 (1245), 'Ludovicus Dei gratia Francorum rex. Noverint universi presentes pariter et futuri quod Nos abbatie monialium Beate Marie Regalis juxta Pontisaram, quam fundavit karissima mater nostra Blancha, illustris Francorum regina, damus et concedimus in puram et perpetuam elemosinam pro anima nostra'. The abbey may have been sited on land belonging to the Premonstratensians; see further discussion in Berman, *The White Nuns*.

[9] Denifle, *Les désolations des églises*; Fossier, *La terre et les hommes*; Fourquin, *Les campagnes de la région parisienne*.

away from elite male religious establishments into the hands of new communities like the Cistercian nunneries, for land received by these women came from older 'establishments': male monastic and clerical institutions, the royal domain, and an impoverished nobility.[10] Given the scale of such transfers of wealth to communities of women, we may ask if resistance to the continued participation of women in the Cistercian Order by thirteenth-century abbots, although couched in terms of the difficulties of providing adequate *cura monialium*, may have been the result of a threat to their own property.[11]

I concentrate here on the archives from three wealthy houses of Cistercian nuns who accumulated granges and seigneuries in the vicinity of Paris. Two of these houses, Port-Royal (Porrois) and Saint-Antoine-des-Champs outside the walls of Paris, were founded in the first decade of the thirteenth century with support from noble families and bishops. The dowager Queen Blanche of Castile founded a third at Maubuisson in the late 1230s; she built its monastic complex and endowed it.[12] All three houses of Cistercian nuns became wealthy and powerful, and their granges from an early date clearly provided sufficient produce to feed their relatively large communities.[13] Markets in Paris must have received considerable amounts of grain, wine, meat, and cheese produced by

[10] Older communities of Cistercian monks had failures of recruitment, if not losses of property, during the later medieval centuries. On the lay-brother crisis, see Donnelly, *The Decline of the Medieval Cistercian Laybrotherhood*; for southern France, Berman, *Medieval Agriculture*, esp. pp. 54–60. If the records for older religious communities do not reveal so clearly the accumulation of wealth in the countryside by the bourgeoisie, it may be because they were no longer producing the numbers of charters which are found for these new communities of religious women; on competition among monasteries, see Ekelund and others, *Sacred Trust*.

[11] Women founders of new houses of nuns, like Queen Blanche of Castile, or her cousins, the sisters Jeanne and Marguerite of Flanders, and Isabelle of Chartres, or the slightly older Blanche of Navarre, countess of Champagne, had considerable local political and economic clout. On requests to the General Chapter from powerful women, see Canivez, *Statuta capitulorum generalium*, for instance, II, years 1221, no. 48, 1224, no. 20, 1227, no. 12, 1236, no. 12, 1238, no. 11, etc. On the attitude of the thirteenth-century General Chapter towards such women's foundations, see de Pontenay Fontette, *Les religieuses à l'âge classique du droit canon*; Degler-Spengler, 'The Incorporation of Cistercian Nuns', but also my discussion in Berman, 'Were There Twelfth-Century Cistercian Nuns?'.

[12] Dutilleux and Depoin, *L'abbaye de Maubuisson*, no. 300 (1239), on her use of dower rights, which were inextricably mixed with her dowry rights.

[13] On size, see Dutilleux and Depoin, *L'abbaye de Maubuisson*, no. 34 (1267), a maximum of 140, and no. 35 (1268), reducing that to 120; for Port-Royal, see de Dion, *Cartulaire de Port-Royal*, no. 144 (1233), which limited that house to sixty. Berman, 'How Much Space Did Medieval Nuns Have?'; I have found no numbers for Saint-Antoine.

those nuns, and we know that they owned property in the vicinity of the great medieval market at Les Halles, from which they could have sold surpluses.[14]

Who founded these new houses of Cistercian women and whom did they recruit? Matilda of Garlande founded Port-Royal with fifteen livres of rents. The rents were intended to benefit the soul of her husband Matthew, lord of Marly, a cadet member of the Montmorency family, who in 1204 was about to depart on Crusade. Matthew died in 1205 before he could fulfill his Crusader vow, and his widow used the revenues to found a house of Cistercian nuns at Port-Royal-les-Champs west of Paris.[15] Gifts for Port-Royal began to flow in 1207 or so, and by 1215 a house of Cistercian nuns had been established in the Chevreuse valley south of Paris.[16] From this rural Port-Royal originated the well-known community of the early modern period in Paris, although from an early date the sisters owned property in the city as well as those in outlying regions.

The abbey of Saint-Antoine was located much closer to Paris itself and had early ties to both local nobles and wealthy burgers.[17] Jacques de Vitry tells us in his *Historia Occidentalis* that this community arose at the very end of the twelfth century just outside the eastern gates of Paris as a result of preaching by Fulk of Neuilly.[18] A charter from 1206 reveals that Saint-Antoine began as a community of both men and women at an existing chapel; it was incorporated into the Cistercian Order between 1204 and 1208.[19] Donors endowed the house with its initial properties and granges, but the nuns of Saint-Antoine soon began consolidating these holdings with purchases. Their earliest patrons were untitled nobles from the region around Paris with close ties to royal administration, including the Montmorency, Montfort, and Mauvoisin; all these families found social advancement in service to the King and in particular in the campaign 'to fight the Albigensian heretics' in the Midi.[20] The widows

[14] Paris, Arch. Nat., LL1595, fols 87^{r}–90^{r}; de Dion, *Cartulaire de Port-Royal*, no. 42 (1219–20), was that abbey's house at Les Halles.

[15] de Dion, *Cartulaire de Port-Royal*, nos 1–4.

[16] de Dion, *Cartulaire de Port-Royal*, nos 42 (1219–20), 51 (1220), 286 and 287 (1262).

[17] See Paris, Arch. Nat., LL1595 and Paris, Arch. Nat., S*4386; Berman, 'Dowries, Private Income'; Berman, 'Cistercian Nuns and the Development of the Order'; Berman, 'Les acquisitions rurales'.

[18] Hinnebusch, *The Historia Occidentalis*, pp. 99–100.

[19] Paris, Arch. Nat., H5 3859–1 (1206) records the gift of 100 solidi in rents by Agnes of Cressonessart to the 'infirmarie sancti antonii parisiensis', granting to 'tam fratrem quam sororem'.

[20] Paris, Arch. Nat., S*4386, fols 3^{v}–4^{v}, of rights at Aulnay purchased for and given

and daughters of these nobles were soon joined at Saint-Antoine by the daughters from families who found wealth as Parisian artisans and merchants or acted as servants in the King's household.[21] The community also cared for the female relatives of Parisian university clerics who granted bequests to Saint-Antoine's nuns for that purpose, as well as for their prayers.[22]

The Queen of France, Blanche of Castile, provided the initial endowment for the third house of Cistercian nuns discussed here, Maubuisson, after a house for monks at Royaumont had been founded for the soul of her late husband, Louis VIII, by Louis IX with her assistance.[23] She began arrangements for founding a house of Cistercian nuns at Pontoise in 1236, although at least part of the site seems to have been in the hands of the Premonstratensian canons until 1241, when the abbot of Joyenval ceded his claims to these properties to the new community of nuns.[24] Blanche purchased many of the lands in the

to the nuns by Lady Agnes of Cressonessart in 1208, 'so that anniversary masses be said for her soul and that of her two late husbands'. She retained usufruct for life of half of her gift, but may have entered the abbey; she appears to have been buried there and may indeed be Abbess Agnes I (1214–21). Her brother was Robert of Mauvoisin, lord of Aulnay and knight on the Albigensian crusade; see Paris, Arch. Nat., S*4386, fols 60^{r} seq., where his executors are recorded to have founded in 1223 the requested chapel for his soul at Saint-Antoine 'in honor of Saint Peter'. Paris, Arch. Nat., S*4386, fol. 5^{v} seq., shows that Simon de Montfort, early leader of the Albigensian crusade, gave five livres annual rent 'for his soul and that of said Robert of Mauvoisin', shortly after the latter's death in 1216; Simon's wife and their son, Amaury, later confirmed and supplemented these gifts. On their participation in the crusade, see Zerner-Chardavoine, 'L'abbé Gui des Vaux-de-Cernay', esp. p. 190; Zerner-Chardavoine, 'L'épouse de Simon de Montfort'; and Sibly and Sibly, *The History of the Albigensian Crusade*, esp. pp. vii–xlvi, and pp. 281 ff.

[21] E.g. Paris, Arch. Nat., LL1595, fols 36^{v}–37^{v} (1261).

[22] Paris, Arch. Nat., S*4386, fol. 9^{r}, and Paris, Arch. Nat., LL1595, fols 5^{r}–5^{v} (1278). Similarly, Sagannus, 'matricularius' of the cathedral of Notre-Dame, made a post-obit gift to Saint-Antoine of half a house in the Clos Brunel 'so that the nuns would celebrate a perpetual anniversary for his soul', Paris, Arch. Nat., LL1595, fol. 42^{r-v} (1210). Roger, canon of Notre-Dame, gave them two arpents of meadow at Bry in 1217, Paris, Arch. Nat., LL1595, fol. 19^{r} (1217). In 1212, the canon Hervé Marshall gave vineyards at Montreuil, again in a post-mortem gift, Paris, Arch. Nat., S*4386, fol. 44^{r} (1212). Similarly, in 1229, John of Paris, master of the scholars from Soissons, made a gift so that the nuns would celebrate an anniversary Mass for his patron, Hugh of Provins, Paris, Arch. Nat., LL1595, fols 28^{v}–29^{r} (1229).

[23] *Septième centenaire*.

[24] Dutilleux and Depoin, *L'abbaye de Maubuisson*, nos 91 (1241) and 92 (1243). The nuns paid 402 livres parisis to tenants there; cf. 'Achatz d'heritages de Maubuisson', fols 40^{v}–41^{r}. Pontoise, Arch. Départ., Val d'Oise, H 58, no. 4, parchment codex 'Achatz d'héritages de

endowment of Maubuisson from noble families in need of cash or from local clergy, and Maubuisson, like other houses of Cistercian women founded in this era, may have profited from increased efforts to recover tithes in lay hands.[25] In Blanche's endowment for Maubuisson we see her carefully distinguishing between the permanent alienation of rents on royal sources of revenue (grants confirmed by Louis IX) and the use of dower income to purchase land.[26]

All three houses of Cistercian nuns, Saint-Antoine, Port-Royal, and Maubuisson, attracted noble recruits whose piety is not in question. However, we may infer that many nuns came from impoverished local noble families from instances of multiple siblings being admitted into these houses and by the limited dowries that noble women brought in comparison to those of bourgeois women. In 1231, two sisters were given places at Port-Royal, and in 1264, four orphaned sisters gave themselves and all their goods to Port-Royal.[27] An impoverished nobility may also be reflected in the entry gifts made to Port-Royal in the form of temporary annuities for the lifetime of an individual nun, rather than permanent transfers of wealth.[28] Moreover, abbesses of these houses did not disdain the wealth of the bourgeoisie as when in the 1260s, for instance, Jean of Lagny, goldsmith, bourgeois of Paris, sent his two underage daughters, Marie and Agnes, to Port-Royal promising the abbey a winepress, eight arpents

Maubuisson', was only partially published by de l'Épinois, 'Comptes relatifs à la fondation de l'abbaye de Maubuisson'.

25 Berman, 'Cistercian Women'.

26 In some cases we can see Blanche receiving into the hand of her manager the income that she has assigned to the nuns and using it for purchasing building supplies. Some acts are very clear, Dutilleux and Depoin, *L'abbaye de Maubuisson*, no. 87 (1237): 'Ego Hugo Tyrelli, dominus Piceii, notum facio omnibus presentes litteras inspecturis quod ego vendidi et quitavi in perpetuum excellentissime domine mee Blanche, Dei gratia Francorum regine Illustri [...] pro nonaginta libris parisis. Que omnia tenebam ab ipsa Regina.'

27 de Dion, *Cartulaire de Port-Royal*, nos 130 (1231), 297 (1263), 303 (1264), and 311 (1267), all concern sisters or daughters.

28 de Dion, *Cartulaire de Port-Royal*, nos 317 (1268), 319 (1269), ten livres for 'as long as my daughter lives'; more ambiguous is the conveyance found in no. 322 (1270/71), 'Voulons et octroyons que l'abaesse et les dessus dits ayent et recoivent cacun an vingt livres en nostre rente de Meurlenc par les termes qu'elle nous est due jusqu'a tant. Que nous aions assis à l'abaesse et au couvent les XX livres de rente illeque ou ailleurs en nostre terre en telle manière que Beatrix notre seure, nonnain du devant dit lieu, ait chaque année quatre livres des deniers dessus dis tant comme elle vivra pour que ses robbes et ce que mestier lui sera'. Were the twenty livres to be permanently held by the nuns, including the four livres of private spending money assigned to his sister?

of vines, and fifty solidi annual '*minute cens*' if the daughters later entered the abbey as nuns.[29]

The phenomenon of bourgeois support is not limited to Port-Royal. In 1261, Peter Coquillarius, citizen of Paris, assigned six livres annual rent to the nuns for his sister Margaret, a nun at Saint-Antoine. In 1296, John of Forrenis, called Imperator, citizen of Paris, gave forty livres cash and three arpents of vineyards when his daughter Jeanette entered Saint-Antoine.[30] Similarly, in 1298, Peter of Inclaustra, citizen of Paris, made a gift when his two daughters, Alice and Jeanne, entered the abbey, and in 1300, Peter the Draper or Wool-seller and his wife Michelle, describing themselves as citizens of Paris, gave rents on Parisian properties to provide for Colette, their daughter, a nun in the same convent.[31] At Maubuisson, too, we see bourgeois donors to the community from an early date.[32]

Women of the artisanal class were important donors, as in the transfer of half a house in the Goldsmithry by Maria, widow of Godefrey Goldsmith.[33] Some donors were recent immigrants to the city, if we are to judge by surnames. Thus, Tostennis of Chartres and Cecily his wife gave Saint-Antoine a house on the Grand Pont in Paris 'for their souls and those of their ancestors'.[34] Robert of Nogent and Christiana his wife gave vineyards and four houses near the abbey.[35] Richard the Scot and his wife Theophania gave property in the Marais, retaining usufruct for life.[36] A family of bankers from Padua, but described as citizens of Paris, gave seventeen livres in annual rents over the bankers' benches on the Grand Pont.[37] And Roger English and his wife Jill gave rents to endow anniversaries for their parents.[38] That gifts from both the laity and ecclesiastics

[29] de Dion, *Cartulaire de Port-Royal*, nos 305 (1266) and 311 (1267).

[30] Paris, Arch. Nat., S*4386, fol. 52^{r-v} (1296).

[31] Paris, Arch. Nat., LL1595, fols 63^{r}–64^{r} (1298) and 64^{v}–66^{v} (1300).

[32] Dutilleux and Depoin, *L'abbaye de Maubuisson*, nos 88 and 89 (1239).

[33] Paris, Arch. Nat., LL1595, fol. 28^{r-v} (1218).

[34] Paris, Arch. Nat., LL1595, fols 38^{r}–39^{r} (1218).

[35] Paris, Arch. Nat., LL1595, fol. 19^{r} (1242).

[36] Paris, Arch. Nat., LL1595, fol. 41^{r-v} (1279).

[37] Paris, Arch. Nat., LL1595, fols 32^{v}–33^{v} (1295); they gave endowment for 'a daily mass at that altar before which their father had been buried'.

[38] Paris, Arch. Nat., LL1595, fol. 32^{v} (1227).

specified anniversary Masses suggests that both clergy and laity had no doubt about the efficacy of prayers for souls said at Saint-Antoine.[39]

Such records as these suggest that feudal families hard up for cash placed multiple daughters in religious houses for which they had once been major patrons, and that wise abbesses chose to compensate for the smaller dowries of noble girls by admitting the daughters of bourgeois families who could make larger gifts. But feudal families of the period must have seen such social mixing behind the doors of these women's monastic communities as evidence of their own progressive impoverishment; like the inability to have their sons knighted, it signified a loss of status. One wonders if this is not related to the outcry among canon-lawyers against the simony of thirteenth-century abbesses who demanded dowries, as many of those clerics must have come from the same families.[40]

The contribution of bourgeois donors and recruits to Saint-Antoine's tremendous success is particularly apparent. Saint-Antoine would become one of the wealthiest houses of religious men or women in all of northern France by the end of the Ancien Régime. Contributions to its nuns from burgers are highlighted in a charter written by the Abbot of Cîteaux in 1277 listing what had been purchased with the cash brought to the abbey by a single, extremely wealthy commoner, Blanche of Paciac. She had given 400 livres parisis as a gift before becoming a nun there and provided an additional 1500 livres tournois after being veiled. The charter itself probably owes its existence to the huge sums that were involved, since cash gifts like Blanche's would not normally have been recorded. This charter may also express concern on Blanche's part about her status as a bourgeois within a community in which the leadership remained in the hands of noblewomen. The document states that it was written 'in order that Blanche be remembered perpetually and included after her death in the prayers of the nuns serving the Lord at this house'.[41] Although no charter records her entrance, other surviving charters reveal something of Blanche's identity. That she brought cash, not land, suggests she was bourgeois rather than noble; her wealth status may also be adduced by the presence in the Saint-Antoine cartu-

[39] Paris, Arch. Nat., S*4386, fol. 23^{r} (1244). Eudes, chaplain of the King's Chapel at Beaumont-sur-Oise, in 1244 gave Saint-Antoine two holdings obtained by purchase in the vineyards of Campagnes 'in pure and perpetual alms for his parents' and his own soul and for celebrating an anniversary Mass annually in the church of those nuns'.

[40] Lynch, *Simoniacal Entry*, pp. 219–20, discusses simony and nuns.

[41] Paris, Arch. Nat., S*4386, fol. 75^{r-v} (1277), which also provides evidence that the nuns of Saint-Antoine were tied directly to the Abbot of Cîteaux; the Latin text is printed in Berman, 'Cistercian Nuns and the Development of the Order'.

lary of a certain Raoul de Paciac (perhaps a relative) who served as executor for the rich Parisian cloth-merchant John of Popiac.[42] Her enormous gifts of cash were used to purchase land at designated places — all of them in suburban areas around Paris. Around 1300, the total revenues from urban and rural rents coming to Saint-Antoine amounted to 1600 livres per annum.[43]

These three houses of nuns amassed and consolidated into granges the lands coming into their hands from impoverished nobles, royals, and earlier monastic and episcopal owners who were experiencing economic crisis. Transfers of property to houses of Cistercian nuns like Saint-Antoine, Port-Royal, or Maubuisson are evidence of the outflow of revenue sources to new groups, which the 'religious establishment' described as economic crisis. As Armelle Bonis in a study of Maubuisson's charters puts it:

> The thirteenth century saw the restitution of a great part of the tithes illegally held for centuries by lay people descended from the great Carolingian families, their vassals or their sub-vassals. This restitution was not motivated by pious reasons, but by a crisis in seigneurial revenues joined with the nobles' increasing need for cash. From that crisis Blanche of Castile benefitted directly.[44]

If so, then Blanche conveyed that benefit onto the Cistercian nuns of Maubuisson, but such shifts are seen for Port-Royal and Saint-Antoine as well, as becomes apparent as we look in more detail at the property acquisitions of each of these houses.

Port-Royal

In its earliest years, Port-Royal primarily received income in the form of rents and tithes, rather than land.[45] The gifts made by founder Lady Matilda of Garlande and confirmed by her son Bouchard, lord of Marly, were typical. In 1215, Bouchard and his brother Matthew confirmed rights in the woods of Molerae, including a rent of twenty solidi, ten arpents of vines, one hundred

[42] Paris, Arch. Nat., LL1595, fols 33^{v} and 50^{v}–51^{r}.

[43] Paris, Arch. Nat., LL1595, fols 87^{v} seq. begins the *censier*.

[44] Bonis, *Abbaye cistercienne de Maubuisson*, p. 32.

[45] de Dion, *Cartulaire de Port-Royal*, no. 190 (1239), in which Guy of Chevreuse sold the nuns an annual rent of five muids of oats for the price of 185 livres; or no. 216 (1242) in which Peter of Beauvoir gave them a rent of two muids of mixed grain, half wheat and half oats, for which they paid him 100 livres, a contract confirmed in no. 217 (1244) by Blanche of Castile and in no. 218 (1244) by Louis IX.

solidi in rents at Marly and in vineyard of Pruniac, fifteen livres annually at Meulan, and ten muids annual rent paid in flour from mills that their mother owned.[46] In the third decade of the thirteenth century, at about the time of Matilda's death, Port-Royal's abbesses changed the direction of their management.[47] This change is epitomized in the transactions of 1221–23 concerning land at Aulnay, located in what had once been royal demesne in the Ile-de-France north of Paris. In 1221 Port-Royal's Abbess ceded to the Abbess of Saint-Antoine ten arpents of land located at a site between Aulnay and Savigny; this land was given to Saint-Antoine's nuns by the Abbess of Port-Royal in return for a rent of twenty sestiers of winter wheat to be paid annually from the tithes at Gratelou. At this point we see the Abbess of Port-Royal seeking sources of income, rather than consolidating landholdings, although the Abbess of Saint-Antoine in this instance was consolidating her property rights.[48] By 1223, when Matthew of Marly established a chapel for his soul, Port-Royal's Abbess, although constrained somewhat by the donor, is moving in the direction of consolidation. He conceded to Port-Royal's nuns the right to a holding located in that same region north of Paris between Aulnay and Savigny, but now the nuns promised never to alienate this holding.[49] Soon thereafter Port-Royal began to consolidate its property rights elsewhere.[50]

We know this because we have a *censier* for Port-Royal dated *c.* 1255 in which fixed annuities and small payments in cash from tenants are mixed with lists of arpents of vines held by the nuns. Donors included Lady Marguerite of Narbonne who made a gift for her daughter who had entered Port-Royal, Master Simon of Gif, Lord Guy of Montfort, Lady Clemencia of Plessy, and so on. Income was paid at quarterly or other terms at a variety of dates and places.[51]

[46] de Dion, *Cartulaire de Port-Royal*, nos 21 and 22 (1214–15); Bouchard of Marly replaced rents from a mill with money rents in no. 175 (1238), a contract confirmed in no. 176 (1238).

[47] Matilda of Garlande who decided to found a house of Cistercian nuns died on 16 March 1224; see de Dion, *Cartulaire de Port-Royal*, no. 68 (1223/24) which must be dated the same year as no. 183, the original of the second charter in the medieval cartulary; its Roman numeral MCCXXIII, must have been misread as MCCXXXVIII.

[48] de Dion, *Cartulaire de Port-Royal*, no. 56 (1221–22), a concession by Saint-Antoine to Port-Royal.

[49] de Dion, *Cartulaire de Port-Royal*, nos 59–61 (all 1223), the confirmation by the Bishop of Paris of the chapel founded.

[50] de Dion, *Cartulaire de Port-Royal*, nos 243 (1247) and 316 (1268).

[51] de Dion, *Cartulaire de Port-Royal*, intro., p. 13, and pp. 15 seq.; the *censier* is dated by no. 263 (1255).

The *censier* and cartulary together suggest that Port-Royal consolidated land into granges at sites where the nuns had originally received income or tithes. For instance, at Saclay rents drawn from tithe income were acquired in 1216 and 1217.[52] In 1224, the tithes themselves were acquired in a contract in which rights to those tithes were granted to the Bishop of Paris by Hugh of Jouiac and his wife Margaret, who asked that the bishop then regrant them to Port-Royal; a confirmation by Bouchard of Marly reveals that the nuns had paid 170 livres to 'donors' of those tithes.[53] Consolidation followed. In 1234 the nuns paid ten livres for eleven arpents of land at Saclay bought from William of Issy, knight, and his wife, Sedilia.[54] Thirty-six arpents at Villeray were purchased in 1241 for 195 livres, and the nuns got four more arpents by exchange, and so on.[55]

Similarly, the sisters of Port-Royal consolidated land around the villa of Saint-Escobille, a site where the abbey had at first held only tithes. A quarter of those tithes, great and small, came to the nuns from the Bishop of Chartres in 1215.[56] In 1220, other donors gave rights to build a grange at Saint-Escobille in which to store the tithes collected; Port-Royal also purchased additional tithes for forty livres at a nearby place called Rupturis (recently cleared land?), which was a large parcel sown with twelve muids of grain.[57] In 1231 and 1233, mortgages made to the nuns for 110 livres brought additional tithes at Saint-Escobille.[58] We can also see the importance of wine production in those years and the profitability of acquiring vineyards in this area in the gifts and purchases of vineyards such as that made in 1228 for the soul of the deceased Ingorrent of Sevres. His widow Odeline gave four arpents of vines in her vineyard of Sevres to Port-Royal where her daughter was a nun.[59]

[52] de Dion, *Cartulaire de Port-Royal*, nos 29 (1216) and 30 (1217), both conveyed tithes, each for 100 solidi.

[53] de Dion, *Cartulaire de Port-Royal*, no. 79 (1224) from the Bishop of Paris, and no. 80 (1224) from Bouchard of Marly.

[54] de Dion, *Cartulaire de Port-Royal*, no. 150 (1234).

[55] de Dion, *Cartulaire de Port-Royal*, nos 205 and 206 (both 1241).

[56] de Dion, *Cartulaire de Port-Royal*, no. 23 (1215).

[57] de Dion, *Cartulaire de Port-Royal*, no. 50 (1220).

[58] de Dion, *Cartulaire de Port-Royal*, nos 127 (1231) and 138 (1233).

[59] de Dion, *Cartulaire de Port-Royal*, no. 98 (1228); she kept a rent of two deniers per arpent paid at the feast of Saint-Rémy and required the nuns to use her winepress unless they constructed their own.

While there is some evidence that the nuns of Port-Royal were acquiring some recently cultivated land in this area on the boundary between the dioceses of Chartres and Paris, many of the nuns' holdings were in long-settled areas where tithes had long existed. Certainly on these lands, if not in those with new tithes as well, the nuns of Port-Royal were displacing earlier owners of rights to those tithes. Whereas we can tell in most cases that these lands were cultivated when they came into Port-Royal's hands, it is difficult to determine exactly how the nuns exploited that property. A list of small *cens* paid to them, found in the mid-thirteenth-century *censier*, suggests that in some cases tenants continued to pay the rents owed to previous owners, but the nuns may also have been letting out larger holdings at farm.[60] On the other hand, some Cistercian-style direct management on their holdings is suggested by the position that the nuns took on disputed tithes. Claiming for themselves the same exemption from tithes that Cistercian monks held, Port-Royal's nuns argued that because they were Cistercians they did not have to pay tithes on land under their own management. Although questions might arise about how long the land had been cultivated, all concerned appear to have accepted this claim.[61]

Maubuisson

Queen Blanche of Castile established Maubuisson in a villa of that name not far from Pontoise. She endowed Maubuisson with a series of holdings at the abbey site and nearby (at Bessancourt, Sognolles, Cergy, Pontoise, Frépillon, and la Vacherie); most of these had been purchased from previous owners, although some were lands previously held from the Queen.[62] For instance,

[60] de Dion, *Cartulaire de Port-Royal*, pp. 13 ff.

[61] de Dion, *Cartulaire de Port-Royal*, no. 121 (1230); the nuns asserted that they did not have to pay tithes because they were Cistercians and therefore had the right to tithes on 'novales' created and cultivated at their own expense, that they had themselves reduced said lands to cultivation ('ad culturam rededi faciunt') and now managed them themselves. The parish priest countered that part of the reclamation had been done by Bouchard of Marly, 'Et dicte moniales responderent quod cum sint Cistercienses privilegiatos sunt in hoc quod de hiis que propriis manibus vel sumptibus excolunt, decimas solvere non tenentur, et ipse dictas terras propriis sumptibus ad culturam redigi faciunt; quare dicto presbytero dictas decimas reddere non tenebantur.' The nuns ended up giving seven arpents of land to the priest in lieu of tithe; see discussion in Berman, 'Cistercian Women and the Development of the Order'; on similar settlements by Cistercian monks in twelfth-century southern France, see Verlaguet, *Cartulaire de l'abbaye de Silvanès*, nos 170 (1154) and 174 (1165).

[62] Dutilleux and Depoin, *L'abbaye de Maubuisson*, no. 93 (1249), one of the first pur-

John of Montmorency gave a third of the woods of Rosières, which had come from the marriage portion of his late wife, Maria Tyrel.[63]

We know that the Queen concentrated her energies and income on the project from 1236 until at least 1242 because, while there is no early *censier* like that for Port-Royal, the abbey's records include a register, 'Achatz d'héritages', recording money sent from the royal treasury at the Temple in Paris and from various rents at Melun, Mantes, Étampes. These accounts show that between 1236 and 1242 she received from the Temple more than 24,430 livres which she expended on Maubuisson, primarily for its construction.[64] These were received into the hands of a Master Roger who was in charge of construction, who presented his accounts of construction expenditures to the Queen several times a year.[65] The amounts expended appear to have been a major portion of her personal revenues for those years.[66]

Blanche's purchases and concessions to Maubuisson included rents in money and kind drawn from royal revenues.[67] There were also rents in grain or designated for the purchase of food, as when an annual thirty livres were granted by Louis IX in 1244 for the purchase of herring at Arques.[68] Blanche also gave

chases by the nuns (rather than by Blanche herself) was rights to a piece of land at the quarry (*carrière*) located within the abbey walls, sold to the nuns for twenty livres. Much of the land was purchased out of current income by Blanche: see no. 87 (dated 1237, but in fact 1239), land and vineyards sold to the queen for 150 livres; no. 89 (1239) of land to the Queen for 64 livres, 16 shillings; the major purchase seems to have been nos 90 and 91 (both 1243) in which the Queen paid 400 livres, 37.5 shillings, for houses and lands adjoining the abbey site, 'ad opus abbatie Beate Marie Regalis'.

[63] Dutilleux and Depoin, *L'abbaye de Maubuisson*, no. 167 (n.s. January 1239).

[64] Berger, *Histoire de Blanche de Castille*, p. 319.

[65] 'Achatz d'héritages de Maubuisson'; Bonis, *Abbaye cistercienne de Maubuisson*, pp. 21–22, in which she assumes that as soon as Royaumont was dedicated, Blanche turned to the establishment of Maubuisson. In fact, there is little evidence for any activity before 1239. This is not so apparent once one sorts out the misdated charters in the printed cartulary; thus Dutilleux and Depoin, *L'abbaye de Maubuisson*, no. 87, is not from 1234, but 1237, and no. 88, although dated in the printed cartulary as 1236, confirms a charter of 1239; except for Pontoise, Arch. Départ., Val d'Oise, 72H132, for Bessancourt, which she dates to 1236, and which I have not been able to verify, the earliest charter is for 1239.

[66] Berman, 'Two Medieval Women's Control'.

[67] Dutilleux and Depoin, *L'abbaye de Maubuisson*, nos 300 (1239) and 532 (1239), are in fact the same gift; numbers in Bonis, *Abbaye cistercienne de Maubuisson*, table 2, p. 33, are thus incorrect.

[68] 'Achatz d'héritages de Maubuisson'; Dutilleux and Depoin, *L'abbaye de Maubuisson*, no. 112 (1244).

eight muids of wheat from her income at Pontoise.[69] In addition, she conveyed tithes in 1239, including all her tithe revenue at Étampes, Dourdan, and les Chastelliers, plus an additional 21.5 muids of grain from tithes at Archemont, Hérouville, and Magnitot, which the Queen had purchased for the abbey.[70] Such endowment provided the fledgling community not only with food for its meals, but with surpluses to convert to cash for additional land purchases.[71]

A community of nuns was sent to Maubuisson from Saint-Antoine in 1241/42, and the church of Maubuisson was dedicated in 1244; the abbey was treated by the Cistercian General Chapter as a direct daughter of Cîteaux.[72] Beyond purchases made by Queen Blanche of Castile for her new foundation, archives and account books show considerable expenditures for its endowment by its first abbess, who appears to have been in charge of those acquisitions from 1242 on. As Bonis describes it:

> By 1244 the nuns of Maubuisson had a demesne of more than 100 arpents of woods, meadows, vineyards, gardens, fish-ponds and mill at the abbey itself; a seigneurie at Bessancourt, and parts other such seigneuries and parcels of land around Pontoise at Frépillon, and at Méry-sur-Oise.[73]

Moreover, Maubuisson gradually also acquired rights further north: in the French Vexin around Epiais, Nonciennes, Gaillon; in the Beauvaisis at Bonfosse and Uny; and in the Parisis at Gonesse, Le Plessis, and Thiessonville.[74] Among the most interesting gifts were rights in Normandy to rents held by Louis IX amounting to more than four hundred livres annually from tenants of assarts (newly cleared lands) in the region of Evreux and Breteuil. Concern over the tithes owed to the church of Evreux on these holdings seems to have led early abbesses to dispose of part of them.[75]

At Maubuisson, as at Port-Royal, we see not only the Queen, but also members of the knightly class, abbots of nearby monasteries, bishops, and priests all

[69] Dutilleux and Depoin, *L'abbaye de Maubuisson*, no. 300 (1239).

[70] Dutilleux and Depoin, *L'abbaye de Maubuisson*, nos 465, 470, 486, and 503 (all 1239).

[71] As is clear from such entries in 'Achatz d'héritages de Maubuisson' as those on fol. 57^{v}.

[72] Dutilleux and Depoin, *L'abbaye de Maubuisson*, nos 3, 5, and 7 (1244).

[73] Bonis, *Abbaye cistercienne de Maubuisson*, p. 35.

[74] Bonis, *Abbaye cistercienne de Maubuisson*, tables and maps, passim.

[75] Dutilleux and Depoin, *L'abbaye de Maubuisson*, no. 329 (1246), a concession by Louis IX which totals over four hundred livres per year in rent (not the forty mentioned in the cartulary); cf. no. 330 (1293).

giving up claims to land in support of the new foundation. However, as at Port-Royal, it is often difficult to ascertain whether these benefactors were giving up land because they were financially pressed. Certainly that was the implication when Blanche purchased woods at Bretignolles for 1500 livres from Matthew of Marly, a grandson of the founder of Port-Royal, which she then used to endow her nuns at Maubuisson. Similar purchases made by Louis IX in the 1240s and transferred to Maubuisson just before his departure on Crusade may also suggest that the nobility was finding itself strapped for cash.[76]

Such transfers of wealth to religious women were neither marginal nor negligible; indeed they had considerable and lasting effects. The redirection of such wealth towards such new religious foundations for women, often effected by such powerful ruling women who chose specifically the prayers of Cistercian nuns, had repercussions for who was thriving (or not) in the late medieval economy; the phenomenon deserves more attention.

Saint-Antoine

The abbey for Cistercian women at Saint-Antoine-des-Champs-lez-Paris, located just outside the eastern gates of the emerging capital, underlines yet another characteristic of religious houses for women: their close ties to urban growth and the expansion of bourgeois ownership in the countryside nearby, as well as their frequent location not far from city walls.[77] Royal confirmations of their acquisitions in both urban and rural properties located 'in censiva domini regis' suggest that urban and suburban property already dispersed from royal control was finding its way into the hands of these nuns.[78] These properties included not only houses and other property in Paris itself, but also land in the great open fields directly north of Paris. The nuns eventually created a great grange at Savigny-le-Temple, virtually underneath the aerogare of Roissy.[79] The initial gifts in the Ile-de-France still owed ground rent to the King; these lands came from nobles like Agnes of Cressonessart and Simon de

[76] Dutilleux and Depoin, *L'abbaye de Maubuisson*, nos 252 (1246) and 256 (1248).

[77] Berman, 'Fashions in Monastic Patronage'.

[78] Royal gifts are mostly confirmations, like Paris, Arch. Nat., S*4386, fol. 22v (1261); I have found no documentation to support Dimier, *Saint Louis et Cîteaux*, p. 155, under 1214, April 25, where he says, 'à la naissance de Saint Louis, son Père Louis, pour fêter cet heureux évènement, fait don à l'abbaye de Saint-Antoine de l'emplacement de l'église et alentour, pour une superficie de 14 arpents', but Branner, *St. Louis and the Court Style*, dates this to 1228.

[79] Paris, Arch. Nat., S*4386, fols 65r–67r seq.

Montfort.[80] However the nuns soon also purchased properties there. Thus in 1211, twelve arpents of land between Aulnay and le Blanc Mésnil were bought for thirty-six livres from the knight Peter of Beaumarchais and his wife Margaret.[81] In a contract from 1234, John of Belfont, Dreux of Montfermiel, and their two brothers gave to Saint-Antoine a fifth of their land at Savigny 'for their souls' and sold the other four-fifths of it to the nuns for three hundred livres.[82] Another purchase was of two arpents for seven livres from Jeanne of Aulnay, niece of 'Brother Bernard of Saint-Antoine'; she had inherited this part from her mother, Erembours, and transferred it by sale along with a gift in pure alms of another three and a half arpents of land inherited from her father.[83]

Similarly, at Beaumont-sur-Oise, north-west of the city, not far from Argenteuil, acquisitions by Saint-Antoine eventually included an entire fief and farm at Champagnes, with associated rents previously held by the lords of Champagnes-sur-Oise.[84] By 1260 their grange would have properties on both sides of the Oise, including rights in a field 'held from the Lord King', a vineyard called the 'Clos de Thoriac', and two arpents of meadow.[85] In 1261 Louis IX confirmed a sale to the nuns who paid 120 livres to the knight Reginald of Champagnes for rents worth eight livres a year.[86] In 1264, a nephew, Jean of Champagnes, knight, with his brothers, Henry and Robert, and their mother, Jeanne, sold three arpents of cultivated land and a quartier of vines, and confirmed the nuns' acquisition of 'A certain manor [...] which included a great hall (*aula*), a smaller hall, a winepress, a barn and smaller stables for cows, all surrounding a courtyard'.[87] In addition the nuns acquired three arpents of planted vineyards, five and a half arpents of land in the open fields, an arpent and a half of meadows, and annual '*minute cens*' at Champagnes amounting to more than thirty-eight shillings per annum paid by more than thirty tenants.[88]

[80] Paris, Arch. Nat., S*4386, fol. 61ᵛ.

[81] Paris, Arch. Nat., S*4386, fol. 60ʳ.

[82] Paris, Arch. Nat., S*4386, fol. 64ʳ.

[83] Paris, Arch. Nat., S*4386, fol. 62ᵛ.

[84] Paris, Arch. Nat., S*4386, fols 21ᵛ seq.

[85] Paris, Arch. Nat., S*4386, fols 24ᵛ seq.

[86] Paris, Arch. Nat., S*4386, fol. 22ᵛ.

[87] Paris, Arch. Nat., S*4386, fols 24ᵛ–26ᵛ, with a small *censier*.

[88] Paris, Arch. Nat., S*4386, fols 24ᵛ–26ʳ. (1264); some of these items were listed as purchased with monies from the gifts of Blanche of Paciac in the 1277 memorandum, discussed above at note 41.

Saint-Antoine's accumulated land at a third site, Montreuil near Vincennes, where the nuns built a grange called le petit-Montreuil; there they practiced both cereal cultivation and intensive cultivation of vineyards.[89] Some contracts conveyed rights from the Countess and Count of Grandpré, who were lords of Montreuil, but more came from Parisian citizens who had begun to invest there in the suburban land market.[90] For instance, Saint-Antoine paid a premium to acquire lands that had been purchased only slightly earlier by Peter of Buciac, citizen of Paris; he expended forty-three livres to purchase rights there from John of Bobigny, draper, citizen of Paris, and his wife Margaret, and from Lord Thomas of Clamartis, knight, and Sedilia his wife.[91] Similarly in 1255, Peter Cambellarius confirmed to Saint-Antoine rights in Montreuil over two houses, nineteen arpents of woodland, sixty-eight arpents of land, two and a half arpents of vineyards, and sixty-two shillings of annual minute *cens*; these were all the rights there that he had accumulated by making purchases.[92]

Saint-Antoine also acquired rights for a grange at Bry-sur-Marne, east of Paris, and in forest areas near the Marne at Fontenay-sur/sous-Bois. The negotiations between Saint-Antoine's nuns and the nearby Premonstratensian canons over woodlands there suggest that the nuns were successfully replacing a rather new community of religious men. Moreover, the administrative power of the nuns is seen when in 1278 the annual rental payments per land unit were reduced to four livres after the abbess successfully claimed that an earlier amount had exceeded the 'just price'.[93] Such rural holdings that included grain-producing lands, vineyards and winepresses, forest areas for animal husbandry, and mills for grinding flour produced most commodities needed for Saint-Antoine's internal consumption needs, as well as surpluses for sale.

But Saint-Antoine's nuns also gained a variety of real estate within the city of Paris from citizens who made gifts and sales to them, and whose daughters, like the Blanche of Paciac discussed earlier, entered the community with large amounts of cash. We know from a rent-roll that comes from the early fourteenth century that the nuns' urban holdings were extensive. That roll or *censier* lists 139 separate holdings producing more than six hundred livres of annual rent:

89 Paris, Arch. Nat., S*4386, fol. 54r (1259); the winepress mentioned in item six of the 1277 memorandum was purchased in 1259 for forty-six livres.

90 Paris, Arch. Nat., S*4386, fols 44v seq.

91 Paris, Arch. Nat., S*4386, fols 54r seq.

92 Paris, Arch. Nat., S*4386, fol. 54r.

93 Paris, Arch. Nat., S*4386, fols 11r seq., rental originally confirmed by the Abbot of Cîteaux.

near the Weavers, the Silk-makers, the Belt-makers, or the Slaughterhouses, near the Petit Pont, in the Marais, near Saint-Médard, near la Grève, in the area between the Baths and Saint-Germain, at the Montmartre gate, across from the King's Palace, in the Cité, at the marketplace where the nuns had 'notre grant maison des Halles', on the Grand Rue Saint-Denis, the Rue de-la-Harpe, the Grand Rue Saint-Jacques, and so on.[94]

But there is also a list of non-Parisian rents: tithes and income from mills, tolls, and granaries in the surrounding region amount to another one thousand livres of annual income.[95] The nuns were using exchanges to consolidate these sources of rent at specific places. Thus an early transfer of five livres annual rent on the port of Mantes given in 1221 by Agnes of Cressonessart was supplemented by purchases from her sons, Thibault and Guy, and later by agreements with her grandchildren. The family would also receive fifty shillings of annual rent from the nuns in exchange for ten arpents of woods at a place called Montjoie at Cressonessart in the Beauvaisis.[96]

Saint-Antoine's close ties to important bourgeois families, the protection of notable noble families from whose ranks it apparently drew its abbesses, along with confirmations and other favours from King and Pope, allowed this abbey of Cistercian women to thrive in the later Middle Ages. While their rents in cash diminished in the suddenly inflationary economy of the late thirteenth and early fourteenth centuries, these nuns managed to stabilize income. They were well aware that rents in kind should not be converted into money in this period.[97] Their houses in Paris, rented to tenants ranging from great ecclesiastics and feudal lords to prosperous Parisian citizens and artisans, paid rents that kept up with inflation. Indeed Saint-Antoine not only increased its overall holdings, it also appears to have invested in improvements. Tenants of Parisian properties granted 'augmentations of rent', permanently increased, probably in return for what we would call 'home-improvement loans'.[98] Transfers of wealth

[94] Paris, Arch. Nat., LL1595, fols 87r seq.

[95] Paris, Arch. Nat., LL1595, fols 88r seq.

[96] Paris, Arch. Nat., S*4386, fols 8r seq.

[97] The nuns of le Lys to Philip IV; BnF, Latin MS 13892, 'Cartulaire du Lys', no. 39 (1311).

[98] Occasionally such increased rents were pious contributions, but more often they must have been given to fund improvements, which are occasionally mentioned. For instance, Paris, Arch. Nat., LL1595, fols 19r–20v (1216) in which Adam Herman and Sancia his wife granted an 'augmentation of rent' to Saint-Antoine on a house in Paris. On fol. 41v (1228) Master William of La Tiniac, a canon of Châlons, made a gift to the nuns of ten livres annual increased rent over a certain house in Paris after his death. Sometimes the augmented rents had been

from earlier owners into the hands of religious women like those of Saint-Antoine contradict claims of overall economic decline.

Conclusion

If we extrapolate from the evidence surviving for the communities of religious women cited in this paper, we find a very different picture of the late medieval economy than that based on the archives and narratives of the great religious communities. Communities of men, the male clerical establishment, and knights and kings needed more and more income over the course of this period and would probably have complained even if things had remained the same. The evidence cited here suggests that the area of land under cultivation as well as the relative value of all the available lands in any one region of France probably actually increased over the later Middle Ages. Land was improved by more intensive cultivation with appropriate crops, by the conversion of poorer agricultural land into pasture or meadow, by the planting of vineyards and gardens in places that were inappropriate to the large open fields and where there was market demand or transport to markets. Far from suffering overall decline, the total value of land and property (particularly if we include such things as tithe barns, farmsteads, mills, and industrial facilities, and particularly if we include the extensive building up of urban properties that produced rents) appears from the records for these nuns to have been actually increasing in northern France in the period we have studied.

Late medieval agricultural production might increase or decline from year to year, and the switch to commercial crops did sometimes contribute to real famine in the early fourteenth century — a time when, in some years, many monastic communities and the nuns we study forwent some of their rents.[99] Nonetheless, there is reason to believe that until the devastations of the Hundred Years War, the French countryside and the Parisian cityscape alike

established before property was conveyed; thus on fol. 16v (1211) there was conveyance of a house sited opposite the house of Adam of Moulent 'cum augmento census'.

[99] In 1279 the Count of Blois fell into arrears on ninety livres of rents (including the forty on the mills) with which Isabelle of Chartres had endowed Eau; eventually the nuns agreed to give up claims to part of the previous three years' rents still unpaid, as well as agreeing to a permanent reduction in income from this source from ninety to sixty livres per annum: Métais, *Cartulaire de Notre-Dame-de-l'Eau*, nos 87 (1279) and 89 (1282); peasants who could not pay rent because of famine are found in Doinel, *Cartulaire de Notre-Dame de Voisins*, no. 60 (1312), a situation discussed at length by Jordan, *The Great Famine*.

were improving their overall productive capacity. How else might we interpret the consolidation of lands, the construction of town dwellings, workshops, and mills, the planting of vineyards, the improvements on buildings, which resulted in higher rents? Little of this activity created only temporarily productive land, and there were real gains in what we would call gross national product.

The examples of Saint-Antoine, Port-Royal, Maubuisson, and a number of other houses of Cistercian women that became wealthy in the late Middle Ages provide an explanation for the complaints emanating from an older 'male religious establishment'. Such complaints arose because property and its income were moving into the hands of new groups, including those of monastic women. Nor is it irrelevant to note that after the Hundred Years War, the Cistercian establishment represented by the abbots of Cîteaux and Clairvaux 'recaptured' some of the revenues and properties by suppressing communities of Cistercian women and taking over properties for the use of communities of monks and to pay their debts. Houses as powerful and well protected by their patrons as Port-Royal, Maubuisson, and Saint-Antoine survived; monks elsewhere, however, would come to suppress smaller communities of Cistercian nuns having attractive holdings.[100] That properties belonging to Cistercian women's houses were valuable enough for abbots to attempt to appropriate them, however, is one more fact pointing towards my conclusion. Thus the transfer of valuable and productive property to women's religious communities like the three houses of Cistercian nuns discussed here was likely an important factor in the 'feudal crisis' of the later Middle Ages.

[100] Berman, 'The Labors of Hercules'; Bondéelle-Souchier, 'Les moniales cisterciennes', item 62; and Skinner, 'The Cartulary of Clairmarais'.

Bibliography

Archives

Paris, Archives Nationales, H5 3859
Paris, Archives Nationales, LL1595
Paris, Archives Nationales, S*4386
Paris, Bibliothèque nationale de France, MS latin 13892, 'Cartulaire du Lys'
Pontoise, Archives Départementales, Val d'Oise, 72H132
Pontoise, Archives Départementales, Val d'Oise, H 58, 'Achatz d'heritages de Maubuisson'

Primary Sources

Septième centenaire de la mort de Saint Louis: Actes des colloques de Royaumont et Paris, 21–27 mai 1970 (Paris: Belles Lettres, 1976)

Canivez, Joseph-Marie, ed., *Statuta capitulorum generalium ordinis cisterciensis ab anno 1116 ad annum 1786*, 8 vols (Louvain: Bureaux de la Revue, 1933)

de Dion, Adolphe, ed., *Cartulaire de l'abbaye de Porrois, au diocèse de Paris, plus connue sous son nom mystique Port-Royal* (Paris: Picard, 1903)

Doinel, Jules, ed., *Cartulaire de Notre-Dame de Voisins de l'Ordre de Cîteaux: (1207–1343)* (Orléans: Herluison, 1887)

Dutilleux, Adolphe, and Joseph Depoin, eds, *L'abbaye de Maubuisson, histoire et cartulaire, publiés d'après les documents inédits*, 4 vols (Pontoise; L. Paris, 1882–90)

Hinnebusch, John Frederick, ed., *The Historia Occidentalis of Jacques de Vitry: A Critical Edition* (Fribourg: Fribourg University Press, 1972)

Métais, Charles, ed., *Cartulaire de l'Abbaye de Notre-Dame-de-l'Eau* (Chartres: C Métais, 1908)

Sibly, W. A., and Michael D. Sibly, trans, *The History of the Albigensian Crusade: Peter of les Vaux-de-Cernay's Historia Albigensis* (Woodbridge: Boydell, 1998)

Verlaguet, P. A., ed., *Cartulaire de l'abbaye de Silvanès* (Rodez: P. Carrère, 1910)

Secondary Sources

Barrière, Bernadette, 'The Cistercian Monastery of Coyroux in the Province of Limousin in Southern France, in the 12th–13th Centuries', *Gesta*, 31 (1992), 76–82

Barrière, Bernadette, and others, eds, *Cîteaux et les femmes: Actes des recontres de Royaumont 1998* (Paris: Éditions Créaphis, 2001)

Berger, Élie, *Histoire de Blanche de Castille, reine de France* (Paris: Écoles francaises d'Athènes et de Rome, 1895)

Berman, Constance H., 'Abbeys for Cistercian Nuns in the Ecclesiastical Province of Sens: Foundation, Endowment and Economic Activities of the Earlier Foundations', *Revue Mabillon*, 73 (1997), 83–113

——, 'Les acquisitions rurales des abbayes cisterciennes féminines en l'Ile-de-France', *Paris et Ile-de-France: Mémoires*, 48 (1997), 113–20

——, *The Cistercian Evolution: The Invention of a Religious Order in Twelfth-Century Europe* (Philadelphia: University of Pennsylvania Press, 2000)

——, 'Cistercian Nuns and the Development of the Order: The Abbey of Saint-Antoine-des-Champs outside Paris', in *The Joy of Learning and the Love of God: Essays in Honor of Jean Leclercq, OSB*, ed. by E. Rozanne Elder (Kalamazoo: Cistercian Publications, 1995), pp. 121–56

——, 'Cistercian Women and Tithes', *Cîteaux*, 49 (1998), 95–128

——, 'Dowries, Private Income, and Anniversary Masses: The Nuns of St. Antoine-des-Champs (Paris)', *Proceedings of the Western Society for French History*, 20 (1993), 3–20

——, 'The Economic Practices of Cistercian Women's Communities: A Preliminary Look', in *Studiosorum Speculum: Studies in Honor of Father Louis J. Lekai, OCSO*, ed. by Francis R. Swietek and John Sommerfeldt, Cistercian Studies Series, 141 (Kalamazoo: Cistercian Publications, 1993), pp. 15–32

——, 'Fashions in Monastic Patronage: The Popularity of Supporting Cistercian Abbeys for Women', *Proceedings of the Western Society for French History*, 17 (1990), 36–45

——, 'How Much Space Did Medieval Nuns Have or Need?', in *Shaping Community: The Art and Archaeology of Monasticism; Papers from a Symposium head at the Frederick R. Weisman Museum at the University of Minnesota, March 10–12, 2000*, ed. by Sheila McNally, BAR International Series, 941 (London: Archaeopress, 2001), pp. 100–116

——, 'The Labors of Hercules, the Cartulary, Church and Abbey for Nuns of La Cour-Notre-Dame-de-Michery', *Journal of Medieval History*, 26 (2000), 33–70

——, *Medieval Agriculture, the Southern-French Countryside, and the Early Cistercians: A Study of Forty-three Monasteries*, Transactions of the American Philosophical Society, 76 (Philadelphia: American Philosophical Society, 1986)

——, 'Two Medieval Women's Control of Property and Religious Benefactions in France: Eleanor of Vermandois and Blanche of Castile', *Viator*, 41.2 (2010), 151–82

——, 'Were There Twelfth-Century Cistercian Nuns?', *Church History*, 68 (1999), 824–64

——, *The White Nuns: Cistercian Abbeys for Women and their Property in Medieval Europe* (forthcoming)

——, *Women and Monasticism in Medieval Europe: Sisters and Patrons of the Cistercian Order* (Kalamazoo: TEAMS, 2002)

Bois, Guy, *Crise du féodalisme: Économie rurale et démographie en Normandie orientale, du début du XIVe s. au milieu du XVIe s.* (Paris: Presses de la fondation nationale des sciences politique, 1976)

Bondéelle-Souchier, Anne, 'Les moniales cisterciennes et leurs livres manuscrits dans la France d'Ancien Régime', *Cîteaux*, 45 (1994), 193–336

Bonis, Armelle, *Abbaye cistercienne de Maubuisson: La formation du Temporel (1236 à 1356)* (Saint-Ouen-l'Aumône: Conseil général du Val-d'Oise, Service départemental d'archéologie du Val-d'Oise, 1990)

Bouchard, Constance B., *Spirituality and Administration: The Role of the Bishop in Twelfth-Century Auxerre* (Cambridge, MA: Medieval Academy, 1979)

Branner, Robert, *St. Louis and the Court Style in Gothic Architecture* (London: A. Zwemmer, 1965)

de Burton, Thomas, *Chronica monasterii de Melsa a fundatione usque ad annum 1396* (London: Rerum Britannicarum, 1866)

Degler-Spengler, Brigitte, 'The Incorporation of Cistercian Nuns into the Order in the Twelfth and Thirteenth Century', in *Hidden Springs*, ed. by John A. Nichols and Lillian Thomas Shank (Kalamazoo: Cistercian Publications, 1995), pp. 85–134

de l'Épinois, Henri, 'Comptes relatifs à la fondation de l'abbaye de Maubuisson, d'après les originaux des archives de Versailles', *Bibliothèque de l'École des Chartes*, 19 (1858), 550–69

Denifle, Heinrich, *Les Désolations des églises, monastères, hopitaux en France vers le milieu du XV*e *siècle* (Paris: Picard, 1897–99)

de Pontenay Fontette, Micheline, *Les religieuses à l'âge classique du droit canon: Recherches sur les structures juridiques des branches féminines des ordres* (Paris: J. Vrin, 1967)

Dimier, Anselm, *Saint Louis et Cîteaux* (Paris: Letouzey & Ané, 1954)

Donnelly, James S., *The Decline of the Medieval Cistercian Laybrotherhood* (New York: Fordham University Press, 1949)

Duby, Georges, *The Early Growth of the European Economy: Warriors and Peasants from the Seventh to the Twelfth Century* (London: Weidenfeld and Nicolson, 1974)

——, *Rural Economy and Country Life in the Medieval West*, trans. by Cynthia Postan (Columbia: University of South Carolina Press, 1968)

Ekelund, Robert B., and others, *Sacred Trust: The Medieval Church as an Economic Firm* (New York: Oxford University Press, 1996)

Evergates, Theodore, 'Aristocratic Women in the County of Champagne', in *Aristocratic Women in Medieval France*, ed. by Theodore Evergates (Philadelphia: University of Pennsylvania Press, 1999), pp. 74–110

Fossier, Robert, *La Terre et les hommes en Picardie jusqu'à la fin du* XIIIe *siècle* (Paris: Nauwelaerts, 1968)

Fourquin, Guy, *Les campagnes de la région parisienne à la fin du Moyen Âge* (Paris: Presses Universitaires de France, 1964)

Grundmann, Herbert, *Religious Movements in the Middle Ages: The Historical Links Between Heresy, the Mendicant Orders, and the Women's Religious Movement in the Twelfth and Thirteenth Century, with the Historical Foundations of German Mysticism*, trans. by Steven Rowan, intro. Robert E. Lerner (South Bend, IN: Notre Dame University Press, 1995)

Johnson, Penelope D., *Equal in Monastic Profession: Religious Women in Medieval France* (Chicago: University of Chicago Press, 1991)

Jordan, Erin, 'Patronage, Prayers and Polders: Assessing Cistercian Foundations in Thirteenth-Century Flanders and Hainaut', *Cîteaux*, 53 (2002), 99–125

Jordan, William Chester, *The Great Famine: Northern Europe in the Early Fourteenth Century* (Princeton: Princeton University Press, 1996)

Lawrence, C. H., *Medieval Monasticism: Forms of Religious Life in Western Europe in the Middle Ages*, 3rd edn (London: Routledge, 2000)

Leclercq, Jean, 'Monachesimo femminile nei secoli XII e XIII', in *Movimento religioso femminile e francescanesimo nel secolo XIII: Atti del VII convegno internazionale di studi francescani, Assisi, 11–13 ottobre 1979* (Assisi: La Società, 1980), pp. 79–92

Lynch, Joseph H., *Simoniacal Entry into Religious Life from 1000 to 1260: A Social, Economic and Legal Study* (Columbus: Ohio State University Press, 1976)

Oliva, Marilyn, *The Convent and the Community in Late Medieval England: Female Monasteries in the Diocese of Norwich 1350–1450* (Woodbridge: Boydell, 1998)

Postan, Michael M., *The Medieval Economy and Society: An Economic History of Britain 1100–1500* (London: Weidenfeld and Nicolson, 1972)

Skinner, Pamela Stucky, 'The Cartulary of Clairmarais, a Monastery of Cistercian Nuns at Reims, France, *c.* 1220–1460: Edition and Commentary' (unpublished doctoral thesis, University of Iowa, 2005)

Spiegel, Gabrielle M., *Romancing the Past; The Rise of Vernacular Prose Historiography in Thirteenth-Century France* (Berkeley: University of California Press, 1993)

Venarde, Bruce L., *Women's Monasticism and Medieval Society: Nunneries in France and England, 890–1215* (Ithaca: Cornell University Press, 1997)

Zerner-Chardavoine, Monique, 'L'abbé Gui des Vaux-de-Cernay, prédicateur de croisade', in *Les Cisterciens de Languedoc (XIIIe–XIVe siècle)*, Cahiers de Fanjeaux, 21 (Toulouse: Privat, 1986), pp. 185–204

——, 'L'épouse de Simon de Montfort et la croisade albigeoise', in *Femmes, Mariages, Lignages: XIIe–XIVe siècles: Mélanges offerts à Georges Duby* (Brussels: De Boeck Université 1992), pp. 449–70

THE MEDIEVAL COUNTRYSIDE

All volumes in this series are evaluated by an Editorial Board, strictly on academic grounds, based on reports prepared by referees who have been commissioned by virtue of their specialism in the appropriate field. The Board ensures that the screening is done independently and without conflicts of interest. The definitive texts supplied by authors are also subject to review by the Board before being approved for publication. Further, the volumes are copyedited to conform to the publisher's stylebook and to the best international academic standards in the field.

Titles in Series

The Rural History of Medieval European Societies: Trends and Perspectives, ed. by Isabel Alfonso (2007)

Eva Svensson, *The Medieval Household: Daily Life in Castles and Farmsteads, Scandinavian Examples in their European Context* (2008)

Land, Power, and Society in Medieval Castile: A Study of Behetría Lordship, ed. by Cristina Jular Pérez-Alfaro and Carlos Estepa Díez (2009)

Survival and Discord in Medieval Society: Essays in Honour of Christopher Dyer, ed. by Richard Goddard, John Langdon, and Miriam Müller (2010)

Feudalism: New Landscapes of Debate, ed. by Sverre Bagge, Michael H. Gelting, and Thomas Lindkvist (2011)

Scale and Scale Change in the Early Middle Ages: Exploring Landscape, Local Society, and the World Beyond, ed. by Julio Escalona and Andrew Reynolds (2011)

José Ramón Díaz de Durana, *Anonymous Noblemen: The Generalization of Hidalgo Status in the Basque Country (1250–1525)* (2011)

Settlement and Lordship in Viking and Early Medieval Scandinavia, ed. by Bjørn Poulsen and Søren Michael Sindbæk (2011)

Britons, Saxons, and Scandinavians: The Historical Geography of Glanville R. J. Jones, ed. by P. S. Barnwell and Brian K. Roberts (2012)

Ferran Garcia-Oliver, *The Valley of the Six Mosques: Work and Life in Medieval Valldigna* (2012)

Town and Countryside in the Age of the Black Death: Essays in Honour of John Hatcher, ed. by Mark Bailey and Stephen Rigby (2012)

In Preparation

Town and Country in Medieval North Western Europe: Dynamic Interactions, edited by Alexis Wilkin, John Naylor, Derek Keene, and Arnoud-Jan Bijsterveld

Alasdair Ross, *Land Assessment and Lordship in Medieval Northern Scotland*

Power and Rural Communities in Al-Andalus: Ideological and Material Representations, ed. by Adela Fábregas and Flocel Sabaté

Peasants and Lords in the Medieval English Economy: Essays in Honour of Bruce M. S. Campbell, ed. by Maryanne Kowaleski, John Langdon, and Phillipp R. Schofield